2015 GUIDE TO LITERARY AGENTS

includes a 1-year online subscription to **Guide to Literary Agents** on

THE ULTIMATE MARKET RESEARCH TOOL FOR WRITERS

To register your *2015 Guide to Literary Agents* book and **start your 1-year online genre-only subscription**, scratch off the block below to reveal your activation code, then go to www.WritersMarket.com. Find the box that says "Have an Activation Code?" then click on "Sign Up Now" and enter your contact information and activation code. It's that easy!

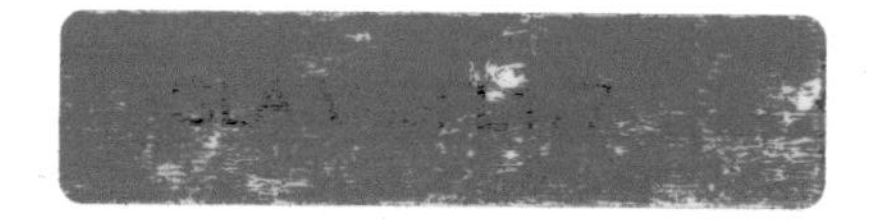

UPDATED MARKET LISTINGS FOR YOUR INTEREST AREA

EASY-TO-USE SEARCHABLE DATABASE • RECORD-KEEPING TOOLS

PROFESSIONAL TIPS & ADVICE • INDUSTRY NEWS

Your purchase of *Guide to Literary Agents* gives you access to updated listings related to this genre of writing (valid through 12/31/15). For just $9.99, you can upgrade your subscription and get access to listings from all of our best-selling Market Books. Visit **www.WritersMarket.com** for more information.

WritersMarket.com

Where & How to Sell What You Write

Activate your WritersMarket.com subscription to get instant access to:

- UPDATED LISTINGS IN YOUR WRITING GENRE: Find additional listings that didn't make it into the book, updated contact information and more. WritersMarket.com provides the most comprehensive database of verified markets available anywhere.
- EASY-TO-USE SEARCHABLE DATABASE: Looking for a specific magazine or book publisher? Just type in its name. Or widen your prospects with the Advanced Search. You can also search for listings that have been recently updated!
- PERSONALIZED TOOLS: Store your best-bet markets, and use our popular recording-keeping tools to track your submissions. Plus, get new and updated market listings, query reminders, and more—every time you log in!
- PROFESSIONAL TIPS & ADVICE: From pay-rate charts to sample query letters, and from how-to articles to Q&A's with literary agents, we have the resources writers need.

YOU'LL GET ALL OF THIS WITH YOUR INCLUDED SUBSCRIPTION TO

GLA15

24TH ANNUAL EDITION

2015 GUIDE TO LITERARY AGENTS

Chuck Sambuchino, Editor

WRITER'S DIGEST
BOOKS
WritersDigest.com
Cincinnati, Ohio

Publisher & Editorial Director, Writing Community: Phil Sexton

Writer's Market website: www.writersmarket.com
Writer's Digest website: www.writersdigest.com
Writer's Digest Bookstore: www.writersdigestshop.com
Guide to Literary Agents Blog: www.guidetoliteraryagents.com/blog

Distributed in Canada by Fraser Direct
100 Armstrong Avenue
Georgetown, Ontario, Canada L7G 5S4
Tel: (905) 877-4411

Distributed in the U.K. and Europe by F&W Media International
Brunel House, Newton Abbot, Devon, TQ12 4PU, England
Tel: (+44) 1626-323200, Fax: (+44) 1626-323319
E-mail: postmaster@davidandcharles.co.uk

Distributed in Australia by Capricorn Link
P.O. Box 704, Windsor, NSW 2756 Australia
Tel: (02) 4577-3555

ISSN: 1078-6945
ISBN-13: 978-1-59963-843-0
ISBN-10: 1-59963-843-6

Attention Booksellers: This is an annual directory of F+W Media, Inc.
Return deadline for this edition is December 31, 2015.

Edited by: Chuck Sambuchino
Cover designed by: Claudean Wheeler
Interior designed by: Claudean Wheeler
Page layout by: Geoff Raker
Production coordinated by: Greg Nock and Debbie Thomas

CONTENTS

RESOURCES

MARKETS

INDEXES

FROM THE EDITOR

This year marks the sixth anniversary of signing with my literary agent, Sorche Fairbank of Fairbank Literary. And in that time, we've sold five books together, and hopefully that number will only continue to grow as time goes on. I mention this simply to illustrate what you likely already know: Literary agents open doors and get your book sold. They still are the key gatekeepers who have access to the biggest and best traditional publishing houses nationwide. Remember: Getting a rep is the biggest step to getting read.

My hope is that someday soon you, too, will celebrate a book deal with your agent (with champagne, preferably!)—and picking up this updated edition of *Guide to Literary Agents* is a key first to-do. Inside you will not only find contact information for more than 1,000 literary agents, but lots more. To help you get your book published, we've pinpointed newer agents actively seeking clients; we've gone into detail regarding how to write query letters, synopses, nonfiction book proposals, blog posts, and more; and we've also examined all the ways you should (and should *not*) begin your novel to get the attention of agents. If you have a question about how to get a literary agent, chances are it's answered in these pages.

Please stay in touch with me through my blog—guidetoliteraryagents.com/blog—or on Twitter (@chucksambuchino) and continue to pass along feedback and success stories. Until we next meet, good luck on your writing journey. (And don't forget to access your free webinar download at www.writersmarket.com/gla15-webinar.)

Chuck Sambuchino
Editor, *Guide to Literary Agents / Children's Writer's & Illustrator's Market*
Author, *How to Survive a Garden Gnome Attack* (2010); *Create Your Writer Platform* (2012)

PHOTO: Al Parrish

HOW TO USE *GUIDE TO LITERARY AGENTS*

Searching for a literary agent can be overwhelming, whether you've just finished your first book or you have several publishing credits on your résumé. More than likely, you're eager to start pursuing agents and anxious to see your name on the spine of a book. But before you go directly to the listings of agencies in this book, take time to familiarize yourself with the way agents work and how you should approach them. By doing so, you will be more prepared for your search, and ultimately save yourself effort and unnecessary grief.

Read the articles

This book begins with feature articles that explain how to prepare for representation, offer strategies for contacting agents, and provide perspectives on the author/agent relationship. The articles are organized into three sections appropriate for each stage of the search process: **Getting Started** and **Contacting Agents**. You may want to start by reading through each article, and then refer back to relevant articles during each stage of your search.

Because there are many ways to make that initial contact with an agent, we've also provided a section called **Perspectives**. These personal accounts from agents and published authors offer information and inspiration for any writer hoping to find representation.

Decide what you're looking for

A literary agent will present your work directly to editors or producers. It's the agent's job to get her client's work published or sold, and to negotiate a fair contract. In the **Literary Agents** section, we list each agent's contact information and explain what type of work the agency represents as well as how to submit your work for consideration.

FREQUENTLY ASKED QUESTIONS

1. **WHY DO YOU INCLUDE AGENTS WHO ARE NOT SEEKING NEW CLIENTS?** Some agents ask that their listings indicate they are currently closed to new clients. We include them so writers know the agents exist and know not to contact them at this time.
2. **WHY DO YOU EXCLUDE FEE-CHARGING AGENTS?** We have received a number of complaints in the past regarding fees, and therefore have chosen to list only those agents who do not charge reading fees.
3. **WHY ARE SOME AGENTS NOT LISTED?** Some agents may not have responded to our requests for information. We have taken others out of the book after receiving serious complaints about them.
4. **DO I NEED MORE THAN ONE AGENT IF I WRITE IN DIFFERENT GENRES?** It depends. If you have written in one genre and want to switch to a new style of writing, ask your agent if she is willing to represent you in your new endeavor. Most agents will continue to represent clients no matter what genre they choose to write. Occasionally, an agent may feel she has no knowledge of a certain genre and will recommend an appropriate agent to her client. Regardless, you should always talk to your agent about any potential career move.
5. **WHY DON'T YOU LIST MORE FOREIGN AGENTS?** Most American agents have relationships with foreign co-agents in other countries. It is more common for an American agent to work with a co-agent to sell a client's book abroad than for a writer to work directly with a foreign agent. We do list agents in the United Kingdom, Australia, Canada and other countries who sell to publishers both internationally and in the United States. If you decide to query a foreign agent, make sure they represent American writers (if you're American). Some may request to only receive submissions from Canadians, for example, or UK residents.
6. **DO AGENTS EVER CONTACT A SELF-PUBLISHED WRITER?** If a self-published author attracts the attention of the media or if his book sells extremely well, an agent might approach the author in hopes of representing him.
7. **WHY WON'T THE AGENT I QUERIED RETURN MY MATERIAL?** An agent may not answer your query or return your manuscript for several reasons. Perhaps you did not include a self-addressed, stamped envelope (SASE). Many agents will discard a submission without a SASE. Or, the agent may have moved. To avoid using expired addresses, use the most current edition of *Guide to Literary Agents* or access the information online at WritersMarket.com. Another possibility is that the

agent is swamped with submissions. An agent can be overwhelmed with queries, especially if the agent recently has spoken at a conference or has been featured in an article or book. Also, some agents specify in their listings that they never return materials of any kind.

For face-to-face contact, many writers prefer to meet agents at **Conferences**. By doing so, writers can assess an agent's personality, attend workshops and have the chance to get more feedback on their work than they get by mailing submissions and waiting for a response. The conferences section lists conferences agents and/or editors attend. In many cases, private consultations are available, and agents attend with the hope of finding new clients to represent.

Utilize the extras

Aside from the articles and listings, this book offers a section of **Resources**. If you come across a term with which you aren't familiar, check out the Resources section for a quick explanation. Also, note the gray tabs along the edge of each page. The tabs block off each section so they are easier to flip to as you conduct your search.

Finally—and perhaps most importantly—are the **Indexes** in the back of the book. These can serve as an incredibly helpful way to start your search because they categorize the listings according to different criteria. For example, you can look for literary agents according to their specialties (fiction/nonfiction genres).

LISTING POLICY AND COMPLAINT PROCEDURE

Listings in *Guide to Literary Agents* are compiled from detailed questionnaires, phone interviews and information provided by agents. The industry is volatile, and agencies change frequently. We rely on our readers for information on their dealings with agents, as well as changes in policies or fees that differ from what has been reported to the editor of this book. Write to us (Guide to Literary Agents, F+W Media, 10151 Carver Road, Suite 200, Cincinnati, OH 45242) or e-mail us (literaryagent@fwmedia.com) if you have new information, questions or problems dealing with the agencies listed.

Listings are published free of charge and are not advertisements. Although the information is as accurate as possible, the listings are not endorsed or guaranteed by the editor or publisher of *Guide to Literary Agents*. If you feel you have not been treated fairly by an agent or representative listed in *Guide to Literary Agents*, we advise you to take the following steps:

- First try to contact the agency. Sometimes one letter or e-mail can clear up the matter. Politely relate your concern.
- Document all your correspondence with the agency. When you write to us with a complaint, provide the name of your manuscript, the date of your first contact with the agency and the nature of your subsequent correspondence.
- We will keep your letter on file and attempt to contact the agency. The number, frequency and severity of complaints will be considered when we decide whether or not to delete an agency's listing from the next edition.
- *Guide to Literary Agents* reserves the right to exclude any agency for any reason.

WHAT AN AGENT DOES

The scoop on day-to-day agent responsibilities.

A writer's job is to write. A literary agent's job is to find publishers for her clients' books. Because publishing houses receive more and more unsolicited manuscripts each year, securing an agent is becoming increasingly necessary. But finding an eager and reputable agent can be a difficult task. Even the most patient writer can become frustrated or disillusioned. As a writer seeking agent representation, you should prepare yourself before starting your search. Learn when to approach agents, as well as what to expect from an author/agent relationship. Beyond selling manuscripts, an agent must keep track of the ever-changing industry, writers' royalty statements, fluctuating market trends—and the list goes on.

So, once again, you face the question: Do I need an agent? The answer, much more often than not, is yes.

WHAT CAN AN AGENT DO FOR YOU?

For starters, today's competitive marketplace can be difficult to break into, especially for unpublished writers. Many larger publishing houses will only look at manuscripts from agents—and rightfully so, as they would be inundated with unsatisfactory writing if they did not. In fact, approximately 80 percent of books published by the six major houses are acquired through agents.

But an agent's job isn't just getting your book through a publisher's door. The following describes the various jobs agents do for their clients, many of which would be difficult for a writer to do without outside help.

AGENTS KNOW EDITORS' TASTES AND NEEDS

An agent possesses information on a complex web of publishing houses and a multitude of editors to ensure her clients' manuscripts are placed in the right hands. This knowledge is gathered through relationships she cultivates with acquisitions editors—the people who decide which books to present to their publisher for possible publication. Through her industry connections, an agent becomes aware of the specializations of publishing houses and their imprints, knowing that one publisher wants only contemporary romances while another is interested solely in nonfiction books about the military. By networking with editors, an agent also learns more specialized information—which editor is looking for a crafty Agatha Christie–style mystery for the fall catalog, for example.

AGENTS TRACK CHANGES IN PUBLISHING

Being attentive to constant market changes and shifting trends is another major requirement of an agent. An agent understands what it may mean for clients when publisher A merges with publisher B and when an editor from house C moves to house D. Or what it means when readers—and therefore editors—are no longer interested in Westerns, but can't get their hands on enough thriller and suspense novels.

AGENTS GET YOUR WORK READ FASTER

Although it may seem like an extra step to send your work to an agent instead of directly to a publishing house, the truth is an agent can prevent you from wasting months sending manuscripts that end up in the wrong place or buried in someone's slush pile. Editors rely on agents to save them time, as well. With little time to sift through the hundreds of unsolicited submissions arriving weekly in the mail, an editor is naturally going to prefer a work that has already been approved by a qualified reader (i.e., the agent) who knows the editor's preferences. For this reason, many of the larger publishers accept agented submissions only.

AGENTS UNDERSTAND CONTRACTS

When publishers write contracts, they are primarily interested in their own bottom line rather than the best interests of the author. Writers unfamiliar with contractual language may find themselves bound to a publisher with whom they no longer want to work. Or, they may find themselves tied to a publisher that prevents them from getting royalties on their first book until subsequent books are written. Agents use their experiences and knowledge to negotiate a contract that benefits the writer while still respecting the publisher's needs. After all, more money for the author will almost always mean more money for the agent—another reason they're on your side.

BEFORE YOU SUBMIT YOUR FICTION BOOK:

1. Finish your novel manuscript or short-story collection. An agent can do nothing for fiction without a finished product. Never query with an incomplete novel.
2. Revise your manuscript. Seek critiques from other writers or an independent editor to ensure your work is as polished as possible.
3. Proofread. Don't ruin a potential relationship with an agent by submitting work that contains typos or poor grammar.
4. Publish short stories or novel excerpts in literary journals, which will prove to prospective agents that editors see quality in your writing.
5. Research to find the agents of writers whose works you admire or are similar to yours.
6. Use the Internet and resources like *Guide to Literary Agents* to construct a list of agents who are open to new writers and looking for your category of fiction. (Jump to the listings sections of this book to start now.)
7. Rank your list according to the agents most suitable for you and your work.
8. Write your novel synopsis.
9. Write your query letter. As an agent's first impression of you, this brief letter should be polished and to the point.
10. Educate yourself about the business of agents so you will be prepared to act on any offer. This guide is a great place to start.

AGENTS NEGOTIATE—AND EXPLOIT—SUBSIDIARY RIGHTS

Beyond publication, a savvy agent keeps in mind other opportunities for your manuscript. If your agent believes your book also will be successful as an audio book, a Book-of-the-Month-Club selection or even a blockbuster movie, she will take these options into consideration when shopping your manuscript. These additional opportunities for writers are called subsidiary rights. Part of an agent's job is to keep track of the strengths and weaknesses of different publishers' subsidiary rights offices to determine the deposition of these rights regarding your work. After contracts are negotiated, agents will seek additional moneymaking opportunities for the rights they kept for their clients.

AGENTS GET ESCALATORS

An escalator is a bonus an agent can negotiate as part of the book contract. It is commonly given when a book appears on a bestseller list or if a client appears on a popular television show. For example, a publisher might give a writer a $30,000 bonus if he is picked for a book club. Both the agent and the editor know such media attention will sell more books, and the agent negotiates an escalator to ensure the writer benefits from this increase in sales.

AGENTS TRACK PAYMENTS

Because an agent receives payment only when the publisher pays the writer, it's in the agent's best interest to make sure the writer is paid on schedule. Some publishing houses are notorious for late payments. Having an agent distances you from any conflict regarding payment and allows you to spend time writing instead of making phone calls.

AGENTS ARE ADVOCATES

Besides standing up for your right to be paid on time, agents can ensure your book gets a better cover design, more attention from the publisher's marketing department or other benefits you may not know to ask for during the publishing process. An agent also can provide advice during each step of the way, as well as guidance about your long-term writing career.

ARE YOU READY FOR AN AGENT?

Now that you know what an agent is capable of, ask yourself if you and your work are at a stage where you need an agent. Look at the to-do lists for fiction and nonfiction writers in this article, and judge how prepared you are for contacting an agent. Have you spent enough time researching or polishing your manuscript? Does your nonfiction book proposal include everything it should? Is your novel completely finished? Sending an agent an incomplete project not only wastes your time, but also may turn off the agent in the process. Is the work thoroughly revised? If you've finished your project, set it aside for a few weeks, then examine it again with fresh eyes. Give your novel or proposal to critique group partners ("beta readers") for feedback. Join up with writing peers in your community or online.

Moreover, your work may not be appropriate for an agent. Most agents do not represent poetry, magazine articles, short stories or material suitable for academic or small presses; the agent's commission does not justify spending time submitting these types of works. Those agents who do take on such material generally represent authors on larger projects first, and then adopt the smaller items as a favor to the client.

If you believe your work is ready to be placed with an agent, make sure you're personally ready to be represented. In other words, consider the direction in which your writing career is headed. Besides skillful writers, agencies want clients with the ability to produce more than one book. Most agents say they're looking to represent careers, not books.

WHEN DON'T YOU NEED AN AGENT?

Although there are many reasons to work with an agent, some authors can benefit from submitting their own work directly to book publishers. For example, if your project focuses on a very specific area, you may want to work with a small or specialized press. These houses usually are open to receiving material directly from writers. Small presses often can give more attention to writers than large houses can, providing editorial help, marketing expertise and other advice. Academic books or specialized nonfiction books (such as a book about the history of Rhode Island) are good bets for unagented writers.

Beware, though, as you will now be responsible for reviewing and negotiating all parts of your contract and payment. If you choose this path, it's wise to use a lawyer or entertainment attorney to review all contracts. Lawyers who specialize in intellectual property can help writers with contract negotiations. Instead of earning a commission on resulting book sales, lawyers are paid for their time only.

And, of course, some people prefer working independently instead of relying on others. If you're one of these people, it's probably better to submit your own work instead of constantly butting heads with an agent. Let's say you manage to sign with one of the few literary agents who represent short-story collections. If the collection gets shopped around to publishers for several months and no one bites, your agent may suggest retooling the work into a novel or novella(s). Agents suggest changes—some bigger than others—and not all writers think their work is malleable. It's all a matter of what you're writing and how you feel about it.

BEFORE YOU SUBMIT YOUR NONFICTION BOOK:

1. Formulate a concrete idea for your book. Sketch a brief outline, making sure you'll have enough material for a book-length manuscript.
2. Research works on similar topics to understand the competition and determine how your book is unique.
3. Write sample chapters. This will help you estimate how much time you'll need to complete the work, and determine whether or not your writing will need editorial help. You will also need to include 1–4 sample chapters in the proposal itself.
4. Publish completed chapters in journals and/or magazines. This validates your work to agents and provides writing samples for later in the process.
5. Polish your nonfiction book proposal so you can refer to it while drafting a query letter—and you'll be prepared when agents contact you.
6. Brainstorm three to four subject categories that best describe your material.
7. Use the Internet and resources like *Guide to Literary Agents* to construct a list of agents who are open to new writers and looking for your category of nonfiction.
8. Rank your list. Research agent websites and narrow your list further, according to your preferences.
9. Write your query. Give an agent an excellent first impression by professionally and succinctly describing your premise and your experience.
10. Educate yourself about the business of agents so you can act on any offer.

ASSESSING CREDIBILITY

Check out agents before you query.

Many people wouldn't buy a used car without at least checking the odometer, and savvy shoppers would consult the blue books, take a test drive and even ask for a mechanic's opinion. Much like the savvy car shopper, you want to obtain the best possible agent for your writing, so you should do some research on the business of agents before sending out query letters. Understanding how agents operate will help you find an agent appropriate for your work, as well as alert you about the types of agents to avoid.

Many writers take for granted that any agent who expresses interest in their work is trustworthy. They'll sign a contract before asking any questions and simply hope everything will turn out all right. We often receive complaints from writers regarding agents *after* they have lost money or have work bound by contract to an ineffective agent. If writers put the same amount of effort into researching agents as they did writing their manuscripts, they would save themselves unnecessary grief.

The best way to educate yourself is to read all you can about agents and other authors. Organizations such as the Association of Authors' Representatives (AAR; aar-online.org), the National Writers Union (NWU; nwu.org), American Society of Journalists and Authors (ASJA; asja.org) and Poets & Writers, Inc. (pw.org), all have informational material on finding and working with an agent.

Publishers Weekly (publishersweekly.com) covers publishing news affecting agents and others in the publishing industry. The Publishers Lunch newsletter (publishersmarketplace.com) comes free via e-mail every workday and offers news on agents and editors, job postings, recent book sales and more.

Even the Internet has a wide range of sites where you can learn basic information about preparing for your initial contact, as well as specific details on individual agents. You can also find online forums and listservs, which keep authors connected and allow them to share experiences they've had with different editors and agents. Keep in mind, however, that not everything printed on the Web is solid fact; you may come across the site of a writer who is bitter because an agent rejected his manuscript. Your best bet is to use the Internet to supplement your other research.

Once you've established what your resources are, it's time to see which agents meet your criteria. Below are some of the key items to pay attention to when researching agents.

LEVEL OF EXPERIENCE

Through your research, you will discover the need to be wary of some agents. Anybody can go to the neighborhood copy center and order business cards that say "literary agent," but that title doesn't mean she can sell your book. She may lack the proper connections with others in the publishing industry, and an agent's reputation with editors can be a major strength or weakness.

Agents who have been in the business awhile have a large number of contacts and carry the most clout with editors. They know the ins and outs of the industry and are often able to take more calculated risks. However, veteran agents can be too busy to take on new clients or might not have the time to help develop an author. Newer agents, on the other hand, may be hungrier, as well as more open to unpublished writers. They probably have a smaller client list and are able to invest the extra effort to make your book a success.

If it's a new agent without a track record, be aware that you're taking more of a risk signing with her than with a more established agent. However, even a new agent should not be new to publishing. Many agents were editors before they were agents, or they worked at an agency as an assistant. This experience is crucial for making contacts in the publishing industry, and learning about rights and contracts. The majority of listings in this book explain how long the agent has been in business, as well as what she did before becoming an agent. You could also ask the agent to name a few editors off the top of her head who she thinks may be interested in your work and why they sprang to mind. Has she sold to them before? Do they publish books in your genre?

If an agent has no contacts in the business, she has no more clout than you do. Without publishing prowess, she's just an expensive mailing service. Anyone can make photocopies, slide them into an envelope and address them to "Editor." Unfortunately, without a contact name and a familiar return address on the envelope, or a phone call from a trusted colleague letting an editor know a wonderful submission is on its way, your work will land in the slush pile with all the other submissions that don't have representation. You can do your own mailings with higher priority than such an agent could.

PAST SALES

Agents should be willing to discuss their recent sales with you: how many, what type of books and to what publishers. Keep in mind, though, that some agents consider this information confidential. If an agent does give you a list of recent sales, you can call the publishers' contracts department to ensure the sale was actually made by that agent. While it's true that even top agents are not able to sell every book they represent, an inexperienced agent who proposes too many inappropriate submissions will quickly lose her standing with editors.

You can also find out details of recent sales on your own. Nearly all of the listings in this book offer the titles and authors of books with which the agent has worked. Some of them also note to which publishing house the book was sold. Again, you can call the publisher and affirm the sale. If you don't have the publisher's information, simply go to your local library or bookstore to see if they carry the book. Consider checking to see if it's available on websites like Amazon.com, too. You may want to be wary of the agent if her books are nowhere to be found or are only available through the publisher's website. Distribution is a crucial component to getting published, and you want to make sure the agent has worked with competent publishers.

TYPES OF FEES

Becoming knowledgeable about the different types of fees agents may charge is vital to conducting effective research. Most agents make their living from the commissions they receive after selling their clients' books, and these are the agents we've listed. Be sure to ask about any expenses you don't understand so you have a clear grasp of what you're paying for. Described below are some types of fees you may encounter in your research.

Office fees

Occasionally, an agent will charge for the cost of photocopies, postage and long-distance phone calls made on your behalf. This is acceptable, so long as she keeps an itemized account of the expenses and you've agreed on a ceiling cost. The agent should only ask for office expenses after agreeing to represent the writer. These expenses should be discussed up front, and the writer should receive a statement accounting for them. This money is sometimes returned to the author upon sale of the manuscript. Be wary if there is an upfront fee amounting to hundreds of dollars, which is excessive.

Reading fees

Agencies that charge reading fees often do so to cover the cost of additional readers or the time spent reading that could have been spent selling. Agents also claim that charging reading fees cuts down on the number of submissions they receive. This practice can save the agent time and may allow her to consider each manuscript more extensively. Whether such promises are kept depends upon the honesty of the agency. You may pay a fee and never receive a response from the agent, or you may pay someone who never submits your manuscript to publishers.

Officially, the Association of Authors' Representatives' (AAR) Canon of Ethics prohibits members from directly or indirectly charging a reading fee, and the Writers Guild of America (WGA) does not allow WGA signatory agencies to charge a reading fee to WGA members, as stated in the WGA's Artists' Manager Basic Agreement. A signatory may charge you a fee if you are not a member, but most signatory agencies do not charge a reading fee as an across-the-board policy.

WARNING SIGNS! BEWARE OF . . .

- Excessive typos or poor grammar in an agent's correspondence.
- A form letter accepting you as a client and praising generic things about your book that could apply to any book. A good agent doesn't take on a new client very often, so when she does, it's a special occasion that warrants a personal note or phone call.
- Unprofessional contracts that ask you for money up front, contain clauses you haven't discussed or are covered with amateur clip-art or silly borders.
- Rudeness when you inquire about any points you're unsure of. Don't employ any business partner who doesn't treat you with respect.
- Pressure, by way of threats, bullying or bribes. A good agent is not desperate to represent more clients. She invites worthy authors but leaves the final decision up to them.
- Promises of publication. No agent can guarantee you a sale. Not even the top agents sell everything they choose to represent. They can only send your work to the most appropriate places, have it read with priority and negotiate you a better contract if a sale does happen.
- A print-on-demand book contract or any contract offering you no advance. You can sell your own book to an e-publisher any time you wish without an agent's help. An agent should pursue traditional publishing routes with respectable advances.
- Reading fees from $25–$500 or more. The fee is usually nonrefundable, but sometimes agents agree to refund the money if they take on a writer as a client, or if they sell the writer's manuscript. Keep in mind, however, that payment of a reading fee does not ensure representation.
- No literary agents who charge reading fees are listed in this book. It's too risky of an option for writers, plus non-fee-charging agents have a stronger incentive to sell your work. After all, they don't make a dime until they make a sale. If you find that a literary agent listed in this book charges a reading fee, please contact the editor at literaryagent@fwmedia.com.

Critique fees

Sometimes a manuscript will interest an agent, but the agent will point out areas requiring further development and offer to critique it for an additional fee. Like reading fees, payment of a critique fee does not ensure representation. When deciding if you will benefit from having someone critique your manuscript, keep in mind that the quality and quantity of comments varies from agent to agent. The critique's usefulness will depend on the agent's knowledge of the market. Also be aware that agents who spend a significant portion of their time commenting on manuscripts will have less time to actively market work they already represent.

In other cases, the agent may suggest an editor who understands your subject matter or genre, and has some experience getting manuscripts into shape. Occasionally, if your story is exceptional, or your ideas and credentials are marketable but your writing needs help, you will work with a ghostwriter or co-author who will share a percentage of your commission, or work with you at an agreed-upon cost per hour.

An agent may refer you to editors she knows, or you may choose an editor in your area. Many editors do freelance work and would be happy to help you with your writing project. Of course, before entering into an agreement, make sure you know what you'll be getting for your money. Ask the editor for writing samples, references or critiques he's done in the past. Make sure you feel comfortable working with him before you give him your business.

An honest agent will not make any money for referring you to an editor. We strongly advise writers not to use critiquing services offered through an agency. Instead, try hiring a freelance editor or joining a writer's group until your work is ready to be submitted to agents who don't charge fees.

PERSPECTIVES

HOW NOT TO START YOUR BOOK

Agents dish about all those things they hate to see in Chapter 1.

by Chuck Sambuchino

Ask literary agents what they're looking for in a first chapter and they'll all say the same thing: "Good writing that hooks me in." Agents appreciate the same elements of good writing that readers do. They want action; they want compelling characters and a reason to read on; they want to see your voice come through in the work and feel an immediate connection with your writing style.

Sure, the fact that agents look for great writing and a unique voice is nothing new. But, for as much as you know about what agents *want* to see in chapter one, what about all those things they *don't* want to see? Obvious mistakes such as grammatical errors and awkward writing aside, writers need to be conscious of first-chapter clichés and agent pet peeves—any of which can sink a manuscript and send a form rejection letter your way.

Have you ever begun a story with a character waking up from a dream? Or opened chapter one with a line of salacious dialogue? Both clichés! Chances are, you've started a story with a cliché or touched on a pet peeve (or many!) in your writing and you don't even know it—and nothing turns off an agent like what agent Cricket Freeman of the August Agency calls "nerve-gangling, major turn-off, ugly-as-sin, nails-on-the-blackboard pet peeves."

To help compile a grand list of these poisonous chapter one no-no's, plenty of established literary agents were more than happy to chime in and vent about everything that they can't stand to see in that all-important first chapter. Here's what they had to say.

DESCRIPTION

"I dislike endless 'laundry list' character descriptions. For example: 'She had eyes the color of a summer sky and long blonde hair that fell in ringlets past her shoulders. Her petite nose was the perfect size for her heart-shaped face. Her azure dress—with the empire waist and long, tight sleeves—sported tiny pearl buttons down the bodice and ivory lace peeked out of the hem in front, blah, blah, blah.' Who cares! Work it into the story."

—LAURIE MCLEAN, *Foreword Literary*

"Slow writing with a lot of description will put me off very quickly. I personally like a first chapter that moves quickly and draws me in so I'm immediately hooked and want to read more."

—ANDREA HURST, *Andrea Hurst & Associates Literary Management*

VOICE AND POINT-OF-VIEW

"A pet peeve of mine is ragged, fuzzy point-of-view. How can a reader follow what's happening? I also dislike beginning with a killer's POV. What reader would want to be in such an ugly place? I feel like a nasty voyeur."

—CRICKET FREEMAN, *The August Agency*

"An opening that's predictable will not hook me in. If the average person could have come up with the characters and situations, I'll pass. I'm looking for a unique outlook, voice, or character and situation."

—DEBBIE CARTER, *formerly of Muse Literary Management*

"Avoid the opening line 'My name is . . .,' introducing the narrator to the reader so blatantly. There are far better ways in chapter one to establish an instant connection between narrator and reader."

—MICHELLE ANDELMAN, *Regal Literary*

"I hate reading purple prose, taking the time to set up—to describe something so beautifully and that has nothing to do with the actual story. I also hate when an author starts something and then says '(the main character) would find out later.' I hate gratuitous sex and violence anywhere in the manuscript. If it is not crucial to the story then I don't want to see it in there, in any chapters."

—CHERRY WEINER, *Cherry Weiner Literary*

"I recently read a manuscript when the second line was something like, 'Let me tell you this, Dear Reader ...' What do *you* think of that?"

—SHEREE BYKOFSKY, *Sheree Bykofsky Literary*

ACTION (OR LACK THEREOF)

"I don't really like first-day-of-school beginnings, or the 'From the beginning of time,' or 'Once upon a time' starts. Specifically, I dislike a chapter one where nothing happens."

—JESSICA REGEL, *Foundry Literary + Media*

" 'The Weather' is always a problem—the author feels he has to take time to set up the scene completely and tell us who the characters are. I like starting a story *in media res*."

—ELIZABETH POMADA, *Larsen/Pomada, Literary Agents*

"I want to feel as if I'm in the hands of a master storyteller, and starting a story with long, flowery, overly descriptive sentences (kind of like this one) makes the writer seem amateurish and the story contrived. Of course, an equally jarring beginning can be nearly as off-putting, and I hesitate to read on if I'm feeling disoriented by the fifth page. I enjoy when writers can find a good balance between exposition and mystery. Too much accounting always ruins the mystery of a novel, and the unknown is what propels us to read further. It is what keeps me up at night saying, 'Just one more chapter, then I'll go to sleep.' If everything is explained away in the first chapter, I'm probably putting the book down and going to sleep."

—**Peter Miller**, *Global Lion Management*

"Characters that are moving around doing little things, but essentially nothing. Washing dishes and thinking, staring out the window and thinking, tying shoes, thinking. Authors often do this to transmit information, but the result is action in a literal sense but no real energy in a narrative sense. The best rule of thumb is always to start the story where the story starts."

—**Dan Lazar**, *Writers House*

CLICHÉS AND FALSE BEGINNINGS

"I *hate* it when a book begins with an adventure that turns out to be a dream at the end of the chapter."

—**Mollie Glick**, *Foundry Literary + Media*

"Anything cliché such as 'It was a dark and stormy night' will turn me off. I hate when a narrator or author addresses the reader (e.g., 'Gentle reader')."

—**Jennie Dunham**, *Dunham Literary*

"Sometimes a reasonably good writer will create an interesting character and describe him in a compelling way, but then he'll turn out to be some unimportant bit player. I also don't want to read about anyone sleeping, dreaming, waking up or staring at anything. Other annoying, unoriginal things I see too often: some young person going home to a small town for a funeral, someone getting a phone call about a death, a description of a psycho lurking in the shadows or a terrorist planting a bomb."

—**Ellen Pepus**, *Signature Literary Agency*

"I don't like it when the main character dies at the end of chapter one. Why did I just spend all this time with this character? I feel cheated."

—**Cricket Freeman**, *The August Agency*

"1. Squinting into the sunlight with a hangover in a crime novel. Good grief—been done a million times. 2. A sci-fi novel that spends the first two pages describing the strange landscape. 3. A trite statement ('Get with the program' or 'Houston, we have a problem' or 'You go girl' or 'Earth to Michael' or 'Are we all on the same page?'), said by a weenie sales guy, usually in the opening paragraph. 4. A rape scene in a Christian novel, especially in the first chapter. 5. 'Years later, Monica would look back and laugh ...' 6. 'The [adjective] [adjective] sun rose in the [adjective] [adjective] sky, shedding its [adjective] light across the [adjective] [adjective] [adjective] land.' "

—CHIP MACGREGOR, *MacGregor Literary*

"A cheesy 'hook' drives me nuts. I know that they say 'Open with a hook!'—something to grab the reader. While that's true, there's a fine line between a hook that's intriguing and a hook that's just silly. An example of a silly hook would be opening with a line of overtly sexual dialogue. Or opening with a hook that's just too convoluted to be truly interesting."

—DAN LAZAR, *Writers House*

"Here are things I can't stand: Cliché openings in fantasy novels can include an opening scene set in a battle (and my peeve is that I don't know any of the characters yet so why should I care about this battle) or with a pastoral scene where the protagonist is gathering herbs (I didn't realize how common this is). Opening chapters where a main protagonist is in the middle of a bodily function (jerking off, vomiting, peeing or what have you) is usually a firm *no* right from the get-go. Gross. Long prologues that often don't have anything to do with the story. (So common in fantasy, again.) Opening scenes that are all dialogue without any context. I could probably go on ..."

—KRISTIN NELSON, *Nelson Literary*

CHARACTERS AND BACKSTORY

"I don't like descriptions of the characters where writers make the characters seem too perfect. Heroines (and heroes) who are described physically as being unflawed come across as unrelatable and boring. No 'flowing, windswept golden locks'; no 'eyes as blue as the sky'; no 'willowy, perfect figures.' "

—LAURA BRADFORD, *Bradford Literary Agency*

"Many writers express the character's backstory before they get to the plot. Good writers will go back and cut that stuff out and get right to the plot. The character's backstory stays with them—it's in their DNA—even after the cut. To paraphrase Bruno Bettelheim: The more the character in a fairy tale is described, the less the audience will identify with him ... The less the character is characterized and described, the more likely the reader is to identify with him."

—ADAM CHROMY, *Movable Type Management*

"I'm really turned off when a writer feels the need to fill in all the backstory before starting the story; a story that opens on the protagonist's mental reflection of their situation is (usually) a red flag."

—STEPHANY EVANS, *FinePrint Literary Management*

"One of the biggest problems I encounter is the 'information dump' in the first few pages, where the author is trying to tell us everything we supposedly need to know to understand the story. Getting to know characters in a story is like getting to know people in real life. You find out their personality and details of their life over time."

—**Rachelle Gardner**, *Books & Such Literary*

OTHER PET PEEVES

"The most common opening is a grisly murder scene told from the killer's point of view. While this usually holds the reader's attention, the narrative drive often doesn't last once we get into the meat of the story. A catchy opening scene is great, but all too often it falls apart after the initial pages. I often refer people to the opening of *Rosemary's Baby* by Ira Levin, which is about nothing more than a young couple getting an apartment. It is masterfully written and yet it doesn't appear to be about anything sinister at all. And it keeps you reading."

—**Irene Goodman**, *Irene Goodman Literary*

"Things I dislike include: 1) Telling me what the weather's like in order to set atmosphere. OK, it was raining. It's *always* raining. 2) Not starting with action. I want to have a sense of dread quite quickly—and not from rain! 3) Sending me anything but the beginning of the book; if you tell me that it 'starts getting good' on page 35, then I will tell you to start the book on page 35, because if even you don't like the first 34, neither will I or any other reader."

—**Josh Getzler**, *Hannigan Salky Getzler Agency.*

"One of my biggest pet peeves is when writers try to stuff too much exposition into dialogue rather than trusting their abilities as storytellers to get information across. I'm talking stuff like the mom saying, 'Listen, Jimmy, I know you've missed your father ever since he died in that mysterious boating accident last year on the lake, but I'm telling you, you'll love this summer camp!' "

—**Chris Richman**, *Upstart Crow Literary*

"I hate to see a whiny character who's in the middle of a fight with one of their parents, slamming doors, rolling eyes, and displaying all sorts of other stereotypical behavior. I also tend to have a hard time bonding with characters who address the reader directly."

—**Kelly Sonnack**, *Andrea Brown Literary*

CHUCK SAMBUCHINO (chucksambuchino.com, @chucksambuchino) edits the *Guide to Literary Agents* (guidetoliteraryagents.com/blog) as well as the *Children's Writer's & Illustrator's Market*. Chuck's other writing books include *Formatting & Submitting Your Manuscript, 3rd. Ed.*, and *Create Your Writer Platform* (fall 2012). Besides that, he is a husband, guitarist, sleep-deprived new father, dog owner, and cookie addict.

RESEARCHING AGENTS

Get personal and establish a connection.

by C. Hope Clark

I clicked from website to website, one blog to another, all telling me my chances of finding an agent were slim in the current publishing environment. Statistics spouted success rates of one half of one percent. One agent read 8,000 queries in a year and only signed five new clients. Some agents even posted the number of queries they received each week versus the number of manuscripts requested. All too often the percentage equaled zero. Hellbent on beating the odds, I devised a plan to find my agent.

Throughout the course of 20 months, I submitted 72 queries, opened 55 rejections and received invitations for seven complete manuscripts. I landed an 88 percent response rate, and finally, a contract with an agent. How did I do it? I got personal.

WHERE TO FIND AGENTS

Many writers cringe at the thought of researching the publishing business. You must be better than that. Embrace the research, especially if it leads to representation. The more you analyze the rules, the players, the successes and failures, the more you increase your chances of signing a contract with a representative. Set aside time (i.e., days, weeks) to educate yourself about these professionals. You have your manuscript, your synopsis, a list of published books like yours and a biography. You've edited and re-edited your query so it's tight as a drum. Now focus. Whom do you see as your handler, your mentor, your guide through the publishing maze? And where do you find him or her?

Agency websites

Most literary houses maintain a website. They post guidelines and books they've pushed into the marketplace. They also inform you about the individual agents on staff—including bios, favorite reads, writing styles they prefer, photos and maybe where they attended school. Read all the website has to offer, taking notes. If any agent represents your type of work, record what they prefer in a query and move on to their blog, if they keep one.

Blogs

Agent blogs reveal clues about what agents prefer. While websites are static in design, blogs allow comments. Here agents offer information about publishing changes, new releases—even their vacations and luncheons with movers and shakers in the industry. Some agents solicit feedback with dynamic dilemmas or ethical obstacles. Kristin Nelson of Nelson Literary, Mary Kole of Movable Type Literary, and Rachelle Gardner of Books & Such Literary have been known to post short contests for their blog readers, if for no other reason than to emphasize what they seek in a client. For a complete list of agent blogs, go to the GLA Blog (guidetoliteraryagents.com/blog) and see them on the right.

Guidebooks and databases

The *Guide to Literary Agents* is a premier example of a guidebook resource. Use it to cull the agents who seek writers just like you. PublishersMarketplace.com and WritersMarket.com offer online, fingertip access to the websites, addresses and desires of most agents—and also point you in other directions to learn more.

Facebook and Twitter

Social networking has enabled writers to see yet another side of agents. These mini-versions of agents' lives can spark ideas for you to use in a query as well as help you digest the publishing world through professional eyes.

Conferences

Margot Starbuck, author of *The Girl in the Orange Dress* and *Unsqueezed: Springing Free from Skinny Jeans*, met her agent at a writers conference. "He had given a seminar that was essentially themed, 'My Perfect Client,' describing the type of writer he'd want to represent. When I got home, I crafted my letter to his own specs!"

It's easier to query an agent you've met, whom you've heard, who has articulated what he likes. That subtle Midwestern accent you would not have heard otherwise might trigger you to pitch about your travel book or romance set in Nebraska. A one-hour class might empower you to query a particular agent after hearing her pet peeves and desires.

Online interviews

Google an agent's name and the word "interview." Authors, writers' organizations, magazines and commercial writing sites post such interviews to attract readers. A current Q&A

might prompt you to reword that query opening and pique an agent's interest. The agent might express a wish to read less women's fiction and more young adult novels these days—information not spelled out on her website profile. She might reveal a weakness for Southern writing. Reps also hop from agency to agency, and a timely interview might let you know she's changed location.

THE PLAN

Not wanting to collaborate with a complete stranger, I began dissecting agents' information to get a better feel for them. After noting 1) name, 2) agency, 3) query preferences, and 4) an address for each potential agent on a spreadsheet column, I dug down more for what I deemed the "zing" factor—the human factor. As a previous human resource director, I knew the power of connection. An applicant attending the same university as the manager often warranted a second glance. A first-time interviewee who played golf might reap a return invitation. Why couldn't this concept apply to literary agents? I was a job seeker; they were hiring. How could I make them take a second look at me and the fabulous writing I offered?

I reread bios and Googled deeper; I studied interviews and deciphered blogs. I read between the lines, earnestly seeking what made these people more than agents. Just like I canvassed the doctors and hairdressers in my life, I investigated these people for characteristics that bridged their preferences with mine.

Zing factors

The human connection between you and an agent is what I call the "zing" factor. These agents receive hundreds of queries per week, most skimmed or unread. You never know when an agent has been up all night with a sick child or arrived at work fighting the flu. You have no control over the timing that places your query in an agent's hands. What you can control is a creative opening that doesn't echo like the 30 before it and the 20 after, and rises to the top even if the reader hasn't had his coffee.

Agents hate to be taken for granted or treated like an anonymous personality (i.e., "Dear Agent"). The attention you give to zing factors will demonstrate that you respect the agent as a person. Suddenly you have that magical connection that holds his attention at least long enough to read your dead-on synopsis.

What makes for a great conduit between you and your agent? Anything and everything.

CLIENTELE—Signing good authors and landing great contracts make an agent proud. If you intend to become part of an agency's stable of authors, become familiar with who occupies the neighboring stalls. Recognize agents for what they have accomplished.

Author Tanya Egan Gibson not only emphasized her knowledge of Susan Golomb's clients, but she contacted one of the authors and asked permission to use him as a reference after meeting at a conference. The query won her representation and, later, a contract with Dutton Publishers.

Christine Chitnis introduced herself to other authors at a retreat where they shared critiques and ideas. Once she completed her manuscript, she pitched to the agents of those authors, knowing they could vouch for the quality of her work. She acquired an agent after two attempts.

PREVIOUS MEETINGS—A dinner table discussion with an agent at a conference could provide the lead for your next query. Make a point to meet and greet agents at these functions. They expect it. Give and take in the conversations. Don't smother them with your views. Listen for advice. Be polite. Afterward, before the experience evaporates, record notes about the topics discussed, the locale, maybe even the jokes or awkward speaker. The zing factor becomes instant recall when you remind an agent you met over dinner, during a fast-pitch or over drinks. You evolve into a person instead of another faceless query.

RECOGNITION—In your query, include where you found the agent's name. Congratulate him or her on recent contracts for books that sound similar to yours. You'll find this information through a website called Publishers Marketplace, or on the agency's website, blog, tweets or Facebook page.

FAVORITE READS—Agents are voracious readers, and, like any word geeks, they have favorite genres, authors and styles. Website bios often mention what sits on their nightstand, and blogs might post writers they admire. Note where you uncovered this information and marvel at your similarities.

GEOGRAPHY—All agents aren't born and reared in New York. With the ease of communication these days, agents live everywhere and telecommute. They also come from other places, and those roots might mirror yours. A New York agent who grew up in Georgia might have a soft spot for Civil War nonfiction.

PERSONAL INTERESTS—Agents have lives and off-duty pastimes. When author Nina Amir first contacted her agent, she also noted a mutual love of horses—in particular, a desire to save ex-racehorses from slaughter. The agent immediately called her.

In pitching to literary agent Verna Dreisbach, I revealed a common interest in mentoring teenage writers, knowing Verna founded Capitol City Young Writers, a nonprofit for youth interested in writing and publishing. Because my proposal was a mystery and I married a federal agent, I also admired her past work in law enforcement. Later, when asked if those initial items caught her attention, Verna responded in the positive. "Of course it made an impact. Writing with a degree of expertise in any field is crucial, including law enforcement. I looked forward to reading your work. I choose to represent authors that

I have a connection with, and your interests and aspirations certainly fit well with mine. As I expected, we hit it off immediately."

PASSION

Nothing, however, replaces the ability to show passion in your work. Genuine excitement over your book is contagious, and agents spot it in an instant. Carole Bartholomeaux unknowingly personalized her query through her passion. Her agent, an expectant father at the time, was touched by her story about a small town putting their lives on the line to save a group of Jewish children during World War II. You are the biggest advocate for your book, with your agent a close second. Everyone in your path should feel that energy. When agents sense it, they jump on your bandwagon knowing that readers will do the same.

When asked which grabbed her attention more, the personalization or the writing, Dreisbach replied diplomatically yet succinctly: "Both are equally important—authors who are personal and professional. Just as in any business, it is important to stand out from the crowd. I do not mean by being bizarre or unusual, but through the expression of a writer's passion, honesty and talent."

Don't cheapen yourself, though. Nathan Bransford, former agent and current award-winning blogger, gives his opinion about personalizing a query: "The goal of personalization isn't to suck up to the agent and score cheap points. As much as some people think we agents just want people to suck up to us, it's really not true. There is an art to personalization. Dedication and diligence are important, so if you query me, I hope you'll do your homework, and sure, if you've read books by my clients, mention that. Just don't try and trick me."

So be genuine. Be your passionate self and the person who obviously has done the research. A relationship with an agent is to be entered seriously and practically, with both parties sharing excitement for a common goal.

C. HOPE CLARK is the founder of FundsforWriters.com, chosen by *Writer's Digest* for its 101 Best Websites for Writers for the past 10 years. Her newsletters reach 40,000 readers weekly. She's published in numerous online and print publications, including *Writer's Digest, The Writer Magazine* and many Chicken Soups. She is the author of the Carolina Slade suspense series from Bell Bridge Books. Hope speaks at several writers conferences each year, and you can find her at hopeclark.blogspot.com, twitter.com/hopeclark, and facebook.com/chopeclark. She writes from the banks of Lake Murray, S.C.

PHOTO: Gary W. Clark

CRAFTING A QUERY

How to write a great letter that gets agents' attention.

by Kara Gebhart Uhl

So you've written a book. And now you want an agent. If you're new to publishing, you probably assume that the next step is to send your finished, fabulous book out to agents, right? Wrong. Agents don't want your finished, fabulous book. In fact, they probably don't even want *part* of your finished, fabulous book—at least, not yet. First, they want your query.

A query is a short, professional way of introducing yourself to an agent. If you're frustrated by the idea of this step, imagine yourself at a cocktail party. Upon meeting someone new, you don't greet them with a boisterous hug and kiss and, in three minutes, reveal your entire life story including the fact that you were late to the party because of some gastrointestinal problems. Rather, you extend your hand. You state your name. You comment on the hors d'oeuvres, the weather, the lovely shade of someone's dress. Perhaps, after this introduction, the person you're talking to politely excuses himself. Or, perhaps, you become best of friends. It's basic etiquette, formality, professionalism—it's simply how it's done.

Agents receive hundreds of submissions every month. Often they read these submissions on their own time—evenings, weekends, on their lunch break. Given the number of writers submitting, and the number of agents reading, it would simply be impossible for agents to ask for and read entire book manuscripts off the bat. Instead, a query is a quick way for you to, first and foremost, pitch your book. But it's also a way to pitch yourself. If an agent is intrigued by your query, she may ask for a partial (say, the first three chapters of your manuscript). Or she may ask for the entire thing.

As troublesome as it may first seem, try not to be frustrated by this process. Because, honestly, a query is a really great way to help speed up what is already a monumentally slow-paced industry. Have you ever seen pictures of slush piles—those piles of unread queries on many well-known agents' desks? Imagine the size of those slush piles if they held full manuscripts instead of one-page query letters. Thinking of it this way, query letters begin to make more sense.

Here we share with you the basics of a query, including its three parts and a detailed list of dos and don'ts.

PART I: THE INTRODUCTION

Whether you're submitting a 100-word picture book or a 90,000-word novel, you must be able to sum up the most basic aspects of it in one sentence. Agents are busy. And they constantly receive submissions for types of work they don't represent. So upfront they need to know that, after reading your first paragraph, the rest of your query is going to be worth their time.

An opening sentence designed to "hook" an agent is fine—if it's good and if it works. But this is the time to tune your right brain down and your left brain up—agents desire professionalism and queries that are short and to-the-point. Remember the cocktail party and always err on the side of formality. Tell the agent, in as few words as possible, what you've written, including the title, genre and length.

In the intro, you also must try to connect with the agent. Simply sending 100 identical query letters out to "Dear Agent" won't get you published. Instead, your letter should be addressed not only to a specific agency but a specific agent within that agency. (And double, triple, quadruple check that the agent's name is spelled correctly.) In addition, you need to let the agent know why you chose her specifically. A good author-agent relationship is like a good marriage. It's important that both sides invest the time to find a good fit that meets their needs. So how do you connect with an agent you don't know personally? Research.

1. Make a connection based on an author or book the agent already represents.

Most agencies have websites that list who and what they represent. Research those sites. Find a book similar to yours and explain that, because such-and-such book has a similar theme or tone or whatever, you think your book would be a great fit. In addition, many agents will list specific genres/categories they're looking for, either on their websites or in interviews. If your book is a match, state that.

2. Make a connection based on an interview you read.

Search agents' names online and read any and all interviews they've participated in. Perhaps they mentioned a love for X and your book is all about X. Perhaps they mentioned that they're looking for Y and your book is all about Y. Mention the specific interview. Prove that you've invested as much time researching them as they're about to spend researching you.

3. Make a connection based on a conference you both attended.

Was the agent you're querying the keynote speaker at a writing conference you were recently at? If so, mention it, and comment on an aspect of his speech you liked. Even better, did you meet the agent in person? Mention it, and if there's something you can say to jog her memory about the meeting, say it. Better yet, did the agent specifically ask you to send your manuscript? Mention it.

Finally, if you're being referred to a particular agent by an author that agent already represents—that's your opening sentence. That referral is guaranteed to get your query placed at the top of the stack.

PART II: THE PITCH

Here's where you really get to sell your book—but in only three to 10 sentences. Consider a book's jacket flap and its role in convincing readers to plunk down $24.95 to buy what's in between those flaps. Like a jacket flap, you need to hook an agent in the confines of very limited space. What makes your story interesting and unique? Is your story about a woman going through a mid-life crisis? Fine, but there are hundreds of stories about women going through mid-life crises. Is your story about a woman who, because of a mid-life crisis, leaves her life and family behind to spend three months in India? Again, fine, but this story, too, already exists—in many forms. Is your story about a woman who, because of a mid-life crisis, leaves her life and family behind to spend three months in India, falls in love with someone new while there and starts a new life—and family? And then has to deal with everything she left behind upon her return? *Now* you have a hook.

Practice your pitch. Read it out loud, not only to family and friends, but to people willing to give you honest, intelligent criticism. If you belong to a writing group, workshop your pitch. Share it with members of an online writing forum. Know anyone in the publishing industry? Share it with them. Many writers spend years writing their books. We're not talking about querying magazines here; we're talking about querying an agent who could become a lifelong partner. Spend time on your pitch. Perfect it. Turn it into jacket-flap material so detailed, exciting and clear that it would be near impossible to read your pitch and not want to read more. Use active verbs. Write your pitch, put it aside for a week, then look at it again. Don't send a query simply because you finished a book. Send a query because you finished your pitch and are ready to take the next steps.

PART III: THE BIO

If you write fiction, unless you're a household name or you've recently been a guest on some very big TV or radio shows, an agent is much more interested in your pitch than in who you are. If you write nonfiction, who you are—more specifically, your platform and publicity—is much more important. Regardless, these are key elements that must be present in every bio:

1. Publishing credits

If you're submitting fiction, focus on your fiction credits—previously published works and short stories. That said, if you're submitting fiction and all your previously published work is nonfiction—magazine articles, essays, etc.—that's still fine and good to mention. Don't be overly long about it. Mention your publications in bigger magazines or well-known literary journals. If you've never had anything published, don't say you lack official credits. Simply skip this altogether and thank the agent for his time.

2. Contests and awards

If you've won many, focus on the most impressive ones and those that most directly relate to your work. Don't mention contests you entered and weren't named in. Also, feel free to leave titles and years out of it. If you took first place at the Delaware Writers Conference for your fiction manuscript, that's good enough. Mentioning details isn't necessary.

3. MFAs

If you've earned or are working toward a Master of Fine Arts in writing, say so and state the program. Don't mention English degrees or online writing courses.

4. Large, recognized writing organizations

Agents don't want to hear about your book club and the fact that there's always great food, or the small critique group you meet with once a week. And they really don't want to hear about the online writing forum you belong to. But if you're a member of something like the Romance Writers of America (RWA), the Mystery Writers of America (MWA), the Society of Children's Book Writers and Illustrators (SCBWI), the Society of Professional Journalists (SPJ), the American Medical Writers, etc., say so. This shows you're serious about what you do and you're involved in groups that can aid with publicity and networking.

5. Platform and publicity

If you write nonfiction, who you are and how you're going to help sell the book once it's published becomes very important. Why are you the best person to write it and what do you have now—public speaking engagements, an active website or blog, substantial cred in your industry—that will help you sell this book?

Finally, be cordial. Thank the agent for taking the time to read your query and consider your manuscript. Ask if you may send more, in the format she desires (partial, full, etc.).

Think of the time you spent writing your book. Unfortunately, you can't send your book to an agent for a first impression. Your query *is* that first impression. Give it the time it deserves. Keep it professional. Keep it formal. Let it be a firm handshake—not a sloppy kiss. Let it be a first meeting that evolves into a lifelong relationship—not a rejection slip. But expect those slips. Just like you don't become best friends with everyone you meet at a cocktail party, you can't expect every agent you pitch to sign you. Be patient. Keep pitching. And in the meantime, start writing that next book.

DOS AND DON'TS FOR QUERYING AGENTS

DO:

- Keep the tone professional.
- Query a specific agent at a specific agency.
- Proofread. Double-check the spelling of the agency and the agent's name.
- Keep the query concise, limiting the overall length to one page (single space, 12-point type in a commonly used font).
- Focus on the plot, not your bio, when pitching fiction.
- Pitch agents who represent the type of material you write.
- Check an agency's submission guidelines to see how to query—for example, via e-mail or mail—and whether or not to include a SASE.
- Keep pitching, despite rejections.

DON'T:

- Include personal info not directly related to the book. For example, stating that you're a parent to three children doesn't make you more qualified than someone else to write a children's book.
- Say how long it took you to write your manuscript. Some bestselling books took 10 years to write—others, six weeks. An agent doesn't care how long it took—an agent only cares if it's good. Same thing goes with drafts—an agent doesn't care how many drafts it took you to reach the final product.
- Mention that this is your first novel or, worse, the first thing you've ever written aside from grocery lists. If you have no other publishing credits, don't advertise that fact. Don't mention it at all.
- State that your book has been edited by peers or professionals. Agents expect manuscripts to be edited, no matter how the editing was done.
- Bring up screenplays or film adaptations—you're querying an agent about publishing a book, not making a movie.
- Mention any previous rejections.
- State that the story is copyrighted with the U.S. Copyright Office or that you own all rights. Of course you own all rights. You wrote it.
- Rave about how much your family and friends loved it. What matters is that the agent loves it.
- Send flowers or anything else except a self-addressed stamped envelope (and only if the SASE is required), if sending through snail mail.
- Follow up with a phone call. After the appropriate time has passed (many agencies say how long it will take to receive a response), follow up in the manner you queried—via e-mail or mail.

KARA GEBHART UHL, formerly a managing editor at *Writer's Digest* magazine, now freelance writers and edits in Fort Thomas, KY. She also blogs about parenting at pleiadesbee.com. Her essays have appeared on The Huffington Post, *The New York Times*' Motherlode and *TIME: Healthland*. Her parenting essay, "Apologies to the Parents I Judged Four Years Ago" was named one of *TIME*'s "Top 10 Opinions of 2012."

PHOTO: Andy Uhl

1 SAMPLE QUERY 1: LITERARY FICTION

Agent's Comments: Jeff Kleinman (Folio Literary)

From: Garth Stein
To: Jeff Kleinman
Subject: Query: "The Art of Racing in the Rain" (1)

Dear Mr. Kleinman:

(2) Saturday night I was participating in a fundraiser for the King County Library System out here in the Pacific Northwest, and I met your client Layne Maheu. He spoke very highly of you and suggested that I contact you.

(3) I am a Seattle writer with two published novels. I have recently completed my third novel, *The Art of Racing in the Rain*, and I find myself in a difficult situation: My new book is narrated by a dog, and my current agent (4) told me that he cannot (or will not) sell it for that very reason. Thus, I am seeking new representation.

(5) *The Art of Racing in the Rain* is the story of Denny Swift, a race car driver who faces profound obstacles in his life, and ultimately overcomes them by applying the same techniques that have made him successful on the track. His story is narrated by his "philosopher dog," Enzo, who, having a nearly human soul (and an obsession with opposable thumbs), believes he will return as a man in his next lifetime.

(6) My last novel, *How Evan Broke His Head and Other Secrets*, won a 2006 Pacific Northwest Booksellers Association Book Award, and since the award ceremony a year ago, I have given many readings, workshops and lectures promoting the book. When time has permitted, I've read the first chapter from *The Art of Racing in the Rain*. Audience members have been universally enthusiastic and vocal in their response, and the first question asked is always: "When can I buy the book about the dog?" Also very positive.

(7) I'm inserting, below, a short synopsis of *The Art of Racing in the Rain*, and my biography. Please let me know if the novel interests you; I would be happy to send you the manuscript.

Sincerely,
Garth Stein

(1) Putting the word "Query" and the title of the book on the subject line of an e-mail often keeps your e-mail from falling into the spam folder. (2) One of the best ways of starting out correspondence is figuring out your connection to the agent. (3) The author has some kind of track record. Who's the publisher, though? Were these both self-published novels, or were there reputable publishers involved? (I'll read on, and hope I find out.) (4) This seems promising, but also know this kind of approach can backfire, because we agents tend to be like sheep—what one doesn't like, the rest of us are wary of, too (or, conversely, what one likes, we all like). But in this case getting in the "two published novels" early is definitely helpful. (5) The third paragraph is the key pitch paragraph and Garth gives a great description of the book—he sums it up, gives us a feel for what we're going to get. This is the most important part of your letter. (6) Obviously it's nice to see the author's winning awards. Also good: The author's not afraid of promoting the book. (7) The end is simple and easy—it doesn't speak of desperation, or doubt, or anything other than polite willingness to help.

2 SAMPLE QUERY 2: YOUNG ADULT

Agent's Comments: Ted Malawer (Upstart Crow Literary)

Dear Mr. Malawer:

I would like you to represent my 65,000-word contemporary teen novel *My Big Nose & Other Natural Disasters.*

1 Seventeen-year-old Jory Michaels wakes up on the first day of summer vacation with her same old big nose, no passion in her life (in the creative sense of the word), and all signs still pointing to her dying a virgin. Plus, her mother is busy roasting a chicken for Day #6 of the Dinner For Breakfast Diet.

2 In spite of her driving record (it was an accident!), Jory gets a job delivering flowers and cakes to Reno's casinos and wedding chapels. She also comes up with a new summer goal: saving for a life-altering nose job. She and her new nose will attract a fabulous boyfriend. Nothing like the shameless flirt Tyler Briggs, or Tom who's always nice but never calls. Maybe she'll find someone kind of like Gideon at the Jewel Café, except better looking and not quite so different. Jory survives various summer disasters like doing yoga after sampling Mom's Cabbage Soup Diet, Enforced Mother Bonding With Crazy Nose Obsessed Daughter Night, and discovering Tyler's big secret. But will she learn to accept herself and maybe even find her passion, in the creative (AND romantic!) sense of the word?

3 I have written for *APPLESEEDS, Confetti, Hopscotch, Story Friends, Wee Ones Magazine,* the *Deseret News, Children's Playmate* and Blooming Tree Press' *Summer Shorts* anthology. I won the Utah Arts Council prize for *Not-A-Dr. Logan's Divorce Book.* My novels *Jungle Crossing* and *Going Native!* each won first prize in the League of Utah Writers contest. I currently serve as an SCBWI Regional Advisor.

4 I submitted *My Big Nose & Other Natural Disasters* to Krista Marino at Delacorte because she requested it during our critique at the summer SCBWI conference (no response yet).

Thank you for your time and attention. I look forward to hearing from you.

Sincerely,
Sydney Salter Husseman

1 With hundreds and hundreds of queries each month, it's tough to stand out. Sydney, however, did just that. First, she has a great title that totally made me laugh. Second, she sets up her main character's dilemma in a succinct and interesting way. In one simple paragraph, I have a great idea of who Jory is and what her life is about—the interesting tidbits about her mother help show the novel's sense of humor, too. 2 Sydney's largest paragraph sets up the plot and the conflict, and introduces some exciting potential love interests and misadventures that I was excited to read about. Again, Sydney really shows off her fantastic sense of humor, and she leaves me hanging with a question that I needed an answer to. 3 She has writing experience and has completed other manuscripts that were prize-worthy. Her SCBWI involvement—while not a necessity—shows me that she has an understanding of and an interest in the children's publishing world. 4 The fact that an editor requested the manuscript is always a good sign. That I knew Krista personally and highly valued her opinion was, as Sydney's main character Jory would say, "The icing on the cake."

3 SAMPLE QUERY 3: NONFICTION (SELF-HELP)

Agent's Comments: Michelle Wolfson (Wolfson Literary)

Dear Ms. Wolfson:

(1) Have you ever wanted to know the best day of the week to buy groceries or go out to dinner? Have you ever wondered about the best time of day to send an e-mail or ask for a raise? What about the best time of day to schedule a surgery or a haircut? What's the best day of the week to avoid lines at the Louvre? What's the best day of the month to make an offer on a house? What's the best time of day to ask someone out on a date? (2)

My book, *Buy Ketchup in May and Fly at Noon: A Guide to the Best Time to Buy This, Do That, and Go There*, has the answers to these questions and hundreds more.

(3) As a long-time print journalist, I've been privy to readership surveys that show people can't get enough of newspaper and magazine stories about the best time to buy or do things. This book puts several hundreds of questions and answers in one place—a succinct, large-print reference book that readers will feel like they need to own. Why? Because it will save them time and money, and it will give them valuable information about issues related to health, education, travel, the workplace and more. In short, it will make them smarter, so they can make better decisions. (4)

Best of all, the information in this book is relevant to anyone, whether they live in Virginia or the Virgin Islands, Portland, Oregon, or Portland, Maine. In fact, much of the book will find an audience in Europe and Australia.

(5) I've worked as a journalist since 1984. In 1999, the Virginia Press Association created an award for the best news writing portfolio in the state—the closest thing Virginia had to a reporter-of-the-year award. I won it that year and then again in 2000. During the summer of 2007, I left newspapering to pursue book projects and long-form journalism.

(6) I saw your name on a list of top literary agents for self-help books, and I read on your website that you're interested in books that offer practical advice. *Buy Ketchup in May and Fly at Noon* offers plenty of that. Please let me know if you'd like to read my proposal.

Sincerely,
Mark Di Vincenzo

(1) I tend to prefer it when authors jump right into the heart of their book, the exception being if we've met at a conference or have some other personal connection. Mark chose clever questions for the opening of the query. All of those questions are, in fact, relevant to my life—with groceries, dinner, e-mail and a raise—and yet I don't have a definitive answer to them. (2) He gets a little more offbeat and unusual with questions regarding surgery, the Louvre, buying a house and dating. This shows a quirkier side to the book and also the range of topics it is going to cover, so I know right away there is going to be a mix of useful and quirky information on a broad range of topics. (3) By starting with "As a long-time print journalist," Mark immediately establishes his credibility for writing on this topic. (4) This helps show that there is a market for this book, and establishes the need for such a book. (5) Mark's bio paragraph offers a lot of good information. (6) It's nice when I feel like an author has sought me out specifically and thinks we would be a good fit.

4 SAMPLE QUERY 4: WOMEN'S FICTION

Agent's Comments: Elisabeth Weed (Weed Literary)

Dear Ms. Weed:

1 Natalie Miller had a plan. She had a goddamn plan. Top of her class at Dartmouth. Even better at Yale Law. Youngest aide ever to the powerful Senator Claire Dupris. Higher, faster, stronger. This? Was all part of the plan. True, she was so busy ascending the political ladder that she rarely had time to sniff around her mediocre relationship with Ned, who fit the three Bs to the max: basic, blond and boring, and she definitely didn't have time to mourn her mangled relationship with Jake, her budding rock star ex-boyfriend.

The lump in her right breast that Ned discovers during brain-numbingly bland morning sex? That? Was most definitely not part of the plan. And Stage IIIA breast cancer? Never once had Natalie jotted this down on her to-do list for conquering the world. When her (tiny-penised) boyfriend has the audacity to dump her on the day after her diagnosis, Natalie's entire world dissolves into a tornado of upheaval, and she's left with nothing but her diary to her ex-boyfriends, her mornings lingering over "The Price is Right," her burnt-out stubs of pot that carry her past the chemo pain, and finally, the weight of her life choices—the ones in which she might drown if she doesn't find a buoy.

2 *The Department of Lost and Found* is a story of hope, of resolve, of digging deeper than you thought possible until you find the strength not to crumble, and ultimately, of making your own luck, even when you've been dealt an unsteady hand.

3 I'm a freelance writer and have contributed to, among others, *American Baby, American Way, Arthritis Today, Bride's, Cooking Light, Fitness, Glamour, InStyle Weddings, Men's Edge, Men's Fitness, Men's Health, Parenting, Parents, Prevention, Redbook, Self, Shape, Sly, Stuff, USA Weekend, Weight Watchers, Woman's Day, Women's Health*, and ivillage.com, msn.com and women.com. I also ghostwrote *The Knot Book of Wedding Flowers*.

If you are interested, I'd love to send you the completed manuscript. Thanks so much! Looking forward to speaking with you soon.

Allison Winn Scotch

1 The opening sentence reads like great jacket copy, and I immediately know who our protagonist is and what the conflict for her will be. (And it's funny, without being silly.) 2 The third paragraph tells me where this book will land: upmarket women's fiction. (A great place to be these days!) 3 This paragraph highlights impressive credentials. While being able to write nonfiction does not necessarily translate over to fiction, it shows me that she is someone worth paying more attention to. And her magazine contacts will help when it comes time to promote the book.

5 SAMPLE QUERY 5: MAINSTREAM/COMEDIC FICTION

Agent's Comments: Michelle Brower (Folio Literary)

Dear Michelle Brower:

1 "I spent two days in a cage at the SPCA until my parents finally came to pick me up. The stigma of bringing your undead son home to live with you can wreak havoc on your social status, so I can't exactly blame my parents for not rushing out to claim me. But one more day and I would have been donated to a research facility."

Andy Warner is a zombie.

After reanimating from a car accident that killed his wife, Andy is resented by his parents, abandoned by his friends, and vilified by society. Seeking comfort and camaraderie in Undead Anonymous, a support group for zombies, Andy finds kindred souls in Rita, a recent suicide who has a taste for consuming formaldehyde in cosmetic products, and Jerry, a 21-year-old car crash victim with an artistic flair for Renaissance pornography.

2 With the help of his new friends and a rogue zombie named Ray, Andy embarks on a journey of personal freedom and self-discovery that will take him from his own casket to the SPCA to a media-driven, class-action lawsuit for the civil rights of all zombies. And along the way, he'll even devour a few Breathers.

Breathers is a contemporary dark comedy about life, or undeath, through the eyes of an ordinary zombie. In addition to *Breathers*, I've written three other novels and more than four dozen short stories—a dozen of which have appeared in small press publications. Currently, I'm working on my fifth novel, also a dark comedy, about fate.

Enclosed is a two-page synopsis and the first chapter of *Breathers*, with additional sample chapters or the entire manuscript available upon request. I appreciate your time and interest in considering my query and I look forward to your response.

Sincerely,
Scott G. Browne

1 What really draws me to this query is the fact that it has exactly what I'm looking for in my commercial fiction—story and style. Scott includes a brief quote from the book that manages to capture his sense of humor as an author and his uniquely relatable main character (hard to do with someone who's recently reanimated). I think this is a great example of how query letters can break the rules and still stand out in the slush pile. I normally don't like quotes as the first line, because I don't have a context for them, but this quote both sets up the main concept of the book *and* gives me a sense of the character's voice. This method won't necessarily work for most fiction, but it absolutely is successful here. 2 The letter quickly conveys that this is an unusual book about zombies, and being a fan of zombie literature, I'm aware that it seems to be taking things in a new direction. I also appreciate how Scott conveys the main conflict of his plot and his supporting cast of characters—we know there is an issue for Andy beyond coming back to life as a zombie, and that provides momentum for the story.

QUERY LETTER FAQS

Here are answers to 19 of the most tricky and confusing query questions around.

by Chuck Sambuchino

Readers and aspiring writers often find querying literary agents to be intimidating and terrifying. Here are some important questions and answers to consider as you craft your query letter.

When contacting agents, the query process isn't as simple as, "Just keep e-mailing until something good happens." There are ins, outs, strange situations, unclear scenarios, and plenty of what-have-you's that block the road to signing with a rep. In short, there are plenty of murky waters out there in the realm of submissions. Luckily, writers have plenty of questions to ask. Here are some of the most interesting (and important) questions and answers regarding protocol during the query process.

When should you query? When is your project ready?

There is no definitive answer, but here's what I suggest. Get other eyes on the material—"beta readers"—people who can give you feedback that is both honest and helpful. These beta readers (usually members of a critique group) will give you feedback. You do not want major concerns, such as, "It starts too slow" or "This character is not likeable." Address these problems through revisions. After rewriting, give it to more beta readers. If they come back with no major concerns, the book is ready, or at least very close.

How should you start your query? Should you begin with a paragraph from the book?

I would not include a paragraph from the book nor would I write the letter in the "voice" of one your characters—those are gimmicks. If you choose, you can just jump right into the pitch—there's nothing wrong with that. But what I recommend is laying out the details of your book in one easy sentence: "I have a completed 78,000-word thriller titled *Dead Cat Bounce*." I suggest this because jumping into a pitch can be jarring and confusing. Think about it. If you started reading an e-mail and the first sentence was simply "Billy has a problem," you don't know if Billy is an adult or a child, or if he is being held captive by terrorists versus being nervous because his turtle is missing. In other words, the agent doesn't know whether to laugh or be worried. He's confused. And when an agent gets confused, he may just stop reading.

Can you query multiple agents at the same agency?

Generally, no. A rejection from one literary agent usually means a rejection from the entire agency. If you query one agent and she thinks the work isn't right for her but still has promise, she will pass it on to fellow agents in the office who can review it themselves.

Should you mention that the query is a simultaneous submission?

You can, but you don't have to. If you say it's exclusive, they understand no other eyes are on the material. If you say nothing, they will assume multiple agents must be considering it. However, some agents will specifically request in their guidelines to be informed if it's a simultaneous submission.

Even if an agent doesn't request it, should you include a few sample pages with your query letter?

This is up to you. When including sample pages, though, remember to paste the pages below the query letter. Do not attach them in a document. Also, do not include much—perhaps 1–5 pages. Most people asking this question probably have more faith in their opening pages than in their query. That's understandable, but keep in mind that while including sample pages may help with an occasional agent who checks out your writing, it doesn't solve the major problem of your query being substandard. Keep working on the query until you have faith in it, regardless of whether you sneak in unsolicited pages or not.

Can your query be more than one page long?

The rise of e-queries removed the dreaded page break, so now it's easy to have your query go over one page. This does not necessarily mean it's a wise move. Going a few sentences over one page is likely harmless, but you don't need a query that trends long. Lengthy letters are a sign of a rambling pitch, which will probably get you rejected. Edit and trim your pitch down as need be. Find beta readers or a freelance query editor to give you ideas and notes. Remember that a succinct letter is preferred, and oftentimes more effective. An exception to this, however, is querying for nonfiction books. Nonfiction queries have to be heavy on author platform, and those notes (with proper names of publications and organizations and websites, etc.) can get long. Feel free to go several sentences over one page if you have to list out platform and marketing notes, as long as the pitch itself is not the item making your letter too long.

How do you follow up with an agent who hasn't responded to your submission?

This is a complicated question, and I'll try to address its many parts.

First, check the agency website for updates and their latest formal guidelines. They might have gone on leave, or they might have switched agencies. They may also have submission guidelines that state how they only respond to submissions if interested. So keep in mind there might be a very good reason as to why you shouldn't follow up or rather why you shouldn't follow up right now.

However, let's say an agent responds to submissions "within three months" and it's been three and a half months with no reply. A few weeks have passed since the "deadline," so now it's time to nicely follow up. All you do is paste your original query into a new e-mail and send it to the agent with a note above the query that says, "Dear [agent], I sent my query below to you [length of time] ago and haven't heard anything. I'm afraid my original note got lost in a spam filter, so I am pasting it below in the hopes that you are still reviewing queries and open to new clients. Thank you for considering my submission. Sincerely, [name]." That's it. Be polite and simply resubmit. If an agent makes it sound like he does indeed respond to submissions but doesn't have a time frame for his reply, I say follow up after three months.

But before you send that follow up, make sure you are not to blame for getting no reply. Perhaps your previous e-mail had an attachment when the agent warned, "No attachments." Perhaps your previous e-mail did not put "Query" in the subject line even though the agent requested just that. Or perhaps your previous e-mail misspelled the agent's e-mail address and the query truly got lost in cyberspace. In other words, double-check everything. If you send that follow up and the agent still doesn't reply, it's probably time to move on.

Can you re-query an agent after she rejects you?

You can, though I'd say you have about a 50/50 shot of getting your work read. Some agents seem to be more than open to reviewing a query letter if it's undergone serious editing. Other agents, meanwhile, believe that a no is a no—period. In other words, you really don't know, so you might as well just query away and hope for the best.

How many query rejections would necessitate a major overhaul of the query?

Submit no more than 10 queries to start. If only 0–1 respond with requests for more, then you've got a problem. Go back to the drawing board and overhaul the query before the next wave of 6–10 submissions. Doing this ensures that you can try to identify where you're going wrong in your submission.

Should you mention that you've self-published books in the past?

In my opinion, you don't have to. If you self-published a few e-books that went nowhere, you don't have to list every one and their disappointing sales numbers. The release of those books should not affect your new novel that you're submitting to agents. However, if your self-published projects experienced healthy sales (3,000-plus print books, 10,000-plus e-books), mention it. Only talk about your self-published projects if they will help your case. Otherwise, just leave them out of the conversation and focus on the new project at hand.

Should you mention your age in a query? Do agents have a bias against older writers and teenagers?

I'm not sure any good can come from mentioning your age in a query. Usually the people who ask this question are either younger than 20 or older than 70. Some literary agents may be hesitant to sign older writers because reps are looking for career clients, not simply individuals with one memoir/book to sell. If you're older, write multiple books to convince an agent that you have several projects in you, and do not mention your age in the query to be safe.

Should you mention in the query that your work is copyrighted and/or has had book editing?

No. All work is copyrighted the moment you write it down in any medium, so saying something that is obvious only comes off as amateurish. On the same note, all work should be edited, so saying that the work is edited (even by a professional editor) also comes off as amateurish.

Is it better to send a query over snail mail or e-mail?

If you have a choice, do not send a snail mail query. They're more of a hassle to physically produce, and they cost money to send. Ninety percent (or more) of queries are sent over e-mail for two very good reasons. E-mail is quicker, in terms of sending submissions and agents' response time, and it's free. Keep in mind that almost all agents have personal, detailed submission guidelines in which they say exactly what they want to receive in a submission and how they want to receive it. So you will almost always not have a choice in how to send materials. Send the agent what they asked for, exactly how they asked for it.

What happens when you're writing a book that doesn't easily fall into one specific genre? How do you handle that problem in a query letter?

Know that you have to bite the bullet and call it *something*. Even if you end up calling it a "middle grade adventure with supernatural elements," then you're at least calling it something. Writers really get into a pickle when they start their pitches with an intro such as, "It's a sci-fi western humorous fantastical suspense romance, set in steampunk Britain ... with erotic werewolf transvestite protagonists." Fundamentally, it must be something, so pick its core genre and just call it that—otherwise your query might not even get read. I'm not a huge fan of writers comparing their work to other projects (saying, "It's X meets Z"—that type of thing), but said strategy—comparing your book to others in the marketplace—is most useful for those authors who have a hard time describing the plot and tone of their tale.

If you're writing a memoir, do you pitch it like a fiction book (complete the whole manuscript) or like a nonfiction book (a complete book proposal with a few sample chapters)?

I'd say 80 percent of agents review memoir like they would a novel. If interested, they ask for the full book and consider it mostly by how well it's written. I have met several agents, however, who want to see a nonfiction book proposal—either with some sample chapters, or sometimes in addition to the whole book. So to answer the question, you can choose to write only the manuscript, and go from there. Or you can choose to complete a proposal, as well, so you have as many weapons as possible as you move forward. (In my opinion, a writer who has both a complete memoir manuscript and nonfiction book proposal seems like a professional who is ahead of the curve and wise to platform matters—and, naturally, people in publishing are often attracted to writers who are ahead of the curve and/or can help sell more books.)

If you're pitching a novel, should the topics of marketing and writer platform be addressed in the query?

Concerning query letters for novels, the pitch is what's paramount, and any mention of marketing or platform is just gravy. If you have some promotional credentials, these skills will definitely be beneficial in selling more books when your title is released. But a decent platform will not get a mediocre novel published. Feel free to list worthwhile, impressive notes about your platform and marketing skills, but don't let them cloud your writing. Remember, the three most crucial elements to a novel selling are *the writing, the writing, the writing.*

Do you need to query conservative agents for a conservative book? A liberal agent for a liberal book?

I asked a few agents this question and some said they were willing to take on any political slant if the book was well written and the author had a great writer platform. A few agents, on the other hand, said they needed to be on the same page politically with the author for a political/religious book, and would only take on books they agreed with. Bottom line: Some will be open-minded; some won't. Look for reps who have taken on books similar to yours, and feel free to query other agents, too. The worst any agent can say is no.

If you're writing a series, does an agent want you to say that in the query?

The old mentality for this was no, you should not discuss a series in the query, and instead just pitch one book and let any discussion naturally progress to the topic of more books, if the agent so inquires. However, I've overheard more and more literary agents say that they do want to know if your book is the potential start of the series. So, the correct answer, it appears, depends on who you ask. In circumstances like these, I recommend crafting an answer to cover all bases: "This book could either be a standalone project or the start of a series." When worded like this, you disclose the series potential, but don't make it sound like you're saying, "I want a 5-book deal or NOTHING." You'll sound like an easy-to-work-with writing professional and leave all options open.

Can you query an agent for a short story collection?

I'd say 95 percent of agents do not accept short story collection queries. The reason? Collections just don't sell well. If you have a collection of short stories, you can do one of three things:

1) Repurpose some or all of the stories into a novel, which is much easier to sell.

2) Write a new book—a novel—and sell that first to establish a reader base. That way, you can have a base that will purchase your next project—the collection—ensuring the publisher makes money on your short stories.

3) Query the few agents who do take collections and hope for the best. If you choose this third route, I suggest you get some of the stories published to help the project gain some momentum. A platform and/or media contacts would help your case, as well.

CHUCK SAMBUCHINO (chucksambuchino.com, @chucksambuchino) edits the *Guide to Literary Agents* (guidetoliteraryagents.com/blog) as well as the *Children's Writer's & Illustrator's Market*. His pop humor books include *How to Survive a Garden Gnome Attack* (film rights optioned by Sony) and *Red Dog / Blue Dog: When Pooches Get Political* (reddog-bluedog.com). Chuck's other writing books include *Formatting & Submitting Your Manuscript, 3rd. Ed.*, and *Create Your Writer Platform* (fall 2012). Besides that, he is a husband, guitarist, sleep-deprived new father, dog owner, and cookie addict.

HOW TO WRITE A SYNOPSIS

6 tips to compose your novel summary.

by Chuck Sambuchino

I've never met a single person who liked writing a synopsis. Seriously—not one. But still, synopses are a necessary part of the submission process (until some brave publishing pro outlaws them), so I wanted to share tips and guidelines regarding how to compose one.

A synopsis is a *summary* of your book. Literary agents and editors may ask to see one if you're writing an adult novel, a memoir, or a kids novel (young adult, middle grade). The purpose of a synopsis request is for the agent or editor to evaluate what happens in the three acts of your story and decide if the characters, plot and conflict warrant a complete read of your manuscript. And if you haven't guessed yet, these summaries can be pretty tough to write.

SYNOPSIS GUIDELINES

Here are some guidelines that will help you understand the basics of synopsis writing, no matter what your novel or memoir is about:

1. Reveal everything major that happens in your book, including the ending. Heck, revealing the story's ending is a synopsis's defining unique characteristic. You shouldn't find a story's ending in a query or in-person pitch, but it does leak out in a synopsis. On this note, know that a synopsis is designed to explain *everything major* that happens, not to tease—so avoid language such as "Krista walks around a corner into a big surprise." Don't say "surprise," but rather just tell us what happens. This touches upon a bigger point. The No. 1 failure of a synopsis is that it confuses the reader. Have no language in your page that is vague and undefined that could lead to multiple interpretations. One of the fundamental purposes of a synopsis is to show your book's narrative arc, and that the story possesses staple elements, such as rising action, the three-act structure, and a satisfying ending.

2. Make your synopsis one page, single-spaced. There is always some disagreement on length. This stems from the fact that synopses used to trend longer (four, six, or even eight pages!). But over the last five years, agents have requested shorter and shorter synopses—with most agents finally settling on 1-2 pages, total. If you write yours as one page, single-spaced, it's the same length as two pages, double-spaced—and either are acceptable. There will be the occasional agent who requests something strange, such as a "five-page synopsis on beige paper that smells of cinnamon!" But trust me, if you turn in a solid one-page work, you'll be just fine across the board. In my opinion, it's the gold standard.

3. Take more care and time if you're writing genre fiction. Synopses are especially difficult to compose if you're writing character-driven (i.e., literary) fiction, because there may not be a whole lot of plot in the book. Agents and editors understand this, and put little (or no) weight into a synopsis for literary or character-driven stories. However, if you're writing genre fiction—specifically categories like romance, fantasy, thriller, mystery, horror or science fiction—agents will quickly want to look over your characters and plot points to make sure your book has a clear beginning, middle and end, as well as some unique aspects they haven't seen before in a story. So if you're getting ready to submit a genre story, don't blow through your synopsis; it's important.

4. Feel free to be dry, but don't step out of the narrative. When you write your prose (and even the pitch in your query letter), there is importance in using style and voice in the writing. A synopsis, thankfully, not only can be dry, but probably *should* be dry. The synopsis has to explain everything that happens in a very small amount of space. So if you find yourself using short sentences like "John shoots Bill and then sits down to contemplate suicide," don't worry. This is normal. Lean, clean language is great. Use active verbs and always strive for clarity. And lastly, do not step out of the narrative. Agents do not want to read things such as "And at the climax of the story," "In a rousing scene," or "In a flashback."

5. Capitalize character names when characters are introduced. Whenever a new character is introduced, make sure to CAPITALIZE them in the first mention and then use normal text throughout. This helps a literary agent immediately recognize each important name. On this subject, avoid naming too many characters, and try to set a limit of five, with no more than six total. I know this may sound tough, but it's doable. It forces you to excise smaller characters and subplots from your summary—actually strengthening your novel synopsis along the way. Sometimes writers fall in love with a minor character or joke or setting, and insist on squeezing in mentions of these elements into the synopsis, even though they are not a piece of the larger plot. These mistakes will water down your summary, and also cause the synopsis to be more than one page.

6. Use third person, present tense. The exception of this is memoir. While you can write your memoir synopsis in third person, it's probably a better idea to write it in first person. "Feeling stifled: I enlist in the Army that very day."

Every agent has a different opinion of the synopsis. Some agents openly state in interviews that they're well aware of how difficult a synopsis is to write, and they put little consideration into them. But we must presume that most or all of the agents who do not openly speak out against synopses put some weight into them, and that's why it's important for you to treat this step with care.

A poor synopsis will confuse the reader, and during the pitching process, confusion = death. A poor synopsis will also reveal big problems in your story, such as strange plot points, how ridiculous acts of God get the main character out of tight situations, or how your romance actually ends in a divorce (a major category no-no).

CHUCK SAMBUCHINO (chucksambuchino.com, @chucksambuchino on Twitter) edits the *Guide to Literary Agents* (guidetoliteraryagents.com/blog) as well as the *Children's Writer's & Illustrator's Market*. His pop-humor books include *How to Survive a Garden Gnome Attack* (film rights optioned by Sony) and *Red Dog / Blue Dog: When Pooches Get Political* (reddog-bluedog.com). Chuck's other writing books include *Formatting & Submitting Your Manuscript, 3rd. Ed.*, as well as *Create Your Writer Platform* (fall 2012). Besides that, he is a husband, sleep-deprived new father, guitarist, dog owner, and cookie addict.

NONFICTION BOOK PROPOSALS

Pitch your nonfiction with confidence.

by Chuck Sambuchino

A *book proposal* is a business plan that explains all the details of a nonfiction book. Since your project is not complete during the pitching stages, the proposal acts as a blueprint and diagram for what the finished product will look like, as well as exactly how you will promote it when the product is in the marketplace.

Better yet, think about it like this: If you wanted to open a new restaurant and needed a bank loan, you would have to make a case to the bank as to why your business will succeed and generate revenue. A book proposal acts in much the same way. You must prove to a publisher that your book idea is a proven means to generate revenue—showing that customers will buy your worthwhile and unique product, and you have the means to draw in prospective customers.

"There are several factors that can help a book proposal's ultimate prospects: great writing, great platform or great information, and ideally all three," says Ted Weinstein, founder of Ted Weinstein Literary. "For narrative works, the writing should be gorgeous, not just functional. For practical works, the information should be insightful, comprehensive and preferably new. And for any work of nonfiction, of course, the author's platform is enormously important."

If you're writing a work of fiction (novel, screenplay, picture book) or memoir, the first all-important step is to simply *finish* the work, because agents and editors will consider it for publication based primarily on how good the writing is. On the other hand, when you have a nonfiction project of any kind, you do *not* need to finish the book to sell it. In fact, even if you're feeling ambitious and knock out the entire text, finishing the book will not help you sell it because all an editor really needs to see are several sample chapters that adequately portray what the rest of the book will be like.

THE STRUCTURE OF A BOOK PROPOSAL

A book proposal is made up of several key sections that flesh out the book, its markets, and information about the author. All of these important sections seek to answer one of the three main questions that every proposal must answer:

1. What is the book, and why is it timely and unique?
2. What is its place in the market?
3. Why are you the best person to write and market it?

"Concerning how to write a compelling nonfiction book proposal: 1) Spill the beans. Don't try to tantalize and hold back the juice. 2) No BS! We agents learn to see right through BS, or we fail rapidly. 3) Get published small. Local papers, literary journals, websites, anything. The more credits you have, the better. And list them all (although not to the point of absurdity) in your query. Why does everyone want to pole-vault from being an unpublished author to having a big book contract? It makes no sense. You have to learn to drive before they'll let you pilot the Space Shuttle."

- Gary Heidt (Signature Literary)

Every book proposal has several sections that allow the author to explain more about their book. Though you can sometimes vary the order of the sections, here are the major elements (and suggested order) that should be addressed before you pitch a nonfiction book to a literary agent.

TITLE PAGE. Keep it simple. Put your title and subtitle in the middle, centered—and put your personal contact information at the bottom right.

TABLE OF CONTENTS (WITH PAGE NUMBERS). A nonfiction book proposal has several sections, and can run many pages, so this is where you explain everything the agent can find in the proposal, in case they want to jump around immediately to peruse different sections at different times.

OVERVIEW. This section gets its name because it's designed to be an overview of the entire proposal to come. It's something of a "greatest hits" of the proposal, where you discuss the concept and content, the evidence of need for this new resource in the market, and your platform. Overviews typically run 1–3 double-spaced pages, and immediately make the case as to why this book is worthwhile for consideration and timely for readers *now.* Another way to think about this section is by imagining as it as an extended query letter, because it serves the same purpose. If an agent likes your overview, they will review the rest of the document to delve deeper into both you and your ideas. The overview is arguably the most important part of the proposal. "Your overview is the sizzle in your nonfiction book proposal," says agent Michael Larsen of Larsen-Pomada Literary Agents. "If it doesn't sell you and your book, agents and editors won't check the bones (the outline of your book) or try the steak (your sample chapter)."

FORMAT. This section explains how the book will be formatted. Remember that your finished, completed product does not physically exist, and all nonfiction books look different from one another in terms of appearance. So spell out exactly what it will look like. What is the physical size of the book? What is your estimated word count when everything is said and done? How long after the contract is signed will you be able to submit the finished product? Will there be sidebars, boxed quotes, or interactive elements? Will there be photos, illustrations or other art? (If so, who will be responsible for collecting this art?)

SPINOFFS (OPTIONAL). Some nonfiction projects lend themselves to things like sequels, spinoffs, subsidiary rights possibilities, and more. For example, when I pitched my political humor book for dog lovers, *Red Dog / Blue Dog,* this is the section where I mentioned the possibility of a tear-off calendar if the book succeeded, as well as a possible sequel, *Red Cat / Blue Cat.* Unlike other sections of a proposal, this one is optional, as some ideas will *not* lend to more variations.

CHAPTER LIST. While you will only be turning over a few completed, polished chapters, agents still want to know exactly what will be in the rest of the book. So list out all your chapter concepts, with a paragraph or so on the content of each. This section is important, as it shows that, although the book is not complete, the author has a very clear path forward in terms of the exact content that will fill all the pages.

SAMPLE CHAPTERS. Although you do not have to finish the book before pitching nonfiction, you do have to complete 2–4 book chapters as an appropriate sample. The goal is to write chapters that you believe give a great representation as to what the book is about. Typical sample chapters include the book's first chapter, and 1–3 more from different sections of the book. Your goal is to make these chapters represent what the final product will be like in both appearance and content. So if the book is going to be funny, your sample chapters better be humorous. If the book will be infused with art and illustrations, gather what images you can to insert in the pages. The sample chapters are the one place in a proposal where the author can step out of "business mode" and into "writer mode"—focusing on things like voice, humor, style, and more.

TARGET AUDIENCES. You've probably heard before that "a book for everyone is a book for no one," so target your work to small, core, focused audience groups. This section is your chance to prove an *evidence of need*. Or, as agent Mollie Glick of Foundry Literary + Media says, "You want an original idea—but not too original."

For example, when I was listing audiences for my book, *How to Survive a Garden Gnome Attack*, they were 1) garden gnome enthusiasts, 2) gardeners, 3) survival guide parody lovers, and 4) humor book lovers. Note how I resisted the urge to say "Everyone everywhere loves a laugh, so I basically see the entire human population snatching this bad boy up at bookstores."

When I was pitching a book on historical theaters around the country, my audiences were 1) theater lovers, 2) historical preservationists in the regions where featured theaters are located, 3) nostalgia lovers, and 4) architecture buffs and enthusiasts. Again, the audiences were concise and focused. I proved I had done my research and honed in on the exact pockets of people who would pay money for what I was proposing.

And once you identify these audiences, you must *quantify* them. If you want to write a book about the history of the arcade game Donkey Kong, a logical target audience would be "Individuals who currently play Donkey Kong"—but you must quantify the audience, because an agent has no idea if that audience size is 1,000 or 500,000. So tell them what it really is—and explain how you came to find that true number. You can find these quantifying numbers by seeing where such audiences get their news. For example, if donkeykongnews.com has a newsletter reach of 12,000 individuals, that is a proven number you can use. If the official Donkey Kong Twitter account has 134,000 followers, that will help you, as well. If *Classic Games Magazine* has a circulation of 52,000, that number can help you, too. "Use round, accurate numbers in your proposal," says Larsen. "If a number isn't round, qualify it by writing nearly, almost or more than (not over). Be ready to provide sources for statistics if asked."

> "Know your market. This is a business, and the more time and effort you expend in studying and understanding the demands of your [niche], the more likely you'll meet with success."
>
> - Gina Panettieri (Talcott Notch Literary Services)

COMPARATIVE TITLES. This is where you list any and all books that are similar to yours in the marketplace. What you're aiming for is showing that many books that have similarities to your title exist and have healthy sales, but no one book accomplishes everything yours will do. If you can show that, you've made an argument that your book is unique (and therefore worthwhile), and also that people have shown a history of buying such a book (and therefore the book is even more worthwhile). You're essentially trying to say "Books exist on Subject A and books exist on Subject B, but no book exists on Subject AB, which is exactly what my book, [*Title*], will do."

You can find comparative titles by searching through the appropriate bookshelf in Barnes & Noble or any local bookstore, as well as by scouring Amazon. Once you have your list, it's your time to write them all down—laying out details such as the publisher, title, year, and any signs of solid sales (such as awards or a good Amazon sales ranking). After you explain a book's specifics, you should quickly say why your book is different from it. At the same time, don't trash competing books. Because your book shares some similarity to it, you don't want your own work to come under fire.

MARKETING / WRITER PLATFORM. This massively important section details all the many avenues you have in place to market the work to the audiences you've already identified. This section will list out your social media channels, contacts in the media, personal marketing abilities, public speaking engagements, and much more. This section is of the utmost importance, as an agent needs to be assured you can currently market your book to thousands of possible buyers, if not more. Otherwise, the agent may stop reading the proposal. "Develop a significant following before you go out with your nonfiction book. If you build it, publishers will come," says agent Jeffery McGraw of The August Agency. "How visible are you to the world? That's what determines your level of platform. Someone with real platform is the 'go to' person in their area of expertise. If you don't make yourself known to the world as the expert in your field, then how will [members of the media] know to reach out to you? Get out there. Make as many connections as you possibly can."

AUTHOR BIO / CREDENTIALS. Now is your chance to explain what makes you qualified to write the content in this book. Tell the agent things such as your degrees, memberships, endorsements, and more. Anything that qualifies you to write this book but is not technically considered "platform" should go in this section.

AN AGENT EXPLAINS 3 COMMON BOOK PROPOSAL PROBLEMS

1. Lack of a story arc. Many failed nonfiction proposals are mere surveys of a subject. The books that sell have strong characters who are engaged in some project that eventually is resolved. Don't do a book about slime mold. Do a book about the Slime Mold Guy who solved the mystery of slime mold.

2. Skimpiness. I like big fat proposals. Writers worry too much about how much reading editors have to do and they self-defeatingly try to keep proposals short. Busy editors are not the problem. A great proposal will hook a reader within a few pages and keep that reader spellbound until the last page no matter how long. Short, skimpy proposals often quit before they can get me, or an editor, truly immersed and engaged. You aren't just informing us about your book; you are recruiting us into joining you on what is going to be a long and expensive expedition. If crazy, fire-eyed Christopher Columbus wants me to join him on his trip to the "Here Be Monsters" part of the ocean, I'd like to inspect his ships very, very carefully before I set sail. Editors are scared to buy books because they are so often wrong. Thoroughness builds confidence.

3. Extrapolation. Many proposals say, in effect, "I don't know all that much about this subject, but give me a six-figure contract and I will go and find out everything there is to know." I understand the problem writers face: How are they supposed to master a subject until after they've done the travels, interviews, and research? Nevertheless, unless you are already an established writer, you can't simply promise to master your subject. Book contracts go to those who have already mastered a subject. If you haven't mastered your subject but you really think you deserve a book contract, try to get a magazine assignment so that you can do at least some of the necessary research, funded by the magazine. But if you're just winging it, I probably can't help you unless you have a superb platform.

Sidebar courtesy of literary agent Russell Galen (Scovil Galen Ghosh Literary Agency).

CHUCK SAMBUCHINO (chucksambuchino.com, @chucksambuchino on Twitter) edits the *Guide to Literary Agents* (guidetoliteraryagents.com/blog) as well as the *Children's Writer's & Illustrator's Market*. His pop-humor books include *How to Survive a Garden Gnome Attack* (film rights optioned by Sony) and *Red Dog / Blue Dog: When Pooches Get Political* (reddog-bluedog.com). Chuck's other writing books include *Formatting & Submitting Your Manuscript, 3rd. Ed.*, as well as *Create Your Writer Platform* (fall 2012). Besides that, he is a husband, sleep-deprived new father, guitarist, dog owner, and cookie addict.

10 REASONS AGENTS REJECT YOUR MANUSCRIPT

by Marie Lamba

A number of years ago, before I became a published novelist and later stepped into my current role as an associate literary agent, I was an unknown writer sending out queries for my first novel, *The Time Passage*. And I was getting a ton of rejections.

But we writers are a persistent bunch. So I kept refining my query, polishing my opening pages, and submitting. Finally agents started requesting that I send my full manuscript for their review. Surely it was only a matter of time before I got an offer for representation, right?

What I got instead were rejections that basically read: "While your novel has merit, I'm afraid I'm going to pass. ..." Why were they declining to represent my work? The agents offered few details. And just like that, I'd hit a wall. Because I couldn't pinpoint what was wrong with *The Time Passage*, I ultimately placed that manuscript on my shelf, where it still sits today, and moved on to other stories that, fortunately, proved to be more successful.

These days, *I'm* the agent sending out the "It has merit, but ..." rejections. Unfortunately, I send out a lot of them. The query sounded great, the opening pages were clean and promising, yet in the end it was a no from me. Why?

When it comes to requested full manuscripts, I always make an effort to spell out why I passed—after all, I know firsthand how important that information is to a writer. And I think it's useful for *all* writers to know that there are common—and avoidable—flaws holding back the majority of the manuscripts agents see. The following are my own top 10 reasons for rejecting a requested full, along with some possible fixes. If you think you're ready to start submitting, see if your manuscript passes this pressure test; if you're already engrossed in submissions but your manuscript isn't getting the results you want, perhaps one of these will strike a chord with you.

REASON #1: IT'S NOT WHAT WAS PROMISED.

When you query an agent, you're drawing her in with a promise of what's to come. But sometimes what I get is *very* different. I've requested what was described as a deep women's fiction story, only to find that it turns into an erotic romance—a category I don't represent. And a touching young adult novel I've been pitched is revealed to be a gory horror tale, another genre I'm not interested in. When I get a manuscript that's completely different from what I was expecting, I'm disappointed. Queries that aren't true representations of the story are a waste of my time *and* the author's (especially when I end up with genres I simply don't represent). Mislead me with your pitch, and you can bet I'll pass.

The fix?

Give your query a closer look. Does it accurately describe your novel?

Sometimes writers fudge their novel's description just to fit what an agent says she wants, thinking that once they have the agent's attention, the manuscript will win her over. Or the author plays up what he thinks is a more marketable element of the story, even though it's a very minor part. And sometimes a query is inaccurate because the author simply doesn't have a solid grip on the book's true slant.

So make your query accurate. Believe me, it matters. Then agents who request your book will truly be interested in what you're sending.

REASON #2: IT'S WRONG FOR THE GENRE / AUDIENCE.

Works that are clearly not a fit for the intended readership get a swift rejection. Like when a novel intended for ages 8–12 ends up dealing with a serious romance. Or when a work of women's fiction has a misogynistic point of view. Or when two-thirds into a contemporary YA novel, it suddenly becomes a paranormal.

In each case, the writer didn't understand the need to meet certain genre conventions or audience expectations, and because of this, has set herself up for failure by creating a novel the agent won't be able to sell.

The fix?

Carefully identify your readership and genre, and study up to know what the marketplace standards are for manuscript content and length. Even writers who have done this up front can lose direction somewhere along the way without realizing it. Make sure your compass is steady. Work within those reader and genre expectations, and you'll help your novel succeed.

So, did your novel turn out to be much longer than what's typical of its category? (Word counts should be revealed in a query letter, but once in a while I'll have the full manuscript in hand before I realize the author failed to mention the "light and fluffy" romance is 175,000 words long.) Is the book's content too mature for its audience? Perhaps your middle-reader novel should actually be a young adult novel, which would require your main character to be a few years older. If you see a reason your book might be outside industry standards and you correct that, it could mean the difference between a no and a yes.

REASON #3: THE STORY LACKS AUTHENTICITY.

Not only must a novel be appropriate for its readership, it also must be smart and authentic enough to appeal strongly to that audience. Errors, false notes and lazy writing will only make agents roll their eyes.

That means if there is humor, it must be memorable and witty. If the book is a medical thriller, then it demands startling twists and mind-blowing science that even a doctor will be impressed with. If a manuscript is set in England, you need real and fresh setting details, not info you could pull out of any guidebook. If the manuscript is YA, then you'd better be up on how teens think and what they do—otherwise, you'll seem out of touch.

The fix?

Get smart. Read widely, and be a huge media consumer in all that is related to your topic so your point of view will be on target.

Also, why not go to the source and test out your material to get your details just right? When I was creating Raina, an Indian teen character for my novel *Over My Head*, I sought out real teenagers living in India who were willing to look over my dialogue and answer my questions. They helped me make Raina convincing and credible. So show your YA manuscript to a plugged-in teen for a fact check. Find a scientist to review your details and "what ifs." Pull together beta readers who read deeply within your intended genre to make sure your point of view is on target. Challenge yourself to strive for authenticity in even the smallest telling details.

REASON #4: THE MANUSCRIPT FALLS TO PIECES.

Writers spend so much time polishing their opening pages and trying to hook the reader that often they overlook the fact that the rest of the book is messy by comparison. There are typos, dropped plot threads, rambling story lines and tense slips. Even character names start changing. It doesn't take long before agents will lose patience and simply stop reading.

The fix?

You may have spit-shined your opening pages, but have you done this for the rest of the book? Don't be so impatient to start submitting that you cut corners. Obviously your entire manuscript should be free of spelling and grammatical errors. But polishing shouldn't stop there. Track your story elements for consistency and continuity. Chart each character's qualities and details so you don't suddenly change their eye color or hometown. And look closely for leftover story fragments that no longer belong—for instance, a dialogue where characters reference a fight that you've cut from the earlier chapters.

REASON #5: IT TAKES YOU TOO LONG TO GET ON WITH IT.

These novels had opening pages that drew me in with lovely imagery, a literary feel, a hint of intrigue or an interesting voice. But when I got the rest of the manuscript, the story never took off and nothing seemed to ever happen—at least, not up to the point where my interest waned and I stopped reading. Lovely elements can hold an agent's interest for only so long.

The fix?

First, ask yourself (and beta readers or critique partners, if possible) if you are starting the novel in the right spot. Many manuscripts begin too early in the tale instead of near the story's inciting incident. Telltale signs are when a character is traveling to where the real story will begin, or waking up and then going through the motions of getting ready.

Next, look closely at your structure. If you don't already have an outline, take the time to make one now, listing what happens scene by scene in each chapter. Is there something plot-related in every scene? Is the tension sustained? Are your characters taking action? Do the challenges grow? If you can find scenes where those answers are no, it's probably time to either cut them or make something happen.

REASON #6: THE WRITING LACKS CONFIDENCE.

When a writer doesn't trust the reader or trust himself, he starts tossing in more and more description, just in case we didn't understand what we were seeing. He tells us what just happened, or how a character is feeling, even though we could have guessed from the context (and should have been allowed to). Instead of letting the main plotline do the job, he adds more and more elements. There's suddenly a murder, a heist, a romance, an elf, a ship from outer space, there's nonstop action. Overwriting can alienate the reader and destroy what promised to be an engrossing tale.

The fix?

Look for large blocks of prose that might harbor over-telling, and pare these sections down. Especially avoid stating emotions, which are best revealed through actions and reactions. One way to find these culprits is to search for the words *feel* and *felt*. When you spot places where you feed readers things like "She felt so angry she wanted to hit him," demonstrate more confidence in your abilities—and give your readers more credit—by instead writing something along the lines of "She glared at him and clenched her fists. Her sharp nails cut into her palms."

Also look at your plotlines—are they more complicated than necessary? How many issues does your main character really need to face? If you find you're resorting to gimmicks just to hold the reader's interest, less really can be more.

REASON #7: TOO FAMILIAR.

I'm seeking fresh and original books, so predictability is a killer. If I see your twist coming well in advance, then you haven't chosen a fresh option. Also not so fresh? Manuscripts that are thinly veiled versions of popular series such as Harry Potter or novels such as *Fight Club.* Relocating the story, renaming the characters, or changing the gender does not an original novel make.

Another side to this "too familiar" coin are the plots that everyone seems to be writing a version of. Example: The woman who is divorced/wronged who starts anew in a ramshackle home by the sea/in the mountains/in a European village and finds love/friendship/her "groove." Here's another: The kid who moves in with a strange older relative in a new town and discovers a huge secret.

The fix?

Follow your own ideas, not knockoffs, and don't create in a void—know what's already out there and make sure your own novel stands apart. To avoid obvious plotting, ask yourself if you chose the first idea that came into your head. If so, can you push yourself further and pick perhaps the fourth idea, or even the eighth? Dig deep and you will probably find a new take on something that was just too obvious before.

REASON #8: YOU HAVEN'T MADE ME CARE.

If my attention starts to wander and I'm skimming pages, that's a bad sign. Another bad sign? If I can put the manuscript down and not feel a nagging urge to pick it up again. When agents aren't invested in the character or intrigued by the stakes, they're definitely passing, even if the manuscript is clean and the plot holds together.

The fix?

Analyze your character's development. Why do we care about her or at least find her interesting? Do these feelings about her deepen as we learn more? Is what's happening throughout the novel significant enough? Or is it too trivial, like when a YA novel centers on a teen whose main goal in life is to be on the prom court? While you're trying to get character and plot details right in your final draft, it's possible to lose sight of the big picture. Take a step back now and make sure you're doing all you can to keep your reader plugged in. If not, it's time to revise before you submit again.

REASON #9: DISAPPOINTING PAYOFF.

If the payoff in the book doesn't justify the read, then I'm going to feel cheated. If I'm flying through the pages of a thriller, you bet I want it to culminate in breathless action and a shocking twist. If I'm engrossed in a heartfelt coming-of-age story, of course I'm expecting deep emotion, perhaps pain, followed by satisfying triumph. If someone has been searching for her mother her whole life, then when that mother finally appears, it should definitely be handled in more than one paragraph! If I finish your manuscript thinking, *That's it? Really?*—even if you had me up to that point—it's ultimately a no from me.

The fix?

Determine what is fueling your story's engine—what most keeps your reader engaged. Now look closely at the climactic moments. Do you answer the book's big question in a satisfying way? For example, if the book is about a guy and girl falling in love but being kept apart, then, when they finally get together, is this moment surprising and so wonderful it's nearly heartbreaking? Do you let readers linger a bit in that heartfelt moment? Or do you rush right past the scene to a quick resolution? Ask yourself if you're rewarding your reader for sticking with your story. If you realize you could do better, you've still got work to do.

REASON #10: IT'S JUST NOT STRONG ENOUGH.

This is the hardest book for me to reject. The author has done so many things correctly, including creating a plot that kept me reading until the end. Yet for reasons I have a hard time qualifying, I'm not jumping out of my chair and dashing to the phone to call with an offer for representation. The problem is, I'm not looking for a good book. I'm looking for an *amazing* book—something that challenges me or astonishes me with its brilliance. Agents go to bat for their clients' projects with big commercial publishers and well-established smaller presses, both of which are extremely competitive markets. If we don't feel dazzled by your novel, then we won't feel confident that a top editor will be motivated enough by it to offer a deal.

The fix?

If the feedback you're getting gives you the sense that your story is good, but might not be *great*, it's time to do some soul-searching. What is your novel's strength? See if you can find a way for that strength to be heightened to make readers sit up and take notice. If it's plot driven, can you imagine ways your plot could be even more innovative, more engaging? If it's character driven, could you make the character more memorable? If it's an emotional read, are you hitting all the high *and* low notes in a remarkable way? If the novel is literary, are your images and language and observations as outstanding as you can make them?

Whatever your novel's special element may be, strive to make the element even stronger as the book progresses. Do this, and you'll be much more likely to finish as strong as you started.

In my experience, these are generally the most common reasons a full manuscript doesn't secure an offer. Remember, though, that another agent might see a novel I just rejected and find it perfect. So don't overreact to each rejection and immediately start revising your work. However, if you continue to have your requested full manuscript rejected again and again, do consider these 10 points.

You might even find that more than one of these reasons applies to your work. That happened to me. Looking back to my old manuscript *The Time Passage*, I can now see a bit of overwriting (No. 6) and that it wasn't quite a standout novel yet (No. 10). Perhaps if I'd applied the suggested fixes, that manuscript would be in bookstores instead of just sitting on my shelf gathering dust. Hmm ... perhaps it's time to get busy and dust it off!

Keep these 10 common flaws in mind, and instead of getting those "It has merit, but ..." emails, just maybe you'll have agents diving for their phones, eager to make "the call" and offer you representation. And who knows? Maybe one of those agents will be me.

Marie Lamba (marielamba.com) is a literary agent at the Jennifer De Chiara Literary Agency (jdlit.com) and author of the YA novels *What I Meant ...*, *Over My Head* and *Drawn*.

8 WAYS TO WRITE A GREAT CHAPTER ONE

Hook an agent or editor fast.

by Elizabeth Sims

Those first few pages have an important job: to whet your readers' appetites for more. Here's how to make sure your opening chapter delivers.

When you decide to go to a restaurant for a special dinner, you enjoy the anticipation. You've committed to spending sufficient time and money, and now you've arrived, and the place looks good and smells good. You smile and order an appetizer. When it comes, you enjoy it as a foretaste of the larger, more complex courses that will follow, but you also savor it for what it is: a delicious dish, complete in itself. If it's a truly great appetizer, you recognize it as an exquisite blend of flavor, texture and temperature. And you're happy, because you know you'll be in good hands for the entire evening.

Isn't that what it's like to begin reading a terrific book?

The first chapter is the appetizer—small, yet so tremendously important. And so full of potential.

As an aspiring author, the prospect of writing Chapter One should not intimidate, but excite the hell out of you. Why? Because no other part of your book can provide you with the disproportionate payoff that an excellent first chapter can. Far more than a great query letter, a great Chapter One can attract the attention of an agent. It can keep a harried editor from yawning and hitting "delete." It can make a bookstore browser keep turning pages during the slow walk to the cash registers. And yes, it can even keep a bleary-eyed owner of one of those electronic thingamajigs touching the screen for more, more, more!

Fiction, like food, is an art and a craft. Here's how to blend inspiration with technique and serve up an irresistible Chapter One.

#1: RESIST TERROR.

Let's be honest: Agents and editors like to make you quiver and sweat as you approach Chapter One. All those warnings: "Grab me from the opening sentence! Don't waste one word! If my attention flags, you've failed—you're down the toilet! In fact, don't even write Chapter One! Start your book at Chapter Four! Leave out all that David Copperfield crap!" From their perspective it's an acid test. They know how important Chapter One is, and if you're weak, they'll scare you into giving up before you begin. (Hey, it makes their jobs easier: one less query in the queue.)

Here's the truth: Agents and editors, all of them, are paper tigers. Every last one is a hungry kitten searching for something honest, original and brave to admire. Now is the time to gather your guts, smile and let it rip.

Your inner genius flees from tension, so first of all, relax. Notice that I did not say agents and editors are looking for perfect writing. Nor are they looking for careful writing. *Honest, original and brave.* That's what they want, and that's what you'll produce if you open up room for mistakes and mediocrity. It's true! Only by doing that will you be able to tap into your wild and free core. Let out the bad with the good now, and you'll sort it out later.

Second, remember who you are and why you're writing this book. What is your book about? What purpose(s) will it serve? Write your answers down and look at them from time to time as you write. (By the way, it's OK to want to write a book simply to entertain people; the noblest art has sprung from just such a humble desire.)

And third, if you haven't yet outlined, consider doing so. Even the roughest, most rustic framework will give you a sharper eye for your beginning and, again, will serve to unfetter your mind. Your outline could be a simple list of things that are gonna happen, or it could be a detailed chronological narrative of all your plot threads and how they relate. I find that knowing where I'm headed frees my mind from everything but the writing at hand. Being prepared makes you calm, and better equipped to tap into your unique voice—which is the most important ingredient in a good Chapter One.

#2: DECIDE ON TENSE AND POINT OF VIEW.

Most readers are totally unconscious of tense and POV; all they care about is the story. Is it worth reading? Fun to read? But you must consider your tense and POV carefully, and Chapter One is go time for these decisions. It used to be simple. You'd choose from any one of the following:

a) First person: *I chased the beer wagon.*

b) Third-person limited: *Tom chased the beer wagon.*

c) Omniscient: *Tom chased the beer wagon while the villagers watched and wondered,* Would all the beer in the world be enough for this oaf?

... and you'd always use past tense.

But today, novels mix points of view and even tenses. In my Rita Farmer novels I shift viewpoints, but limit all POVs to the good guys. By contrast, John Grisham will shift out of the main character's POV to the bad guy's for a paragraph or two, then back again. (Some critics have labeled this practice innovative, while others have called it lazy; in the latter case, I'm sure Grisham is crying all the way to the bank.) It's also worth noting that studies have shown that older readers tend to prefer past tense, while younger ones dig the present. (If that isn't a statement with larger implications, I don't know what is.)

Many writing gurus tell you to keep a first novel simple by going with first person, past tense. This approach has worked for thousands of first novels (including mine, 2002's *Holy Hell*), but I say go for whatever feels right to you, simple or not. I do, however, recommend that you select present or past tense and stick with it. Similarly, I advise against flashbacks and flash-forwards for first novels. Not that they can't work, but they seem to be off-putting to agents and editors, who will invariably ask, "Couldn't this story be told without altering the time-space continuum?"

The point is, you want your readers to feel your writing is smooth; you don't want them to see the rivets in the hull, so to speak. And the easiest way to do that is to create fewer seams.

If you're still unsure of your tense or POV choices, try these techniques:

- **Go to your bookshelf and take a survey of your favorite novels**. What POVs and tenses are selected, and why do you suppose the authors chose those approaches?
- **Rehearse**. Write a scene using first person, then third-person limited, then omniscient. What feels right?
- **Don't forget to consider the needs of your story**. If you plan to have simultaneous action in Fresno, Vienna and Pitcairn, and you want to show it all in living color, you almost certainly need more than one POV.

And if you're still in doubt, don't freeze up—just pick an approach and start writing. Remember, you can always change it later if you need to.

#3: CHOOSE A NATURAL STARTING POINT.

When you read a good novel, it all seems to unfold so naturally, starting from the first sentence. But when you set out to write your own, you realize your choices are limitless, and this can be paralyzing. Yet your novel must flow from the first scene you select.

Let's say you've got an idea for a novel that takes place in 1933. There's this pair of teenagers who figure out what really happened the night the Lindbergh baby was abducted, but before they can communicate with the police, they themselves are kidnapped. Their captives take them to proto-Nazi Germany, and it turns out there's some weird relationship between Col. Lindbergh and the chancellor—or is there? Is the guy with the haircut really Lindbergh? The teens desperately wonder: *What do they want with us?*

Sounds complicated. Where should you start? A recap of the Lindbergh case? The teenagers on a date where one of them stumbles onto a clue in the remote place they go to make out? A newspaper clipping about a German defense contract that should have raised eyebrows but didn't?

Basically, write your way in.

Think about real life. Any significant episode in your own life did not spring whole from nothing; things happened beforehand that shaped it, and things happened afterward as a result of it. Think about your novel in this same way. The characters have pasts and futures (unless you plan to kill them); places, too, have pasts and futures. Therefore, every storyteller jumps into his story midstream. Knowing this can help you relax about picking a starting point. The Brothers Grimm did not begin by telling about the night Hansel and Gretel were conceived; they got going well into the lives of their little heroes, and they knew we wouldn't care about anything but what they're doing right now.

If you're unsure where to begin, pick a scene you know you're going to put in—you just don't know where yet—and start writing it. You might discover your Chapter One right there. And even if you don't, you'll have fodder for that scene when the time comes.

Here are a few other strategies that can help you choose a starting point:

- Write a character sketch or two. You need them anyway, and they're great warm-ups for Chapter One. Ask yourself: What will this character be doing when we first meet him? Write it. Again, you might find yourself writing Chapter One.
- Do a Chapter-One-only brainstorm and see what comes out.
- The truth is, you probably can write a great story starting from any of several places. If you've narrowed it down to two or three beginnings and still can't decide, flip a coin and get going. In my hypothetical Lindbergh thriller, I'd probably pick the date scene, with a shocking clue revealed. Why? Action!

It's OK to be extremely loose with your first draft of your first chapter. In fact, I recommend it. The important thing at this point is to begin.

#4: PRESENT A STRONG CHARACTER RIGHT AWAY.

This step might seem obvious, but too many first-time novelists try to lure the reader into a story by holding back the main character. Having a couple of subsidiary characters talking about the protagonist can be a terrific technique for character or plot development at some point, but not at the beginning of your novel.

When designing your Chapter One, establish your characters' situation(s). What do they know at the beginning? What will they learn going forward? What does their world mean to them?

Who is the strongest character in your story? Watch out; that's a trick question. Consider Kazuo Ishiguro's *The Remains of the Day*. The main character, Stevens, is a weak man, yet his presence is as strong as a hero. How? Ishiguro gave him a voice that is absolutely certain, yet absolutely vacant of self-knowledge. We *know* Stevens, and because we see his limitations, we know things will be difficult for him. Don't be afraid to give all the depth you can to your main character early in your story. You'll discover much more about him later, and can always revise if necessary.

#5: BE SPARING OF SETTING.

Another common error many aspiring novelists make is trying to set an opening scene in too much depth. You've got it all pictured in your head: the colors, sounds, flavors and feelings. You want everybody to be in the same place with the story you are. But you're too close: A cursory—but poignant!—introduction is what's needed. Readers will trust you to fill in all the necessary information later. They simply want to get a basic feel for the setting, whether it's a lunar colony or a street in Kansas City.

Pack punch into a few details. Instead of giving the history of the place and how long the character has been there and what the weather's like, consider something like this:

> *He lived in a seedy neighborhood in Kansas City. When the night freight passed, the windows rattled in their frames and the dog in the flat below barked like a maniac.*

Later (if you want) you'll tell all about the house, the street, the neighbors and maybe even the dog's make and model, but for now a couple of sentences like that are all you need.

But, you object, what of great novels that opened with descriptions of place, like John Steinbeck's *The Grapes of Wrath* or Edna Ferber's *Giant*? Ah, in those books the locale has been crafted with the same care as a character, and effectively used as one. Even so, the environment is presented *as the characters relate to it*: in the former case, man's mark on the land (by indiscriminate agriculture), and in the latter, man's mark on the sky (the jet plumes of modern commerce).

Another way to introduce a setting is to show how a character feels about it. In Dostoyevsky's *Crime and Punishment*, Raskolnikov seethes with resentment at the opulence around him in St. Petersburg, and this immediately puts us on the alert about him. The setting serves the character; it does not stand on its own.

#6: USE CAREFULLY CHOSEN DETAIL TO CREATE IMMEDIACY.

Your Chapter One must move along smartly, but in being economical you cannot become vague. Difficult, you say? It's all in the context.

The genius of books as diverse as Miguel de Cervantes' *Don Quixote* and Robin Cook's *Coma* lies in the authors' generosity with good, authentic detail. Cervantes knew that a suit of armor kept in a junk locker for years wouldn't merely be dusty, it would be corroded to hell—and that would be a problem to overcome. Likewise, Cook, himself a doctor, knew that a patient prepped for surgery would typically be given a calming drug before the main anesthetic—and that some patients, somehow, do not find peace even under the medication, especially if they have reason not to.

If you're an expert on something, go ahead and show that you know what you're talking about. One of the reasons my novel *Damn Straight*, a story involving a professional golfer, won a Lambda Award is that I know golf, and let my years of (painful) experience inform the book. I felt I'd done a good job when reviewer after reviewer wrote, "I absolutely hate golf, but I love how Sims writes about it in this novel."

Let's say your Chapter One begins with your main character getting a root canal. You could show the dentist nattering on and on as dentists tend to do, and that would be realistic, but it could kill your chapter, as in this example:

> *Dr. Payne's running commentary included the history of fillings, a story about the first time he ever pulled a tooth and a funny anecdote about how his college roommate got really drunk every weekend.*

Bored yet? Me too. Does that mean there's too much detail? No. It means there's too much extraneous detail.

How about this:

Dr. Payne paused in his running commentary on dental history and put down his drill. "Did you know," he remarked, "that the value of all the gold molars in a city this size, at this afternoon's spot price of gold, would be something on the order of half a million dollars?" He picked up his drill again. "Open."

If the detail serves the story, you can hardly have too much.

#7: GIVE IT A MINI-PLOT.

It's no accident that many great novels have first chapters that were excerpted in magazines, where they essentially stood as short stories. I remember being knocked to the floor by the gorgeous completeness of Ian McEwan's first chapter of *On Chesil Beach* when it was excerpted in *The New Yorker*.

Every chapter should have its own plot, none more important than Chapter One. Use what you know about storytelling to:

- **Make trouble.** I side with the writing gurus who advise you to put in a lot of conflict early. Pick your trouble and make it big. If it can't be big at first, make it ominous.
- **Focus on action.** Years ago I got a rejection that said, "Your characters are terrific and I love the setting, but not enough happens." A simple and useful critique! Bring action forward in your story; get it going quick. This is why agents and editors tell you to start your story in the middle: They've seen too many Chapter Ones bogged down by backstory. Put your backstory in the back, not the front. Readers will stick with you if you give them something juicy right away. I make a point of opening each of my Rita Farmer novels with a violent scene, which is then revealed to be an audition, or a film shoot or a rehearsal. Right away, the reader gets complexity, layers and a surprise shift of frame of reference.
- **Be decisive.** A good way to do that is to make a character take decisive action.
- **Don't telegraph too much; let action develop through the chapter**. It's good to end Chapter One with some closure. Because it is Chapter One, your readers will trust that the closure will turn out to be deliciously false.

#8: BE BOLD.

The most important thing to do when writing Chapter One is put your best material out there. Do not humbly introduce your story—present it with a flourish. Don't hold back! Set your tone and own it. You're going to write a whole book using great material; have confidence that you can generate terrific ideas for action and emotion whenever you want.

If you do your job creating a fabulous appetizer in Chapter One and follow it up well, your readers will not only stay through the whole meal, they'll order dessert, coffee and maybe even a nightcap—and they won't want to leave until you have to throw them out at closing time.

ELIZABETH SIMS (elizabethsims.com) is a *WD* contributing editor who holds degrees in English from Michigan State University and Wayne State University. She's the author of several popular novels, including the Lambda Award-winning *Damn Straight*.

GREAT CHAPTER ONES IN HISTORY

Jane Eyre, **BY CHARLOTTE BRONTË (1847)**

How bad is Jane's life? Bad! From the first page, Jane gets trodden down again and again, until you know something's gonna give.

Crime and Punishment, **BY FYODOR DOSTOYEVSKY (1866)**

A man in debt, feeling sorry for himself, already rationalizing immoral behavior.

Dracula, **BY BRAM STOKER (1897)**

After a thimbleful of history, we get frightened peasants crossing themselves, a castle, moonlight, shadows, howling wolves and an unmistakable feeling of impending evil.

Little House in the Big Woods, **BY LAURA INGALLS WILDER (1932)**

Chapter One actually begins, "Once upon a time …" Children love this book because it's made of stuff adults don't expect them to like—it opens with a pig-slaughtering, wildcats, bears and even deer ready for butchering hanging in trees.

The Violent Bear It Away, **BY FLANNERY O'CONNOR (1960)**

Chapter One cuts right to the bone of what so many other authors dance around and never get to: ultimate motivations, absolute morality and the harsh requirements of a fundamental God. Primal fury!

Coma, **BY ROBIN COOK (1977)**

Deft character development plus unsettling medical detail forms a breakthrough idea—and a big what if?

The Remains of the Day, **BY KAZUO ISHIGURO (1988)**

You feel bludgeoned by Stevens' moral and emotional cluelessness; when you realize with horror that he's going to be at your side through the whole story, you cannot walk away.

On Chesil Beach, **BY IAN MCEWAN (2007)**

A long Chapter One that quietly presents enormous conflict, sharpened by the fact that only one of the two characters knows it.

CRAFTING A NOVEL AGENTS WILL LOVE

How to grab an agent with voice and flair.

by Donald Maass

You'll never meet an author who admits to publishing a "failed" novel. You will, though, encounter authors in bars and on blogs who will loudly tell you what's wrong with the book industry. They'll chronicle in detail how their titles languished on the shelves because their publishers screwed up and failed *them*.

But accept blame? No way. If sales were disappointing or an option was dropped, it's the fault of weak "support," a lousy cover, awful back-panel copy, bad timing, distribution mistakes, lack of subsidiary rights sales, or a host of other common publishing woes.

How can it be the author's fault? After all, he wrote a book that was *good enough*. It was published. It met the standard—one that sometimes seems impossibly high. Any poor performance was therefore not the author's doing but someone else's, right?

But if that's true, then why do some novels become successful *in spite of* the sting of small deals, minimal press runs, little promotion, forgettable covers, bland copy, distribution snafus, and the absence of movie deals or translation sales?

Take timing and distribution troubles, for instance. In a recent interview in *Writer's Digest*, British author Chris Cleave related that due to a terrorist attack in London on the publication day of his first novel, *Incendiary*—which happened to be about a terrorist attack in London—the book was yanked from bookshop shelves after only about 90 minutes on sale. Talk about disasters! Yet that book later found its audience and was successful, even becoming a feature film. Cleave went on to write the mega-sellers *Little Bee* and *Gold*.

And what about awful covers? Do you remember what was on the covers of *Mystic River* or *Empire Falls*? I didn't think so. It didn't matter. In fact, think about any great novel you read in the last decade and ask yourself this: Was the reason you bought or loved that novel the flap copy, the Italian edition, the movie option, the author's Twitter feed, or the news of her honking big advance? Probably not.

I'm not saying that the industry is perfect, or that authors can't help their sales with smart self-promotion. (Although my experience has been that the boost is typically smaller than evangelists would like you to believe.) If you want to distract yourself with those issues, go ahead. I won't stop you. But you'll be missing a critical point.

As a literary agent who's helped guide fiction careers for more than 30 years, here's what I've learned: Runaway success comes from great fiction, period. The publishing industry may help or hinder but cannot stop a powerful story from being powerful. Conversely, the book business cannot magically transform an adequate novel into a great one.

You may not like every bestseller (*Fifty Shades of Grey*, anyone?), but if a book is selling well then it's doing things right for many readers. By the same token, less commercially successful novels are not doing enough of those things, even if they were good enough to get into print.

What are those critical factors, then? Let's take a look at some of the most common.

CULPRIT NO. 1: TIMID VOICES

Great novels not only draw us in immediately but command our attention. They not only hold our interest but hold us rapt. They cast a spell. A snappy premise and meaty plot can hook us and keep us reading but cannot by themselves work that magic. It takes something extra: voice.

What is voice, anyway? Narrative style? Character diction? A set of subject matter or a singular setting? All of the above? Pinning it down can be difficult, but start with this: We primarily experience stories through point-of-view characters.

To put it differently, voice in a novel is not the author's thoughts or vocabulary but the sum total of what her characters observe, think, feel and express in their own unique ways.

First-person narrators automatically have a voice, but that doesn't necessarily mean it's strong. Victims, whiners and passive daughters often have weak voices. On the flip side, snappy narrators who fire off zingers every page or so don't always leave a lasting impression, either. Have you ever met a government-issue alpha male or central-casting kick-ass heroine whose name you forgot as soon as you turned the final page? Then you know what I mean.

Lorrie Moore's bestselling literary novel *A Gate at the Stairs* is the coming-of-age story of Tassie Keltjin, a 20-year-old student and daughter of a potato farmer. As the novel opens, Tassie is on a term break and needs money. She is looking for babysitting jobs.

> *I was looking in December for work that would begin at the start of the January term. I'd finished my exams and was answering ads from the student job board, ones for*

"childcare provider." I liked children—I did!—or rather, I liked them OK. They were sometimes interesting.

Tassie is about as ordinary as characters get. She's a student. She needs a job. She has no odd talent, paranormal ability or backstory secret. The only reason we're compelled to read about her is her voice, her take on things. Her take on herself is wry. She's a future babysitter trying to talk herself into liking kids. That wry voice makes her engaging enough to lure us forward into the rest of her tragi-comic story.

Third-person narrators are a step removed from the reader, true enough, but when their inner experiences are both vivid and different, then their voices can become strong. It's not just language. It's not only getting into a character's head. It's how you use both of those things to create a strong voice.

Erin Morgenstern's bestselling literary fantasy *The Night Circus* is a three-ring carnival of voice that's all the more remarkable for using not only the third person but the often icy present tense. Open her novel at random and see. Here's Lefèvre, the circus manager, practicing knife throwing by aiming at the byline of a reviewer in a newspaper clipping:

The sentence that holds his name is the particular one that has incensed M. Lefèvre to the point of knife throwing. A single sentence that reads thusly: "M. Chandresh Christophe Lefèvre continues to push the boundaries of the modern stage, dazzling his audiences with spectacle that is almost transcendent."

Most theatrical producers would likely be flattered by such a remark. They would clip the article for a scrapbook of reviews, quote it for references and referrals.

But not this particular theatrical producer. No, M. Chandresh Christophe Lefèvre instead focuses on that penultimate word. Almost. **Almost.**

How often do you use the words *thusly* and *penultimate* in your fiction? Not often? That's OK. I'm not saying that stuffy diction is the way to craft a strong voice. But in this case, it makes the repressed anger and obsessive perfectionism of M. Chandresh Christophe Lefèvre wonderfully distinctive.

STRENGTHEN THAT HARD-TO-DEFINE VOICE:

- What's your protagonist's initial view of the main story problem? Evolve that understanding in three steps. How is it different at the end? Put each stage on the page.
- What's your protagonist's opening opinion of a secondary character, the story's locale, or era? Open with that ... then change it by the end.
- Pick anything ordinary in the world of your story: for example, a vehicle, a sport, or a topic of public debate. Give your protagonist a fanatic view. Write his rant.

CULPRIT NO. 2: UNTESTED CHARACTERS

If voice comes from a character's way of looking at the world, a character's continuing grip on the reader comes from what she does, why she does it, and who she is. It's not enough for your characters to simply have actions, motives and principles. Those drivers can be weak or they can be strong.

Let's start with actions. The weakest action is inaction. You'd think this is obvious, yet many scenes, indeed whole novels (yes, even published ones), can pass without a character actually doing something. Reacting, observing, and bearing what is hard or painful are not actions. Running away is active, technically speaking, but it isn't as strong as facing up, confronting and fighting.

More compelling are actions that show spine, take courage, spring from high principles or bring characters face to face with their deepest fears. Strongest of all are self-sacrifice, forgiveness and other actions that demonstrate growth, grace and love.

What about motives? In life our motives are many, deep and intertwined. Unfortunately, in many novels characters are motivated in ways that are single-minded and simplistic. Generic motives make for cartoonish characters.

You can see that in some genre novels. Detectives have codes, romance heroines seek love, and fantasy heroes fight evil. Is that bad? No. Codes, yearning for love and fighting evil are good—but as characters' lone motives they're also generic.

What makes characters' motivations genuinely gripping, then? There's a hierarchy. Mixed motives make characters real. Conflicting motives make characters complex. Most gripping of all are motives that reveal to us characters' innermost cores. We're shaped by our hurts. When a character's hurts are unique and specific, what propels them on their journeys—motivates them—paradoxically becomes universal.

Think of it this way: The deeper you dig into what drives your protagonist, the more readers will be able to connect.

What about principles? They are the rules we live by and the beliefs we hold. These too can be weak or strong. Generic principles are common and obvious. *Do unto others* is a fine but commonplace rule for living. Compelling principles are personal, a twist on what's familiar. *Build a bridge to everyone you meet—then walk across it*, is somewhat more personal. That's especially true if the protagonist who lives by that rule is a bridge inspector.

When actions, motives and principles come together the effect can be profound. Jamie Ford's longtime bestseller *Hotel on the Corner of Bitter and Sweet* is set largely in Seattle in 1942. It's the story of Henry Lee, a sixth-grade Chinese-American boy who falls in love with Keiko Okabe, a Japanese-American girl in his class. When Keiko and her family are removed to an internment camp, Henry is distraught. That would be enough for many literary novels. The romantic tragedy has happened. The political point is made.

But Ford has his protagonist *do something*: Henry gets a job as a kitchen assistant to the school cook who has been contracted to feed the prisoners at the internment camp. He goes looking for Keiko.

> *Another language barrier Henry ran into was within Camp Harmony. Just seeing a Chinese kid standing on an apple crate behind the serving counter was strange enough. But the more he questioned those who came through his chow line about the Okabes, the more frustrated he became. Few cared, and those who did never seemed to understand. Still, like a lost ship occasionally sending out an SOS, Henry kept peppering those he served with questions.*
>
> *"Okabes? Does anyone know the Okabes?"*

Henry's search poignantly shows the strength of his character. He rejects his father (who tries to force a Chinese Nationalist identity on Henry), ignores social prejudice and defies the odds. His actions, motives and principles are high, more so because he's only a kid.

PUT YOUR PROTAGONIST TO THE TEST:

- What's the biggest thing your protagonist could possibly do, but can't? By the end of the story, have her do it.
- The story problem bugs your protagonist like it bugs no one else. The real reason connects back to something from childhood—what? Build that into a dramatic, character-defining backstory event. Let it underlie every scene, but reveal what happened only late in the story.
- In what way are your protagonist's operating principles unlike anyone else's? Boil them down to one precept. Drop that in early, and then depict, challenge and deepen that axiom at least three times by the story's end.

CULPRIT NO. 3: OVERLY INTERIOR OR EXTERIOR STORIES

You're the god of your story world. So there's no reason not to play god with your story.

Certain story patterns are pretty much guaranteed to lead to fiction of underwhelming force. That's often true of novels built on delay, suffering and being stuck. Even plot-heavy yarns can leave us yawning. Stupendous plot turns don't necessarily have a stupendous effect.

Quiet authors need to create a disturbance in church. At the other end of the spectrum, razzle-dazzle storytellers need to recognize that a burst of flash powder doesn't cause the audience to feel deeply. More simply, interior stories need more dramatic outward events; by the same token, dramatic outward events need to create a more devastating interior impact.

If you shy away from that cheap gimmick called plot, I applaud your integrity—but try focusing on the inner state of your main character at any given moment and finding a way to externalize it. Make something happen. If, conversely, you focus on keeping your pages turning at a mile a minute, good for you—but try sending your protagonist on a mission not just to save the world but also to save himself.

In a practical sense, playing god with your story means making your characters do bigger things and, conversely, *feel* bigger things when they experience something small.

Earlier I mentioned *Fifty Shades of Grey*. It's hard to find anyone who thinks this mainstream erotica is especially well written, yet its blockbuster status suggests that millions nevertheless find it easy to surrender to it. Why is that, then?

The novel's heroine, student Anastasia Steele, falls under the spell of a man with a dark sexual side, entrepreneur Christian Grey. Anastasia at first resists his magnetic appeal. The slow breakdown of that resistance generates the tension in the novel's early chapters. It's an internal tension, though, and to work it must infuse every routine encounter.

In an early scene Grey comes into the hardware store where Anastasia works and he buys cable ties, masking tape and rope. Anastasia renders polite customer service, but inside is intrigued, confused and quivering. When he leaves, she narrates her feelings in this passage:

> *Okay, I like him. There, I've admitted it to myself. I cannot hide from my feelings anymore. I've never felt like this before. I find him attractive, very attractive. But it's a lost cause, I know, and I sigh with bittersweet regret. It was just a coincidence, his coming here. But still, I can admire him from afar, surely. No harm can come of that.*

While the prose may not be the most artful ever written, notice in this passage the push-pull of Anastasia's feelings. She submits to her attraction but immediately rejects it. She dismisses his visit to the hardware store as a fluke. (Really? Masking tape?) Her decision to admire him from afar is an amusing piece of foreshadowing. Most significantly, her response to Grey's hardware shopping is overly large, as if a godlike master has dropped into a humble hardware store from on high—which for Anastasia is true.

PLAY GOD WITH YOUR STORY:

- Your character is stymied, suffering and stuck. She phones a crisis hotline. You answer. You're trained to convince callers to get help. What should your protagonist do? Make her do it ... then make it fail.
- Your action hero races ahead at top speed. Throw up a roadblock. Force a one-hour delay. During that hour, ask your hero the following: Why are you racing? Why does it matter? You're racing but also running from—what? Write it down. Fold it in. There's time to deepen your character.
- Rain a punishment on your protagonist, and simultaneously test his inner conviction. What's the hardest possible test for him? Add it. What's being tested? Make that clear.

A MEASURE OF SUCCESS

If there are no pink slips for published authors, how do you know you've "failed"? The fact is that there is no failure per se; there are only disappointing sales, dropped options, unreturned calls, panic and anger. A bruised self-image is painful.

Recovery starts with examining first how it is that you define success. If it's by *selling a lot of copies*, then you're setting yourself up for failure, because you'll always lose to the heavy hitters like Harlan Coben. Indeed, I've found that focusing on selling a lot of copies is almost a guarantee that you won't.

Likewise, blaming the publishing industry for your disappointment will not heal or strengthen you. It's a mental trap. Book publishing is a big industry. It's dominated by a handful of big conglomerates that put out roughly 6,000 new works of fiction every year. Things are bound to go wrong.

While the industry isn't without blame, the fact is that you can't change the business. You can only change your writing.

When you make it to that happy place called *published*, remember that as a writer you have the same strengths and weaknesses that you did before. Your strengths have grown strong enough to get you over the first hurdle; your weaknesses have lessened enough that they didn't stop you from jumping over the bar. But you still have growing to do.

If you encounter disappointments in your publishing career, don't despair. That happens to pretty much every author. The trick is not to simmer but to learn. Learn what? How to become a more powerful storyteller.

The good news is that when you do, industry flaws become less bothersome. In fact, you'll run into fewer of them and finally none at all. Your books will succeed—not because you've beat the odds but because you've become a great novelist.

DONALD MAASS'S literary agency sells more than 150 novels every year to major publishers in the U.S. and overseas. He is the author of several books on writing, most recently *Writing 21st Century Fiction* (WD Books).

YOUR FUTURE AGENT'S WISH LIST

by Kimiko Nakamura

All agents, admittedly or not, have a wish list—markers that help us determine which writers are primed for our representation. With hundreds of projects flooding our inboxes daily, writers who follow these simple guidelines can catch the eye of an agent and rise like a lotus blossom out of the slush pile. Here's how to do it.

YOUR PLATFORM

Think of your platform as the foundation you're building for success. It's made up of everything that qualifies you to write and speak about your chosen topic (even if that topic is fiction) and that demonstrates your popularity with potential book-buying readers. It comprises ongoing relationships with publications your writing has appeared in, leadership/public involvement in associations with a tie to your work's focus, classes you teach or talks you regularly give/present and, more and more important these days, a social media presence. Publishing houses think authors with success in social media are a good financial investment because they can see that these writers have a ready-made audience. Think of your social media platform as your virtual business card. People aren't looking for you in an office building anymore; they're looking for you online.

Here's a breakdown of popular ways you can effectively elevate your platform and visibility.

Your Website:

Essential for all writers, published and unpublished.

A website is the best place to give people a point of reference for your work and connect them to your social media presence elsewhere. Things to include are: contact info, a professional-looking headshot or photo of yourself, blurbs about your projects, a bio, a list of any awards and writing credits, and your social media links.

Who does it well: Geraldine Brooks, geraldinebrooks.com

Facebook:

Essential for nonfiction writers building an audience, or for published fiction writers cultivating readerships.

Facebook is like a public bulletin board. [Note: Creating a Facebook page for a writer or (soon-to-be) public figure is different from creating a personal Facebook page. To create a writer or public figure page, visit facebook.com/pages/create.] Promote yourself by offering posts that entertain and inform your audience. People who enjoy your posts can "like" your page and automatically get notified every time you post something new. But every "like" isn't an instant book sale, which is why agents look for nonfiction writers with around 3,000 "likes" to start. We're hoping you'll double that number (or better) before publication.

Who does it well: Jack Canfield, facebook.com/jackcanfieldfan

Twitter:

Good for nonfiction writers building an audience, or for published fiction writers cultivating readerships.

Twitter is a way to update and engage followers multiple times a day in rapid-fire bursts of short text. Users pick which Twitter accounts they want updates from and receive a news feed where they can click through to interesting articles you've posted, see funny comments you've made, and know what you're doing in real time.

Who does it well: Sarah Dessen, twitter.com/sarahdessen

Blog:

Great for nonfiction writers building an audience, or for published fiction writers cultivating readerships.

A blog can be a phenomenal way to build an audience, but you need a specific focus that directly relates to the book you want to publish. This will show agents that subscribers to your blog have interest in purchasing your book. So remember, unless you're looking to score a cookbook deal, we're not curious about what you had for breakfast. Also, before you launch a blog, make sure you have the time and stamina to make a minimum of one post every week or two; it's necessary to regularly provide new content in order to build and retain a strong readership.

Who does it well: Deb Perelman, smittenkitchen.com

Self-Publishing:

Let's clear up a misconception about platform and self-publishing. For the average first-time writer, self-publishing is not a reliable way to expand your platform. It's simply a way to publish on your own, without the help of an agent or the resources of a traditional publishing house. Agents do not see self-published authors as any more serious about finding an agent than non-self-published writers.

Authors with well-established platforms have better odds of self-publishing lucratively and successfully, but it's important to have a realistic mindset about where you want to go from there. It's a full-time job to sell books without the backing of a publisher. Selling (not giving away for free) fewer than 10,000 books and/or e-books can demonstrate that your project lacks strong audience appeal. If you then try shopping that self-published book to agents or publishers, they're likely to view it as "sloppy seconds." Self-publishing is not a precursor to publishing for writers hoping to secure agent representation. It is the real thing. Once a book or e-book is published and given an ISBN (an industry tracking number), it has a traceable sales history. If your book sales are not a selling point, your work, not the medium used to publish it, will be seen as the cause. Self-publishing can benefit some writers, but if you choose this route make sure you are OK with the possibility that that project very well may not be traditionally published later.

The good news is that even if you have already self-published and those sales were not brag-worthy, most agents will not be deterred from considering submissions for your new, unpublished projects. Just make sure you are transparent about your self-publishing history (without overemphasizing it) and that the new project isn't intended to piggyback on the self-published work in any way.

YOUR QUERY

Agents look for queries that make us want to turn the pages of your story. That means you need to think of your query as the first and most important page of your manuscript. Not only are you introducing your manuscript or proposal, you're also introducing yourself as a writer—and as with any first meeting, you'll want to make a good impression.

A query is a map of your manuscript or proposal, and agents need the keys to understand what direction you're headed in and decide if we want to come along for the ride.

For fiction, orient agents by stating your manuscript's stats: title, word count and genre. If you're not sure what your genre is, pick the one closest to the theme of your manuscript and, if necessary, reference one supporting subcategory. When done well, your query should read like a movie trailer version of your manuscript, not a synopsis. So keep the details short. Identify your main characters and tell us why we're rooting for them, and include only the most important conflict and action points.

For nonfiction, show agents the scope of your platform and what qualifies you to write about your subject. Also, tell us the clever things we will learn and briefly mention audience potential.

Whether you are writing fiction or nonfiction, highlight the unique points of your project—especially if elements of your work are similar to popular books already in circulation. Agents aren't looking for carbon copies of pre-existing books, but they are looking for new twists on trends that haven't already peaked. Stay current by reading your genre's trendsetters and bestsellers. It's not essential to compare your title to a bestseller, but do let your description show you've taken the thread of a popular or emerging market and spun a story all your own.

Whatever you do, don't blindly pitch your work. Know which agents you are pitching and why. Your job as a querying writer is not to change the mind of an agent who doesn't rep your genre, but to find agents who do—and demonstrate to them that your work is ready for representation.

Thank us for our time and consideration before signing your query, and avoid the following query sins, or you might find yourself so far at the bottom of an agent's list, you've fallen off:

1. Don't say your friends and family loved your manuscript. Unless they are industry professionals, this doesn't mean anything to us.
2. Know that querying via mass email will lead to mass rejections.
3. Stay away from negative statements like, "I know it needs a lot of work," or, "I don't have any writing experience." You might as well say, "Don't bother."
4. Don't send agents links to websites that host your query or sample pages, expecting us to go on a scavenger hunt.
5. If you've self-published Book 1 of a trilogy and want our help selling Book 2 to a publishing house, it won't happen. You can't mix and match one series using different publishing models (unless you have mind-blowingly phenomenal numbers on Book 1, in which case you should be pitching us that one first).

YOUR MANUSCRIPT

The biggest trick to rising up on an agent's wish list is to wow us from the beginning, but not for the reasons you may be thinking. The truth is that most agents rarely read manuscripts from front to back, and even more rarely in a single sitting. As a writer, you have no control over which pages an agent will read more thoroughly than others, with one exception—without fail, we will always look closely at the beginning pages of your work. Manuscripts and proposals are then set aside into one of two categories: rejection or possible representation. Get past this initial screening and you've placed yourself on a shorter list of work that an agent will take more time to consider.

There are tremendous resources available for writers looking to improve their opening pages. If you want an agent, you'll need to exhaust every one of them. The essentials to have in those make-or-break pages—in any genre—are a clear POV with a strong voice, fantastic language and prose, and a solid emotional connection between your main character and the reader.

Almost every agent agrees that poorly executed prologues are the quickest route back to slushville. Prologues reflexively cause agents to skip to Chapter 1 without a look back. Most have backstory that is too often "told" instead of "shown." We've seen so many terrible prologues, we reason reading yours will only do you a disservice. If you insist on including a prologue, assume that it might not be read, and carefully craft Chapter 1 as if it's the first thing an agent will read. Take any shortcuts by renaming your prologue as Chapter 1, and we will know!

After you've taken care to craft an exceptional beginning, don't let rookie mistakes break the spell of an agent reading your work. Typos happen; no writer is immune. If you can't afford to have a copy editor proofread your work, be extra vigilant about self-editing. Or consider hiring someone to proofread your first 25 pages and then using their corrections as a model of what to look for in polishing the rest of the manuscript.

Lastly, avoid getting too inspired with formatting. Save the creativity for your writing. We need clean, easy-to-read pages to avoid premature graying and permanent frown lines. Misguided "finishing touches" may actually detract from your writing. Please don't break our immersive reading experience with bizarre formatting, distracting fonts, and more italicized words than we know what to do with. If an agent has not stated a personal preference, pick a simple default-style font to showcase your work.

HANDLING REJECTIONS AND RESUBMISSIONS

As disappointing as it is to receive a rejection, how you conduct yourself post-rejection will set the stage for any future communication with that agent. The quickest cure for anger is compassionate forgiveness. The Dalai Lama can back me up on this. Please forgive us for rejecting you. It feels personal, but it's not. Neither was sending you a standard rejection. We don't enjoy sending them, and rejections—thank goodness—are not our main job. Our main job is to help promote and sell the authors who we've made commitments to, and to find new authors we know we can do right by. Email us a nasty response and we'll never look at your work again.

Know that every time an agent does give feedback beyond a form rejection, you've struck gold—in no way have you come away empty-handed. Some of the advice may seem simplistic or trite. You want specifics! What do they mean the character development was weak? Yes, often the feedback seems basic, but that doesn't mean the suggestions should be easily discarded. Take these critiques seriously and you may be able to create an opportunity for resubmission.

Sometimes writers take an encouraging rejection and unknowingly use it to their disadvantage. If an agent invites you to resubmit or points out aspects of your work that made an impression, you've grabbed her attention. However, after we've taken the time to give you constructive feedback, don't tell us you were thinking the same thing! Why then did you submit your material to us, if you felt it still needed work? Of course, disagreeing won't go over well either. Get defensive about feedback and you're showing how you'll conduct yourself once you really get comfortable with us. Even a rebuttal couched in niceties burns bridges.

To create an opportunity for resubmission, respond to rejections graciously, promptly thanking the agent for his time and consideration. That's it. Don't detail other pro-jects you'd like to submit, or say you were hoping we would come to a different conclusion. Just take a breath. Unless an agent has specifically inquired about your other writing, wait at least two weeks before querying a new project. To resubmit the same project, say you've used our exceptional feedback to improve your work and would appreciate us taking another look. In either case, trust that the next time we see your name, we'll remember your thoughtful note.

If an agent comes out and invites you to resubmit a revised manuscript, she might be considering you as a client. Now, assuming you find merit in her feedback and would like to take advantage of the opportunity to incorporate it, you'll have to show her you're ready. The biggest mistake a writer can make when sending revised materials is underestimating the amount of revisions an agent was expecting. Make sure you send back a proposal or manuscript that is a significantly improved incarnation of your previous work. But act quickly. If you wait more than six to eight months you risk the market changing and, with it, the interest of your future agent.

SEALING THE DEAL

What agents won't tell you is that every email and conversation with us is a testing ground. Can we trust you to handle communications professionally—not just with us, but also with our publishing contacts who would be involved in seeing your book through to publication and beyond? We are well aware that the behavior of our clients can reflect upon us. We want to know you're polite, open to suggestions, and enjoyable to work with.

To gauge your flexibility, we'll ask you some questions, and we also expect you to show that you're thoughtful and savvy by asking a few of your own. This conversation is the final step in making the leap from wish list to client list.

Questions an agent may ask:

- Are you willing to further expand your platform?
- Are you open to revisions? (Basically that's a trap—say yes and mean it!)
- Do you have the time to revise prior to publication?

Questions you should ask:

- What kind of revisions do you foresee?
- Who do you see as a potential audience for my work?
- Do you have experience selling in my genre? And do you have specific publishers in mind for my book?

If there are other agents you're waiting to hear from, this is the time to let us know. We're hoping you can't imagine anyone else representing you, but we understand that partnering with an agent is an important decision. Out of consideration, set a reasonable timeline of up to three weeks to make a final choice.

OUR WISH FOR YOU ...

Ultimately you are our compass. We're hunting for buried treasure, so please point us in the right direction. Establish an image, craft your best work, connect with us on a personal level, and your future will shine ahead of you like a sea of glossy book jackets. You can find an agent. We know this because we're hoping to find you, too. WD

QUERY LETTER CHECKLIST

- Hit us with your logline and manuscript stats right away.
- Mention how you found us.
- Give a movie trailer version of your book, not the spoilers.
- For fiction (and some narrative nonfiction), tell us about your main characters and why we're rooting for them.
- Mention the major points of conflict in your story.
- For nonfiction, give highlights of your platform and explain what we'll learn from your proposal.
- Tell us about yourself in a brief bio paragraph.
- Indicate that you've enclosed any other materials requested in our submission guidelines (opening chapters, synopsis, etc.).
- Make sure we have all of your contact info: telephone and email.
- Thank us for our time and consideration.

KIMIKO NAKAMURA is an agent with Dee Mura Literary (deemuraliterary.com), where she represents both fiction and nonfiction titles, and looks for writers with unique voices and inspiring stories.

SERIES WRITING

How to plan for multiple books.

by Karen S Wiesner

"The disease of writing is dangerous and contagious," Abelard famously said to Heloise. So, too, can a book series become a relentless obsession: It's why readers follow series devotedly to the last, why writers write them for years on end, and why publishers contract them in spades. In our trend-driven world, series are hotter than ever.

But if writing a novel can seem overwhelming, the idea of creating a whole series of them can be exponentially more so. Whether you've been pondering starting a series from Page 1, or you've finished a book and don't want to let the characters go, there are plenty of simple things you can implement now to lay a strong foundation for what's to come.

TIES

If a series doesn't have a "tie" that connects each book, it could hardly be called a series. Ties can be any (or even all) of the following:

- A recurring character or couple (think Aloysius Pendergast in Douglas Preston and Lincoln Child's Pendergast series, or J.D. Robb's Eve and Roarke from the In Death series)
- A central group of characters (George R.R. Martin's *A Song of Ice and Fire*, Kate Jacobs' *Friday Night Knitting Club*)
- A plot or premise (Robin Cook's Jack Stapleton medical mysteries, Dan Brown's treasure hunts starring Robert Langdon)
- A setting (*Twilight*'s Forks, Wash., Harry Potter's Hogwarts School of Witchcraft and Wizardry)

Series can be open-ended—in which each book stands on its own, and the series could continue indefinitely (Langdon)—or closed, in which an underlying plot continues in each book and resolves in the last (Harry Potter).

What connects the books in a series should be evident from Book 1. Ensuring this kind of continuity requires advance planning, starting as early as possible.

STORY ARCS & SERIES ARCS

Every work of fiction, series or otherwise, has a contained story line. That story arc is introduced, developed and concluded within each individual book. Series books often have a series arc as well: a long-term plot thread that is introduced in the first book; developed, expanded and/or alluded to in some way in each subsequent book; and resolved only in the final installment of the series.

Series arcs can be prominent, or can be more subtly defined. The series arc is generally separate from each individual story arc, though they must fit together seamlessly in each book to provide logical progression throughout the series. For example, in *Harry Potter and the Sorcerer's Stone,* the story arc is the Sorcerer's Stone plotline. The series arc, in the most simplified terms, is good overcoming evil among this set group of characters in the fantasy world of the series. The series arc runs progressively and cohesively beneath the individual story arcs in all the successive books.

Unless a series is completely open-ended, it is imperative that you pay off promises made early in your series arc in the concluding book. You've presented a nagging situation in the first book that *must* be settled satisfactorily in the last. Without that, readers who have invested time, money and passion will feel cheated. If, in the course of Brandon Mull's Fablehaven Series, Kendra and Seth didn't defeat the evil threatening the Fablehaven preserve and stop the plague that could have led to a hoard of imprisoned demons escaping into the world, Mull would have left his fans crying foul because he broke the pledge of a satisfactory resolution implied in the first book.

Take the time to map out your series arc as much as you can up front, so you can work through that premise from the start and ensure you'll reward readers at the finish.

C-S-P SERIES POTENTIAL

Readers fall in love with characters, settings and plots. They want conflict but don't want you to hurt their heroes. They want something different but don't want things to change. But a character, setting or plot that doesn't evolve doesn't remain lifelike, and eventually becomes boring.

Series characters, settings and plots should have longevity and intriguing potential that continues to grow, never stagnate or wane, throughout the course of a series. While none of these should ever have a radical transplant from one book to the next, it's crucial they're affected by changes. Consider the three P's that make characters (and just as certainly settings and plots) three-dimensional:

1) **Personality:** always multifaceted, with strengths and weaknesses, and capable of growing—being molded, deeply delved, and stretched.

2) **Problems:** combining light and dark, good and evil, simple and complex—not necessarily in equal parts.

3) **Purpose:** evolving goals and motivations broad enough to introduce new and unpredictable themes throughout the series, but narrow enough to maintain focus in each individual story.

Without the introduction of something new for series characters, settings and plots in each book, your readers will lose motivation to read all the way to the end.

To plant seeds for future growth in your series, nurture your C-S-P (Character-Setting-Plot) potential by establishing "plants" in early books that can be cultivated at any time during the life of the series to expand on one or all three of these components. Naturally, the sooner you incorporate these, the more believable they'll be when it's time to fully develop them.

In Dan Brown's novels, for example, Robert Langdon frequently mentions the Mickey Mouse watch he wears—not something most grown men would be caught dead in. It was a gift from his parents on his ninth birthday, and it's rife with sentimental value. Considering that his plots involve racing against the clock, the significance of this object is heightened.

The watch becomes pivotal when Langdon is thrust in a tank of breathable oxygenated liquid in *The Lost Symbol* (Book 3). If that were the first time it was mentioned, the story's believability would have been drowned as a consequence. But Brown planted the item early enough in Book 1—during an appropriate time for passive reflection—that its later role in life-or-death action scenes doesn't feel contrived or overly convenient to the plot.

Most authors include numerous "plants" in the first book in a series without even realizing it. That's good news for you if your first book is already well under way. But that doesn't mean you shouldn't deliberately insert them. When developing your C-S-P series potential, do free-form summaries for the following questions. Don't worry if you can't come up with much right away; simply use these as a jumping-off point as the series progresses, assuming that these seeds may be planted (and left mostly unexplored) in the early books for development in later titles:

- How can you outfit *all* series characters, even minor ones, with heroic traits and habits in addition to flaws and vices that can lead to natural growth as well as interesting plots and subplots?
- How can you give them occupations, hobbies, interests and idiosyncrasies that might be gradually developed?

- What relationships and potential enemies/villains can you add to expand the potential for subplots, characters or ongoing conflicts or rivalries that might play a bigger role in a later book?
- What lessons, backstory or experiences can be hinted at for later revelation and development that may lead to suspenseful plots or emotional crises?
- What life conditions, challenges, trials, grudges, grief, betrayals, threats, heartaches or obsessions can characters face that may lead to compelling situations throughout the series? (Think romance, marriage, divorce, parents/children, illness, medical ailment or death.)
- What locations can you set the series and individual books in to expand characters and plots?
- What world, regional or local events, holidays, important dates or disasters (natural or man-made) can provide a catalyst?
- What quest—fortuitous, cursed or anywhere in between—can be undertaken?
- What item or object might become the basis for plot, setting or character development?

Always leave plenty of plants unexplored to give your series longevity and your characters and story lines flexibility. In the early books in the Pendergast series, it was revealed that the protagonist's wife had been killed years earlier. Superficial details about this death were alluded to but kept sparse and flexible enough that, when the authors moved into their Helen Trilogy quite a few books later, they could easily mold this event any way they needed to and maintain believability. Had they locked down specific details early on, the trilogy might never have seen the light of day.

Hints and allusions are essential when implementing C-S-P potential. In real life, no one walks around with a list to show others of the people they know, the places they've been, or the things they've done. These are shared a little at a time. In the same way, from one book to the next, explore the facets of C-S-P slowly. If you give too much detail too soon, you may find it hard to change or adapt when the time comes to use a plant.

Remember: If no one wants to see more of these characters, settings and plots over the long haul, the series is doomed. Always spin established facts on their axis so the reader will have a new, emotional and unexpected journey in each story. Every offering must be *at least* as exciting as the one before. These are the ingredients that bring readers back for more.

ORGANIZATION OF DETAILS

The best way to learn how *not* to write a series is to do so with no organization whatsoever. You'll likely miss countless opportunities to plant and grow seeds for C-S-P series potential, be forced to backtrack to clear up issues that arise, and maybe even write yourself into a corner.

While some authors may be capable of outlining every book in a series before writing a word, that's not possible for everyone. Maybe the only way for you to figure out where you're going with your series is to complete the first book, then set it aside while you think about what might lie ahead: Which characters will take the lead? What story will be told, and which conflicts will arise? What seeds can you go back and plant in the first manuscript to prepare readers for the next installments? Even if you're not much of a planner, try answering the C-S-P potential questions (on the previous page) as much as you can. Never underestimate the value of the key story (and series!) questions percolating in your mind.

How much preplanning you do is up to you, but at minimum, I recommend you at least attempt to build on your C-S-P potential by writing summary blurbs for the series and its individual books. Just see how far you can get. Play with them and don't expect perfection the first time. You can work with them more as your series progresses.

For a series blurb, you're not focusing on individual stories but on the gist of what the series *as a whole* is about. If the series blurb is done well enough, it'll accurately reflect what every book in the series is about in a concise, intriguing summary. Remember your series ties while you're working; they'll help you figure out what your series arc should be. In no more than four sentences, define your series arc by using "leads to" logic (note that the components don't have to be in order, nor is a resolution required since you may not want to defuse the intrigue or tension):

Introduction → Change → Conflicts → Choices

Crisis → Resolutions

Here's an example from my Incognito series:

> *The Network is the world's most covert organization. Having unchallenged authority and skill to disable criminals, the Network takes over where regular law enforcement leaves off in the mission for absolute justice (***Introduction***). The price: Men and women who have sacrificed their personal identities (***Choices***) to live in the shadows (***Change***) and uphold justice for all (***Conflicts***)—no matter the cost (***Crisis***).*

Next, try blurbing the individual stories you foresee comprising the series. It's all right if you've only gotten as far as brainstorming one or two books. Start with what you have and add later, as more comes to you. Even if you don't think you know enough to get started planning this way, you'll likely find that the process of putting your ideas into words helps your concepts multiply.

Focus on which characters will take the lead in individual stories and what each story arc (conflict) will be. Write free-form summaries covering the who, what, where, when and why of each story. Then try creating a more compelling blurb using this equation (if you have more than one main character, do this for each):

> (**Name of Character**) *wants* (**Goal to be Achieved**) *because* (**Motivation for Acting**), *but faces* (**Conflict Standing in the Way**).

As before, you can mix up the order of the components. Here's the story blurb from *Dark Approach*, the 12th in my Incognito series:

> *Network operatives and lovers Lucy Carlton and Vic Leventhal* (**Names of Characters**) *have spent years living in the shadows, the property of the covert organization they gave their loyalty to in the lofty pursuit of justice for all* (**Motivation for Acting**). *Disillusioned, they're now determined to live their lives on their own terms. When the Network's archenemy secretly approaches the two about defecting—freedom for information that will disable the Network* (**Goal to be Achieved**)*—the couple must choose between love and loyalty. In the process, they jeopardize the Network's anonymity ... and its very existence* (**Conflict Standing in the Way**).

Blurbing in this way will help you develop your series—and get you excited about writing it.

The appeal of writing a series is obvious: You don't have to leave characters, places or premises you've grown to love behind when you finish a single book. While each story should stand on its own, remember that no series book should feel quite complete without the others since readers will be emotionally invested in your story even more than they would with a stand-alone novel. Keep the above factors at the forefront as you work, and you'll keep your series satisfying for your fans—and for you.

KAREN S. WIESNER is a multi-genre author of more than 100 published books—including five trilogies and 12 series, ranging from three to 12 books each—which have been nominated for and/or won 125 awards. Her latest is *Writing the Fiction Series* (Writer's Digest Books).

READING WITH A WRITER'S EYE

Read to gain insight into your craft.

by Tania Casselle

"What's your best tip for new writers?" That's a question I've asked more than fifty authors in radio interviews, and they're often quick to reply: "Read! Read a lot. Read with a writer's eye."

It's advice that newer writers sometimes take with a grain of salt, perhaps suspecting that those already on the publishing ladder are just trying to sell more books. And even if we do take their advice, what does it mean to read with a writer's eye? We don't want to sound like someone else, we have our own voice and style. So how can reading other people's work practically help with our own writing?

First, there's the sheer inspiration of reading wonderful fiction, the motivation it gives us to jump up from the armchair and hit the keyboard. Then there's the osmosis factor—just by reading widely we absorb the art of writing, which emerges intuitively in our work. But when our intuition fails, when we're stuck in a project or realize that we need to polish up a craft area, that's the time to turn our writer's eye to our favorite fiction. Examining objectively what works successfully in a story, and how and why it works, helps us pick up tips, tricks, and techniques we can bring to our own writing problems or just give a gentle nudge to open our minds to possibilities we haven't seen before.

After all, every challenge we face in fiction has already been solved by someone else. Why reinvent the wheel? As author John Nichols says: "See how other people do it, the same way that painters go to museums and reproduce the great masters in order to understand how Rembrandt or Picasso used color and construction. The tools of the writing trade are essentially what's been written before."

DEVELOPING YOUR WRITER'S EYE

"Read the first pages of five books to see what's in common in the first pages, or the first chapters," says Lisa Tucker, author of *The Promised World* and *The Winters in Bloom*. "This is after you've read the whole book, and you understand what the story is, and you want to see how it's made, the nuts and bolts."

Study how the writer creates and establishes her characters. "A lot of new writers think 'If I kill somebody on page one, I'll really have the reader.' But you won't, unless the person you kill is somebody we already care about. You need to bring characters to life quickly, especially if you're going to murder them. Then the threat is so much more important. It's a real person that's going to be killed."

Tucker noticed how Kate Atkinson's *When Will There Be Good News?* created a vivid impression of a family in the first pages, setting up the tragedy that soon befalls them. The mother, for example, is "An artist, divorced, a sort of a wild woman. You get the feeling that she has a passionate personality, there's maybe one sentence about the painting she used to do ... and the fact that she used to do it... Why doesn't she do it anymore? You want to give us enough about the character that we're curious about them."

Also consider how the backstory is handled. "How much backstory must be told? Writers feel that they have to introduce everything about their backstory before they can do anything, which is not true." Tucker suggests charting out what we're told in the first pages about front story and backstory, noting the interplay between them, and writing down what we're told about every character.

If your characters feel flat, Robin Romm (*The Mother Garden*) says "Look at the way Andre Dubus or Joy Williams create character. They're using very particular traits, staying consistent, and they don't say very much. It's not a list of 'blonde hair, blue eyes, six foot five.' It's more likely to be the way somebody puts a beer can on the counter."

Romm points to Flannery O'Connor's *The Life You Save May Be Your Own*, when Mr. Shiflet strikes a match. The flame creeps closer to his skin till he puts it out just before it burns him. "O'Connor never says this is a dangerous man, but the fact that he let the match burn that long, that tiny detail is all you need."

"You read a story once and it affects you, it's a great story, but you probably don't know how or why," says Antonya Nelson, author of *Nothing Right* and *Bound*. "So you read it again and again, and you start to see how the writer has been manipulating your experience. How the writer has made conscious decisions about how to place its emphasis, how to inflect certain themes or moments." Nelson suggests looking at why a story ended where it did, and how motifs move through it. "I was struck in an Edith Wharton novel by the patient way she described a character, and realized that I was trying shortcuts with a piece I was working on."

WORD BY WORD

John Nichols (*The Empanada Brotherhood*) observes that we learn by imitation—it's how children learn language and behavior. He's taken chapters from writers he admires and typed them up, word by word. "In the process you demystify them, and you also learn a lot about how that person writes."

Lisa Tucker recalls typing out a scene from Jane Smiley's "A Thousand Acres." "It helped me see how she moved from dialogue to action. I had a problem at first thinking about incorporating gestures into dialogue. Sometimes I'd have floating heads—two characters having a discussion—and I had to remember 'Oh wait, they're doing something!' It made me understand how people look away, pick things up, make expressions, and how to fit that in with dialogue in such a smooth way."

Robert Wilder typed out Ethan Canin's story "The Year of Getting to Know Us" when he was learning to write fiction. He liked Canin's economy and wanted to understand the structure. "I was figuring it out from the inside out. It helped me enormously about scene and summary, and fed into my understanding of what makes a scene, dialogue, description, setting, details. And to literally feel what it's like to have those words coming out of your hands. Hopefully some of the structure of the prose and sentence-making ability will enter into your body." Wilder's two essay collections include *Tales From The Teachers' Lounge*, and his fiction has appeared in *The Greensboro Review*, *Colorado Review*, and *Hayden's Ferry Review*.

MENTORS & MODELS

"A lot of professors in my grad program were not crazy about my work, so I found mentorship in books," says Pam Houston, whose latest novel is *Contents May Have Shifted*. Houston read Ron Carlson, Richard Ford, Lorrie Moore, and Amy Bloom. "My contemporaries, but ahead of me in their careers. Writers who were doing things that seemed similar to what I was trying to do. I studied how they used metaphors, how they structured stories, how they made sentences."

When Houston started writing her novel *Sight Hound*, she was struggling with voice. Her previous books were essentially written in her own personal voice, but she couldn't see that approach working for *Sight Hound*. Yet it was a big leap to imagine it told from a different voice.

Houston laughs as she remembers. "I felt, God, I'm sick to death of this girl. Have you no range, Pam?" Then she saw *The Laramie Project* on stage, based on interviews with people around the murder of Matthew Shepard. "The bartender, the cop, the doctor, his parents, everybody, and they created monologues for all these characters. It's so moving, the idea of a choral community telling the story together." Houston bought the play that night and read it. "Seeing how a bunch of different voices could tell the story in the first person gave me permission to tiptoe into this idea of other voices. That's how *Sight Hound* wound up having twelve first-person narratives."

Novels from two very different writers were helpful studies for Tara Ison's debut novel. "*The Bluest Eye* by Toni Morrison was the first time I was consciously aware of the device of multiple points of view. The texture that gave the story, to use that shifting lens so seamlessly and beautifully... It was really inspiring to me." As a teen, Ison read Stephen King's *Carrie*. "It's a narrative collage, with newspaper articles and interviews, and he takes all of these elements, and weaves them together." Both informed Ison's *A Child Out of Alcatraz*.

Ison's second novel *The List* was originally written in first-person narrative voice, alternating between two characters. "It felt too claustrophobic," says Ison, so she switched gears and revisited Brian Moore's *The Lonely Passion of Judith Hearne* to see how he'd achieved a close third-person voice. (So close, in fact, that on earlier readings Ison had remembered it written in first person; she'd been surprised to realize it was in third person.) "I went back to study how he was able to make me feel so intimate to the character, yet he had the flexibility of third person. He could leave her mind when he needed to, to give us insights that the character could not have on her own."

FIRST IMPRESSIONS

"If you find a writer you love, go back and read their first novel. It's easier to see how they're made, they show their structure more clearly because the writer is not as good at hiding it. If you read *The Song Reader*, my first novel, I think it's more clear how I did it. You could make an outline and think about what I was working with, because I wasn't able to hide the bones." —Lisa Tucker

Pamela Erens found a model structure for her first novel *The Understory* in William Trevor's *Reading Turgenev*, where chapters of past story are interspersed with chapters of current story, and the two gradually converge.

"Trevor's book starts with a character in a bad spot, in an institution, but you don't know why. After a short chapter, you immediately jump way back in time, but the past chapters keep getting closer to the present."

Erens' character was in a different kind of institution, a Buddhist monastery, and her past story didn't sprawl back as far as Trevor's, but she immediately intuited that this was a good way to marry her material with form. "It was a very enjoyable way to bring the reader incrementally toward the present moment and explain how he got to where he was when you opened to the first page. It's reassuring to have some sort of structure to follow."

The Understory has an ominous tone which builds turn-the-page tension. Erens had already pared the writing in revisions, but during her final draft she read Camus' *The Stranger*.

"It's a very short book, with a creepy sense of omission—what's being left out." Reading that made her trim back even more.

SCENE VS. SUMMARY

"Pay attention to where the writer is slowing down to put us in the moment with the character, versus when the writer is doing a summarizing sweep of time, to move us along. Identify moments of discovery, confrontation, and decision making, because I think those are the moments that express character so well, and those are the moments rich in conflict, and that's when I think it's really valuable to slow down, as opposed to summarizing for the reader." —Tara Ison

OPEN TO ENLIGHTENMENT

John Dufresne (*Requiem, Mass.*) believes that reading writers who don't write the way you do is especially useful to open up new vistas. "It snaps you out of your habitual way you write."

Dufresne's greatest difficulty as a writer is usually in finding his plot. "I start with characters, give them some trouble, then after one hundred pages of the novel ask myself: 'Well, what's the plot?'"

In turning our writer's eye on other authors' story plots, Dufresne suggests a few questions. "The first time you read it you were surprised at everything but when you got to the end you realized it was inevitable, it had to happen this way. So how did he effect that? Do you know why the character is doing what he's doing at any moment? What does he want? Why does he want it? Why is he doing this to get it? The plot emanates from the behavior of the characters ... here's where the struggle begins, here's where the character tried to get what she wanted.

"I pay attention to my own emotions. Why do I love this character so much? Why do I feel so sad at this point? The writer made me feel this way or think that way, how did she do it? When was I surprised? How did she pull that surprise off?"

One way to pick up tricks of the trade is to diagram a story you admire. You can even follow that model, using your own characters and story.

"I've done this with Alice Munro," says Dufresne. "I took a story of hers and diagrammed it out and tried to write a story in exactly the same way, as an exercise... just trying to intuit what she was thinking."

INSPIRATIONS

"Dennis Cooper opened my mind on what you can actually do in a novel," says Don Waters, winner of the Iowa Short Fiction Award for his collection *Desert Gothic*. "Cooper began writing as a poet first, a novelist later. I love how in his sentences things are working! Several things can be happening in the same sentence. It's that weird thing that happens when you're striving for something, and then you see somebody else who's already done it, and something in you just physically bursts open and you think: This is it! And Cooper walks a very risky line in what he writes about. It opened my mind to what you could actually write about in terms of subject matter."

Waters recommends reading plays to study dialogue. "Like David Mamet, the master of hyperrealistic dialogue. Everything happens through dialogue in a play, characterization and how to move a plot."

While obviously it's plagiarism to copy other writers' words, there's a difference between form and content, and everyone's techniques and approaches to craft and structure are all up for grabs.

"Hemingway and Fitzgerald, they never had workshops!" says Robert Westbrook, whose novels include the series of Howard Moon Deer Mysteries. "They just read and read and loved books. If you do imitate, consciously or unconsciously, your own effort is going to come out different. It comes out with your own slant."

"What I discovered is the wonderful truth that it never sounds like the other writer," says Pamela Erens. "It sounds like yourself, and learning that really freed me up. While you're working on a story, things mutate so much that you end up with something that's your own. Every writer has a completely different consciousness and inflection. How else are you going to learn? It's a great resource. You have the whole library of literature to go to for help.

TANIA CASSELLE is freelance writer with nearly two decades of experience contributing to magazines and news media in the United States and Europe. She contributed to *Now Write! Fiction Writing Exercises from Today's Best Writers and Teachers* (Tarcher), and her fiction has appeared in lit journals including *New York Stories, The Saint Ann's Review, South Dakota Review, Bitter Oleander, Carve Magazine*, and anthologies including *Harlot Red* (Serpent's Tail Press) and *Online Writing: The Best of the First Ten Years* (Snowvigate Press). She hosts the *Writers on Radio* show for NPR-affiliate KRZA in New Mexico and Colorado, also broadcast on other stations.

CREATE YOUR WRITER PLATFORM

8 fundamental rules for author visibility.

by Chuck Sambuchino

The chatter about the importance of a writer platform builds each year. Having an effective platform has never been more important than right now. With so many books available and few publicists left to help promote, the burden now lies upon the author to make sure copies of their book fly off bookshelves. In other words, the pressure is on for writers to act as their own publicist and chief marketer, and very few can do this successfully.

Know that if you're writing nonfiction, a damn good idea won't cut it. You need to prove that people will buy your book by showing a comprehensive ability to market yourself through different channels such as social networking sites and traditional media. If you can't do that, a publisher won't even consider your idea.

WHAT IS PLATFORM?

Platform, simply put, is your visibility as an author. In other words, platform is your personal ability to sell books right this instant. Better yet, I've always thought of platform like this: When you speak, who listens? In other words, when you have a something to say, what legitimate channels exist for you to release your message to audiences who will consider buying your books/services?

Platform will be your key to finding success as an author, especially if you're writing nonfiction. Breaking the definition down, realize that platform is your personal ability to sell books through:

1. Who you are
2. Personal and professional connections you have
3. Any media outlets (including personal blogs and social networks) that you can utilize to sell books

In my opinion, the following are the most frequent building blocks of a platform:

1. A blog of impressive size
2. A newsletter of impressive size
3. Article/column writing (or correspondent involvement) for the media—preferably for larger publications, radio, and TV shows
4. Contributions to successful websites, blogs and periodicals helmed by others
5. A track record of strong past book sales that ensures past readers will buy your future titles
6. Networking, and your ability to meet power players in your community and subject area
7. Public speaking appearances—especially national ones; the bigger the better
8. An impressive social media presence (such as on Twitter or Facebook)
9. Membership in organizations that support the successes of their own
10. Recurring media appearances and interviews—in print, on the radio, on TV, or online
11. Personal contacts (organizational, media, celebrity, relatives) who can help you market at no cost to yourself, whether through blurbs, promotion or other means.

Not all of these methods will be of interest/relevance to you. As you learn more about to how to find success in each one, some will jump out at you as practical and feasible, while others will not. And to learn what constitutes "impressive size" in a platform plank, check out this article: tinyurl.com/8d2hnrj.

"PLATFORM" VS. "PUBLICITY"

Platform and publicity are interconnected yet very different. Platform is what you do before a book comes out to make sure that when it hits shelves, it doesn't stay there long. Publicity is an active effort to acquire media attention for a book that already exists. In other words, platform falls upon the author, whereas (hopefully) publicity will be handled by a publicist, either in-house or contracted for money.

Do something right now: Go to Amazon.com and find a book for sale that promises to teach you how to sell more books. Look at the comparable titles below it and start scrolling left to right using the arrows. (Do it now. I'll wait.) Tons of them, aren't there? It's because so many authors are looking for any way possible to promote their work, especially the many self-published writers out there. They've got a book out—and now they realize copies aren't selling. Apparently having your work online to buy at places like Amazon isn't enough to have success as a writer. That's why we must take the reins on our own platform and marketing.

As a last thought, perhaps consider it like this: Publicity is about asking and wanting: gimme gimme gimme. Platform is about giving first, then receiving because of what you've given and the goodwill it's earned you.

THE FUNDAMENTAL PRINCIPLES OF PLATFORM

1. It is in giving that we receive.

In my experience, this concept—*it is in giving that we receive*—is the fundamental rule of platform. Building a platform means that people follow your updates, listen to your words, respect and trust you, and, yes, will consider buying whatever it is you're selling. But they will only do that if they like you—and the way you get readers to like you is by legitimately helping them. Answer their questions. Give them stuff for free. Share sources of good, helpful information. Make them laugh and smile. Inform them and make their lives easier and/or better. Do what they cannot: cull together information or entertainment of value. Access people and places they want to learn more about. Help them achieve their goals. Enrich their lives. After they have seen the value you provide, they will want to stay in contact with you for more information. They begin to like you, and become a follower. And the more followers you have, the bigger your platform becomes.

2. You don't have to go it alone.

Creating a large and effective platform from scratch is, to say the least, a daunting task. But you don't have to swim out in the ocean alone; you can—and are encouraged to—work with others. There are many opportunities to latch on to bigger publications and groups in getting your words out. And when your own platform outlets—such as a blog—get large enough, they will be a popular source for others seeking to contribute guest content. You will find yourself constantly teaming with others on your way up, and even after you've found some success.

3. Platform is what you are *able* to do, not what you are *willing* to do.

I review nonfiction book proposals for writers, and in each of these proposals there is a marketing section. Whenever I start to read a marketing section and see bullet points such as "I am happy to go on a book tour" or "I believe that Fox News and MSNBC will be interested in this book because it is controversial," then I stop reading—because the proposal has a big problem. Understand this immediately: Your platform is not pie-in-the-sky thinking. It is not what you hope will happen or maybe could possibly hopefully happen sometime if you're lucky and all the stars align when your publicist works really hard. It's also not what you are willing to do, such as "be interviewed by the media" or "sign books at trade events." (Everyone is willing to do these things, so by mentioning them, you are making no case for your book because you're demonstrating no value.) The true distinction for writer platform is that it must be absolutely what you can make happen right now.

4. You can only learn so much about writer platform by instruction, which is why you should study what others do well and learn by example.

I don't know about you, but, personally, I learn from watching and doing better than I learn from reading. On that note, don't be afraid to study and mimic what others are doing. If you are looking for totally original ideas on how to blog and build your platform, I'll just tell you right now there likely are few or none left. So if you want to see what's working, go to the blogs and websites and Twitter feeds and newspaper columns of those you admire—then take a page from what they're doing. If you start to notice your favorite large blogs include all their social networking links at the top ("Find me on Twitter," "Find me on Facebook"), then guess what? Do the same. If people are getting large followings doing book reviews of young adult fantasy novels, why not do the same?

5. You must make yourself easy to contact.

I have no idea why people make themselves difficult to contact without a website and/or e-mail listed online. Besides "visibility," another way to think about platform is to examine your reach. And if your goal is reach, you do not want to limit people's abilities to find and contact you much if at all. You want people to contact you. You want other writers to e-mail from out of the blue. I love it when a member of the media finds my info online and writes me. I don't even mind it when a writer sends me an e-mail with a random question. I've made long-term friends that way—friends who have bought my book and sung my praises to others. It's called networking—and networking starts by simply making yourself available, and taking the next step to encourage people with similar interests or questions to contact you.

6. Start small and start early.

A true writer platform is something that's built before your book comes out, so that when the book hits your hands, you will be above the masses for all to see. I won't lie—the beginning is hard. It's full of a lot of effort and not a whole lot of return. Fear not; this will pass. Building a platform is like building a structure—every brick helps. Every brick counts. Small steps are not bad. You must always be considering what an action has to offer and if it can lead to bigger and better things. "What frustrates most people is that they want to have platform now," says literary agent Roseanne Wells of the Marianne Strong Literary Agency. "It takes time and a lot of effort, and it builds on itself. You can always have more platform, but trying to sell a book before you have it will not help you."

7. Have a plan, but feel free to make tweaks.

At first, uncertainty will overwhelm you. What are you going to blog about? How should you present yourself when networking? Should your Twitter handle be your name or the title of your book/brand? All these important questions deserve careful thought early on. The earlier you have a plan, the better off you will be in the long run—so don't just jump in blind. The more you can diagram and strategize at the beginning, the clearer your road will be.

As you step out and begin creating a writer platform, make sure to analyze how you're doing, then slowly transition so you're playing to your strengths and eliminating your weakest elements. No matter what you want to write about, no matter what platform elements you hone in on, don't ignore the importance of analysis and evolution in your journey. Take a look at what you're doing right and wrong to make sure you're not throwing good money after bad. And feel free to make all kinds of necessary tweaks and changes along the way to better your route.

8. Numbers matter—so quantify your platform

If you don't include specific numbers or details, editors and agents will be forced to assume the element of platform is unimpressive, which is why you left out the crucial detail of its size/reach. Details are sexy; don't tease us. Try these right and wrong approaches below:

WRONG: "I am on Twitter and just love it."
CORRECT: "I have more than 10,000 followers on Twitter."

WRONG: "I do public speaking on this subject."
CORRECT: "I present to at least 10 events a year—sometimes as a keynote. The largest events have up to 1,200 attendees."

WRONG: "I run a blog that has won awards from other friendly bloggers."
CORRECT: "My blog averages 75,000 page views each month and has grown at a rate of 8 percent each month over the past year."

Also, analyzing numbers will help you see what's working and not working in your platform plan—allowing you to make healthy changes and let the strategy evolve. Numbers reflect the success you're having, and it's up to you to figure out why you're having that success.

CHUCK SAMBUCHINO (chucksambuchino.com, @chucksambuchino on Twitter) edits the *Guide to Literary Agents* (guidetoliteraryagents.com/blog) as well as the *Children's Writer's & Illustrator's Market*. His pop humor books include *How to Survive a Garden Gnome Attack* (film rights optioned by Sony) and *Red Dog / Blue Dog: When Pooches Get Political* (reddog-bluedog.com). Chuck's other writing books include *Formatting & Submitting Your Manuscript, 3rd. Ed.*, and *Create Your Writer Platform* (fall 2012). Besides that, he is a husband, guitarist, sleep-deprived new father, dog owner, and cookie addict.

"PLATFORM" VS. "CREDENTIALS"

The most important question you will be asked as you try to get your nonfiction book published is: "Why are you the best person to write this book?" This question is two-fold, as it speaks to both your credentials and your platform. To be a successful author, you will need both, not just the former.

Your credentials encompass your education and experience to be considered as an expert in your category. For example, if you want to write a book called *How to Lose 10 Pounds in 10 Weeks*, then my first thought would be to wonder if you are a doctor or a dietician. If not, what position do you hold that would give you solid authority to speak on your subject and have others not question the advice you're presenting? Or maybe you want to write a book on how to sell real estate in a challenging market. To have the necessary gravitas to compose such a book, you would likely have to have worked as an agent for decades and excelled in your field—hopefully winning awards over the years and acting in leadership roles within the real estate agent community.

Would you buy a book on how to train a puppy from someone whose only credential was that they owned a dog? I wouldn't. I want to see accolades, leadership positions, endorsements, educational notes and more. I need to make sure I'm learning from an expert before I stop questioning the text and take it as helpful fact.

All this—all your authority—comes from your credentials. That's why they're so necessary. But believe it or not, credentials are often easier to come by than platform.

Platform, as we now know, is your ability to sell books and market yourself to target audience(s). There are likely many dieticians out there who can teach people interesting ways to lower their weight. But a publishing company is not interested in the 90 percent of them who lack any platform. They want the 10 percent of experts who have the ability to reach readers. Publishing houses seek experts who possess websites, mailing lists, media contacts, a healthy number of Twitter followers and a plan for how to grow their visibility.

It's where credentials meet platform—*that's* where book authors are born.

PERSPECTIVES

BLOGGING BASICS:

Get the most out of your site.

by Robert Lee Brewer

In these days of publishing and media change, writers have to build platforms and learn how to connect to audiences if they want to improve their chances of publication and overall success. There are many methods of audience connection available to writers, but one of the most important is blogging.

Since I've spent several years successfully blogging—both personally and professionally—I figure I've got a few nuggets of wisdom to pass on to writers who are curious about blogging or who are already doing it.

Here's my quick list of tips:

1. **START BLOGGING TODAY.** If you don't have a blog, use Blogger, WordPress, or some other blogging software to start your blog today. It's free, and you can start off with your very personal "Here I am, world" post.
2. **START SMALL.** Blogs are essentially very simple, but they can get very complicated (for people who like complications). However, I advise bloggers start small and evolve over time.
3. **USE YOUR NAME IN YOUR URL.** This will make it easier for search engines to find you when your audience eventually starts seeking you out by name. For instance, my URL is http://robertleebrewer.blogspot.com. If you try Googling "Robert Lee Brewer," you'll notice that My Name Is Not Bob is one of the top five search results (behind my other blog: Poetic Asides).
4. **UNLESS YOU HAVE A REASON, USE YOUR NAME AS THE TITLE OF YOUR BLOG.** Again, this helps with search engine results. My Poetic Asides blog includes my name in the title, and it ranks higher than My Name Is Not Bob. However, I felt the play on my name was worth the trade-off.

5. **FIGURE OUT YOUR BLOGGING GOALS.** You should return to this step every couple months, because it's natural for your blogging goals to evolve over time. Initially, your blogging goals may be to make a post a week about what you have written, submitted, etc. Over time, you may incorporate guests posts, contests, tips, etc.
6. **BE YOURSELF.** I'm a big supporter of the idea that your image should match your identity. It gets too confusing trying to maintain a million personas. Know who you are and be that on your blog, whether that means you're sincere, funny, sarcastic, etc.
7. **POST AT LEAST ONCE A WEEK.** This is for starters. Eventually, you may find it better to post once a day or multiple times per day. But remember: Start small and evolve over time.
8. **POST RELEVANT CONTENT.** This means that you post things that your readers might actually care to know.
9. **USEFUL AND HELPFUL POSTS WILL ATTRACT MORE VISITORS.** Talking about yourself is all fine and great. I do it myself. But if you share truly helpful advice, your readers will share it with others, and visitors will find you on search engines.
10. **TITLE YOUR POSTS IN A WAY THAT GETS YOU FOUND IN SEARCH ENGINES.** The more specific you can get the better. For instance, the title "Blogging Tips" will most likely get lost in search results. However, the title "Blogging Tips for Writers" specifies which audience I'm targeting and increases the chances of being found on the first page of search results.
11. **LINK TO POSTS IN OTHER MEDIA.** If you have an e-mail newsletter, link to your blog posts in your newsletter. If you have social media accounts, link to your blog posts there. If you have a helpful post, link to it in relevant forums and on message boards.

Don't spend a week writing each post. Try to keep it to an hour or two tops and then post.

12. **WRITE WELL, BUT BE CONCISE.** At the end of the day, you're writing blog posts, not literary manifestos. Don't spend a week writing each post. Try to keep it to an hour or two tops and then post. Make sure your spelling and grammar are good, but don't stress yourself out too much.
13. **FIND LIKE-MINDED BLOGGERS.** Comment on their blogs regularly and link to them from yours. Eventually, they may do the same. Keep in mind that blogging is a form of social media, so the more you communicate with your peers the more you'll get out of the process.

14. **RESPOND TO COMMENTS ON YOUR BLOG.** Even if it's just a simple "Thanks," respond to your readers if they comment on your blog. After all, you want your readers to be engaged with your blog, and you want them to know you care that they took time to comment.
15. **EXPERIMENT.** Start small, but don't get complacent. Every so often, try something new. For instance, the biggest draw to my Poetic Asides blog are the poetry prompts and challenges I issue to poets. Initially, that was an experiment—one that worked very well. I've tried other experiments that haven't panned out, and that's fine. It's all part of a process.

SEO TIPS FOR WRITERS

Most writers may already know what SEO is. If not, SEO stands for *search engine optimization*. Basically, a site or blog that practices good SEO habits should improve its rankings in search engines, such as Google and Bing. Most huge corporations have realized the importance of SEO and spend enormous sums of time, energy, and money on perfecting their SEO practices. However, writers can improve their SEO without going to those same extremes.

In this section, I will use the terms of *site pages* and *blog posts* interchangeably. In both cases, you should be practicing the same SEO strategies (when it makes sense).

Here are my top tips on ways to improve your SEO starting today:

1. **USE APPROPRIATE KEYWORDS.** Make sure that your page displays your main keyword(s) in the page title, content, URL, title tags, page header, image names and tags (if you're including images). All of this is easy to do, but if you feel overwhelmed, just remember to use your keyword(s) in your page title and content (especially in the first and last fifty words of your page).
2. **USE KEYWORDS NATURALLY.** Don't kill your content and make yourself look like a spammer to search engines by overloading your page with your keyword(s). You don't get SEO points for quantity but for quality. Plus, one of the main ways to improve your page rankings is when you...
3. **DELIVER QUALITY CONTENT.** The best way to improve your SEO is by providing content that readers want to share with others by linking to your pages. Some of the top results in search engines are years old, because the content is so good that people keep coming back. So, incorporate your keywords in a smart way, but make sure it works organically with your content.
4. **UPDATE CONTENT REGULARLY.** If your site looks dead to visitors, then it'll appear that way to search engines, too. So update your content regularly. This should be very easy for writers who have blogs. For writers who have sites, incorporate your blog into your site. This will make it easier for visitors to your blog to discover more about you on your site (through your site navigation tools).

5. **LINK BACK TO YOUR OWN CONTENT.** If I have a post titled Blogging Tips for Writers, for instance, I'll link back to it if I have a platform-building post, because the two complement each other. This also helps clicks on my blog, which helps SEO. The one caveat is that you don't go crazy with your linking and that you make sure your links are relevant. Otherwise, you'll kill your traffic, which is not good for your page rankings.
6. **LINK TO OTHERS YOU CONSIDER HELPFUL.** Back in 2000, I remember being ordered by my boss at the time (who didn't last too much longer afterward) to ignore any competitive or complementary websites—no matter how helpful their content—because they were our competitors. You can try basing your online strategy on these principles, but I'm nearly 100 percent confident you'll fail. It's helpful for other sites and your own to link to other great resources. I shine a light on others to help them out (if I find their content truly helpful) in the hopes that they'll do the same if ever they find my content truly helpful for their audience.
7. **GET SPECIFIC WITH YOUR HEADLINES.** If you interview someone on your blog, don't title your post with an interesting quotation. While that strategy may help get readers in the print world, it doesn't help with SEO at all. Instead, title your post as "Interview With (insert name here)." If you have a way to identify the person further, include that in the title, too. For instance, when I interview poets on my Poetic Asides blog, I'll title those posts like this: Interview With Poet Erika Meitner. Erika's name is a keyword, but so are the terms *poet* and *interview*.

If you interview someone on your blog, don't title your post with an interesting quotation. While that strategy may help get readers in the print world, it doesn't help with SEO at all.

8. **USE IMAGES.** Many expert sources state that the use of images can improve SEO, because it shows search engines that the person creating the page is spending a little extra time and effort on the page than a common spammer. However, I'd caution anyone using images to make sure those images are somehow complementary to the content. Don't just throw up a lot of images that have no relevance to anything. At the same time...
9. **OPTIMIZE IMAGES THROUGH STRATEGIC LABELING.** Writers can do this by making sure the image file is labeled using your keyword(s) for the post. Using the Erika Meitner example above (which does include images), I would label the file "Erika Meitner headshot.jpg"—or whatever the image file type happens to be. Writers can

also improve image SEO through the use of captions and ALT tagging. Of course, at the same time, writers should always ask themselves if it's worth going through all that trouble for each image or not. Each writer has to answer that question for him (or her) self.

10. **USE YOUR SOCIAL MEDIA PLATFORM TO SPREAD THE WORD.** Whenever you do something new on your site or blog, you should share that information on your other social media sites, such as Twitter, Facebook, LinkedIn, online forums, etc. This lets your social media connections know that something new is on your site/blog. If it's relevant and/or valuable, they'll let others know. And that's a great way to build your SEO.

Programmers and marketers could get much deeper into the dynamics of SEO optimization, but I think these tips will help most writers out immediately and effectively while still allowing plenty of time and energy for the actual work of writing.

BLOG DESIGN TIPS FOR WRITERS

Design is an important element to any blog's success. But how can you improve your blog's design if you're not a designer? I'm just an editor with an English Lit degree and no formal training in design. However, I've worked in media for more than a decade now and can share some very fundamental and easy tricks to improve the design of your blog.

Here are my seven blog design tips for writers:

1. **USE LISTS.** Whether they're numbered or bullet points, use lists when possible. Lists break up the text and make it easy for readers to follow what you're blogging.
2. **BOLD MAIN POINTS IN LISTS.** Again, this helps break up the text while also highlighting the important points of your post.
3. **USE HEADINGS.** If your posts are longer than three hundred words and you don't use lists, then please break up the text by using basic headings.
4. **USE A READABLE FONT.** Avoid using fonts that are too large or too small. Avoid using cursive or weird fonts. Times New Roman or Arial works, but if you want to get "creative," use something similar to those.
5. **LEFT ALIGN.** English-speaking readers are trained to read left to right. If you want to make your blog easier to read, avoid centering or right aligning your text (unless you're purposefully calling out the text).
6. **USE SMALL PARAGRAPHS.** A good rule of thumb is to try and avoid paragraphs that drone on longer than five sentences. I usually try to keep paragraphs to around three sentences.
7. **ADD RELEVANT IMAGES.** Personally, I shy away from using too many images. My reason is that I only like to use them if they're relevant. However, images are very

powerful on blogs, so please use them. Just make sure they're relevant to your blog post.

If you're already doing everything on my list, keep it up! If you're not, then you might want to rethink your design strategy on your blog. Simply adding a header here and a list there can easily improve the design of a blog post.

GUEST POSTING TIPS FOR WRITERS

Recently, I've broken into guest posting as both a guest poster and as a host of guest posts (over at my Poetic Asides blog). So far, I'm pretty pleased with both sides of the guest posting process. As a writer, it gives me access to an engaged audience I may not usually reach. As a blogger, it provides me with fresh and valuable content I don't have to create. Guest blogging is a rare win-win scenario.

That said, writers could benefit from a few tips on the process of guest posting:

1. **PITCH GUEST POSTS LIKE ONE WOULD PITCH ARTICLES TO A MAGAZINE.** Include what your hook is for the post, what you plan to cover, and a little about who you are. Remember: Your post should somehow benefit the audience of the blog you'd like to guest post.
2. **OFFER PROMOTIONAL COPY OF BOOK (OR OTHER GIVEAWAYS) AS PART OF YOUR GUEST POST.** Having a random giveaway for people who comment on a blog post can help spur conversation and interest in your guest post, which is a great way to get the most mileage out of your guest appearance.
3. **CATER POSTS TO AUDIENCE.** As the editor of *Writer's Market* and *Poet's Market*, I have great range in the topics I can cover. However, if I'm writing a guest post for a fiction blog, I'll write about things of interest to a novelist, not a poet.
4. **MAKE PERSONAL, BUT PROVIDE NUGGET.** Guest posts are a great opportunity for you to really show your stuff to a new audience. You could write a very helpful and impersonal post, but that won't connect with readers the way a very helpful and personal post will. Getting more personal makes readers want to learn more about you (and your blog, your book, your Twitter account, etc.). Speaking of which...
5. **SHARE LINKS TO YOUR WEBSITE, BLOG, SOCIAL NETWORKS, ETC.** After all, you need to make it easy for readers who enjoyed your guest post to learn more about you and your projects. Start the conversation in your guest post and keep it going on your own sites, profiles, etc. And related to that...
6. **PROMOTE YOUR GUEST POST THROUGH YOUR NORMAL CHANNELS ONCE THE POST GOES LIVE.** Your normal audience will want to know where you've been and what you've been doing. Plus, guest posts lend a little extra "street cred" to your projects. But don't stop there...

7. **CHECK FOR COMMENTS ON YOUR GUEST POST AND RESPOND IN A TIMELY MANNER.** Sometimes the comments are the most interesting part of a guest post (no offense). This is where readers can ask more in-depth or related questions, and it's also where you can show your expertise on the subject by being as helpful as possible. And guiding all seven of these tips is this one:
8. **PUT SOME EFFORT INTO YOUR GUEST POST.** Part of the benefit to guest posting is the opportunity to connect with a new audience. Make sure you bring your A-game, because you need to make a good impression if you want this exposure to actually help grow your audience. Don't stress yourself out, but put a little thought into what you submit.

ONE ADDITIONAL TIP: Have fun with it. Passion is what really drives the popularity of blogs. Share your passion and enthusiasm, and readers are sure to be impressed.

ROBERT LEE BREWER is the editor of *Writer's Market* and *Poet's Market*, as well as a published poet. He is the former Poet Laureate of the Blogosphere.

DEBUT AUTHORS TELL ALL

14 first-time authors discuss their journeys.

compiled by Chuck Sambuchino

MAINSTREAM FICTION

1 SUSAN RIEGER

TINYURL.COM/RIEGERAUTHOR

The Divorce Papers (MARCH 2014, CROWN)

QUICK TAKE: The story of a very messy, contentious, high-profile divorce, and the smart, funny and sometimes prickly young woman lawyer dragooned into handling it, told entirely through emails, memos, letters, invitations, interviews, laws, and the like."

WRITES FROM: New York City.

PRE-PAPERS: As a newly minted lawyer, I had taught a Moot Court course which required me to make up a case for my students to brief and argue. I thought then that writing a novel using real documents might be an interesting way of telling a story. Years later, after my own divorce, I decided to follow up on the idea. I also spent years freelancing by writing articles on law and the way it intersects with daily life.

TIME FRAME: The total time span was about 12 years, but mainly I wrote the book in two chunks, from 1999-2001, and from 2009 to 2011.

ENTER THE AGENT: I asked a young novelist acquaintance if she would read the book and tell me if she thought it might be publishable. She liked the book a lot, and this important step gave me the confidence to look for an agent. My [second] husband, who's a journalist, approached his agent, Kathy Robbins of The Robbins Office, for her advice. After reading it, she said *she'd* like to be my agent—so long as my husband and I didn't see problems in sharing an agent. We didn't. He thinks of her as his agent, and I think of her as mine.

WHAT I LEARNED: I was naïve about the vulnerabilities it creates. I had to learn to take criticism and figure out from my agent's and my editor's suggestions how to rethink characters and situations I had known so long.

ADVICE FOR WRITERS: Remember TIC, or tush in chair. It's crucial.

NEXT UP: I've started a second novel.

PSYCHOLOGICAL FICTION

2 JENNI FAGAN

THEDEADQUEENOFBOHEMIA.WORDPRESS.COM

The Panopticon **(JULY 2013, HOGARTH)**

QUICK TAKE: The story of 16-year-old panopticon prisoner Anais Hendricks, who seeks the outlawed concepts of identity and spirit.

WRITES FROM: Scotland.

BEFORE PANOPTICON: I did quite a lot of playwriting, film scripting, poetry, short stories, and wrote my first novel at 21 (which I put in a drawer and never looked at again). In my late 20s, I departed from theater and embraced my first love (the only form I knew had no boundaries), which is fiction. I returned to studying [the craft] and won awards. This all helped me to get an agent and publication deal.

TIME FRAME: I wrote my first draft over a summer, averaging 12 hours a day, roughly seven days a week. It came in at around 160,000 words. I cut it almost in half and changed it from third person to first person.

ENTER THE AGENT: I had just been shortlisted for the Dundee International Book Prize, and at the same time the author Ali Smith had been writing to me about my poetry. She was kind enough to take a look at my novel [and] suggest a few agents. When I met my agent, Tracy Bohan of The Wylie Agency, I knew straight away that I wanted to work with her.

WHAT I DID RIGHT: I kept working exceptionally hard, and I often thought it might be a small thing that makes a difference. You know, you meet someone at a reading one day, they like [your work], they recommend your poetry to someone else. Or, you enter a small competition, it gives you confidence, you enter another.

NEXT UP: I am just finishing [a new] novel. I completed a short-story collection a few months ago, and I am finally collating all the poetry I've written over the last few years.

LITERARY HORROR

3 PETER STENSON

PETERCSTENSON.COM

Fiend **(JULY 2013, CROWN)**

QUICK TAKE: A love story between two methamphetamine addicts during the zombie apocalypse.

WRITES FROM: Denver.

BEFORE FIEND: I was in my second year of grad school at Colorado State University when I started writing *Fiend*. I had the good fortune of landing a few short stories in literary journals, which eventually served to give me the confidence to start on a novel.

TIME FRAME: The first draft of *Fiend* took about six weeks to write. From the opening sentence, I had a pretty good handle on my first-person narrator (fears, desires, history, insecurities, etc.), and just wrote without worrying about what was happening or why.

ENTER THE AGENT: I met my agent, James McGinniss of McGinniss Associates, at the 2011 AWP convention in Washington D.C. I was working at *The Colorado Review* table when he walked up and we started talking. He gave me his card and told me to send something over. The next week I sent the first chapter of *Fiend* and I signed with him a few days later.

WHAT I LEARNED: 1) It takes forever. 2) An editor makes a manuscript so much better with the harsh-yet-necessary words, "This part isn't working." I was under the impression that once you sold a book, the work was pretty much done. My editor guided me through two rewrites of *Fiend*'s ending, which I'm immensely grateful for.

WHAT I DID RIGHT: Taking risks. It probably sounds corny and cliché, but it's true. I think I took a chance with the book itself. The voice is rather raw, the subject matter vulgar at times, and it merges two seemingly incongruent genres.

IF I COULD DO IT AGAIN: Been more aware/grateful of each step along the way.

BEST ADVICE: Write books you would want to read.

NEXT UP: My agent is about to start shopping around my new novel, *A Lesson on Invisibility*.

SCIENCE FICTION

4 ANDY WEIR

GALACTANET.COM/WRITING.HTML

The Martian (**FEBRUARY 2014, CROWN**)

QUICK TAKE: An astronaut must use his wits to survive after being accidentally left behind on Mars.

WRITES FROM: Mountain View, Calif., Earth

PRE-MARTIAN: I've been writing fiction for years and posting it in serial form to my website. *The Martian* was one such story. Before that, I wrote and drew two webcomics: "Casey and Andy" and "Cheshire Crossing."

TIME FRAME: It took me three years to write *The Martian*. I posted it chapter by chapter to my website as a serial story. The feedback from my readers kept my motivation up and made for a better story as they pointed out problems and plot holes.

ENTER THE AGENT: It started with me self-publishing *The Martian* to Amazon Kindle. It sold very well and caught the interest of publishers. An editor at a major publishing house recommended the book to his literary agent colleague, David Fugate [of Launchbooks Literary Agency]. David then contacted me to ask if I was looking for representation.

BIGGEST SURPRISE: I was surprised at how long traditional publishing takes. I guess the Internet and the instant gratification it offers have spoiled me.

WHAT I DID RIGHT: Self-publishing on Kindle was the key. It's amazing the reach Amazon has. It was available for free on my website, while, at the same time, it was 99 cents on Kindle, but ten times as many people bought the Kindle version as downloaded the free version. Once it got in to the top-ten rankings, it snowballed from there.

PLATFORM: I have a website and a mailing list where I post short stories and serials for free. I slowly built up a few thousand readers. Those core readers are great, because I get immediate feedback.

ADVICE FOR WRITERS: The Internet is your friend. Create a website, or just a blog if you don't want the hassle of site maintenance. Post your stories there and you will build up a reader base.

NEXT UP: I have a sci-fi epic that I've been posting in serial form to my website.

NONFICTION (HISTORY)

5 JAMES B. CONROY

JAMESBCONROY.COM

Our One Common Country **(JANUARY 2014, LYONS PRESS)**

QUICK TAKE: The story of when Abraham Lincoln secretly met with three Confederate leaders in 1865 in the hopes to bring the Civil War to a peaceful conclusion.

WRITES FROM: Hingham, Mass.

PRE-COUNTRY: While practicing law for 32 years and serving as a Senate and Congressional aide for years before that, I always wanted to write history. After many starts and stops, I tripped across the idea of a book on the Hampton Roads Peace Conference. I was amazed to learn that no one had written a book about it and thrilled to find my subject.

TIME FRAME: While working full time as a litigator, it took me four and a half years to research and write the book—considerably longer than it took to fight the Civil War. Having finished almost all of the research, I worked my way through four progressively tighter drafts in a year and a half.

ENTER THE AGENT: Before she became my agent, the brilliant Alice Martell [of The Martell Agency] represented my son, Scott Conroy, who co-authored a book on Sarah Palin's presidential campaign. Scott referred me to Alice, and shamed me into getting serious about writing a book of my own. Alice was taken with the proposal from the start, confirmed my belief in it, and made it all happen.

BIGGEST SURPRISE: I evaded the surrender of the manuscript until it was ripped from my tight little hand—always looking for another detail to research. Parting is such sweet sorrow.

WHAT I DID RIGHT: I was fortunate to generate a burst of energy to pursue the career I always wanted, at an age when my contemporaries are retiring.

DO DIFFERENT NEXT TIME: I would have followed my dream and taken my chances much sooner in life than I did.

ADVICE FOR WRITERS: Write what you are good at, on an unexhausted subject, and ask yourself if you are putting down your pen or taking your hands off the keyboard out of laziness or necessity.

NEXT UP: If I told you, I would have to shoot you.

NEW ADULT

6 LAURA KRUGHOFF

LAURAKRUGHOFF.COM

My Brother's Name **(SEPTEMBER 2013, SCARLETTA PRESS)**

QUICK TAKE: When Jane's brother suffers a psychotic break, she chooses to assume his identity with the mad hope that living her life as her brother will keep the version of the brother she idolized alive in the world.

WRITES FROM: Chicago

BEFORE THE BOOK: I wrote and published short stories in literary magazines and journals for the past 10 years. The success of having stories published, and on occasion receiving awards and recognition, gave me the motivation and faith to pursue writing a novel.

TIME FRAME: I began writing some version of this novel in 2005, so it has been many years in the making.

ENTER THE AGENT: I did not have an agent for this book. I previously had an agent who shopped a proposal for this novel, but no one picked up the project and she eventually left the field. While I was trying to find a new agent and working on academic projects, I sent the manuscript unsolicited to Scarletta Press. When the first reader at Scarletta replied and said, "I fell in love with this novel," I felt like the book had found the right home and the right hands.

WHAT I DID RIGHT: I was willing to imagine alternatives to the New York book scene. I think it's a great time to be a writer looking for an audience. Also, serendipity.

DO DIFFERENT NEXT TIME: I would've started networking with writers and editors and other industry professionals earlier to develop a sense of how this project could best be pitched and positioned for the market.

PLATFORM: The very best decision I've made about doing this was to hire a publicist. I needed professional guidance in terms of how to think about social media, how to conceptualize the audience for this book, and how to reach out to that audience.

ADVICE FOR WRITERS: Stay in touch with mentors, editors, and writer friends—not just by adding to an ever-growing list of contacts or social media friends, but by reading and supporting their work. Read the novels of the writers who mentor you, the journals and magazines that publish you, and pay attention to the careers of the editors who take an interest in your work.

NEXT UP: I'm working on a novel-in-stories based on the characters from my short story "Halley's Comet."

YOUNG ADULT

7 LIVIA BLACKBURNE

LIVIABLACKBURNE.COM

Midnight Thief (JULY 2014, DISNEY-HYPERION)

QUICK TAKE: An acrobatic thief takes a mysterious job with the Assassins Guild, and a young knight stumbles upon her trail.

WRITES FROM: Los Angeles.

BEFORE THE BOOK: I published a nonfiction essay, "From Words to Brain," with a small digital press on the neuroscience of reading.

TIME FRAME: I started writing a novel in high school. Eventually I got to about 60 pages. Then I went to college and stopped writing. When I turned 25, I took out the old manuscript. The most interesting character was the heroine's best friend, Kyra. So I took Kyra and rewrote the manuscript to be about her. It took me about two years to finish.

ENTER THE AGENT: I initially wanted to self-publish my novel, but my writer friends suggested I query a few agents. As irony would have it, I got an offer fairly quickly, and decided to give the traditional pathway a try. My agent is Jim McCarthy of Dystel & Goderich Literary Management.

WHAT I LEARNED: Just how important your first book is to your career. The sales numbers color your record from then on, and it also determines the books you write after that.

WHAT I DID RIGHT: I didn't start querying until the manuscript was absolutely ready. I got a few full requests at conferences, but I waited a year before I sent it to those agents. It was hard to wait, but I knew I only had one chance. My manuscript went through my critique group and beta readers (about 20 total) before I started querying.

WHAT I WISH I WOULD HAVE DONE DIFFERENT: I would've revised even more before the manuscript went on submission to editors. Because the more offers you have for your manuscript, the higher your advance, and the more support and publicity your book will ultimately get.

PLATFORM: To gain readers for my fiction, I recently self-published a novella called *Poison Dance* that's related to *Midnight Thief*. I've been doing a lot of promotion for the novella, as well as giving it away for reviews in hopes of building buzz and gaining readers.

ADVICE FOR WRITERS: Get critique partners that you can trust.

NEXT UP: I'm exploring the possibility of a sequel to *Midnight Thief*, as well as some ideas for unrelated works.

LITERARY FICTION

8 NATALIA SYLVESTER

NATALIASYLVESTER.COM

Chasing the Sun **(MAY 2014, NEW HARVEST)**

QUICK TAKE: A tense family drama about a husband's quest to save his wife, who's been kidnapped in Lima, Peru, in 1992, and how far he'll go to save their imperfect marriage.

WRITES FROM: Austin, Texas

BEFORE THE BOOK: I worked as an editor at a start-up magazine on Miami Beach before deciding to freelance full-time. I worked on magazine assignments by day, and wrote fiction by night/morning.

TIME FRAME: *Chasing the Sun* was my "drawer novel." It began as my senior thesis when I was a Creative Writing undergrad at the University of Miami, but when I graduated in 2006, I didn't feel ready to take it any further. I tucked it away and wrote a new story—a novel that, five years later, led to me signing with my agent. While we waited and hoped for that novel to sell (it didn't), I went back to *Chasing the Sun* and revised it some more. Seven years after I first started writing it, the story sold.

ENTER THE AGENT: I met Brandi Bowles of Foundry Literary + Media at the Writer's League of Texas Agent & Editors Conference in 2010. Brandi and I saw eye-to-eye on so many things; I was delighted to sign with her.

WHAT I LEARNED: That there are no guarantees. I'd heard about many authors who landed an agent and then the book didn't sell, but I didn't want to think it'd happen to me. Success isn't just the multiple offers of representation, or the luck of a bestseller; it's not giving up when rejection comes.

WHAT I WISH I WOULD HAVE DONE DIFFERENT: Managing my expectations would've saved me a lot of hardship. There's no point where things suddenly become easy. Writing a book, landing an agent, getting a book deal and then having that book sell to readers—it's all hard work. But it's incredibly rewarding every step of the way.

PLATFORM: I blog at TheDebutanteBall.com, a group blog made up of five first-time novelists, and I attend as many signings and events as I can within my local literary community.

ADVICE FOR WRITERS: If you can write your way into a problem, you can write your way out of it. It's like building a puzzle: You can't figure out where the pieces go by staring at it. You have to try one piece after another until the right one fits.

NEXT UP: I've started writing a new novel.

MYSTERY

9 CAROL MILLER

CAROLMILLERAUTHOR.COM

Murder & Moonshine **(MAY 2014, MINOTAUR BOOKS)**

QUICK TAKE: When a dead body turns up at the local diner in sleepy southwestern Virginia, Daisy McGovern, a young, recently-separated waitress, learns that some secrets are more dangerous to keep than others, especially when there's money and moonshine involved.

WRITES FROM: Roanoke, Va.

TIME FRAME: I wrote the bulk of the book over several months in a remote log cabin located in Pittsylvania County, Va. It was scenic and very isolated.

ENTER THE AGENT: Kari Stuart at ICM Partners represents me, and she is wonderful to work with! I sent her a short, simple query letter.

WHAT I LEARNED: I've learned patience. And more patience.

WHAT I DID RIGHT: I started writing, and I kept on writing. Although that may sound obvious, it's true. People are always telling me that they would like to become a writer, but they don't actually write anything. You have to write and continue to write.

DO DIFFERENT NEXT TIME: Buy a good dictionary earlier! I initially wrote much of the manuscript by hand, so I didn't have spellcheck.

ADVICE FOR WRITERS: Always keep a bottle of whiskey nearby.

NEXT UP: The novel's sequel: *Mayhem and Moonshine.*

NONFICTION (CRAFT/HOBBIES)

10 ALLISON HOFFMAN LARK

CRAFTISCOOL.COM

AmiguruME: Make Cute Crocheted People **(OCT. 2013, LARK CRAFT BOOKS)**

QUICK TAKE: This book enables the reader to crochet a custom doll to look like anyone he or she would like, famous or familiar, using a selection of many different patterns from head to toe.

WRITES FROM: Austin, Texas

BEFORE THE BOOK: I'd done a lot of designing for my personal website as well as several yarn companies, magazines and websites. I was constantly getting requests for this celebrity or that character, so I recognized the demand for a DIY guide to designing custom dolls.

TIME FRAME: I began writing the book in the summer of 2011 and had everything completed within a year. My biggest challenge was narrowing down the number of dolls that would actually be pictured in the book. I had almost too many ideas and spent hours trying to squeeze all of my designs into the number of dolls I was aiming to finish.

ENTER THE AGENT: Through my research, one name—Kate McKean of Howard Morhaim Literary—kept popping up. I sent her a query and talked to her on the phone. She was excited about my project and knew so much about the genre and what certain publishers were looking for. It was a perfect match.

BIGGEST SURPRISE: I was not prepared for how long it would take to write this book! Writing, rewriting, making everything consistent and thorough—all of that took a lot of time.

WHAT I DID RIGHT: Lots of people can write excellent crochet patterns and many more can crochet amazingly, but to get recognition in this craft, I think you need a signature style and niche. I started crocheting people and soon became recognized for that very skill. I also got lots of celebrity endorsements. Conan O'Brien showed my work on his show and handpicked me to be part of his Conan Fan Art gallery shows in San Diego and New York. Martha Stewart became familiar with my work and invited me to be on her show. Lots of celebrities have tweeted and shown support online for what I'm doing, so I've gotten a fan base just through their kind words and photos.

ADVICE FOR WRITERS: Don't compare your work to another's. In crafting, there is a lot of comparing and competition sometimes, but if you try not to focus on "one-upping," and follow your own instincts instead, it will come a lot easier.

NEXT UP: I have many ideas for more books. I've been designing for galleries and several art shows around the country.

LITERARY THRILLER

11 ADAM STERNBERGH

ADAMSTERNBERGH.COM

Shovel Ready **(JAN. 2014, CROWN)**

QUICK TAKE: Spademan, a former garbageman turned hitman who's living in a post-dirty-bomb New York, is hired to kill the daughter of America's most famous evangelist.

WRITES FROM: Brooklyn, N.Y.

BEFORE THE BOOK: I've been a journalist for 15 years, the last three at *The New York Times Magazine*. *Shovel Ready* is my first published novel, but not my first novel. My first novel, which was not hardboiled, dystopian, or thrilling, now lives in quiet retirement in a very comfortable desk drawer.

TIME FRAME: The first draft was finished very quickly after just a few months of writing. Then came an extensive editing process, with notes first from my wife (who's a playwright), and then, later, from my editor.

ENTER THE AGENT: My agent is David McCormick of McCormick & Williams. He approached me about becoming my agent back in 2006 actually, because he'd been interested in some of my nonfiction journalism work. But he's been terrifically supportive of my fiction writing as well.

WHAT I LEARNED: Just how many people are involved in making a single book. It's humbling and gratifying to have such a large team of talented people, from the cover designer to the copy editors to the sales force, all working together on something that sprang out of your brain.

WHAT I DID RIGHT: For starters, I had to stop worrying, or even thinking, about getting published. My first novel (shelved) and second one (abandoned) were both strangulated, to some degree, by my inability to let go of notions I had about how each novel might eventually be received.

PLATFORM: As a journalist, I already have some kind of public profile, and I've long been very active on Twitter, since I enjoy it.

BEST ADVICE: Write the book you want to read. It's the only way you'll write anything that's any good.

NEXT UP: A sequel to *Shovel Ready*. So I'm at work on that right now.

FANTASY

12 E.L. TETTENSOR

ELTETTENSOR.COM

Darkwalker: A Nicolas Lenoir Novel (DEC. 2013, ROC)

QUICK TAKE: To solve a series of disturbing crimes, a cynical detective is forced to confront the demons of his past—literally.

WRITES FROM: New York City and Bujumbura, Burundi.

BEFORE THE BOOK: A short story of mine appeared in a Wizards of the Coast anthology ("Realms of the Dragons II") back in 2005. It gave me confidence to start taking writing a bit more seriously. I started on *Darkwalker* shortly after that, but for a variety of reasons, it ended up getting put on hold.

TIME FRAME: The first half was written back in 2008, but I spent the next few years bouncing around the world, often in some very remote places where it wasn't so easy to sit down and write. It took a long time to come back to the manuscript, but when I did, I had gathered a lot of new experiences and ideas, many of which found their way onto the pages.

ENTER THE AGENT: I approached Jabberwocky Literary Agency back in 2007. The agent I originally queried moved on shortly afterward, but Joshua Bilmes agreed to take me on in 2008. These days, I'm working with both Joshua and [his co-agent] Lisa Rodgers.

WHAT I LEARNED: Patience. Finishing a novel is an exciting experience; you want to share it with the world right away. But typing "the end" on the first draft is just the beginning.

WHAT I DID RIGHT: I did my homework. I sought advice from published authors, many of whom were generous enough to give it. Most of all, I stuck with it.

IF I COULD DO IT AGAIN: I wouldn't have let my writing lapse for as long as I did. Taking time away can be a good thing, especially if you come back to a project with fresh eyes. But letting too much time pass makes getting back into the rhythm a lot harder.

BEST ADVICE: Try to find a way of getting good, structured criticism from people who are not afraid to tell you where yours misses the mark.

NEXT UP: The sequel to *Darkwalker* is well underway. It should hit shelves December 2014.

MEMOIR

13 MARIA MUTCH

MARIAMUTCH.COM

Know the Night: A Memoir **(MARCH 2014, SIMON & SCHUSTER)**

QUICK TAKE: My experience of being up at night with my oldest son, who has Down syndrome and autism, combined with the 1930s Antarctic adventure of Admiral Richard Byrd.

WRITES FROM: Rhode Island.

BEFORE THE BOOK: I was deeply involved with both of my young sons' care, as well as writing poetry, which seemed to work with my schedule. I had had a number of poems and a short story published in literary journals. In 2008, I took a writing workshop that focused on personal essays and memoir. The work I began in that class eventually became *Know the Night.*

TIME FRAME: The entire process was close to four years, including the final edits with the publisher. I wrote for well over two years without a structure. I was working with various subjects: my son's insomnia, Admiral Byrd and Antarctica, jazz, and other smaller but potent things, and I really wasn't sure how I was going to bring them all together. After I received the structural lightning bolt, it was time to lay all my previous work, two years worth, on the kitchen table and do major surgery.

ENTER THE AGENT: I attended a writers' conference and one of the faculty who read an early excerpt of my manuscript ended up telling an agent about it many months later. When the agent, Nathaniel Jacks of Inkwell Management, contacted me, I wasn't remotely finished. But Nathaniel patiently waited for me to finish. Knowing that he was on the other end, and receiving his feedback, was tremendously helpful.

DO DIFFERENT NEXT TIME: I would go to conferences and workshops sooner than I did. I worked in solitude for a very long time, without supportive peers and not a lot of feedback.

PLATFORM: Once the book was sold, I was lucky enough to participate in Grub Street's Launch Lab program in Boston. The group consisted of 14 authors whose books were about to come out, and the program coaches opened up many of the mysteries surrounding book launches and the various kinds of promotion, how to use tools like social media and align those tools with personal goals. It gave me friendships and a community I wouldn't have had otherwise. It's the kind of program that should be commonplace but somehow is not.

ADVICE FOR WRITERS: "Write what fascinates you." I would love to thank the person who said this, but I can't remember where I read it.

NEXT UP: I'm working on a collection of short stories.

CHUCK SAMBUCHINO (chucksambuchino.com, @chucksambuchino on Twitter) edits the *Guide to Literary Agents* (guidetoliteraryagents.com/blog) as well as the *Children's Writer's & Illustrator's Market*. His pop-humor books include *How to Survive a Garden Gnome Attack* (film rights optioned by Sony) and *Red Dog / Blue Dog: When Pooches Get Political* (reddog-bluedog.com). Chuck's other writing books include *Formatting & Submitting Your Manuscript, 3rd. Ed.*, as well as *Create Your Writer Platform* (fall 2012). Besides that, he is a husband, sleep-deprived new father, guitarist, dog owner, and cookie addict.

GLA SUCCESS STORIES

Those who came before and succeeded.

I realize there are other places you can turn to for information on agents, but the *Guide to Literary Agents* has always prided itself as being the biggest (we list almost every agent) and the most thorough (guidelines, sales, agent-by-agent breakdowns, etc.). That's why it's sold more than 250,000 copies. It *works*—and if you keep reading, I'll prove it to you. Here are testimonials from a handful of writers who have used this book to find an agent and publishing success.

❶ **MARISHA CHAMBERLAIN**, *The Rose Variations* (Soho)

"*Guide to Literary Agents* oriented me, the lowly first-time novelist, embarking on an agent search. The articles and the listings gave insight into the world of literary agents that allowed me to comport myself professionally and to persist. And I did find a terrific agent."

❷ **Eugenia Kim**, *The Calligrapher's Daughter* (Holt)
"After so many years working on the novel, the relative speed of creating the query package prodded the impetus to send it out ... As a fail-safe measure, I bought the *Guide to Literary Agents* [and] checked who might be a good fit for my novel..."

❸ **Eve Brown-Waite**, *First Comes Love, Then Comes Malaria* (Broadway)
"I bought the *Guide To Literary Agents* ... and came across Laney Katz Becker. So I sent off a very funny query. On March 15, 2007, Laney called. 'I love your book,' she said. 'I'd like to represent you.' Three months later, Laney sold my book—at auction—in a six-figure deal."

❹ **Mara Purnhagen**, *Tagged* (Harlequin Teen)
"I trusted the *Guide to Literary Agents* to provide solid, up-to-date information to help me with the process. I now have a wonderful agent and a four-book deal."

❺ **Richard Harvell**, *The Bells* (Crown)
"*Guide to Literary Agents* was crucial in my successful search for an agent. I found a great agent and my book has now been translated into a dozen languages."

❻ **Patrick Lee**, *The Breach* (Harper)
"The *GLA* has all the info you need for narrowing down a list of agencies to query."

❼ **Karen Dionne**, *Freezing Point* and *Boiling Point* (Jove)
"I'm smiling as I type this, because I actually got my agent via the *Guide to Literary Agents*. I certainly never dreamed that I'd tell my [success] story in the same publication!"

❽ **Heather Newton**, *Under the Mercy Trees* (Harper)
"I found my literary agent through the *Guide to Literary Agents*!"

❾ **Michael Wiley,** *The Last Striptease* and *The Bad Kitty Lounge* (Minotaur)
"*GLA* was very useful to me when I started. I always recommend it to writers."

❿ **Les Edgerton,** *Hooked* and 11 more books
"Just signed with literary agent Chip MacGregor and I came upon him through the *Guide to Literary Agents*. If not for *GLA*, I'd probably still be looking."

⓫ **Jennifer Cervantes,** *Tortilla Sun* (Chronicle)
"Within 10 days of submitting, I found an amazing agent—and it's all thanks to *GLA*."

⓬ **Carson Morton,** *Stealing Mona Lisa* (St. Martin's / Minotaur)
"I wanted to thank you for the *Guide to Literary Agents*. After contacting 16 literary agencies, number 17 requested my historical novel. Within a few weeks, they offered to represent me. Hard work and good, solid, accurate information makes all the difference. Thanks again."

⓭ **darien gee,** *Friendship Bread: A Novel* (Ballantine)
"The *Guide to Literary Agents* was an indispensable tool for me when I was querying agents. I highly recommend it for any aspiring author."

⓮ **lexi george,** *Demon Hunting in Dixie* (Brava)
"The *Guide to Literary Agents* is an invaluable resource for writers."

⓯ **stephanie barden,** *Cinderella Smith* (HarperCollins)
"When I felt my book was finally ready for eyes other than mine to see it, I got some terrific advice: Go buy the *Guide to Literary Agents*. By the time I was through with it, it looked like it had gone to battle—it was battered and dog-eared and highlighted and Post-It-Noted. But it was victorious; I had an agent. Huge thanks, *GLA*—I couldn't have done it without you!"

⓰ **BILL PESCHEL,** *Writers Gone Wild: The Feuds, Frolics, and Follies of Literature's Great Adventurers, Drunkards, Lovers, Iconoclasts, and Misanthropes* (Perigee)

"The *Guide to Literary Agents* gave me everything I needed to sell *Writers Gone Wild*. It was the personal assistant who found me the right agents to pitch, the publicist who suggested conferences to attend and the trusted adviser who helped me negotiate the path to publication."

⓱ **LAURA GRIFFIN,** *Unforgivable* (Pocket Books)

"Writing the book is only the first step. Then it's time to find a home for it. The *Guide to Literary Agents* is filled with practical advice about how to contact literary agents who can help you market your work."

⓲ **DEREK TAYLOR KENT (A.K.A. DEREK THE GHOST),** *Scary School* (HarperCollins)

"The *Guide to Literary Agents* was absolutely instrumental to my getting an agent and subsequent three-book deal with HarperCollins."

⓳ **TAMORA PIERCE,** *Alanna: The First Adventure: The Song of the Lioness* (Atheneum)

"The best guide to literary agents is the *Guide to Literary Agents*, published by Writer's Market Books ... These listings will tell you the names and addresses of the agencies; if an agency is made up of more than one agent, they will list the different agents and what kinds of book they represent; they will include whether or not the agent will accept simultaneous submissions (submitting a manuscript to more agents than one)."

⓴ **WADE ROUSE,** *It's All Relative: Two Families, Three Dogs, 34 Holidays, and 50 Boxes of Wine: A Memoir* (Crown)

"And when you think you're done writing your book? Write some more. And when you think you're finished? Set it aside for a while, go back, redraft, edit, rewrite, and redraft ... Then pick up the Writer's Digest *Guide to Literary Agents*."

㉑ **Dianna Dorisi Winget**, *A Smidgen of Sky* (Harcourt)

"*Guide to Literary Agents* is simply the best writing reference book out there. I don't think I would have landed an agent without it."

㉒ **Carole Brody Fleet**, *Happily Even After: A Guide to Getting Through (and Beyond!) the Grief of Widowhood* (Viva Editions)

"I am not overstating it when I say that *Guide to Literary Agents* was absolutely instrumental in my landing an agent. Moreover, I wound up with numerous agents from which to choose—how often does *that* happen to an unknown and unpublished author? Thank you again for this book. It not only changed my life forever, but it led to our being able to serve the widowed community around the world."

㉓ **Guinevere Durham**, *Teaching Test-Taking Skills: Proven Techniques to Boost Your Student's Scores* (R&L Education)

"I was looking for an agent for my book. I had been trying for 7 years. I have enough rejection letters to wallpaper my office. Finally, I researched the *Guide to Literary Agents*. Three months later I had a contract."

㉔ **Adam Brownlee**, *Building a Small Business That Warren Buffett Would Love* (John Wiley and Sons)

"The *Guide to Literary Agents* was invaluable for me in many ways. Specifically, the sections on 'Write a Killer Query Letter' and 'Nonfiction Book Proposals' enabled me to put together a package that led to the publication of my book."

㉕ **Kim Baker**, *Pickle: The (Formerly) Anonymous Prank Club of Fountain Point Middle School* (Roaring Brook)

"I read the *Guide to Literary Agents* religiously when I was planning submissions."

㉖ **Jeri Westerson,** *Blood Lance: A Medieval Noir* (Pocket Books)
"The whole writing industry is so confusing. Where to start? I started with the Writer's Digest *Guide to Literary Agents,* where I not only created my list of agents and game plan, I received all sorts of excellent information in crafting my winning query letter. I recommend it to anyone starting out. And yes, I did get an agent through the Guide."

㉗ **Noelle Sterne,** *Trust Your Life: Forgive Yourself and Go After Your Dreams* (Unity)
"Your *Guide to Literary Agents* and the features from authors on the often-hard lessons learned from the dream of publishing have helped me immensely to keep my feet on the ground, butt in the chair, and fingers on the keyboard. Thank you, Chuck, for taking all the time and effort and for caring."

㉘ **Lynne Raimondo,** *Dante's Wood: A Mark Angelotti Novel* (Seventh Street Books)
"*Guide to Literary Agents* is how I found my agent, so I owe you one."

㉙ **Gennifer Albin,** *Crewel* (Pocket Books)
"I got a lot of mileage out of *Guide to Literary Agents* when I was looking for an agent, and I frequently recommend it."

NEW AGENT SPOTLIGHTS

Learn about new reps seeking clients.

by Chuck Sambuchino

One of the most common recurring blog items I get complimented on is my "New Agent Alerts," a series where I spotlight new/newer literary reps who are open to queries and looking for clients right now.

This is due to the fact that newer agents are golden opportunities for aspiring authors because they are actively building their client lists. They're hungry to sign new clients and start the ball rolling with submissions to editors and get books sold. Whereas an established agent with 40 clients may have little to no time to consider new writers' work (let alone help them shape it), a newer agent may be willing to sign a promising writer whose work is not a guaranteed huge payday.

THE CONS AND PROS OF NEWER AGENTS

At writing conferences, a frequent question I get is "Is it OK to sign with a new agent?" The question comes about because people value experience and wonder about the skill of someone who's new to the scene. The concern is an interesting one, so let me try to list the downsides and upsides to choosing a rep who's in her first few years agenting.

Probable cons

- They are less experienced in contract negotiations.
- They know fewer editors at this point than a rep who's been in business a while, meaning there is a less likely chance they can help you get published. This is a big, justified point—and writers' foremost concern.
- They are in a weaker position to demand a high advance for you.

- New agents come and some go. This means if your agent is in business for a year or two and doesn't find the success for which they hoped, they could bail on the biz altogether. That leaves you without a home. If you sign with an agent who's been in business for 14 years, however, chances are they won't quit tomorrow.

Probable pros

- They are actively building their client lists—and that means they are anxious to sign new writers and lock in those first several sales.
- They are willing to give your work a longer look. They may be willing to work with you on a project to get it ready for submission, whereas a more established agent has lots of clients and no time—meaning they have no spare moments to help you with shaping your novel or proposal.
- With fewer clients under their wing, you will get more attention than you would with an established rep.
- If they've found their calling and don't seem like they're giving up any time soon (and keep in mind, most do continue on as agents), you can have a decades-long relationship that pays off with lots of books.
- They have little going against them. An established agent once told me that a new agent is in a unique position because they have no duds under their belt. Their slates are clean.

HOW CAN YOU DECIDE FOR YOURSELF?

1. Factor in if they're part of a larger agency. Agents share contacts and resources. If your agent is the new girl at an agency with five people, those other four agents will help her (and you) with submissions. In other words, she's new, but not alone.

2. Learn where the agent came from. Has she been an apprentice at the agency for two years? Was she an editor for seven years and just switched to agenting? If they already have a few years in publishing under their belt, they're not as green as you may think. Agents don't become agents overnight.

3. Ask where she will submit the work. This is a big one. If you fear the agent lacks proper contacts to move your work, ask straight out: "What editors do you see us submitting this book to, and have you sold to them before?" The question tests their plan for where to send the manuscript and get it in print.

4. Ask them, "Why should I sign with you?" This is another straight-up question that gets right to the point. If she's new and has little/no sales at that point, she can't respond with "I sell tons of books and I make it rain cash money!! Dolla dolla bills, y'all!!!" She can't rely on her track record to entice you. So what's her sales pitch? Weigh her enthusiasm, her plan for the book, her promises of hard work and anything else she tells you. In the publishing business, you want communication and enthusiasm from agents (and editors). Both are invaluable. What's the point of signing with a huge agent when they don't return your e-mails and consider your book last on their list of priorities for the day?

5. If you're not sold, you can always say no. It's as simple as that. Always query new/newer agents because, at the end of the day, just because they offer representation doesn't mean you have to accept.

NEW AGENT SPOTLIGHTS

Peppered throughout this book's large number of agency listings are sporadic "New Agent Alert" sidebars. Look them over to see if these newer reps would be a good fit for your work. Always read personal information and submission guidelines carefully. Don't let an agent reject you because you submitted work incorrectly. Wherever possible, we have included a website address for their agency, as well as their Twitter handle for those reps that tweet.

Also please note that as of when this book went to press in 2014, all these agents were still active and looking for writers. That said, I cannot guarantee every one is still in their respective position when you read this, nor that they have kept their query inboxes open. I urge you to visit agency websites and double check before you query. (This is always a good idea in any case.) Good luck!

CHUCK SAMBUCHINO (chucksambuchino.com, @chucksambuchino) edits the *Guide to Literary Agents* (guidetoliteraryagents.com/blog) as well as the *Children's Writer's & Illustrator's Market*. His pop humor books include *How to Survive a Garden Gnome Attack* (film rights optioned by Sony) and *Red Dog / Blue Dog: When Pooches Get Political* (reddog-bluedog.com). Chuck's other writing books include *Formatting & Submitting Your Manuscript, 3rd. Ed.*, and *Create Your Writer Platform* (fall 2012). Besides that, he is a husband, guitarist, sleep-deprived new father, dog owner, and cookie addict.

GLOSSARY OF INDUSTRY TERMS

Your guide to every need-to-know term.

#10 ENVELOPE. A standard, business-size envelope.

ACKNOWLEDGMENTS PAGE. The page of a book on which the author credits sources of assistance—both individuals and organizations.

ACQUISITIONS EDITOR. The person responsible for originating and/or acquiring new publishing projects.

ADAPTATION. The process of rewriting a composition (novel, story, film, article, play) into a form suitable for some other medium, such as TV or the stage.

ADVANCE. Money a publisher pays a writer prior to book publication, usually paid in installments, such as one-half upon signing the contract and one-half upon delivery of the complete, satisfactory manuscript. An advance is paid against the royalty money to be earned by the book. Agents take their percentage off the top of the advance as well as from the royalties earned.

ADVENTURE. A genre of fiction in which action is the key element, overshadowing characters, theme and setting.

AUCTION. Publishers sometimes bid for the acquisition of a book manuscript with excellent sales prospects. The bids are for the amount of the author's advance, guaranteed dollar amounts, advertising and promotional expenses, royalty percentage, etc. Auctions are conducted by agents.

AUTHOR'S COPIES. An author usually receives about 10 free copies of his hardcover book from the publisher; more from a paperback firm. He can obtain additional copies at a price that has been reduced by an author's discount (usually 50 percent of the retail price).

AUTOBIOGRAPHY. A book-length account of a person's entire life written by the subject himself.

BACKLIST. A publisher's list of books that were not published during the current season, but that are still in print.

BACKSTORY. The history of what has happened before the action in your story takes place, affecting a character's current behavior.

BIO. A sentence or brief paragraph about the writer; includes work and educational experience.

BIOGRAPHY. An account of a person's life (or the lives of a family or close-knit group) written by someone other than the subject(s). The work is set within the historical framework (i.e., the unique economic, social and political conditions) existing during the subject's life.

BLURB. The copy on paperback book covers or hardcover book dust jackets, either promoting the book and the author or featuring testimonials from book reviewers or well-known people in the book's field. Also called flap copy or jacket copy.

BOILERPLATE. A standardized publishing contract. Most authors and agents make many changes on the boilerplate before accepting the contract.

BOOK DOCTOR. A freelance editor hired by a writer, agent or book editor who analyzes problems that exist in a book manuscript or proposal, and offers solutions to those problems.

BOOK PACKAGER. Someone who draws elements of a book together—from initial concept to writing and marketing strategies—and then sells the book package to a book publisher and/or movie producer. Also known as book producer or book developer.

BOUND GALLEYS. A prepublication, often paperbound, edition of a book, usually prepared from photocopies of the final galley proofs. Designed for promotional purposes, bound galleys serve as the first set of review copies to be mailed out. Also called bound proofs.

CATEGORY FICTION. A term used to include all types of fiction. See *genre*.

CLIMAX. The most intense point in the story line of a fictional work.

CLIPS. Samples, usually from newspapers or magazines, of your published work. Also called tearsheets.

COMMERCIAL FICTION. Novels designed to appeal to a broad audience. These are often broken down into categories such as western, mystery and romance. See *genre*.

CONFESSION. A first-person story in which the narrator is involved in an emotional situation that encourages sympathetic reader identification, concluding with the affirmation of a morally acceptable theme.

CONFLICT. A prime ingredient of fiction that usually represents some obstacle to the main character's (i.e., the protagonist's) goals.

CONTRIBUTOR'S COPIES. Copies of the book sent to the author. The number of contributor's copies is often negotiated in the publishing contract.

CO-PUBLISHING. Arrangement where author and publisher share publication costs and profits of a book. Also called co-operative publishing.

COPYEDITING. Editing of a manuscript for writing style, grammar, punctuation and factual accuracy.

COPYRIGHT. A means to protect an author's work. A copyright is a proprietary right designed to give the creator of a work the power to control that work's reproduction, distribution and public display or performance, as well as its adaptation to other forms.

COVER LETTER. A brief letter that accompanies the manuscript being sent to an agent or publisher.

CREATIVE NONFICTION. Type of writing where true stories are told by employing the techniques usually reserved for novelists and poets, such as scenes, character arc, a three-act structure and detailed descriptions. This category is also called narrative nonfiction or literary journalism.

CRITIQUING SERVICE. An editing service offered by some agents in which writers pay a fee for comments on the salability or other qualities of their manuscript. Sometimes the critique includes suggestions on how to improve the work. Fees vary, as does the quality of the critique.

CURRICULUM VITAE (CV). Short account of one's career or qualifications.

DEADLINE. A specified date and/or time that a project or draft must be turned into the editor. A deadline factors into a preproduction schedule, which involves copyediting, typesetting and production.

DEAL MEMO. The memorandum of agreement between a publisher and author that precedes the actual contract and includes important issues such as royalty, advance, rights, distribution and option clauses.

DEUS EX MACHINA. A term meaning "God from the machine" that refers to any unlikely, contrived or trick resolution of a plot in any type of fiction.

DIALOGUE. An essential element of fiction. Dialogue consists of conversations between two or more people, and can be used heavily or sparsely.

DIVISION. An unincorporated branch of a publishing house/company.

ELECTRONIC RIGHTS. Secondary or subsidiary rights dealing with electronic/multimedia formats (the Internet, CD-ROMs, electronic magazines).

EL-HI. Elementary to high school. A term used to indicate reading or interest level.

EROTICA. A form of literature or film dealing with the sexual aspects of love. Erotic content ranges from subtle sexual innuendo to explicit descriptions of sexual acts.

ETHNIC. Stories and novels whose central characters are African American, Native American, Italian American, Jewish, Appalachian or members of some other specific cultural group. Ethnic fiction usually deals with a protagonist caught between two conflicting ways of life: mainstream American culture and his ethnic heritage.

EVALUATION FEES. Fees an agent may charge to simply evaluate or consider material without further guarantees of representation. Paying upfront evaluation fees to agents is never recommended and strictly forbidden by the Association of Authors' Representations. An agent makes money through a standard commission—taking 15 percent of what you earn through advances and, if applicable, royalties.

EXCLUSIVE. Offering a manuscript, usually for a set period of time such as one month, to just one agent and guaranteeing that agent is the only one looking at the manuscript.

EXPERIMENTAL. Type of fiction that focuses on style, structure, narrative technique, setting and strong characterization rather than plot. This form depends largely on the revelation of a character's inner being, which elicits an emotional response from the reader.

FAMILY SAGA. A story that chronicles the lives of a family or a number of related or interconnected families over a period of time.

FANTASY. Stories set in fanciful, invented worlds or in a legendary, mythic past that rely on outright invention or magic for conflict and setting.

FILM RIGHTS. May be sold or optioned by the agent/author to a person in the film industry, enabling the book to be made into a movie.

FLOOR BID. If a publisher is very interested in a manuscript, he may offer to enter a floor bid when the book goes to auction. The publisher sits out of the auction, but agrees to take the book by topping the highest bid by an agreed-upon percentage (usually 10 percent).

FOREIGN RIGHTS. Translation or reprint rights to be sold abroad.

FOREIGN RIGHTS AGENT. An agent who handles selling the rights to a country other than that of the first book agent. Usually an additional percentage (about 5 percent) will be added on to the first book agent's commission to cover the foreign rights agent.

GENRE. Refers to either a general classification of writing, such as a novel, poem or short story, or to the categories within those classifications, such as problem novels or sonnets.

GENRE FICTION. A term that covers various types of commercial novels, such as mystery, romance, Western, science fiction, fantasy, thriller and horror.

GHOSTWRITING. A writer puts into literary form the words, ideas or knowledge of another person under that person's name. Some agents offer this service; others pair ghostwriters with celebrities or experts.

GOTHIC. Novels characterized by historical settings and featuring young, beautiful women who win the favor of handsome, brooding heroes while simultaneously dealing with some life-threatening menace—either natural or supernatural.

GRAPHIC NOVEL. Contains comic-like drawings and captions, but deals more with everyday events and issues than with superheroes.

HIGH CONCEPT. A story idea easily expressed in a quick, one-line description.

HI-LO. A type of fiction that offers a high level of interest for readers at a low reading level.

HISTORICAL. A story set in a recognizable period of history. In addition to telling the stories of ordinary people's lives, historical fiction may involve political or social events of the time.

HOOK. Aspect of the work that sets it apart from others and draws in the reader/viewer.

HORROR. A story that aims to evoke some combination of fear, fascination and revulsion in its readers—either through supernatural or psychological circumstances.

HOW-TO. A book that offers the reader a description of how something can be accomplished. It includes both information and advice.

IMPRINT. The name applied to a publisher's specific line of books.

IN MEDIAS RES. A Latin term, meaning "into the midst of things," that refers to the literary device of beginning a narrative at a dramatic point in a story well along in the sequence of events to immediately convey action and capture reader interest.

IRC. International Reply Coupon. Buy at a post office to enclose with material sent outside the country to cover the cost of return postage. The recipient turns them in for stamps in their own country.

ISBN. This acronym stands for International Standard Book Number. ISBN is a tool used for both ordering and cataloging purposes.

JOINT CONTRACT. A legal agreement between a publisher and two or more authors that establishes provisions for the division of royalties their co-written book generates.

JUVENILE. Category of children's writing that can be broken down into easy-to-read books (ages 7–9), which run 2,000–10,000 words, and middle-grade books (ages 9–12), which run 20,000–40,000 words.

LIBEL. A form of defamation, or injury to a person's name or reputation. Written or published defamation is called *libel*, whereas spoken defamation is known as *slander*.

LITERARY. A book where style and technique are often as important as subject matter. In literary fiction, character is typically more important than plot, and the writer's voice and skill with words are both very essential. Also called serious fiction.

LOGLINE. A one-sentence description of a plot.

MAINSTREAM FICTION. Fiction on subjects or trends that transcend popular novel categories like mystery or romance. Using conventional methods, this kind of fiction tells stories about people and their conflicts.

MARKETING FEE. Fee charged by some agents to cover marketing expenses. It may be used to cover postage, telephone calls, faxes, photocopying or any other legitimate expense incurred in marketing a manuscript. Recouping expenses associated with submissions and marketing is the one and only time agents should ask for out-of-pocket money from writers.

MASS MARKET PAPERBACKS. Softcover books, usually 4×7 inches, on a popular subject directed at a general audience and sold in groceries, drugstores and bookstores.

MEMOIR. An author's commentary on the personalities and events that have significantly influenced one phase of his life.

MIDLIST. Those titles on a publisher's list expected to have limited sales. Midlist books are mainstream, not literary, scholarly or genre, and are usually written by new or relatively unknown writers.

MULTIPLE CONTRACT. Book contract that includes an agreement for a future book(s).

MYSTERY. A form of narration in which one or more elements remain unknown or unexplained until the end of the story. Subgenres include: amateur sleuth, caper, cozy, heist, malice domestic, police procedural, etc.

NET RECEIPTS. One method of royalty payment based on the amount of money a book publisher receives on the sale of the book after the booksellers' discounts, special sales discounts and returned copies.

NOVELIZATION. A novel created from the script of a popular movie and published in paperback. Also called a movie tie-in.

NOVELLA. A short novel or long short story, usually 20,000–50,000 words. Also called a novelette.

OCCULT. Supernatural phenomena, including ghosts, ESP, astrology, demonic possession, paranormal elements and witchcraft.

ONE-TIME RIGHTS. This right allows a short story or portions of a fiction or nonfiction book to be published again without violating the contract.

OPTION. The act of a producer buying film rights to a book for a limited period of time (usually six months or one year) rather than purchasing said rights in full. A book can be optioned multiple times by different production companies.

OPTION CLAUSE. A contract clause giving a publisher the right to publish an author's next book.

OUTLINE. A summary of a book's content (up to 15 double-spaced pages); often in the form of chapter headings with a descriptive sentence or two under each one to show the scope of the book.

PICTURE BOOK. A type of book aimed at ages 2–9 that tells the story partially or entirely with artwork, with up to 1,000 words. Agents interested in selling to publishers of these books often handle both artists and writers.

PLATFORM. A writer's speaking experience, interview skills, website and other abilities that help form a following of potential buyers for his book.

PROOFREADING. Close reading and correction of a manuscript's typographical errors.

PROPOSAL. An offer to an editor or publisher to write a specific work, usually a package consisting of an outline and sample chapters.

PROSPECTUS. A preliminary written description of a book, usually one page in length.

PSYCHIC/SUPERNATURAL. Fiction exploiting—or requiring as plot devices or themes—some contradictions of the commonplace natural world and materialist assumptions about it (including the traditional ghost story).

QUERY. A letter written to an agent or a potential market to elicit interest in a writer's work.

READER. A person employed by an agent or buyer to go through the slush pile of manuscripts and scripts, and select those worth considering.

REGIONAL. A book faithful to a particular geographic region and its people, including behavior, customs, speech and history.

RELEASE. A statement that your idea is original, has never been sold to anyone else, and that you are selling negotiated rights to the idea upon payment. Some agents may ask that you sign a release before they request pages and review your work.

REMAINDERS. Leftover copies of an out-of-print or slow-selling book purchased from the publisher at a reduced rate. Depending on the contract, a reduced royalty or no royalty is paid to the author on remaindered books.

REPRINT RIGHTS. The right to republish a book after its initial printing.

ROMANCE. A type of category fiction in which the love relationship between a man and a woman pervades the plot. The story is told from the viewpoint of the heroine, who meets a man (the hero), falls in love with him, encounters a conflict that hinders their relationship, and then resolves the conflict with a happy ending.

ROYALTIES. A percentage of the retail price paid to the author for each copy of the book that is sold. Agents take their percentage from the royalties earned and from the advance.

SASE. Self-addressed, stamped envelope. It should be included with all mailed correspondence.

SCHOLARLY BOOKS. Books written for an academic or research audience. These are usually heavily researched, technical and often contain terms used only within a specific field.

SCIENCE FICTION. Literature involving elements of science and technology as a basis for conflict, or as the setting for a story.

SERIAL RIGHTS. The right for a newspaper or magazine to publish sections of a manuscript.

SIMULTANEOUS SUBMISSION. Sending the same query or manuscript to several agents or publishers at the same time.

SLICE OF LIFE. A type of short story, novel, play or film that takes a strong thematic approach, depending less on plot than on vivid detail in describing the setting and/or environment, and the environment's effect on characters involved in it.

SLUSH PILE. A stack of unsolicited submissions in the office of an editor, agent or publisher.

STANDARD COMMISSION. The commission an agent earns on the sales of a manuscript. The commission percentage (usually 15 percent) is taken from the advance and royalties paid to the writer.

SUBAGENT. An agent handling certain subsidiary rights, usually working in conjunction with the agent who handled the book rights. The percentage paid the book agent is increased to pay the subagent.

SUBSIDIARY. An incorporated branch of a company or conglomerate (for example, Crown Publishing Group is a subsidiary of Random House, Inc.).

SUBSIDIARY RIGHTS. All rights other than book publishing rights included in a book publishing contract, such as paperback rights, book club rights and movie rights. Part of an agent's job is to negotiate those rights and advise you on which to sell and which to keep.

SUSPENSE. The element of both fiction and some nonfiction that makes the reader uncertain about the outcome. Suspense can be created through almost any element of a story, including the title, characters, plot, time restrictions and word choice.

SYNOPSIS. A brief summary of a story, novel or play. As a part of a book proposal, it is a comprehensive summary condensed in a page or page-and-a-half, single-spaced. Unlike a query letter or logline, a synopsis is a front-to-back explanation of the work—and will give away the story's ending.

TERMS. Financial provisions agreed upon in a contract, whether between writer and agent, or writer and editor.

TEXTBOOK. Book used in school classrooms at the elementary, high school or college level.

THEME. The point a writer wishes to make. It poses a question—a human problem.

THRILLER. A story intended to arouse feelings of excitement or suspense. Works in this genre are highly sensational, usually focusing on illegal activities, international espionage, sex and violence.

TOC. Table of Contents. A listing at the beginning of a book indicating chapter titles and their corresponding page numbers. It can also include chapter descriptions.

TRADE BOOK. Either a hardcover or softcover book sold mainly in bookstores. The subject matter frequently concerns a special interest for a more general audience.

TRADE PAPERBACK. A soft-bound volume, usually 5×8 inches, published and designed for the general public; available mainly in bookstores.

TRANSLATION RIGHTS. Sold to a foreign agent or foreign publisher.

UNSOLICITED MANUSCRIPT. An unrequested full manuscript sent to an editor, agent or publisher.

VET. A term used by editors when referring to the procedure of submitting a book manuscript to an outside expert (such as a lawyer) for review before publication. Memoirs are frequently vetted to confirm factually accuracy before the book is published.

WESTERNS/FRONTIER. Stories set in the American West, almost always in the 19th century, generally between the antebellum period and the turn of the century.

YOUNG ADULT (YA). The general classification of books written for ages 12–15. They run 40,000–80,000 words and include category novels—adventure, sports, paranormal, science fiction, fantasy, multicultural, mysteries, romance, etc.

LITERARY AGENTS

Literary Agents generate 98–100 percent of their income from commission on sales. They do not charge for reading, critiquing or editing your manuscript or book proposal. It's the goal of an agent to find salable manuscripts: Her income depends on finding the best publisher for your manuscript.

Since an agent's time is better spent meeting with editors, she will have little or no time to critique your writing. Agents who don't charge fees must be selective and often prefer to work with established authors, celebrities or those with professional credentials in a particular field.

Some agents in this section may charge clients for office expenses such as photocopying, foreign postage, long-distance phone calls or express mail services. Make sure you have a clear understanding of what these expenses are before signing any agency agreement.

SUBHEADS

Each agency listing is broken down into subheads to make locating specific information easier. In the first section, you'll find contact information for each agency. You'll also learn if the agents within the agency belong to any professional organizations; membership in these organizations can tell you a lot about an agency. For example, members of the Association of Authors' Representatives (AAR) are prohibited from charging reading or evaluating fees. Additional information in this section includes the size of each agency, its willingness to work with new or unpublished writers, and its general areas of interest.

Member Agents: Agencies comprised of more than one agent list member agents and their individual specialties. This information will help you determine the appropriate person to whom you should send your query letter.

Represents: This section allows agencies to specify what nonfiction and fiction subjects they represent. Make sure you query only those agents who represent the type of material you write.

Look for the key icon to quickly learn an agent's areas of specialization. In this portion of the listing, agents mention the specific subject areas they're currently seeking, as well as those subject areas they do not consider.

How to Contact: Most agents open to submissions prefer an initial query letter that briefly describes your work. While some agents may ask for an outline and a specific number of sample chapters, most don't. You should send these items only if the agent requests them. In this section, agents also mention if they accept queries by fax or e-mail, if they consider simultaneous submissions, and how they prefer to obtain new clients.

Recent Sales: To give you a sense of the types of material they represent, the agents list specific titles they've sold, as well as a sampling of clients' names. Note that some agents consider their client list confidential and may only share client names once they agree to represent you.

At the beginning of some listings, you will find one or more of the following symbols:

- ⊕ agency new to this addition
- ⊘ agency not currently seeking new clients
- Canadian agency
- agency located outside of the U.S. and Canada
- comment from the editor of *Guide to Literary Agents*
- ○ newer agency actively seeking clients
- ◐ agency seeking both new and established writers
- ● agency seeking mostly established writers through referrals
- ◎ agency has a specialized focus
- tips on agency's specializations

Find a pull-out bookmark with a key to symbols on the inside cover of this book.

Terms: Provided here are details of an agent's commission, whether a contract is offered and for how long, and what additional office expenses you might have to pay if the agent agrees to represent you. Standard commissions range from 10–15 percent for domestic sales and 15–20 percent for foreign or dramatic sales (with the difference going to the co-agent who places the work).

Writers' Conferences: A great way to meet an agent is at a writers' conference. Here agents list the conferences they usually attend. For more information about a specific conference, check the Conferences section starting on page 297.

Tips: In this section, agents offer advice and additional instructions for writers.

SPECIAL INDEXES

Literary Agents Specialties Index: This index (page 338) organizes agencies according to the subjects they are interested in receiving. This index should help you compose a list of agents specializing in your areas. Cross-referencing categories and concentrating on agents interested in two or more aspects of your manuscript might increase your chances of success.

Agents Index: This index (page 332) provides a list of agents' names in alphabetical order, along with the name of the agency for which they work. Find the name of the person you would like to contact, and then check the agency listing.

A+B WORKS

E-mail: query@aplusbworks.com. **Website:** aplusbworks.com. **Contact:** Amy Jameson, Brandon Jameson. Estab. 2004.

Prior to her current position, Ms. Jameson worked at Janklow & Nesbit Associates.

REPRESENTS nonfiction books, novels. **Considers these nonfiction areas:** creative nonfiction. **Considers these fiction areas:** middle grade, women's, young adult.

HOW TO CONTACT Query via e-mail only. "Please review our submissions policies first. Send queries to query@aplusbworks.com."

DOMINICK ABEL LITERARY AGENCY, INC.

146 W. 82nd St., #1A, New York NY 10024. (212)877-0710. **E-mail:** agency@dalainc.com. **Website:** dalainc.com/. Estab. 1975. Member AAR. Represents 100 clients. Currently handles: adult fiction and nonfiction.

REPRESENTS Considers these nonfiction areas: business, creative nonfiction. **Considers these fiction areas:** mystery, suspense.

HOW TO CONTACT Query via e-mail. Check website to learn when this agency reopens to new submissions.

TERMS Agent receives 15% commission on domestic sales. Agent receives 20% commission on foreign sales.

ABOUT WORDS AGENCY

E-mail: query@aboutwords.org. **Website:** aboutwords.org. **Contact:** Felice Gums. Currently handles: nonfiction books 40%, novels 60%.

MEMBER AGENTS Felice Gums (multicultural, African American, chick lit, commercial, literary, suspense/thrillers, women's fiction, urban fiction, memoir); **Idaliz Seymour** (adventure, mystery/thrillers, suspense, romance, and paranormal).

REPRESENTS Considers these nonfiction areas: memoirs. **Considers these fiction areas:** adventure, commercial, ethnic, literary, multicultural, paranormal, romance, suspense, thriller, urban fantasy, women's.

About Words Agency is looking for commercial fiction and nonfiction. Does not want poetry, religious/Christian, true crime, screenplays or children's fiction.

HOW TO CONTACT Only accepts e-mail queries. This agency has very specific guidelines on how to submit your work, so check the agency's submission page on their website.

TERMS Agent receives 15% commission on domestic sales. Agent receives 20% commission on foreign sales. Offers written contract.

ADAMS LITERARY

7845 Colony Rd., C4 #215, Charlotte NC 28226. (704)542-1440. **Fax:** (704)542-1450. **E-mail:** info@adamsliterary.com. **E-mail:** submissions@adamsliterary.com. **Website:** www.adamsliterary.com. **Contact:** Tracey Adams, Josh Adams, Quinlan Lee. Member of AAR. Other memberships include SCBWI and WNBA. Currently handles: juvenile books.

MEMBER AGENTS Tracey Adams, Josh Adams, Quinlan Lee.

REPRESENTS Considers these fiction areas: middle grade, picture books, young adult.

Represents "the finest children's book authors and artists."

HOW TO CONTACT Contact through online form on website only. Send e-mail if that is not operating correctly. All submissions and queries should first be made through the online form on website. Will not review—and will promptly recycle—any unsolicited submissions or queries received by mail. Before submitting work for consideration, review complete guidelines. Responds in 6 weeks. "While we have an established client list, we do seek new talent—and we accept submissions from both published and aspiring authors and artists."

TERMS Agent receives 15% commission on domestic sales; 20% on foreign sales. Offers written contract.

RECENT SALES *Exposed*, by Kimberly Marcus (Random House); *The Lemonade Crime*, by Jacqueline Davies (Houghton Mifflin); *Jane Jones: Worst Vampire Ever*, by Caissie St. Onge (Random House).

TIPS "Guidelines are posted (and frequently updated) on our website."

THE AGENCY GROUP, LLC

142 W 57th St., 6th Floor, New York NY 10019. (212)581-3100. **Website:** www.theagencygroup.com. **Contact:** Marc Gerald, agent.

Prior to becoming an agent, Mr. Gerald owned and ran an independent publishing and entertainment agency.

REPRESENTS nonfiction books, novels. **Considers these nonfiction areas:** anthropology, archeology, architecture, art, autobiography, biography, business, child guidance, cooking, cultural interests, dance, decorating, design, economics, environment, ethnic, finance, foods, government, health, history, how-to, humor, interior design, investigative, law, medicine, memoirs, money, nature, nutrition, parenting, personal improvement, popular culture, politics, psychology, satire, self-help, sports, true crime. **Considers these fiction areas:** action, adventure, cartoon, comic books, commercial, confession, contemporary issues, crime, detective, erotica, ethnic, experimental, family saga, feminist, frontier, gay, glitz, hi-lo, historical, horror, humor, inspirational, juvenile, lesbian, literary, mainstream, metaphysical, military, multicultural, multimedia, mystery, New Age, occult, picture books, plays, poetry, poetry in translation, police, psychic, regional, religious, romance, satire, short story collections, spiritual, sports, supernatural, suspense, thriller, translation, war, Westerns, women's, young adult.

This agency is only taking on new clients through referrals.

HOW TO CONTACT "We are currently not accepting submissions except by referral." Accepts simultaneous submissions. Obtains most new clients through recommendations from others.

TERMS Agent receives 15% commission on domestic sales. Agent receives 20% commission on foreign sales. Offers written contract.

THE AHEARN AGENCY, INC.

2021 Pine St., New Orleans LA 70118. (504)861-8395. **Fax:** (504)866-6434. **E-mail:** pahearn@aol.com. **Website:** www.ahearnagency.com. **Contact:** Pamela G. Ahearn. Other memberships include MWA, RWA, ITW. Represents 35 clients. 20% of clients are new/unpublished writers.

Prior to opening her agency, Ms. Ahearn was an agent for 8 years and an editor with Bantam Books.

REPRESENTS **Considers these fiction areas:** romance, suspense, thriller, women's.

Handles women's fiction and suspense fiction only. Does not want to receive category romance, science fiction or fantasy.

HOW TO CONTACT Query with SASE or via e-mail. Please send a one page query letter stating the type of book you're writing, word length, where you feel your book fits into the current market, and any writing credentials you may possess. Please do not send manuscript pages or synopses if they haven't been previously requested. If you're querying via e-mail, send no attachments. Accepts simultaneous submissions. Responds in 2-3 months to queries & mss. Obtains most new clients through recommendations from others, solicitations, conferences.

TERMS Agent receives 15% commission on domestic sales. Agent receives 20% commission on foreign sales. Offers written contract, binding for 1 year; renewable by mutual consent.

RECENT SALES *To the Grave*, by Carlene Thompson; *The Spanish Revenge*, by Allan Topol; *Final Crossing*, by Carter Wilson; *The Incense Game*, by Laura Joh Rowland.

TIPS "Be professional! Always send in exactly what an agent/editor asks for—no more, no less. Keep query letters brief and to the point, giving your writing credentials and a very brief summary of your book. If 1 agent rejects you, keep trying—there are a lot of us out there!"

ALIVE LITERARY AGENCY

7680 Goddard St., Suite 200, Colorado Springs CO 80920. (719)260-7080. Established: 1989. **Fax:** (719)260-8223. **E-mail:** bhaugh@aliveliterary.com [for general purposes]; submissions@aliveliterary.com [for submissions]. **Website:** www.aliveliterary.com. Member of AAR. Other memberships include Authors Guild. Represents 125+ clients. This agency's total book sales top 200 million. The agency serces an elite group of authors who are critically acclaimed and commercially successful in both Christian and general markets.

MEMBER AGENTS **Rick Christian**, president (blockbusters, bestsellers); **Andrea Heinecke** (adult fiction and nonfiction, particularly memoir, religion/spirituality, practical advice, social issues); **Joel Kneedler** (nonfiction narrative, memoir, Christian living, leadership); **Bryan Norman** (spiritual growth, Christian living, biography and autobiography).

This agency specializes in fiction, Christian living, how-to and commercial nonfiction. Actively seeking inspirational, literary and mainstream fiction, and work from authors with established track records and platforms. Does not want to receive poetry, scripts or dark themes.

HOW TO CONTACT "Query via e-mail. "Be advised that this agency works primarily with well-established, best-selling, and career authors. Always looking for a breakout, blockbuster author with genuine talent."

TERMS Agent receives 15% commission on domestic sales. Offers written contract; 2-month notice must be given to terminate contract.

RECENT SALES Sold 100 titles in the last year. Alive's bestselling titles include: *Heaven is for Real*, by Todd Burpo with Lynn Vincent (Nelson); *Everyman's Battle*, by Steve Arterburn (WaterBrook/Multnomah); *The Message Bible*, translated by Eugene Peterson; *A Hole in our Gospel*, by Rich Stearns (Nelson); *15 Minutes*, by Karen Kingsbury (Howard); *The Ragamuffin Gospel*, by Brennan Manning (WaterBrook/Multnomah); *Blue Like Jazz*, by Donald Miller; *The Pastor: A Memoir*, by Eugene Peterson (Harper One); *Life Recovery Bible* by Steve Arterburn and Dave Stoop (Tyndale); *7*, by Jen Hatmaker (B&H); *C.S. Lewis: A Life*, by Alister McGrath (Tyndale); *Successful Women Think Differently*, by Valorie Burton (Harvest House); *Same Kind of Different as Me*, by Ron Hall and Denver Moore (Nelson); *Living in God's Love: The New York Crusade*, by Billy Graham (Penguin); Left Behind series by Tim LaHaye and Jerry B. Jenkins (Tyndale).

TIPS "Rewrite and polish until the words on the page shine. Endorsements and great connections may help, provided you can write with power and passion. Network with publishing professionals by making contacts, joining critique groups, and attending writers' conferences in order to make personal connections and to get feedback."

ALLEN O'SHEA LITERARY AGENCY

615 Westover Rd., Stamford CT 06902. (203)359-9965. **Fax:** (203)357-9909. **E-mail:** marilyn@allenoshea.com; coleen@allenoshea.com. **Website:** www.allenoshea.com. **Contact:** Marilyn Allen. Represents 100 clients. 20% of clients are new/unpublished writers. Currently handles: nonfiction books 99%.

Prior to becoming agents, both Ms. Allen and Ms. O'Shea held senior positions in publishing.

MEMBER AGENTS Marilyn Allen; Coleen O'Shea.

REPRESENTS nonfiction books. **Considers these nonfiction areas:** biography, business, cooking, crafts, current affairs, health, history, how-to, humor, military, money, popular culture, psychology, science, interior design/decorating.

"This agency specializes in practical nonfiction including health, cooking, business, pop culture, etc. We look for clients with strong marketing platforms and new ideas coupled with strong writing ability." Actively seeking narrative nonfiction, health, popular science, cookbooks, and history writers; very interested in writers who have large media platforms following and interesting topics. Does not want to receive fiction, memoirs, poetry, textbooks or children's.

HOW TO CONTACT Query via e-mail or mail with SASE. Submit book proposal with sample chapters, competitive analysis, outline, author bio, marketing page. No phone or fax queries. Accepts simultaneous submissions. Responds in 1 week to queries; 1-2 months to mss. Obtains most new clients through recommendations from others, conferences.

TERMS Agent receives 15% commission on domestic sales. Offers written contract, binding for 2 years; 1-month notice must be given to terminate contract. Charges for photocopying large mss, and overseas postage—"typically minimal costs."

RECENT SALES Sold 90 titles in the last year. "This agency prefers not to share information about specific sales, but see our website."

WRITERS CONFERENCES ASJA, Publicity Submit for Writers, Meet the Agents, PNWA Conference, Cape Cod Writer's Conference, Willamette Writer's Conference, Connecticut Authors and Publishers, Mark Victor Hansen Mega Book Conference.

TIPS "Prepare a strong overview, with competition, marketing and bio. We will consider when your proposal is ready."

MIRIAM ALTSHULER LITERARY AGENCY

53 Old Post Rd. N, Red Hook NY 12571. (845)758-9408. **E-mail:** query@maliterary.com. **Website:** www.miriamaltshulerliteraryagency.com. **Contact:** Miriam Altshuler. Estab. 1994. Member of AAR. Represents 40 clients. Currently handles: nonfiction books 45%, novels 45%, story collections 5%, juvenile books 5%.

Ms. Altshuler has been an agent since 1982.

MEMBER AGENTS **Miriam Altshuler** (literary and commercial fiction, nonfiction, and children's books); **Reiko Davis** (literary fiction, well-told commercial fiction, narrative nonfiction, and young adult).

REPRESENTS nonfiction books, novels, short story collections, juvenile. **Considers these nonfiction ar-**

eas: creative nonfiction, how-to, memoirs, self-help, spirituality, women's issues. **Considers these fiction areas:** commercial, literary, middle grade, picture books, young adult.

Literary commercial fiction and general nonfiction. Does not want mystery, romance, horror, spiritual, fantasy, poetry, screenplays, science fiction or techno-thriller, western.

HOW TO CONTACT Query through e-mail or snail mail. "A query should include a brief author bio, a synopsis of the work, and the first chapter pasted within the body of the e-mail only. (For security purposes, we do not open attachments.)" Accepts simultaneous submissions. Obtains most new clients through recommendations from others.

TERMS Agent receives 15% commission on domestic sales. Agent receives 20% commission on foreign sales. Charges clients for overseas mailing, photocopies, overnight mail when requested by author.

WRITERS CONFERENCES Bread Loaf Writers' Conference; Washington Independent Writers Conference; North Carolina Writers' Network Conference.

TIPS See the website for specific submission details.

AMBASSADOR LITERARY AGENCY & SPEAKERS BUREAU

P.O. Box 50358, Nashville TN 37205. (615)370-4700. **Website:** www.ambassadoragency.com. **Contact:** Wes Yoder. Represents 25-30 clients. 10% of clients are new/unpublished writers. Currently handles: nonfiction books 95%, novels 5%.

Prior to becoming an agent, Mr. Yoder founded a music artist agency in 1973; he established a speakers bureau division of the company in 1984.

REPRESENTS nonfiction books, novels. **Considers these nonfiction areas:** biography, current affairs, ethnic, government, history, inspirational, memoirs, popular culture.

"This agency specializes in religious market publishing dealing primarily with A-level publishers." Actively seeking popular nonfiction themes, including the following: practical living; Christian spirituality; literary fiction. Does not want to receive short stories, children's books, screenplays, or poetry.

HOW TO CONTACT Authors should e-mail a short description of their manuscript with a request to submit their work for review. Official submission guidelines will be sent if we agree to review a manuscript. Speakers should submit a bio, headshot, and speaking demo. Direct all inquiries and submissions to info@ambassadorspeakers.com. Accepts simultaneous submissions. Obtains most new clients through recommendations from others.

TERMS Agent receives 15% commission on domestic sales. Agent receives 20% commission on foreign sales. Offers written contract.

MARCIA AMSTERDAM AGENCY

41 W. 82nd St., Suite 9A, New York NY 10024-5613. (212)873-4945. **Contact:** Marcia Amsterdam. Signatory of WGA. Currently handles: nonfiction books 15%, novels 70%, movie scripts 5%, TV scripts 10%.

Prior to opening her agency, Ms. Amsterdam was an editor.

REPRESENTS novels, movie scripts, feature film, sitcom. **Considers these fiction areas:** adventure, detective, horror, mainstream, mystery, romance (contemporary, historical), science, thriller, young adult. **Considers these script areas:** comedy, romantic comedy.

HOW TO CONTACT Query with SASE. Responds in 1 month to queries.

TERMS Agent receives 15% commission on domestic sales. Agent receives 20% commission on foreign sales. Agent receives 10% commission on film sales. Offers written contract, binding for 1 year. Charges clients for extra office expenses, foreign postage, copying, legal fees (when agreed upon).

RECENT SALES *Hidden Child* by Isaac Millman (FSG); *Lucky Leonardo*, by Jonathan Canter (Sourcebooks).

TIPS "We are always looking for interesting literary voices."

BETSY AMSTER LITERARY ENTERPRISES

6312 SW Capitol Hwy #503, Portland OR 97239. **Website:** www.amsterlit.com. **Contact:** Betsy Amster (adult); Mary Cummings (children's and YA). Estab. 1992. Member of AAR. Represents more than 65 clients. 35% of clients are new/unpublished writers. Currently handles: nonfiction books 65%, novels 35%.

Prior to opening her agency, Ms. Amster was an editor at Pantheon and Vintage for 10 years, and served as editorial director for the Globe Pequot Press for 2 years.

REPRESENTS nonfiction books, novels. **Considers these nonfiction areas:** art & design, biography,

NEW AGENT SPOTLIGHT

ALLISON HUNTER

(INKWELL MANAGEMENT)

inkwellmanagement.com

@AllisonSHunter

ABOUT ALLISON: Allison Hunter, a native of the San Francisco Bay Area, began her publishing career in 2005 working for the Los Angeles-based literary publicity firm, Kim-from-L.A. She joined the InkWell Management team in New York City in 2010. She has a B.A. in American Studies and Creative Writing from Stanford University and a J.D. from the University of Chicago Law School.

SHE IS SEEKING: literary and commercial fiction (including romance), memoir, narrative nonfiction, cultural studies, pop culture and prescriptive titles, including cookbooks. She is always looking for funny female authors, great love stories and family epics, and for nonfiction projects that speak to the current cultural climate.

HOW TO QUERY: submissions@inkwellmanagement.com. Put "Query for Allison: (Title)" in the subject line. In the body of your email, please also include a short writing sample (1-2 chapters). Due to the volume of queries we receive, response times may take up to two months."

business, child guidance, cooking/nutrition, current affairs, ethnic, gardening, health/medicine, history, memoirs, money, parenting, popular culture, psychology, science/technology, self-help, sociology, travelogues, social issues, women's issues. **Considers these fiction areas:** ethnic, literary, women's, high quality.

🗝 "Actively seeking strong narrative nonfiction, particularly by journalists; outstanding literary fiction (the next Jennifer Haigh or Jess Walter); witty, intelligent commerical women's fiction (the next Elinor Lipman); mysteries that open new worlds to us; and high-profile self-help and psychology, preferably research based." Does not want to receive poetry, children's books, romances, western, science fiction, action/adventure, screenplays, fantasy, techno-thrillers, spy capers, apocalyptic scenarios, or political or religious arguments.

HOW TO CONTACT For adult titles: b.amster.assistant@gmail.com. "For fiction or memoirs, please embed the first three pages in the body of your e-mail. For nonfiction, please embed your proposal." For children's and YA: b.amster.kidsbooks@gmail.com. See submission requirements online at website. "For picture books, please embed the entire text in the body of your e-mail. For novels, please embed the first three pages." Accepts simultaneous submissions. Responds in 1 month to queries. Responds in 2 months to mss. Obtains most new clients through recommendations from others, solicitations, conferences.

TERMS Agent receives 15% commission on domestic sales. Agent receives 20% commission on foreign sales.

Offers written contract, binding for 1 year; 3-month notice must be given to terminate contract. Charges for photocopying, postage, messengers, galleys/books used in submissions to foreign and film agents and to magazines for first serial rights.

WRITERS CONFERENCES Los Angeles Times Festival of Books; USC Masters in Professional Writing; San Diego State University Writers' Conference; UCLA Extension Writers' Program; The Loft Literary Center; Willamette Writers Conference.

THE ANDERSON LITERARY AGENCY

435 Convent Ave., Suite 5, New York NY 10031. (646)783-9736. **E-mail:** contact@andersonliteraryagency.com. **Website:** www.andersonliteraryagency.com. **Contact:** Giles Anderson.

Owner and founder Giles Anderson started the agency in 2000 after working several years at The Waxman Literary Agency, Zephyr Press, and The Carnegie Council for Ethics in International Affairs.

MEMBER AGENTS Kathleen Anderson.

REPRESENTS nonfiction books. **Considers these nonfiction areas:** business, education, history, psychology, religious, self-help, spirituality.

Biography, business/investing/finance, history, religious, mind/body/spirit, science.

HOW TO CONTACT Send brief query via e-mail. No attachments.

RECENT SALES *The Myths of Creativity*, by David Burkus; *9 Things Successful People Do Differently*, by Heidi Grant Halverson; *Own the Room*, by Amy Jen Su and Muriel Maignan Wilkins.

ANNE EDELSTEIN LITERARY AGENCY

404 Riverside Dr., #12D, New York NY 10025. (212)414-4923. **Fax:** (212)414-2930. **E-mail:** submissions@aeliterary.com. **Website:** www.aeliterary.com. Member of AAR.

MEMBER AGENTS Anne Edelstein.

REPRESENTS nonfiction, fiction. **Considers these nonfiction areas:** history, memoirs, psychology, religious, cultural history. **Considers these fiction areas:** commercial, literary.

This agency specializes in fiction and narrative nonfiction.

HOW TO CONTACT E-mail queries only; consult website for submission guidelines.

RECENT SALES *Amsterdam*, by Russell Shorto (Doubleday); *The Story of Beautiful Girl*, by Rachel Simon (Grand Central).

ARCADIA

31 Lake Place N., Danbury CT 06810. **E-mail:** arcadialit@sbcglobal.net. **Contact:** Victoria Gould Pryor. Member of AAR.

REPRESENTS nonfiction books. **Considers these nonfiction areas:** biography, current affairs, health, history, psychology, science, investigative journalism, culture, classical music, life transforming self-help.

"I'm a very hands-on agent, which is necessary in this competitive marketplace. I work with authors on revisions until whatever we present to publishers is as strong as possible. Arcadia represents talented, dedicated, intelligent and ambitious writers who are looking for a long-term relationship based on professional success and mutual respect." Does not want to receive fiction, true crime, business science fiction/fantasy, horror, memoirs about addiction or abuse, humor or children's/YA.

HOW TO CONTACT No unsolicited submissions. Query with SASE. This agency accepts e-queries (no attachments).

THE AXELROD AGENCY

55 Main St., P.O. Box 357, Chatham NY 12037. (518)392-2100. **E-mail:** steve@axelrodagency.com. **Website:** www.axelrodagency.com. **Contact:** Steven Axelrod. Member of AAR. Represents 15-20 clients. Currently handles: novels 95%.

Prior to becoming an agent, Mr. Axelrod was a book club editor.

REPRESENTS novels. **Considers these fiction areas:** crime, mystery, new adult, romance, women's.

This agency specializes in women's fiction and romance.

HOW TO CONTACT Query. Accepts simultaneous submissions. Obtains most new clients through recommendations from others.

TERMS Agent receives 15% commission on domestic sales. Agent receives 20% commission on foreign sales. No written contract.

WRITERS CONFERENCES RWA National Conference.

JENNIFER AZANTIAN LITERARY AGENCY

E-mail: queries@azantianlitagency.com. **Website:** www.azantianlitagency.com. Estab. 2013.

Prior to her current position, Ms. Azantian was with Sandra Dijkstra Literary Agency.

REPRESENTS Considers these fiction areas: fantasy, horror, middle grade, new adult, science fiction, young adult. She seeks all subgenres of fantasy and science fiction. She particularly likes horror, and it is horror submissions she wants to see in young adult, middle grade and new adult submissions.

Horror. Does not want picture books.

HOW TO CONTACT To submit, send your query letter and 1-2 page synopsis, and first 10-15 pages all pasted in an e-mail (no attachments). Please note in the e-mail subject line if your work was requested at a conference, is an exclusive submission, or if your work was referred from a current client. Accepts simultaneous submissions. Responds within 6 weeks. Feel free to follow up if you have heard nothing by then.

BARER LITERARY, LLC

20 W. 20th St., Suite 601, New York NY 10011. (212)691-3513. **E-mail:** submissions@barerliterary.com. **Website:** www.barerliterary.com. **Contact:** Julie Barer. Estab. 2004. Member of AAR.

Before becoming an agent, Julie worked at Shakespeare & Co. Booksellers in New York City. She is a graduate of Vassar College.

MEMBER AGENTS Julie Barer, Anna Geller, William Boggess (literary fiction and narrative nonfiction).

REPRESENTS nonfiction books, novels, short story collections. Julie Barer is especially interested in working with emerging writers and developing long-term relationships with new clients. **Considers these nonfiction areas:** biography, ethnic, history, memoirs, popular culture, women's. **Considers these fiction areas:** contemporary issues, ethnic, historical, literary, mainstream.

This agency actively seeks most genres of fiction and nonfiction. This agency no longer accepts young adult submissions. No health/fitness, business/investing/finance, sports, mind/body/spirit, reference, thrillers/suspense, military, romance, children's books/picture books, screenplays.

HOW TO CONTACT Query; no attachments if query by e-mail. "We do not respond to queries via phone or fax."

TERMS Agent receives 15% commission on domestic sales. Agent receives 20% commission on foreign sales. Offers written contract. Charges for photocopying and books ordered.

RECENT SALES *The Unnamed*, by Joshua Ferris (Reagan Arthur Books); *Tunneling to the Center of the Earth*, by Kevin Wilson (Ecco Press); *A Disobedient Girl*, by Ru Freeman (Atria Books); *A Friend of the Family*, by Lauren Grodstein (Algonquin); *City of Veils*, by Zoe Ferraris (Little, Brown).

LORETTA BARRETT BOOKS, INC.

220 E. 23rd St., 11th Floor, New York NY 10010. (212)242-3420. **E-mail:** query@lorettabarrettbooks.com. **Website:** www.lorettabarrettbooks.com. **Contact:** Loretta A. Barrett; Nick Mullendore; Gabriel Davis. Estab. 1990. Member of AAR. Currently handles: nonfiction books 50%, novels 50%.

Prior to opening her agency, Ms. Barrett was vice president and executive editor at Doubleday and editor-in-chief of Anchor Books.

MEMBER AGENTS Loretta A. Barrett; Nick Mullendore.

REPRESENTS nonfiction books, novels. **Considers these nonfiction areas:** biography, cooking, creative nonfiction, current affairs, gardening, health, history, humor, memoirs, politics, psychology, science, spirituality, sports, true crime, women's issues. **Considers these fiction areas:** commercial, literary, mainstream, metaphysical, mystery, romance, thriller, women's.

"Loretta Barrett Books, Inc. represents a wide variety of fiction and nonfiction for general audiences."

HOW TO CONTACT Query via snail mail or e-mail. No e-mail attachments. Paste all materials into the e-mail. "For hard-copy fiction queries, please send a 1-2 page query letter and a synopsis or chapter outline for your project. For hard-copy nonfiction queries, please send a 1-2 page query letter and a brief overview or chapter outline for your project." Accepts simultaneous submissions. Responds in 3-6 weeks to queries.

TERMS Agent receives 15% commission on domestic sales. Agent receives 20% commission on foreign sales. Offers written contract. Charges clients for shipping and photocopying.

BARRON'S LITERARY MANAGEMENT

4615 Rockland Dr., Arlington TX 76016. **E-mail:** barronsliterary@sbcglobal.net. **Contact:** Adele Brooks, president.

REPRESENTS Considers these nonfiction areas: business, cooking, health, money, psychology, true crime. **Considers these fiction areas:** crime, detective, historical, horror, mystery, paranormal, police, romance, suspense, thriller.

Barron's Literary Management is a small Dallas/Fort Worth-based agency with good publishing contacts. Seeks tightly written, fast moving fiction, and nonfiction authors with a significant platform or subject area expertise.

HOW TO CONTACT Contact by e-mail initially. Send bio and a brief synopsis of story (fiction) or a nonfiction book proposal. Obtains most new clients through e-mail submissions.

TIPS "Have your book tightly edited, polished, and ready to be seen before contacting agents. I respond quickly and if interested may request an electronic or hard copy mailing."

FAYE BENDER LITERARY AGENCY

19 Cheever Place, Brooklyn NY 11231. **E-mail:** info@fbliterary.com. **Website:** www.fbliterary.com. **Contact:** Faye Bender. Estab. 2004. Member of AAR.

MEMBER AGENTS Faye Bender.

REPRESENTS nonfiction books, novels, juvenile. **Considers these nonfiction areas:** biography, memoirs, popular culture, women's issues, women's studies, young adult, narrative, health, popular science. **Considers these fiction areas:** commercial, literary, middle grade, women's, young adult.

"I choose books based on the narrative voice and strength of writing. I work with previously published and first-time authors." Faye does not represent picture books, genre fiction for adults (western, romance, horror, science fiction, fantasy), business books, spirituality, or screenplays.

HOW TO CONTACT Please submit a query letter and ten sample pages to info@fbliterary.com (no attachments). "Due to the volume of e-mails, we can't respond to everything. If we are interested, we will be in touch as soon as we possibly can. Otherwise, please consider it a pass."

RECENT SALES Liane Moriarty's *The Husband's Secret* (Amy Einhorn Books); Rebecca Stead's *Liar & Spy* (Wendy Lamb Books); Kristin Cashore's *Bitterblue* (Dial); Dayna Lorentz's No Safety in Numbers series (Dial).

TIPS "Please keep your letters to the point, include all relevant information, and have a bit of patience."

THE BENT AGENCY

Bent Agency, The, 159 20th St., #2B, Brooklyn NY 11232. **E-mail:** info@thebentagency.com. **Website:** www.thebentagency.com. **Contact:** Jenny Bent; Susan Hawk; Molly Ker Hawn; Gemma Cooper; Louise Fury; Brooks Sherman; Beth Phelan; Victoria Lowes. Estab. 2009.

Prior to forming her own agency, Ms. Bent was an agent and vice president at Trident Media.

MEMBER AGENTS **Jenny Bent** (adult fiction including women's fiction, romance and crime/suspense, she particularly likes novels with magical or fantasy elements that fall outside of genre fiction; young adult and middle grade fiction; memoir; humor); **Susan Hawk** (young adult and middle grade and picture books; within the realm of kids stories, she likes contemporary, mystery, fantasy, science fiction, and historical fiction); **Molly Ker Hawn** (young adult and middle grade books, including contemporary, historical science fiction, fantasy, thrillers, mystery); **Gemma Cooper** (all ages of children's and young adult books, including picture books, likes historical, contemporary, thrillers, mystery, humor, and science fiction); **Louise Fury** (picture books, literary middle grade, all young adult, speculative fiction, suspense/thriller, commercial fiction, all subgenres of romance including erotic, nonfiction: cookbooks, pop culture); **Brooks Sherman** (speculative and literary adult fiction, select narrative nonfiction; all ages of children's and young adult books, including picture books; likes historical, contemporary, thrillers, humor, fantasy, and horror); **Beth Phelan** (young adult, thrillers, suspense and mystery, romance and women's fiction, literary and general fiction, cookbooks, lifestyle and pets/animals); **Victoria Lowes** (romance and women's fiction, thrillers and mystery, and young adult).

REPRESENTS Considers these nonfiction areas: animals, cooking, creative nonfiction, popular culture. **Considers these fiction areas:** commercial, crime, fantasy, historical, horror, literary, mystery, picture books, romance, suspense, thriller, women's, young adult.

HOW TO CONTACT For Jenny Bent, e-mail: queries@thebentagency.com; for Susan Hawk, e-mail: kidsqueries@thebentagency.com; for Molly Ker Hawn, e-mail: hawnqueries@thebentagency.com; for Gemma Cooper, e-mail: cooperqueries@thebentagency.com; for Louise Fury, e-mail: furyqueries@thebentagency.com; for Brooks Sherman, e-mail: shermanqueries@thebentagency.com; for Beth Phelan, e-mail: phelanagencies@thebentagency.com; for Victoria Lowes, e-mail: lowesqueries@thebentagency.com. "Tell us briefly who you are, what your book is, and why you're the one to write it. Then include the first 10 pages of your material in the body of your e-mail. We respond to all queries; please resend your query if you haven't had a response within 4 weeks." Accepts simultaneous submissions.

RECENT SALES *The Pocket Wife*, by Susan Crawford (Morrow); *The Smell of Other People's Houses*, by Bonnie-Sue Hitchcock (Wendy Lamb Books); *The Graham Cracker Plot*, by Shelley Tougas (Roaring Brook); *Murder Is Bad Manners*, by Robin Stevens (Simon & Schuster); The Inside Out Series, by Lisa Renee Jones (Simon & Schuster); *True North*, by Liora Blake (Pocket Star).

BIDNICK & COMPANY

E-mail: bidnick@comcast.net. **Website:** www.publishersmarketplace.com/members/bidnick/. Currently handles: 100% nonfiction books.

Founding member of Collins Publishers. Vice president of HarperCollins, San Francisco.

MEMBER AGENTS Carole Bidnick.

REPRESENTS **Considers these nonfiction areas:** cooking, creative nonfiction.

This agency specializes in cookbooks and narrative nonfiction.

HOW TO CONTACT Send queries via e-mail only.

RECENT SALES *The Mexican Slow Cooker*, by Deborah Schneider (Ten Speed); *Around the Southern Table*, by Rebecca Lang (Oxmoor House); *Mac & Cheese Please*, by Laura Werlin (Andrews McMeel).

DAVID BLACK LITERARY AGENCY

335 Adams St., Suite 2707, Brooklyn NY 11201. (718)852-5500. **Fax:** (718)852-5539. **Website:** www.davidblackagency.com. **Contact:** David Black, owner. Member of AAR. Represents 150 clients. Currently handles: nonfiction books 90%, novels 10%.

MEMBER AGENTS David Black; Susan Raihofer; Gary Morris; Joy E. Tutela (general nonfiction, literary fiction, commercial fiction, YA, MG); Linda Loewenthal; Antonella Iannarino; David M. Larabell; Susan Raihofer; Sarah Smith; Gary Morris; Luke Thomas.

REPRESENTS nonfiction books, novels. **Considers these nonfiction areas:** biography, business, creative nonfiction, current affairs, gay/lesbian, health, history, humor, memoirs, money, parenting, politics, self-help, women's issues. **Considers these fiction areas:** commercial, literary, middle grade, thriller, young adult.

HOW TO CONTACT "To query an individual agent, please follow the specific query guidelines outlined in the agent's profile on our website. Not all agents are currently accepting unsolicited queries. To query the agency, please send a 1-2 page query letter describing your book, and include information about any previously published works, your audience, and your platform." Note that some agents prefer e-queries whereas some prefer snail mail queries. Accepts simultaneous submissions. Responds in 2 months to queries.

TERMS Agent receives 15% commission on domestic sales. Charges clients for photocopying and books purchased for sale of foreign rights.

RECENT SALES Some of the agency's best-selling authors include: Mitch Albom, Erik Larson, Ken Davis, Bruce Feiler, Dan Coyle, Jane Leavy, Randy Pausch, Steve Lopez, Jenny Sanford, David Kidder and Noah Oppenheim.

BLEECKER STREET ASSOCIATES, INC.

217 Thompson St., #519, New York NY 10012. (212)677-4492. **Fax:** (212)388-0001. **E-mail:** bleeckerst@hotmail.com. **Contact:** Agnes Birnbaum. Member of AAR. Other memberships include RWA, MWA. Represents 60 clients. 20% of clients are new/unpublished writers. Currently handles: nonfiction books 75%, novels 25%.

Prior to becoming an agent, Ms. Birnbaum was a senior editor at Simon & Schuster, Dutton/Signet, and other publishing houses.

Does not want to receive science fiction, westerns, poetry, children's books, academic/scholarly/professional books, plays, scripts, or short stories.

HOW TO CONTACT Query by referral only. Accepts simultaneous submissions. Responds in 2 weeks to queries. Responds in 1 month to mss. "Obtains most new clients through recommendations from others, solicitations, conferences."

TERMS Agent receives 15% commission on domestic sales. Agent receives 25% commission on foreign sales. Offers written contract; 1-month notice must be given to terminate contract. Charges for postage, long distance, fax, messengers, photocopies (not to exceed $200).

RECENT SALES Sold 14 titles in the last year. *Following Sarah*, by Daniel Brown (Morrow); *Biology of the Brain*, by Paul Swingle (Rutgers University Press); *Santa Miracles*, by Brad and Sherry Steiger (Adams); *Surviving the College Search*, by Jennifer Delahunt (St. Martin's).

TIPS "Keep query letters short and to the point; include only information pertaining to the book or background as a writer. Try to avoid superlatives in description. Work needs to stand on its own, so how much editing it may have received has no place in a query letter."

JUDY BOALS, INC.

307 W. 38th St., #812, New York NY 10018. (212)500-1424. **Fax:** (212)500-1426. **E-mail:** info@judyboals.com. **Website:** www.judyboals.com. **Contact:** Judy Boals.

HOW TO CONTACT Query by referral or invitation only.

REID BOATES LITERARY AGENCY

69 Cooks Crossroad, Pittstown NJ 08867. (908)797-8087. **Fax:** (908)788-3667. **E-mail:** reid.boates@gmail.com; boatesliterary@att.net. **Contact:** Reid Boates. Represents 45 clients.

HOW TO CONTACT **No unsolicited queries of any kind**. Obtains new clients by personal referral only. This agency, at the current time, is handling 100% nonfiction.

TERMS Agent receives 15% commission on domestic sales. Agent receives 20% commission on foreign sales.

RECENT SALES New sales include placements at HarperCollins, Wiley, Random House, and other major general-interest publishers.

BOND LITERARY AGENCY

4340 E. Kentucky Ave., Suite 471, Denver CO 80246. (303)781-9305. **E-mail:** queries@bondliteraryagency.com. **Website:** www.bondliteraryagency.com. **Contact:** Sandra Bond.

Prior to her current position, Ms. Bond worked with agent Jody Rein.

REPRESENTS nonfiction books, novels. **Considers these nonfiction areas:** biography, business, creative nonfiction, health, memoirs, science. **Considers these fiction areas:** commercial, literary, mystery, women's, young adult.

Does not represent romance, adult fantasy, poetry, and children's picture books.

HOW TO CONTACT Submit query by mail or e-mail (no attachments). "She will let you know if she is interested in seeing more material. *No unsolicited mss.* No phone calls, please." Accepts simultaneous submissions.

RECENT SALES *Claws of the Cat*, by Susan Spann (a mystery); *Fatal Descent*, by Beth Groundwater; *Death in the 12th House*, by Mitch Lewis.

BOOK CENTS LITERARY AGENCY, LLC

P.O. Box 11826, Charleston WV 25339. **E-mail:** cw@bookcentsliteraryagency.com. **Website:** www.bookcentsliteraryagency.com. **Contact:** Christine Witthohn. Member of AAR, RWA, MWA, SinC, KOD.

MEMBER AGENTS Christine Witthohn (represents both published and unpublished authors); Kristina Smith.

"Single-title romance (contemporary, romantic comedy, paranormal, mystery/suspense), women's lit (must have a strong hook), mainstream mystery/suspense, thrillers (high octane, psychological), literary fiction and new adult. For nonfiction, seeking women's issues/experiences, fun/quirky topics (particularly those of interest to women), cookbooks (fun, ethnic, etc.), gardening (herbs, plants, flowers, etc.), books with a "save-the-planet" theme, how-to books, travel and outdoor adventure." Does not want to receive category romance, erotica, inspirational, historical, sci-fi/fantasy, horror/dark thrillers (serial killers), short stories/novella, children's picture books, poetry, screenplays.

HOW TO CONTACT E-queries only. You can submit via this agency's online form.

TIPS "Sponsors *International Women's Fiction Festival* in Matera, Italy. See: www.womensfictionfestival.com for more information. Christine is also the U.S. rights and licensing agent for leading French publisher, Bragelonne, Egmont-Germany. For a list of upcoming publications, leading clients and sales, visit: www.publishersmarketplace.com/members/BookCents."

BOOKENDS, LLC

136 Long Hill Rd., Gillette NJ 07933. **Website:** www.bookends-inc.com. **Contact:** Kim Lionetti, Jessica Alvarez, Beth Campbell. Member of AAR, RWA, MWA. Represents 50+ clients. 10% of clients are new/unpublished writers. Currently handles: nonfiction books 50%, novels 50%.

MEMBER AGENTS **Jessica Faust** (no longer accepting unsolicited material); **Kim Lionetti** (only currently considering romance, women's fiction, cozies, and contemporary young adult queries. "If your book is in any of these 3 categories, please be sure to specify 'Romance,' 'Women's Fiction,' or 'Young Adult' in your e-mail subject line. Any queries that do not follow these guidelines will not be considered."); **Jessica Alvarez** (romance, cozies, women's fiction, erotica, romantic suspense); **Beth Campbell.**

REPRESENTS nonfiction books, novels. **Considers these nonfiction areas:** business, ethnic, how-to, money, sex, true crime. **Considers these fiction areas:** detective, cozies, mainstream, mystery, romance, thrillers, women's.

"BookEnds is currently accepting queries from published and unpublished writers in the areas of romance (and all its subgenres), erotica, mystery, suspense, women's fiction, and literary fiction." BookEnds does not want to receive children's books, screenplays, science fiction, poetry, or technical/military thrillers.

HOW TO CONTACT Review website for guidelines, as they change. BookEnds is no longer accepting unsolicited proposal packages or snail mail queries. Send query in the body of e-mail to only 1 agent.

BOOKS & SUCH LITERARY AGENCY

52 Mission Circle, Suite 122, PMB 170, Santa Rosa CA 95409. **E-mail:** representation@booksandsuch.com. **Website:** www.booksandsuch.biz. **Contact:** Janet Kobobel Grant, Wendy Lawton, Rachel Kent, Mary Keeley, Rachelle Gardner. Member of AAR. Member of CBA (associate), American Christian Fiction Writers. Represents 150 clients. 5% of clients are new/unpublished writers. Currently handles: nonfiction books 50%, novels 50%.

Prior to becoming an agent, Ms. Grant was an editor for Zondervan and managing editor for *Focus on the Family*; Ms. Lawton was an author, sculptor, and designer of porcelein dolls. Ms. Keeley accepts both nonfiction and adult fiction. She previously was an acquisition editor for Tyndale publishers.

REPRESENTS nonfiction books, novels. **Considers these nonfiction areas:** humor, religion, self-help, women's. **Considers these fiction areas:** historical, literary, mainstream, new adult, religious, romance, young adult.

This agency specializes in general and inspirational fiction, romance, and in the Christian booksellers market. Actively seeking well-crafted material that presents Judeo-Christian values, if only subtly.

HOW TO CONTACT Query via e-mail only; no attachments. Accepts simultaneous submissions. Responds in 1 month to queries. "If you don't hear from us asking to see more of your writing within 30 days after you have sent your e-mail, please know that we have read and considered your submission but determined that it would not be a good fit for us." Obtains most new clients through recommendations from others, conferences.

TERMS Agent receives 15% commission on domestic sales. Agent receives 20% commission on foreign sales. Offers written contract; 2-month notice must be given to terminate contract. No additional charges.

RECENT SALES *One Perfect Gift*, by Debbie Macomber (Howard Books); *Greetings from the Flipside*, by Rene Gutteridge and Cheryl Mckay (B&H Publishing); *Key on the Quilt*, by Stephanie Grace Whitson (Barbour Publishing); *Annotated Screwtape Letters, Annotations*, by Paul Mccusker (Harper One). Other clients include: Lauraine Snelling, Lori Copeland, Rene Gutteridge, Dale Cramer, BJ Hoff, Diann Mills. A full list of this agency's clients (and the awards they have won) is on the agency website.

WRITERS CONFERENCES Mount Hermon Christian Writers' Conference; Writing for the Soul; American Christian Fiction Writers' Conference; San Francisco Writers' Conference.

TIPS "The heart of our agency's motivation is to develop relationships with the authors we serve, to do what we can to shine the light of success on them, and to help be a caretaker of their gifts and time."

BOOKSTOP LITERARY AGENCY

67 Meadow View Rd., Orinda CA 94563. (925)254-2664. **Fax:** (925)254-2668. **E-mail:** kendra@bookstopliterary.com; info@bookstopliterary.com. **Website:** www.bookstopliterary.com. Estab. 1983.

"Special interest in Hispanic, Asian American, and African American writers; quirky picture books; clever adventure/mystery novels; and authentic and emotional young adult voices."

HOW TO CONTACT Send: cover letter, entire ms for picture books; first 30 pages of novels; proposal and sample chapters OK for nonfiction. E-mail submissions: Paste cover letter and first 10 pages of ms into body of e-mail, send to info@bookstopliterary.com. Send sample illustrations only if you are an illustrator.

TERMS Agent receives 15% commission on domestic sales. Offers written contract, binding for 1 year.

THE BARBARA BOVA LITERARY AGENCY

3951 Gulf Shore Blvd. N., Unit PH 1-B, Naples FL 34103. (239)649-7263. **Fax:** (239)649-7263. **E-mail:** michaelburke@barbarabovaliteraryagency.com. **Website:** www.barbarabovaliteraryagency.com. **Contact:** Ken Bova, Michael Burke. Represents 30 clients. Currently handles: nonfiction books 20%, fiction 80%.

REPRESENTS nonfiction books, novels. **Considers these nonfiction areas:** biography, history, science, self-help, true crime, women's, social sciences. **Considers these fiction areas:** adventure, crime, detective, mystery, police, science fiction, suspense, thriller, women's, young adult, teen lit.

This agency specializes in fiction and nonfiction, hard and soft science. "We also handle foreign, movie, television, and audio rights." No scripts, poetry, or children's books.

HOW TO CONTACT Query through website. No attachments. "We accept short (3-5 pages) e-mail queries. All queries should have the word 'Query' in the subject line. Include all information as you would in a standard, snail mail query letter, such as pertinent credentials, publishing history, and an overview of the book. Include a word count of your project. You may include a short synopsis. We're looking for quality fiction and nonfiction." Obtains most new clients through recommendations from others.

TERMS Agent receives 15% commission on domestic sales. Agent receives 20% commission on foreign sales. Charges clients for overseas postage, overseas calls, photocopying, shipping.

BRADFORD LITERARY AGENCY

5694 Mission Center Rd., #347, San Diego CA 92108. (619)521-1201. **E-mail:** queries@bradfordlit.com. **Website:** www.bradfordlit.com. **Contact:** Laura Bradford, Natalie Lakosil, Sarah LaPolla. Estab. 2001. Member of AAR, RWA, SCBWI, ALA. Represents 50 clients. 20% of clients are new/unpublished writers. Currently handles: nonfiction books 5%, novels 95%.

REPRESENTS **Considers these nonfiction areas:** biography, business, creative nonfiction, humor, memoirs, parenting, self-help. **Considers these fiction areas:** erotica, middle grade, mystery, paranormal, picture books, romance, thriller, women's, young adult.

Actively seeking many types of romance (historical, romantic suspense, paranormal, category, contemporary, erotic). Does not want to receive poetry, screenplays, short stories, westerns, horror, new age, religion, crafts, cookbooks, gift books.

HOW TO CONTACT Accepts e-mail queries only; send to queries@bradfordlit.com (or sarah@bradfordlit if contacting Sarah LaPolla). The entire submission must appear in the body of the e-mail and not as an attachment. The subject line should begin as follows: QUERY: (the title of the ms or any short message that is important should follow). For fiction: e-mail a query letter along with the first chapter of ms and a synopsis. Include the genre and word count in cover letter. Nonfiction: e-mail full nonfiction proposal including a query letter and a sample chapter. Accepts simultaneous submissions. Responds in 2-4 weeks to queries. Responds in 10 weeks to mss. Obtains most new clients through solicitations.

TERMS Agent receives 15% commission on domestic sales. Agent receives 20% commission on foreign sales. Offers written contract, non-binding for 2 years; 45-day notice must be given to terminate contract. Charges for extra copies of books for foreign submissions.

RECENT SALES Sold 68 titles in the last year. *All Fall Down*, by Megan Hart (Mira Books); *Body and Soul*, by Stacey Kade (Hyperion Children's); *All Things Wicked*, by Karina Cooper (Avon); *Circle Eight: Matthew*, by Emma Lang (Kensington Brava); *Midnight Enchantment*, by Anya Bast (Berkley Sensation); *Outpost*, by Ann Aguirre (Feiwel and Friends); *The One That I Want*, by Jennifer Echols (Simon Pulse); *Catch Me a Cowboy*, by Katie Lane (Grand Central); *Back in a Soldier's Arms*, by Soraya Lane (Harlequin); *Enraptured*, by Elisabeth Naughton (Sourcebooks); *Wicked Road to Hell*, by Juliana Stone (Avon); *Master of Sin*, by Maggie Robinson (Kensington Brava); *Chaos Burning*, by Lauren Dane

NEW AGENT SPOTLIGHT

REBECCA PODOS
(REES LITERARY AGENCY)

reesagency.com

@RebeccaPodos

ABOUT REBECCA: Rebecca Podos (Rees Literary Agency) is a graduate of the MFA Writing, Literature and Publishing program at Emerson College, whose own fiction has appeared in *Glimmer Train, Glyph, CAJE, Bellows American Review, Paper Darts*, and *SmokeLong Quarterly*.

SHE IS SEEKING: young adult fiction of all kinds, including contemporary, emotionally driven stories, mystery, romance, urban and historical fantasy, horror, and sci-fi. Occasionally, she also considers literary and commercial adult fiction, new adult, and narrative nonfiction.

HOW TO QUERY: Send a query letter and the first few chapters (pasted in the e-mail) to Rebecca@reesagency.com.

(Berkley Sensation); *If I Lie*, by Corrine Jackson (Simon Pulse); *Renegade*, by J.A. Souders (Tor).

WRITERS CONFERENCES RWA National Conference; Romantic Times Booklovers Convention.

◐ BRANDT & HOCHMAN LITERARY AGENTS, INC.

1501 Broadway, Suite 2310, New York NY 10036. (212)840-5760. **Fax:** (212)840-5776. **Website:** brandthochman.com. **Contact:** Gail Hochman. Member of AAR. Represents 200 clients.

MEMBER AGENTS Gail Hochman; Marianne Merola; Charles Schlessiger; Bill Contardi; Emily Forland (graphic novels); Emma Patterson (anything about the Yankees, stories set in Brooklyn); Jody Klein; Henry Thayer. The e-mail addresses and specific likes of each of these agents is listed on the agency website.

REPRESENTS Considers these nonfiction areas: biography, cooking, creative nonfiction, foods, history, memoirs, music, sports, young adult. **Considers these fiction areas:** commercial, crime, family saga, fantasy, historical, literary, middle grade, mystery, suspense, thriller, women's.

No screenplays or textbooks.

HOW TO CONTACT "We accept queries by e-mail and regular mail; however, we cannot guarantee a response to e-mailed queries. For queries via regular mail, be sure to include a self-addressed stamped envelope for our reply. Query letters should be no more than two pages and should include a convincing overview of the book project and information about the author and his or her writing credits. Address queries to the specific Brandt & Hochman agent whom you would like to consider your work. Agent e-mail addresses and query preferences may be found at the end of each agent profile on the AGENTS page of our website." Accepts simultaneous submissions. Responds in 1 month to queries. Obtains most new clients through recommendations from others.

TERMS Agent receives 15% commission on domestic sales. Agent receives 20% commission on foreign sales.
RECENT SALES This agency sells 40-50 new titles each year. A full list of their hundreds of clients is on the agency website.
TIPS "Write a letter which will give the agent a sense of you as a professional writer—your long-term interests as well as a short description of the work at hand."

THE JOAN BRANDT AGENCY

788 Wesley Dr., Atlanta GA 30305. (404)351-8877. **Contact:** Joan Brandt.

Prior to her current position, Ms. Brandt was with Sterling Lord Literistic.

REPRESENTS nonfiction books, novels, short story collections. **Considers these nonfiction areas:** creative nonfiction, investigative, popular culture, true crime. **Considers these fiction areas:** commercial, crime, family saga, historical, literary, mystery, suspense, thriller, women's.
HOW TO CONTACT Query letter with SASE. Accepts simultaneous submissions.
TERMS Agent receives 15% commission on domestic sales. Agent receives 20% commission on foreign sales. No written contract.

THE HELEN BRANN AGENCY, INC.

94 Curtis Rd., Bridgewater CT 06752. **Fax:** (860)355-2572. Member of AAR.
HOW TO CONTACT Query with SASE.

THE BRATTLE AGENCY

P.O. Box 380537, Cambridge MA 02238. (617)721-5375. **E-mail:** christopher.vyce@thebrattleagency.com. **E-mail:** submissions@thebrattleagency.com. **Website:** thebrattleagency.com/. **Contact:** Christopher Vyce.

Prior to being an agent Mr. Vyce worked for the Beacon Press in Boston as an acquisitions editor.

MEMBER AGENTS Christopher Vyce.
HOW TO CONTACT Query by e-mail. Include cover letter, brief synopsis, brief CV. Responds in 2 days. If asked to see mss, responds in 6-8 weeks.

BARBARA BRAUN ASSOCIATES, INC.

7 E. 14th St., Suite 19F, New York NY 10003. **Fax:** (212)604-9023. **Website:** www.barbarabraunagency.com. **Contact:** Barbara Braun. Member of AAR.
MEMBER AGENTS Barbara Braun; John F. Baker.
REPRESENTS nonfiction books, novels. **Considers these nonfiction areas:** architecture, art, biography, design, film, history, photography, psychology, women's issues. **Considers these fiction areas:** commercial, literary.

"Our fiction is strong on women's stories, historical and multicultural stories, as well as mysteries and thrillers. We're interested in narrative nonfiction and books by journalists. Look online for more details." We do not represent poetry, science fiction, fantasy, horror, or screenplays.

HOW TO CONTACT "We no longer accept submissions by regular mail. Please send all queries to bbasubmissions@gmail.com, marked 'Query' in the subject line. Your query should include: a brief summary of your book, word count, genre, any relevant publishing experience, and the first 5 pages of your manuscript pasted into the body of the e-mail. (NO attachments—we will not open these.)"
TERMS Agent receives 15% commission on domestic sales. Agent receives 20% commission on foreign sales.
RECENT SALES *Clara and Mr. Tiffany*, by Susan Vreeland.
TIPS "Our clients' books are represented throughout Europe, Asia, and Latin America by various sub-agents. We are also active in selling motion picture rights to the books we represent, and work with various Hollywood agencies."

BRESNICK WEIL LITERARY AGENCY

115 W. 29th St., Third Floor, New York NY 10001. (212)239-3166. **Fax:** (212)239-3165. **E-mail:** paul@bresnickagency.com. **Website:** bresnickagency.com. **Contact:** Paul Bresnick, Polly Bresnick.

Prior to becoming an agent, Mr. Bresnick spent 25 years as a trade book editor.

REPRESENTS nonfiction books, novels. **Considers these nonfiction areas:** autobiography/memoir, biography, health, history, humor, memoirs, multicultural, popular culture, sports, travel, true crime, celebrity-branded books, narrative nonfiction, pop psychology, relationship issues. **Considers these fiction areas:** general fiction.
HOW TO CONTACT For fiction, submit query and 2 chapters. For nonfiction, submit query with proposal. Electronic submissions only (for both).
RECENT SALES Sales include *Heads: A Subcultural Biography Of Psychedelic America*, by Jesse Jarnow (Da Capo Press, 2014); *Mafia Summit: J. Edgar Hoover, The Kennedy Brothers, And The Meeting That Unmasked The Mob*, by Gil Reavill (Thomas Dunne

Books, 2013); *Crossroads: How The Blues Shaped Rock 'N' Roll (And Rock Saved The Blues)*, by John Milward (University Press of New England, 2013). A complete list of sales is available on agency website.

BRET ADAMS LTD. AGENCY

448 W. 44th St., New York NY 10036. (212)765-5630. **E-mail:** literary@bretadamsltd.net. **Website:** bretadamsltd.net. **Contact:** Colin Hunt, Mark Orsini. Member of AAR. Currently handles: movie scripts, TV scripts, stage plays.

MEMBER AGENTS Bruce Ostler, Mark Orsini, Alexis Williams.

REPRESENTS movie scripts, TV scripts, TV movie of the week, theatrical stage play.

Handles theatre/film and TV projects. No books. Cannot accept unsolicited material.

HOW TO CONTACT Use the online submission form. Because of this agency's submission policy and interests, it's best to approach with a professional recommendation from a client.

M. COURTNEY BRIGGS

Derrick & Briggs, LLP, 100 N. Broadway Ave., 28th Floor, Oklahoma City OK 73102-8806. (405)235-1900. **Fax:** (405)235-1995. **Website:** www.derrickandbriggs.com.

Prior to becoming an agent, Ms. Briggs was in subsidiary rights at Random House for 3 years; an associate agent and film rights associate with Curtis Brown, Ltd.; and an attorney for 16 years.

REPRESENTS nonfiction books, novels, juvenile. **Considers these nonfiction areas:** young adult.

"I work primarily, but not exclusively, with children's book authors and illustrators. I will also consult or review a contract on an hourly basis." Actively seeking children's fiction, children's picture books (illustrations and text), young adult novels, fiction, nonfiction.

HOW TO CONTACT Query with SASE. Only published authors should submit queries. Obtains most new clients through recommendations from others.

TERMS Agent receives 15% commission on domestic sales. Agent receives 25% commission on foreign sales. Offers written contract; 60-day notice must be given to terminate contract.

WRITERS CONFERENCES SCBWI Annual Winter Conference.

CURTIS BROWN (AUST) PTY LTD

P.O. Box 19, Paddington NSW 2021 Australia. (+61)(2)9361-6161. **Fax:** (+61)(2)9360-3935. **E-mail:** reception@curtisbrown.com.au. **Website:** www.curtisbrown.com.au. 10% of clients are new/unpublished writers. Currently handles: nonfiction books 30%, novels 30%, juvenile books 25%, other 15%.

"Prior to joining Curtis Brown, most of our agents worked in publishing or the film/theatre industries in Australia and the United Kingdom."

MEMBER AGENTS **Fiona Inglis** (managing director/agent); **Fran Moore** (deputy managing director / agent); **Tara Wynne** (agent); **Pippa Masson** (agent); Clare Forster (agent).

"We are Australia's oldest and largest literary agency representing a diverse range of Australian and New Zealand writers and Estates."

HOW TO CONTACT "Please refer to our website for information regarding ms submissions, permissions, theatre rights requests, and the clients and Estates we represent. We are not currently looking to represent poetry, short stories, stage/screenplays, picture books, or translations. We do not accept e-mailed or faxed submissions. No responsibility is taken for the receipt or loss of mss."

ANDREA BROWN LITERARY AGENCY, INC.

1076 Eagle Dr., Salinas CA 93905. (831)422-5925. **E-mail:** andrea@andreabrownlit.com; caryn@andreabrownlit.com; lauraqueries@gmail.com; jennifer@andreabrownlit.com; kelly@andreabrownlit.com; jennL@andreabrownlit.com; jamie@andreabrownlit.com; jmatt@andreabrownlit.com; lara@andreabrownlit.com. **Website:** www.andreabrownlit.com. **Contact:** Andrea Brown, president. Member of AAR. 10% of clients are new/unpublished writers.

Prior to opening her agency, Ms. Brown served as an editorial assistant at Random House and Dell Publishing and as an editor with Knopf.

MEMBER AGENTS **Andrea Brown** (President); **Laura Rennert** (Senior Agent); **Caryn Wiseman** (Senior Agent); Kelly Sonnack (Agent); **Jennifer Rofé** (Agent); **Jennifer Laughran** (Agent); **Jamie Weiss Chilton** (Agent); **Jennifer Mattson** (Associate Agent); **Lara Perkins** (Associate Agent, Digital Manager).

REPRESENTS nonfiction, fiction, juvenile books. **Considers these nonfiction areas:** juvenile nonfiction, memoirs, young adult, narrative. **Considers these fiction areas:** juvenile, literary, picture books, women's, young adult, middle grade, all juvenile genres.

8—π Specializes in "all kinds of children's books—illustrators and authors." 98% juvenile books. Considers: nonfiction, fiction, picture books, young adult.

HOW TO CONTACT For picture books, submit complete ms. For fiction, submit query letter, first 10 pages. For nonfiction, submit proposal, first 10 pages. Illustrators: submit a query letter and 2-3 illustration samples (in jpeg format), link to online portfolio, and text of picture book, if applicable. "We only accept queries via e-mail. No attachments, with the exception of jpeg illustrations from illustrators." Visit the agents' bios on our website and choose only one agent to whom you will submit your e-query. Send a short e-mail query letter to that agent with QUERY in the subject field. Accepts simultaneous submissions. If we are interested in your work, we will certainly follow up by e-mail or by phone. However, if you haven't heard from us within 6 to 8 weeks, please assume that we are passing on your project. Obtains most new clients through referrals from editors, clients and agents. Check website for guidelines and information.

TERMS Agent receives 15% commission on domestic sales. Agent receives 25% commission on foreign sales. Offers written contract.

RECENT SALES *The Scorpio Races*, by Maggie Stiefvater (Scholastic); *The Raven Boys*, by Maggie Stiefvater (Scholastic); *Wolves of Mercy Falls* series, by Maggie Stiefvater (Scholastic); *The Future of Us*, by Jay Asher; *Triangles*, by Ellen Hopkins (Atria); *Crank*, by Ellen Hopkins (McElderry/S&S); *Burned*, by Ellen Hopkins (McElderry/S&S); *Impulse*, by Ellen Hopkins (McElderry/S&S); *Glass*, by Ellen Hopkins (McElderry/S&S); *Tricks*, by Ellen Hopkins (McElderry/S&S); *Fallout*, by Ellen Hopkins (McElderry/S&S); *Perfect*, by Ellen Hopkins (McElderry/S&S); *The Strange Case of Origami Yoda*, by Tom Angleberger (Amulet/Abrams); *Darth Paper Strikes Back*, by Tom Angleberger (Amulet/Abrams); *Becoming Chloe*, by Catherine Ryan Hyde (Knopf); Sasha Cohen autobiography (HarperCollins); *The Five Ancestors*, by Jeff Stone (Random House); *Thirteen Reasons Why*, by Jay Asher (Penguin); *Identical*, by Ellen Hopkins (S&S).

WRITERS CONFERENCES SCBWI; Asilomar; Maui Writers' Conference; Southwest Writers' Conference; San Diego State University Writers' Conference; Big Sur Children's Writing Workshop; William Saroyan Writers' Conference; Columbus Writers' Conference; Willamette Writers' Conference; La Jolla Writers' Conference; San Francisco Writers' Conference; Hilton Head Writers' Conference; Pacific Northwest Conference; Pikes Peak Conference.

TIPS "ABLA is consistently ranked #1 in juvenile sales in Publishers Marketplace. Several clients have placed in the top 10 of the NY Times Bestseller List in the last year, including Tom Angleberger, Jay Asher, Ellen Hopkins, and Maggie Stiefvater. Awards recently won by ABLA clients include the Michael L. Printz Honor, the APALA Asian/Pacific Award and Honor, Charlotte Zolotow Honor, Cybils Award, EB White Read Aloud Award and Honor, Edgar Award Nominee, Indies Choice Honor Award, Jack Ezra Keats New Writer Award, Odyssey Honor Audiobook, Orbis Pictus Honor, Pura Belpré Illustrator Honor Book; SCBWI Golden Kite Award; Stonewall Honor; Texas Bluebonnet Award; Theodore Seuss Geisel Honor; William C. Morris YA Debut Award."

O MARIE BROWN ASSOCIATES, INC.

412 W. 154th St., New York NY 10032. (212)939-9725. **Fax:** (212)939-9728. **E-mail:** mbrownlit@aol.com. **Contact:** Marie Brown. Estab. 1984. Represents 60 clients. Currently handles: nonfiction books 75%, juvenile books 10%, other 15%.

REPRESENTS nonfiction books, juvenile. **Considers these nonfiction areas:** biography, business, ethnic, history, music, religious, women's issues. **Considers these fiction areas:** commercial, ethnic, juvenile, literary, mainstream, middle grade, multicultural, young adult.

8—π This agency specializes in multicultural and African-American writers.

HOW TO CONTACT Query with SASE. Prefers to read materials exclusively. Obtains most new clients through recommendations from others.

TERMS Agent receives 15% commission on domestic sales. Agent receives 20% commission on foreign sales. Offers written contract.

MARSAL LYON LITERARY AGENCY, LLC

PMB 121, 665 San Rodolfo Dr. 124, Solana Beach CA 92075. **E-mail:** Kevan@MarsalLyonLiteraryAgency.com; Jill@MarsalLyonLiteraryAgency.com; **Website:** www.marsallyonliteraryagency.com. **Contact:** Kevan Lyon, Jill Marsal.

REPRESENTS nonfiction books, novels. **Considers these nonfiction areas:** animals, biography, business, cooking, current affairs, diet/nutrition, foods, health, history, investigative, memoirs, music, parenting, popular culture, politics, psychology, science, self-help, sports, women's issues, relationships, advice. **Considers these fiction areas:** commercial, mainstream, multicultural, mystery, romance, suspense, thriller, women's, young adult.

HOW TO CONTACT Query by e-mail to either Jill Marsal at jill@marsallyonliteraryagency.com, Kevan Lyon at kevan@marsallyonliteraryagency.com, Kathleen Rushall at Kathleen@marsallyonliteraryagency.com, Shannon Hassan at shannon@marsallyonliteraryagency.com. "Please visit our website to determine who is best suited for your work. Write 'query' in the subject line of your e-mail. Please allow up to several weeks to hear back on your query."

TIPS "Our agency's mission is to help writers achieve their publishing dreams. We want to work with authors not just for a book but for a career; we are dedicated to building long-term relationships with our authors and publishing partners. Our goal is to help find homes for books that engage, entertain, and make a difference."

THE BUKOWSKI AGENCY

14 Prince Arthur Ave., Suite 202, Toronto Ontario M5R 1A9 Canada. (416)928-6728. **Fax:** (416)963-9978. **E-mail:** assistant@thebukowskiagency.com; info@thebukowskiagency.com. **Website:** www.thebukowskiagency.com. **Contact:** Denise Bukowski. Estab. 1986.

Prior to becoming an agent, Ms. Bukowski was a book editor.

REPRESENTS nonfiction books, novels.

"The Bukowski Agency specializes in international literary fiction and upmarket nonfiction for adults. Bukowski looks for Canadian writers whose work can be marketed in many media and territories, and who have the potential to make a living from their work." Actively seeking nonfiction and fiction works from Canadian writers. Does not want submissions from American authors, nor genre fiction, poetry, children's literature, picture books, film scripts, or TV scripts.

HOW TO CONTACT Query with SASE. (No e-queries.) See online guidelines for nonfiction and fiction specifics. No unsolicited fiction. "The Bukowski Agency is currently accepting nonfiction submissions from prospective authors who are residents in Canada. We ask for exclusivity for 6 weeks after receipt to allow time for proper consideration. Please see our nonfiction submission guidelines on our agency website for more details on submitting proposals for nonfiction. Submissions should be sent by mail, in hard copy only. We also consider fiction submissions, by mail only, from prospective authors who are residents in Canada. Please send the first 50 pages of your novel (double-spaced in 12-point type, printed on one side of the sheet only) with a BRIEF synopsis and a self-addressed stamped envelope (SASE). Note that if you do not include an SASE, a response to your submission will not be possible." Responds in 6 weeks to queries.

SHEREE BYKOFSKY ASSOCIATES, INC.

PO Box 706, Brigantine NJ 08203. **E-mail:** shereebee@aol.com. **E-mail:** submitbee@aol.com. **Website:** www.shereebee.com. **Contact:** Sheree Bykofsky. Member of AAR. Memberships include Author's Guild, Atlantic City Chamber of Commerce, WNBA. Currently handles: nonfiction books 80%, novels 20%.

Prior to opening her agency, Ms. Bykofsky served as executive editor of the Stonesong Press and managing editor of Chiron Press. She is also the author or coauthor of more than 20 books, including *The Complete Idiot's Guide to Getting Published*. As an adjunct professor, Ms. Bykofsky teaches publishing at Rosemont College, NYU, and SEAK, Inc.

MEMBER AGENTS Janet Rosen, associate; Thomas V. Hartmann, associate.

REPRESENTS nonfiction, novels. **Considers these nonfiction areas:** Americana, animals, architecture, art, autobiography, biography, business, child guidance, cooking, crafts, creative nonfiction, cultural interests, current affairs, dance, design, economics, education, environment, ethnic, film, finance, foods, gardening, gay, government, health, history, hobbies, humor, language, law, lesbian, memoirs, metaphysics, military, money, multicultural, music, nature, New Age, nutrition, parenting, philosophy, photography, popular culture, politics, psychology, recreation, regional, religious, science, sex, sociology, spirituality, sports, translation, travel, true crime, war, anthropology; creative nonfiction. **Considers these fiction**

areas: contemporary issues, literary, mainstream, mystery, suspense.

This agency specializes in popular reference nonfiction, commercial fiction with a literary quality, and mysteries. "I have wide-ranging interests, but it really depends on quality of writing, originality, and how a particular project appeals to me (or not). I take on fiction when I completely love it—it doesn't matter what area or genre." Does not want to receive poetry, material for children, screenplays, westerns, horror, science fiction, or fantasy.

HOW TO CONTACT "We only accept e-queries now and will only respond to those in which we are interested. E-mail short queries to submitbee@aol.com. Please, no attachments, snail mail, or phone calls. One-page query, one-page synopsis, and first page of ms in the body of the e-mail. Nonfiction: One-page query in the body of the e-mail. We cannot open attached Word files or any other types of attached files. These will be deleted." Accepts simultaneous submissions. Responds in 1 month to requested mss. Obtains most new clients through recommendations from others.

TERMS Agent receives 15% commission on domestic sales. Agent receives 20% commission on foreign sales. Offers written contract, binding for 1 year. Charges for postage, photocopying, fax.

RECENT SALES *ADHD Does Not Exist*, by Dr. Richard Saul (Harper Collins); *Be Bold and Win the Sale*, by Jeff Shore (McGraw-Hill); *Idea to Invention*, by Patricia Nolan-Brown (Amacom); *The Hour of Lead*, by Bruce Holbert (Counterpoint); *Slimed! An Oral History of Nickelodeon's Golden Age*, by Matthew Klickstein (Plume); *Bang the Keys: Four Steps to a Lifelong Writing Practice*, by Jill Dearman (Alpha, Penguin); *Signed, Your Student: Celebrities on the Teachers Who Made Them Who They Are Today*, by Holly Holbert (Kaplan); *The Five Ways We Grieve*, by Susan Berger (Trumpeter/Shambhala).

WRITERS CONFERENCES Truckee Meadow Community College, Keynote; ASJA Writers Conference; Asilomar; Florida Suncoast Writers' Conference; Whidbey Island Writers' Conference; Florida First Coast Writers' Festival; Agents and Editors Conference; Columbus Writers' Conference; Southwest Writers' Conference; Willamette Writers' Conference; Dorothy Canfield Fisher Conference; Maui Writers' Conference; Pacific Northwest Writers' Conference; IWWG.

TIPS "Read the agent listing carefully and comply with guidelines."

KIMBERLEY CAMERON & ASSOCIATES

1550 Tiburon Blvd., #704, Tiburon CA 94920. **Fax:** (415)789-9191. **E-mail:** info@kimberleycameron.com. **Website:** www.kimberleycameron.com. **Contact:** Kimberley Cameron. Member of AAR. 30% of clients are new/unpublished writers.

Kimberley Cameron & Associates (formerly The Reece Halsey Agency) has had an illustrious client list of established writers, including the estate of Aldous Huxley, and has represented Upton Sinclair, William Faulkner, and Henry Miller.

MEMBER AGENTS **Kimberley Cameron**; **Elizabeth Kracht**, liz@kimberleycameron.com (literary, commercial, women's, thrillers, mysteries, and YA with crossover appeal); **Pooja Menon**, pooja@kimberleycameron.com (international stories, literary, historical, commercial, fantasy and high-end women's fiction; in nonfiction, she's looking for adventure & travel memoirs, journalism & human-interest stories, and self-help books addressing relationships and the human psychology from a fresh perspective); **Amy Cloughley**, amyc@kimberleycameron.com (literary and upmarket fiction, women's, mystery, narrative nonfiction); **Mary C. Moore** (literary fiction; she also loves a good commercial book; commercially she is looking for unusual fantasy, grounded science fiction, and atypical romance; strong female characters and unique cultures especially catch her eye); **Ethan Vaughan** (no submissions).

REPRESENTS **Considers these nonfiction areas:** creative nonfiction, psychology, self-help, travel. **Considers these fiction areas:** commercial, fantasy, historical, literary, mystery, romance, science fiction, thriller, women's, young adult.

"We are looking for a unique and heartfelt voice that conveys a universal truth."

HOW TO CONTACT We accept e-mail queries only. Please address all queries to one agent only. Please send a query letter in the body of the e-mail, written in a professional manner and clearly addressed to the agent of your choice. Attach a one-page synopsis and the first fifty pages of your manuscript as separate Word or PDF documents. We have difficulties opening other file formats. Include "Author Submission" in the subject line. If submitting nonfiction, attach a nonfiction proposal. Obtains new clients through recommendations from others, solicitations.

TERMS Agent receives 15% on domestic sales; 10% on film sales. Offers written contract, binding for 1 year.

WRITERS CONFERENCES Texas Writing Retreat; Pacific Northwest Writers Association Conference; Women's Fiction Festival in Matera, Italy; Willamette Writers Conference; San Francisco Writers Conference; Book Passage Mystery and Travel Writers Conferences; Chuckanut Writers Conference; many others.

TIPS "Please consult our submission guidelines and send a polite, well-written query to our e-mail address."

CYNTHIA CANNELL LITERARY AGENCY

833 Madison Ave., New York NY 10021. (212)396-9595. **Website:** www.cannellagency.com. **Contact:** Cynthia Cannell. Estab. 1997. Member of AAR. Other memberships include the Women's Media Group.

Prior to forming the Cynthia Cannell Literary Agency, Ms. Cannell was, for 12 years, vice president of Janklow & Nesbit Associates.

REPRESENTS Considers these nonfiction areas: biography, history, memoirs, science, self-help, spirituality. **Considers these fiction areas:** literary.

Does not represent screenplays, children's books, illustrated books, cookbooks, romance, category mystery, or science fiction.

HOW TO CONTACT "Please query us with an e-mail or letter. If querying by e-mail, send a brief description of your project with relevant biographical information including publishing credits (if any) to info@cannellagency.com. Do not send attachments. If querying by conventional mail, enclose an SASE." Responds if interested.

RECENT SALES *Song of the Shank*, by Jeffery Renard Allen (Graywolf Press); *100 Places That Can Change Your Child's Life*, by Keith Bellows (Nat. Geo Books); *Brilliant: The Evolution of Artificial Light*, by Jane Brox (HMH).

MARIA CARVAINIS AGENCY, INC.

Rockefeller Center, 1270 Avenue of the Americas, Suite 2320, New York NY 10020. (212)245-6365. **Fax:** (212)245-7196. **E-mail:** mca@mariacarvainisagency.com. **Website:** mariacarvainisagency.com. **Contact:** Maria Carvainis. Estab. 1977. Member of AAR. Signatory of WGA. Other memberships include Authors Guild, Women's Media Group, ABA, MWA, RWA. Represents 75 clients.

Prior to opening her agency, Ms. Carvainis spent more than 10 years in the publishing industry as a senior editor with Macmillan Publishing, Basic Books, Avon Books, and Crown Publishers. Ms. Carvainis has served as a member of the AAR Board of Directors and AAR Treasurer, as well as serving as chair of the AAR Contracts Committee. She presently serves on the AAR Royalty Committee.

REPRESENTS nonfiction books, novels. **Considers these nonfiction areas:** biography, business, history, memoirs, popular culture, psychology, science. **Considers these fiction areas:** historical, literary, mainstream, middle grade, mystery, suspense, thriller, women's.

The agency does not represent screenplays, children's picture books, science fiction, or poetry.

HOW TO CONTACT You can query via e-mail or snail mail. If by snail mail, send your submission "ATTN: Query Department." Please send a query letter, a synopsis of the work, two sample chapters, and note any writing credentials. Obtains most new clients through recommendations from others, conferences, query letters.

TERMS Agent receives 15% commission on domestic sales. Agent receives 20% commission on foreign sales. Offers written contract. Charges clients for foreign postage and bulk copying.

RECENT SALES *A Secret Affair*, by Mary Balogh (Delacorte); *Tough Customer*, by Sandra Brown (Simon & Schuster); *A Lady Never Tells*, by Candace Camp (Pocket Books); *The King James Conspiracy*, by Phillip Depoy (St. Martin's Press).

WRITERS CONFERENCES BookExpo America; Frankfurt Book Fair; London Book Fair; Mystery Writers of America; Thrillerfest; Romance Writers of America.

CASTIGLIA LITERARY AGENCY

1155 Camino Del Mar, Suite 510, Del Mar CA 92014. **E-mail:** castigliaagency-query@yahoo.com. **Website:** www.castigliaagency.com. Member of AAR. Other memberships include PEN. Represents 65 clients. Currently handles: nonfiction books 55%, novels 45%.

MEMBER AGENTS **Julie Castiglia** (not accepting queries at this time); **Win Golden** (fiction: thrillers, mystery, crime, science fiction, YA, commercial/literary fiction; nonfiction: narrative nonfiction, current events, science, journalism).

REPRESENTS nonfiction books, novels. **Considers these nonfiction areas:** creative nonfiction, current affairs, investigative, science. **Considers these fiction areas:** commercial, crime, literary, mystery, science fiction, thriller, young adult.

"We'd particularly like to hear from you if you are a journalist or published writer in magazines and newspapers, have expertise on the subject you're writing, together with media exposure and/or a speaking schedule. We'd like to hear from anyone who has had success with a previous novel. We do look at debut novels and it helps if you've been published in literary anthologies or magazines, if you have studied under well-known authors, or have an MFA. It's all about the writing of course but if great writing is accompanied by a marketing hook, that's a seductive combination." Does not want to receive horror, screenplays, poetry, or academic nonfiction.

HOW TO CONTACT Query via e-mail to CastigliaAgency-query@yahoo.com. Send no materials at first contact besides a one-page query. No snail mail submissions accepted. Obtains most new clients through recommendations from others, solicitations, conferences.

TERMS Agent receives 15% commission on domestic sales. Agent receives 25% commission on foreign sales. Offers written contract; 6-week notice must be given to terminate contract.

RECENT SALES *Germs Gone Wild*, by Kenneth King (Pegasus); *The Insider*, by Reece Hirsch (Berkley/Penguin); *The Leisure Seeker*, by Michael Zadoorian (Morrow/HarperCollins); *Beautiful: The Life of Hedy Lamarr*, by Stephen Shearer (St. Martin's Press); *American Libre*, by Raul Ramos y Sanchez (Grand Central); *The Two Krishnas*, by Ghalib Shiraz Dhalla (Alyson Books).

WRITERS CONFERENCES Santa Barbara Writers' Conference; Southern California Writers' Conference; Surrey International Writers' Conference; San Diego State University Writers' Conference; Willamette Writers' Conference.

TIPS "Be professional with submissions. Attend workshops and conferences before you approach an agent."

CHALBERG & SUSSMAN

115 West 29th St, Third Floor, New York NY 10001. (917)261-7550. **Website:** www.chalbergsussman.com.

Prior to her current position, Ms. Chalberg held a variety of editorial positions, and was an agent with The Susan Golomb Literary Agency. Ms. Sussman was an agent with Zachary Shuster Harmsworth. Ms. James was with The Aaron Priest Literary Agency.

REPRESENTS **Considers these nonfiction areas:** history, how-to, humor, memoirs, popular culture, psychology, self-help. **Considers these fiction areas:** commercial, literary, thriller, women's, young adult.

"Rachel Sussman represents a wide range of voice- and idea-driven nonfiction and a select list of literary fiction. Her nonfiction list spans both serious and 'unserious' subject matter, from history, psychology, and memoir to humor and pop culture. Nicole James is looking for novels celebrated in other countries but unknown here in the U.S. as well as literary and commercial fiction, including action-packed thrillers with great heroes. She is eager to find a female-driven thriller; a fantastic beach read for women; and a smart and thoughtfully written young adult series. On the nonfiction side, Nicole is looking out for a book about weddings ('how-to' or memoir); a hip and intelligent 'self-help' book; and anything topical that calls to her."

HOW TO CONTACT To query by e-mail, please contact one of the following: terra@chalbergsussman.com, rachel@chalbergsussman.com, nicole@chalbergsussman.com. To query by regular mail, please address your letter to one agent and include a self-addressed stamped envelope.

RECENT SALES The agents' sales and clients are listed on their website.

CHASE LITERARY AGENCY

236 W. 26th St., Suite 801, New York NY 10001. (212)477-5100. **E-mail:** farley@chaseliterary.com. **Website:** www.chaseliterary.com. **Contact:** Farley Chase.

MEMBER AGENTS Farley Chase.

REPRESENTS **Considers these fiction areas:** commercial, historical, literary.

NEW AGENT SPOTLIGHT

ALLISON DEVEREUX
(WOLF LITERARY SERVICES)

wolflit.com

@AllisonDevereux

ABOUT ALLISON: A Texas native, Allison earned her B.A. at the University of Texas at Austin, where she graduated from the Plan II Honors Program. Before coming to WLS, Allison worked at Macmillan in Tor Books' managing editorial department; prior to that, she was an editorial and design assistant at the Institute of Classical Archaeology in Austin, as well as an intern at the Harry Ransom Center.

SHE IS SEEKING: literary and upmarket commercial fiction with fresh, unique voices and tight prose. She is also passionate about magical realism (more real than magic), and idiosyncratic, picaresque characters. For nonfiction: narrative nonfiction, compelling memoir, and books on popular and contemporary culture with a strong, original premise. She is looking for illustrated/graphic books for adults (both fiction and non), as well as blog-to-book projects. She also loves a good humor book.

HOW TO QUERY: Send a query letter addressed to Allison along with a 50-page writing sample (for fiction) or a detailed proposal (for nonfiction) to queries@wolflit.com. Samples may be submitted as an attachment or embedded in the e-mail.

Wants: General fiction, reference, biography, business/investing/finance, history, health, travel, lifestyle, cookbooks, sports, African-American, science, humor, pop-culture, popular science, natural history, military history, memoir. "I'm interested in humor books and pop culture projects, photo, graphic, and otherwise illustrated books; books that can be adapted out of blogs or websites." No romance, science fiction, supernatural or young adult.

HOW TO CONTACT Query. Include first few pages of ms with query.

RECENT SALES *Loopers*, by John Dunn; *The Afrika Reich*, by Guy Saville; *Top of the First: The End of Word War II*, by Robert Weintraub; *Heads in Beds*, by Jacob Tomsky; *A Bintel Brief*, by Liana Finck; and *Devil in the Grove*, by Gilbert King.

JANE CHELIUS LITERARY AGENCY

548 Second St., Brooklyn NY 11215. (718)499-0236. **Fax:** (718)832-7335. **E-mail:** queries@janechelius.com. **Website:** www.janechelius.com. Member of AAR.

MEMBER AGENTS Jane Chelius, Mark Chelius.

REPRESENTS nonfiction books, novels. **Considers these nonfiction areas:** biography, humor, medicine, parenting, popular culture, satire, women's issues, women's studies, natural history; narrative. **Considers these fiction areas:** literary, mystery, suspense, women's.

Does not want to receive children's books, fantasy, science fiction, stage plays, screenplays, or poetry.

HOW TO CONTACT E-query. Does not consider e-mail queries with attachments. No unsolicited sample chapters or mss. Responds if interested. Responds in 3–4 weeks usually.

ELYSE CHENEY LITERARY ASSOCIATES, LLC

78 Fifth Avenue, 3rd Floor, New York NY 10011. (212)277-8007. **Fax:** (212)614-0728. **E-mail:** submissions@cheneyliterary.com. **Website:** www.cheneyliterary.com. **Contact:** Elyse Cheney; Adam Eaglin; Alex Jacobs.

Prior to her current position, Ms. Cheney was an agent with Sanford J. Greenburger Associates.

REPRESENTS nonfiction, novels. **Considers these nonfiction areas:** biography, business, creative nonfiction, current affairs, economics, memoirs, politics, science, journalism. **Considers these fiction areas:** commercial, family saga, historical, literary, short story collections, suspense, women's.

HOW TO CONTACT Query by e-mail or snail mail. For a snail mail responses, include an SASE. If you e-query, feel free to paste up to 25 pages of your work in the e-mail below your query.

RECENT SALES *Moonwalking with Einstein: The Art and Science of Remembering Everything*, by Joshua Foer; *The Possessed: Adventures with Russian Books and the People Who Read Them*, by Elif Batuman (Farrar, Strauss & Giroux); *The Coldest Winter Ever*, by Sister Souljah (Atria); *A Heartbreaking Work of Staggering Genius*, by Dave Eggers (Simon and Schuster); *No Easy Day*, by Mark Owen; *Malcom X: A Life of Reinvention*, by Manning Marable.

THE CHUDNEY AGENCY

72 North State Rd., Suite 501, Briarcliff Manor NY 10510. (201)758-8739. **E-mail:** steven@thechudneyagency.com. **Website:** www.thechudneyagency.com. **Contact:** Steven Chudney. Estab. 2001. Memberships include SCBWI. 90% of clients are new/unpublished writers.

Prior to becoming an agent, Mr. Chudney held various sales positions with major publishers.

REPRESENTS novels, juvenile. **Considers these nonfiction areas:** juvenile. **Considers these fiction areas:** historical, juvenile, literary, mystery, suspense, young adult.

This agency specializes in children's and teens' books, and wants to find authors who are illustrators as well. "At this time, the agency is only looking for author/illustrators (one individual), who can both write and illustrate wonderful picture books. The author/illustrator must really know and understand the needs and wants of the child reader! Storylines should be engaging, fun, with a hint of a life lesson and cannot be longer than 800 words. With chapter books, middle grade and teen novels, I'm primarily looking for quality, contemporary literary fiction: novels that are exceedingly well-written, with wonderful settings and developed, unforgettable characters. I'm looking for historical fiction that will excite me, young readers, editors, and reviewers, and will introduce us to unique characters in settings and situations, countries, and eras we haven't encountered too often yet in children's and teen literature." Does not want to receive any fantasy or science fiction; board books or lift-the-flap books; fables; folklore or traditional fairytales; poetry or mood pieces; stories for all ages (as these ultimately are too adult oriented); message-driven stories that are heavy-handed; and didactic or pedantic writing.

HOW TO CONTACT No snail-mail submissions. Queries only. Submit proposal package, 4-6 sample chapters. For children's, submit full text and 3-5 illustrations. Accepts simultaneous submissions. Responds in 2-3 weeks to queries. Responds in 3-4 weeks to mss.

TERMS Agent receives 15% commission on domestic sales. Agent receives 20% commission on foreign sales. Offers written contract, binding for 1 year; 30-day notice must be given to terminate contract.

TIPS "If an agent has a website, review it carefully to make sure your material is appropriate for that agent. Read lots of books within the genre you are writing;

work hard on your writing; don't follow trends—most likely, you'll be too late."

CINE/LIT REPRESENTATION

P.O. Box 802918, Santa Clarita CA 91380-2918. (661)513-0268. **Fax:** (661)513-0915. **Contact:** Mary Alice Kier. Member of AAR.

MEMBER AGENTS Mary Alice Kier; Anna Cottle.

HOW TO CONTACT Send query letter with SASE. Or e-query to cinelit@att.net. Note this agency's specialized nature.

EDWARD B. CLAFLIN LITERARY AGENCY, LLC

128 High Ave., Suite #2, Nyack NY 10960. (845)358-1084. **E-mail:** edclaflin@aol.com. **Contact:** Edward Claflin. Represents 30 clients. 10% of clients are new/unpublished writers.

Prior to opening his agency, Mr. Claflin worked at Banbury Books, Rodale, and Prentice Hall Press. He is the co-author of 13 books.

REPRESENTS nonfiction books. **Considers these nonfiction areas:** business, cooking, current affairs, economics, finance, food, health, history, how-to, medicine, military, money, nutrition, psychology, sports, war.

This agency specializes in consumer health, narrative history, psychology/self-help, and business. Actively seeking compelling and authoritative nonfiction for specific readers. Does not want to receive fiction.

HOW TO CONTACT Query with synopsis, bio, SASE or e-mail attachment in Word. Responds in 1 month to queries. Obtains most new clients through recommendations from others.

TERMS Agent receives 15% commission on domestic sales.

FRANCES COLLIN, LITERARY AGENT

P.O. Box 33, Wayne PA 19087-0033. **E-mail:** queries@francescollin.com. **Website:** www.francescollin.com. **Contact:** Sarah Yake, associate agent. Member of AAR. Represents 90 clients. 1% of clients are new/unpublished writers. Currently handles: nonfiction books 50%, fiction 50%.

Does not want to receive cookbooks, craft books, poetry, screenplays, or books for young children.

HOW TO CONTACT Query via e-mail describing project (text in the body of the e-mail only, no attachments) to queries@francescollin.com. "Please note that all queries are reviewed by both agents." No phone or fax queries. Accepts simultaneous submissions.

TERMS Agent receives 15% commission on domestic sales. Agent receives 20% commission on foreign sales. Offers written contract.

COMPASS TALENT

6 East 32nd Street, 6th Floor, New York NY 10016. (646)376-7718. **E-mail:** query@compasstalent.com. **Website:** www.compasstalent.com. **Contact:** Heather Schroder.

REPRESENTS Considers these nonfiction areas: cooking, creative nonfiction, foods, history, memoirs, science. **Considers these fiction areas:** commercial, juvenile, literary, mainstream.

HOW TO CONTACT Please send a query describing your project, along with a sample chapter and some information about yourself to query@compasstalent.com. Allow eight weeks for a response. Please do not send your material to us through the mail.

RECENT SALES A full list of agency clients is available on the website.

DON CONGDON ASSOCIATES INC.

110 William St., Suite 2202, New York NY 10038. (212)645-1229. **Fax:** (212)727-2688. **E-mail:** dca@doncongdon.com. **Website:** doncongdon.com. **Contact:** Michael Congdon, Susan Ramer, Cristina Concepcion, Maura Kye Casella, Katie Kotchman, Katie Grimm. Member of AAR. Represents 100 clients.

REPRESENTS Considers these nonfiction areas: anthropology, archeology, autobiography, biography, child guidance, cooking, creative nonfiction, current affairs, dance, environment, film, foods, government, health, history, humor, language, law, literature, medicine, memoirs, military, music, parenting, popular culture, politics, psychology, satire, science, technology, theater, travel, true crime, war, women's issues, women's studies. **Considers these fiction areas:** action, adventure, contemporary issues, crime, detective, literary, mainstream, middle grade, mystery, police, short story collections, suspense, thriller, women's, young adult.

Especially interested in narrative nonfiction and literary fiction.

HOW TO CONTACT "For queries via e-mail, you must include the word 'Query' and the agent's full name in your subject heading. Please also include your query and sample chapter in the body of the e-mail, as we do not open attachments for security reasons. Please query only one agent within the agency at a time." Responds in 3 weeks to queries. Responds in 1 month to mss. Obtains most new clients through recommendations from other authors.

TERMS Agent receives 15% commission on domestic sales. Agent receives 19% commission on foreign sales. Charges client for extra shipping costs, photocopying, copyright fees, book purchases.

RECENT SALES This agency represents many best-selling clients such as David Sedaris and Kathryn Stockett.

TIPS "Writing a query letter with an SASE is a must. We cannot guarantee replies to foreign queries via standard mail. No phone calls. We never download attachments to e-mail queries for security reasons, so please copy and paste material into your e-mail."

CONNOR LITERARY AGENCY

2911 W. 71st St., Minneapolis MN 55423. (612)866-1486. **E-mail:** connoragency@aol.com; coolmkc@aol.com. **Website:** www.connorliteraryagency.webs.com. **Contact:** Marlene Connor Lynch; Deborah Connor Coker. Represents 50 clients. 30% of clients are new/unpublished writers.

Prior to opening her agency, Ms. Connor served at the Literary Guild of America, Simon & Schuster, and Random House. She is author of *Welcome to the Family: Memories of the Past for a Bright Future* (Broadway Books) and *What is Cool: Understanding Black Manhood in America* (Crown).

MEMBER AGENTS **Marlene Connor Lynch** (all categories of mainstream nonfiction and fiction); **Deborah Coker** (young adult and mainstream fiction and nonfiction, suspense, historical fiction, humor, illustrated books, children's books).

REPRESENTS nonfiction books, novels. **Considers these fiction areas:** historical, literary, mainstream, picture books, suspense, young adult.

HOW TO CONTACT Query with 1 page and synopsis; include SASE. All unsolicited mss returned unopened. There is also an online submission form on the agency website. Obtains most new clients through recommendations from others, conferences, grapevine.

TERMS Agent receives 15% commission on domestic sales. Agent receives 25% commission on foreign sales. Offers written contract, binding for 1 year.

RECENT SALES *Beautiful Hair at Any Age*, by Lisa Akbari; *12 Months of Knitting*, by Joanne Yordanou; *The Warrior Path: Confessions of a Young Lord*, by Felipe Luciano.

WRITERS CONFERENCES National Writers Union, Midwest Chapter; Agents, Agents, Agents; Texas Writers' Conference; Detroit Writers' Conference; Annual Gwendolyn Brooks Writers' Conference for Literature and Creative Writing; Wisconsin Writers' Festival.

TIPS "Previously published writers are preferred; new writers with national exposure or potential to have national exposure from their own efforts preferred."

THE DOE COOVER AGENCY

P.O. Box 668, Winchester MA 01890. (781)721-6000. **E-mail:** info@doecooveragency.com. **Website:** www.doecooveragency.com. Represents 150+ clients. Currently handles: nonfiction books 80%, novels 20%.

MEMBER AGENTS **Doe Coover** (general nonfiction, including business, cooking/food writing, health and science); **Colleen Mohyde** (literary and commercial fiction, general nonfiction); Associate: Frances Kennedy.

REPRESENTS **Considers these nonfiction areas:** autobiography, biography, business, cooking, economics, foods, gardening, health, history, nutrition, science, technology, social issues, narrative nonfiction. **Considers these fiction areas:** commercial, literary.

The agency specializes in narrative nonfiction, particularly biography, business, cooking and food writing, health, history, popular science, social issues, gardening, and humor; literary and commercial fiction. The agency does not represent poetry, screenplays, romance, fantasy, science fiction or unsolicited children's books.

HOW TO CONTACT Accepts queries by e-mail only. Check website for submission guidelines. No unsolicited mss. Accepts simultaneous submissions. Responds within 4–6 weeks, only if additional material is required. Obtains most new clients through solicitation and recommendation.

TERMS Agent receives 15% commission on domestic sales, 10% of original advance commission on foreign sales. No reading fees.

RECENT SALES *Vegetable Literacy*, by Deborah Madison (Ten Speed Press); *L.A. Son: My Life, My City, My Food*, by Roy Choi (Anthony Bourdain/Ecco); *The*

Big-Flavor Grill, by Chris Schlesinger and John Willoughby (Ten Speed Press); *The Shape Of The Eye: A Memoir*, by George Estreich (Tarcher). *Frontera: Margaritas, Guacamoles, and Snacks*, by Rick Bayless and Deann Groen Bayless (W.W. Norton); *The Essay*, by Robin Yocum (Arcade Publishing); *The Flower of Empire*, by Tatiana Holway (Oxford University Press); Dulcie Schwartz mystery series, by Clea Simon (Severn House UK). Other clients include: WGBH, New England Aquarium, Duke University, Cheryl & Bill Jamison, Blue Balliett, David Allen, Jacques Pepin, Cindy Pawlcyn, Joann Weir, Suzanne Berne, Paula Poundstone, Anita Silvey, Marjorie Sandor, Tracy Daugherty, Carl Rollyson, and Joel Magnuson.

CORNERSTONE LITERARY, INC.

4525 Wilshire Blvd., Suite 208, Los Angeles CA 90010. (323)930-6039. **Fax:** (323)930-0407. **E-mail:** info@cornerstoneliterary.com. **Website:** www.cornerstoneliterary.com. **Contact:** Helen Breitwieser. Member of AAR. Other memberships include Author's Guild, MWA, RWA, PEN, Poets & Writers. Represents 40 clients. 30% of clients are new/unpublished writers.

Prior to founding her own boutique agency, Ms. Breitwieser was a literary agent at The William Morris Agency.

REPRESENTS novels. **Considers these nonfiction areas:** creative nonfiction. **Considers these fiction areas:** commercial, literary.

"We do not respond to unsolicited e-mail inquiries. All unsolicited snail mail mss will be returned unopened." Does not want to receive how-to, photography books, science fiction, Western, poetry, screenplays, fantasy, gay/lesbian, horror, self-help, psychology, business, or diet.

HOW TO CONTACT "Submissions should consist of a one-page query letter detailing the book as well as the qualifications of the author. For fiction, submissions may also include the first ten pages of the novel pasted in the e-mail or one short story from a collection. We receive hundreds of queries each month, and make every effort to give each one careful consideration. We cannot guarantee a response to queries submitted electronically due to the volume of queries received." Obtains most new clients through recommendations from others.

TERMS Agent receives 15% commission on domestic sales. Agent receives 20% commission on foreign sales. Offers written contract, binding for 1 year; 2-month notice must be given to terminate contract.

CORVISIERO LITERARY AGENCY

275 Madison Ave., 14th Floor, New York NY 10016. (646)942-8396. **Fax:** (646)217-3758. **E-mail:** contact@corvisieroagency.com. **E-mail:** query@corvisieroagency.com. **Website:** www.corvisieroagency.com. **Contact:** Marisa A. Corvisiero, senior agent and literary attorney.

MEMBER AGENTS **Marisa A. Corvisiero**, senior agent and literary attorney; **Saritza Hernandez**, senior agent; **Sarah Negovetich**, junior agent; **Doreen McDonald**, junior agent; **Rebecca Simas**, junior agent; **Cate Hart**, junior agent.

HOW TO CONTACT Accepts submissions via e-mail only. Include 5 pages of complete and polished ms pasted into the body of an e-mail, and a 1-2 page synopsis. For nonfiction, include a proposal instead of the synopsis. All sample pages must be properly formatted into 1 inch margins, double-spaced lines, Times New Roman black font size 12.

TIPS "For tips and discussions on what we look for in query letters and submissions, please take a look at Marisa A. Corvisiero's blog: Thoughts From A Literary Agent."

CRAWFORD LITERARY AGENCY

92 Evans Rd., Barnstead NH 03218. (603)269-5851. **E-mail:** crawfordlit@att.net. **Contact:** Susan Crawford. Winter Office: 3920 Bayside Rd., Fort Myers Beach FL 33931. (239)463-4651. **Fax:** (239)463-0125.

REPRESENTS nonfiction books, commercial fiction.

Actively seeking action/adventure stories; medical, legal, and psychological thrillers; true crime; romance and romantic suspense; self-help; inspirational; how-to; women's issues. No short stories, or poetry.

HOW TO CONTACT Query with cover letter, SASE. Accepts simultaneous submissions. Responds in 3-6 weeks. Obtains most new clients through recommendations from others and conferences.

TERMS Agent receives 15% commission on domestic sales. Agent receives 20% commission on foreign sales. Offers written contract.

RECENT SALES *Sexy Star Cooking: An Astrology Cookbook for Lovers*, by Sabra Ricci; *Date with the*

Devil, by Don Lasseter; *Petals from the Sky*, by Mingmei Yip.

WRITERS CONFERENCES Hawaii Spellbinders Conference; Love is Murder Mystery Conference; Puerto Villarta Writers Conference; International Film & Television Workshops; Maui Writers Conference; Emerson College Conference; Suncoast Writers Conference; San Diego Writers Conference; Simmons College Writers Conference; Cape Cod Writers Conference; Maui-Writers Alaskan Cruise; Western Caribbean Cruise and Fiji Island Writers Retreat.

TIPS "Keep learning to improve your craft. Attend conferences and network."

THE CREATIVE CULTURE, INC.

47 E. 19th St., 3rd Floor, New York NY 10003. (212)680-3510. **Fax:** (212)680-3509. **E-mail:** submissions@thecreativeculture.com. **Website:** www.thecreativeculture.com. **Contact:** Debra Goldstein. Estab. 1998. Member of AAR.

Prior to opening her agency, Ms. Goldstein and Ms. Gerwin were agents at the William Morris Agency; Ms. Naples was a senior editor at Simon & Schuster.

MEMBER AGENTS **Debra Goldstein** (self-help, creativity, fitness, inspiration, lifestyle); **Mary Ann Naples** (health/nutrition, lifestyle, narrative nonfiction, practical nonfiction, literary fiction, animals/vegetarianism); **Laura Nolan** (literary fiction, parenting, self-help, psychology, women's studies, current affairs, science); **Karen Gerwin** (pop culture, lifestyle, parenting, humor, memoir/narrative nonfiction, women's interests, and a very limited selection of fiction [no genre categories, i.e. thrillers, romance, sci-fi/fantasy, etc.]); **Matthew Elblonk** (literary fiction, humor, pop culture, music and young adult; interests also include commercial fiction, narrative nonfiction, science, and he is always on the lookout for something slightly quirky or absurd).

REPRESENTS nonfiction books, novels. **Considers these nonfiction areas:** animals, creative nonfiction, health, humor, inspirational, memoirs, music, parenting, popular culture, self-help, women's issues, women's studies. **Considers these fiction areas:** humor, literary, young adult.

"We are known for our emphasis on lifestyle books that enhance readers' overall well-being—be it through health, inspiration, entertainment, thought-provoking ideas, life management skills, beauty and fashion, or food." Does not want to receive children's books, poetry, screenplays, or science fiction.

HOW TO CONTACT Query by e-mail or snail mail. "If you are submitting fiction, please send four to seven pages of the novel with the query. If you are submitting by mail, be sure to include a self-addressed, stamped envelope. All submissions will be read; however, because of the volume received, we will reply to e-mail submissions only if we are interested in seeing more material."

RECENT SALES *Not That Kind of Girl*, by Carlene Bauer (Harper); *Kiss My Math*, by Danica McKellar (Hudson Street Press); *The Wow Factor*, by Frances Cole Jones (Ballantine).

CREATIVE TRUST, INC.

5141 Virginia Way, Suite 320, Brentwood TN 37027. (615)297-5010. **Fax:** (615)297-5020. **E-mail:** info@creativetrust.com. **Website:** www.creativetrust.com. New York Office: 39 Broadway, 3rd Floor, New York NY 10006. Currently handles: novella graphic novels, movie scripts, multimedia, other video scripts.

HOW TO CONTACT "Creative Trust Literary Group does not accept unsolicited mss or book proposals from unpublished authors. We do accept unsolicited inquiries from previously published authors under the following requisites: e-mail inquiries only, which must not be accompanied by attachments of any kind. If we're interested, we'll e-mail you an invitation to submit additional materials and instructions on how to do so."

CRICHTON & ASSOCIATES

6940 Carroll Ave., Takoma Park MD 20912. (301)495-9663. **Fax:** (202)318-0050. **E-mail:** query@crichton-associates.com. **Website:** www.crichton-associates.com. **Contact:** Sha-Shana Crichton. 90% of clients are new/unpublished writers. Currently handles: nonfiction books 50%, fiction 50%.

Prior to becoming an agent, Ms. Crichton did commercial litigation for a major law firm.

REPRESENTS nonfiction books, novels. **Considers these nonfiction areas:** child guidance, cultural interests, ethnic, gay, government, investigative, law, lesbian, parenting, politics, true crime, women's issues, women's studies, African-American studies. **Considers these fiction areas:** ethnic, feminist, inspirational, literary, mainstream, mystery, religious, romance, suspense, chick lit.

Actively seeking women's fiction, romance, and chick lit. Looking also for multicultural fiction and nonfiction. Does not want to receive poetry, children's, YA, science fiction, or screenplays.

HOW TO CONTACT "In the subject line of e-mail, please indicate whether your project is fiction or nonfiction. Please do not send attachments. Your query letter should include a description of the project and your biography. If you wish to send your query via snail mail, please include your telephone number and e-mail address. We will respond to you via e-mail. For fiction, include short synopsis and first 3 chapters with query. For nonfiction, send a book proposal." Responds in 3-5 weeks to queries.

TERMS Agent receives 15% commission on domestic sales. Agent receives 20% commission on foreign sales. Offers written contract, binding for 45 days. Only charges fees for postage and photocopying.

RECENT SALES *The African American Entrepreneur*, by W. Sherman Rogers (Praeger); *The Diversity Code*, by Michelle Johnson (Amacom); *Secret & Lies*, by Rhonda McKnight (Urban Books); *Love on the Rocks*, by Pamela Yaye (Harlequin). Other clients include Kimberley White, Beverley Long, Jessica Trap, Altonya Washington, Cheris Hodges.

WRITERS CONFERENCES Silicon Valley RWA; BookExpo America.

RICHARD CURTIS ASSOCIATES, INC.

171 E. 74th St., New York NY 10021. (212)772-7363. **Fax:** (212)772-7393. **Website:** www.curtisagency.com. Memberships include RWA, MWA, ITW, SFWA. Represents 100 clients. 1% of clients are new/unpublished writers.

Prior to being an agent, Mr. Curtis authored blogs, articles and books on the publishing business and help for authors.

REPRESENTS **Considers these fiction areas:** commercial, fantasy, romance, science fiction, thriller, young adult.

HOW TO CONTACT Considers only authors published by national houses.

TERMS Agent receives 15% commission on domestic sales. Agent receives 25% commission on foreign sales. Offers written contract. Charges for photocopying, express mail, international freight, book orders.

RECENT SALES Sold 100 titles in the last year: *Sylo*, by DJ MacHale; *War Dogs*, by Greg Bear; *Ever After*, by Kim Harrison.

WRITERS CONFERENCES RWA National Conference.

CURTIS BROWN, LTD.

10 Astor Place, New York NY 10003-6935. (212)473-5400. **E-mail:** gknowlton@cbltd.com. **Website:** www.curtisbrown.com. **Contact:** Ginger Knowlton. Alternate address: Peter Ginsberg, president at CBSF, 1750 Montgomery St., San Francisco CA 94111; (415)954-8566. Member of AAR. Signatory of WGA.

MEMBER AGENTS **Ginger Clark** (science fiction, fantasy, paranormal romance, literary horror, and young adult and middle grade fiction); **Katherine Fausset** (adult fiction and nonfiction, including literary and commercial fiction, journalism, memoir, lifestyle, prescriptive and narrative nonfiction); **Holly Frederick**; **Peter Ginsberg**, President; **Elizabeth Harding**, Vice President (represents authors and illustrators of juvenile, middle grade and young adult fiction); **Steve Kasdin** (commercial fiction, including mysteries/thrillers, romantic suspense—emphasis on the suspense, and historical fiction; narrative nonfiction, including biography, history and current affairs; and young adult fiction, particularly if it has adult crossover appeal); **Ginger Knowlton**, Executive Vice President (authors and illustrators of children's books in all genres); **Timothy Knowlton**, Chief Executive Officer; **Jonathan Lyons** (biographies, history, science, pop culture, sports, general narrative nonfiction, mysteries, thrillers, science fiction and fantasy, and young adult fiction); **Laura Blake Peterson**, Vice President (memoir and biography, natural history, literary fiction, mystery, suspense, women's fiction, health and fitness, children's and young adult, faith issues and popular culture); **Maureen Walters**, Senior Vice President (working primarily in women's fiction and nonfiction projects on subjects as eclectic as parenting & child care, popular psychology, inspirational/motivational volumes as well as a few medical/nutritional books); **Mitchell Waters** (literary and commercial fiction and nonfiction, including mystery, history, biography, memoir, young adult, cookbooks, self-help and popular culture).

REPRESENTS nonfiction books, novels, short story collections, juvenile. **Considers these nonfiction areas:** animals, anthropology, art, biography, business, computers, cooking, crafts, creative nonfiction, current affairs, education, ethnic, film, gardening, government, health, history, how-to, humor, language, memoirs, military, money, multicultural, music, New Age, philosophy, photography, popular culture, psychology, recreation, regional, science, self-help, sex, sociology, software, spirituality, sports, translation, travel, true crime. **Considers these fiction areas:** adventure, confession, detective, erotica, ethnic, experimental, fantasy, feminist, gay, historical, horror, humor, juvenile, literary, mainstream, middle grade, military, multicultural, multimedia, mystery, New Age, occult, picture books, regional, religious, romance, spiritual, sports, thriller, translation, women's, young adult.

HOW TO CONTACT "Send us a query letter, a synopsis of the work, a sample chapter and a brief resume. Illustrators should send 1-2 samples of published work, along with 6-8 color copies (no original art). Please send all book queries to our address, Attn: Query Department. Please enclose a stamped, self-addressed envelope for our response and return postage if you wish to have your materials returned to you. We typically respond to queries within 6 to 8 weeks." Note that some agents list their e-mail on the agency website and are fine with e-mail submissions. Note if the submission/query is being considered elsewhere. Responds in 3 weeks to queries; 5 weeks to mss. Obtains most new clients through recommendations from others, solicitations, conferences.

TERMS Agent receives 15% commission on domestic sales; 20% on foreign sales. Offers written contract. 75-day notice must be given to terminate contract. Charges for some postage (overseas, etc.).

RECENT SALES This agency prefers not to share information on specific sales.

D4EO LITERARY AGENCY

7 Indian Valley Rd., Weston CT 06883. (203)544-7180. **Fax:** (203)544-7160. **Website:** www.d4eoliteraryagency.com. **Contact:** Bob Diforio. Represents 100+ clients. 50% of clients are new/unpublished writers. Currently handles: nonfiction books 70%, novels 25%, juvenile books 5%.

Prior to opening his agency, Mr. Diforio was a publisher.

MEMBER AGENTS **Bob Diforio** (referrals only); **Mandy Hubbard** (middle grade, young adult, and genre romance); **Kristin Miller-Vincent** (closed to queries); **Bree Odgen** (children's, young adult, juvenile nonfiction, graphic novels, pop culture, art books, genre horror, noir, genre romance, historical, hard sci-fi); **Samantha Dighton** (closed to queries); **Joyce Holland** (currently closed to submissions).

REPRESENTS nonfiction books, novels. **Considers these nonfiction areas:** juvenile, art, biography, business, child, current affairs, gay, health, history, how-to, humor, memoirs, military, money, psychology, religion, science, self-help, sports, true crime, women's. **Considers these fiction areas:** adventure, detective, erotica, historical, horror, humor, juvenile, literary, mainstream, middle grade, mystery, picture books, romance, sports, thriller.

HOW TO CONTACT Each of these agents has a different submission e-mail and different tastes regarding how they review material. See all on their individual agent pages on the agency website. Responds in 1 week to queries. Obtains most new clients through recommendations from others.

TERMS Agent receives 15% commission on domestic sales. Agent receives 25% commission on foreign sales. Offers written contract, binding for 2 years; 60-day notice must be given to terminate contract. Charges for photocopying and submission postage.

LAURA DAIL LITERARY AGENCY, INC.

350 Seventh Ave., Suite 2003, New York NY 10001. (212)239-7477. **Fax:** (212)947-0460. **E-mail:** queries@ldlainc.com. **Website:** www.ldlainc.com. Member of AAR.

MEMBER AGENTS Laura Dail; Tamar Rydzinski.

REPRESENTS nonfiction books, novels. **Considers these nonfiction areas:** humor. **Considers these fiction areas:** commercial, historical, young adult.

Specializes in historical, literary and some young adult fiction, as well as both practical and idea-driven nonfiction. "Tamar is not interested in prescriptive or practical nonfiction, humor, coffee table books or children's books (meaning anything younger than middle grade). She is interested in everything else that is well-written and has great characters, including graphic novels." "Due to the volume of queries and mss received, we apologize for not answering every e-mail and letter. None of us handles children's picture books or chapter books. No New Age. We do not handle screenplays or poetry."

HOW TO CONTACT "If you would like, you may include a synopsis and no more than 10 pages. If you are mailing your query, please be sure to include a self-addressed, stamped envelope; without it, you may not hear back from us. To save money, time and trees, we prefer queries by e-mail (queries@ldlainc.com).We get a lot of spam and are wary of computer viruses, so please use the word 'Query' in the subject line and include your detailed materials in the body of your message, not as an attachment."

DANIEL LITERARY GROUP

1701 Kingsbury Dr., Suite 100, Nashville TN 37215. (615)730-8207. **E-mail:** submissions@danielliterarygroup.com. **Website:** www.danielliterarygroup.com. **Contact:** Greg Daniel. Represents 45 clients. 30% of clients are new/unpublished writers.

Prior to becoming an agent, Mr. Daniel spent 10 years in publishing—6 at the executive level at Thomas Nelson Publishers.

REPRESENTS nonfiction. **Considers these nonfiction areas:** autobiography, biography, business, child guidance, current affairs, economics, environment, film, health, history, how-to, humor, inspirational, medicine, memoirs, nature, parenting, personal improvement, popular culture, religious, satire, self-help, sports, theater, women's issues, women's studies.

"We take pride in our ability to come alongside our authors and help strategize about where they want their writing to take them in both the near and long term. Forging close relationships with our authors, we help them with such critical factors as editorial refinement, branding, audience, and marketing." The agency is open to submissions in almost every popular category of nonfiction, especially if authors are recognized experts in their fields. No fiction, screenplays, poetry, science fiction/fantasy, romance, children's, or short stories.

HOW TO CONTACT Query via e-mail only. Submit publishing history, author bio, key selling points; no attachments. Check Submissions Guidelines before querying or submitting. Please do not query via telephone. Responds in 2-3 weeks to queries.

DARHANSOFF & VERRILL LITERARY AGENTS

236 W. 26th St., Suite 802, New York NY 10001. (917)305-1300. **Fax:** (917)305-1400. **E-mail:** submissions@dvagency.com. **Website:** www.dvagency.com. Member of AAR. Represents 120 clients. 10% of clients are new/unpublished writers. Currently handles: nonfiction books 25%, novels 60%, story collections 15%.

MEMBER AGENTS Liz Darhansoff; Chuck Verrill; Michele Mortimer; Catherine Luttinger (science fiction, fantasy, historical fiction, YA, thrillers, mysteries).

REPRESENTS **Considers these nonfiction areas:** creative nonfiction, memoirs. **Considers these fiction areas:** fantasy, historical, literary, mystery, science fiction, suspense, thriller, young adult.

HOW TO CONTACT Send queries via e-mail (submissions@dvagency.com) or by snail mail with SASE. Obtains most new clients through recommendations from others.

RECENT SALES A full list of clients is available on their website.

CAROLINE DAVIDSON LITERARY AGENCY

5 Queen Anne's Gardens, London England W4 ITU United Kingdom. (44)(208)995-5768. **Fax:** (44)(208)994-2770. **E-mail:** enquiries@cdla.co.uk. **Website:** www.cdla.co.uk. **Contact:** Ms. Caroline Davidson.

REPRESENTS nonfiction books, serious material only, novels.

Does not consider autobiographies, chick lit, children's, crime, erotica, fantasy, horror, local history, murder mysteries, occult, self-help, short stories, sci-fi, thrillers, individual short stories, or memoir.

HOW TO CONTACT Handles novels and nonfiction of originality and high quality (12.5%). Send preliminary letter with CV and detailed, well-thought-out book proposal/synopsis and/or first 50pp of novel in hard copy only. No e-mail submissions will be accepted or replied to. No reply without large SAE with correct return postage/IRC. No reading fee. CDLA does not consider plays, films, scripts, poetry, children's/YA, thrillers, fantasy, horror, crime, erotica, occult or sci-fi. Obtains most new clients through recommendations from others. Please refer to website for further information. CDLA does not acknowledge or reply to e-mail enquiries. No telephone enquiries. Responds in 2 weeks to queries. Obtains most new clients through recommendations from others, solicitations.

TIPS "Please visit our website before submitting any work to us."

LIZA DAWSON ASSOCIATES

350 Seventh Ave., Suite 2003, New York NY 10001. (212)465-9071. **Website:** www.lizadawsonassociates.com. **Contact:** Anna Olswanger. Member of AAR. Other memberships include MWA, Women's Media Group. Represents 50+ clients. 30% of clients are new/unpublished writers.

Prior to becoming an agent, Ms. Dawson was an editor for 20 years, spending 11 years at William Morrow as vice president and 2 years at Putnam as executive editor. Ms. Blasdell was a senior editor at HarperCollins and Avon. Ms. Olswanger is an author.

MEMBER AGENTS **Liza Dawson** (plot-driven literary fiction, historicals, thrillers, suspense, parenting books, history, psychology [both popular and clinical], politics, narrative nonfiction and memoirs); **Caitlin Blasdell** (science fiction, fantasy (both adult and young adult), parenting, business, thrillers and women's fiction); **Anna Olswanger** (gift books for adults, young adult fiction and nonfiction, children's illustrated books, and Judaica); **Havis Dawson** (business books, how-to and practical books, spirituality, fantasy, Southern-culture fiction and military memoirs); **Hannah Bowman** (commercial fiction, especially science fiction and fantasy; women's fiction; cozy mysteries; romance; young adult; also nonfiction in the areas of mathematics, science, and spirituality); **Monica Odom** (literary fiction, women's fiction, voice-driven memoir, nonfiction in the areas of pop culture, food and cooking, history, politics, and current affairs).

REPRESENTS nonfiction books, novels and gift books (Olswanger only). **Considers these nonfiction areas:** autobiography, biography, business, cooking, current affairs, health, history, medicine, memoirs, parenting, popular culture, politics, psychology, sociology, women's issues, women's studies. **Considers these fiction areas:** commercial, fantasy, historical, literary, mystery, regional, romance, science fiction, suspense, thriller, women's, young adult, fantasy and science fiction (Blasdell only).

This agency specializes in readable literary fiction, thrillers, mainstream historicals, women's fiction, academics, historians, business, journalists, and psychology.

HOW TO CONTACT Query by e-mail only. No phone calls. Each of these agents has their own specific submission requirements, which you can find online at their website. querymonica@LizaDawsonAssociates.com; queryHannah@LizaDawsonAssociates.com; queryhavis@LizaDawsonAssociates.com; queryanna@LizaDawsonAssociates.com; queryCaitlin@LizaDawsonAssociates.com; queryliza@LizaDawsonAssociates.com. Responds in 4 weeks to queries; 8 weeks to mss. Obtains most new clients through recommendations from others, conferences.

TERMS Agent receives 15% commission on domestic sales. Agent receives 20% commission on foreign sales. Offers written contract.

THE JENNIFER DECHIARA LITERARY AGENCY

31 East 32nd St., Suite 300, New York NY 10016. (212)481-8484. **Fax:** (212)481-9582. **Website:** www.jdlit.com.

MEMBER AGENTS **Jennifer DeChiara**, jenndec@aol.com (literary, commercial, women's fiction [no bodice-rippers, please], chick-lit, mysteries, suspense, thrillers; for nonfiction: LGBTQ, memoirs, books about the arts and performing arts, behind-the-scenes-type books, and books about popular culture); **Stephen Fraser**, stephenafraser@verizon.net (one-of-a-kind picture books; strong chapter book series; whimsical, dramatic, or humorous middle grade; dramatic or high-concept young adult; powerful and unusual nonfiction; nonfiction with a broad audience on topics as far-reaching as art history, theater, film, literature, and travel); **Marie Lamba**, marie.jdlit@gmail.com (young adult and middle grade fiction, along with general and women's fiction and some memoir); **Linda Epstein**, linda.p.epstein@gmail.com (young adult, middle grade, literary fiction, quality upscale commercial fiction, vibrant narrative nonfiction, compelling memoirs, health and parenting books, cookbooks); **Roseanne Wells**, queryroseanne@gmail.com (literary fiction, YA, middle grade, narrative nonfiction, select memoir, science [popular or trade, not academic], history, religion [not inspirational], travel, humor, food/cooking, and similar subjects).

REPRESENTS nonfiction books, novels, juvenile. **Considers these nonfiction areas:** art, cooking, creative nonfiction, film, foods, gay/lesbian, health, history, humor, literature, memoirs, parenting, popular culture, religious, science, theater, travel. **Considers these fiction areas:** commercial, literary, middle grade, mystery, picture books, suspense, thriller, women's, young adult.

HOW TO CONTACT Each agent has their own e-mail submission address and submission instructions. Accepts simultaneous submissions. Obtains most new clients through recommendations from others, conferences, query letters.

TERMS Agent receives 15% commission on domestic sales. Agent receives 20% commission on foreign sales. Offers written contract.

DEFIORE & CO.

47 E. 19th St., 3rd Floor, New York NY 10003. (212)925-7744. **Fax:** (212)925-9803. **E-mail:** info@defioreandco.com; submissions@defioreandco.com. **Website:** www.defioreandco.com. Member of AAR.

Prior to becoming an agent, Mr. DeFiore was publisher of Villard Books (1997-1998), editor-in-chief of Hyperion (1992-1997), and editorial director of Delacorte Press (1988-1992).

MEMBER AGENTS Brian DeFiore (popular nonfiction, business, pop culture, parenting, commercial fiction); **Laurie Abkemeier** (memoir, parenting, business, how-to/self-help, popular science); **Kate Garrick** (literary fiction, memoir, popular nonfiction); **Matthew Elblonk** (young adult, popular culture, narrative nonfiction); **Caryn Karmatz-Rudy** (popular fiction, self-help, narrative nonfiction); **Adam Schear** (commercial fiction, humor, YA, smart thrillers, historical fiction, and quirky debut literary novels. For nonfiction: popular science, politics, popular culture, and current events); **Meredith Kaffel** (smart upmarket women's fiction, literary fiction [especially debut] and literary thrillers, narrative nonfiction, nonfiction about science and tech, sophisticated pop culture/humor books); **Rebecca Strauss** (literary and commercial fiction, women's fiction, urban fantasy, romance, mystery, YA, memoir, pop culture, and select nonfiction); **Debra Goldstein** (nonfiction books on how to live better).

REPRESENTS nonfiction books, novels. **Considers these nonfiction areas:** autobiography, biography, business, child guidance, cooking, economics, foods, how-to, inspirational, money, multicultural, parenting, popular culture, politics, psychology, religious, science, self-help, sports, young adult. **Considers these fiction areas:** ethnic, literary, mainstream, middle grade, mystery, paranormal, romance, short story collections, suspense, thriller, women's, young adult.

"Please be advised that we are not considering children's picture books, poetry, adult science fiction and fantasy, romance, or dramatic projects at this time."

HOW TO CONTACT Query with SASE or e-mail to submissions@defioreandco.com. "Please include the word 'Query' in the subject line. All attachments will be deleted; please insert all text in the body of the e-mail. For more information about our agents, their individual interests, and their query guidelines, please visit our 'About Us' page on our website." There is more information (details, sales) for each agent on the agency website. Accepts simultaneous submissions. Obtains most new clients through recommendations from others.

TERMS Agent receives 15% commission on domestic sales. Agent receives 20% commission on foreign sales. Offers written contract; 10-day notice must be given to terminate contract. Charges clients for photocopying and overnight delivery (deducted only after a sale is made).

WRITERS CONFERENCES Maui Writers Conference; Pacific Northwest Writers Conference; North Carolina Writers' Network Fall Conference.

JOELLE DELBOURGO ASSOCIATES, INC.

101 Park St., 3rd Floor, Montclair NJ 07042. (973)773-0836. **Fax:** (973)783-6802. **E-mail:** submissions@delbourgo.com. **Website:** www.delbourgo.com. Represents more than 100 clients. Currently handles: nonfiction books 75%, novels 25%.

Prior to becoming an agent, Ms. Delbourgo was an editor and senior publishing executive at HarperCollins and Random House.

MEMBER AGENTS Joelle Delbourgo, joelle@delbourgo.com (broad range of adult nonfiction and fiction, as well as a select and growing list of young adult and middle grade fiction and nonfiction); **Jacqueline Flynn**, jacqueline@delbourgo.com (thought-provoking nonfiction in business, history, self-help, memoir, current events, science, and more as well as very select fiction and children's titles); **Carrie Cantor**, carrie@delbourgo.com (current events, politics, history, popular science and psychology, memoir, and narrative nonfiction).

REPRESENTS nonfiction books, novels. **Considers these nonfiction areas:** creative nonfiction, current affairs, history, memoirs, politics, psychology, science, self-help. **Considers these fiction areas:** literary, mainstream, middle grade, young adult.

"We are former publishers and editors with deep knowledge and an insider perspective. We have a reputation for individualized attention to clients, strategic management of authors' careers, and creating strong partnerships with publishers for our clients."

HOW TO CONTACT It's preferable if you submit via e-mail to a specific agent. Query one agent only. No attachments. More submission tips on agency website. Accepts simultaneous submissions.

TERMS Agent receives 15% commission on domestic sales. Agent receives 20% commission on foreign sales. Offers written contract. Charges clients for postage and photocopying.

RECENT SALES *Alexander the Great*, by Philip Freeman; *The Big Book of Parenting Solutions*, by Dr. Michele Borba; *The Secret Life of Ms. Finkelman*, by Ben H. Wintners; *Not Quite Adults*, by Richard Settersten Jr. and Barbara Ray; *Tabloid Medicine*, by Robert Goldberg, PhD; *Table of Contents*, by Judy Gerlman and Vicky Levi Krupp.

TIPS "Do your homework. Do not cold call. Read and follow submission guidelines before contacting us. Do not call to find out if we received your material. No e-mail queries. Treat agents with respect, as you would any other professional, such as a doctor, lawyer or financial advisor."

SANDRA DIJKSTRA LITERARY AGENCY

1155 Camino del Mar, PMB 515, Del Mar CA 92014. (858)755-3115. **Fax:** (858)794-2822. **E-mail:** elise@dijkstraagency.com. **Website:** www.dijkstraagency.com. Member of AAR. Other memberships include Authors Guild, PEN West, PEN USA, Organization of American Historians, Poets and Editors, MWA. Represents 100+ clients. 30% of clients are new/unpublished writers.

MEMBER AGENTS **Sandra Dijkstra**, president (adult only). Other acquiring agents: **Elise Capron** (adult only), **Jill Marr** (adult only), **Thao Le** (adult and YA), **Roz Foster** (adult and YA), **Jessica Watterson** (adult and YA).

REPRESENTS nonfiction books, novels. **Considers these nonfiction areas:** biography, business, creative nonfiction, design, history, memoirs, psychology, science, self-help, narrative. **Considers these fiction areas:** commercial, horror, literary, middle grade, science fiction, suspense, thriller, women's, young adult.

HOW TO CONTACT "Please see guidelines on our website, and note that we only accept e-mail submissions. Due to the large number of unsolicited submissions we receive, we are only able to respond to those submissions in which we are interested." Accepts simultaneous submissions. Responds to queries of interest within 6 weeks.

TERMS Works in conjunction with foreign and film agents. Agent receives 15% commission on domestic sales and 20% commission on foreign sales. Offers written contract. No reading fee.

TIPS "Remember that publishing is a business. Do your research and present your project in as professional a way as possible. Only submit your work when you are confident that it is polished and ready for prime-time. Make yourself a part of the active writing community by getting stories and articles published, networking with other writers, and getting a good sense of where your work fits in the market."

DONADIO & OLSON, INC.

121 W. 27th St., Suite 704, New York NY 10001. (212)691-8077. **Fax:** (212)633-2837. **E-mail:** mail@donadio.com. **Website:** donadio.com. **Contact:** Neil Olson. Member of AAR.

MEMBER AGENTS **Neil Olson** (no queries); **Edward Hibbert** (no queries); **Carrie Howland** (represents literary fiction and nonfiction as well as young adult fiction. She can be reached at carrie@donadio.com.).

REPRESENTS nonfiction books, novels. **Considers these fiction areas:** literary, young adult.

This agency represents mostly fiction, and is very selective.

HOW TO CONTACT Please send a query letter, full synopsis, and the first three chapters/first 25 pages of the manuscript to mail@donadio.com. Please allow a few weeks for a reply. Obtains most new clients through recommendations from others.

JANIS A. DONNAUD & ASSOCIATES, INC.

525 Broadway, Second Floor, New York NY 10012. (212)431-2664. **Fax:** (212)431-2667. **E-mail:** jdonnaud@aol.com; donnaudassociate@aol.com. **Website:** www.publishersmarketplace.com/members/JanisDonnaud/. **Contact:** Janis A. Donnaud. Mem-

NEW AGENT SPOTLIGHT

MARIA VICENTE
(P.S. LITERARY AGENCY)

psliterary.com

@MsMariaVicente

ABOUT MARIA: Maria has a B.A. in English Literature from Carleton University and a B.Ed. from The University of Western Ontario.

SHE IS SEEKING: literary and commercial fiction, new adult, young adult, middle grade, high-concept picture books, and nonfiction proposals in the pop culture, pop psychology, design, and lifestyle categories. She has a particular interest in magical realism, fiction with visual components, and nonfiction inspired by online culture.

HOW TO QUERY: query@psliterary.com. Limit your query to one page and include the following: an introduction (the title and category of your work and an estimated word count), a brief overview (similar to back-cover copy), and a writer's bio (a little bit about yourself and your background). Do not send attachments or submit a full-length manuscript/proposal unless requested. In your e-mail subject line, have it read "Query for Maria: [Book Title]."

ber of AAR. Signatory of WGA. Represents 40 clients. 5% of clients are new/unpublished writers. Currently handles: nonfiction books 100%.

Prior to opening her agency, Ms. Donnaud was vice president and associate publisher of Random House Adult Trade Group.

REPRESENTS nonfiction books. **Considers these nonfiction areas:** biography, business, cooking, creative nonfiction, ethnic, health, history, money, sports.

Does not want to receive "fiction, poetry, mysteries, juvenile books, romances, science fiction, young adult, religious or fantasy."

HOW TO CONTACT Query. For nonfiction, send a proposal. Prefers exclusive submissions. Responds in 1 month to queries and mss. Obtains most new clients through recommendations from others.

TERMS Agent receives 15% commission on domestic and film sales; 20% commission on foreign sales. Offers written contract; 1-month notice must be given to terminate contract.

RECENT SALES Stephane Stiavetti and Garrett McCord for *Melt*, their book on mac and cheese; Jennifer Klinec for her memoir, *The Temporary Bride*; Amy Thielen for 2 books including *The New Midwestern Table*; Jacquy Pfeiffer, for *The French Pastry Primer*; Catherine Crawford for her book *Why French Children Don't Talk Back*; Jaden Hair's *Steamy Kitchen* book; Also: Paula Deen's books, Pat and Gina Neely's books, Anne Burrell's books, Suzanne Goin's books.

JIM DONOVAN LITERARY

5635 SMU Blvd., Suite 201, Dallas TX 75206. **E-mail:** jdliterary@sbcglobal.net. **Contact:** Melissa Shultz, agent. Represents 30 clients. 10% of clients are new/unpublished writers. Currently handles: nonfiction books 75%, novels 25%.

MEMBER AGENTS **Jim Donovan** (history—particularly American, military and Western; biography; sports; popular reference; popular culture; fiction—literary, thrillers and mystery); **Melissa Shultz** (parenting, women's issues, memoir).

This agency specializes in commercial fiction and nonfiction. "Does not want to receive poetry, children's, sci-fi, fantasy, short stories, inspirational or anything else not listed above."

HOW TO CONTACT "For nonfiction, I need a well thought out query letter telling me about the book: What it does, how it does it, why it's needed now, why it's better or different than what's out there on the subject, and why the author is the perfect writer for it. For fiction, the novel has to be finished, of course; a short (2 to 5 page) synopsis—not a teaser, but a summary of all the action, from first page to last—and the first 30-50 pages is enough. This material should be polished to as close to perfection as possible." Accepts simultaneous submissions. Responds in 2 weeks to queries. Responds in 1 month to mss. Obtains most new clients through recommendations from others.

TERMS Agent receives 15% commission on domestic sales. Agent receives 20% commission on foreign sales. Offers written contract, binding for 1 year; 30-day notice must be given to terminate contract. This agency charges for things such as overnight delivery and manuscript copying. Charges are discussed beforehand.

RECENT SALES *Below*, by Ryan Lockwood (Kensington); *The Dead Lands*, by Joe McKinney (Kensington); *Perfect: Don Larsen's Miraculous World Series Game and the Men Who Made It Happen*, by Lew Paper (NAL); *Untouchable: The Life and Times of Elliott Ness, America's Greatest Crime Fighter* (Viking); *Last Stand at Khe Sanh*, by Gregg Jones (DaCapo); *Soldier of Misfortune*, by Richard Bak; *Powerless* by Tim Washburn.

TIPS "Get published in short form—magazine reviews, journals, etc.—first. This will increase your credibility considerably, and make it much easier to sell a full-length book."

DOYEN LITERARY SERVICES, INC.

1931-660th St., Newell IA 50568-7613. **Website:** www.barbaradoyen.com. **Contact:** (Ms.) B.J. Doyen, president. Represents over 100 clients. 20% of clients are new/unpublished writers. Currently handles: nonfiction books 100%.

Prior to opening her agency, Ms. Doyen worked as a published author, teacher, and guest speaker, and wrote and appeared in her own weekly TV show airing in 7 states. She is also the coauthor of *The Everything Guide to Writing a Book Proposal* (Adams 2005) and *The Everything Guide to Getting Published* (Adams 2006).

REPRESENTS nonfiction for adults, no children's. **Considers these nonfiction areas:** agriculture, Americana, animals, anthropology, archeology, architecture, art, autobiography, biography, business, child guidance, computers, cooking, crafts, cultural interests, current affairs, diet/nutrition, design, economics, education, environment, ethnic, film, foods, gardening, government, health, history, hobbies, horticulture, language, law, medicine, memoirs, metaphysics, military, money, multicultural, music, parenting, photography, popular culture, politics, psychology, recreation, regional, science, self-help, sex, sociology, software, technology, theater, true crime, women's issues, women's studies, creative nonfiction, computers, electronics.

This agency specializes in nonfiction. Actively seeking business, health, science, how-to, self-help—all kinds of adult nonfiction suitable for the major trade publishers. Does not want to receive pornography, screenplays, children's books, fiction, or poetry.

HOW TO CONTACT Send a query letter initially. "Do not send us any attachments. Your text must be in the body of the e-mail. Please read the website before submitting a query. Include your background information in a bio. Send no unsolicited attachments." Reach this agency through its current e-mail, which is posted on the agency website. Accepts simultaneous submissions. Responds immediately to queries. Responds in 3 weeks to mss.

TERMS Agent receives 15% commission on domestic sales. Agent receives 20% commission on foreign sales. Offers written contract, binding for 2 years.

RECENT SALES *Stem Cells for Dummies*, by Lawrence S.B. Goldstein and Meg Schneider; *The Complete Idiot's Guide to Country Living*, by Kimberly Willis; *The Complete Illustrated Pregnancy Companion*, by Robin Elise Weiss; *The Complete Idiot's Guide* *to Playing the Fiddle*, by Ellery Klein; *Healthy Aging for Dummies*, by Brent Agin, MD and Sharon Perkins, RN.

TIPS "Our authors receive personalized attention. We market aggressively, undeterred by rejection. We get the best possible publishing contracts. We are very interested in nonfiction book ideas at this time and will consider most topics. Many writers come to us from referrals, but we also get quite a few who initially approach us with query letters. Do not call us regarding queries. It is best if you do not collect editorial rejections prior to seeking an agent, but if you do, be upfront and honest about it. Do not submit your manuscript to more than 1 agent at a time—querying first can save you (and us) much time. We're open to established or beginning writers—just send us a terrific letter!"

DREISBACH LITERARY MANAGEMENT

PO Box 5379, El Dorado Hills CA 95762. (916)804-5016. **E-mail:** verna@dreisbachliterary.com. **Website:** www.dreisbachliterary.com. **Contact:** Verna Dreisbach. Estab. 2007.

Prior to opening her own agency, Ms. Dreisbach was with Andrea Hurst Literary.

REPRESENTS **Considers these nonfiction areas:** animals, biography, business, health, memoirs, multicultural, parenting, travel, true crime, women's issues. **Considers these fiction areas:** commercial, literary, mystery, thriller, young adult.

The agency has a particular interest in books with a political, economic, or social context. Open to most types of nonfiction. Fiction interests include literary, commercial, and YA. Verna's first career as a law enforcement officer gives her a genuine interest and expertise in the genres of mystery, thriller, and true crime. Does not want to receive sci-fi, fantasy, horror, poetry, screenplay, Christian, or children's books.

HOW TO CONTACT E-mail queries only. No attachments in the query; they will not be opened. No unsolicited mss. *Accepting new nonfiction clients only through a writers conference or a personal referral. Not accepting fiction.*

RECENT SALES *How to Blog a Book* (Writer's Digest Books); *Quest for Justice* (New Horizon Press); *Walnut Wine and Truffle Groves* (Running Press); *Coming to the Fire* (BenBella Books); *Off the Street* (Behler Publications); *Lowcountry Bribe* (Bell Bridge Books).

DUNHAM LITERARY, INC.

110 William St., Suite 2202, New York NY 10038. (212)929-0994. **E-mail:** dunhamlit@yahoo.com. **E-mail:** query@dunhamlit.com. **Website:** www.dunhamlit.com. **Contact:** Jennie Dunham. Member of AAR. SCBWI Represents 50 clients. 15% of clients are new/unpublished writers. Currently handles: nonfiction books 25%, novels 25%, juvenile books 50%.

Prior to opening her agency, Ms. Dunham worked as a literary agent for Russell & Volkening. The Rhoda Weyr Agency is now a division of Dunham Literary, Inc.

REPRESENTS nonfiction, fiction, novels, juvenile books. **Considers these nonfiction areas:** anthropology, archeology, biography, cultural interests, environment, ethnic, health, history, language, literature, medicine, popular culture, politics, psychology, science, technology, women's issues, women's studies. **Considers these fiction areas:** ethnic, juvenile, literary, mainstream, picture books, young adult.

HOW TO CONTACT Query with SASE. Responds in 3 weeks to queries; 2 months to mss. Obtains most new clients through recommendations from others, solicitations.

TERMS Agent receives 15% commission on domestic sales. Agent receives 20% commission on foreign sales.

RECENT SALES Sales include The Bad Kitty Series, by Nick Bruel (Macmillan); *The Little Mermaid*, by Robert Sabuda (Simon & Schuster); *Transformers*, by Matthew Reinhart (Little, Brown); *The Gollywhopper Games* and Sequels, by Jody Feldman (HarperCollins); *Learning Not to Drown*, by Anna Shinoda (Simon & Schuster); *The Things You Kiss Goodbye*, by Leslie Connor (HarperCollins); *Gangsterland*, by Tod Goldberg (Counterpoint); *Ancestors and Others*, by Fred Chappell (Macmillan), *Forward From Here*, by Reeve Lindbergh (Simon & Schuster).

DUNOW, CARLSON, & LERNER AGENCY

27 W. 20th St., Suite 1107, New York NY 10011. (212)645-7606. **E-mail:** mail@dclagency.com. **Website:** www.dclagency.com. Member of AAR.

MEMBER AGENTS **Jennifer Carlson** (narrative nonfiction writers and journalists covering current events and ideas and cultural history, as well as literary and upmarket commercial novelists); **Henry**

Dunow (quality fiction—literary, historical, strongly written commercial—and voice-driven nonfiction across a range of areas—narrative history, biography, memoir, current affairs, cultural trends and criticism, science, sports); **Erin Hosier** (nonfiction: popular culture, music, sociology and memoir); **Betsy Lerner** (nonfiction writers in the areas of psychology, history, cultural studies, biography, current events, business; fiction: literary, dark, funny, voice driven); **Yishai Seidman** (broad range of fiction: literary, postmodern, and thrillers; nonfiction: sports, music, and pop culture); **Amy Hughes** (nonfiction in the areas of history, cultural studies, memoir, current events, wellness, health, food, pop culture, and biography; also literary fiction); **Eleanor Jackson** (literary, commercial, memoir, art, food, science and history); **Julia Kenny** (fiction—adult, middle grade and YA—and is especially interested in dark, literary thrillers and suspense).

REPRESENTS nonfiction books, novels, juvenile. **Considers these nonfiction areas:** art, biography, creative nonfiction, cultural interests, current affairs, foods, health, history, memoirs, music, popular culture, psychology, science, sociology, sports. **Considers these fiction areas:** commercial, literary, mainstream, middle grade, mystery, picture books, thriller, young adult.

HOW TO CONTACT Query via snail mail with SASE, or by e-mail. No attachments. Responds if interested.

RECENT SALES A full list of agency clients is on the website.

DYSTEL & GODERICH LITERARY MANAGEMENT

1 Union Square W., Suite 904, New York NY 10003. (212)627-9100. **Fax:** (212)627-9313. **Website:** www.dystel.com. Estab. 1994. Member of AAR. Other membership includes SCBWI. Represents 600+ clients.

MEMBER AGENTS **Jane Dystel**; **Miriam Goderich** (literary and commercial fiction as well as some genre fiction, narrative nonfiction, pop culture, psychology, history, science, art, business books, and biography/memoir); **Stacey Kendall Glick** (narrative nonfiction including memoir, parenting, cooking and food, psychology, science, health and wellness, lifestyle, current events, pop culture, YA, middle grade, and select adult contemporary fiction); **Michael Bourret** (middle grade and young adult fiction, commercial adult fiction, and all sorts of nonfiction, from practical to narrative; he's especially interested in food- and cocktail-related books, memoir, popular history, politics, religion [though not spirituality], popular science, and current events); **Jim McCarthy** (literary women's fiction, underrepresented voices, mysteries, romance, paranormal fiction, narrative nonfiction, memoir, and paranormal nonfiction); **Jessica Papin** (literary and smart commercial fiction, narrative nonfiction, history with a thesis, medicine, science and religion, health, psychology, women's issues); **Lauren E. Abramo** (smart commercial fiction and well-paced literary fiction with a unique voice, including middle grade, YA, and adult and a wide variety of narrative nonfiction including science, interdisciplinary cultural studies, pop culture, psychology, reportage, media, contemporary culture, and history); **John Rudolph** (picture book author/illustrators, middle grade, YA, commercial fiction for men, nonfiction); **Rachel Stout** (literary fiction, narrative nonfiction, and believable and thought-provoking YA as well as magical realism); **Sharon Pelletier** (witty literary fiction and smart commercial fiction featuring female characters, narrative nonfiction).

REPRESENTS nonfiction books, novels, cookbooks. **Considers these nonfiction areas:** animals, anthropology, archeology, autobiography, biography, business, child guidance, cultural interests, current affairs, economics, ethnic, gay/lesbian, health, history, humor, inspirational, investigative, medicine, metaphysics, military, New Age, parenting, popular culture, psychology, religious, science, technology, true crime, women's issues, women's studies. **Considers these fiction areas:** action, adventure, commercial, crime, detective, ethnic, family saga, gay, lesbian, literary, mainstream, middle grade, mystery, picture books, police, suspense, thriller, women's, young adult.

"We are actively seeking fiction for all ages, in all genres." No plays, screenplays, or poetry.

HOW TO CONTACT Query via e-mail. The varying e-mail addresses for each agent are on the agency website under "Who We Are and What We're Looking For." Accepts simultaneous submissions. Responds in 6 to 8 weeks to queries; within 8 weeks to mss. Obtains most new clients through recommendations from others, solicitations, conferences.

TERMS Agent receives 15% commission on domestic sales. Agent receives 19% commission on foreign sales. Offers written contract.

WRITERS CONFERENCES Backspace Writers' Conference; Pacific Northwest Writers' Association; Pike's Peak Writers' Conference; Writers League of Texas; Love Is Murder; Surrey International Writers Conference; Society of Children's Book Writers and Illustrators; International Thriller Writers; Willamette Writers Conference; The South Carolina Writers Workshop Conference; Las Vegas Writers Conference; Writer's Digest; Seton Hill Popular Fiction; Romance Writers of America; Geneva Writers Conference.

TIPS "DGLM prides itself on being a full-service agency. We're involved in every stage of the publishing process, from offering substantial editing on mss and proposals, to coming up with book ideas for authors looking for their next project, negotiating contracts and collecting monies for our clients. We follow a book from its inception through its sale to a publisher, its publication, and beyond. Our commitment to our writers does not, by any means, end when we have collected our commission. This is one of the many things that makes us unique in a very competitive business."

EAST/WEST LITERARY AGENCY, LLC

1158 26th St., Suite 462, Santa Monica CA 90403. (310)573-9303. **Fax:** (310)453-9008. **E-mail:** dwarren@eastwestliteraryagency.com. **Contact:** Deborah Warren. Estab. 2000. Currently handles: juvenile books 90%, adult books 10%.

MEMBER AGENTS Deborah Warren, founder.

REPRESENTS Considers these fiction areas: middle grade, picture books, young adult.

HOW TO CONTACT By referral only. Submit proposal and first 3 sample chapters, table of contents (2 pages or fewer), synopsis (1 page). For picture books, submit entire ms. Requested submissions should be sent by mail as a Word document in Courier, 12-pt., double-spaced with 1.20-inch margin on left, ragged right text, 25 lines per page, continuously paginated, with all your contact info on the first page. Only responds if interested, no need for SASE. Responds in 60 days. Obtains new clients through recommendations from others.

TERMS Agent receives 15% commission on domestic sales. Agent receives 25% commission on foreign sales. Offers written contract; 30-day notice must be given to terminate contract. Charges for out-of-pocket expenses, such as postage and copying.

EBELING & ASSOCIATES

P.O. Box 2529, Lyons CO 80540. (303)823-6963. **E-mail:** ebothat@yahoo.com. **Website:** www.ebelingagency.com. **Contact:** Michael Ebeling. Represents 6 clients. 50% of clients are new/unpublished writers. Currently handles: nonfiction books 100%.

Prior to becoming an agent, Mr. Ebeling established a career in the publishing industry through long-term author management. He has expertise in sales, platforms, publicity and marketing.

REPRESENTS nonfiction books. **Considers these nonfiction areas:** animals, business, cooking, diet/nutrition, environment, foods, history, how-to, humor, inspirational, medicine, money, music, parenting, psychology, religious, satire, self-help, spirituality, sports.

"We accept very few clients for representation. To be considered, an author needs a very strong platform and a unique book concept. We represent nonfiction authors, most predominantly in the areas of business and self-help. We are very committed to our authors and their messages, which is a main reason we have such a high placement rate. We are always looking at new ways to help our authors gain the exposure they need to not only get published, but develop a successful literary career." Actively seeking well-written nonfiction material with fresh perspectives written by writers with established platforms. Does not want to receive fiction, poetry or children's lit.

HOW TO CONTACT We accept queries and proposals by e-mail only. Accepts simultaneous submissions. Responds in 4-6 weeks to queries. Obtains most new clients through referrals and queries.

TERMS Agent receives 15% commission on domestic sales. Agent receives 20% commission on foreign sales. Offers written contract; 60-day notice must be given to terminate contract. There is a charge for normal out-of-pocket fees, not to exceed $200 without client approval.

RECENT SALES *Naked: How to Find Your Perfect Partner by Revealing Your True Self* by David Wygant (Hay House 2012); *The One Command: Command Your Wealth* by Asara Lovejoy (Berkley/Penguin 2012); *Growing Happy Kids* by Maureen Healy (Health Communications, Inc. 2012).

WRITERS CONFERENCES BookExpo America; San Francisco Writers' Conference.

TIPS "Approach agents when you're already building your platform, you have a well-written book, you have a firm understanding of the publishing process, and you have come up with a complete competitive proposal. Know the name of the agent you are contacting. You're essentially selling a business plan to the publisher. Make sure you've made a convincing pitch throughout your proposal, as ultimately, publishers are taking a financial risk by investing in your project."

ANNE EDELSTEIN LITERARY AGENCY

404 Riverside Dr., #12D, New York NY 10025. (212)414-4923. **Fax:** (212)414-2930. **E-mail:** submissions@aeliterary.com. **Website:** www.aeliterary.com. Member of AAR.

MEMBER AGENTS Anne Edelstein.

REPRESENTS nonfiction, fiction. **Considers these nonfiction areas:** history, memoirs, psychology, religious, cultural history. **Considers these fiction areas:** commercial, literary.

This agency specializes in fiction and narrative nonfiction.

HOW TO CONTACT E-mail queries only; consult website for submission guidelines.

RECENT SALES *Amsterdam*, by Russell Shorto (Doubleday); *The Story of Beautiful Girl*, by Rachel Simon (Grand Central).

EDUCATIONAL DESIGN SERVICES LLC

5750 Bou Ave, Suite 1508, N. Bethesda MD 20852. **E-mail:** blinder@educationaldesignservices.com. **Website:** www.educationaldesignservices.com. **Contact:** B. Linder. Estab. 1981. 80% of clients are new/unpublished writers.

"We specialize in educational materials to be used in classrooms (in class sets), for staff development or in teacher education classes." Actively seeking educational, text materials. Not looking for picture books, story books, fiction; no illustrators.

HOW TO CONTACT Query by e-mail or with SASE or send outline and 1 sample chapter. Considers simultaneous queries and submissions if so indicated. Returns material only with SASE. Responds in 6-8 weeks to queries/mss. Obtains clients through recommendations from others, queries/solicitations, or through conferences.

TERMS Agent receives 15% commission on domestic sales; 25% on foreign sales. Offers written contract, binding until any party opts out. Terminate contract through certified letter.

RECENT SALES *How to Solve Word Problems in Mathematics*, by Wayne (McGraw-Hill); *Preparing for the 8th Grade Test in Social Studies*, by Farran-Paci (Amsco); *Minority Report*, by Gunn-Singh (Scarecrow Education); *No Parent Left Behind*, by Petrosino & Spiegel (Rowman & Littlefield); *Teaching Test-taking Skills* (R&L Education); *10 Languages You'll Need Most in the Classroom*, by Sundem, Krieger, Pickiewicz (Corwin Press); *Kids, Classrooms & Capital Hill*, by Flynn (R&L Education); *Bully Nation*, by Susan Eva Porter (Paragon House).

JUDITH EHRLICH LITERARY MANAGEMENT, LLC

880 Third Ave., 8th Floor, New York NY 10022. (646)505-1570. **Fax:** (646)505-1570. **E-mail:** jehrlich@judithehrlichliterary.com. **Website:** www.judithehrlichliterary.com. Member of the Author's Guild and the American Society of Journalists and Authors.

Prior to her current position, Ms. Ehrlich was a senior associate at the Linda Chester Agency and is an award-winning journalist; she is the co-author of *The New Crowd: The Changing of the Jewish Guard on Wall Street* (Little, Brown).

MEMBER AGENTS **Judith Ehrlich**; **Sophia Seidner**: sseidner@judithehrlichliterary.com (strong literary fiction and nonfiction including self-help, narrative nonfiction, memoir, and biography. Areas of special interest include medical and health-related topics, science [popular, political and social], animal welfare, current events, politics, law, history, ethics, parody and humor, sports, art and business self-help).

REPRESENTS **Considers these nonfiction areas:** biography, business, creative nonfiction, cultural interests, current affairs, health, history, memoirs, parenting, psychology, science, women's issues. **Considers these fiction areas:** commercial, literary.

Does not want to receive novellas, poetry, textbooks, plays, or screenplays.

HOW TO CONTACT Queries should include a synopsis and some sample pages. Send e-queries to jehrlich@judithehrlichliterary.com. The agency will respond only if interested.

RECENT SALES *Power Branding: Leveraging the Success of the World's Best Brands* by Steve McKee (Palgrave Macmillan); *What Was the Underground Railroad?* by Yona Zeldis McDonough (Grosset & Dunlap); *Confessions of a Sociopath: A Life Spent Hiding in Plain Sight* by M.E. Thomas (Crown); *The Last Kiss* by Leslie Brody (TitleTown); *Love, Loss, and Laughter: Seeing Alzheimer's Differently* (Lyons Press); *Luck and Circumstance: A Coming of Age in New York, Hollywood, and Points Beyond* by Michael Lindsay-Hogg (Knopf); *Paris Under Water: How the City of Light Survived the Great Flood of 1910* by Jeffrey H. Jackson (Palgrave Macmillan). Fiction titles: *Two of a Kind* by Yona Zeldis McDonough (NAL, September 2013); *Once We Were* by Kat Zhang (HarperCollins, September 2013).

EINSTEIN THOMPSON AGENCY

27 West 20th Street, Suite 1003, New York NY 10011. (212)221-8797. **E-mail:** submissions@einsteinthompson.com. Estab. 2011. Member of AAR.

MEMBER AGENTS Susanna Einstein, Meg Thompson, Molly Reese Lerner (associate agent).

REPRESENTS **Considers these nonfiction areas:** cooking, creative nonfiction, history, memoirs, popular culture, politics, science, sports. **Considers these fiction areas:** commercial, crime, historical, literary, middle grade, women's, young adult.

No picture books.

HOW TO CONTACT For fiction, send a query letter and the first 25 pages pasted into an e-mail. Address your query to your targeted agent. Please send a query and full proposal for nonfiction. Submit to submissions@einsteinthompson.com.

RECENT SALES A full list of agency clients is available on the website.

E.J. MCCARTHY AGENCY

(415)383-6639. **E-mail:** ejmagency@gmail.com. **Website:** www.publishersmarketplace.com/members/ejmccarthy/.

Prior to his current position, Mr. McCarthy was a former executive editor with more than twenty years book-publishing experience (Bantam Doubleday Dell, Presidio Press, Ballantine/Random House).

REPRESENTS **Considers these nonfiction areas:** biography, history, memoirs, military, sports.

This agency specializes in nonfiction. No fiction.

HOW TO CONTACT Query first by e-mail.

RECENT SALES *One Bullet Away* by Nathaniel Fick; *The Unforgiving Minute* by Craig Mullaney; *The Sling And the Stone* by Thomas X. Hammes; *Arms Of Little Value* by G. L. Lamborn (Casemate). Leading clients include Nathaniel Fick, Craig Mullaney, Eric Greitens, Thomas X. Hammes, Daniel P. Bolger, John S. D. Eisenhower, Jay Stout, Ryan A. Conklin, Benjamin Runkle, Brian Steed.

THE LISA EKUS GROUP, LLC

57 North St., Hatfield MA 01038. (413)247-9325. **Fax:** (413)247-9873. **E-mail:** lisaekus@lisaekus.com. **Website:** www.lisaekus.com. **Contact:** Lisa Ekus-Saffer. Member of AAR.

MEMBER AGENTS Lisa Ekus; Sally Ekus.

REPRESENTS nonfiction books. **Considers these nonfiction areas:** cooking, diet/nutrition, foods, occasionally health/well-being and women's issues.

HOW TO CONTACT Submit a one-page query via e-mail or submit complete hard copy proposal with title page, proposal contents, concept, bio, marketing, TOC, etc. Include SASE for the return of materials.

RECENT SALES "Please see the regularly updated client listing on our website."

TIPS "Please do not call. No phone queries."

ETHAN ELLENBERG LITERARY AGENCY

548 Broadway, #5-E, New York NY 10012. (212)431-4554. **Fax:** (212)941-4652. **E-mail:** agent@ethanellenberg.com. **Website:** ethanellenberg.com. **Contact:** Ethan Ellenberg. Estab. 1984. Represents 80 clients. 10% of clients are new/unpublished writers. Currently handles: nonfiction books 25%, novels 75%.

Prior to opening his agency, Mr. Ellenberg was contracts manager of Berkley/Jove and associate contracts manager for Bantam.

MEMBER AGENTS **Denise Little**: deniselitt@aol.com. (accepts romance, paranormal, YA, science fiction, fantasy, Christian fiction, and commercial nonfiction. Send a short query letter telling about your writing history, and including the first 15 pages of the work you want her to represent. If she is interested in your work, she'll reply to you within four weeks); **Evan Gregory** (accepting clients).

REPRESENTS nonfiction books, novels, children's books. **Considers these nonfiction areas:** biography, current affairs, health, history, medicine, military, science, technology, war, narrative. **Considers these**

fiction areas: commercial, fantasy, literary, mystery, romance, science fiction, suspense, thriller, women's, young adult, children's (all types).

"This agency specializes in commercial fiction—especially thrillers, romance/women's, and specialized nonfiction. We also do a lot of children's books." "Actively seeking commercial fiction as noted above—romance/fiction for women, science fiction and fantasy, thrillers, suspense and mysteries. Our other two main areas of interest are children's books and narrative nonfiction. We are actively seeking clients, follow the directions on our website." Does not want to receive poetry, short stories, or screenplays.

HOW TO CONTACT Query by e-mail. Paste the query, synopsis and first 50 pages into the e-mail. For nonfiction, paste the proposal. For picture books, paste the entire text. Accepts simultaneous submissions. Responds in 2 weeks to queries (no attachments); 4-6 weeks to mss.

TERMS Agent receives 15% commission on domestic sales. Agent receives 10% commission on foreign sales. Offers written contract. Charges clients (with their consent) for direct expenses limited to photocopying and postage.

WRITERS CONFERENCES RWA National Conference; Novelists, Inc.; and other regional conferences.

TIPS We do consider new material from unsolicited authors. Write a good, clear letter with a succinct description of your book. We prefer the first 3 chapters when we consider fiction. For all submissions, you must include an SASE or the material will be discarded. It's always hard to break in, but talent will find a home. Check our website for complete submission guidelines. We continue to see natural storytellers and nonfiction writers with important books.

EMPIRE LITERARY

50 Davis Lane, Roslyn NY 11576. (917)213-7082. **E-mail:** abarzvi@empireliterary.com. **Website:** www.empireliterary.com. Estab. 2013.

Prior to opening her own agency, Ms. Barzvi was an agent at ICM Partners for 13 years.

REPRESENTS **Considers these nonfiction areas:** cooking, creative nonfiction, diet/nutrition, health, how-to, memoirs, parenting. **Considers these fiction areas:** women's.

This agency specializes in commercial nonfiction, and women's fiction.

HOW TO CONTACT E-query. No attachments,. Put "Query" in the subject line.

THE ELAINE P. ENGLISH LITERARY AGENCY

4710 41st St. NW, Suite D, Washington DC 20016. (202)362-5190. **Fax:** (202)362-5192. **E-mail:** queries@elaineenglish.com. **E-mail:** elaine@elaineenglish.com. **Website:** www.elaineenglish.com/literary.php. **Contact:** Elaine English, Lindsey Skouras. Member of AAR. Represents 20 clients. 25% of clients are new/unpublished writers. Currently handles: novels 100%.

Ms. English has been working in publishing for more than 20 years. She is also an attorney specializing in media and publishing law.

MEMBER AGENTS Elaine English (novels).

REPRESENTS novels. **Considers these fiction areas:** historical, multicultural, mystery, suspense, thriller, women's, romance (single title, historical, contemporary, romantic, suspense, chick lit, erotic), general women's fiction. The agency is slowly but steadily acquiring in all mentioned areas.

Actively seeking women's fiction, including single-title romances. Does not want to receive any science fiction, time travel, or picture books.

HOW TO CONTACT Not accepting queries as of 2014. Keep checking the website for further information and updates. Responds in 4-8 weeks to queries; 3 months to requested submissions. Obtains most new clients through recommendations from others, conferences, submissions.

TERMS Agent receives 15% commission on domestic sales. Agent receives 20% commission on foreign sales. Offers written contract; 30-day notice must be given to terminate contract. Charges only for shipping expenses; generally taken from proceeds.

RECENT SALES Have been to Sourcebooks, Tor, Harlequin.

WRITERS CONFERENCES RWA National Conference; Novelists, Inc.; Malice Domestic; Washington Romance Writers Retreat, among others.

FELICIA ETH LITERARY REPRESENTATION

555 Bryant St., Suite 350, Palo Alto CA 94301-1700. (650)375-1276. **E-mail:** feliciaeth.literary@gmail.com. **Website:** ethliterary.com. **Contact:** Felicia Eth. Member of AAR. Represents 25-35 clients. Currently handles: nonfiction books 75%, novels 25% adult.

REPRESENTS nonfiction books, novels. **Considers these nonfiction areas:** animals, anthropology, autobiography, biography, business, child guidance, cultural interests, current affairs, economics, health, history, investigative, law, medicine, parenting, popular culture, politics, psychology, science, sociology, technology, women's issues, women's studies. **Considers these fiction areas:** literary, mainstream.

This agency specializes in high-quality fiction (preferably mainstream/contemporary) and provocative, intelligent, and thoughtful nonfiction on a wide array of commercial subjects.

HOW TO CONTACT Query with SASE. Accepts simultaneous submissions. Responds in 3 weeks to queries. Responds in 4-6 weeks to mss.

TERMS Agent receives 15% commission on domestic sales. Agent receives 20% commission on foreign sales. Agent receives 20% commission on film sales. Charges clients for photocopying and express mail service.

RECENT SALES *Bumper Sticker Philosophy*, by Jack Bowen (Random House); *Boys Adrift* by Leonard Sax (Basic Books; *The Memory Thief*, by Emily Colin (Ballantine Books); *The World is a Carpet*, by Anna Badkhen (Riverhead).

WRITERS CONFERENCES "Wide array—from Squaw Valley to Mills College."

TIPS "For nonfiction, established expertise is certainly a plus—as is magazine publication—though not a prerequisite. I am highly dedicated to those projects I represent, but highly selective in what I choose."

MARY EVANS INC.

242 E. Fifth St., New York NY 10003. (212)979-0880. **Fax:** (212)979-5344. **E-mail:** info@maryevansinc.com. **Website:** maryevansinc.com. Member of AAR.

MEMBER AGENTS **Mary Evans** (no unsolicited queries); **Julia Kardon** (literary and upmarket fiction, narrative nonfiction, journalism, and history); **Mary Gaule** (picture books, middle grade, and YA fiction).

REPRESENTS nonfiction books, novels.

No screenplays or stage plays.

HOW TO CONTACT Query by mail or e-mail. If querying by mail, include a proper SASE. If querying by e-mail, put "Query" in the subject line. For fiction: Include the first few pages, or opening chapter of your novel as a single Word attachment. For nonfiction: Include your book proposal as a single Word attachment. Responds within 8 weeks. Obtains most new clients through recommendations from others, solicitations.

EVATOPIA, INC.

8447 Wilshire Blvd., Suite 401, Beverly Hills CA 90211. **E-mail:** submissions@evatopia.com. **Website:** www.evatopia.com. **Contact:** Margery Walshaw. Represents 15 clients. 85% of clients are new/unpublished writers. Currently handles: movie scripts and book to film adaptations.

Prior to becoming an agent, Ms. Walshaw was a writer and publicist for the entertainment industry.

MEMBER AGENTS Mary Kay (story development); Jamie Davis (story editor); Jill Jones (story editor).

REPRESENTS movies. **Considers these fiction areas:** projects aimed at women, teens and children. **Considers these script areas:** projects aimed at women, teens and children. "In addition to representing screenplays, we specialize in book to film adaptations with particular emphasis on middle grade, young adult fiction, and women's fiction."

"We specialize in promoting and developing the careers of first-time screenwriters. All of our staff members have strong writing and entertainment backgrounds, making us sympathetic to the needs of our clients." Actively seeking dedicated and hard-working writers.

HOW TO CONTACT Submit via online submission form. Accepts simultaneous submissions. Responds in 4-6 weeks to queries. Responds in 4 weeks to mss. Obtains most new clients through recommendations from others, solicitations.

TERMS Agent receives 15% commission on domestic sales. Agent receives 15% commission on foreign sales. Offers written contract; 30-day notice must be given to terminate contract.

TIPS "Remember that you only have 1 chance to make that important first impression. Make your loglines original and your synopses concise. The secret to a screenwriter's success is creating an original story and telling it in a manner that we haven't heard before."

FAIRBANK LITERARY REPRESENTATION

P.O. Box 6, Hudson NY 12534-0006. (617)576-0030. **Fax:** (617)576-0030. **E-mail:** queries@fairbankliterary.com. **Website:** www.fairbankliterary.com. **Contact:** Sorche Fairbank. Member of AAR. Represents 45 clients. 20% of clients are new/unpublished writers. Currently handles: nonfiction books 60%, novels 22%, story collections 3%, other 15% illustrated.

MEMBER AGENTS Sorche Fairbank (narrative nonfiction, commercial and literary fiction, memoir, food and wine); Matthew Frederick, matt@fairbankliterary.com (scout for sports nonfiction, architecture, design).

REPRESENTS nonfiction books, novels, short story collections. **Considers these nonfiction areas:** agriculture, architecture, art, autobiography, biography, cooking, crafts, cultural interests, current affairs, decorating, diet/nutrition, design, environment, ethnic, foods, gay/lesbian, government, hobbies, horticulture, how-to, interior design, investigative, law, memoirs, photography, popular culture, politics, science, sociology, sports, technology, true crime, women's issues, women's studies. **Considers these fiction areas:** action, adventure, feminist, gay, lesbian, literary, mainstream, mystery, sports, suspense, thriller, women's, Southern voices.

"I have a small agency in Harvard Square, where I tend to gravitate toward literary fiction and narrative nonfiction, with a strong interest in women's issues and women's voices, international voices, class and race issues, and projects that simply teach me something new about the greater world and society around us. We have a good reputation for working closely and developmentally with our authors and love what we do." Actively seeking literary fiction, international and culturally diverse voices, narrative nonfiction, topical subjects (politics, current affairs), history, sports, architecture/design and pop culture. Does not want to receive romance, poetry, science fiction, pirates, vampire, young adult, or children's works.

HOW TO CONTACT Query with SASE. Submit author bio. Accepts simultaneous submissions. Responds in 6 weeks to queries. Responds in 10 weeks to mss. Obtains most new clients through recommendations from others, solicitations, conferences, ideas generated in-house.

TERMS Agent receives 15% commission on domestic sales. Agent receives 20% commission on foreign sales. Offers written contract, binding for 12 months; 45-day notice must be given to terminate contract.

RECENT SALES *How to Survive a Clown Attack*, by Chuck Sambuchino (Running Press); 101 Things I Learned in School series, by Matthew Frederick; all recent sales available on website.

WRITERS CONFERENCES San Francisco Writers' Conference, Muse and the Marketplace/Grub Street Conference, Washington Independent Writers' Conference, Murder in the Grove, Surrey International Writers' Conference.

TIPS "Be professional from the very first contact. There shouldn't be a single typo or grammatical flub in your query. Have a reason for contacting me about your project other than I was the next name listed on some website. Please do not use form query software! Believe me, we can get a dozen or so a day that look identical—we know when you are using a form. Show me that you know your audience—and your competition. Have the writing and/or proposal at the very, very best it can be before starting the querying process. Don't assume that if someone likes it enough they'll 'fix' it. The biggest mistake new writers make is starting the querying process before they—and the work—are ready. Take your time and do it right."

THE FIELDING AGENCY, LLC

269 S. Beverly Dr., No. 341, Beverly Hills CA 90212. (323)461-4791. **E-mail:** wlee@fieldingagency.com; query@fieldingagency.com. **Website:** www.fieldingagency.com. **Contact:** Whitney Lee.

Prior to her current position, Ms. Lee worked at other agencies in different capacities.

REPRESENTS nonfiction books, novels, short story collections, juvenile. **Considers these nonfiction areas:** animals, anthropology, archeology, architecture, art, autobiography, biography, business, child guidance, cooking, crafts, cultural interests, current affairs, decorating, diet/nutrition, design, economics, education, environment, ethnic, foods, gay/lesbian, government, health, history, hobbies, how-to, humor, investigative, juvenile nonfiction, language, law, literature, medicine, memoirs, military, money, parenting, popular culture, politics, psychology, satire, science, self-help, sociology, sports, technology, translation, true crime, war, women's issues, women's studies. **Considers these fiction areas:** action, adventure, cartoon, comic books, crime, detective, ethnic, family saga, fantasy, feminist, gay, glitz, historical, horror, humor, juvenile, lesbian, literary, mainstream, mystery, picture books, police, romance, satire, suspense, thriller, women's, young adult.

"We specialize in representing books published abroad and have strong relationships with foreign co-agents and publishers. For books we

NEW AGENT SPOTLIGHT

BETH PHELAN
(BENT LITERARY)

thebentagency.com

@beth_phelan

ABOUT BETH: "After graduating from New York University, I found my footing as an intern with the Levine Greenberg Literary Agency. Since then, I've held positions at Waxman Leavell Literary and Howard Morhaim Literary Agency. As a literary agent, my favorite stories are told with humor and sprinkled with surprises. I live in Brooklyn with a neurotic chihuahua."

SHE IS SEEKING: fiction for young adults and middle grade readers, select commercial and literary adult fiction, and nonfiction by way of lifestyle, cooking/food writing, humor, pop culture, LGBT and pets/animals. For adult fiction, she leans toward new adult, suspense, thriller, and mystery.

HOW TO QUERY: Review any online submissions guideline updates on the agency website, then e-mail phelanqueries@thebentagency.com.

represent in the U.S., we have to be head-over-heels passionate about it because we are involved every step of the way." Does not want to receive scripts for TV or film.

HOW TO CONTACT Query with SASE. Submit synopsis, author bio. Accepts queries by e-mail and snail mail. Accepts simultaneous submissions. Obtains most new clients through recommendations from others.

TERMS Agent receives 15% commission on domestic sales. Agent receives 20% commission on foreign sales. Offers written contract, binding for 9-12 months.

WRITERS CONFERENCES London Book Fair; Frankfurt Book Fair; Bologna Book Fair.

DIANA FINCH LITERARY AGENCY

116 W. 23rd St., Suite 500, New York NY 10011. (917)544-4470. **E-mail:** diana.finch@verizon.net. **Website:** dianafinchliteraryagency.blogspot.com. **Contact:** Diana Finch. Member of AAR. Represents 40 clients. 20% of clients are new/unpublished writers. Currently handles: nonfiction books 85%, novels 15%, juvenile books 5%, multimedia 5%.

Seeking to represent books that change lives. Prior to opening her agency in 2003, Ms. Finch worked at Ellen Levine Literary Agency for 18 years.

REPRESENTS nonfiction books, novels, scholarly. **Considers these nonfiction areas:** autobiography, biography, business, child guidance, computers, cultural interests, current affairs, dance, economics, environment, ethnic, film, government, health, history, how-to, humor, investigative, juvenile nonfiction, law, medicine, memoirs, military, money, music, parenting, photography, popular culture, politics, psychology, satire, science, self-help, sports, technology, theater, translation, true crime, war, women's issues, women's studies. **Considers these fiction areas:** action, adventure, crime, detective, ethnic, historical, literary, mainstream, police, thriller, young adult.

"Does not want romance, mysteries, or children's picture books."

HOW TO CONTACT This agency prefers submissions via its online form: dianafinchliteraryagency.submittable.com/submit. Accepts simultaneous submissions. Obtains most new clients through recommendations from others.

TERMS Agent receives 15% commission on domestic sales. Agent receives 20% commission on foreign sales. Offers written contract. "I charge for photocopying, overseas postage, galleys, and books purchased, and try to recoup these costs from earnings received for a client, rather than charging outright."

RECENT SALES *Heidegger's Glasses*, by Thaisa Frank; *Genetic Rounds*, by Robert Marion, MD (Kaplan); *Honeymoon in Tehran*, by Azadeh Moaveni (Random House); *Darwin Slept Here*, by Eric Simons (Overlook); *Black Tide*, by Antonia Juhasz (HarperCollins); *Stalin's Children*, by Owen Matthews (Bloomsbury); *Radiant Days*, by Michael Fitzgerald (Shoemaker & Hoard); *The Queen's Soprano*, by Carol Dines (Harcourt Young Adult); *What to Say to a Porcupine*, by Richard Gallagher (Amacom); *The Language of Trust*, by Michael Maslansky et al.

TIPS "Do as much research as you can on agents before you query. Have someone critique your query letter before you send it. It should be only 1 page and describe your book clearly—and why you are writing it—but also demonstrate creativity and a sense of your writing style."

FINEPRINT LITERARY MANAGEMENT

115 W. 29th, 3rd Floor, New York NY 10001. (212)279-1282. **E-mail:** stephany@fineprintlit.com. **Website:** www.fineprintlit.com. Member of AAR.

MEMBER AGENTS **Peter Rubie**, CEO (nonfiction interests include narrative nonfiction, popular science, spirituality, history, biography, pop culture, business, technology, parenting, health, self-help, music, and food; fiction interests include literate thrillers, crime fiction, science fiction and fantasy, military fiction and literary fiction, middle grade and YA fiction and nonfiction for boys); **Stephany Evans** (Nonfiction: health and wellness, especially women's health; spirituality, environment/sustainability, food and wine, memoir, and narrative nonfiction; Fiction: stories with a strong and interesting female protagonist, both literary and upmarket commercial/book club fiction, romance—all subgenres; mysteries); **Janet Reid** (Nonfiction: narrative nonfiction, history and biography; Fiction: thrillers); **Laura Wood** (Nonfiction: nonfiction books, business, dance, economics, history, humor, law,science, narrative nonfiction, popular science; Fiction: fantasy, science fiction, suspense); **June Clark** (see juneclark.com); **Rachel Coyne**, (young adult novels of all stripes [historical, fantasy, romance, contemporary, literary, humorous], as well as middle grade novels, especially with a humorous voice. She's also looking for adult historical, fantasy, urban fantasy and science fiction).

REPRESENTS **Considers these nonfiction areas:** biography, business, creative nonfiction, foods, health, history, humor, law, memoirs, music, parenting, popular culture, science, self-help, spirituality, technology. **Considers these fiction areas:** commercial, crime, fantasy, middle grade, military, mystery, romance, science fiction, suspense, thriller, women's, young adult.

HOW TO CONTACT Query with SASE. Submit synopsis and first 3-5 pages of ms embedded in an e-mail proposal for nonfiction. Do not send attachments or manuscripts without a request. See contact page online at website for e-mails. Obtains most new clients through recommendations from others, solicitations.

TERMS Agent receives 15% commission on domestic sales. Agent receives 20% commission on foreign sales.

JAMES FITZGERALD AGENCY

118 Waverly Place #1B, New York NY 10011. (212)308-1122. **E-mail:** submissions@jfitzagency.com. **Website:** www.jfitzagency.com. **Contact:** James Fitzgerald.

Prior to his current position, Mr. Fitzgerald was an editor at St. Martin's Press, Doubleday, and the *New York Times*.

MEMBER AGENTS James Fitzgerald; Christopher Rhodes.

James is a nonfiction generalist, meaning that he doesn't represent certain nonfiction categories as much as he simply connects with projects. Does not want to receive poetry or screenplays.

HOW TO CONTACT Query via e-mail or snail mail. This agency's online submission guidelines page explains all the elements they want to see when you submit a nonfiction book proposal.

RECENT SALES *Gimme Something Better: The Profound, Progressive, and Occasionally Pointless History of Punk in the Bay Area*, by Jack Boulware and Silke Tudor (Viking/Penguin); *Black Dogs: The Possibly True Story of Classic Rock's Greatest Robbery*, by Jason Buhrmester (Three Rivers/Crown); *Theo Gray's Mad Science: Experiments You Can Do at Home—But Probably Shouldn't* (Black Dog and Loenthal).

TIPS "Please submit all information in English, even if your manuscript is in Spanish."

FLANNERY LITERARY

1140 Wickfield Ct., Naperville IL 60563. (630)428-2682. **Fax:** (630)428-2683. **E-mail:** jennifer@flannery-literary.com. **Contact:** Jennifer Flannery. Represents 40 clients. 50% of clients are new/unpublished writers. Currently handles: juvenile books 100%.

REPRESENTS Considers these fiction areas: juvenile, middle grade, young adult.

This agency specializes in children's and young adult fiction and nonfiction. It also accepts picture books. 100% juvenile books.

HOW TO CONTACT Query by mail with SASE. "Multiple queries are fine, but please inform us. Mail that requires a signature will be returned to sender, as we are not always available to sign for mail." Responds in 2 weeks to queries; 1 month to mss. Obtains new clients through referrals and queries.

TERMS Agent receives 15% commission on domestic sales. Agent receives 20% commission on foreign sales. Offers written contract, binding for life of book in print; 1-month notice must be given to terminate contract.

TIPS "Write an engrossing, succinct query describing your work. We are always looking for a fresh new voice."

PETER FLEMING AGENCY

P.O. Box 458, Pacific Palisades CA 90272. (310)454-1373. **E-mail:** peterfleming@earthlink.net. **Contact:** Peter Fleming. Currently handles: nonfiction books 100%.

This agency specializes in nonfiction books that unearth innovative and uncomfortable truths with bestseller potential. "Greatly interested in journalists in the free press (the Internet)."

HOW TO CONTACT Query with SASE. Obtains most new clients through a different, one-of-a-kind idea for a book often backed by the writer's experience in that area of expertise.

TERMS Agent receives 15% commission on domestic sales. Agent receives 25% commission on foreign sales. Offers written contract, binding for 1 year. Charges clients only those fees agreed to in writing.

RECENT SALES *Stop Foreclosure*, by Lloyd Segol; *Rulers of Evil*, by F. Tupper Saussy (HarperCollins); *Why Is It Always About You—Saving Yourself from the Narcissists in Your Life*, by Sandy Hotchkiss (Free Press).

TIPS "You can begin by starting your own blog."

FLETCHER & COMPANY

78 Fifth Ave., 3rd Floor, New York NY 10011. (212)614-0778. **Fax:** (212)614-0728. **E-mail:** info@fletcherandco.com. **Website:** www.fletcherandco.com. **Contact:** Christy Fletcher. Estab. 2003. Member of AAR.

MEMBER AGENTS **Christy Fletcher**; **Melissa Chinchillo**; **Rebecca Gradinger** (literary fiction, up-market commercial fiction, narrative nonfiction, self-help, memoir, women's studies, humor, and pop culture); **Gráinne Fox** (literary fiction and quality commercial authors, award-winning journalists and food writers); **Lisa Grubka** (fiction—literary, upmarket women's, and young adult; and nonfiction—narrative, food, science, and more); **Donald Lamm** (nonfiction—history, biography, investigative journalism, politics, current affairs, and business); **Todd Sattersten** (business books); **Sylvie Greenberg** (literary fiction, humor, history, sports writing and anything California-related); **Rachel Crawford** (international fiction, smart novels with a sci-fi/fantasy bent, big ideas, and great science writing).

REPRESENTS nonfiction books, novels. **Considers these nonfiction areas:** biography, business, creative nonfiction, foods, history, humor, investigative, memoirs, popular culture, politics, science, self-help, sports, women's issues, women's studies. **Considers these fiction areas:** commercial, fantasy, literary, science fiction, women's, young adult.

HOW TO CONTACT To query, please send a letter, brief synopsis, and an SASE to our address, or you may also send queries to info@fletcherandco.com. Please do not include e-mail attachments with your initial query, as they will be deleted. Responds in 6 weeks to queries.

RECENT SALES *Happier at Home*, by Gretchen Rubin; *Astonish Me*, by Maggie Shipstead; *Elusion*, by Claudia Gabel & Cheryl Klam.

THE FOLEY LITERARY AGENCY

34 E. 38th St., New York NY 10016-2508. (212)686-6930. **Contact:** Joan Foley, Joseph Foley. Estab. 1956. Represents 10 clients. Currently handles: nonfiction books 75%, novels 25%.

REPRESENTS nonfiction books, novels. **Considers these nonfiction areas:** business services.

HOW TO CONTACT Query with letter, brief outline, SASE. Responds promptly to queries. Obtains most new clients through recommendations from others (rarely taking on new clients).

TERMS Agent receives 10% commission on domestic sales. Agent receives 15% commission on foreign sales.

FOLIO LITERARY MANAGEMENT, LLC

The Film Center Building, 630 Ninth Ave., Suite 1101, New York NY 10036. (212)400-1494. **Fax:** (212)967-0977. **Website:** www.foliolit.com. Member of AAR. Represents 100+ clients.

Prior to creating Folio Literary Management, Mr. Hoffman worked for several years at another agency; Mr. Kleinman was an agent at Graybill & English; Ms. Wheeler was an agent at Creative Media Agency.

MEMBER AGENTS Scott Hoffman; Jeff Kleinman; Paige Wheeler; Frank Weimann; Michelle Brower; Claudia Cross; Jita Fumich; Michael Harriot; Molly Jaffa; Erin Harris; Erin Niumata; Katherine Latshaw; Ruth Pomerance; Marcy Posner; Steve Troha; Emily van Beek; Melissa Sarver White; Maura Teitelbaum.

REPRESENTS nonfiction books, novels, short story collections. **Considers these nonfiction areas:** animals, art, biography, business, child guidance, cooking, creative nonfiction, economics, environment, foods, health, history, how-to, humor, inspirational, memoirs, military, parenting, popular culture, politics, psychology, religious, satire, science, self-help, technology, war, women's issues, women's studies. **Considers these fiction areas:** commercial, erotica, fantasy, horror, literary, middle grade, mystery, picture books, religious, romance, thriller, women's, young adult.

No poetry, stage plays, or screeplays.

HOW TO CONTACT Query via e-mail only (no attachments). Read agent bios online for specific submission guidelines and e-mail addresses. Responds in 1 month to queries.

TIPS "Please do not submit simultaneously to more than one agent at Folio. If you're not sure which of us is exactly right for your book, don't worry. We work closely as a team, and if one of our agents gets a query that might be more appropriate for someone else, we'll always pass it along. It's important that you check each agent's bio page for clear directions as to how to submit, as well as when to expect feedback."

FOREWORD LITERARY

E-mail: info@forewordliterary.com. **Website:** forewordliterary.com/. **Contact:** Laurie McLean.

MEMBER AGENTS **Laurie McLean** (referrals only); **Gordon Warnock**, querygordon@forewordliterary.com (nonfiction: memoir [adult, new adult, YA, graphic], cookbooks and food studies, political and current events, pop-science, pop-culture [also punk culture and geek culture], self-help, how-to, humor, pets, business and career; Fiction: high-concept commercial fiction, literary fiction, new adult, contemporary YA, graphic novels); **Pam van Hylckama Vlieg**, querypam@forewordliterary.com (young adult, middle grade, romance, genre fiction [urban fantasy, paranormal, and epic/high fantasy], pop culture nonfiction and adult picture books); **Connor Goldsmith**, queryconnor@forewordliterary.com (sci-fi, fantasy, horror, thrillers, upmarket commercial, literary, LGBT, many nonfiction categories); **Jen Karsbaek**, queryjen@forewordliterary.com (women's fiction, upmarket commercial fiction, historical fiction, and literary fiction); **Emily Keyes**, queryemily@forewordliterary.com (mostly YA and MG, but also commercial fiction which includes fantasy & science fiction, women's fiction, new adult fiction, along with pop culture and humor titles); **Sara Sciuto** (juvenile books, picture books).

REPRESENTS **Considers these nonfiction areas:** animals, film, gay/lesbian, history, how-to, humor, memoirs, music, popular culture, politics, science, theater. **Considers these fiction areas:** commercial, fantasy, gay, horror, lesbian, literary, mainstream, middle grade, mystery, new adult, paranormal, picture books, romance, science fiction, suspense, thriller, women's, young adult.

HOW TO CONTACT E-query. Each agent has a different query e-mail and style. Check their individual pages on the website for the latest updated info. Accepts simultaneous submissions.

RECENT SALES *Hollow World*, by Michael J. Sullivan; *Looking For Home: Hope Springs*, by Sarah M. Eden; *Free Agent*, by J.C. Nelson.

WRITERS CONFERENCES San Diego State University Writers' Conference, San Francisco Writers Conference, WNBA Pitch-O-Rama, LDS Storymakers Conference, SFWA Nebula Awards, Book Expo America, Ellen Hopkins' Ventana Sierra, Romance Writers of America Conference, Central Coast Writers Conference, World Fantasy Con, and many more. The agency website lists all.

FOUNDRY LITERARY + MEDIA

33 West 17th St., PH, New York NY 10011. (212)929-5064. **Fax:** (212)929-5471. **Website:** www.foundrymedia.com.

MEMBER AGENTS **Peter McGuigan**, pmsubmissions@foundrymedia.com; **Yfat Reiss Gendell**, yrgsubmissions@foundrymedia.com (practical nonfiction projects in the areas of health and wellness, diet, lifestyle, how-to, and parenting and a broad range of narrative nonfiction that includes humor, memoir, history, science, pop culture, psychology, and adventure/travel stories); **Stéphanie Abou**, sasubmissions@foundrymedia.com; **Mollie Glick**, mgsubmissions@foundrymedia.com (literary fiction, young adult fiction, narrative nonfiction, and a bit of practical nonfiction in the areas of popular science, medicine, psychology, cultural history, memoir and current events); **Stephen Barbara**, sbsubmissions@foundrymedia.com (books for young readers, and adult fiction and nonfiction); **David Patterson**, dpsubmissions@foundrymedia.com (narrative and idea-driven nonfiction, with an emphasis on journalists, public figures, and scholars); **Chris Park**, cpsubmissions@foundrymedia.com (memoirs, narrative nonfiction, sports books, Christian nonfiction and character-driven fiction); **Hannah Brown Gordon**, hbgsubmissions@foundrymedia.com (stories and narratives that blend genres, including thriller, suspense, historical, literary, speculative, memoir, pop-science, psychology, humor, and pop culture); **Brandi Bowles**, bbsubmissions@foundrymedia.com (literary and commercial fiction, especially high-concept novels that feature strong female bonds and psychological or scientific themes); **Kirsten Neuhaus**, knsubmissions@foundrymedia.com (platform-driven narrative nonfiction, in the areas of lifestyle [beauty/fashion/relationships], memoir, business, current events, history and stories with strong female voices, as well as smart, upmarket, and commercial fiction); **Jessica Regel**, jrsubmissions@foundrymedia.com (young adult and middle grade books, as well as a select list of adult general fiction, women's fiction, and adult nonfiction); **Anthony Mattero**, amsubmissions@foundrymedia.com (smart, platform-driven, nonfiction particularly in the genres of pop-culture, humor, music, sports, and pop-business).

REPRESENTS **Considers these nonfiction areas:** creative nonfiction, current affairs, diet/nutrition, health, history, how-to, humor, medicine, memoirs, music, parenting, popular culture, psychology, science, sports, travel. **Considers these fiction areas:** commercial, historical, humor, literary, middle grade, suspense, thriller, women's, young adult.

HOW TO CONTACT Target one agent only. Send queries to the specific submission e-mail of the agent. For fiction: send query, synopsis, author bio, first three chapters—all pasted in the e-mail. For nonfiction, send query, sample chapters, table of contents, author bio (all pasted).

RECENT SALES *Tell the Wolves I'm Home*, by Carol Rifka Blunt; *The Rathbones*, by Janice Clark; *This is Your Captain Speaking*, by Jon Methven; *The War Against the Assholes* and *The November Criminals*, by Sam Munson; *Ready Player One*, by Ernest Cline.

TIPS "Consult website for each agent's submission instructions."

FOX LITERARY

110 W. 40th St., Suite 410, New York NY 10018. **E-mail:** submissions@foxliterary.com. **Website:** www.publishersmarketplace.com/members/fox/.

REPRESENTS **Considers these nonfiction areas:** biography, creative nonfiction, history, memoirs, popular culture. **Considers these fiction areas:** fantasy, historical, literary, mainstream, romance, science fiction, thriller, young adult, graphic novels.

"I am actively seeking the following: young adult fiction (all genres), science fiction/fantasy, romance, historical fiction, thrillers, and graphic novels. I'm always interested in books that cross genres and reinvent popular concepts with an engaging new twist (especially when there's a historical and/or speculative element involved). On the nonfiction side I'm interested in memoirs, biography, and smart narrative nonfiction; I particularly enjoy memoirs and other nonfiction about sex work, addiction and recovery, and pop culture." Does not want to receive screenplays, poetry, category westerns, horror, Christian/inspirational, or children's picture books.

HOW TO CONTACT E-mail query and first 5 pages in body of e-mail. E-mail queries preferred. For snail mail queries, must include an e-mail address for response and no response means NO. Do not send SASE.

RECENT SALES *Black Ships* by Jo Graham (Orbit); Evernight series by Claudia Gray (HarperCollins); October Daye series by Seanan McGuire (DAW); *Salt and Silver* by Anna Katherine (Tor); *Alcestis* by Katharine Beutner (Soho Press); *Shadows Cast by Stars* by Catherine Knutsson (Atheneum); *Saving June* and *Speechless* by Hannah Harrington (Harlequin Teen); Spellcaster trilogy by Claudia Gray (HarperCollins).

LYNN C. FRANKLIN ASSOCIATES, LTD.

1350 Broadway, Suite 2015, New York NY 10018. (212)868-6311. **Fax:** (212)868-6312. **E-mail:** agency@fsainc.com. **E-mail:** agency@franklinandsiegal.com. **Contact:** Lynn Franklin, president; Claudia Nys, foreign rights. Other memberships include PEN America.

REPRESENTS nonfiction books, novels. **Considers these nonfiction areas:** biography, current affairs, memoirs, psychology, self-help, spirituality, alternative medicine.

"This agency specializes in general nonfiction with a special interest in self-help, biography/memoir, alternative health, and spirituality."

HOW TO CONTACT Query via e-mail to agency@franklinandsiegal.com. No unsolicited mss. No attachments. For nonfiction, query letter with short outline and synopsis. For fiction, query letter with short synopsis and a maximum of 10 sample pages (in the body of the e-mail). Please indicate "query adult" or "query children's" in the subject line. Accepts simultaneous submissions. Obtains most new clients through recommendations from others, solicitations.

TERMS Agent receives 15% commission on domestic sales. Agent receives 20% commission on foreign sales. Offers written contract.

RECENT SALES *The Wahls Protocol: How I Beat Progressive MS Using Paleo Principles And Functional Medicine* by Terry Wahls, M.D. (Avery/Penguin); *The Book Of Forgiving: The Four-Fold Path To Healing For Ourselves And Our World* by Archbishop Desmond Tutu and Reverend Mpho Tutu (US: HarperOne, UK: Collins); *The Customer Rules: 39 Essential Practices For Delivering Sensational Service* by Lee Cockerell (Crown Business/Random House); *My Name Is Jody Williams* by Jody Williams (University of California Press-Berkeley); *Everybody Matters: A Memoir* by Mary Robinson (US: Bloomsbury, UK and Ireland: Hodder).

JEANNE FREDERICKS LITERARY AGENCY, INC.

221 Benedict Hill Rd., New Canaan CT 06840. (203)972-3011. **Fax:** (203)972-3011. **E-mail:** jeanne.fredericks@gmail.com. **Website:** www.jeannefredericks.com. **Contact:** Jeanne Fredericks. Estab. 1997. Member of AAR. Other memberships include Authors Guild. Represents 90 clients. 10% of clients are new/unpublished writers. Currently handles: nonfiction books 100%.

Prior to opening her agency in 1997, Ms. Fredericks was an agent and acting director with the Susan P. Urstadt, Inc. Agency.

REPRESENTS nonfiction books. **Considers these nonfiction areas:** animals, autobiography, biography, child guidance, cooking, decorating, foods, gardening, health, history, how-to, interior design, medicine, parenting, photography, psychology, self-help, women's issues.

This agency specializes in quality adult nonfiction by authorities in their fields. We do **not** handle: fiction, true crime, juvenile, textbooks, poetry, essays, screenplays, short stories, science fiction, pop culture, guides to computers and software, politics, horror, pornography, books on overly depressing or violent topics, romance, teacher's manuals, or memoirs.

HOW TO CONTACT Query first with SASE, then send outline/proposal, 1-2 sample chapters, SASE, or by e-mail, if requested. See submission guidelines online first. Accepts simultaneous submissions. Responds in 3-5 weeks to queries. Responds in 2-4 months to mss. Obtains most new clients through recommendations from others, solicitations, conferences.

TERMS Agent receives 15% commission on domestic sales. Agent receives 25% commission on foreign sales with co-agent. Offers written contract, binding for 9 months; 2-month notice must be given to terminate contract. Charges client for photocopying of whole proposals and mss, overseas postage, priority mail, express mail services.

RECENT SALES *The Creativity Cure*, by Carrie Alton, M.D., and Alton Barron, M.D. (Scribner); *Lilias! Yoga*, by Lilias Folan (Skyhorse); *The Epidural Book*, by Rich Siegenfeld, M.D. (Johns Hopkins University Press); *A Place in the Sun*, by Stephen Snyder (Rizzoli); *Margaret Mitchell's Gone with the Wind*, by Ellen F. Brown and John Wiley, Jr. (Taylor); *World Class Marriage*, by Patty Howell and Ralph Jones (Rowman and Littlefield); *Teenage as a Second Language*, by Barbara Greenberg, Ph.D. and Jennifer Powell-Lunder, Psy.D.; *The Small Budget Gardener*, by Maureen Gilmer (Cool Springs Press); *Palm Beach Gardens and Terraces*, by Kathleen Quigley (Rizzoli); *Step Ahead of Autism*, by Anne Burnett (Sunrise River); *Electrified*, by Bob Shaw (Sterling); *The Green Market Baking Book* by Laura Martin (Sterling); *Tales of the Seven Seas*, by Dennis Powers (Taylor); *The Generosity Plan* by Kathy LeMay (Beyond Words/Atria); *Canadian Vegetable Gardening* by Doug Green (Cool Springs).

WRITERS CONFERENCES Connecticut Authors and Publishers Association-University Conference; ASJA Writers' Conference; BookExpo America; Garden Writers' Association Annual Symposium; Harvard Medical School CME Course in Publishing.

TIPS "Be sure to research competition for your work and be able to justify why there's a need for your book. I enjoy building an author's career, particularly if he/she is professional, hardworking, and courteous. Aside from 20 years of agenting experience, I've had 10 years of editorial experience in adult trade book publishing that enables me to help an author polish a proposal so that it's more appealing to prospective editors. My MBA in marketing also distinguishes me from other agents."

○ GRACE FREEDSON'S PUBLISHING NETWORK

375 N. Broadway, Suite 102, Jericho NY 11753. (516)931-7757. **Fax:** (516)931-7759. **E-mail:** gfreedson@worldnet.att.net. **Contact:** Grace Freedson. 17 Center Dr., Syosset NY 11791. Represents 100 clients. 10% of clients are new/unpublished writers. Currently handles: nonfiction books 90%, juvenile books 10%.

Prior to becoming an agent, Ms. Freedson was a managing editor and director of acquisitions for Barron's Educational Series.

REPRESENTS nonfiction books, juvenile. **Considers these nonfiction areas:** animals, business, cooking, crafts, current affairs, diet/nutrition, economics, education, environment, foods, health, history, hobbies, how-to, humor, medicine, money, popular culture, psychology, satire, science, self-help, sports, technology.

"In addition to representing many qualified authors, I work with publishers as a packager of unique projects—mostly series." Does not want to receive fiction.

HOW TO CONTACT Query with SASE. Submit synopsis, SASE. Responds in 2-6 weeks to queries. Obtains most new clients through recommendations from others.

TERMS Agent receives 15% commission on domestic sales. Offers written contract; 30-day notice must be given to terminate contract.

RECENT SALES Sold 50 titles in the last year. *The Dangers Lurking Beyond the Glass Ceiling*, by D. Sherr bourierg Carter (Prometheus); *Threats, Lies and Intimidation: Inside Debt Collection*, by Fred Williams (FT Press); *Plastic Planet*, by Kathryn Jones (FT Press).

WRITERS CONFERENCES BookExpo of America.

TIPS "At this point, I am only reviewing proposals on nonfiction topics by credentialed authors with platforms."

FRESH BOOKS LITERARY AGENCY

231 Diana St., Placerville CA 95667. **E-mail:** matt@fresh-books.com. **Website:** www.fresh-books.com. **Contact:** Matt Wagner. Represents 30+ clients. 5% of clients are new/unpublished writers. Currently handles: nonfiction books 95%, multimedia 5%.

Prior to becoming an agent, Mr. Wagner was with Waterside Productions for 15 years.

REPRESENTS nonfiction books. **Considers these nonfiction areas:** animals, anthropology, archeology, architecture, art, business, child guidance, computers, cooking, crafts, cultural interests, current affairs, dance, design, economics, education, environment, ethnic, gay/lesbian, government, health, history, hobbies, humor, law, medicine, military, money, music, parenting, photography, popular culture, politics, psychology, satire, science, sports, technology.

"I specialize in tech and how-to. I love working with books and authors, and I've repped many of my clients for upwards of 15 years now." Actively seeking popular science, natural history, adventure, how-to, business, education and reference. Does not want to receive fiction, children's books, screenplays, or poetry.

HOW TO CONTACT Plain text e-mail query (with no attachments) to matt@fresh-books.com. Accepts simultaneous submissions. Responds in 1-4 weeks to queries. Responds in 1-4 weeks to mss. Obtains most new clients through recommendations from others.

TERMS Agent receives 15% commission on domestic sales. Agent receives 20% commission on foreign sales.

RECENT SALES *The Myth of Multitasking: How Doing It All Gets Nothing Done* (Jossey-Bass); *Wilderness Survival for Dummies* (Wiley); and *The Zombie Combat Manual* (Berkley).

TIPS "Do your research. Find out what sorts of books and authors an agent represents. Go to conferences. Make friends with other writers—most of my clients come from referrals."

SARAH JANE FREYMANN LITERARY AGENCY

59 W. 71st St., Suite 9B, New York NY 10023. (212)362-9277. **E-mail:** sarah@sarahjanefreymann.com; Submissions@SarahJaneFreymann.com. **Website:** www.sarahjanefreymann.com. **Contact:** Sarah Jane Freymann, Steve Schwartz. Represents 100 clients. 20% of clients are new/unpublished writers. Currently handles: nonfiction books 75%, novels 23%, juvenile books 2%.

MEMBER AGENTS **Sarah Jane Freymann** (nonfiction books, novels, illustrated books); **Jessica Sinsheimer,** Jessica@sarahjanefreymann.com (young adult fiction, literary fiction); **Steven Schwartz**, steve@sarahjanefreymann.com; **Katharine Sands**.

REPRESENTS **Considers these nonfiction areas:** animals, anthropology, architecture, art, autobiography, biography, business, child guidance, cooking, current affairs, decorating, diet/nutrition, design, economics, ethnic, foods, health, history, interior design, medicine, memoirs, parenting, psychology, self-help, women's issues, women's studies, lifestyle. **Considers these fiction areas:** ethnic, literary, mainstream, young adult.

HOW TO CONTACT Query with SASE. Responds in 2 weeks to queries. Responds in 6 weeks to mss. Obtains most new clients through recommendations from others.

TERMS Agent receives 15% commission on domestic sales. Agent receives 20% commission on foreign sales. Offers written contract. Charges clients for long distance, overseas postage, photocopying. 100% of business is derived from commissions on ms sales.

RECENT SALES *How to Make Love to a Plastic Cup: And Other Things I Learned While Trying to Knock Up My Wife*, by Greg Wolfe (Harper Collins); *I Want to Be Left Behind: Rapture Here on Earth*, by Brenda Peterson (a Merloyd Lawrence Book); *That Bird Has My Name: The Autobiography of an Innocent Man on Death Row*, by Jarvis Jay Masters with an introduction by Pema Chodrun (HarperOne); *Perfect One-Dish Meals*, by Pam Anderson (Houghton Mifflin); *Birdology*, by Sy Montgomery (Simon & Schuster); *Emptying the Nest: Launching Your Reluctant Young Adult*, by Dr. Brad Sachs (Macmillan); *Tossed & Found*, by Linda and John Meyers (Steward, Tabori & Chang); *32 Candles*, by Ernessa Carter; *God and Dog*, by Wendy Francisco.

TIPS "I love fresh, new, passionate works by authors who love what they are doing and have both natural talent and carefully honed skill."

FREDRICA S. FRIEDMAN AND CO., INC.

136 E. 57th St., 14th Floor, New York NY 10022. (212)829-9600. **Fax:** (212)829-9669. **E-mail:** info@fredricafriedman.com; submissions@fredricafriedman.com. **Website:** www.fredricafriedman.com. **Contact:** Ms. Chandler Smith.

Prior to establishing her own literary management firm, Ms. Friedman was the Editorial Director, Associate Publisher and Vice President of Little, Brown & Co., a division of Time Warner, and the first woman to hold those positions.

REPRESENTS nonfiction books, novels, anthologies. **Considers these nonfiction areas:** art, biography, business, child, cooking, current affairs, education, ethnic, gay, government, health, history, how to, humor, language, memoirs, money, music, photography, popular culture, psychology, self-help, sociology, film, true crime, women's, interior design/decorating. **Considers these fiction areas:** literary.

"We represent a select group of outstanding nonfiction and fiction writers. We are partic-

NEW AGENT SPOTLIGHT

JESSICA NEGRON
(TALCOTT NOTCH LITERARY)

talcottnotch.net

ABOUT JESSICA: She attended University of New Haven. For five years she interned with various local publications in both an editorial and design capacity until finally she found a place with Talcott Notch.

SHE IS SEEKING: all kinds of young adult and adult fiction, but leans toward science fiction and fantasy (and all the little subgenres), romance (the steamier, the better), and thrillers.

HOW TO QUERY: jnegron@talcottnotch.net. Paste the first 10 pages of your manuscript in the e-mail after your query. Address your query to Jessica.

ularly interested in helping writers expand their readership and develop their careers." Does not want poetry, plays, screenplays, children's books, sci-fi/fantasy, or horror.

HOW TO CONTACT Submit e-query, synopsis; be concise, and include any pertinent author information, including relevant writing history. If you are a fiction writer, we also request a one-page sample from your manuscript to provide its voice. We ask that you keep all material in the body of the e-mail. Accepts simultaneous submissions. Responds in 4-6 weeks to queries. Responds in 4-6 weeks to mss. Obtains most new clients through recommendations from others.

TERMS Agent receives 15% commission on domestic sales. Agent receives 25% commission on foreign sales. Offers written contract. Charges for photocopying and messenger/shipping fees for proposals.

RECENT SALES *A World of Lies: The Crime and Consequences of Bernie Madoff*, by Diana B. Henriques (Times Books/Holt); *Polemic and Memoir: The Nixon Years* by Patrick J. Buchanan (St. Martin's Press); *Angry Fat Girls: Five Women, Five Hundred Pounds, and a Year of Losing It . . . Again*, by Frances Kuffel (Berkley/Penguin); *Life with My Sister Madonna*, by Christopher Ciccone with Wendy Leigh (Simon & Schuster Spotlight); *The World Is Curved: Hidden Dangers to the Global Economy*, by David Smick (Portfolio/Penguin); *Going to See the Elephant*, by Rodes Fishburne (Delacorte/Random House); *Seducing the Boys Club: Uncensored Tactics from a Woman at the Top*, by Nina DiSesa (Ballantine/Random House); *The Girl from Foreign: A Search for Shipwrecked Ancestors, Forgotten Histories, and a Sense of Home*, by Sadia Shepard (Penguin Press).

TIPS "Spell the agent's name correctly on your query letter."

THE FRIEDRICH AGENCY

19 W. 21st St., Suite 201, New York NY 10010. **E-mail:** mfriedrich@friedrichagency.com; lcarson@friedrichagency.com; nichole@friedrichagency.com; mmoretti@friedrichagency.com. **Website:** www.friedrichagency.com. **Contact:** Molly Friedrich; Lucy Carson. Member of AAR. Signatory of WGA. Represents 50+ clients.

Prior to her current position, Ms. Friedrich was an agent at the Aaron Priest Literary Agency.

MEMBER AGENTS **Molly Friedrich**, founder and agent (open to queries); **Lucy Carson**, foreign rights director and agent (open to queries); **Maggie Riggs** (new as of 2014); **Nichole LeFebvre** (foreign rights manager).

REPRESENTS full-length fiction and nonfiction. **Considers these nonfiction areas:** creative nonfiction, memoirs. **Considers these fiction areas:** commercial, literary.

HOW TO CONTACT Query by e-mail (strongly preferred), or by mail with SASE. See guidelines on website. Please query only one agent at this agency.

RECENT SALES *W is For Wasted*, by Sue Grafton; *Don't Go*, by Lisa Scottoline; *Olive Kitteridge*, by Elizabeth Strout. Other clients include Frank McCourt, Jane Smiley, Esmeralda Santiago, Terry McMillan, Cathy Schine, Ruth Ozeki, Karen Joy Fowler and more.

REBECCA FRIEDMAN LITERARY AGENCY

E-mail: Abby@rfliterary.com. **Website:** www.rfliterary.com/. Estab. 2013.

Prior to opening her own agency in 2013, Ms. Friedman was with Sterling Lord Literistic from 2006 to 2011, then with Frederick Hill Bonnie Nadell.

REPRESENTS Considers these nonfiction areas: memoirs. **Considers these fiction areas:** commercial, literary, romance, suspense, women's, young adult.

The agency is interested in commercial and literary fiction with a focus on literary novels of suspense, women's fiction, contemporary romance, and young adult, as well as journalistic nonfiction and memoir. Most of all, we are looking for great stories told in strong voices.

HOW TO CONTACT Please submit your query letter and first chapter (no more than fifteen pages, double-spaced) to Abby@rfliterary.com.

RECENT SALES *So Much Pretty*, by Cara Hoffman; *The Black Nile*, by Dan Morrison; *Maybe One Day*, by Melissa Kantor; *Devoured*, by Emily Snow. A complete list of agency authors is available online.

FULL CIRCLE LITERARY, LLC

7676 Hazard Center Dr., Suite 500, San Diego CA 92108. **E-mail:** submissions@fullcircleliterary.com. **Website:** www.fullcircleliterary.com. **Contact:** Lilly Ghahremani, Stefanie Von Borstel. Represents 55 clients. 60% of clients are new/unpublished writers. Currently handles: nonfiction books 70%, novels 10%, juvenile books 20%.

Before forming Full Circle, Ms. Von Borstel worked in both marketing and editorial capacities at Penguin and Harcourt; Ms. Ghahremani received her law degree from UCLA, and has experience in representing authors on legal affairs.

MEMBER AGENTS Lilly Ghahremani; Stefanie Von Borstel; Adriana Dominguez; Taylor Martindale (multicultural voices).

REPRESENTS nonfiction books, juvenile. **Considers these nonfiction areas:** creative nonfiction, design, how-to, popular culture, women's issues. **Considers these fiction areas:** literary, middle grade, picture books, women's, young adult.

"Our full-service boutique agency, representing a range of nonfiction and children's books (limited fiction), provides a one-stop resource for authors. Our extensive experience in the realms of law and marketing provide Full Circle clients with a unique edge." "Actively seeking nonfiction by authors with a unique and strong platform, projects that offer new and diverse viewpoints, and literature with a global or multicultural perspective. We are particularly interested in books with a Latino or Middle Eastern angle and books related to pop culture." Does not want to receive "screenplays, poetry, commercial fiction or genre fiction (horror, thriller, mystery, Western, sci-fi, fantasy, romance, historical fiction)."

HOW TO CONTACT Agency accepts e-queries. Put "Query for [Agent]" in the subject line. Send a 1-page query letter (in the body of the e-mail) including a description of your book, writing credentials and author highlights. Following your query, please include the first 10 pages or complete picture book manuscript text within the body of the e-mail. For nonfiction, include a proposal with one sample chapter. Accepts simultaneous submissions. Obtains most new clients through recommendations from others, solicitations, conferences.

TERMS Agent receives 15% commission on domestic sales. Agent receives 20% commission on foreign sales. Offers written contract; up to 30-day notice must be given to terminate contract. Charges for copying and postage.

TIPS "Put your best foot forward. Contact us when you simply can't make your project any better on your own, and please be sure your work fits with what the agent you're approaching represents. Little things count, so copyedit your work. Join a writing group and attend conferences to get objective and constructive feedback before submitting. Be active about building your platform as an author before, during, and after publication. Remember this is a business and your agent is a business partner."

THE G AGENCY, LLC

P.O. Box 374, Bronx NY 10471. (718)664-4505. **E-mail:** gagencyquery@gmail.com. **Website:** www.publishersmarketplace.com/members/jeffg/. **Contact:** Jeff Gerecke. Estab. 2012.

MEMBER AGENTS Jeff Gerecke.

REPRESENTS Considers these nonfiction areas: biography, business, computers, history, military, money, popular culture, technology. **Considers these fiction areas:** mainstream, mystery.

"I am interested in commercial and literary fiction, as well as serious nonfiction and pop culture. My focus as an agent has always been on working with writers to shape their work for its greatest commercial potential. I provide lots of editorial advice in sharpening manuscripts and proposals before submission." Does not want screenplays, sci-fi/fantasy or romance.

HOW TO CONTACT E-mail submissions preferred—attach sample chapters or proposal if you wish. Send to gagencyquery@gmail.com. Enter "QUERY" along with the title in the subject line of e-mail or on the envelope of snail mail.

RECENT SALES *Killing The Cranes,* by Edward Girardet (Chelsea Green); *Islam Without Extremes,* by Mustafa Akyol (Norton); *The Race to the New World,* by Douglas Hunter (Palgrave); *Intelligence and US Foreign Policy,* by Paul Pillar (Columbia UP); *Transforming Darkness to Light,* by Travis Vining (Bella Rosa); *Faith Misplaced: The Broken Promise of US-Arab Relations,* by Ussama Makdisi (Public Affairs); *Drinking Arak Off An Ayatollah's Beard,* by Nick Jubber (DaCapo); *The Rule of Empires,* by Tim Parsons (Oxford).

TIPS "I've been a member of the Royalty Committee of the Association of Authors Representatives since its founding and am always keen to challenge publishers for their willfully obscure royalty reporting. Also I have recently taken over the position of Treasurer of the A.A.R. My publishing background includes working at the University of California Press so I am always intrigued by academic subjects which are given a commercial spin to reach an audience outside academia. I've also worked as a foreign scout for publishers like Hodder & Stoughton in England and Wilhelm Heyne in Germany, which gives me a good sense of how American books can be successfully translated overseas."

NANCY GALLT LITERARY AGENCY

273 Charlton Ave., South Orange NJ 07079. (973)761-6358. **Fax:** (973)761-6318. **E-mail:** submissions@nancygallt.com. **Website:** www.nancygallt.com. **Contact:** Nancy Gallt, Marietta Zacker. Represents 40 clients. 30% of clients are new/unpublished writers. Currently handles: juvenile books 100%.

Prior to opening her agency, Ms. Gallt was subsidiary rights director of the children's book division at Morrow, Harper and Viking.

MEMBER AGENTS Nancy Gallt; Marietta Zacker.

REPRESENTS juvenile. **Considers these fiction areas:** juvenile, middle grade, picture books, young adult.

"We only handle children's books." Actively seeking picture books, middle grade, and young adult novels. Does not want to receive rhyming picture book texts.

HOW TO CONTACT Submit through online submission form on agency website. Accepts simultaneous submissions. Obtains most new clients through recommendations from others, solicitations.

TERMS Agent receives 15% commission on domestic sales. Agent receives 20% commission on foreign sales. Offers written contract; 30-day notice must be given to terminate contract.

RECENT SALES Rick Riordan's books (Hyperion); *Something Extraordinary* by Ben Clanton (Simon & Schuster); *The Baby Tree* by Sophie Blackall (Nancy Paulsen Books/Penguin); *Fenway And Hattie* by Victoria J Coe (Putnam/Penguin); *The Meaning Of Maggie* by Megan Jean Sovern (Chronicle); *The Misadventures Of The Family Fletcher* By Dana Alison Levy (Random House); *Abrakapow!* by Isaiah Campbell (Simon & Schuster); *Subway Love* by Nora Raleigh Baskin (Candlewick).

TIPS "Writing and illustrations stand on their own, so submissions should tell the most compelling stories possible--whether visually, in words, or both."

THE GARAMOND AGENCY, INC.

1840 Columbia Rd. NW, #503, Washington DC 20009. **E-mail:** query@garamondagency.com. **Website:** www.garamondagency.com. Other memberships include Author's Guild.

MEMBER AGENTS Lisa Adams; David Miller.

REPRESENTS nonfiction books. **Considers these nonfiction areas:** business, current affairs, economics, history, law, politics, psychology, science, technology, social science, narrative nonfiction.

"We work closely with our authors through each stage of the publishing process, first in developing their books and then in presenting themselves and their ideas effectively to publishers and to readers. We represent our clients throughout the world in all languages, media, and territories through an extensive network of subagents." No proposals for children's or young adult books, fiction, poetry, or memoir.

HOW TO CONTACT Queries sent by e-mail may not make it through the spam filters on our server. Please e-mail a brief query letter only, we do not read unsolicited manuscripts submitted by e-mail under any circumstances. See website.

RECENT SALES *Big Data*, by Viktor Mayer-Schoenberger and Kenneth Cukier (Houghton Mifflin Harcourt); *Nature's Fortune*, by Mark R. Tercek and Jonathan S. Adams (Basic Books); *The Depths* by Jonathan Rottenberg (Basic Books); *Outsiders* by William Thorndike (Harvard Business Press); *Personal Intelligence* by John D. Mayer, (Scientific American/Farrar, Straus & Giroux). See website for other clients.

TIPS "Query us first if you have any questions about whether we are the right agency for your work."

MAX GARTENBERG LITERARY AGENCY

912 N. Pennsylvania Ave., Yardley PA 19067. (215)295-9230. **Website:** www.maxgartenberg.com. **Contact:** Anne Devlin (fiction and nonfiction). Estab. 1954. Represents 100 clients. 20% of clients are new/unpublished writers. Currently handles: nonfiction books 80%, novels 20%.

MEMBER AGENTS **Anne G. Devlin** (current events, politics, true crime, women's issues, sports, parenting, biography, environment, narrative nonfiction, health, lifestyle, literary fiction, romance, and celebrity); **Dirk Devlin** (thrillers, science fiction, mysteries, and humor).

REPRESENTS nonfiction books, novels. **Considers these nonfiction areas:** agriculture horticulture, animals, art, biography, child, current affairs, health, history, money, music, nature, psychology, science, self-help, sports, film, true crime, women's.

HOW TO CONTACT Writers desirous of having their work handled by this agency may query by e-mail to agdevlin@aol.com. Accepts simultaneous submissions. Responds in 2 weeks to queries. Responds in 6 weeks to mss. Obtains most new clients through recommendations from others, following up on good query letters.

TERMS Agent receives 15% commission on domestic sales. Agent receives 20% commission on foreign sales.

RECENT SALES *Blazing Ice: Pioneering the 21st Century's Road to the South Pole*, by John H. Wright; *Beethoven for Kids: His Life and Music*, by Helen Bauer; *Slaughter on North LaSalle*, by Robert L. Snow; *What Patients Taught Me*, by Audrey Young, MD (Sasquatch Books); *Unorthodox Warfare: The Chinese Experience*, by Ralph D. Sawyer (Westview Press); *Encyclopedia of Earthquakes and Volcanoes*, by Alexander E. Gates (Facts on File); *Homebirth in the Hospital*, by Stacey Kerr, M.D. (Sentient Publications).

TIPS "We have recently expanded to allow more access for new writers."

GELFMAN SCHNEIDER / ICM PARTNERS

850 7th Ave., Suite 903, New York NY 10019. (212)245-1993. **Fax:** (212)245-8678. **E-mail:** mail@gelfmanschneider.com. **Website:** www.gelfmanschneider.com. **Contact:** Jane Gelfman, Deborah Schneider. Member of AAR. Represents 300+ clients. 10% of clients are new/unpublished writers.

MEMBER AGENTS Jane Gelfman, Victoria Marini, Heather Mitchell.

REPRESENTS fiction and nonfiction books. **Considers these nonfiction areas:** creative nonfiction, popular culture. **Considers these fiction areas:** historical, literary, mainstream, middle grade, mystery, suspense, women's, young adult.

Does not want to receive romance, science fiction, westerns, or illustrated children's books.

HOW TO CONTACT Query. Send queries via snail mail only. No unsolicited mss. Please send a query letter, a synopsis, and a SAMPLE CHAPTER ONLY. Consult website for each agent's submission requirements. Responds in 1 month to queries. Responds in 2 months to mss.

TERMS Agent receives 15% commission on domestic sales. Agent receives 20% commission on foreign sales. Agent receives 15% commission on film sales. Offers written contract. Charges clients for photocopying and messengers/couriers.

GEORGES BORCHARDT, INC.

136 E. 57th St., New York NY 10022. (212)753-5785. **Website:** www.gbagency.com. Estab. 1967. Member of AAR. Represents 200+ clients.

MEMBER AGENTS Anne Borchardt; Georges Borchardt; Valerie Borchardt; Samantha Shea.

This agency specializes in literary fiction and outstanding nonfiction.

HOW TO CONTACT *No unsolicited mss.* Obtains most new clients through recommendations from others.

TERMS Agent receives 15% commission on domestic sales. Agent receives 20% commission on foreign sales. Offers written contract.

RECENT SALES John Ashbery's *Selected Translations* (FSG); Evelyn Barish's *The Double Life of Paul de Man* (Norton); Louis Begley's *Memories of a Marriage* (Nan A. Talese); W. Michael Blumenthal's *From Exile to Leadership* (Overlook).

THE GERNERT COMPANY

136 East 57th St., 18th Floor, New York NY 10022. (212)838-7777. **Fax:** (212)838-6020. **E-mail:** info@thegernertco.com. **Website:** www.thegernertco.com. **Contact:** Sarah Burnes.

Prior to her current position, Ms. Burnes was with Burnes & Clegg, Inc.

MEMBER AGENTS **Sarah Burnes** (commercial fiction, adventure and true story); **Stephanie Cabot** (literary fiction, commercial fiction, historical fiction); **Chris Parris-Lamb**; **Seth Fishman** (accepts graphic novels); **Logan Garrison**; **Will Roberts**; **Erika Storella; Anna Worrall; Andy Kifer; Ellen Goodson**. At this time, Courtney Gatewood and Rebecca Gardner are closed to queries. See the website to find out the tastes of each agent.

REPRESENTS nonfiction books, novels. **Considers these nonfiction areas:** art, crafts, creative nonfiction, foods, history, memoirs, politics, sociology, travel. **Considers these fiction areas:** fantasy, historical, literary, middle grade, science fiction, thriller, women's, young adult.

HOW TO CONTACT Queries should be addressed to a specific agent via the e-mail subject line. Please send a query letter, either by mail or e-mail, describing the work you'd like to submit, along with some information about yourself and a sample chapter if appropriate. Please do not send e-mails to individual agents; use info@thegernertco.com and indicate which agent you're querying. See company website for more instructions. Obtains most new clients through recommendations from others, solicitations.

RECENT SALES *Sycamore Row* by John Grisham; *The Night Guest* by Fiona McFarlane; *Someone* by Alice Mcdermott; *Ancillary Justice* by Ann Leckie; *Beatles Vs Stones* by John Mcmillian; *Bargain Fever* by Mark Ellwood.

GLOBAL LION INTELLECTUAL PROPERTY MANAGEMENT, INC.

PO BOX 669238, Pompano Beach FL 33066. **E-mail:** assistantpma@gmail.com. **Website:** www.globallionmanagement.com. **Contact:** Peter Miller. Represents more than 100 clients. 50% of clients are new/unpublished writers.

In his time in the literary world, Mr. Miller has successfully managed more than 1,000 books and dozens of motion picture and television properties. He is the author of *Author! Screenwriter!*

MEMBER AGENTS Peter Miller (big nonfiction, business, true crime, religion).

REPRESENTS nonfiction books, novels, juvenile, movie, tv, tv movie. **Considers these nonfiction areas:** autobiography, biography, business, child guidance, cooking, cultural interests, current affairs, diet/nutrition, economics, ethnic, foods, humor, inspirational, investigative, memoirs, money, parenting, popular culture, religious, satire, self-help, sports, true crime. **Considers these fiction areas:** action, adventure, crime, detective, erotica, ethnic, experimental, gay, historical, humor, inspirational, juvenile, lesbian, literary, mainstream, mystery, police, psychic, religious, romance, satire, supernatural, suspense, thriller, women's, young adult. **Considers these script areas:** action/adventure, comedy, mainstream, romantic comedy, romantic drama, thriller.

Does not want to receive poetry, stage plays, picture books and clichés.

HOW TO CONTACT E-query. Include a 1-page synopsis, about 20 pages of your work (pasted), an author bio, and any social media links of value. Accepts simultaneous submissions. Obtains most new clients through recommendations from others, solicitations, conferences.

TERMS Agent receives 15% commission on domestic sales. Agent receives 25% commission on foreign sales. Offers written contract; 30-day notice must be given to terminate contract. This agency charges for approved expenses, such as photocopies and overnight delivery.

RECENT SALES *For the Sake of Liberty*, by M. William Phelps (Thomas Dunne Books); *The Haunting of Cambria*, by Richard Taylor (Tor); *Cover Girl Confidential*, by Beverly Bartlett (5 Spot); *Ten Prayers God Always Says Yes To!*, by Anthony DeStefano (Doubleday); *Miss Fido Manners: The Complete Book of Dog Etiquette*, by Charlotte Reed (Adams Media); film rights to *Murder in the Heartland*, by M. William Phelps (Mathis Entertainment); film rights to *The Killer's Game*, by Jay Bonansinga (Andrew Lazar/Mad Chance, Inc.).

TIPS "Don't approach agents before your work is ready, and always approach them as professionally as possible. Don't give up."

BARRY GOLDBLATT LITERARY LLC

320 Seventh Ave. #266, Brooklyn NY 11215. (718)832-8787. **E-mail:** query@bgliterary.com. **Website:** www.bgliterary.com/. **Contact:** Barry Goldblatt. Estab. 2000.

MEMBER AGENTS Barry Goldblatt.

REPRESENTS **Considers these fiction areas:** middle grade, young adult.

"Please see our website for specific submission guidelines and information on our particular tastes."

HOW TO CONTACT Obtains clients through referrals, queries, and conferences.

TERMS Agent receives 15% commission on domestic sales; 20% on foreign and dramatic sales. Offers written contract. 60 days notice must be given to terminate contract.

RECENT SALES *Read Between the Lines*, by Jo Knowles; *Bright Before Sunrise*, by Tiffany Schmidt; *The Infamous Ratsos*, by Kara LaReau; *Wonders of the Invisible World*, by Christopher Barzak.

TIPS "We're a hands-on agency, focused on building an author's career, not just making an initial sale. We don't care about trends or what's hot; we just want to sign great writers."

FRANCES GOLDIN LITERARY AGENCY, INC.

57 E. 11th St., Suite 5B, New York NY 10003. (212)777-0047. **Fax:** (212)228-1660. **E-mail:** agency@goldinlit.com. **Website:** www.goldinlit.com. Estab. 1977. Member of AAR. Represents over 100 clients.

MEMBER AGENTS **Frances Goldin**, principal/agent; **Ellen Geiger**, agent (commercial and literary fiction and nonfiction, cutting-edge topics of all kinds); **Matt McGowan**, agent/rights director (innovative works of fiction and nonfiction); **Sam Stoloff**, agent (literary fiction, memoir, history, accessible sociology and philosophy, cultural studies, serious journalism, narrative and topical nonfiction with a progressive orientation); **Sarah Bridgins**, agent/office manager, sb@goldinlit.com (voice-driven fiction and narrative nonfiction).

REPRESENTS nonfiction books, novels. **Considers these nonfiction areas:** creative nonfiction, cultural interests, investigative, memoirs, philosophy, sociology. **Considers these fiction areas:** literary, mainstream.

"We are hands on and we work intensively with clients on proposal and manuscript development." Does not want anything that is racist, sexist, agist, homophobic, or pornographic. No screenplays, children's books, art books, cookbooks, business books, diet books, romance, self-help, or genre fiction.

HOW TO CONTACT Query by letter or e-mail. No unsolicited mss or work previously submitted to publishers. Prefers hard-copy queries. If querying by e-mail, put word "query" in subject line. For queries to Sam Stoloff or Ellen Geiger, please use online submission form. Responds in 4-6 weeks to queries.

THE SUSAN GOLOMB LITERARY AGENCY

540 President St., 3rd Floor, Brooklyn NY 11215. **Fax:** (212)239-9503. **E-mail:** susan@sgolombagency.com; krista@sgolombagency.com. **Contact:** Susan Golomb; Krista Ingebretson. Currently handles: nonfiction books 50%, novels 40%, story collections 10%.

MEMBER AGENTS Susan Golomb (accepts queries); Krista Ingebretson (accepts queries).

REPRESENTS nonfiction, novels, short story collections. **Considers these nonfiction areas:** animals, anthropology, biography, business, current affairs, economics, environment, health, history, law, memoirs, military, money, popular culture, politics, psychology, science, sociology, technology, women's issues, women's studies. **Considers these fiction areas:** ethnic, historical, humor, literary, mainstream, satire, thriller, women's, young adult, chick lit.

"We specialize in literary and upmarket fiction and nonfiction that is original, vibrant and of excellent quality and craft. Nonfiction should be edifying, paradigm-shifting, fresh and entertaining." Actively seeking writers with strong voices. Does not want to receive genre fiction.

HOW TO CONTACT Query via mail with SASE or by e-mail. Will respond if interested. Submit outline/proposal, synopsis, 1 sample chapter, author bio. Obtains most new clients through recommendations from others, solicitations, and unsolicited queries.

TERMS Offers written contract.

RECENT SALES *The Kraus Project*, by Jonathan Franzen (FSG); *The Word Exchange*, by Alena Graedon (Doubleday); *The Flamethrowers*, by Rachel Kushner (Scribner); *The Book of Jonah*, by Joshua Feldman (Holt); *Last Stories* and *Other Stories* and *The Dying Grass*, by William T. Vollmann (Viking).

GOODMAN ASSOCIATES

500 West End Ave., New York NY 10024. (212)873-4806. **Contact:** Arnold P. Goodman. Member of AAR.

Accepting new clients by recommendation only.

IRENE GOODMAN LITERARY AGENCY

27 W. 24th St., Suite 700B, New York NY 10010. **E-mail:** irene.queries@irenegoodman.com. **Website:** www.irenegoodman.com. **Contact:** Irene Goodman, Miriam Kriss. Member of AAR.

MEMBER AGENTS Irene Goodman; Beth Vesel; Miriam Kriss; Barbara Poelle; Rachel Ekstrom.

REPRESENTS nonfiction, novels. **Considers these nonfiction areas:** narrative nonfiction dealing with social, cultural and historical issues; an occasional memoir and current affairs book, parenting, social issues, francophilia, anglophilia, Judaica, lifestyles, cooking, memoir. **Considers these fiction areas:** crime, detective, historical, mystery, romance, thriller, women's, young adult.

"Specializes in the finest in commercial fiction and nonfiction. We have a strong background in women's voices, including mysteries, romance, women's fiction, thrillers, suspense. Historical fiction is one of Irene's particular passions and Miriam is fanatical about modern urban fantasies. In nonfiction, Irene is looking for topics on narrative history, social issues and trends, education, Judaica, Francophilia, Anglophilia, other cultures, animals, food, crafts, and memoir." Barbara is looking for commercial thrillers with strong female protagonists; Miriam is looking for urban fantasy and edgy sci-fi/young adult. No children's picture books, screenplays, poetry, or inspirational fiction.

HOW TO CONTACT Query. Submit synopsis, first 10 pages. E-mail queries only! See the website submission page. No e-mail attachments. Responds in 2 months to queries. Consult website for each agent's submission guidelines.

RECENT SALES *The Ark*, by Boyd Morrison; *Isolation*, by C.J. Lyons; *The Sleepwalkers*, by Paul Grossman; *Dead Man's Moon*, by Devon Monk; *Becoming Marie Antoinette*, by Juliet Grey; *What's Up Down There*, by Lissa Rankin; *Beg for Mercy*, by Toni Andrews; *The Devil Inside*, by Jenna Black.

TIPS "We are receiving an unprecedented amount of e-mail queries. If you find that the mailbox is full, please try again in two weeks. E-mail queries to our personal addresses will not be answered. E-mails to our personal inboxes will be deleted."

GOUMEN & SMIRNOVA LITERARY AGENCY

Nauki pr., 19/2 fl. 293, St. Petersburg 195220 Russia. **E-mail:** info@gs-agency.com. **Website:** www.gs-agency.com. **Contact:** Julia Goumen, Natalia Smirnova. Represents 20 clients. 10% of clients are new/unpublished writers. Currently handles: nonfiction books 10%, novels 80%, story collections 5%, juvenile books 5%.

Prior to becoming agents, both Ms. Goumen and Ms. Smirnova worked as foreign rights managers with an established Russian publisher selling translation rights for literary fiction.

MEMBER AGENTS **Julia Goumen** (translation rights, Russian language rights, film rights); **Natalia Smirnova** (translation rights, Russian language rights, film rights).

REPRESENTS nonfiction books, novels, short story collections, novellas, movie, TV, TV movie, sitcom. **Considers these nonfiction areas:** biography, current affairs, ethnic, humor, memoirs, music. **Considers these fiction areas:** adventure, experimental, family, historical, horror, literary, mainstream, mystery, romance, thriller, young adult, womens. **Considers**

these script areas: action, comedy, detective, family, mainstream, romantic comedy, romantic drama, teen, thriller.

"We are the first full-service agency in Russia, representing our authors in book publishing, film, television, and other areas. We are also the first agency representing Russian authors worldwide, based in Russia. The agency also represents international authors, agents and publishers in Russia. Our philosophy is to provide an individual approach to each author, finding the right publisher both at home and across international cultural and linguistic borders, developing original marketing and promotional strategies for each title." Actively seeking manuscripts written in Russian, both literary and commercial; and foreign publishers and agents with the high-profile fiction and general nonfiction lists to represent in Russia. Does not want to receive unpublished manuscripts in languages other than Russian, or any information irrelevant to our activity.

HOW TO CONTACT Submit synopsis, author bio. Accepts simultaneous submissions. Responds in 14 days to mss. Obtains most new clients through recommendations from others, solicitations.

TERMS Agent receives 20% commission on domestic sales. Agent receives 20% commission on foreign sales. Offers written contract, binding for 1 year; 2-month notice must be given to terminate contract.

DOUG GRAD LITERARY AGENCY, INC.

68 Jay Street, Suite W11, Brooklyn NY 11201. (718)788-6067. **E-mail:** doug.grad@dgliterary.com. **E-mail:** query@dgliterary.com. **Website:** www.dgliterary.com. **Contact:** Doug Grad. Estab. 2008.

Prior to being an agent, Doug Grad spent the last 22 years as an editor at 4 major publishing houses.

MEMBER AGENTS Doug Grad (narrative nonfiction, military, sports, celebrity memoir, thrillers, mysteries, historical fiction, young adult fiction, romance, music, style, business, home improvement, cookbooks, self-help, science and theater); **George Bick** (science fiction [no fantasy!], narrative nonfiction, business, thrillers, mysteries, military, pop science, pop culture, and travel).

REPRESENTS Considers these nonfiction areas: business, cooking, creative nonfiction, military, music, popular culture, science, self-help, sports, theater, travel. **Considers these fiction areas:** historical, mystery, science fiction, thriller, young adult.

HOW TO CONTACT Query by e-mail first at query@dgliterary.com. No sample material unless requested; no printed submissions by mail.

RECENT SALES *The Earthend Saga*, by Gillian Anderson and Jeff Rovin (Simon451); *Written Off: The Heroic Ordeal of Medal of Honor Nominee Captain William Albracht,* by William Albracht and Marvin Wolf (Berkley/Caliber); *Gordie Howe's Sun: A Hall of Fame Life in the Shadow of Mr. Hockey*, by Mark Howe with Jay Greenberg (HarperCanada/Triumph Books US).

ASHLEY GRAYSON LITERARY AGENCY

1342 W. 18th St., San Pedro CA 90732. **E-mail:** graysonagent@earthlink.net. **Website:** www.publishersmarketplace.com/members/CGrayson/. Estab. 1976. Member of AAR. Represents 100 clients. 5% of clients are new/unpublished writers. Currently handles: nonfiction books 20%, novels 50%, juvenile books 30%.

MEMBER AGENTS Ashley Grayson (fantasy, mystery, thrillers, young adult); **Carolyn Grayson** (chick lit, mystery, children's, nonfiction, women's fiction, romance, thrillers); **Lois Winston** (women's fiction, chick lit, mystery).

REPRESENTS nonfiction books, novels. **Considers these nonfiction areas:** business, computers, economics, history, investigative, popular culture, science, self-help, sports, technology, true crime. **Considers these fiction areas:** fantasy, juvenile, middle grade, multicultural, mystery, romance, science fiction, suspense, women's, young adult.

"We represent literary and commercial fiction, as well as nonfiction for adults (self-help, parenting, pop culture, mind/body/spirit, true crime, business, science). We also represent fiction for younger readers (chapter books through YA). We are seeking more mysteries and thrillers." Actively seeking previously published fiction authors.

HOW TO CONTACT The agency is temporarily closed to queries from *fiction* writers who are not published at book length (self-published or print-on-demand do not count). There are only three exceptions to this policy: (1) Unpublished authors who have received an offer from a reputable publisher, who need an agent before beginning contract negotiations; (2)

NEW AGENT SPOTLIGHT

SARAH NEGO
(CORVISIERO LITERARY)

corvisieroagency.com

@sarahnego

ABOUT SARAH: She divides her time between her own writing and working with amazing authors. Her background is in marketing, and she uses her experience to help authors build their platforms and promote their work.

SHE IS SEEKING: middle grade and young adult fiction manuscripts—open to any genre within those age groups, but prefers speculative fiction. Contemporary is not her favorite, but she will look at it.

HOW TO QUERY: Send your letter, 1-2 page synopsis and the first 5 pages pasted into the body of an e-mail to Query@CorvisieroAgency.com. Please use "Query for Sarah" as your subject line.

Authors who are recommended by a published author, editor or agent who has read the work in question; (3) Authors whom we have met at conferences and from whom we have requested submissions. Nonfiction authors who are recognized within their field or area may still query with proposals. Note: We cannot review self-published, subsidy-published, and POD-published works to evaluate moving them to mainstream publishers.

TERMS Agent receives 15% commission on domestic sales. Agent receives 20% commission on foreign sales.

RECENT SALES *Juliet Dove, Queen of Love*, by Bruce Coville (Harcourt); *Alosha*, by Christopher Pike (TOR); *Sleeping Freshmen Never Lie*, by David Lubar (Dutton); *Ball Don't Lie*, by Matt de la Peña (Delacorte); *Wiley & Grampa's Creature Features*, by Kirk Scroggs (10-book series, Little Brown); *Snitch*, by Allison van Diepen (Simon Pulse). Also represents: J.B. Cheaney (Knopf), Bruce Wetter (Atheneum).

TIPS "We do request revisions as they are required. We are long-time agents, professional and known in the business. We perform professionally for our clients and we ask the same of them."

O SANFORD J. GREENBURGER ASSOCIATES, INC.

55 Fifth Ave., New York NY 10003. (212)206-5600. **Fax:** (212)463-8718. **Website:** www.greenburger.com. Member of AAR. Represents 500 clients.

MEMBER AGENTS **Matt Bialer**, LRibar@sjga.com (fantasy, science fiction, thrillers, and mysteries as well as a select group of literary writers, and also loves smart narrative nonfiction including books about current events, popular culture, biography, history, music, race, and sports); **Brenda Bowen**, queryBB@sjga.com (literary fiction, writers and illustrators of picture books, chapter books, and middle grade and teen fiction); **Lisa Gallagher**, lgsubmissions@sjga.com (accessible literary fiction, quality commercial women's fiction, crime fiction, lively narrative nonfiction); **Faith Hamlin**, fhamlin@sjga.com (receives submissions by referral); **Heide Lange**, queryHL@sjga.com; **Daniel Mandel**, querydm@sjga.com (literary and commercial fiction, as well as memoirs and nonfiction about business, art, history, politics, sports, and popular culture); **Courtney Miller-Callihan**, cmiller@sjga.com (YA, middle grade, women's fiction, romance, and historical novels, as well as nonfiction projects on unusual topics, humor, pop culture, and lifestyle books); **Nicholas Ellison**, nellison@sjga.com; **Chelsea Lindman**, clindman@sjga.com (playful literary fiction, upmarket crime fiction, and forward thinking or boundary-pushing nonfiction); **Rachael Dillon Fried**, rfried@sjga.com (both fiction and nonfiction authors, with a keen interest in unique literary voices, women's fiction, narrative nonfiction, memoir, and comedy); **Lindsay Ribar**, co-agents with Matt Bailer (young adult and middle grade fiction).

REPRESENTS nonfiction books and novels. **Considers these nonfiction areas:** art, biography, business, creative nonfiction, current affairs, ethnic, history, humor, memoirs, music, popular culture, politics, sports. **Considers these fiction areas:** crime, fantasy, historical, literary, middle grade, mystery, picture books, romance, science fiction, thriller, women's, young adult.

No Westerns. No screenplays.

HOW TO CONTACT E-query. "Please look at each agent's profile page for current information about what each agent is looking for and for the correct e-mail address to use for queries to that agent. Please be sure to use the correct query e-mail address for each agent." Accepts simultaneous submissions. Responds in 2 months to queries and mss. Obtains most new clients through recommendations from others.

TERMS Agent receives 15% commission on domestic sales. Agent receives 20% commission on foreign sales. Charges for photocopying and books for foreign and subsidiary rights submissions.

RECENT SALES *Inferno*, by Dan Brown; *Hidden Order*, by Brad Thor; *The Chalice*, by Nancy Bilveau; *Horns*, by Joe Hill.

THE GREENHOUSE LITERARY AGENCY

11308 Lapham Dr., Oakton VA 22124. **E-mail:** submissions@greenhouseliterary.com. **Website:** www.greenhouseliterary.com. Member of AAR. Other memberships include SCBWI. Represents 20 clients. 100% of clients are new/unpublished writers. Currently handles: juvenile books 100%.

Sarah Davies has had an editorial and management career in children's publishing spanning 25 years; for 5 years prior to launching the Greenhouse she was Publishing Director of Macmillan Children's Books in London, and publishing leading authors from both sides of the Atlantic.

MEMBER AGENTS **Sarah Davies**, vice president (middle grade and young adult); **John M. Cusick**, agent (picture books, middle grade, YA, and boy books for kids); **Polly Nolan**, agent (fiction by UK, Irish, Commonwealth—including Australia, NZ and India—authors, from picture books to young fiction series, through middle grade and young adult).

REPRESENTS juvenile. **Considers these fiction areas:** juvenile, middle grade, picture books, young adult.

"We exclusively represent authors writing fiction for children and teens. The agency has offices in both the USA and UK, and Sarah Davies (who is British) personally represents authors to both markets. The agency's commission structure reflects this—taking 15% for sales to both US and UK, thus treating both as 'domestic' markets.' " All genres of children's and YA fiction—ages 5+. Does not want to receive nonfiction, poetry, picture books (text or illustration) or work aimed at adults; short stories, educational or religious/inspirational work, pre-school/novelty material, or screenplays.

HOW TO CONTACT Query one agent only. Put the target agent's name in the subject line. Paste the first 5 pages of your story (or your complete picture book) after the query. Obtains most new clients through recommendations from others, solicitations, conferences.

TERMS Agent receives 15% commission on domestic sales. Agent receives 25% commission on foreign sales. Offers written contract. This agency occasionally charges for submission copies to film agents or foreign publishers.

RECENT SALES *Fracture*, by Megan Miranda (Walker); *Paper Valentine*, by Brenna Yovanff (Razorbill); *Uses for Boys*, by Erica L. Scheidt (St Martin's); *Dark Inside*, by Jeyn Roberts (Simon & Schuster); *Breathe*, by Sarah Crossan (HarperCollins); *After the Snow*, by SD Crockett (Feiwel/Macmillan); *Sean Griswold's Head*, by Lindsey Leavitt (Hyperion).

WRITERS CONFERENCES Bologna Children's Book Fair, ALA and SCBWI conferences, BookExpo America.

TIPS "Before submitting material, authors should read the Greenhouse's 'Top 10 Tips for Authors of Children's Fiction' and carefully follow our submission guidelines which can be found on the website."

KATHRYN GREEN LITERARY AGENCY, LLC

250 West 57th St., Suite 2302, New York NY 10107. (212)245-4225. **Fax:** (212)245-4042. **E-mail:** query@kgreenagency.com. **Contact:** Kathy Green. Memberships include Women's Media Group. Represents approximately 20 clients. 50% of clients are new/unpublished writers. Currently handles: nonfiction books 50%, novels 25%, juvenile books 25%.

Prior to becoming an agent, Ms. Green was a book and magazine editor.

REPRESENTS nonfiction books, novels, short story collections, juvenile, middle grade and young adult only). **Considers these nonfiction areas:** autobiography, biography, business, child guidance, cooking, current affairs, diet/nutrition, economics, education, foods, history, how-to, humor, interior design, investigative, juvenile nonfiction, memoirs, parenting, popular culture, psychology, satire, self-help, sports, true crime, women's issues, women's studies, juvenile. **Considers these fiction areas:** crime, detective, family saga, historical, humor, juvenile, literary, mainstream, middle grade, mystery, police, romance, satire, suspense, thriller, women's, young adult.

Keeping the client list small means that writers receive my full attention throughout the process of getting their project published. Does not want to receive science fiction or fantasy.

HOW TO CONTACT Query to query@kgreenagency.com. Send no samples unless requested. Accepts simultaneous submissions. Responds in 1-2 months to mss. Obtains most new clients through recommendations from others, solicitations, conferences.

TERMS Agent receives 15% commission on domestic sales. Agent receives 20% commission on foreign sales. No written contract.

RECENT SALES *Welcome To The Dark House*; *Extinct For A Reason*; *The Arnifour Affair*; *The Civil War In Color*; *The Racecar Book.*

TIPS "This agency offers a written agreement."

BLANCHE C. GREGORY, INC.

2 Tudor City Place, New York NY 10017. (212)697-0828. **E-mail:** info@bcgliteraryagency.com. **Website:** www.bcgliteraryagency.com. Member of AAR.

REPRESENTS nonfiction books, novels, juvenile.

This agency specializes in adult fiction and nonfiction; children's literature is also considered. Does not want to receive screenplays, stage plays or teleplays.

HOW TO CONTACT Submit via snail mail—query, brief synopsis, bio, SASE. No e-mail queries. Obtains most new clients through recommendations from others.

GREYHAUS LITERARY

3021 20th St., PL SW, Puyallup WA 98373. **E-mail:** scott@greyhausagency.com. **Website:** www.greyhausagency.com. **Contact:** Scott Eagan, member RWA. Estab. 2003.

REPRESENTS Considers these fiction areas: romance, women's.

"Greyhaus only focuses on romance and women's fiction. Please review submission information found on the website to know exactly what Greyhaus is looking for. Stories should be 75,000-120,000 words in length or meet the word count requirements for Harlequin or Entangled found on their respective websites." Does not want sci-fi, fantasy, literary, futuristic, erotica, writers targeting e-pubs, young adult, nonfiction, memoirs, how-to books, self-help, screenplays, novellas, poetry.

HOW TO CONTACT Submissions to Greyhaus can be done in one of three ways: 1) Send a query, the first 3 pages and a synopsis of no more than 3 pages (and a SASE), using a snail mail submission. 2) A standard query letter via e-mail. If using this method, do not attach documents or send anything else other than a query letter. Or 3) use the Submission Form found on the website on the Contact page.

JILL GRINBERG LITERARY AGENCY

16 Court St., Suite 3306, Brooklyn NY 11241. (212)620-5883. **Fax:** (212)627-4725. **E-mail:** info@grinbergliterary.com. **Website:** www.jillgrinbergliterary.com. Estab. 1999.

Prior to her current position, Ms. Grinberg was at Anderson Grinberg Literary Management.

MEMBER AGENTS Jill Grinberg, jill@jillgrinbergliterary.com; **Cheryl Pientka**, cheryl@jillgrinber gliterary.com; **Katelyn Detweiler**, katelyn@jillgrinbergliterary.com.

REPRESENTS nonfiction books, novels. **Considers these nonfiction areas:** biography, cooking, ethnic, history, science, travel. **Considers these fiction areas:** fantasy, juvenile, literary, mainstream, romance, science fiction, young adult.

HOW TO CONTACT Please send your query letter to info@jillgrinbergliterary.com and attach the first 50 pages (fiction) or proposal (nonfiction) as a Word doc file. All submissions will be read, but electronic mail is preferred.

RECENT SALES *Cinder*, Marissa Meyer; *The Hero's Guide to Saving Your Kingdom*, Christopher Healy; *Kiss and Make Up*, Katie Anderson; i, T.J. Stiles; *Eon* and *Eona*, Alison Goodman; *American Nations*, Colin Woodard; HALO Trilogy, Alexandra Adornetto; *Babymouse*, Jennifer & Matthew Holm; Uglies/Leviathan Trilogy, Scott Westerfeld; *Liar*, Justine Larbalestier; *Turtle in Paradise*, Jennifer Holm; *Wisdom's Kiss* and *Dairy Queen*, Catherine Gilbert Murdock.

TIPS "We prefer submissions by mail."

JILL GROSJEAN LITERARY AGENCY

1390 Millstone Rd., Sag Harbor NY 11963. (631)725-7419. **E-mail:** JillLit310@aol.com. **Contact:** Jill Grosjean. Estab. 1999. No No

Prior to becoming an agent, Ms. Grosjean managed an independent bookstore. She also worked in publishing and advertising.

REPRESENTS Considers these fiction areas: literary, mainstream, mystery.

Actively seeking literary novels and mysteries.

HOW TO CONTACT E-mail queries preferred, no attachments. No cold calls, please. Accepts simultaneous submissions, though when manuscript requested, requires exclusive reading time. Accepts simultaneous submissions. Responds in 1 week to queries; month to mss. Obtains most new clients through recommendations and solicitations.

TERMS Agent receives 15% commission on domestic sales; 20% commission on foreign and film sales.

RECENT SALES *A Spark of Death*, *Fatal Induction*, and *Capacity for Murder*, by Bernadette Pajer (Poison Pen Press); *Neutral Ground*, by Greg Garrett (Bondfire Books); *Threading the Needle*, by Marie Bostwick (Kensington Publishing); *Tim Cratchit's Christmas Carol: A Novel of Scrooge's Legacy*, by Jim Piecuch (Simon & Schuster).

WRITERS CONFERENCES Thrillerfest; Texas Writer's League; Book Passage Mystery's Writer's Conference.

LAURA GROSS LITERARY AGENCY

P.O. Box 610326, Newton Highlands MA 02461. (617)964-2977. **Fax:** (617)964-3023. **E-mail:** query@lg-la.com. **Website:** www.lg-la.com. **Contact:** Laura Gross. Estab. 1988. Represents 30 clients. Currently handles: nonfiction books 40%, novels 50%, scholarly books 10%.

Prior to becoming an agent, Ms. Gross was an editor.

REPRESENTS nonfiction books, novels. **Considers these nonfiction areas:** autobiography, biography, child guidance, cultural interests, current affairs, ethnic, government, health, history, law, medicine, memoirs, parenting, popular culture, politics, psychology, sports, women's issues, women's studies. **Considers these fiction areas:** historical, literary, mainstream, mystery, suspense, thriller.

HOW TO CONTACT Queries accepted online via online form on LGLA website. Responds in several days to queries. Obtains most new clients through recommendations from others.

TERMS Agent receives 15% commission on domestic sales. Agent receives 20% commission on foreign sales. Offers written contract.

THE MITCHELL J. HAMILBURG AGENCY

149 S. Barrington Ave., #732, Los Angeles CA 90049. (310)471-4024. **Fax:** (310)471-9588. **Contact:** Michael Hamilburg. Estab. 1937. Signatory of WGA. Represents 70 clients. Currently handles: nonfiction books 70%, novels 30%.

REPRESENTS nonfiction books, novels. **Considers these nonfiction areas:** anthropology, biography, business, child, cooking, current affairs, education, government, health, history, memoirs, military, money, psychology, recreation, regional, self-help, sex, sociology, spirituality, sports, travel, women's, creative nonfiction; romance; architecture; inspirational; true crime. **Considers these fiction areas:** glitz, New Age, adventure, experimental, feminist, humor, military, mystery, occult, regional, religious, romance, sports, thriller, crime; mainstream; psychic.

HOW TO CONTACT Query with outline, 2 sample chapters, SASE. Responds in 1 month to mss. Obtains most new clients through recommendations from others, conferences, personal search.

TERMS Agent receives 10-15% commission on domestic sales.

THE JOY HARRIS LITERARY AGENCY, INC.

381 Park Avenue S, Suite 428, New York NY 10016. (212)924-6269. **Fax:** (212)725-5275. **E-mail:** submissions@jhlitagent.com; contact@jhlitagent.com. **Website:** joyharrisliterary.com. **Contact:** Joy Harris. Estab. 1990. Member of AAR. Represents more than 100 clients. Currently handles: nonfiction books 50%, novels 50%.

MEMBER AGENTS **Joy Harris** (most interested in literary fiction and narrative nonfiction); **Adam Reed** (arts, literary fiction, science and technology, and pop culture).

REPRESENTS **Considers these nonfiction areas:** art, creative nonfiction, popular culture, science, technology. **Considers these fiction areas:** literary.

We do not accept unsolicited manuscripts, and are not accepting poetry, screenplays, or self-help submissions at this time.

HOW TO CONTACT "Please send by regular mail a query letter, outline or sample chapter, and self-addressed stamped envelope to the address below. You may e-mail your submission to submissions@jhlitagent.com; however, we will only reply if interested." Do not send your full manuscript before it is requested. Accepts simultaneous submissions. Responds in 2 months to queries. Obtains most new clients through recommendations from clients and editors.

TERMS Agent receives 15% commission on domestic sales. Agent receives 20% commission on foreign sales. Charges clients for some office expenses.

RECENT SALES *Carry the One*, by Carol Anshaw; *Kill You Twice,* by Chelsea Cain; *Fire in the Belly*, by Cynthia Carr; *Radiance*, by Louis Jones; *Saved by Beauty,* by Roger Housden.

HARTLINE LITERARY AGENCY

123 Queenston Dr., Pittsburgh PA 15235-5429. (412)829-2483. **Fax:** (412)829-2432. **E-mail:** joyce@hartlineliterary.com. **Website:** www.hartlineliterary.com. **Contact:** Joyce A. Hart. Represents 40 clients. 20% of clients are new/unpublished writers. Currently handles: nonfiction books 40%, novels 60%.

MEMBER AGENTS **Joyce A. Hart**, principal agent (no unsolicited queries); **Jim Hart**; **Terry Burns**, terry@hartlineliterary.com (some YA and middle grade along with his other interests); **Diana Flegal**, diana@hartlineliterary.com; **Linda Glaz**, linda@hartlineliterary.com; **Andy Scheer**, andy@hartlineliterary.com.

REPRESENTS nonfiction books, novels.

"This agency specializes in the Christian bookseller market." Actively seeking adult fiction, self-help, nutritional books, devotional, and business. Does not want to receive erotica, gay/lesbian, fantasy, horror, etc.

HOW TO CONTACT E-query only. Target one agent only. "All e-mail submissions sent to Hartline Agents should be sent as a MS Word doc (or in rich text file format from another word processing program) attached to an e-mail with "submission: title, author's name and word count" in the subject line. A proposal is a single document, not a collection of files. Place the query letter in the e-mail itself. Do not send the entire proposal in the body of the e-mail or send PDF files." Further guidelines online. Accepts simultaneous submissions. Responds in 2 months to queries. Responds in 3 months to mss. Obtains most new clients through recommendations from others.

TERMS Agent receives 15% commission on domestic sales. Offers written contract.

RECENT SALES *Aurora, An American Experience in Quilt, Community and Craft*, and *A Flickering Light*, by Jane Kirkpatrick (Waterbrook Multnomah); *Oprah Doesn't Know My Name* by Jane Kirkpatrick (Zondervan); *Paper Roses, Scattered Petals, and Summer Rains*, by Amanda Cabot (Revell Books); *Blood Ransom*, by Lisa Harris (Zondervan); *I Don't Want a Divorce*, by David Clark (Revell Books); *Love Finds You in Hope, Kansas*, by Pamela Griffin (Summerside Press); Journey to the Well, by Diana Wallis Taylor (Revell Books); *Paper Bag Christmas, The Nine Lessons* by Kevin Milne (Center Street); *When Your Aging Parent Needs Care* by Arrington & Atchley (Harvest House); *Katie at Sixteen* by Kim Vogel Sawyer (Zondervan); *A Promise of Spring*, by Kim Vogel Sawyer (Bethany House); *The Big 5-OH!*, by Sandra Bricker (Abingdon Press); A *Silent Terror & A Silent Stalker,* by Lynette Eason (Steeple Hill); Extreme Devotion series, by Kathi Macias (New Hope Publishers); *On the Wings of the Storm*, by Tamira Barley (Whitaker House); *Tribute*, by Graham Garrison (Kregel Publications); *The Birth to Five Book*, by Brenda Nixon (Revell Books); *Fat to Skinny Fast and Easy*, by Doug Varrieur (Sterling Publishers).

JOHN HAWKINS & ASSOCIATES, INC.

71 W. 23rd St., Suite 1600, New York NY 10010. (212)807-7040. **Fax:** (212)807-9555. **E-mail:** jha@jhalit.com. **Website:** www.jhalit.com. **Contact:** Moses Cardona (rights and translations); Liz Free (permissions); Warren Frazier, literary agent; Anne Hawkins, literary agent. Member of AAR. Represents 100+ clients. 5-10% of clients are new/unpublished writers. Currently handles: nonfiction books 40%, novels 40%, juvenile books 20%.

MEMBER AGENTS **Moses Cardona**, moses@jhalit.com (commercial fiction, suspense, business, science, and multicultural fiction); **William Reiss**, reiss@jhalit.com (historical narratives, biography, slightly off-beat fiction, suspense fiction and children's books); **Warren Frazier**, frazier@jhalit.com (nonfiction—technology, history, world affairs and foreign policy); **Anne Hawkins,** ahawkins@jhalit.com (thrillers to literary fiction to serious nonfiction; she also has particular interests in science, history, public policy, medicine and women's issues).

REPRESENTS nonfiction books, novels. **Considers these nonfiction areas:** biography, business, history, medicine, politics, science, technology, women's issues. **Considers these fiction areas:** commercial, historical, literary, multicultural, suspense, thriller.

HOW TO CONTACT Query. Include the word "Query" in the subject line. For fiction, include 1-3 chapters of your book as a single Word attachment. For nonfiction, include your proposal as a single attachment. E-mail a particular agent directly if you are targeting one. Accepts simultaneous submissions. Responds in 1 month to queries. Obtains most new clients through recommendations from others.

TERMS Agent receives 15% commission on domestic sales. Agent receives 20% commission on foreign sales. Charges clients for photocopying.

RECENT SALES *The Doll*, by Taylor Stevens; *Flora*, by Gail Godwin; *The Affairs of Others*, by Amy Loyd.

HEACOCK HILL LITERARY AGENCY, INC.

West Coast Office, 1020 Hollywood Way, #439, Burbank CA 91505. (818)951-6788. **E-mail:** agent@heacockhill.com. **Website:** www.heacockhill.com. **Contact:** Catt LeBaigue or Tom Dark. Estab. 2009. Member of AAR. Other memberships include SCBWI.

Prior to becoming an agent, Ms. LeBaigue spent 18 years with Sony Pictures and Warner Bros.

MEMBER AGENTS **Tom Dark** (adult fiction, nonfiction); **Catt LeBaigue** (juvenile fiction, adult nonfiction including arts, crafts, anthropology, astronomy, nature studies, ecology, body/mind/spirit, humanities, self-help).

REPRESENTS nonfiction, fiction. **Considers these nonfiction areas:** art, business, gardening, politics. **Considers these fiction areas:** juvenile, middle grade, picture books, young adult.

Not presently accepting new clients for adult fiction. Please check the website for updates.

HOW TO CONTACT E-mail queries only. No unsolicited manuscripts. No e-mail attachments. Responds in 1 week to queries. Obtains most new clients through recommendations from others, solicitations.

TERMS Offers written contract.

TIPS "Write an informative original e-query expressing your book idea, your qualifications, and short excerpts of the work. No unfinished work, please."

HELEN HELLER AGENCY INC.

4-216 Heath Street W, Toronto Ontario M5P 1N7 Canada. (416)489-0396. **E-mail:** info@helenhelleragency.com. **Website:** www.helenhelleragency.com. **Contact:** Helen Heller. Represents 30+ clients.

Prior to her current position, Ms. Heller worked for Cassell & Co. (England), was an editor for Harlequin Books, a senior editor for Avon Books, and editor-in-chief for Fitzhenry & Whiteside.

MEMBER AGENTS **Helen Heller**, helen@helenhelleragency.com (crime fiction and front-list general fiction); **Daphne Hart**, daphne@helenhelleragency.com (clients range from masters of literary nonfiction, academics, journalists, critics, and wordsmiths to professionals who write prescriptively on their areas of expertise); **Sarah Heller**, sarah@helenhelleragency.com (front list commercial YA and adult fiction, with a particular interest in high concept historical fiction).

REPRESENTS nonfiction books, novels. **Considers these fiction areas:** commercial, crime, historical, literary, mainstream, young adult.

Actively seeking adult fiction and nonfiction (excluding children's literature, screenplays or genre fiction). Does not want to receive

NEW AGENT SPOTLIGHT

CLAIRE ANDERSON-WHEELER
(REGAL LITERARY)

regal-literary.com

ABOUT CLAIRE: Claire previously worked at Anderson Literary Management in New York, and at Christine Green Authors' Agent in London, UK. She holds an LLB from Trinity College, Dublin, and a Master's in Creative Writing from the University of East Anglia, UK. Claire is Irish, was born in DC, and grew up in Dublin, Geneva, and Brussels.

SHE IS SEEKING: YA with a strong voice (realistic or high-concept), works of narrative nonfiction and pop culture/pop psychology, literary fiction, and commercial women's fiction driven by strong contemporary issues.

HOW TO QUERY: E-mail your query, attaching a synopsis and the first three chapters as MS Word documents. Send to submissions@regal-literary.com, and put "Query for Claire: [Title]" in the subject line.

screenplays, poetry, or young children's picture books.

HOW TO CONTACT Submit synopsis, publishing history, author bio. Online submission form available at website. No attachments with e-queries. Responds in 6 weeks. Obtains most new clients through recommendations from others, solicitations.

RECENT SALES *Break on Through*, by Jill Murray (Doubleday Canada); *Womankind: Faces of Change Around the World*, by Donna Nebenzahl (Raincoast Books); *One Dead Indian: The Premier, The Police, and the Ipperwash Crisis*, by Peter Edwards (McClelland & Stewart); a full list of deals is available online.

TIPS "Whether you are an author searching for an agent, or whether an agent has approached you, it is in your best interest to first find out who the agent represents, what publishing houses has that agent sold to recently and what foreign sales have been made. You should be able to go to the bookstore, or search online and find the books the agent refers to. Many authors acknowledge their agents in the front or back or their books."

RICHARD HENSHAW GROUP

145 W. 28th St., 12th Floor, New York NY 10001. (212)414-1172. **E-mail:** submissions@henshaw.com. **Website:** www.richardhenshawgroup.com. **Contact:** Rich Henshaw. Member of AAR. Other memberships include SinC, MWA, HWA, SFWA, RWA. 20% of clients are new/unpublished writers. Currently handles: nonfiction books 35%, novels 65%.

Prior to opening his agency, Mr. Henshaw served as an agent with Richard Curtis Associates, Inc.

REPRESENTS nonfiction books, novels. **Considers these nonfiction areas:** animals, autobiography, biography, business, child guidance, cooking, current affairs, dance, economics, environment, foods, gay/lesbian, health, humor, investigative, money, music, New Age, parenting, popular culture, politics, psychology, science, self-help, sociology, sports, technology, true crime, women's issues, women's studies. **Considers these fiction areas:** crime, detective, fantasy, historical, horror, literary, mainstream, mystery, police, science fiction, supernatural, suspense, thriller, young adult.

This agency specializes in thrillers, mysteries, science fiction, fantasy and horror. "We only consider works between 65,000-150,000 words." We do not represent children's books, screenplays, short fiction, poetry, textbooks, scholarly works or coffee-table books.

HOW TO CONTACT "Please feel free to submit a query letter in the form of an e-mail of fewer than 250 words to submissions@henshaw.com address. As of December 1, 2013, we will no longer accept letters or partials at our physical address unless we have agreed in advance to make an exception." Responds in 3 weeks to queries. Responds in 6 weeks to mss. Obtains most new clients through recommendations from others, solicitations, conferences.

TERMS Agent receives 15% commission on domestic sales. Agent receives 20% commission on foreign sales. No written contract. Charges clients for photocopying and book orders.

RECENT SALES *Though Not Dead*, by Dana Stabenow; *The Perfect Suspect*, by Margaret Coel; *City of Ruins*, by Kristine Kathryn Rusch; *A Dead Man's Tale*, by James D. Doss; *Wickedly Charming*, by Kristine Grayson, History of the World series by Susan Wise Bauer; *Notorious Pleasures*, by Elizabeth Hoyt.

TIPS "While we do not have any reason to believe that our submission guidelines will change in the near future, writers can find up-to-date submission policy information on our website. Always include an SASE with correct return postage."

HERMAN AGENCY

350 Central Park West, New York NY 10025. (212)749-4907. **E-mail:** Ronnie@HermanAgencyInc.com. **Website:** www.hermanagencyinc.com. Estab. 1999. Currently handles: books for young readers.

MEMBER AGENTS Ronnie Ann Herman.

REPRESENTS children's.

HOW TO CONTACT Submit via e-mail to one of our agents. See website for specific agents' specialties.

TIPS "Check our website to see if you belong with our agency."

THE JEFF HERMAN AGENCY, LLC

P.O. Box 1522, Stockbridge MA 01262. (413)298-0077. **Fax:** (413)298-8188. **E-mail:** jeff@jeffherman.com. **Website:** www.jeffherman.com. **Contact:** Jeffrey H. Herman. Represents 100 clients. 10% of clients are new/unpublished writers. Currently handles: nonfiction books 85%, scholarly books 5%, textbooks 5%.

Prior to opening his agency, Mr. Herman served as a public relations executive.

MEMBER AGENTS Deborah Levine, vice president (nonfiction book doctor); Jeff Herman.

REPRESENTS nonfiction books. **Considers these nonfiction areas:** business, economics, government, health, history, how-to, law, medicine, politics, psychology, self-help, spirituality, technology, popular reference.

This agency specializes in adult nonfiction.

HOW TO CONTACT Query with SASE. Accepts simultaneous submissions.

TERMS Agent receives 15% commission on domestic sales. Offers written contract. Charges clients for copying and postage.

RECENT SALES *Days of Our Lives* book series; *H&R Block* book series. Sold 35 titles in the last year.

HIDDEN VALUE GROUP

27758 Santa Margarita Pkwy #361, Mission Viejo CA 92691. **E-mail:** bookquery@hiddenvaluegroup.com. **Website:** www.hiddenvaluegroup.com. **Contact:** Nancy Jernigan. Represents 55 clients. 10% of clients are new/unpublished writers.

MEMBER AGENTS **Jeff Jernigan**, jjernigan@hiddenvaluegroup.com (men's nonfiction, fiction, Bible studies/curriculum, marriage and family); **Nancy Jernigan**, njernigan@hiddenvaluegroup.com (nonfiction, women's issues, inspiration, marriage and family, fiction).

REPRESENTS nonfiction books and adult fiction; no poetry.

We are currently interested in receiving proposals in a variety of genres such as family/parenting/marriage, inspirational, self-help, men's and women's issues, business and fiction. No poetry or short stories. Actively seeking established fiction authors, and authors who are focusing on women's issues. Does not want to receive poetry or short stories.

HOW TO CONTACT Query with SASE. Submit synopsis, 2 sample chapters, author bio, and marketing and speaking summary. Accepts queries to bookquery@hiddenvaluegroup.com. No fax queries. Responds in 1 month to queries. Responds in 1 month to mss. Obtains most new clients through recommendations from others, solicitations.

TERMS Agent receives 15% commission on domestic sales. Agent receives 15% commission on foreign sales. Offers written contract.

WRITERS CONFERENCES Glorieta Christian Writers' Conference; CLASS Publishing Conference.

JULIE A. HILL AND ASSOCIATES, LLC

12997 Caminto del Pasaje, #530, Del Mar CA 92014. (858)259-2595. **Fax:** (858)259-2777. **E-mail:** Hillagent@aol.com. **Website:** www.publishersmarketplace/members/hillagent. **Contact:** Julie Hill. Represents 50+ clients. 20% of clients are new/unpublished writers. Currently handles: nonfiction books 90%, story collections 5%, other 5% books that accompany films.

MEMBER AGENTS Julie Hill, agent and principal.

REPRESENTS nonfiction books. **Considers these nonfiction areas:** biography, cooking, ethnic, health, history, how-to, language, memoirs, music, New Age, popular culture, psychology, religious, self-help, travel, women's issues, technology books, both for professionals and laypersons.

Currently interested in finding memoir from wives and adult children of drug lords, known criminals, and those in polygamist marriages. Currently developing a memoir from one of the largest Mexican drug cartels. Actively seeking travel, health, and media tie-ins. Does not want to receive horror, juvenile, scifi, thrillers or autobiographies of any kind.

HOW TO CONTACT Snail mail: Query with SASE. Submit outline/proposal, SASE. E-submissions, please send to: HIllagent@aol.com. Accepts simultaneous submissions. Responds in 4-6 weeks to queries. Obtains most new clients through recommendations from other authors, editors, and agents.

RECENT SALES Sales (many of which are available in languages such as Chinese, Russian, Spanish, and more) include *Data Crush*, by Chris Surdak; *Hikes on the Pacific Crest Trail*, by Marlise Kast-Myers; Bestselling *Publish This Book,* by Stephen Markley (reviewed by *PW*, *Huffington Post* and many others. "Soon to be a feature film; rights sold in Decemeber 2011 in a major deal, including percentage of gross receipts."); *Cracking Up*, from the book *The Happy Neurotic*, by David Granirer, to GRBTV. Travel: multiple titles to Frommers (Wiley) for kids travel and theme parks guides, including *Walt Disney World for Dummies*, by Laura Lea Miller, Barnes and Noble travel bestsellers. Falcon (Globe Pequot) hiking guides: *Best Easy Day Hikes to Long Island*, and others by Susan Finch. Insiders Guides, Off the Beaten Path, Best Day Trips to multiple US cities by multiple authors, including New York City, Chicago, Seattle, Houston, Palm Beaches (Fla) and many more.

TIPS A secondary website for this agency is www.publishersmarketplace.com/members/destiny, dealing with astrology for writers.

HILL NADELL LITERARY AGENCY

8899 Beverly Blvd., Suite 805, Los Angeles CA 90048. (310)860-9605. **Fax:** (310)860-9672. **E-mail:** queries.hillnadell@gmail.com. **Website:** www.hillnadell.com. Represents 100 clients.

MEMBER AGENTS **Bonnie Nadell** (Her nonfiction books include works on current affairs and food as well as memoirs and other narrative nonfiction. In fiction, she represents thrillers along with upmarket women's and literary fiction); **Dara Hyde** (literary and genre fiction, narrative nonfiction, graphic novels, memoir and the occasional young adult novel).

REPRESENTS nonfiction books, novels. **Considers these nonfiction areas:** biography, current affairs, environment, government, health, history, language, literature, medicine, popular culture, politics, science, technology, biography; government/politics, narrative. **Considers these fiction areas:** literary, mainstream, thriller, women's, young adult.

HOW TO CONTACT Send a query and SASE. If you would like your materials returned, please include adequate postage. To submit electronically: Send your query letter and the first chapter (no more than fifteen pages double-spaced) to queries@hillnadell.com. No attachments. Due to the high volume of submissions the agency receives, we cannot guarantee a response to all e-mailed queries. Accepts simultaneous submissions.

TERMS Agent receives 15% commission on domestic sales. Agent receives 20% commission on foreign sales. Agent receives 15% commission on film sales. Charges clients for photocopying and foreign mailings.

RECENT SALES *Living the Sweet Life in Paris* by David Lebovitz (memoir); *Next Stop, Reloville: Inside America's New Rootless Professional Class* by Peter Kilborn.

HOLLOWAY LITERARY

Washington DC **E-mail:** submissions@hollowayliteraryagency.com. **Website:** hollowayliteraryagency.

com. **Contact:** Nikki Terpilowski. Estab. 2011. Memberships include International Thriller Writers and Romance Writers of America.

REPRESENTS Considers these nonfiction areas: foods, history, military, spirituality, travel. **Considers these fiction areas:** erotica, ethnic, fantasy, middle grade, multicultural, regional, romance, thriller, women's, young adult, graphic novels and manga of all types.

Note to self-published authors: While we are happy to receive submissions from authors who have previously self-published novels, we do not represent self-published works. Send us your unpublished manuscripts only. Please note, we do not represent horror, true crime or novellas.

HOW TO CONTACT Send us your query and the first fifteen pages of your novel in the body of your e-mail, or attach your nonfiction proposal as a PDF and e-mail to the attention of: Submissions Editor, at submissions@hollowayliteraryagency.com. In the subject header, write: Query: (insert your title/genre). You can expect a response to your query in one to two weeks. Please note, we do not represent previously published material.

RECENT SALES A list of agency clients is available on the website.

THE HOLMES AGENCY

1942 Broadway, Suite 314, Boulder CO 80302. (720)443-8550. **E-mail:** kristina@holmesliterary.com. **Website:** www.holmesliterary.com. **Contact:** Kristina A. Holmes.

MEMBER AGENTS Kristina A. Holmes.

REPRESENTS Considers these nonfiction areas: business, cooking, environment, foods, health, memoirs, psychology, science, sex, spirituality, women's issues.

HOW TO CONTACT To submit your book for consideration, please e-mail your query and full book proposal to submissions@holmesliterary.com. (Please note that this agency does not represent fiction of any kind, true crime, poetry, or children's books.) In your query, please briefly describe your book (content, vision, purpose, and audience), as well as a bit about your background as an author (including notable platform highlights such as national media, a popular blog or website, speaking career, etc.).

RECENT SALES *Virtual Freedom: How To Work With Virtual Assistants To Create More Time, Increase Your Productivity, And Build Your Dream Business*, by Chris Ducker (Benbella Books 2014); *Recipes For A Sacred Life: True Stories And A Few Miracles*, by Rivvy Neshama (Divine Arts, Fall 2013); *50 Ways To Say You're Awesome*, by Alexandra Franzen (Sourcebooks, Fall 2013); *The Cosmic View Of Albert Einstein: His Reflections On Humanity And The Universe*, by Editors Walt Martin And Magda Ott (Sterling, Fall 2013); *Go Green, Spend Less, Live Better: The Ultimate Guide To Saving The Planet, Saving Money, And Protecting Your Health*, by Crissy Trask (Skyhorse, Spring 2013); *Pinfluence: The Complete Guide To Marketing Your Business With Pinterest*, by Beth Hayden (John Wiley & Sons, Summer 2012); *Stillpower: Excellence with Ease in Sports—and Life*, by Garret Kramer (Beyond Words/Atria/Simon & Schuster, Summer 2012); *Kissed by a Fox: And Other Stories of Friendship in Nature*, by Priscilla Stuckey (Counterpoint Press, Fall 2012); *The Mother's Wisdom Deck*, by Niki Dewart and Elizabeth Marglin (Sterling Publishing, Spring 2012).

TIPS "With seven years of experience as a literary agent, I have had the privilege of working with many gifted and inspiring writers. Some of them are bestselling authors and well-known experts in their field, but what makes them truly special, from my perspective, is their deep passion for their work, and their commitment to guiding, educating, and inspiring people around the world. At The Holmes Agency, I'm looking for considered and intelligent writing on a variety of nonfiction subjects. I am seeking authors focused on inspiring and helping positively transform readers' lives. I am open to queries, including from first time authors. However, please be aware that I don't generally represent authors without a platform."

HOPKINS LITERARY ASSOCIATES

2117 Buffalo Rd., Suite 327, Rochester NY 14624-1507. (585)352-6268. **Contact:** Pam Hopkins. Member of AAR. Other memberships include RWA. Represents 30 clients. 5% of clients are new/unpublished writers. Currently handles: novels 100%.

REPRESENTS novels. **Considers these fiction areas:** romance, women's.

This agency specializes in women's fiction, particularly historical, contemporary, and category romance, as well as mainstream work.

NEW AGENT SPOTLIGHT

AMY CLOUGHLEY
(KIMBERLEY CAMERON & ASSOCIATES)

kimberleycameron.com

@AmyCloughley

ABOUT AMY: Amy studied creative writing and literature and holds a B.S. in magazine journalism. She worked in editorial and marketing roles in magazine publishing and corporate business before shifting her professional focus to her lifelong love of books.

SHE IS SEEKING: literary and commercial fiction, mystery/suspense, narrative nonfiction, travel or adventure memoir.

HOW TO QUERY: For fiction, please send your query with a one-page synopsis and the first 50 pages of your manuscript as separate Word or .pdf attachments to amyc@kimberleycameron.com. For nonfiction, please send your query and include a well-researched proposal and three sample chapters in the same format. Include "Author Submission" in the subject line.

HOW TO CONTACT Regular mail with synopsis, 3 sample chapters (or first 50 pages), SASE. Accepts simultaneous submissions. Obtains most new clients through recommendations from others, solicitations, conferences.

TERMS Agent receives 15% commission on domestic sales. Agent receives 20% commission on foreign sales. No written contract.

RECENT SALES *The Wilting Bloom Series* by Madeline Hunter (Berkley); *The Dead Travel Fast*, by Deanna Raybourn; *Baggage Claim*, by Tanya Michna (NAL).

WRITERS CONFERENCES RWA National Conference.

HORNFISCHER LITERARY MANAGEMENT

P.O. Box 50544, Austin TX 78763. **E-mail:** queries@hornfischerlit.com. **Website:** www.hornfischerlit.com. **Contact:** James D. Hornfischer, president. Represents 45 clients. 10% of clients are new/unpublished writers. Currently handles: nonfiction books 100%.

Prior to opening his agency, Mr. Hornfischer held editorial positions at HarperCollins and McGraw-Hill. "My New York editorial background is useful in this regard. In 17 years as an agent, I've handled 12 *New York Times* nonfiction bestsellers, including 3 No. 1's."

REPRESENTS nonfiction books. **Considers these nonfiction areas:** anthropology, archeology, autobiography, biography, business, child guidance, current affairs, economics, environment, government, health, history, how-to, humor, inspirational, investigative, law, medicine, memoirs, military, money, multicultural, parenting, popular culture, politics, psychology, religious, satire, science, self-help, sociology, sports, technology, true crime, war.

Actively seeking commercial nonfiction. Does not want poetry or genre fiction.

HOW TO CONTACT E-mail queries only. Responds if interested. Accepts simultaneous submissions. Responds in 5-6 weeks to submissions. Obtains most new clients through referrals from clients, reading books and magazines, pursuing ideas with New York editors.

TERMS Agent receives 15% commission on domestic sales. Agent receives 25% commission on foreign sales. Offers written contract. Reasonable expenses deducted from proceeds after book is sold.

TIPS "When you query agents and send out proposals, present yourself as someone who's in command of his material and comfortable in his own skin. Too many writers have a palpable sense of anxiety and insecurity. Take a deep breath and realize that—if you're good—someone in the publishing world will want you."

HSG AGENCY

287 Spring St., New York NY 10013. **E-mail:** channigan@hsgagency.com; jsalky@hsgagency.com; jgetzler@hsgagency.com. **Website:** hsgagency.com. **Contact:** Carrie Hannigan; Jesseca Salky; Josh Getzler. Estab. 2011.

Prior to opening HSG Agency, Ms. Hannigan, Ms. Salky and Mr. Getzler were agents at Russell & Volkening.

MEMBER AGENTS Carrie Hannigan, Jesseca Salky, Josh Getzler.

REPRESENTS **Considers these nonfiction areas:** business, creative nonfiction, current affairs, education, foods, memoirs, photography, politics, psychology, science. **Considers these fiction areas:** commercial, crime, historical, literary, middle grade, mystery, picture books, thriller, women's, young adult.

Ms. Hannigan is actively seeking both fiction and nonfiction children's books in the picture book and middle grade age range, as well as adult women's fiction and select photography projects that would appeal to a large audience. Ms. Salky is actively seeking literary and commercial fiction that appeals to women and men; "all types of nonfiction, with a particular interest in memoir and narrative nonfiction in the areas of science, pop-psychology, politics, current affairs, business, education, food, and any other topic that is the vehicle for a great story." Mr. Getzler is actively seeking adult historical and crime-related fiction (mystery, thriller), select nonfiction and YA projects (particularly those that fit within historical or crime fiction). He is also interested in smart women's fiction.

HOW TO CONTACT Electronic submission only. Send query letter, first 5 pages of ms within e-mail to appropriate agent. Avoid submitting to multiple agents within the agency. Picture books: include entire ms. Responds in 4-6 weeks.

RECENT SALES *The Beginner's Goodbye*, by Anne Tyler (Knopf); *Blue Sea Burning*, by Geoff Rodkey (Putnam); *The Partner Track*, by Helen Wan (St. Martin's Press); *The Thrill of the Haunt*, by E.J. Copperman (Berkley); *Aces Wild*, by Erica Perl (Knopf Books for Young Readers); *Steve & Wessley: The Sea Monster*, by Jennifer Morris (Scholastic); *Infinite Worlds*, by Michael Soluri (Simon & Schuster).

ANDREA HURST LITERARY MANAGEMENT

P.O. Box 1467, Coupeville WA 98239. **E-mail:** andrea@andreahurst.com. **Website:** www.andreahurst.com. **Contact:** Andrea Hurst. Represents 100+ clients. 50% of clients are new/unpublished writers. Currently handles: nonfiction books 50%, novels 50%.

Prior to becoming an agent, Ms. Hurst was an acquisitions editor as well as a freelance editor and published writer.

MEMBER AGENTS **Andrea Hurst**, andrea@andreahurst.com (adult fiction, women's fiction, nonfiction, including personal growth, health and wellness, science, business, parenting, relationships, women's issues, animals, spirituality, metaphysical, psychological, cookbooks, and self-help); **Katie Reed**, kate@andreahurst.com (YA fiction and nonfiction and adult nonfiction); **Amberley Finnarelli** (not accepting new clients).

REPRESENTS nonfiction, novels, juvenile books. **Considers these nonfiction areas:** crafts, inspirational, memoirs, parenting, self-help, true crime. **Considers these fiction areas:** fantasy, inspirational, juvenile, literary, mainstream, psychic, religious, romance, science fiction, supernatural, suspense, thriller, women's, young adult.

"We work directly with our signed authors to help them polish their work and their platform for optimum marketability. Our staff is always available to answer phone calls and e-mails from our authors and we stay with a project until we have exhausted all publishing avenues." Actively seeking "well written nonfiction by authors with a strong platform; superbly crafted fiction with depth that touches the mind and heart and all of our listed subjects." Does not want to receive sci-fi, horror, Western, poetry, or screenplays.

HOW TO CONTACT E-mail query with SASE. Submit outline/proposal, synopsis, 2 sample chapters, author bio. Query a specific agent after reviewing website. Use (agentfirstname)@andreahurst.com. Accepts simultaneous submissions. Obtains most new clients through recommendations from others, solicitations, conferences.

TERMS Agent receives 15% commission on domestic sales. Agent receives 20% commission on foreign sales. Offers written contract, binding for 6 to 12 months; 30-day notice must be given to terminate contract. This agency charges for postage. No reading fees.

RECENT SALES *Art of Healing*, by Bernie Siegel; *Truly, Madly, Deadly*, by Hannah Jayne; *Ultimate Poultry Cookbook*, by Chef John Ash; *The Guestbook*, by Andrea Hurst; *No Buddy Left Behind*, by Terrir Crisp and Cindy Hurn (Lyons Press); *A Year of Miracles*, by Dr. Bernie Siegel (NWL); *Selling Your Crafts on Etsy* (St. Martin's); *The Underground Detective Agency* (Kensington); *Alaskan Seafood Cookbook* (Globe Pequot); *Faith, Hope and Healing*, by Dr. Bernie Siegel (Rodale); *Code Name: Polar Ice*, by Jean-Michel Cousteau and James Fraioli (Gibbs Smith); *How to Host a Killer Party*, by Penny Warner (Berkley/Penguin).

WRITERS CONFERENCES San Francisco Writers' Conference; Willamette Writers' Conference; PNWA; Whidbey Island Writers Conference.

TIPS "Do your homework and submit a professional package. Get to know the agent you are submitting to by researching their website or meeting them at a conference. Perfect your craft: Write well and edit ruthlessly over and over again before submitting to an agent. Be realistic: Understand that publishing is a business and be prepared to prove why your book is marketable and how you will market it on your own. Be persistent! Andrea Hurst is no longer accepting unsolicited query letters. Unless you have been referred by one of our authors, an agent or publisher, please check our website for another appropriate agent. www.andreahurst.com."

INKWELL MANAGEMENT, LLC

521 Fifth Ave., 26th Floor, New York NY 10175. (212)922-3500. **Fax:** (212)922-0535. **E-mail:** submissions@inkwellmanagement.com. **Website:** www.inkwellmanagement.com. Represents 500 clients.

MEMBER AGENTS **Monika Woods** (literary and commercial fiction, young adult, memoir, and compelling nonfiction in popular culture, science, and current affairs); **Lauren Smythe** (smart narrative nonfiction [narrative journalism, modern history, biography, cultural criticism, personal essay, humor], personality-driven practical nonfiction [cookbooks, fashion and style], and contemporary literary fiction); **David Hale Smith**; **Hannah Schwartz**; **Eliza Rothstein** (literary and commercial fiction, narrative nonfiction, memoir, popular science, and food writing); **Charlie Olsen** (fiction, children's books, graphic novels and illustrated works, and compelling narrative nonfiction); **Jacqueline Murphy**; **Alyssa Mozdzen**; **Nathaniel Jacks** (memoir, narrative nonfiction, social sciences, health, current affairs, business, religion, and popular history, as well as fiction—literary and commercial, women's, young adult, historical, short story, among others); **Alexis Hurley** (literary and commercial fiction, memoir, narrative nonfiction and more); **Allison Hunter** (literary and commercial fiction [including romance], memoir, narrative nonfiction, cultural studies, pop culture and prescriptive titles, including cookbooks); **David Forrer** (literary, commercial, historical and crime fiction to suspense/thriller, humorous nonfiction and popular history); **Catherine Drayton** (bestselling authors of books for children, young adults and women readers); **William Callahan** (nonfiction of all stripes, especially American history and memoir, pop culture and illustrated books, as well as voice-driven fiction that stands out from the crowd); **Lizz Blaise** (literary fiction, women's and young adult fiction, suspense, and psychological thriller); **Kimberly Witherspoon**; **Michael V Carlisle**; **Richard Pine**.

REPRESENTS nonfiction books, novels. **Considers these nonfiction areas:** biography, business, cooking, creative nonfiction, current affairs, foods, health, history, humor, memoirs, popular culture, religious, science. **Considers these fiction areas:** commercial, crime, historical, literary, middle grade, picture books, romance, short story collections, suspense, thriller, women's, young adult.

HOW TO CONTACT In the body of your e-mail, please include a query letter and a short writing sample (1-2 chapters). We currently accept submissions in all genres except screenplays. Due to the volume of queries we receive, our response time may take up to two months. Feel free to put "Query for [Agent Name]: [Your Book Title]" in the e-mail subject line. Obtains most new clients through recommendations from others.

TERMS Agent receives 15% commission on domestic sales. Agent receives 20% commission on foreign sales. Offers written contract.

TIPS "We will not read mss before receiving a letter of inquiry."

ICM PARTNERS

730 Fifth Ave., New York NY 10019. (212)556-5600. **Website:** www.icmtalent.com. **Contact:** Literary Department. Member of AAR. Signatory of WGA.

REPRESENTS nonfiction, fiction, novels, juvenile books.

We do not accept unsolicited submissions.

HOW TO CONTACT This agency is generally not open to unsolicited submissions. However, some agents do attend conferences and meet writers then. The agents take referrals, as well. Obtains most new clients through recommendations from others.

TERMS Agent receives 15% commission on domestic sales. Agent receives 20% commission on foreign sales.

JABBERWOCKY LITERARY AGENCY

49 West 45th St., New York NY 10036. (718)392-5985. **Website:** www.awfulagent.com. **Contact:** Joshua Bilmes. Memberships include SFWA. Represents 40 clients. 15% of clients are new/unpublished writers. Currently handles: nonfiction books 15%, novels 75%, scholarly books 5%, other 5% other.

MEMBER AGENTS Joshua Bilmes; Eddie Schneider; Lisa Rodgers; Sam Morgan.

REPRESENTS novels. **Considers these nonfiction areas:** autobiography, biography, business, cooking, current affairs, diet/nutrition, economics, film, foods, gay/lesbian, government, health, history, humor, language, law, literature, medicine, money, popular culture, politics, satire, science, sociology, sports, theater, war, women's issues, women's studies, young adult. **Considers these fiction areas:** action, adventure, contemporary issues, crime, detective, ethnic, family saga, fantasy, gay, glitz, historical, horror, humor, lesbian, literary, mainstream, middle grade, police, psychic, regional, satire, science fiction, sports, supernatural, thriller, young adult.

This agency represents quite a lot of genre fiction and is actively seeking to increase the amount of nonfiction projects. It does not handle children's or picture books. Book-length material only—no poetry, articles, or short fiction.

HOW TO CONTACT "We are currently open to unsolicited queries. No e-mail, phone, or fax queries, please. Query with SASE. Please check our website, as there may be times during the year when we are not accepting queries. Query letter only; no manuscript material unless requested." Accepts simultaneous submissions. Responds in 3 weeks to queries. Obtains most new clients through solicitations, recommendation by current clients.

TERMS Agent receives 15% commission on domestic sales. Agent receives 20% commission on foreign sales. Offers written contract, binding for 1 year. Charges clients for book purchases, photocopying, international book/ms mailing.

RECENT SALES Sold 30 US and 100 foreign titles in the last year. *Dead Ever After*, by Charlaine Harris; *Words of Radiance*, by Brandon Sanderson; *The Daylight War*, by Peter V. Brett; *Limits of Power*, by Elizabeth Moon. Other clients include Tanya Huff, Simon Green, Jack Campbell, Myke Cole, William C. Dietz, and Marie Brennan.

TIPS "In approaching with a query, the most important things to us are your credits and your biographical background to the extent it's relevant to your work. I (and most agents) will ignore the adjectives you may choose to describe your own work."

JAMES PETER ASSOCIATES, INC.

P.O. Box 358, New Canaan CT 06840. (203)972-1070. **E-mail:** gene_brissie@msn.com. **Website:** www.jamespeterassociates.com. **Contact:** Gene Brissie. Represents 75 individual and 6 corporate clients. 15% of clients are new/unpublished writers. Currently handles: nonfiction books 100%.

REPRESENTS nonfiction books. **Considers these nonfiction areas:** anthropology, archeology, architecture, art, biography, business, current affairs, dance, design, ethnic, film, gay/lesbian, government, health, history, language, literature, medicine, military, money, music, popular culture, psychology, self-help, theater, travel, war, women's issues, women's studies, memoirs (political, business).

"We are especially interested in general, trade, and reference nonfiction." Does not want to receive children's/young adult books, poetry, or fiction.

HOW TO CONTACT Submit proposal package, outline, SASE. Prefers to read materials exclusively. Responds in 1 month to queries. Obtains most new clients through recommendations from others, solicitations, contact with people who are doing interesting things.

TERMS Agent receives 15% commission on domestic sales. Agent receives 20% commission on foreign sales. Offers written contract.

JANKLOW & NESBIT ASSOCIATES

445 Park Ave., New York NY 10022. (212)421-1700. **Fax:** (212)980-3671. **E-mail:** submissions@janklow.com. **Website:** www.janklowandnesbit.com. Estab. 1989.

MEMBER AGENTS **Morton L. Janklow; Anne Sibbald; Lynn Nesbit; Luke Janklow; Cullen Stanley; PJ Mark** (interests are eclectic, including short stories and literary novels. His nonfiction interests include journalism, popular culture, memoir/narrative, essays and cultural criticism); **Richard Morris** (books that challenge our common assumptions, be it in the fields of cultural history, business, food, sports, science or faith); **Paul Lucas** (literary and commercial fiction, focusing on literary thrillers, science fiction and fantasy; also seeks narrative histories of ideas and objects, as well as biographies and popular science); **Emma Parry** (nonfiction by experts, but will consider outstanding literary fiction and upmarket commercial fiction. I'm not looking for children's books, middle grade, or fantasy); **Alexandra Machinist; Kirby Kim** (formerly of WME).

REPRESENTS nonfiction, fiction.

Does not want to receive unsolicited submissions or queries.

HOW TO CONTACT Query via snail mail or e-mail. Include a synopsis and the first 10 pages if sending fiction. For nonfiction, send a query and full outline. Accepts simultaneous submissions. Responds in 8 weeks to queries/mss. Obtains most new clients through recommendations from others.

TIPS "Please send a short query with first 10 pages or artwork."

J DE S ASSOCIATES, INC.

9 Shagbark Road, Wilson Point, South Norwalk CT 06854. (203)838-7571. **E-mail:** Jdespoel@aol.com. **Website:** www.jdesassociates.com. **Contact:** Jacques de Spoelberch. Represents 50 clients. Currently handles: nonfiction books 50%, novels 50%.

Prior to opening his agency, Mr. de Spoelberch was an editor with Houghton Mifflin.

REPRESENTS nonfiction books, novels. **Considers these nonfiction areas:** biography, business, cultural interests, current affairs, economics, ethnic, government, health, history, law, medicine, metaphysics, military, New Age, personal improvement, politics, self-help, sociology, sports, translation. **Considers these fiction areas:** crime, detective, frontier, historical, juvenile, literary, mainstream, mystery, New Age, police, suspense, westerns, young adult.

HOW TO CONTACT Brief queries by regular mail and e-mail are welcomed for fiction and nonfiction, but kindly do not include sample proposals or other material unless specifically requested to do so. Responds in 2 months to queries. Obtains most new clients through recommendations from authors and other clients.

TERMS Agent receives 15% commission on domestic sales. Agent receives 20% commission on foreign sales. Charges clients for foreign postage and photocopying.

RECENT SALES Joshilyn Jackson's new novel *A Grown-Up Kind of Pretty* (Grand Central), Margaret George's final Tudor historical *Elizabeth I* (Penguin), the fifth in Leighton Gage's series of Brazilian thrillers *A Vine in the Blood* (Soho), Genevieve Graham's romance *Under the Same Sky* (Berkley Sensation), Hilary Holladay's biography of the early Beat Herbert Huncke, *American Hipster* (Magnus), Ron Rozelle's *My Boys and Girls Are In There: The 1937 New London School Explosion* (Texas A&M), the concluding novel in Dom Testa's YA science fiction series, *The Galahad Legacy* (Tor), and Bruce Coston's new collection of animal stories *The Gift of Pets* (St. Martin's Press).

THE CAROLYN JENKS AGENCY

30 Cambridge Park Dr., #3150, Cambridge MA 02140. (617)354-5099. **E-mail:** queries@carolynjenksagency.com. **Website:** www.carolynjenksagency.com. **Contact:** Carolyn Jenks. Estab. 1987. Signatory of WGA

MEMBER AGENTS Carolyn Jenks; Eric Wing. "See agency website for current member preferences" as well as a list of junior agents.

REPRESENTS **Considers these nonfiction areas:** architecture, art, autobiography, biography, business, cultural interests, current affairs, design, education, ethnic, gay/lesbian, government, history, juvenile nonfiction, language, law, literature, memoirs, metaphysics, military, money, music, New Age, religious, science, technology, translation, true crime, women's issues, women's studies. **Considers these fiction areas:** action, adventure, ethnic, experimental, family saga, fantasy, feminist, frontier, gay, historical, horror, humor, inspirational, juvenile, lesbian, literary, mainstream, mystery, psychic, regional, religious, science fiction, supernatural, thriller, westerns, women's, young adult. **Considers these script areas:** autobiography, biography, contemporary issues, ethnic, experimental, family saga, fantasy, feminist, frontier, gay, historical, horror, inspirational, lesbian, mainstream, mystery, psychic, religious, romantic comedy, romantic drama, science fiction, supernatural, suspense, thriller, western.

HOW TO CONTACT Please submit a one page query including a brief bio via the form on the agency website. "Due to the high volume of queries we receive, we are unable to respond to everyone. Queries are reviewed on a rolling basis, and we will follow up directly with the author if there is interest in a full manuscript." Accepts simultaneous submissions. Obtains new clients by recommendations from others, queries/submissions, agency outreach.

TERMS Offers written contract, 1-3 years depending on the project. Requires 60 day notice before terminating contract.

TIPS "Do not make cold calls to the agency. E-mail contact only. Do not query for more than one property at a time. If possible, have a professional photograph of yourself ready to submit with your query, as it is important to be media-genic in today's marketplace. Be ready to discuss platform."

JET LITERARY ASSOCIATES

941 Calle Mejia, #507, Santa Fe NM 87501. (505)780-0721. **E-mail:** etp@jetliterary.com. **Website:** www.jetliterary.com. **Contact:** Liz Trupin-Pulli. Represents 75 clients. 35% of clients are new/unpublished writers.

MEMBER AGENTS **Liz Trupin-Pulli** (adult and YA fiction/nonfiction; romance, mysteries, parenting); **Jim Trupin** (adult fiction/nonfiction, military history, pop culture); **Jessica Trupin**, associate agent based in Seattle (adult fiction and nonfiction, children's and young adult, memoir, pop culture).

REPRESENTS nonfiction books, novels, short story collections. **Considers these nonfiction areas:** autobiography, biography, business, child guidance, cultural interests, current affairs, economics, ethnic, gay/lesbian, government, humor, investigative, law, memoirs, military, parenting, popular culture, politics, satire, sports, true crime, war, women's issues, women's studies. **Considers these fiction areas:** action, adventure, crime, detective, erotica, ethnic, gay, glitz, historical, humor, lesbian, literary, mainstream, mystery, police, romance, suspense, thriller, women's, young adult.

"JET was founded in New York in 1975, so we bring a wealth of knowledge and contacts, as well as quite a bit of expertise to our representation of writers." Actively seeking women's fiction, mysteries and narrative nonfiction. JET represents the full range of adult and YA fiction and nonfiction, including humor and cookbooks. Does not want to receive sci-fi, fantasy, horror, poetry, children's or religious.

HOW TO CONTACT An e-query only is accepted. Responds in 1 week to queries. Responds in 8 weeks to mss. Obtains most new clients through recommendations from others, solicitations, conferences.

TERMS Agent receives 15% commission on domestic sales. Agent receives 10% commission on foreign sales. Offers written contract, binding for 3 years. This agency charges for reimbursement of mailing and any photocopying.

RECENT SALES *Mom-in-chief*, by Jamie Woolf (Wiley, 2009); *Dangerous Games* by Charlotte Mede (Kensington, 2009); *So You Think You Can Spell!* by David Grambs and Ellen Levine (Perigee, 2009); *Cut, Drop & Die*, by Joanna Campbell Slan (Midnight Ink, 2009).

WRITERS CONFERENCES Women Writing the West; Southwest Writers Conference; Florida Writers Association Conference.

TIPS Do not write cute queries—stick to a straightforward message that includes the title and what your book is about, why you are suited to write this particular book, and what you have written in the past (if anything), along with a bit of a bio.

KELLER MEDIA INC.

578 Washington Blvd., No. 745, Marina del Rey CA 90292. (800)278-8706. **Website:** www.KellerMedia.com. **Contact:** Wendy Keller, senior agent; Elise Howard, editorial assistant; Laura Rensing, editorial assistant. Estab. 1989. Member of the National Speak-

NEW AGENT SPOTLIGHT

ROZ FOSTER
(SANDRA DIJKSTRA LITERARY AGENCY)

dijkstraagency.com

@RozFoster

ABOUT ROZ: Roz has a B.A. in English Literature from UC San Diego, studied philosophy for a year at the University of Sheffield, UK, and earned her M.A. in English, with an emphasis in Composition & Rhetoric and Creative Writing, from Portland State University. She's been learning French since 2009.

SHE IS SEEKING: Roz is interested in literary and commercial fiction, women's fiction, literary sci-fi, and literary YA. She loves novels that make her feel like the author is tuned into a rising revolution—cultural, political, literary, or whatnot—that's about to burst on the scene. Nonfiction: current affairs, design, business, cultural anthropology/social science, politics, psychology and memoir.

HOW TO QUERY: roz@dijkstraagency.com. Please send a query, a 1-page synopsis, a brief bio (including a description of your publishing history), and the first 10-15 pages of your manuscript. Please send all items in the body of the e-mail, not as an attachment.

ers Association. 25% of clients are new/unpublished writers. Currently handles: nonfiction books 100%.

Prior to becoming an agent, Ms. Keller was an award-winning journalist and worked for PR Newswire.

REPRESENTS nonfiction. **Considers these nonfiction areas:** business, current affairs, health, history, politics, psychology, science, self-help, sociology, women's issues.

"All of our authors are highly credible experts, who have or want a significant platform in media, academia, politics, paid professional speaking, syndicated columns, or regular appearances on radio/TV. Does not want (and absolutely will not respond to) fiction, true crime, scripts, teleplays, poetry, juvenile, anything Christian, picture books, illustrated books, first-person stories of mental or physical illness, wrongful incarceration, abduction by aliens, books channeled by aliens, demons, or dead celebrities (I wish I was kidding!)."

HOW TO CONTACT "To query, just go to www.KellerMedia.com/query and fill in the simple form; it takes 1 minute or less. You'll get a fast, courteous response. Please do not mail us anything unless requested to do so by a staff member." Accepts simultaneous submissions. Responds in 7 days. Obtains most new clients through referrals.

TERMS Agent receives 15% commission on domestic sales. Agent receives 20% commission on foreign, dramatic, sponsorship, appearance fees, audio, and merchandising deals. "30% on speaking engagements we book for the author."

TIPS "Don't send a query to any agent unless you're certain they handle the type of book you're writing. 90% of all rejections happen because what you offered us doesn't fit our established, advertised, printed, touted and shouted guidelines. Be organized! Have your proposal in order before you query. Never make apologies for 'bad writing' or sloppy content. Please just get it right before you waste your 1 shot with us. Have something new, different or interesting to say and be ready to dedicate your whole heart to marketing it. Marketing is everything."

NATASHA KERN LITERARY AGENCY

P.O. Box 1069, White Salmon WA 98672. (509)493-3803. **E-mail:** agent@natashakern.com. **Website:** www.natashakern.com. **Contact:** Natasha Kern. Memberships include RWA, MWA, SinC, The Authors Guild, and American Society of Journalists and Authors.

Prior to opening her agency, Ms. Kern worked as an editor and publicist for Simon & Schuster, Bantam, and Ballantine. This agency has sold more than 700 books.

MEMBER AGENTS Natasha Kern.

REPRESENTS Considers these nonfiction areas: animals, child guidance, cultural interests, current affairs, environment, ethnic, gardening, health, inspirational, medicine, metaphysics, New Age, parenting, popular culture, psychology, religious, self-help, spirituality, women's issues, women's studies, investigative journalism. **Considers these fiction areas:** commercial, historical, inspirational, mainstream, multicultural, mystery, religious, romance, suspense, thriller, women's.

"This agency specializes in commercial fiction and nonfiction for adults. We are a full-service agency." Historical novels from any country or time period; contemporary fiction including novels with romance or suspense elements; and multi-cultural fiction. We are also seeking inspirational fiction in a broad range of genres including: suspense and mysteries, historicals, romance, and contemporary novels. Does not represent horror, true crime, erotica, children's books, short stories or novellas, poetry, screenplays, technical, photography or art/craft books, cookbooks, travel, or sports books.

HOW TO CONTACT See submission instructions online. Send query to queries@natashakern.com. Please include the word "QUERY" in the subject line. "We do not accept queries by snail mail or phone." Accepts simultaneous submissions. Responds in 3 weeks to queries.

TERMS Agent receives 15% commission on domestic sales. Agent receives 20% commission on foreign sales. Agent receives 15% commission on film sales.

RECENT SALES Sold 43 titles in the last year. *China Dolls*, by Michelle Yu and Blossom Kan (St. Martin's); *Bastard Tongues*, by Derek Bickerton (Farrar Strauss); *Bone Rattler*, by Eliot Pattison; *Wicked Pleasure*, by Nina Bangs (Berkley); *Inviting God In*, by David Aaron (Shambhala); *Unlawful Contact*, by Pamela Clare (Berkley); *Dead End Dating*, by Kimberly Raye (Ballantine); *A Scent of Roses*, by Nikki Arana (Baker Book House); *The Sexiest Man Alive*, by Diana Holquist (Warner Books).

WRITERS CONFERENCES RWA National Conference; MWA National Conference; ACFW Conference; and many regional conferences.

TIPS "Your chances of being accepted for representation will be greatly enhanced by going to our website first. Our idea of a dream client is someone who participates in a mutually respectful business relationship, is clear about needs and goals, and communicates about career planning. If we know what you need and want, we can help you achieve it. A dream client has a storytelling gift, a commitment to a writing career, a desire to learn and grow, and a passion for excellence. We want clients who are expressing their own unique voice and truly have something of their own to communicate. This client understands that many people have to work together for a book to succeed and that everything in publishing takes far longer than one imagines. Trust and communication are truly essential."

VIRGINIA KIDD LITERARY AGENCY, INC.

P.O. Box 278, Milford PA 18337. (570)296-6205. **Fax:** (570)296-7266. **Website:** www.vk-agency.com. Memberships include SFWA, SFRA. Represents 80 clients.

REPRESENTS novels. **Considers these fiction areas:** fantasy, science fiction, speculative.

This agency specializes in science fiction and fantasy. "The Virginia Kidd Literary Agency is one of the longest established, science fiction specialized literary agencies in the world—with almost half a century of rich experience in the science fiction and fantasy genres. Our client list reads like a top notch 'who's-who' of science fiction: Beth Bernobich, Gene Wolfe, Anne McCaffrey, Ted Chiang, Alan Dean Foster and others set the bar very high indeed. Our authors have won Hugos, Nebulas, World Fantasy, Tiptree, National Book Award, PEN Malamud, SFWA Grandmaster, Gandalf, Locus Award, Margaret Edwards Award, IAMTW Lifetime Achievement Award (Grand Master), Rhysling Award, Author Emeritus SFWA, BSFA Award — and more. The point is, we represent the best of the best.We welcome queries from prospective and published authors."

HOW TO CONTACT Snail mail queries only.

TERMS Agent receives 15% commission on domestic sales. Agent receives 20-25% commission on foreign sales. Agent receives 20% commission on film sales. Offers written contract; 2-month notice must be given to terminate contract. Charges clients occasionally for extraordinary expenses.

RECENT SALES *Sagramanda*, by Alan Dean Foster (Pyr); *Incredible Good Fortune*, by Ursula K. Le Guin (Shambhala); *The Wizard and Soldier of Sidon*, by Gene Wolfe (Tor); *Voices and Powers*, by Ursula K. Le Guin (Harcourt); *Galileo's Children*, by Gardner Dozois (Pyr); *The Light Years Beneath My Feet* and *Running From the Deity*, by Alan Dean Foster (Del Ray); *Chasing Fire*, by Michelle Welch. Other clients include Eleanor Arnason, Ted Chiang, Jack Skillingstead, Daryl Gregory, Patricia Briggs, and the estates for James Tiptree, Jr., Murray Leinster, E.E. "Doc" Smith, R.A. Lafferty.

TIPS "If you have a completed novel that is of extraordinary quality, please send us a query."

KIRCHOFF/WOHLBERG, INC.

897 Boston Post Rd., Madison CT 06443. (203)245-7308. **Fax:** (203)245-3218. **Website:** www.kirchoffwohlberg.com. **Contact:** Ronald Zollshan. Memberships include SCBWI, Society of Illustrators, SPAR, Bookbuilders of Boston, New York Bookbinders' Guild, AIGA.

Kirchoff/Wohlberg has been in business for more than 35 years.

REPRESENTS Considers these fiction areas: juvenile, middle grade, picture books, young adult.

This agency specializes in juvenile fiction and nonfiction through young adult.

HOW TO CONTACT "Submit by mail to address above. We welcome the submission of mss from first-time or established children's book authors. Please enclose an SASE, but note that while we endeavor to read all submissions, we cannot guarantee a reply or their return." Accepts simultaneous submissions.

TERMS Offers written contract, binding for at least 1 year. Agent receives standard commission, depending upon whether it is an author only, illustrator only, or an author/illustrator.

HARVEY KLINGER, INC.

300 W. 55th St., Suite 11V, New York NY 10019. (212)581-7068. **Website:** www.harveyklinger.com. **Contact:** Harvey Klinger. Member of AAR. Represents 100 clients. 25% of clients are new/unpublished writers. Currently handles: nonfiction books 50%, novels 50%.

MEMBER AGENTS Harvey Kliinger; David Dunton (popular culture, music-related books, literary fiction, young adult, fiction, and memoirs); **Sara Crowe** (children's and young adult authors, adult fiction and nonfiction, foreign rights sales); **Andrea Somberg** (literary fiction, commercial fiction, romance, sci-fi/fantasy, mysteries/thrillers, young adult, middle grade, quality narrative nonfiction, popular culture, how-to, self-help, humor, interior design, cookbooks, health/fitness).

REPRESENTS nonfiction books, novels. **Considers these nonfiction areas:** autobiography, biography, cooking, diet/nutrition, foods, health, investigative, medicine, psychology, science, self-help, spirituality, sports, technology, true crime, women's issues, women's studies. **Considers these fiction areas:** action, adventure, crime, detective, family saga, glitz, literary, mainstream, mystery, police, suspense, thriller.

This agency specializes in big, mainstream, contemporary fiction and nonfiction.

HOW TO CONTACT Use online e-mail submission form on the website, or query with SASE via snail mail. No phone or fax queries. Don't send unsolicited manuscripts or e-mail attachments. Responds in 2 months to queries and mss. Obtains most new clients through recommendations from others.

TERMS Agent receives 15% commission on domestic sales. Agent receives 25% commission on foreign sales. Offers written contract. Charges for photocopying mss and overseas postage for mss.

RECENT SALES *Woman of a Thousand Secrets*, by Barbara Wood; *I Am Not a Serial Killer*, by Dan Wells; untitled memoir, by Bob Mould; *Children of the Mist*, by Paula Quinn; *Tutored*, by Allison Whittenberg; *Will You Take Me As I Am*, by Michelle Mercer. Other clients include: George Taber, Terry Kay, Scott Mebus, Jacqueline Kolosov, Jonathan Maberry, Tara Altebrando, Alex McAuley, Eva Nagorski, Greg Kot, Justine Musk, Nick Tasler, Ashley Kahn, Barbara De Angelis.

KNEERIM, WILLIAMS & BLOOM

90 Canal St., Boston MA 02114. **E-mail:** submissions@kwlit.com. **Website:** www.kwlit.com. Also located in New York and Washington D.C. Estab. 1990.

Prior to becoming an agent, Mr. Williams was a lawyer; Ms. Kneerim was a publisher and editor; Mr. Wasserman was an editor and journalist; Ms. Bloom worked in magazines; Ms. Flynn in academia.

MEMBER AGENTS **Brettne Bloom**, bloom@kwblit.com (memoir, history, current events, biography, travel, adventure, science, parenting, popular culture, cooking and food narratives, personal growth and women's issues, adult commercial and literary fiction and young adult fiction); **Hope Denekamp**; **Katherine Flynn**, flynn@kwblit.com (history, biography, politics, current affairs, adventure, nature, pop culture, science, and psychology for nonfiction and particularly loves exciting narrative nonfiction; she also represents both literary and commercial fiction, and is fond of urban or foreign locales, crime novels, insight into women's lives, biting wit, and historical settings); **Jill Kneerim; Ike Williams; Carol Franco; Gerald Gross.**

Actively seeking distinguished authors, experts, professionals, intellectuals, and serious writers.

HOW TO CONTACT E-query an individual agent. Send no attachments. Put "Query" in the subject line. Accepts simultaneous submissions. Obtains most new clients through recommendations from others.

LINDA KONNER LITERARY AGENCY

10 W. 15th St., Suite 1918, New York NY 10011. (212)691-3419. **E-mail:** ldkonner@cs.com. **Website:** www.lindakonnerliteraryagency.com. **Contact:** Linda Konner. Member of AAR. Signatory of WGA. Other memberships include ASJA. Represents 85 clients. 30-35% of clients are new/unpublished writers. Currently handles: nonfiction books 100%.

REPRESENTS nonfiction books. **Considers these nonfiction areas:** gay/lesbian, health, medicine, money, parenting, popular culture, psychology, science, self-help, women's issues, biography (celebrity), African American and Latino issues, relationships, popular science.

This agency specializes in health, self-help, and how-to books. Authors/co-authors must be top experts in their field with a substantial media platform.

HOW TO CONTACT Query by e-mail or by mail with SASE, synopsis, author bio, sufficient return postage. Prefers to read materials exclusively for 2 weeks. Accepts simultaneous submissions. Obtains most new clients through recommendations from others, occasional solicitation among established authors/journalists.

TERMS Agent receives 15% commission on domestic sales. Agent receives 25% commission on foreign sales. Offers written contract. Charges one-time fee for domestic expenses; additional expenses may be incurred for foreign sales.

RECENT SALES *The Calorie Myth* (New York Times best-seller) by Jonathan Bailor (Harper Wave); *Outsmarting Anger* (finalist, Books for a Better Life award) by Joseph Shrand, MD, with Leigh Devine and the editors of Harvard Health Publications (Jossey-Bass/Wiley); *Lucky Me: My Life With And Without My Mother, Shirley Maclaine* by Sachi Parker with Frederick Stroppel (Gotham/ Penguin); *80/20 Running* by Matt Fitzgerald (NAL/Penguin).

WRITERS CONFERENCES ASJA Writers Conference, Harvard Medical School's "Publishing Books, Memoirs, and Other Creative Nonfiction" Annual Conference.

ELAINE KOSTER LITERARY AGENCY, LLC

55 Central Park W., Suite 6, New York NY 10023. (212)362-9488. **Fax:** (212)712-0164. **Website:** www.publishersmarketplace.com/members/ElaineKoster/. **Contact:** Elaine Koster, Stephanie Lehmann, Ellen Twaddell. Estab. 1998. Member of AAR. Other memberships include MWA, Author's Guild, Women's Media Group. Represents 40 clients. 10% of clients are new/unpublished writers. Currently handles: nonfiction books 10%, novels 90%.

Prior to opening her agency, Ms. Koster was president and publisher of Dutton-NAL, part of the Penguin Group.

REPRESENTS nonfiction books, novels. **Considers these nonfiction areas:** autobiography, biography, business, child guidance, cooking, current affairs, diet/nutrition, economics, environment, ethnic, foods, health, history, how-to, medicine, money, parenting, popular culture, psychology, self-help, spirituality, women's issues, women's studies. **Considers these fiction areas:** contemporary issues, crime, detective, ethnic, family saga, feminist, historical, literary, mainstream, mystery, police, regional, suspense, thriller, young adult, chick lit.

This agency specializes in quality fiction and nonfiction. Does not want to receive juvenile, screenplays, or science fiction.

HOW TO CONTACT This agency is currently closed to submissions. Responds in 3 weeks to queries. Responds in 1 month to mss. Obtains most new clients through recommendations from others.

TERMS Agent receives 15% commission on domestic sales. Bills back specific expenses incurred doing business for a client.

RECENT SALES *After You* by Julie Buxbaum (Dial Press); *Lady Jasmine* by Victoria Christopher Murray (Touchstone); *If You Were My Man* by Francis Ray (St. Martin's Press); *Silencing Sam* by Julie Kramer (Atria); *Love, Honor And Betray* by Kimberla Lawson Roby (Grand Central).

TIPS "We prefer exclusive submissions. Don't e-mail or fax submissions. Please include biographical information and publishing history."

BARBARA S. KOUTS, LITERARY AGENT

P.O. Box 560, Bellport NY 11713. (631)286-1278. **Fax:** (631) 286-1538. **Contact:** Barbara S. Kouts. Member of AAR. Represents 50 clients. 10% of clients are new/unpublished writers.

REPRESENTS juvenile.

This agency specializes in children's books.

HOW TO CONTACT Query with SASE. Accepts queries by mail only. Accepts simultaneous submissions. Responds in 1 week to queries; 2 months to mss. Obtains most new clients through recommendations from others, solicitations, conferences.

TERMS Agent receives 10% commission on domestic sales. Agent receives 20% commission on foreign sales. This agency charges clients for photocopying.

RECENT SALES *Code Talker*, by Joseph Bruchac (Dial); *The Penderwicks*, by Jeanne Birdsall (Knopf); *Froggy's Baby Sister*, by Jonathan London (Viking).

TIPS "Write, do not call. Be professional in your writing."

KRAAS LITERARY AGENCY

E-mail: irenekraas@sbcglobal.net. **Website:** www.kraasliteraryagency.com. **Contact:** Irene Kraas. Represents 35 clients. 75% of clients are new/unpublished writers. Currently handles: novels 100%.

MEMBER AGENTS Irene Kraas, principal.

REPRESENTS novels. **Considers these fiction areas:** literary, thriller, young adult.

This agency is interested in working with published writers, but that does not mean self-published writers. "The agency is ONLY accepting new manuscripts in the genre of adult thrillers and mysteries. Submissions should be the first ten pages of a completed manuscript embedded in an e-mail. I do not open attachments or go to websites." Does not want to receive short stories, plays, or poetry. This agency no longer represents adult fantasy or science fiction.

HOW TO CONTACT Query and e-mail the first 10 pages of a completed ms. Requires exclusive read on mss. Attachments aren't accepted. Accepts simultaneous submissions.

TERMS Offers written contract.

TIPS "I am interested in material—in any genre—that is truly, truly unique."

STUART KRICHEVSKY LITERARY AGENCY, INC.

381 Park Ave. S., Suite 428, New York NY 10016. (212)725-5288. **Fax:** (212)725-5275. **Website:** www.skagency.com. Member of AAR.

MEMBER AGENTS **Stuart Krichevsky** (query@skagency.com); **Shana Cohen** (SCquery@skagency.com); **Ross Harris** (RHquery@skagency.com; voice-driven humor and memoir, books on popular culture and our society, narrative nonfiction and select contemporary fiction).

REPRESENTS nonfiction books, novels. **Considers these nonfiction areas:** creative nonfiction, humor, memoirs, popular culture. **Considers these fiction areas:** contemporary issues.

"Areas of interest include history, adventure, politics and current affairs, biography, science & natural history, technology & culture, business and memoir. Our fiction list includes authors of literary and commercial fiction, science fiction and fantasy, and young adult fiction."

HOW TO CONTACT Please send a query letter and the first few (up to 10) pages of your manuscript or proposal in the body of an e-mail (not an attachment) to one of the addresses here. For security reasons, we do not open attachments. Responds if interested. Obtains most new clients through recommendations from others, solicitations.

EDITE KROLL LITERARY AGENCY, INC.

20 Cross St., Saco ME 04072. (207)283-8797. **Fax:** (207)283-8799. **E-mail:** ekroll@maine.rr.com. **Contact:** Edite Kroll. Represents 45 clients. 20% of clients are new/unpublished writers. Currently handles: nonfiction books 40%, novels 5%, juvenile books 40%, scholarly books 5%, other.

Prior to opening her agency, Ms. Kroll served as a book editor and translator.

REPRESENTS nonfiction books, novels, juvenile, scholarly. **Considers these nonfiction areas:** juvenile, biography, current affairs, ethnic, gay, government, health, no diet books, humor, memoirs, popular culture, psychology, religion, self-help, women's, issue-oriented nonfiction. **Considers these fiction areas:** juvenile, literary, picture books, young adult, middle grade, adult.

"We represent writers and writer-artists of both adult and children's books. We have a special focus on international feminist writers, women writers and artists who write their own books (including children's and humor books)." Actively seeking artists who write their own books and international feminists who write in English. Does not want to receive genre (mysteries, thrillers, diet, cookery, etc.), photography books, coffee table books, romance, or commercial fiction.

HOW TO CONTACT Query with SASE. Submit outline/proposal, synopsis, 1-2 sample chapters, author bio, entire ms if sending picture book. No phone queries. Responds in 2-4 weeks to queries. Responds in 4-8 weeks to mss. Obtains most new clients through recommendations from others.

TERMS Agent receives 15% commission on domestic sales. Agent receives 20% commission on foreign sales. Offers written contract; 30-day notice must be given to terminate contract. Charges clients for photocopying and legal fees with prior approval from writer.

RECENT SALES Sold 12 domestic/30 foreign titles in the last year. This agency prefers not to share information on specific sales. Clients include Shel Silverstein estate, Suzy Becker, Geoffrey Hayes, Henrik Drescher, Charlotte Kasl, Gloria Skurzynski, Fatema Mernissa.

TIPS "Please do your research so you won't send me books/proposals I specifically excluded."

KT LITERARY, LLC

9249 S. Broadway, #200-543, Highlands Ranch CO 80129. (720)344-4728. **Fax:** (720)344-4728. **E-mail:** queries@ktliterary.com. **Website:** ktliterary.com. **Contact:** Kate Schafer Testerman. Member of AAR. Other memberships include SCBWI. Represents 20 clients. 60% of clients are new/unpublished writers.

Prior to her current position, Ms. Schafer was an agent with Janklow & Nesbit.

MEMBER AGENTS Kate Schafer Testerman, Renee Nyon.

REPRESENTS **Considers these fiction areas:** middle grade, young adult.

"I'm bringing my years of experience in the New York publishing scene, as well as my life-long love of reading, to a vibrant area for writers, proving that great work can be found, and sold, from anywhere." "We're thrilled to be actively seeking new clients writing brilliant, funny, original middle grade and young adult fiction, both literary and commercial." Does not want picture books, serious nonfiction, and adult literary fiction.

HOW TO CONTACT "To submit to kt literary, please e-mail us a query letter with the first three pages of your manuscript in the body of the e-mail. The subject line of your e-mail should include the word 'Query' along with the title of your manuscript. Queries should not contain attachments. Attachments will not be read, and queries containing attachments will be deleted unread. We aim to reply to all queries within two weeks of receipt. No snail mail queries." Responds in 2 weeks to queries. Responds in 2 months to mss. Obtains most new clients through recommendations from others, solicitations, conferences.

TERMS Agent receives 15% commission on domestic sales. Agent receives 20% commission on foreign sales. Offers written contract; 30-day notice must be given to terminate contract.

NEW AGENT SPOTLIGHT

CONNOR GOLDSMITH
(FOREWORD LITERARY)

forewordliterary.com

@dreamoforgonon

ABOUT CONNOR: Connor began his career in publishing at Lowenstein Associates and also spent a year as a full-time intern and relief assistant at Abrams Artists Agency. Born and raised in New York, Connor lived for a brief stint in the Midwest studying English and the Classics at Oberlin College in Ohio. He is passionate about narrative fiction across all media as a vehicle for social progress, and received his Master's degree in Media Studies from The New School for Public Engagement in 2014.

HE IS SEEKING: In fiction, Connor is seeking adult sci-fi/fantasy/horror, thrillers, upmarket commercial fiction, and literary fiction with a unique and memorable hook. He is especially interested in books by and about people from marginalized perspectives, such as LGBT people and/or racial minorities. In nonfiction, fields of interest include history (particularly of the ancient world), theater, cinema, music, television, mass media, popular culture, feminism and gender studies, LGBT issues, race relations, and the sex industry.

HOW TO QUERY: Send your query, a 1-2 page plot synopsis, and the first ten pages of your manuscript to queryconnor@forewordliterary.com. Please paste all content into the body of the e-mail.

RECENT SALES *Albatross*, by Julie Bloss; *The Last Good Place of Lily Odilon*, by Sara Beitia; *Texting the Underworld*, by Ellen Booraem. A full list of clients is available on the agency website.

WRITERS CONFERENCES Various SCBWI conferences, BookExpo.

TIPS "If we like your query, we'll ask for (more). Continuing advice is offered regularly on my blog 'Ask Daphne,' which can be accessed from my website."

THE LA LITERARY AGENCY

P.O. Box 46370, Los Angeles CA 90046. (323)654-5288. **E-mail:** ann@laliteraryagency.com; mail@laliteraryagency.com. **Website:** www.laliteraryagency.com. **Contact:** Ann Cashman.

Prior to becoming an agent, Eric Lasher worked in broadcasting and publishing in New York and Los Angeles. Prior to opening the agency, Maureen Lasher worked in New York at Prentice-Hall, Liveright, and Random House.

MEMBER AGENTS Ann Cashman, Eric Lasher, Maureen Lasher.

REPRESENTS nonfiction books, novels. **Considers these nonfiction areas:** biography, business, cooking, creative nonfiction, health, history, memoirs, parenting, psychology, science, sports. **Considers these fiction areas:** commercial, literary.

HOW TO CONTACT Prefers submissions by mail, but welcomes e-mail submissions as well. Nonfiction: query letter and book proposal. Fiction: Query with outline and first 50 pages as an attachment, 1 sample chapter. Accepts simultaneous submissions.

RECENT SALES *The Fourth Trimester*, by Susan Brink (University of California Press); *Rebels in Paradise*, by Hunter Drohojowska-Philp (Holt); *La Cucina Mexicana*, by Marilyn Tausend (UC Press); *Degas, Renoir and the Orpheus Clock*, by Simon Goodman (Scribner); *Cake Balls*, by DeDe Wilson (Harvard Common Press); *Michael Jackson: Before He Was King*, by Todd Gray (Chronicle).

PETER LAMPACK AGENCY, INC.

The Empire State Building, 350 Fifth Ave., Suite 5300, New York NY 10118. (212)687-9106. **Fax:** (212)687-9109. **E-mail:** andrew@peterlampackagency.com. **Website:** www.peterlampackagency.com. **Contact:** Andrew Lampack.

REPRESENTS nonfiction books, novels. **Considers these fiction areas:** adventure, commercial, crime, detective, family saga, literary, mainstream, mystery, police, suspense, thriller.

"This agency specializes in commercial fiction, and nonfiction by recognized experts." Actively seeking literary and commercial fiction, thrillers, mysteries, suspense, and psychological thrillers. Does not want to receive horror, romance, science fiction, westerns, historical literary fiction or academic material.

HOW TO CONTACT The Peter Lampack Agency no longer accepts material through conventional mail. E-queries only. When submitting, you should include a cover letter, author biography and a one- or two-page synopsis. Please do not send more than one sample chapter of your manuscript at a time. Due to the extremely high volume of submissions, we ask that you allow 4-6 weeks for a response. Accepts simultaneous submissions. Obtains most new clients through referrals made by clients.

TERMS Agent receives 15% commission on domestic sales. Agent receives 20% commission on foreign sales.

RECENT SALES *Spartan Gold*, by Clive Cussler with Grant Blackwood; *The Wrecker*, by Clive Cussler with Justin Scott; *Medusa*, by Clive Cussler and Paul Kemprecos; *Silent Sea* by Clive Cussler with Jack Dubrul; *Summertime*, by J.M. Coetzee; *Dreaming in French*, by Megan McAndrew; *Time Pirate*, by Ted Bell.

WRITERS CONFERENCES BookExpo America; Mystery Writers of America.

TIPS "Submit only your best work for consideration. Have a very specific agenda of goals you wish your prospective agent to accomplish for you. Provide the agent with a comprehensive statement of your credential—educational and professional accomplishments."

LAURA LANGLIE, LITERARY AGENT

147-149 Green St., Hudson NY 12534. (518)828-4708. **Fax:** (518)828-4787. **E-mail:** laura@lauralanglie.com. **Contact:** Laura Langlie. Represents 25 clients. 50% of clients are new/unpublished writers. Currently handles: nonfiction books 15%, novels 58%, story collections 2%, juvenile books 25%.

Prior to opening her agency, Ms. Langlie worked in publishing for 7 years and as an agent at Kidde, Hoyt & Picard for 6 years.

REPRESENTS Considers these nonfiction areas: autobiography, biography, cultural interests, current affairs, environment, film, history, language, law, literature, memoirs, popular culture, politics, psychology, theater, women's studies. **Considers these fiction areas:** crime, detective, ethnic, feminist, historical, humor, juvenile, literary, mainstream, mystery, police, suspense, thriller, young adult, mainstream.

"I'm very involved with and committed to my clients. Most of my clients come to me via recommendations from other agents, clients and editors. I've met very few at conferences. I've often sought out writers for projects, and I still find new clients via the traditional query letter." Does not want to receive how-to, children's picture books, hardcore science fiction, poetry, men's adventure, or erotica.

HOW TO CONTACT Query with SASE. Accepts queries via fax. Accepts simultaneous submissions. Responds in 1 week to queries. Responds in 1 month to mss. Obtains most new clients through recommendations, submissions.

TERMS Agent receives 15% commission on domestic sales. Agent receives 20% commission on foreign and dramatic sales. No written contract.

RECENT SALES Sold 15 titles in the last year. *As Close As Hands and Feet*, by Emily Arsenault (William Morrow); *The Aviator's Wife*, by Melanie Benjamin (Delacorte Press); *Free Verse* and *Ashes to Ashe-*

ville, by Sarah Dooley (G.P. Putnam's Son's/Penguin Young Reader's Group); *Miss Dimple Suspects*, by Mignon F. Ballard (St. Martin's Press); *Awaken*, by Meg Cabot (Scholastic, Inc.); *Size 12 and Ready to Rock*, by Meg Cabot (William Morrow); *Adaptation* and *Inheritance*, by Malinda Lo (Little, Brown & Co Books for Young Readers); *One Tough Chick*, by Leslie Margolis (Bloomsbury); *The Elite Gymnasts*, by Dominique Moceanu and Alicia Thompson (Disney/Hyperion); *The Lighthouse Road*, by Peter Geye (Unbridled Books); *The Nazi and the Psychiatrist*, by Jack El-Hai (Public Affairs Books); *The Last Animal*, by Abby Geni (Counterpoint Press); *Something Resembling Love*, by Mary Hogan (William Morrow); *Little Wolves*, by Thomas Maltman (Soho Press).

TIPS "Be complete, forthright and clear in your communications. Do your research as to what a particular agent represents."

MICHAEL LARSEN/ELIZABETH POMADA, LITERARY AGENTS

1029 Jones St., San Francisco CA 94109. (415)673-0939. **E-mail:** larsenpoma@aol.com. **Website:** www.larsen-pomada.com. **Contact:** Mike Larsen, Elizabeth Pomada. Member of AAR. Other memberships include Authors Guild, ASJA, PEN, WNBA, California Writers Club, National Speakers Association. Represents 100 clients. 40-45% of clients are new/unpublished writers. Currently handles: nonfiction books 70%, novels 30%.

Prior to opening their agency, Mr. Larsen and Ms. Pomada were promotion executives for major publishing houses. Mr. Larsen worked for Morrow, Bantam, and Pyramid (now part of Berkley); Ms. Pomada worked at Holt, David McKay and Dial Press. Mr. Larsen is the author of the 4th edition of *How to Write a Book Proposal* and *How to Get a Literary Agent* as well as the coauthor of *Guerilla Marketing for Writers: 100 Weapons for Selling Your Work*, which was republished in September 2009.

MEMBER AGENTS **Michael Larsen** (nonfiction); **Elizabeth Pomada** (fiction & narrative nonfiction); **Lynn Brown** (associate agent, new in 2014).

REPRESENTS **Considers these nonfiction areas:** anthropology, archeology, architecture, art, autobiography, biography, business, current affairs, diet/nutrition, design, economics, environment, ethnic, film, foods, gay/lesbian, health, history, how-to, humor, inspirational, investigative, law, medicine, memoirs, metaphysics, money, music, New Age, popular culture, politics, psychology, religious, satire, science, self-help, sociology, sports, travel, women's issues, women's studies, futurism. **Considers these fiction areas:** action, adventure, contemporary issues, crime, detective, ethnic, experimental, family saga, feminist, gay, glitz, historical, humor, inspirational, lesbian, literary, mainstream, mystery, police, religious, romance, satire, suspense.

We have diverse tastes. We look for fresh voices and new ideas. We handle literary, commercial and genre fiction, and the full range of nonfiction books. Actively seeking commercial, genre, and literary fiction. Does not want to receive children's books, plays, short stories, screenplays, pornography, poetry or stories of abuse.

HOW TO CONTACT Query with SASE. **Elizabeth Pomada** handles literary and commercial fiction, romance, thrillers, mysteries, narrative nonfiction and mainstream women's fiction. If you have completed a novel, please e-mail the first 10 pages and 2-page synopsis to larsenpoma@aol.com. Use 14-point typeface, double-spaced, as an e-mail letter with no attachments. For nonfiction, please read Michael's *How to Write a Book Proposal* book—available through your library or bookstore, and through our website—so you will know exactly what editors need. Then, before you start writing, send him the title, subtitle, and your promotion plan via conventional mail (with SASE) or e-mail. If sent as e-mail, please include the information in the body of your e-mail with NO attachments. Please allow up to 2 weeks for a response. See each agent's page on the website for contact and submission information. Responds in 8 weeks to pages or submissions.

TERMS Agent receives 15% commission on domestic sales. Agent receives 20% (30% for Asia) commission on foreign sales. May charge for printing, postage for multiple submissions, foreign mail, foreign phone calls, galleys, books, legal fees.

RECENT SALES Sold at least 15 titles in the last year. *Secrets of the Tudor Court*, by D. Bogden (Kensington); *Zen & the Art of Horse Training*, by Allan Hamilton, MD (Storey Pub.); *The Solemn Lantern Maker* by Merlinda Bobis (Delta); *Bite Marks*, the fifth book in an urban fantasy series by J.D. Rardin (Orbit/Grand Central); *The Iron King*, by Julie Karawa (Harlequin Teen).

WRITERS CONFERENCES This agency organizes the annual San Francisco Writers' Conference (www.sfwriters.org).

TIPS "We love helping writers get the rewards and recognition they deserve. If you can write books that meet the needs of the marketplace and you can promote your books, now is the best time ever to be a writer. We must find new writers to make a living, so we are very eager to hear from new writers whose work will interest large houses, and nonfiction writers who can promote their books. For a list of recent sales, helpful info, and three ways to make yourself irresistible to any publisher, please visit our website."

THE STEVE LAUBE AGENCY

5025 N. Central Ave., #635, Phoenix AZ 85012. (602)336-8910. **E-mail:** krichards@stevelaube.com. **Website:** www.stevelaube.com. **Contact:** Steve Laube, president, Karen Ball, or Dan Balow. Memberships include CBA. Represents 60+ clients. 5% of clients are new/unpublished writers.

Prior to becoming an agent, Mr. Laube worked 11 years as a Christian bookseller and 11 years as editorial director of nonfiction with Bethany House Publishers. Mrs. Murray was an accomplished novelist and agent. Mrs. Ball was an executive editor with Tyndale, Multnomah, Zondervan, and B&H. Mr. Balow was marketing director for the Left Behind series at Tyndale.

REPRESENTS nonfiction books, novels. **Considers these nonfiction areas:** religious. **Considers these fiction areas:** inspirational, religious.

Primarily serves the Christian market (CBA). Actively seeking Christian fiction and religious nonfiction. Does not want to receive children's picture books, poetry, or cookbooks.

HOW TO CONTACT Submit proposal package, outline, 3 sample chapters, SASE. For e-mail submissions, attach as Word doc or PDF. Consult website for guidelines. Accepts simultaneous submissions. Responds in 6-8 weeks to queries. Obtains most new clients through recommendations from others, solicitations, conferences.

TERMS Agent receives 15% commission on domestic sales. Agent receives 20% commission on foreign sales. Offers written contract; 30-day notice must be given to terminate contract.

RECENT SALES Sold 200 titles in the last year. Other clients include Deborah Raney, Allison Bottke, H. Norman Wright, Ellie Kay, Jack Cavanaugh, Karen Ball, Susan May Warren, Lisa Bergren, Cindy Woodsmall, Karol Ladd, Judith Pella, Margaret Daley, William Lane Craig, Ginny Aiken, Kim Vogel Sawyer, Mesu Andrews, Mary Hunt, Hugh Ross, Bill & Pam Farrel, Ronie Kendig.

WRITERS CONFERENCES Mount Hermon Christian Writers' Conference; American Christian Fiction Writers' Conference;.

LAUNCHBOOKS LITERARY AGENCY

566 Sweet Pea Place, Encinitas CA 92024. (760)944-9909. **E-mail:** david@launchbooks.com. **Website:** www.launchbooks.com. **Contact:** David Fugate. Represents 45 clients. 35% of clients are new/unpublished writers.

David Fugate has been an agent for 20 years and has successfully represented more than 1,000 book titles. He left another agency to found LaunchBooks in 2005.

REPRESENTS Considers these nonfiction areas: business, creative nonfiction, current affairs, environment, history, humor, popular culture, politics, science, sociology, sports, technology. **Considers these fiction areas:** mainstream.

We're looking for genre-breaking fiction. Do you have the next *The Martian*? Or maybe the next *The Remaining, Ready Player One*, or *Wool*, or *Monster Hunter International*? The next *Never Let Me Go*, or perhaps the next *Ender's Game, Snow Crash*, or *The Brief Wondrous Life of Oscar Wao*? What about the next *The Amazing Adventures of Kavalier and Clay, Robopocalypse*, or *World War Z*? We're on the lookout for fun, engaging, contemporary novels that appeal to a broad audience.

HOW TO CONTACT Query via e-mail. Submit outline/proposal, synopsis, 1 sample chapter, author bio. Accepts simultaneous submissions. Responds in 1 week to queries. Responds in 4 weeks to mss. Obtains most new clients through recommendations from others, solicitations.

TERMS Agent receives 15% commission on domestic sales. Agent receives 25% commission on foreign sales. Offers written contract; 30-day notice must be given to terminate contract. Charges occur very seldom. This agency's agreement limits any charges to $50 unless the author gives a written consent.

RECENT SALES *Ex-Heroes and Ex-Patriots*, by Peter Clines (Crown); *We Are Anonymous*, by Parmy Olson (Little, Brown); *The $100 Startup*, by Chris Guillebeau (Crown); *Ghost in the Wires*, by Kevin Mitnick (Little, Brown); *Kingpin*, by Kevin Poulsen (Crown); *Powering the Dream*, by Alexis Madrigal (Da Capo); *Countdown to Zero Day*, by Kim Zetter (Crown); *Rogue Code*, by Mark Russinovich (Thomas Dunne Books); *Beyond Human*, by Mark McClusky (Hudson Street Press); *Mad Science*, by Wired Magazine (Little, Brown); *You Can Buy Happiness (And It's Cheap)*, by Tammy Strobel (New World Library); *The Automatic Year*, by Scott Berkun (Jossey-Bass); *The Big Tiny*, by Dee Williams (Blue Rider Press).

SARAH LAZIN BOOKS

121 W. 27th St., Suite 704, New York NY 10001. (212)989-5757. **Fax:** (212)989-1393. **E-mail:** manuela@lazinbooks.com; slazin@lazinbooks.com. **Website:** www.lazinbooks.com. **Contact:** Sarah Lazin. Estab. 1983. Member of AAR. Represents 75+ clients. Currently handles: nonfiction books 80%, novels 20%.

MEMBER AGENTS Sarah Lazin; Manuela Jessel.

REPRESENTS nonfiction books, novels. **Considers these nonfiction areas:** biography, history, investigative, memoirs, parenting, popular culture. **Considers these fiction areas:** commercial, literary, short story collections.

Works with companies who package their books; handles some photography.

HOW TO CONTACT As of 2014: "We accept submissions through referral only." Only accepts queries on referral.

TERMS Agent receives 15% commission on domestic sales. Agent receives 20% commission on foreign sales.

THE NED LEAVITT AGENCY

70 Wooster St., Suite 4F, New York NY 10012. (212)334-0999. **Website:** www.nedleavittagency.com. **Contact:** Ned Leavitt; Jillian Sweeney. Member of AAR. Represents 40+ clients.

MEMBER AGENTS Ned Leavitt, founder and agent; Britta Alexander, agent; Jillian Sweeney, agent.

REPRESENTS nonfiction books, novels.

"We are small in size, but intensely dedicated to our authors and to supporting excellent and unique writing."

HOW TO CONTACT This agency now only takes queries/submissions through referred clients. Do *not* cold query.

TIPS Look online for this agency's recently changed submission guidelines."We strongly recommend the following books: *Writing Down the Bones* by Nathalie Goldberg; *Bird By Bird* by Anne Lamott.

ROBERT LECKER AGENCY

4055 Melrose Ave., Montreal QC H4A 2S5 Canada. (514)830-4818. **Fax:** (514)483-1644. **E-mail:** robert.lecker@gmail.com. **Website:** www.leckeragency.com. **Contact:** Robert Lecker. Represents 20 clients. 20% of clients are new/unpublished writers. Currently handles: nonfiction books 80%, novels 10%, scholarly books 10%.

Prior to becoming an agent, Mr. Lecker was the cofounder and publisher of ECW Press and professor of English literature at McGill University. He has 30 years of experience in book and magazine publishing.

MEMBER AGENTS **Robert Lecker** (popular culture, music); **Mary Williams** (travel, food, popular science).

REPRESENTS nonfiction books, novels, scholarly, syndicated material. **Considers these nonfiction areas:** autobiography, biography, cooking, cultural interests, dance, diet/nutrition, ethnic, film, foods, how-to, language, literature, music, popular culture, science, technology, theater. **Considers these fiction areas:** action, adventure, crime, detective, erotica, literary, mainstream, mystery, police, suspense, thriller.

RLA specializes in books about popular culture, popular science, music, entertainment, food, and travel. The agency responds to articulate, innovative proposals within 2 weeks. We do not represent children's literature, screenplays, poetry, self-help books, or spiritual guides.

HOW TO CONTACT E-query. In the subject line, write: "New Submission QUERY." Accepts simultaneous submissions. Responds in 2 weeks to queries. Responds in 1 month to mss. Obtains most new clients through recommendations from others, conferences, interest in website.

TERMS Agent receives 15% commission on domestic sales. Agent receives 15-20% commission on foreign sales. Offers written contract, binding for 1 year; 6-month notice must be given to terminate contract.

THE LESHNE AGENCY

16 W. 23rd St., 4th Floor, New York NY 10010. **E-mail:** info@leshneagency.com. **E-mail:** submissions@leshneagency.com. **Website:** www.leshneagency.com. **Contact:** Lisa Leshne, agent and owner.

Prior to founding the Leshne Agency, Lisa was a literary agent at publishing leader, Larry Kirshbaum's, LJK Literary.

MEMBER AGENTS Lisa Leshne, agent and owner; Sandy Hodgman, director of foreign rights.

REPRESENTS **Considers these nonfiction areas:** creative nonfiction, health, memoirs, parenting, politics, sports. **Considers these fiction areas:** commercial, middle grade.

Wants "authors across all genres. We are interested in narrative, memoir, and prescriptive nonfiction, with a particular interest in sports, wellness, business, political and parenting topics. We will also look at truly terrific commercial fiction and young adult and middle grade books."

HOW TO CONTACT "Submit all materials in the body of an e-mail; no attachments. Be sure to include the word 'QUERY' and the title of your ms in the subject line. Include brief synopsis, TOC or chapter outline, 10 sample pages, bio, any previous publications, word count, how much of the ms is complete, and the best way to reach you."

LEVINE GREENBERG ROSTAN LITERARY AGENCY, INC.

307 Seventh Ave., Suite 2407, New York NY 10001. (212)337-0934. **Fax:** (212)337-0948. **E-mail:** submit@levinegreenberg.com. **Website:** www.levinegreenberg.com. Member of AAR. Represents 250 clients. 33% of clients are new/unpublished writers. Currently handles: nonfiction books 70%, novels 30%.

Prior to opening his agency, Mr. Levine served as vice president of the Bank Street College of Education.

MEMBER AGENTS **Jim Levine**; **Stephanie Rostan** (adult fiction, nonfiction, YA); **Melissa Rowland**; **Daniel Greenberg** (literary fiction; nonfiction: popular culture, narrative nonfiction, memoir, and humor); **Victoria Skurnick**; **Danielle Svetcov**; **Elizabeth Fisher**; **Lindsay Edgecombe** (narrative nonfiction, memoir, lifestyle and health, illustrated books, as well as literary fiction); **Monika Verma** (nonfiction: humor, pop culture, memoir, narrative nonfiction and style and fashion titles); **Kerry Sparks** (young adult and middle grade); **Tim Wojcik**; **Jamie Maurer**; **Miek Coccia**; **Arielle Eckstut**; **Kirsten Wolf**.

REPRESENTS nonfiction books, novels. **Considers these nonfiction areas:** animals, art, biography, business, computers, cooking, creative nonfiction, gardening, health, humor, memoirs, money, New Age, science, sociology, spirituality, sports. **Considers these fiction areas:** literary, mainstream, middle grade, mystery, thriller, women's, young adult.

This agency specializes in business, psychology, parenting, health/medicine, narrative nonfiction, spirituality, religion, women's issues, and commercial fiction.

HOW TO CONTACT See website for full submission procedure at "How to Submit." Or use our e-mail address (submit@levinegreenberg.com) if you prefer, or online submission form. Do not submit directly to agents. Prefers electronic submissions. Cannot respond to submissions by mail. Do not attach more than 50 pages. Obtains most new clients through recommendations from others.

TERMS Agent receives 15% commission on domestic sales. Agent receives 20% commission on foreign sales. Offers written contract. Charges clients for out-of-pocket expenses—telephone, fax, postage, photocopying—directly connected to the project.

RECENT SALES *Gone Girl*, by Gillian Flynn; *Hyperbole and a Half*, by Allie Brosh; *Our Dumb Century*, by editors of the *The Onion*; *Predictably Irrational*, by Dan Ariely.

WRITERS CONFERENCES ASJA Writers' Conference.

TIPS "We focus on editorial development, business representation, and publicity and marketing strategy."

PAUL S. LEVINE LITERARY AGENCY

1054 Superba Ave., Venice CA 90291. (310)450-6711. **Fax:** (310)450-0181. **E-mail:** paul@paulslevinelit.com. **Website:** www.paulslevinelit.com. **Contact:** Paul S. Levine. Memberships include the State Bar of California. Represents over 100 clients. 75% of clients are new/unpublished writers. Currently handles: nonfiction books 60%, novels 10%, movie scripts 10%, TV scripts 5%, juvenile books 5%.

MEMBER AGENTS **Paul S. Levine** (children's and young adult fiction and nonfiction, adult fiction and nonfiction except sci-fi, fantasy, and horror); **Loren R.**

NEW AGENT SPOTLIGHT

LAURA ZATS
(RED SOFA LITERARY)

redsofaliterary.com

@LZats

ABOUT LAURA: Laura graduated from Grinnell College with degrees in English and Anthropology. She's been working as an editor for several years and has held positions at companies in both the US and the UK. In her free time, Laura likes to craft, swing dance, bake, and binge on Netflix marathons of "Buffy the Vampire Slayer" and "Doctor Who."

SHE IS SEEKING: young adult and middle grade (especially contemporary for both), romance, new adult, contemporary women's fiction, sci-fi, fantasy, and erotica.

HOW TO QUERY: laura@redsofaliterary.com. Put "Query" in the subject line.

Grossman (archaeology, art/photography/architecture, gardening, education, health, medicine, science).

REPRESENTS nonfiction books, novels, episodic drama, movie, TV, movie scripts, feature film, TV movie of the week, sitcom, animation, documentary, miniseries, syndicated material, reality show. **Considers these nonfiction areas:** architecture, art, autobiography, biography, business, child guidance, computers, cooking, crafts, cultural interests, current affairs, diet/nutrition, design, economics, education, ethnic, film, foods, gay/lesbian, government, health, history, hobbies, how-to, humor, investigative, language, law, medicine, memoirs, military, money, music, New Age, parenting, photography, popular culture, politics, psychology, science, self-help, sociology, sports, theater, true crime, women's issues, women's studies, creative nonfiction, animation. **Considers these fiction areas:** action, adventure, comic books, confession, crime, detective, erotica, ethnic, experimental, family saga, feminist, frontier, gay, glitz, historical, humor, inspirational, lesbian, literary, mainstream, mystery, police, regional, religious, romance, satire, sports, suspense, thriller, westerns. **Considers these script areas:** action, biography, cartoon, comedy, contemporary, detective, erotica, ethnic, experimental, family, feminist, gay, glitz, historical, horror, juvenile, mainstream, multimedia, mystery, religious, romantic comedy, romantic drama, sports, teen, thriller, western.

Does not want to receive science fiction, fantasy, or horror.

HOW TO CONTACT Query with SASE. Accepts simultaneous submissions. Responds in 1 day to queries. Responds in 6-8 weeks to mss. Obtains most new clients through conferences, referrals, listings on various websites, and in directories.

TERMS Agent receives 15% commission on domestic sales. Offers written contract. Charges for postage and actual, out-of-pocket costs only.

RECENT SALES Sold 8 books in the last year.

WRITERS CONFERENCES Willamette Writers Conference; San Francisco Writers Conference; Santa Barbara Writers Conference and many others.

TIPS "Write good, sellable books."

ROBERT LIEBERMAN ASSOCIATES

400 Nelson Rd., Ithaca NY 14850-9440. (607)273-8801. **E-mail:** rhl10@cornell.edu. **Website:** www.people.cornell.edu/pages/rhl10. **Contact:** Robert Lieberman. Currently handles: nonfiction books 100%.

REPRESENTS nonfiction books, trade, scholarly, college-level textbooks. **Considers these nonfiction areas:** agriculture, anthropology, archeology, architecture, art, business, computers, design, economics, education, environment, film, health, horticulture, medicine, music, psychology, science, sociology, technology, theater, memoirs by authors with high public recognition.

This agency only accepts nonfiction ideas and specializes in university/college-level textbooks, CD-ROM/software for the university/college-level textbook market, and popular trade books in math, engineering, economics, and other subjects. Does not want to receive any fiction, self-help, or screenplays.

HOW TO CONTACT Prefers to read materials exclusively. Responds in 2 weeks to queries. Responds in 1 month to mss. Obtains most new clients through referrals.

TERMS Agent receives 15% commission on domestic sales. Agent receives 20% commission on foreign sales. Offers written contract; 1-month notice must be given to terminate contract. Fees are sometimes charged to clients for shipping and when special reviewers are required.

TIPS "The trade books we handle are by authors who are highly recognized in their fields of expertise. Our client list includes Nobel Prize winners and others with high name recognition, either by the public or within a given area of expertise."

LIPPINCOTT MASSIE MCQUILKIN

27 West 20th Street, Suite 305, New York NY 10011. **Fax:** (212)352-2059. **E-mail:** info@lmqlit.com. **Website:** www.lmqlit.com.

MEMBER AGENTS **Shannon O'Neill** (writing that informs, intrigues, or inspires: special interests include narrative nonfiction, popular science, current affairs, the history of ideas, and literary and upmarket fiction); **Laney Katz Becker**; **Kent Wolf** (literary fiction, upmarket women's fiction, memoir, pop culture, all types of narrative nonfiction, and select YA); **Ethan Bassoff** (emerging and established writers of literary and crime fiction and narrative nonfiction including history, science, humor, and sports writing); **Jason Anthony** (specializes in young adult and commercial fiction and most areas of nonfiction, including pop culture, memoir, true crime, and general psychology); **Will Lippincott** (politics, current events, narrative nonfiction and history); **Maria Massie** (literary fiction, memoir, and cultural history); **Rob McQuilkin** (fiction, memoir, history, sociology, psychology, and graphic works).

REPRESENTS nonfiction books, novels, short story collections, scholarly, graphic novels. **Considers these nonfiction areas:** animals, anthropology, archeology, architecture, art, autobiography, biography, business, child guidance, cultural interests, current affairs, design, economics, ethnic, film, gay/lesbian, government, health, history, inspirational, language, law, literature, medicine, memoirs, military, money, music, parenting, popular culture, politics, psychology, religious, science, self-help, sociology, technology, true crime, women's issues, women's studies, young adult. **Considers these fiction areas:** action, adventure, cartoon, comic books, confession, family saga, feminist, gay, historical, humor, lesbian, literary, mainstream, regional, satire.

"LMQ focuses on bringing new voices in literary and commercial fiction to the market, as well as popularizing the ideas and arguments of scholars in the fields of history, psychology, sociology, political science, and current affairs. Actively seeking fiction writers who already have credits in magazines and quarterlies, as well as nonfiction writers who already have a media platform or some kind of a university affiliation." Does not want to receive romance, genre fiction, or children's material.

HOW TO CONTACT E-query. "Include the word 'Query' as well as the agent you are querying in the subject line of your e-mail (i.e., 'Query for Maria Massie'). If your project is fiction, please also include the first 5-10 pages pasted into the body of your e-mail. We look forward to reviewing your work." Accepts simultaneous submissions. Obtains most new clients through recommendations from others, solicitations, conferences.

TERMS Agent receives 15% commission on domestic sales. Agent receives 20% commission on foreign sales. Offers written contract; 30-day notice must be given to terminate contract. Only charges for reasonable business expenses upon successful sale.

RECENT SALES Clients include: Peter Ho Davies, Kim Addonizio, Natasha Trethewey, Anne Carson, David Sirota, Katie Crouch, Uwen Akpan, Lydia Millet, Tom Perrotta, Jonathan Lopez, Chris Hayes, Caroline Weber.

LITERARY AND CREATIVE ARTISTS, INC.

3543 Albemarle St., N.W., Washington D.C. 20008-4213. (202)362-4688. **Fax:** (202)362-8875. **E-mail:** lca9643@lcadc.com. **Website:** www.lcadc.com. **Contact:** Muriel Nellis. Member of AAR. Other memberships include Authors Guild, American Bar Association, American Booksellers Association. Currently handles: nonfiction books 50%, novels 50%.

MEMBER AGENTS Prior to becoming an agent, Mr. Powell was in sales and contract negotiation.

REPRESENTS nonfiction books, novels, art, biography, business, photography, popular culture, religion, self-help, literary, regional, religious, satire. **Considers these nonfiction areas:** autobiography, biography, business, cooking, diet/nutrition, economics, foods, government, health, how-to, law, medicine, memoirs, philosophy, politics.

"Actively seeking quality projects by authors with a vision of where they want to be in 10 years and a plan of how to get there." We do not handle poetry, or purely academic/technical work.

HOW TO CONTACT Query via e-mail first and include a synopsis. No attachments. **We do not accept unsolicited manuscripts, faxed manuscripts, manuscripts sent by e-mail or manuscripts on computer disk.** Accepts simultaneous submissions. Responds in 3 weeks to queries. Responds in 1 week to mss. Obtains new clients through recommendations from others.

TERMS Agent receives 15% commission on domestic sales. Agent receives 25% commission on foreign sales. Offers written contract. Charges clients for long-distance phone/fax, photocopying, shipping.

TIPS "If you are an unpublished author, join a writers group, even if it is on the Internet. You need good honest feedback. Don't send a manuscript that has not been read by at least five people. Don't send a manuscript cold to any agent without first asking if they want it. Try to meet the agent face to face before signing. Make sure the fit is right."

THE LITERARY GROUP INTERNATIONAL

1357 Broadway, Suite 316, New York NY 10018. (212)400-1494, ext. 380. **Website:** www.theliterarygroup.com. **Contact:** Frank Weimann. 1900 Ave. of the Stars, 25 Fl., Los Angeles, CA 90067; Tel: (310)282-8961; **Fax:** (310) 282-8903. 65% of clients are new/unpublished writers. Currently handles: nonfiction books 50%, 50% fiction.

MEMBER AGENTS Frank Weimann.

REPRESENTS nonfiction books, novels, graphic novels. **Considers these nonfiction areas:** animals, anthropology, biography, business, child guidance, crafts, creative nonfiction, current affairs, education, ethnic, film, government, health, history, humor, juvenile nonfiction, language, memoirs, military, multicultural, music, nature, popular culture, politics, psychology, religious, science, self-help, sociology, sports, travel, true crime, women's issues, women's studies. **Considers these fiction areas:** adventure, contemporary issues, detective, ethnic, experimental, family saga, fantasy, feminist, historical, horror, humor, literary, multicultural, mystery, psychic, regional, romance, sports, thriller, young adult, graphic novels.

This agency specializes in nonfiction (memoir, military, history, biography, sports, how-to).

HOW TO CONTACT Query. Prefers to read materials exclusively. Only responds if interested. Obtains most new clients through referrals, writers conferences, query letters.

TERMS Agent receives 15% commission on domestic sales. Agent receives 20% commission on foreign sales. Offers written contract; 30-day notice must be given to terminate contract.

RECENT SALES *Living With Honor* by Sal Giunta (Simon and Schuster) *Siempre,* by JR Darhower (Pocket Books); *Wear Your Dreams: My Life in Tattoos,* by Ed Hardy (St. Martin's Press); *The New Jewish Table: Modern Seasonal Recipes for Traditional Dishes,* by Todd Gray and Ellen Kassoff Gray (St. Martin's Press); *Grace, Gold, and Glory: My Leap of Faith,* by Gabby Douglas (HarperCollins).

WRITERS CONFERENCES San Diego State University Writers' Conference; Agents and Editors Conference; NAHJ Convention in Puerto Rico, others.

LITERARY SERVICES, INC.

P.O. Box 888, Barnegat NJ 08005. **E-mail:** john@literaryservicesinc.com; shane@literaryservicesinc.

com. **Website:** www.LiteraryServicesInc.com. **Contact:** John Willig. Memberships include Author's Guild. Represents 90 clients. 25% of clients are new/unpublished writers. Currently handles: nonfiction books 100%. Beginning to accept and consider historical, crime and literary fiction projects.

MEMBER AGENTS John Willig (business, personal growth, narratives, history, health, science and technology, politics, current events).

REPRESENTS nonfiction books. **Considers these nonfiction areas:** architecture, art, biography, business, child guidance, cooking, crafts, design, economics, health, history, humor, language, literature, money, popular culture, psychology, satire, science, self-help, sports, technology, true crime.

We work primarily with nonfiction and mystery/crime fiction authors. "Our publishing experience and 'inside' knowledge of how companies and editors really work sets us apart from many agencies; our specialties are noted above, but we are open to unique presentations in all nonfiction topic areas." Actively seeking business, work/life topics, story-driven narratives. Does not want to receive fiction (except crime fiction), children's books, science fiction, religion or memoirs.

HOW TO CONTACT Query with SASE. For starters, a one-page outline sent via e-mail is acceptable. See our website and our Submissions section to learn more about our questions. Do not send manuscript unless requested. Accepts simultaneous submissions. Responds in 3-4 weeks to queries. Responds in 4 weeks to mss. Obtains most new clients through recommendations from others, solicitations, conferences.

TERMS Agent receives 15% commission on domestic sales. Agent receives 15% commission on foreign sales. Offers written contract. This agency charges administrative fees for copying, postage, etc.

RECENT SALES Sold 20 titles in the last year. A full list of new and award-winning books is noted on the agency website.

WRITERS CONFERENCES ASJA; Publicity Summit; Writer's Digest Conference (NYC); Thrillerfest.

TIPS "Be focused. In all likelihood, your work is not going to be of interest to 'a very broad audience' or 'every parent,' so I appreciate when writers research and do some homework, i.e., positioning, special features and benefits of your work. Be a marketer. How have you tested your ideas and writing (beyond your inner circle of family and friends)? Have you received any key awards for your work or endorsements from influential persons in your field? What steps, especially social media, have you taken to increase your presence in the market?"

LIVING WORD LITERARY AGENCY

P.O. Box 40974, Eugene OR 97414. **E-mail:** livingwordliterary@gmail.com. **Website:** livingwordliterary.wordpress.com. **Contact:** Kimberly Shumate, agent. Estab. 2009. Member Evangelical Christian Publishers Association

Kimberly began her employment with Harvest House Publishers as the assistant to the National Sales Manager as well as the International Sales Director, continued into the editorial department.

REPRESENTS Considers these nonfiction areas: health, parenting, self-help, relationships. **Considers these fiction areas:** inspirational, adult fiction, Christian living.

Does not want to receive YA fiction, cookbooks, children's books, science fiction or fantasy, memoirs, screenplays or poetry.

HOW TO CONTACT Submit a query with short synopsis and first chapter via Word document. Agency only responds if interested.

LOWENSTEIN ASSOCIATES INC.

121 W. 27th St., Suite 501, New York NY 10001. (212)206-1630. **Fax:** (212)727-0280. **E-mail:** assistant@bookhaven.com. **Website:** www.lowensteinassociates.com. **Contact:** Barbara Lowenstein. Member of AAR. Represents 150 clients.

MEMBER AGENTS **Barbara Lowenstein**, president (nonfiction interests include narrative nonfiction, health, money, finance, travel, multicultural, popular culture, and memoir; fiction interests include literary fiction and women's fiction); **Emily Gref** (young adult, middle grade, fantasy, science fiction, literary, commercial, various nonfiction).

REPRESENTS nonfiction books, novels. **Considers these nonfiction areas:** creative nonfiction, health, memoirs, money, multicultural, popular culture, travel. **Considers these fiction areas:** commercial, fantasy, literary, middle grade, science fiction, women's, young adult.

Barbara Lowenstein is currently looking for writers who have a platform and are leading experts in their field, including business, women's issues, psychology, health, science and social issues, and is particularly interested in strong new voices in fiction and narrative nonfiction. Does not want Westerns, textbooks, children's picture books and books in need of translation.

HOW TO CONTACT "For fiction, please send us a one-page query letter, along with the first ten pages pasted in the body of the message by e-mail to assistant@bookhaven.com. If nonfiction, please send a one-page query letter, a table of contents, and, if available, a proposal pasted into the body of the e-mail to assistant@bookhaven.com. Please put the word QUERY and the title of your project in the subject field of your e-mail and address it to the agent of your choice. Please do not send an attachment as the message will be deleted without being read and no reply will be sent." Accepts simultaneous submissions. Responds in 6 weeks to queries. Obtains most new clients through recommendations from others, solicitations, conferences.

TERMS Agent receives 15% commission on domestic sales. Agent receives 20% commission on foreign sales. Offers written contract. Charges for large photocopy batches, messenger service, international postage.

WRITERS CONFERENCES Malice Domestic.

TIPS "Know the genre you are working in and read! Also, please see our website for details on which agent to query for your project."

ANDREW LOWNIE LITERARY AGENCY, LTD.

36 Great Smith St., London SW1P 3BU England. (44) (207)222-7574. **Fax:** (44)(207)222-7576. **E-mail:** lownie@globalnet.co.uk; david.haviland@andrewlownie.co.uk. **Website:** www.andrewlownie.co.uk. **Contact:** Andrew Lownie (nonfiction); David Haviland (fiction). Member of AAA. Represents 130 clients. 20% of clients are new/unpublished writers. Currently handles: nonfiction books 90%, novels 10%.

Prior to becoming an agent, Mr. Lownie was a journalist, bookseller, publisher, author of 12 books, and director of the Curtis Brown Agency. Short-listed for Literary Agent of the Year 2013 by *Bookseller Magazine* and the top selling agent in the world on Publishers Marketplace 2013-2014. Mr. Haviland is a writer and has worked in advertising, script development, and was co-founder of Sirius Television.

REPRESENTS nonfiction books. **Considers these nonfiction areas:** autobiography, biography, current affairs, government, history, investigative, law, memoirs, military, popular culture, politics, true crime, war. **Considers these fiction areas:** commercial, crime, horror, literary, science fiction, thriller, women's.

This agent has wide publishing experience, extensive journalistic contacts, and a specialty in showbiz/celebrity memoir. Showbiz memoirs, narrative histories, and biographies. No poetry, short stories, children's fiction, academic or scripts.

HOW TO CONTACT Query by e-mail only. Submit outline, 1 sample chapter. Accepts simultaneous submissions. Responds in 1 week to queries. Responds in 1 month to mss. Obtains most new clients through recommendations from others and unsolicited through website.

TERMS Agent receives 15% commission on domestic sales. Agent receives 20% commission on foreign sales. Offers written contract; 30-day notice must be given to terminate contract.

RECENT SALES Sold 60 titles in the last year, with over a dozen top 10 bestsellers including many number ones, as well as the memoirs of Queen Elizabeth II's Press Officer Dickie Arbiter, Lance Armstrong's masseuse Emma O'Reilly, actor Warwick Davis, Multiple Personality Disorder sufferer Alice Jamieson, round-the-world yachtsman Mike Perham, poker player Dave 'Devilfish' Ulliott, David Hasselhoff, Sam Faiers and Kirk Norcross from *TOWIE*, Spencer Matthews from *Made in Chelsea*, singer Kerry Katona. Other clients: Juliet Barker, Guy Bellamy, Joyce Cary estate, Roger Crowley, Duncan Falconer, Marius Gabriel, Laurence Gardner, the actress Paula Hamilton, Cathy Glass, Timothy Good, Robert Hutchinson, Lawrence James, Leslie Kenton, Christopher Lloyd, Sian Rees, Desmond Seward, Daniel Tammet, Casey Watson, and Christian Wolmar.

DONALD MAASS LITERARY AGENCY

121 W. 27th St., Suite 801, New York NY 10001. (212)727-8383. **E-mail:** info@maassagency.com. **Website:** www.maassagency.com. Estab. 1980. Member of AAR. Other memberships include SFWA, MWA, RWA. Represents more than 100 clients. 5% of clients are new/unpublished writers. Currently handles: novels 100%.

Prior to opening his agency, Mr. Maass served as an editor at Dell Publishing (New York) and as a reader at Gollancz (London). He also served as the president of AAR.

MEMBER AGENTS **Donald Maass** (mainstream, literary, mystery/suspense, science fiction, romance); **Jennifer Jackson** (commercial fiction, romance, science fiction, fantasy, mystery/suspense); **Cameron McClure** (literary, mystery/suspense, urban, fantasy, narrative nonfiction and projects with multicultural, international, and environmental themes, gay/lesbian); **Stacia Decker** (fiction, memoir, narrative nonfiction, pop-culture [cooking, fashion, style, music, art], smart humor, upscale erotica/erotic memoir and multicultural fiction/nonfiction); **Amy Boggs** (fantasy and science fiction, especially urban fantasy, paranormal romance, steampunk, YA/children's, and alternate history, historical fiction, multicultural fiction, westerns); **Katie Shea Boutillier** (women's fiction/book club; edgy/dark, realistic/contemporary YA; commercial-scale literary fiction; and celebrity memoir); **Jennifer Udden** (speculative fiction [both science fiction and fantasy], urban fantasy, and mysteries, as well as historical, erotic, contemporary, and paranormal romance).

REPRESENTS nonfiction, novels. **Considers these nonfiction areas:** creative nonfiction, memoirs, popular culture. **Considers these fiction areas:** crime, detective, fantasy, historical, horror, literary, mainstream, multicultural, mystery, paranormal, police, psychic, romance, science fiction, supernatural, suspense, thriller, westerns, women's, young adult.

This agency specializes in commercial fiction, especially science fiction, fantasy, mystery and suspense. Actively seeking to expand in literary fiction and women's fiction. We are fiction specialists. All genres are welcome.

HOW TO CONTACT E-query. All the agents have different submission addresses and instructions. See the website and each agent's online profile for exact submission instruction. Accepts simultaneous submissions.

TERMS Agent receives 15% commission on domestic sales. Agent receives 20% commission on foreign sales.

RECENT SALES *Codex Alera 5: Princep's Fury*, by Jim Butcher (Ace); *Fonseca 6: Bright Futures*, by Stuart Kaimsky (Forge): *Fathom*, by Cherie Priest (Tor); *Gospel Grrls 3: Be Strong and Curvaceous*, by Shelly Adina (Faith Words); *Ariane 1: Peacekeeper*, by Laura Reeve (Roc); *Execution Dock*, by Anne Perry (Random House).

WRITERS CONFERENCES Donald Maass: World Science Fiction Convention; Frankfurt Book Fair; Pacific Northwest Writers Conference; Bouchercon. Jennifer Jackson: World Science Fiction Convention; RWA National Conference.

TIPS We are fiction specialists, also noted for our innovative approach to career planning. Few new clients are accepted, but interested authors should query with a SASE. Works with subagents in all principle foreign countries and Hollywood. No prescriptive nonfiction, picture books, or poetry will be considered.

GINA MACCOBY LITERARY AGENCY

P.O. Box 60, Chappaqua NY 10514. (914)238-5630. **E-mail:** query@maccobylit.com. **Contact:** Gina Maccoby. Member of AAR. AAR Board of Directors; Ethics and Contracts subcommittees; Authors Guild. Represents 25 clients. Currently handles: nonfiction books 33%, novels 33%, juvenile books 33%.

MEMBER AGENTS Gina Maccoby.

REPRESENTS nonfiction books, novels, juvenile. **Considers these nonfiction areas:** autobiography, biography, cultural interests, current affairs, ethnic, history, juvenile nonfiction, popular culture, women's issues, women's studies. **Considers these fiction areas:** juvenile, literary, mainstream, mystery, thriller, young adult.

HOW TO CONTACT Query by e-mail only. Accepts simultaneous submissions. Owing to volume of submissions, may not respond to queries unless interested. Obtains most new clients through recommendations from clients and publishers.

TERMS Agent receives 15% commission on domestic sales. Agent receives 20-25% commission on foreign sales, which includes subagents commissions. Charges clients for photocopying. May recover certain costs, such as legal fees or the cost of shipping books by air to Europe or Japan.

RECENT SALES *The Perfect Ghost*, by Linda Barnes (St. Martin's Minotaur, April 2013); *Supreme City: How Jazz Age Manhattan Gave Birth to Modern America* by Donald L. Miller (Simon & Schuster, May 2014); *Stripes of All Types* by Susan Stockdale (Peachtree, April 2013); *You Read to Me, I'll Read to You: Very Short Tall Tales to Read Aloud* by Mary Ann Hoberman (Little Brown, April 2014); *True Colors* by Natalie Kinsey-Warnock (Yearling, November 2013).

NEW AGENT SPOTLIGHT

NIKKI TERPILOWSKI
(HOLLOWAY LITERARY)

hollowayliteraryagency.com

@HollowayLit, @AWomanReading

ABOUT NIKKI: Nikki has degrees in English and International Relations and is a member of Romance Writers of America and International Thriller Writers. Readers can follow her blog at AWomanReading.wordpress.com.

SHE IS SEEKING: women's fiction, Southern fiction, multicultural literary fiction, upmarket African-American fiction, steam funk, romance (all kinds except category), military and espionage thrillers, historical fiction, nonfiction with a strong platform and academic assessments of popular culture. Additionally, Nikki seeks graphic novels, Manga, YA, MG and children's picture books. Nikki is especially interested in time travel, reincarnation, mythology, ancient civilizations, magical and animist realism, Japan, American history (especially hidden African-American history, interesting women in history, as well as the antebellum period, and the Civil and Revolutionary wars), the military (all branches, but especially the U.S. Marine Corp, Army and all Special Forces), espionage, martial arts, narrative nonfiction about food and beverage (especially organic food, wine and coffee), travel or expat life, international relations and foreign policy, and prescriptive nonfiction on spirituality, parenting, health and well-being.

HOW TO QUERY: submissions@hollowayliteraryagency.com. For fiction: send a one-page query and the first 15 pages of your ms in the body of the e-mail. For nonfiction: send a proposal (and if relevant, link to related blog). Include a brief bio and social media links.

⊘◎ MACGREGOR LITERARY INC.

2373 N.W. 185th Ave., Suite 165, Hillsboro OR 97124. (503)277-8308. **Website:** www.macgregorliterary.com. **Contact:** Chip MacGregor. Signatory of WGA. Represents 40 clients. 10% of clients are new/unpublished writers. Currently handles: nonfiction books 40%, novels 60%.

Prior to his current position, Mr. MacGregor was the senior agent with Alive Communications. Most recently, he was associate publisher for Time-Warner Book Group's Faith Division, and helped put together their Center Street imprint.

MEMBER AGENTS Chip MacGregor, Sandra Bishop, Amanda Luedeke; Holly Lorincz; Erin Buterbaugh.

REPRESENTS nonfiction books, novels. **Considers these nonfiction areas:** business, current affairs, economics, history, how-to, humor, inspirational, parenting, popular culture, satire, self-help, sports, marriage. **Considers these fiction areas:** crime, detective, historical, inspirational, mainstream, mystery, police, religious, romance, suspense, thriller, women's, chick lit.

"My specialty has been in career planning with authors—finding commercial ideas, then helping authors bring them to market, and in the midst of that assisting the authors as they get firmly established in their writing careers. I'm probably best known for my work with Christian books over the years, but I've done a fair amount of general market projects as well." Actively seeking authors with a Christian worldview and a growing platform. Does not want to receive fantasy, sci-fi, children's books, poetry or screenplays.

HOW TO CONTACT Do not query this agency without an invitation or referral. Accepts simultaneous submissions. Responds in 3 weeks to queries. Obtains most new clients through recommendations from others. Not looking to add unpublished authors except through referrals from current clients.

TERMS Agent receives 15% commission on domestic sales. Agent receives 15% commission on foreign sales. Offers written contract; 30-day notice must be given to terminate contract. Charges for exceptional fees after receiving authors' permission.

WRITERS CONFERENCES Blue Ridge Christian Writers' Conference; Write to Publish.

TIPS "Seriously consider attending a good writers' conference. It will give you the chance to be face-to-face with people in the industry. Also, if you're a novelist, consider joining one of the national writers' organizations. The American Christian Fiction Writers (ACFW) is a wonderful group for new as well as established writers. And if you're a Christian writer of any kind, check into The Writers View, an online writing group. All of these have proven helpful to writers."

KIRSTEN MANGES LITERARY AGENCY

115 W. 29th St., Third Floor, New York NY 10001. **Website:** www.mangeslit.com. **Contact:** Kirsten Manges.

Prior to her current position, Ms. Manges was an agent at Curtis Brown.

REPRESENTS nonfiction books, novels.

HOW TO CONTACT Closed to submissions. Obtains most new clients through recommendations from others, solicitations.

CAROL MANN AGENCY

55 Fifth Ave., New York NY 10003. (212)206-5635. **Fax:** (212)675-4809. **E-mail:** submissions@carolmannagency.com. **Website:** www.carolmannagency.com. **Contact:** Lydia Blyfield. Member of AAR. Represents roughly 200 clients. 15% of clients are new/unpublished writers.

MEMBER AGENTS **Carol Mann** (health/medical, religion, spirituality, self-help, parenting, narrative nonfiction, current affairs); **Laura Yorke; Gareth Esersky; Myrsini Stephanides** (nonfiction areas of interest: pop culture and music, humor, narrative nonfiction and memoir, cookbooks; fiction areas of interest: offbeat literary fiction, graphic works, and edgy YA fiction); **Joanne Wyckoff** (nonfiction areas of interest: memoir, narrative nonfiction, personal narrative, psychology, women's issues, education, health and wellness, parenting, serious self-help, natural history; also accepts fiction).

REPRESENTS nonfiction books, novels. **Considers these nonfiction areas:** anthropology, archeology, architecture, art, autobiography, biography, business, child guidance, cultural interests, current affairs, design, ethnic, government, health, history, law, medicine, money, music, parenting, popular culture, politics, psychology, self-help, sociology, sports, women's issues, women's studies. **Considers these fiction areas:** commercial, literary, young adult, graphic works.

Does not want to receive genre fiction (romance, mystery, etc.).

HOW TO CONTACT Please see website for submission guidelines. Responds in 4 weeks to queries.

TERMS Agent receives 15% commission on domestic sales. Agent receives 20% commission on foreign sales. Offers written contract.

MANSION STREET LITERARY MANAGEMENT

E-mail: mansionstreet@gmail.com. **E-mail:** querymansionstreet@gmail.com (Jean); querymichelle@mansionstreet.com. **Website:** mansionstreet.com. **Contact:** Jean Sagendorph; Michelle Witte.

MEMBER AGENTS **Jean Sagendorph** (pop culture, gift books, cookbooks, general nonfiction, lifestyle, design, brand extensions), **Michelle Witte** (young adult, middle grade, juvenile nonfiction).

REPRESENTS **Considers these nonfiction areas:** cooking, design, popular culture. **Considers these fiction areas:** juvenile, middle grade, young adult.

HOW TO CONTACT Send a query letter and no more than the first 10 pages of your manuscript in the body of an e-mail. Query one specific agent at this agency. No attachments. You must list the genre in the subject line. If the genre is not in the subject line, your query will be deleted. Responds in up to 6 weeks.

RECENT SALES Authors: Paul Thurlby, Steve Ouch, Steve Seabury, Gina Hyams, Sam Pocker, Kim Siebold, Jean Sagendorph, Heidi Antman, Shannon O'Malley, Meg Bartholomy, Dawn Sokol, Hollister Hovey, Porter Hovey, Robb Pearlman.

MANUS & ASSOCIATES LITERARY AGENCY, INC.

425 Sherman Ave., Suite 200, Palo Alto CA 94306. (650)470-5151. **Fax:** (650)470-5159. **E-mail:** manuslit@manuslit.com. **Website:** www.manuslit.com. **Contact:** Jillian Manus, Jandy Nelson, Penny Nelson. NYC address: 444 Madison Ave., 29th Floor, New York, NY 10022. Member of AAR. Represents 75 clients. 30% of clients are new/unpublished writers.

Prior to becoming an agent, Ms. Manus was associate publisher of two national magazines and director of development at Warner Bros. and Universal Studios; she has been a literary agent for 20 years.

MEMBER AGENTS **Jandy Nelson** (currently not taking on new clients); **Jillian Manus**, jillian@manuslit.com (political, memoirs, self-help, history, sports, women's issues, thrillers); **Penny Nelson,** penny@manuslit.com (memoirs, self-help, sports, nonfiction); **Janet Wilkens Manus** (narrative fact-based crime books, religion, pop psychology, inspiration, memoirs, cookbooks).

REPRESENTS nonfiction books, novels. **Considers these nonfiction areas:** cooking, history, inspirational, memoirs, politics, psychology, religious, self-help, sports, women's issues. **Considers these fiction areas:** thriller.

"Our agency is unique in the way that we not only sell the material, but we edit, develop concepts, and participate in the marketing effort. We specialize in large, conceptual fiction and nonfiction, and always value a project that can be sold in the TV/feature film market." Actively seeking high-concept thrillers, commercial literary fiction, women's fiction, celebrity biographies, memoirs, multicultural fiction, popular health, women's empowerment and mysteries. No horror, romance, science fiction, fantasy, western, young adult, children's, poetry, cookbooks, or magazine articles.

HOW TO CONTACT Query via snail mail. Include proper SASE for a reply. Send print queries to the California address. Accepts simultaneous submissions. Responds in 3 months to queries. Responds in 3 months to mss. Obtains most new clients through recommendations from others, solicitations, conferences.

TERMS Agent receives 15% commission on domestic sales. Agent receives 20-25% commission on foreign sales. Offers written contract, binding for 2 years; 60-day notice must be given to terminate contract. Charges for photocopying and postage/UPS.

RECENT SALES *Nothing Down for the 2000s* and *Multiple Streams of Income for the 2000s*, by Robert Allen; *Missed Fortune 101*, by Doug Andrew; *Cracking the Millionaire Code*, by Mark Victor Hansen and Robert Allen; *Stress Free for Good*, by Dr. Fred Luskin and Dr. Ken Pelletier; *The Mercy of Thin Air*, by Ronlyn Domangue; *The Fine Art of Small Talk*, by Debra Fine; *Bone Men of Bonares*, by Terry Tamoff.

WRITERS CONFERENCES Maui Writers' Conference; San Diego State University Writers' Conference; Willamette Writers' Conference; BookExpo America; MEGA Book Marketing University.

TIPS "Research agents using a variety of sources."

MARCH TENTH, INC.

24 Hillside Terrace, Montvale NJ 07645. (201)387-6551. **Fax:** (201)387-6552. **E-mail:** hchoron@aol.com; schoron@aol.com. **Website:** www.marchtenthinc.com. **Contact:** Harry Choron, vice president. Represents 40 clients. 30% of clients are new/unpublished writers. Currently handles: nonfiction books 100%.

REPRESENTS nonfiction books. **Considers these nonfiction areas:** autobiography, biography, current affairs, film, health, history, humor, language, literature, medicine, music, popular culture, satire, theater.

8—ᴛ "We prefer to work with published/established writers." Does not want to receive children's or young adult novels, plays, screenplays or poetry.

HOW TO CONTACT "Query with SASE. Include your proposal, a short bio, and contact information." You can also query via e-mail. Detailed submission guidelines on agency website. Accepts simultaneous submissions. Responds in 1 month to queries.

TERMS Agent receives 15% commission on domestic sales. Agent receives 20% commission on foreign sales. Agent receives 20% commission on film sales. Does not require expense money upfront.

○◎ THE DENISE MARCIL LITERARY AGENCY, INC.

483 Westover Road, Stamford CT 06902. (203)327-9970. **E-mail:** dmla@DeniseMarcilAgency.com; AnneMarie@denisemarcilagency.com. **Website:** www.denisemarcilagency.com. **Contact:** Denise Marcil, Anne Marie O'Farrell. Address for Anne Marie O'Farrell: 86 Dennis Street, Manhasset, NY 11030. Member of AAR. –

Prior to opening her agency, Ms. Marcil served as an editorial assistant with Avon Books and as an assistant editor with Simon & Schuster.

MEMBER AGENTS Denise Marcil (self-help and popular reference books such as health, women's issues, business, and parenting); **Anne Marie O'Farrell** (is interested in helping to convey and promote innovative, practical and cutting edge information and ideas which help people increase their self-awareness and fulfillment and maximize their potential in whatever area they choose; she is dying to represent a great basketball book).

REPRESENTS Considers these nonfiction areas: business, health, parenting, self-help, women's issues.

8—ᴛ "In nonfiction we are looking for self-help, business, and popular reference; we want to represent books that help people's lives."

HOW TO CONTACT E-query. At this time, the agency is no longer taking on new, unsolicited *fiction* clients that have not been referred or met at a conference. New nonfiction writers are welcome to query the appropriate agent.

TERMS Agent receives 15% commission on domestic sales. Agent receives 20% commission on foreign sales. Offers written contract, binding for 2 years. Charges $100/year for postage, photocopying, long-distance calls, etc.

RECENT SALES For Denise Marcil: *A Chesapeake Shores Christmas*, by Sherryl Woods; *Prime Time Health*, by William Sears, M.D. and Martha Sears, R.N.; *The Autism Book*, by Robert W. Sears, M.D.; *The Yellow House and The Linen Queen* by Patricia Falvey; *The 10-Minute Total Body Breakthrough*, by Sean Foy. For Anne Marie O'Farrell: *Think Confident, Be Confident*, by Leslie Sokol Ph.d and Marci G. Fox, Ph.d; *Hell Yes*, by Elizabeth Baskin; *Breaking Into the Boys Club*, by Molly Shepard, Jane K. Stimmler, and Peter Dean.

○ THE EVAN MARSHALL AGENCY

Roseland NJ 07068-1121. (973)287-6216. **Fax:** (973)488-7910. **E-mail:** evan@evanmarshallagency.com. **Contact:** Evan Marshall. Member of AAR. Other memberships include MWA, Sisters in Crime. Currently handles: novels 100%.

REPRESENTS novels. **Considers these fiction areas:** action, adventure, erotica, ethnic, frontier, historical, horror, humor, inspirational, literary, mainstream, mystery, religious, satire, science fiction, suspense, western, romance (contemporary, gothic, historical, regency).

HOW TO CONTACT Do not query. Currently accepting clients only by referal from editors and our own clients. Responds in 1 week to queries. Responds in 1 month to mss. Obtains most new clients through recommendations from others.

TERMS Agent receives 15% commission on domestic sales. Agent receives 20% commission on foreign sales. Offers written contract.

RECENT SALES *If You Could See What I See*, by Cathy Lamb (Kensington); *Rebecca's Christmas Gift*, by Emma Miller (Love Inspired); *If He's Wicked*, by Hannah Howell (Kensington); *Amanda Weds a Good Man*, by Naomi King (NAL); *Born in Blood*, by Alexandra Ivy (Kensington).

○ THE MARTELL AGENCY

1350 Avenue of the Americas, Suite 1205, New York NY 10019. **Fax:** (212)317-2676. **E-mail:** submissions@themartellagency.com. **Website:** www.themartellagency.com. **Contact:** Alice Martell.

REPRESENTS nonfiction, novels. **Considers these nonfiction areas:** business, economics, health, history, medicine, memoirs, multicultural, psychology, self-help, women's issues, women's studies,. **Considers these fiction areas:** commercial, mystery, suspense, thriller.

HOW TO CONTACT E-query. Please send a query first to Alice Martell, by mail or e-mail. This should include a summary of the project and a short biography and any information, if appropriate, as to why you are qualified to write on the subject of your book, including any publishing credits. submissions@themartellagency.com.

RECENT SALES *Peddling Peril: The Secret Nuclear Arms Trade* by David Albright and Joel Wit (Five Press); *America's Women: Four Hundred Years of Dolls, Drudges, Helpmates, and Heroines*, by Gail Collins (William Morrow). Other clients include Serena Bass, Janice Erlbaum, David Cay Johnston, Mark Derr, Barbara Rolls, PhD.

MARTIN LITERARY MANAGEMENT

7683 SE 27th St., #307, Mercer Island WA 98040. (206)466-1773. **E-mail:** sharlene@martinliterarymanagement.com. **Website:** www.MartinLiteraryManagement.com. **Contact:** Sharlene Martin.

Prior to becoming an agent, Ms. Martin worked in film/TV production and acquisitions.

MEMBER AGENTS **Sharlene Martin** (nonfiction); **Clelia Martin** (picture books, middle grade, young adult).

REPRESENTS **Considers these nonfiction areas:** autobiography, biography, business, child guidance, current affairs, economics, health, history, how-to, humor, inspirational, investigative, medicine, memoirs, parenting, popular culture, psychology, satire, self-help, true crime, women's issues, women's studies. **Considers these fiction areas:** middle grade, picture books, young adult.

This agency has strong ties to film/TV. Actively seeking nonfiction that is highly commercial and that can be adapted to film. "We are being inundated with queries and submissions that are wrongfully being submitted to us, which only results in more frustration for the writers."

HOW TO CONTACT Query via e-mail with MS Word attachments only. No attachments on queries; place letter in body of e-mail. Accepts simultaneous submissions. Responds in 2 weeks to queries. Responds in 3-4 weeks to mss. Obtains most new clients through recommendations from others.

TERMS Agent receives 15% commission on domestic sales. Agent receives 25% commission on foreign sales. Offers written contract, binding for 1 year; 1-month notice must be given to terminate contract. Charges author for postage and copying if material is not sent electronically. 99% of materials are sent electronically to minimize charges to author for postage and copying.

RECENT SALES *Honor Bound: My Journey to Hell and Back with Amanda Knox*, by Raffaele Sollecito; *Impossible Odds: The Kidnapping of Jessica Buchanan and Dramatic Rescue by SEAL Team Six*, by Jessica Buchanan, Erik Landemalm and Anthony Flacco; *Walking on Eggshells*, by Lisa Chapman; *Publish Your Nonfiction*, by Sharlene Martin and Anthony Flacco.

TIPS "Have a strong platform for nonfiction. Please don't call. (I can't tell how well you write by the sound of your voice.) I welcome e-mail. I'm very responsive when I'm interested in a query and work hard to get my clients' materials in the best possible shape before submissions. Do your homework prior to submission and only submit your best efforts. Please review our website carefully to make sure we're a good match for your work. If you read my book, *Publish Your Nonfiction Book: Strategies For Learning the Industry, Selling Your Book and Building a Successful Career* (Writer's Digest Books), you'll know exactly how to charm me."

MARGRET MCBRIDE LITERARY AGENCY

P.O. Box 9128, La Jolla CA 92038. (858)454-1550. **Fax:** (858)454-2156. **E-mail:** staff@mcbridelit.com. **Website:** www.mcbrideliterary.com. **Contact:** Michael Daley, submissions manager. Member of AAR. Other memberships include Authors Guild.

Prior to opening her agency, Ms. McBride worked at Random House, Ballantine Books, and Warner Books.

REPRESENTS nonfiction books, novels. **Considers these nonfiction areas:** autobiography, biography, business, cooking, cultural interests, current affairs, economics, ethnic, foods, government, health, history, how-to, law, medicine, money, popular culture, politics, psychology, science, self-help, sociology, technology, women's issues, style. **Considers these fiction areas:** action, adventure, crime, detective, historical, humor, literary, mainstream, mystery, police, satire, suspense, thriller.

This agency specializes in mainstream fiction and nonfiction. Actively seeking commercial fiction and nonfiction, business, health, self-help. PLEASE DO NOT SEND: screenplays, romance, poetry, or children's.

HOW TO CONTACT Query via snail mail with SASE. Send a query and 1-2 page synopsis (for fiction). Accepts simultaneous submissions. Responds in 8 weeks to queries. Responds in 6-8 weeks to mss.

TERMS Agent receives 15% commission on domestic sales. Agent receives 25% commission on foreign sales. Charges for overnight delivery and photocopying.

RECENT SALES *Value Tales Treasure: Stories for Growing Good People*, by Spencer Johnson, MD. (Simon & Schuster Children's); *The 6 Reasons You'll Get the Job: What Employers Really Want—Whether They Know it or Not*, by Debra MacDougall and Elisabeth Harney Sanders-Park (Tarcher); *The Solution: Conquer Your Fear, Control Your Future*, by Lucinda Bassett (Sterling).

TIPS "Our office does not accept e-mail queries!"

THE MCCARTHY AGENCY, LLC

7 Allen St., Rumson NJ 07660. Phone/**Fax:** (732)741-3065. **E-mail:** McCarthylit@aol.com; ntfrost@hotmail.com. **Contact:** Shawna McCarthy. Member of AAR. Currently handles: nonfiction books 25%, novels 75%.

MEMBER AGENTS Shawna McCarthy, Nahvae Frost.

REPRESENTS nonfiction books, novels. **Considers these nonfiction areas:** biography, history, philosophy, science. **Considers these fiction areas:** fantasy, juvenile, mystery, romance, women's.

HOW TO CONTACT Query via e-mail or regular mail to The McCarthy Agency, c/o Nahvae Frost, 101 Clinton Avenue, Apartment #2, Brooklyn, NY 11205. Accepts simultaneous submissions.

SEAN MCCARTHY LITERARY AGENCY

E-mail: submissions@mccarthylit.com. **Website:** www.mccarthylit.com. **Contact:** Sean McCarthy.

Prior to his current position, Sean McCarthy began his publishing career as an editorial intern at Overlook Press and then moved over to the Sheldon Fogelman Agency.

REPRESENTS Considers these fiction areas: juvenile, middle grade, picture books, young adult.

Sean is drawn to flawed, multifaceted characters with devastatingly concise writing in YA, and boy-friendly mysteries or adventures in MG. In picture books, he looks more for unforgettable characters, off-beat humor, and especially clever endings. He is not currently interested in high fantasy, message-driven stories, or query letters that pose too many questions.

HOW TO CONTACT E-query. "Please include a brief description of your book, your biography, and any literary or relevant professional credits in your query letter. If you are a novelist: Please submit the first three chapters of your manuscript (or roughly 25 pages) and a one page synopsis in the body of the e-mail or as a Word or PDF attachment. If you are a picture book author: Please submit the complete text of your manuscript. We are not currently accepting picture book manuscripts over 1,000 words. If you are an illustrator: Please attach up to 3 JPEGs or PDFs of your work, along with a link to your website."

THE MCGILL AGENCY, INC.

10000 N. Central Expressway, Suite 400, Dallas TX 75231. (214)390-5970. **E-mail:** info.mcgillagency@gmail.com. **Contact:** Jack Bollinger. Estab. 2009. Represents 10 clients. 50% of clients are new/unpublished writers.

MEMBER AGENTS Jack Bollinger (eclectic tastes in nonfiction and fiction); **Amy Cohn** (nonfiction interests include women's issues, gay/lesbian, ethnic/cultural, memoirs, true crime; fiction interests include mystery, suspense and thriller).

REPRESENTS Considers these nonfiction areas: biography, business, child guidance, current affairs, education, ethnic, gay, health, history, how-to, memoirs, military, psychology, self-help, true crime, women's issues. **Considers these fiction areas:** historical, mainstream, mystery, romance, thriller.

HOW TO CONTACT Query via e-mail. Responds in 2 weeks to queries and 6 weeks to mss. Obtains new clients through conferences.

TERMS Agent receives 15% commission.

MCINTOSH & OTIS, INC.

353 Lexington Ave., New York NY 10016. (212)687-7400. **Fax:** (212)687-6894. **E-mail:** info@mcintoshandotis.com. **Website:** www.mcintoshandotis.com. **Contact:** Eugene H. Winick, Esq. Estab. 1927.

Member of AAR, SCBWI Currently handles: juvenile books.

MEMBER AGENTS **Elizabeth Winick Rubinstein**, EWRquery@mcintoshandotis.com (literary fiction, women's fiction, historical fiction, and mystery/suspense, along with narrative nonfiction, spiritual/self-help, history and current affairs); **Shira Hoffman**, SHquery@mcintoshandotis.com (young adult, MG, mainstream commercial fiction, mystery, literary fiction, women's fiction, romance, urban fantasy, fantasy, science fiction, horror and dystopian); **Christa Heschke**, CHquery@mcintoshandotis.com (picture books, middle grade, young adult and new adult projects); **Adam Muhlig**, AMquery@mcintoshandotis.com (music—from jazz to classical to punk—popular culture, natural history, travel and adventure, and sports); **Eugene Winick**; **Ira Winick**.

REPRESENTS **Considers these nonfiction areas:** creative nonfiction, current affairs, history, popular culture, self-help, spirituality, sports, travel. **Considers these fiction areas:** fantasy, historical, horror, literary, middle grade, mystery, new adult, paranormal, picture books, romance, science fiction, suspense, urban fantasy, women's, young adult.

Actively seeking "books with memorable characters, distinctive voices, and great plots."

HOW TO CONTACT Prefers e-mail submissions. Each agent has their own e-mail address for subs. For fiction: Please send a query letter, synopsis, author bio, and the first three consecutive chapters (no more than 30 pages) of your novel. For nonfiction: Please send a query letter, proposal, outline, author bio, and three sample chapters (no more than 30 pages) of the manuscript. For children's & young adult: Please send a query letter, synopsis and the first three consecutive chapters (not to exceed 25 pages) of the manuscript. Obtains clients through recommendations from others, editors, conferences and queries.

TERMS Agent receives 15% commission on domestic sales; 20% on foreign sales.

WRITERS CONFERENCES Attends Bologna Book Fair, in Bologna Italy in April; SCBWI Conference in New York in February; and regularly attends other conferences and industry conventions.

SALLY HILL MCMILLAN & ASSOCIATES, INC.

429 E. Kingston Ave., Charlotte NC 28203. (704)334-0897. **Website:** www.publishersmarketplace.com/members/McMillanAgency/. **Contact:** Sally Hill McMillan. Member of AAR.

REPRESENTS **Considers these nonfiction areas:** creative nonfiction, health, history, women's issues, women's studies. **Considers these fiction areas:** commercial, literary, mainstream, mystery.

Do not send science fiction, military, horror, fantasy/adventure, children's or cookbooks.

HOW TO CONTACT "Please query first with SASE and await further instructions. E-mail queries will be read, but not necessarily answered."

RECENT SALES Fiction: Lynne Hinton, Linda Lenhoff, Jennifer Manske Fenske, Joe Martin, Nancy Peacock, Mike Stewart. Nonfiction: Lois Trigg Chaplin, Rose Clayton, Tanya Denckla, Andrea Engber, Ray Jones, Dr. Leah Klungness, Dr. Sally Kneidel, Katie Lyle, Bruce Roberts, Nancy Roberts, Dr. Bryan Robinson, Martha Woodham, John Yow, Victoria Zak.

BOB MECOY LITERARY AGENCY

66 Grand St., Suite 1, New York NY 10013. (212)226-1398. **E-mail:** mecoy@aol.com. **Website:** www.grandstreetliterary.com. **Contact:** Bob Mecoy.

MEMBER AGENTS Bob Mecoy.

Fiction (literary, crime, romance); nonfiction (true crime, finance, memoir, literary, prescriptive self-help & graphic novelists). No Westerns.

HOW TO CONTACT Query with sample chapters and synopsis.

MENDEL MEDIA GROUP, LLC

115 W. 30th St., Suite 800, New York NY 10001. (646)239-9896. **Fax:** (212)685-4717. **E-mail:** scott@mendelmedia.com. **Website:** www.mendelmedia.com. Member of AAR. Represents 40-60 clients.

Prior to becoming an agent, Mr. Mendel was an academic. "I taught American literature, Yiddish, Jewish studies, and literary theory at the University of Chicago and the University of Illinois at Chicago while working on my PhD in English. I also worked as a freelance technical writer and as the managing editor of a healthcare magazine. In 1998, I began working for the late Jane Jordan Browne, a long-time agent in the book publishing world."

REPRESENTS nonfiction books, novels, scholarly, with potential for broad/popular appeal. **Considers these nonfiction areas:** Americana, animals, anthropology, architecture, art, biography, business, child guidance, cooking, current affairs, dance, diet/nutrition, education, environment, ethnic, foods, gardening, gay/lesbian, government, health, history, how-to, humor, investigative, language, medicine, memoirs, military, money, multicultural, music, parenting, philosophy, popular culture, psychology, recreation, regional, religious, science, self-help, sex, sociology, software, spirituality, sports, true crime, war, women's issues, women's studies, Jewish topics, creative nonfiction. **Considers these fiction areas:** action, adventure, contemporary issues, crime, detective, erotica, ethnic, feminist, gay, glitz, historical, humor, inspirational, juvenile, lesbian, literary, mainstream, mystery, picture books, police, religious, romance, satire, sports, thriller, young adult, Jewish fiction.

"I am interested in major works of history, current affairs, biography, business, politics, economics, science, major memoirs, narrative nonfiction, and other sorts of general nonfiction." Actively seeking new, major or definitive work on a subject of broad interest, or a controversial, but authoritative, new book on a subject that affects many people's lives. I also represent more light-hearted nonfiction projects, such as gift or novelty books, when they suit the market particularly well." Does not want "queries about projects written years ago that were unsuccessfully shopped to a long list of trade publishers by either the author or another agent. I am specifically not interested in reading short, category romances (regency, time travel, paranormal, etc.), horror novels, supernatural stories, poetry, original plays, or film scripts."

HOW TO CONTACT Query with SASE. Do not e-mail or fax queries. For nonfiction, include a complete, fully edited book proposal with sample chapters. For fiction, include a complete synopsis and no more than 20 pages of sample text. Responds in 2 weeks to queries. Responds in 4-6 weeks to mss. Obtains most new clients through recommendations from others.

TERMS Agent receives 15% commission on domestic sales. Agent receives 20% commission on foreign sales.

WRITERS CONFERENCES BookExpo America; Frankfurt Book Fair; London Book Fair; RWA National Conference; Modern Language Association Convention; Jerusalem Book Fair.

TIPS "While I am not interested in being flattered by a prospective client, it does matter to me that she knows why she is writing to me in the first place. Is one of my clients a colleague of hers? Has she read a book by one of my clients that led her to believe I might be interested in her work? Authors of descriptive nonfiction should have real credentials and expertise in their subject areas, either as academics, journalists, or policy experts, and authors of prescriptive nonfiction should have legitimate expertise and considerable experience communicating their ideas in seminars and workshops, in a successful business, through the media, etc."

SCOTT MEREDITH LITERARY AGENCY

200 W. 57th St., Suite 904, New York NY 10019. (646)274-1970. **Fax:** (212)977-5997. **E-mail:** info@scottmeredith.com. **Website:** www.scottmeredith.com. **Contact:** Arthur Klebanoff, CEO. Adheres to the AAR canon of ethics. Represents 20 clients. 5% of clients are new/unpublished writers. Currently handles: nonfiction books 85%, novels 5%, textbooks 5%.

Prior to becoming an agent, Mr. Klebanoff was a lawyer.

REPRESENTS nonfiction books, textbooks.

This agency's specialty lies in category nonfiction publishing programs. Actively seeking category leading nonfiction. Does not want to receive first fiction projects.

HOW TO CONTACT Query with SASE. Submit proposal package, author bio. Accepts simultaneous submissions. Responds in 1 week to queries. Responds in 2 weeks to mss. Obtains most new clients through recommendations from others.

TERMS Agent receives 15% commission on domestic sales. Offers written contract.

RECENT SALES *The Conscience of a Liberal*, by Paul Krugman; *The King of Oil: The Secret Lives of Marc Rich*, by Daniel Ammann; *Ten*, by Sheila Lukins; *Peterson Field Guide to Birds of North America*.

DORIS S. MICHAELS LITERARY AGENCY, INC.

1841 Broadway, Suite 903, New York NY 10023. (212)265-9474. **Fax:** (212)265-9480. **E-mail:** query@dsmagency.com. **Website:** www.dsmagency.com. **Contact:** Doris S. Michaels, President. Member of AAR. Other memberships include WNBA.

REPRESENTS novels. **Considers these fiction areas:** commercial, literary.

No romance, coffee table books, art books, trivia, pop culture, humor, westerns, occult and

NEW AGENT SPOTLIGHT

LARA PERKINS
(ANDREA BROWN LITERARY AGENCY)

andreabrownlit.com

@lara_perkins

ABOUT LARA: Lara has a B.A. in English and Art History from Amherst College and an M.A. in English Literature from Columbia University, where she studied Victorian Brit Lit. In her pre-publishing life, she trained to be an architect, before deciding that books, not bricks, are her true passion. She spent over a year at the B.J. Robbins Literary Agency in Los Angeles before coming to Andrea Brown Literary.

SHE IS SEEKING: smart and raw young adult fiction, character-driven middle grade fiction with a totally original, hilarious voice, and so-adorable-she-can't-stand-it picture books, preferably with some age-appropriate emotional heft. She's a sucker for a great mystery and is passionate about stories that teach her new things or open up new worlds.

HOW TO QUERY: lara@andreabrownlit.com. ABLA only allows writers to query one agent per agency, so please do not query Lara if you have queried other ABLA agents in the past. There are various submission instructions depending on what you are submitting, and everything is laid out nicely on the agency submission page online.

supernatural, horror, poetry, textbooks, children's books, picture books, film scripts, articles, cartoons, and professional manuals.

HOW TO CONTACT As of early 2014, they are not taking new clients. Check the website to see if this agency reopens to queries. Obtains most new clients through recommendations from others, conferences.

TERMS Agent receives 15% commission on domestic sales. Agent receives 20% commission on foreign sales. Offers written contract, binding for 1 year; 1-month notice must be given to terminate contract. Charges clients for office expenses, not to exceed $150 without written permission.

WRITERS CONFERENCES BookExpo America; Frankfurt Book Fair; London Book Fair; Maui Writers Conference.

⊘ MARTHA MILLARD LITERARY AGENCY

50 W.67th St., #1G, New York NY 10023. **Contact:** Martha Millard. Estab. 1980. Member of AAR. Other memberships include SFWA. Represents 50 clients. Currently handles: nonfiction books 25%, novels 65%, story collections 10%.

Prior to becoming an agent, Ms. Millard worked in editorial departments of several publishers and was vice president at another agency for more than four years.

REPRESENTS nonfiction books, novels. **Considers these nonfiction areas:** architecture, art, autobiography, biography, business, child guidance, cooking, cultural interests, current affairs, design, economics, education, ethnic, film, health, history, how-to, memoirs, metaphysics, money, music, New Age, parenting, photography, popular culture, psychology, self-help, theater, true crime, women's issues, women's studies. **Considers these fiction areas:** fantasy, mystery, romance, science fiction, suspense.

HOW TO CONTACT No unsolicited queries. **Referrals only.** Obtains most new clients through recommendations from others.

TERMS Agent receives 15% commission on domestic sales. Agent receives 20% commission on foreign sales. Offers written contract.

THE MILLER AGENCY

Film Center, 630 Ninth Ave., Suite 1102, New York NY 10036. (212) 206-0913. **Fax:** (212) 206-1473. **E-mail:** info@milleragency.net. **Website:** www.milleragency.net. Represents 100 clients. 5% of clients are new/unpublished writers.

REPRESENTS nonfiction books. **Considers these nonfiction areas:** child guidance, cooking, design, foods, health, parenting.

This agency specializes in nonfiction, multicultural arts, psychology, self-help, cookbooks, biography, travel, memoir, and sports. Fiction is considered selectively.

HOW TO CONTACT Accepts simultaneous submissions. Obtains most new clients through referrals.

TERMS Agent receives 15% commission on domestic sales. Agent receives 20-25% commission on foreign sales. Offers written contract, binding for 2 years; 2-month notice must be given to terminate contract. Charges clients for postage (express mail or messenger services) and photocopying.

MOORE LITERARY AGENCY

10 State St., #309, Newburyport MA 01950. (978)465-9015. **Fax:** (978)465-8817. **E-mail:** cmoore@moorelit.com. **Contact:** Claudette Moore. Estab. 1989. 10% of clients are new/unpublished writers. Currently handles: nonfiction books 100%.

REPRESENTS nonfiction books. **Considers these nonfiction areas:** computers, technology.

This agency specializes in trade computer books (90% of titles).

HOW TO CONTACT Query with SASE. Submit proposal package. Query by e-mail. Send proposals by snail mail. Obtains most new clients through recommendations from others, conferences.

TERMS Agent receives 15% commission on domestic sales. Agent receives 15% commission on foreign sales. Agent receives 15% commission on film sales. Offers written contract.

HOWARD MORHAIM LITERARY AGENCY

30 Pierrepont St., Brooklyn NY 11201. (718)222-8400. **Fax:** (718)222-5056. **Website:** www.morhaimliterary.com. Member of AAR.

MEMBER AGENTS **Howard Morhaim, Kate McKean; Paul Lamb** (new as of 2014); **Maria Ribas** (new as of 2014).

REPRESENTS **Considers these nonfiction areas:** cooking, crafts, creative nonfiction, design, humor, sports. **Considers these fiction areas:** fantasy, historical, literary, middle grade, new adult, romance, science fiction, women's, young adult, LGBTQ young adult, magical realism, fantasy should be high fantasy, historical fiction should be no earlier than the 20th century.

Kate McKean is open to many subgenres and categories of YA and MG fiction. Check the website for the most details. Actively seeking fiction, nonfiction, and young adult novels. Kate does not want "mysteries, thrillers, crime, paranormal romance, or urban fantasy. She is not the best reader of fiction that features: cops/private detectives/FBI/CIA, fairy tale retellings, dragons, werewolves/vampires/zombies etc., satire, spoof, or the picaresque. No novellas."

HOW TO CONTACT Query via e-mail with cover letter and three sample chapters. See each agent's listing for specifics.

WILLIAM MORRIS ENDEAVOR ENTERTAINMENT

1325 Avenue of the Americas, New York NY 10019. (212)586-5100. **Fax:** (212)246-3583. **Website:** www.wma.com. **Contact:** Literary Department Coordinator. Member of AAR.

REPRESENTS nonfiction books, novels, tv, movie scripts, feature film.

HOW TO CONTACT This agency is generally closed to unsolicited literary submissions. Meet an agent at a conference, or query through a referral. Accepts simultaneous submissions.

TERMS Agent receives 15% commission on domestic sales. Agent receives 20% commission on foreign sales.

TIPS "If you are a prospective writer interested in submitting to the William Morris Agency in **London**, please follow these guidelines: For all queries, please send a cover letter, synopsis, and the first three chapters (up to 50 pages) by e-mail only to: dkar@wmeentertainment.com."

MOVEABLE TYPE MANAGEMENT

244 Madison Ave., Suite 334, New York NY 10016. (646)431-6134. **Website:** www.mtmgmt.net.

MEMBER AGENTS Adam Chromy.

REPRESENTS Considers these nonfiction areas: business, creative nonfiction, history, how-to, humor, memoirs, money, popular culture. **Considers these fiction areas:** commercial, literary, mainstream, romance, women's, young adult.

Mr. Chromy is a generalist, meaning that he accepts fiction submissions of virtually any kind (except juvenile books aimed for middle grade and younger) as well as nonfiction. He has sold books in the following categories: new adult, women's, romance, memoir, pop culture, young adult, lifestyle, horror, how-to, general fiction, and more.

RECENT SALES *The Gin Lovers* by Jamie Brenner (St. Martin's Press); *Miss Chatterley* by Logan Belle (Pocket/S&S); *Sons Of Zeus*, by Noble Smith (Thomas Dunne Books); *World Made By Hand And Too Much Magic* by James Howard Kunstler (Grove/Atlantic Press); *Dirty Rocker Boys* by Bobbie Brown (Gallery/S&S).

DEE MURA LITERARY

P.O. Box 131, Massapequa NY 11762. (516)795-1616. **Fax:** (516)795-8797. **E-mail:** query@deemuraliterary.com. **Website:** www.deemuraliterary.com. **Contact:** Dee Mura. Member of WGA.

Prior to opening her agency, Mura was a public relations executive with a roster of film and entertainment clients. She is the president and CEO of both Dee Mura Literary and Dee Mura Entertainment.

MEMBER AGENTS Dee Mura, Kimiko Nakamura, Kaylee Davis.

REPRESENTS Considers these nonfiction areas: animals, anthropology, archeology, art, biography, business, cooking, current affairs, entertainment, environmental issues, ethnic, health, history, home/garden, humor, inspirational, Jewish, LGBTQ, memoir, mind/body, motivational, narrative nonfiction, nature, New Age, parenting, photography, popular culture, psychology, religious, science, self-help, spirituality, sports, technology, travel. **Considers these fiction areas:** adventure, commercial, contemporary, crime, espionage, erotica, family saga, fantasy, historical, literary, magical realism, middle grade, mystery, new adult, paranormal, romance, satire, science fiction, speculative fiction, suspense, thriller, urban fantasy, women's, young adult.

We are currently not seeking screenplays, poetry, or children's picture books. "We focus on developing our clients' careers from day one through to publication and beyond by providing personalized editorial feedback, social media and platform marketing, and thorough rights management. Both new and experienced writers are welcome to submit."

HOW TO CONTACT Query with SASE or e-mail query@deemuraliterary.com (e-mail queries are preferred). Please include the first 25 pages in the body of the e-mail as well as a short author bio and synopsis of the work. Responds to queries in 3-4 weeks. Responds to mss in 8 weeks. Accepts simultaneous submissions. Obtains new clients through recommendations, solicitation, and conferences.

TERMS Agent receives 15% commission on domestic sales. Agent receives 20% commission on foreign sales. Offers written contract.

WRITERS CONFERENCES Alaska Writers Guild Conference, BookExpo America, Hampton Roads Writers Conference, NESCBWI Regional Conference, Books Alive! Conference, Writer's Digest Conference East, LVW's Writers Meet Agents Conference, James River Writers Conference, New England Crime Bake.

ERIN MURPHY LITERARY AGENCY

2700 Woodlands Village, #300-458, Flagstaff AZ 86001. **Fax:** (928)525-2480. **Website:** emliterary.com. **Contact:** Erin Murphy, president; Ammi-Joan Paquette, senior agent; Tricia Lawrence, associate agent. 25% of clients are new/unpublished writers. Currently handles: juvenile books.

REPRESENTS Considers these fiction areas: middle grade, picture books, young adult.

Specializes in children's books only.

TERMS Agent receives 15% commission on domestic sales; 20-30% on foreign sales. Offers written contract. 30 days notice must be given to terminate contract.

JEAN V. NAGGAR LITERARY AGENCY, INC.

216 E. 75th St., Suite 1E, New York NY 10021. (212)794-1082. **E-mail:** jweltz@jvnla.com; atasman@jvnla.com. **Website:** www.jvnla.com. **Contact:** Jean Naggar. Member of AAR. Other memberships include PEN, Women's Media Group, Women's Forum, SCBWI. Represents 450 clients. 20% of clients are new/unpublished writers.

Ms. Naggar has served as president of AAR.

MEMBER AGENTS **Jennifer Weltz** (well researched and original historicals, thrillers with a unique voice, wry dark humor, and magical realism; enthralling narrative nonfiction; young adult, middle grade); **Jean Naggar** (taking no new clients); **Alice Tasman** (literary, commercial, YA, middle grade, and nonfiction in the categories of narrative, biography, music or pop culture); **Elizabeth Evans** (narrative nonfiction, memoir, current affairs, pop science, journalism, health and wellness, psychology, history, pop culture, and humor); **Laura Biagi** (literary fiction, magical realism, young adult novels, middle grade novels, and picture books).

REPRESENTS nonfiction books, novels. **Considers these nonfiction areas:** biography, creative nonfiction, current affairs, health, history, humor, memoirs, music, popular culture, psychology, science. **Considers these fiction areas:** commercial, fantasy, literary, middle grade, picture books, thriller, young adult.

This agency specializes in mainstream fiction and nonfiction and literary fiction with commercial potential.

HOW TO CONTACT This agency now has an online submission form on its website. Accepts simultaneous submissions. Obtains most new clients through recommendations from others.

TERMS Agent receives 15% commission on domestic sales. Agent receives 20% commission on foreign sales. Offers written contract. Charges for overseas mailing, messenger services, book purchases, long-distance telephone, photocopying—all deductible from royalties received.

RECENT SALES *Night Navigation*, by Ginnah Howard; *After Hours at the Almost Home*, by Tara Yelen; *An Entirely Synthetic Fish: A Biography of Rainbow Trout*, by Anders Halverson; *The Patron Saint of Butterflies*, by Cecilia Galante; *Wondrous Strange*, by Lesley Livingston; *6 Sick Hipsters*, by Rayo Casablanca; *The Last Bridge*, by Teri Coyne; *Gypsy Goodbye*, by Nancy Springer; *Commuters*, by Emily Tedrowe; *The Language of Secrets*, by Dianne Dixon; *Smiling to Freedom*, by Martin Benoit Stiles; *The Tale of Halcyon Crane*, by Wendy Webb; *Fugitive*, by Phillip Margolin; *BlackBerry Girl*, by Aidan Donnelley Rowley; *Wild Girls*, by Pat Murphy.

WRITERS CONFERENCES Willamette Writers Conference; Pacific Northwest Writers Conference; Bread Loaf Writers Conference; Marymount Manhattan Writers Conference; SEAK Medical & Legal Fiction Writing Conference.

TIPS "Use a professional presentation. Because of the avalanche of unsolicited queries that flood the agency every week, we have had to modify our policy. We will now only guarantee to read and respond to queries from writers who come recommended by someone we know. Our areas are general fiction and nonfiction—no children's books by unpublished writers, no multimedia, no screenplays, no formula fiction, and no mysteries by unpublished writers. We recommend patience and fortitude: the courage to be true to your own vision, the fortitude to finish a novel and polish it again and again before sending it out, and the patience to accept rejection gracefully and wait for the stars to align themselves appropriately for success."

NELSON LITERARY AGENCY

1732 Wazee St., Suite 207, Denver CO 80202. (303)292-2805. **E-mail:** query@nelsonagency.com. **Website:** www.nelsonagency.com. **Contact:** Kristin Nelson, president and senior literary agent; Sara Megibow, associate literary agent. Estab. 2002. Member of AAR, RWA, SCBWI, SFWA.

Prior to opening her own agency, Ms. Nelson worked as a literary scout and subrights agent for agent Jody Rein.

MEMBER AGENTS Kristin Nelson; Sara Megibow.

REPRESENTS **Considers these fiction areas:** commercial, fantasy, literary, mainstream, middle grade, new adult, romance, science fiction, women's, young adult.

NLA specializes in representing commercial fiction and high-caliber literary fiction. They represent many pop genre categories, including things like historical romance, steampunk, and all subgenres of YA. Does not want short story collections, mysteries, thrillers, Christian, horror, children's picture books, or screenplays.

HOW TO CONTACT Query by e-mail. Put the word "Query" in the e-mail subject line. No attachments. Address your query to Sara or Kristin. Responds within 1 month.

RECENT SALES *Champion*, by Marie Lu (young adult); *Wool*, by Hugh Howey (science fiction); *The Whatnot*, by Stefan Bachmann (middle grade); *Catching Jordan*, by Miranda Kenneally (young adult); *Broken Like This*, by Monica Trasandes (debut literary fiction); *The Darwin Elevator*, by Jason Hough (debut science fiction). A full list of clients is available online.

NEW LEAF LITERARY & MEDIA, INC.

110 W. 40th St., Suite 410, New York NY 10018. (646)248-7989. **Fax:** (646)861-4654. **E-mail:** query@newleafliterary.com. **Contact:** Joanna Volpe; Kathleen Ortiz; Suzie Townsend; Pouya Shahbazian. Member of AAR.

MEMBER AGENTS **Joanna Volpe** (women's fiction, thriller, horror, speculative fiction, literary fiction and historical fiction, young adult, middle grade, art-focused picture books); **Kathleen Ortiz**, director of subsidiary rights (new voices in YA and animator/illustrator talent); **Suzie Townsend** (new adult, young adult, middle grade, romance [all subgenres], fantasy [urban fantasy, science fiction, steampunk, epic fantasy] and crime fiction [mysteries, thrillers]; **Pouya Shahbazian**, film and television agent.

REPRESENTS **Considers these fiction areas:** crime, fantasy, historical, horror, literary, mainstream, middle grade, mystery, new adult, paranormal, picture books, romance, thriller, women's, young adult.

HOW TO CONTACT E-mail queries only. "Put the word QUERY in subject line, plus the agent's name." No attachments. Responds only if interested.

RECENT SALES *Allegiant*, by Veronica Roth; *The Sharpest Blade*, by Sandy Williams (Ace); *Siege and Storm*, by Leigh Bardugo (Henry Holt); *Erased*, by Jennifer Rush (Little Brown Books for Young Readers).

DANA NEWMAN LITERARY

9720 Wilshire Blvd., 5th Floor, Beverly Hills CA 90212. (323)974-4334. **Fax:** (866)636-7585. **E-mail:** dananewmanliterary@gmail.com. **Website:** www.about.me/dananewman. **Contact:** Dana Newman. Estab. 2009. Member of Author's Guild. Represents 15 clients. 50% of clients are new/unpublished writers. Currently handles: 85% nonfiction books, 15% novels.

Prior to being an agent, Ms. Newman was an attorney in the entertainment industry for 14 years.

MEMBER AGENTS **Dana Newman** (narrative nonfiction, business, biography, lifestyle, current affairs, parenting, memoir, pop culture, health, literary, and upmarket fiction).

REPRESENTS nonfiction, fiction. **Considers these nonfiction areas:** architecture, art, autobiography, biography, business, child guidance, cooking, cultural interests, current affairs, design, education, ethnic, film, foods, gay/lesbian, government, health, history, how-to, language, law, literature, medicine, memoirs, metaphysics, music, popular culture, politics, science, self-help, sociology, sports, technology, theater, women's issues, women's studies. **Considers these fiction areas:** historical, literary, women's.

Ms. Newman has a background in contracts, licensing, and intellectual property law. She is experienced in digital content creation and distribution and embraces the changing publishing environment. Actively seeking narrative nonfiction, historical, or upmarket fiction. Does not want religious, children's, poetry, horror, mystery, science fiction.

HOW TO CONTACT Submit query letter, outline, synopsis, 2 sample chapters, biography, and proposal. Accepts simultaneous submissions. Responds to queries/proposals in 2 weeks; mss in 1 month. Obtains new clients through recommendations from others, queries, submissions.

TERMS Obtains 15% commission on domestic sales; 20% on foreign sales. Offers 1-year written contract. Notice must be given 30 days prior to terminate a contract.

RECENT SALES *Home Sweet Anywhere*, by Lynne Martin (Sourcebooks); *Cracked, Not Broken*, by Kevin Hines (Roman and Littlefield); *How to Read a Client*, by Brandy Mychals (McGraw-Hill); *The King of Style*, by Michael Bush (Insight Editions); *An Atomic Love Story*, by Shirley Streshinsky (Turner Publishing); *Combined Destinies*, by Ann Todd Jealous (Potomac Books).

WRITERS CONFERENCES Writer's Digest Conference (L.A., NYC); San Francisco Writers Conference; Santa Barbara Writers Conference.

HAROLD OBER ASSOCIATES

425 Madison Ave., New York NY 10017. (212)759-8600. **Fax:** (212)759-9428. **Website:** www.haroldober.com. **Contact:** Appropriate agent. Member of AAR. Represents 250 clients. 10% of clients are new/unpublished writers. Currently handles: nonfiction books 35%, novels 50%, juvenile books 15%.

Mr. Elwell was previously with Elwell & Weiser.

MEMBER AGENTS **Phyllis Westberg**; **Pamela Malpas**; **Craig Tenney** (few new clients, mostly Ober backlist); **Jake Elwell** (previously with Elwell & Weiser).

HOW TO CONTACT Submit concise query letter addressed to a specific agent with the first 5 pages of the ms or proposal and SASE. No fax or e-mail. Does not handle filmscripts or plays. Responds as promptly as possible. Obtains most new clients through recommendations from others.

TERMS Agent receives 15% commission on domestic sales. Agent receives 20% commission on foreign sales. Charges clients for express mail/package services.

PARADIGM TALENT AND LITERARY AGENCY

360 Park Avenue South, 16th floor, New York NY 10010. (212)897-6400. **Fax:** (212)764-8941. **Website:** www.paradigmagency.com.

MEMBER AGENTS Lydia Wills, others.

REPRESENTS movie scripts, feature film, theatrical stage plays.

Paradigm Talent and Literary Agency is a Los-Angeles-based talent agency with additional offices in New York City, Nashville, and Monterey. The firm acquired Writers & Artists Group International in 2004. The acquisition of WAGI added both talent and agents to Paradigm's roster, bolstering its New York office with legit agents representing playwrights and theatre directors.

HOW TO CONTACT *No unsolicited queries.* Do not query unless meeting an agent at an event, or through a referral.

PARK LITERARY GROUP, LLC

270 Lafayette St., Suite 1504, New York NY 10012. (212)691-3500. **Fax:** (212)691-3540. **E-mail:** queries@parkliterary. **Website:** www.parkliterary.com. Estab. 2005.

MEMBER AGENTS **Theresa Park** (plot-driven fiction and serious nonfiction); **Abigail Koons** (popular science, history, politics, current affairs and art, and women's fiction); **Peter Knapp** (middle grade and young adult fiction, as well as suspense and thrillers for all ages).

REPRESENTS nonfiction books, novels. **Considers these nonfiction areas:** art, current affairs, history, politics, science. **Considers these fiction areas:** middle grade, suspense, thriller, women's, young adult.

The Park Literary Group represents fiction and nonfiction with a boutique approach: an emphasis on servicing a relatively small number of clients, with the highest professional standards and focused personal attention. Does not want to receive poetry or screenplays.

HOW TO CONTACT Please specify the first and last name of the agent to whom you are submitting in the subject line of the e-mail and send your query letter and accompanying material to queries@parkliterary.com. All materials must be in the body of the e-mail. Responds if interested. For fiction submissions to Abigail Koons or Theresa Park, please include a query letter with short synopsis and the first three chapters of your work. For middle grade and young adult submissions to Peter Knapp, please include a query letter and the first three chapters or up to 10,000 words of your novel (no synopsis necessary). For nonfiction submissions, please send a query letter, proposal, and sample chapter(s).

RECENT SALES This agency's client list is on their website. It includes bestsellers Nicholas Sparks and Debbie Macomber.

THE RICHARD PARKS AGENCY

P.O. Box 693, Salem NY 12865. (518)854-9466. **Fax:** (518)854-9466. **E-mail:** rp@richardparksagency.com. **Website:** www.richardparksagency.com. **Contact:** Richard Parks. Member of AAR. Currently handles: nonfiction books 55%, novels 40%, story collections 5%.

REPRESENTS nonfiction books, novels. **Considers these nonfiction areas:** animals, anthropology, archeology, art, autobiography, biography, business, child guidance, cooking, crafts, cultural interests, current affairs, dance, diet/nutrition, economics, environment, ethnic, film, foods, gardening, gay/lesbian, government, health, history, hobbies, how-to, humor, language, law, memoirs, military, money, music, parenting, popular culture, politics, psychology, science, self-help, sociology, technology, theater, travel, women's issues, women's studies.

Actively seeking nonfiction. Considers fiction by referral only. Does not want to receive unsolicited material.

HOW TO CONTACT Query with SASE. Does not accept queries by e-mail or fax. Responds in 2 weeks to queries. Obtains most new clients through recommendations/referrals.

TERMS Agent receives 15% commission on domestic sales. Agent receives 20% commission on foreign sales. Charges clients for photocopying or any unusual expense incurred at the writer's request.

KATHI J. PATON LITERARY AGENCY

P.O. Box 2236 Radio City Station, New York NY 10101. (212)265-6586. **E-mail:** KJPLitBiz@optonline.net. **Website:** www.PatonLiterary.com. **Contact:** Kathi Paton.

REPRESENTS Considers these nonfiction areas: biography, business, computers, current affairs, health, history, humor, investigative, money, parenting, popular culture, science, sports, technology. **Considers these fiction areas:** literary.

This agency specializes in adult nonfiction. No science fiction, fantasy, horror, category romance, juvenile, young adult or self-published books.

HOW TO CONTACT E-mail queries only. Please include a brief description. If interested, we'll ask for the nonfiction proposal or fiction synopsis and sample chapter. Do not send attachments or referrals to websites, they will not be opened or visited. Responds if interested. Accepts simultaneous submissions. Accepts new clients through recommendations from current clients.

TERMS Agent receives 15% commission on domestic sales. Agent receives 20% commission on foreign sales. Offers written contract. Charges clients for photocopying.

RECENT SALES Byron Acohido, Jon Swartz—*Zero Day Threat: The Shocking Truth of How Banks and Credit Bureaus Help Cyber Crooks*; Mary Collins—*American Idle: A Journey Through Our Sedentary Culture*; Raphael Ezekiel—*The Racist Mind: Portraits of American Neo-Nazis and Klansmen.*

WRITERS CONFERENCES Attends major regional panels, seminars, and conferences.

PAVILION LITERARY MANAGEMENT

660 Massachusetts Ave., Suite 4, Boston MA 02118. (617)792-5218. **E-mail:** jeff@pavilionliterary.com. **Website:** www.pavilionliterary.com. **Contact:** Jeff Kellogg.

Prior to his current position, Mr. Kellogg was a literary agent with The Stuart Agency, and an acquiring editor with HarperCollins.

REPRESENTS nonfiction books, novels, memoir. **Considers these nonfiction areas:**, narrative nonfiction (topical and historical) and cutting-edge popular science from experts in their respective fields. **Considers these fiction areas:** adventure, fantasy, juvenile, mystery, thriller, general fiction, genre-blending fiction.

"We are presently accepting fiction submissions only from previously published authors and/or by client referral. Nonfiction projects, specifically narrative nonfiction and cutting-edge popular science from experts in their respective fields, are most welcome."

HOW TO CONTACT Query first by e-mail (no attachments). The subject line should specify fiction or nonfiction and include the title of the work. If submitting nonfiction, include a book proposal (no longer than 75 pages), with sample chapters.

L. PERKINS AGENCY

5800 Arlington Ave., Riverdale NY 10471. (718)543-5344. **Fax:** (718)543-5354. **E-mail:** submissions@lperkinsagency.com. **Website:** lperkinsagency.com. Member of AAR. Represents 90 clients. 10% of clients are new/unpublished writers.

Ms. Perkins has been an agent for 20 years. She is also the author of *The Insider's Guide to Getting an Agent* (Writer's Digest Books), as well as three other nonfiction books. She has also edited 12 erotic anthologies, and is also the editorial director of Ravenousromance.com, an e-publisher.

MEMBER AGENTS Tish Beaty, ePub agent (erotic romance—including paranormal, historical, gay/lesbian/bisexual, and light-BDSM fiction; also, she seeks new adult and YA); **Lori Perkins** (not currently taking new clients); **Sandy Lu**.

REPRESENTS nonfiction books, novels. **Considers these nonfiction areas:** biography, creative nonfiction, film, foods, history, humor, music, popular culture, psychology, science, theater. **Considers these fic-**

tion areas: commercial, erotica, gay, historical, horror, lesbian, mystery, new adult, paranormal, thriller, urban fantasy, young adult.

"Most of my clients write both fiction and nonfiction. This combination keeps my clients publishing for years. I am also a published author, so I know what it takes to write a good book." Does not want to receive anything outside of the above categories (westerns, romance, etc.).

HOW TO CONTACT E-queries only. Include your query, a 1-page synopsis, and the first 5 pages from your novel pasted into the e-mail. No attachments. Submit to only one agent at the agency. No snail mail queries. Accepts simultaneous submissions. Responds in 12 weeks to queries. Responds in 3-6 months to mss. Obtains most new clients through recommendations from others, solicitations, conferences.

TERMS Agent receives 15% commission on domestic sales. Agent receives 20% commission on foreign sales. No written contract. Charges clients for photocopying.

WRITERS CONFERENCES NECON, Killercon, BookExpo America, World Fantasy Convention, RWA, Romantic Times.

TIPS "Research your field and contact professional writers' organizations to see who is looking for what. Finish your novel before querying agents. Read my book, *An Insider's Guide to Getting an Agent*, to get a sense of how agents operate. Read agent blogs—agentinthemiddle.blogspot.com and ravenous romance.blogspot.com."

PFD GROUP LTD.

Drury House, 34-43 Russell St., London WC2B 5HA United Kingdom. (44)(207)344-1000. **Fax:** (44) (207)836-9539. **E-mail:** info@pfd.co.uk. **Website:** www.pfd.co.uk.

"Peters Fraser and Dunlop offers its clients something unique in British agenting. Calling on our many areas of expertise, we work closely together to deliver an unparalleled full service, covering all aspects of publishing and media businesses. We have an active Television Division that represents broadcasters. We work with TV companies to come up with complementary programming as well selling film and television rights for our book clients. We have a Public Speaking Division for clients who wish to give lectures and speak at events. Our Foreign Rights Division is there to make sure that our authors' work is sold and published in foreign language markets. We have a Digital Division that represents our clients in the rapidly changing online world. Overall this team ensures that all our clients' talents and opportunities are given the fullest possible professional attention."

MEMBER AGENTS **Rowan Lawton** (books), **Caroline Michel** (books), **Michael Sissons** and **Fiona Petheram** (books), **Annabel Merullo** (books), **Claire Daniel** (foreign rights), **Robert Caskie** (books and journalism).

PIPPIN PROPERTIES, INC.

110 w. 40th Street, Suite 1704, New York NY 10018. (212)338-9310. **Fax:** (212)338-9579. **E-mail:** info@pippinproperties.com. **Website:** www.pippinproperties.com. **Contact:** Holly McGhee. Represents 52 clients. Currently handles: juvenile books 100%.

Prior to becoming an agent, Ms. McGhee was an editor for 7 years and in book marketing for 4 years.

MEMBER AGENTS Holly McGhee, Elena Giovinazzo.

REPRESENTS Juvenile. **Considers these fiction areas:** middle grade, picture books, young adult.

"We are strictly a children's literary agency devoted to the management of authors and artists in all media. We are small and discerning in choosing our clientele." Actively seeking middle grade and young adult novels.

HOW TO CONTACT Query via e-mail. Include a synopsis of the work(s), your background and/or publishing history, and anything else you think is relevant. Accepts simultaneous submissions. Responds in 3 weeks to queries if interested. Responds in 10 weeks to mss. Obtains most new clients through recommendations from others.

TERMS Agent receives 15% commission on domestic sales. Agent receives 25% commission on foreign sales. Offers written contract; 30-day notice must be given to terminate contract. Charges for color copying and UPS/FedEx.

TIPS "Please do not start calling after sending a submission."

AARON M. PRIEST LITERARY AGENCY

708 3rd Ave., 23rd Floor, New York NY 10017. (212)818-0344. **Fax:** (212)573-9417. **E-mail:** info@aar

onpriest.com. **Website:** www.aaronpriest.com. Estab. 1974. Member of AAR. Currently handles: nonfiction books 25%, novels 75%.

MEMBER AGENTS Aaron Priest, querypriest@aaronpriest.com (thrillers, commercial fiction, biographies); **Lisa Erbach Vance**, queryvance@aaronpriest.com (contemporary fiction, especially women's fiction, thoughtful fiction about families and friends, thrillers/suspense, psychological suspense, contemporary gothic fiction, unique ghost stories, international fiction [not translation], narrative nonfiction, current or historical topics); **Lucy Childs Baker**, querychilds@aaronpriest.com (commercial fiction [women's and mystery], and especially literary fiction [including historical], as well as narrative nonfiction).

Does not want to receive poetry, screenplays, horror or sci-fi.

HOW TO CONTACT Query one of the agents using the appropriate e-mail listed on the website. "Please do not submit to more than 1 agent at this agency. We urge you to check our website and consider each agent's emphasis before submitting. Your query letter should be about one page long and describe your work as well as your background. You may also paste the first chapter of your work in the body of the e-mail. Do not send attachments." Accepts simultaneous submissions. Responds in 4 weeks, only if interested.

TERMS Agent receives 15% commission on domestic sales.

RECENT SALES *The Hit*, by David Baldacci; *Six Years*, by Harlan Coben; *Suspect*, by Robert Crais; *Permanent Record*, by Leslie Stella; *Eye for an Eye*, by Ben Coes.

PROSPECT AGENCY

551 Valley Road, PMB 377, Upper Montclair NJ 07043. (718)788-3217. **Fax:** (718)360-9582. **Website:** www.prospectagency.com. Estab. 2005. Member of AAR. Currently handles: 60% of material handled is books for young readers.

MEMBER AGENTS Emily Sylvan Kim, esk@prospectagency.com; **Rachel Orr**, rko@prospectagency.com (no new clients); **Becca Stumpf**, becca@prospectagency.com (young adult, middle grade, fantasy, sci-fi, literary mysteries, literary thrillers, spicy romance); **Carrie Pestritto**, carrie@prospectagency.com (narrative nonfiction, general nonfiction, biography, and memoir; commercial fiction with a literary twist, historical fiction, "new adult," YA, and middle grade); **Teresa Kietlinski**, tk@prospectagency.com (picture book artists and illustrators).

REPRESENTS Considers these nonfiction areas: biography, memoirs. **Considers these fiction areas:** commercial, historical, juvenile, middle grade, mystery, new adult, picture books, romance, thriller, young adult.

"We're looking for strong, unique voices and unforgettable stories and characters."

HOW TO CONTACT Note that each agent at this agency has a different submission e-mail address and different submission policies. Check the agency website for the latest formal guideline per each agent. Obtains new clients through conferences, recommendations, queries, and some scouting.

TERMS Agent receives 15% on domestic sales, 20% on foreign sales sold directly and 25% on sales using a subagent. Offers written contract.

RECENT SALES Recent sales include: *Ollie and Claire* (Philomel), *Vicious* (Bloomsbury), *Tempest Rising* (Walker Books), *Where Do Diggers Sleep at Night* (Random House Children's), *A DJ Called Tomorrow* (Little, Brown), *The Princesses of Iowa* (Candlewick).

P.S. LITERARY AGENCY

20033 - 520 Kerr St., Oakville ON L6K 3C7 Canada. **E-mail:** query@psliterary.com. **Website:** www.psliterary.com. **Contact:** Curtis Russell, principal agent; Carly Watters, agent; Maria Vincente, associate agent. Estab. 2005. Currently handles: nonfiction books 50%, novels 50%.

REPRESENTS nonfiction, novels, juvenile books. **Considers these nonfiction areas:** autobiography, biography, business, child guidance, cooking, current affairs, diet/nutrition, economics, environment, foods, government, health, history, how-to, humor, law, memoirs, military, money, parenting, popular culture, politics, science, self-help, sports, technology, true crime, war, women's issues, women's studies. **Considers these fiction areas:** action, adventure, detective, erotica, ethnic, family saga, historical, horror, humor, juvenile, literary, mainstream, middle grade, mystery, new adult, picture books, romance, sports, thriller, women's, young adult, biography/autobiography, business, child guidance/parenting, cooking/food/nutrition, current affairs, government/politics/law, health/medicine, history, how-to, humor, memoirs, military/war, money/finance/economics, nature/environment, popular culture, science/technology, self-help/personal improvement, sports, true crime/investigative, women's issues/women's studies.

"What makes our agency distinct: We take on a small number of clients per year in order to provide focused, hands-on representation. We pride ourselves in providing industry-leading client service." Actively seeking both fiction and nonfiction. Seeking both new and established writers. Does not want to receive poetry or screenplays.

HOW TO CONTACT Queries by e-mail only. Submit query, and bio. "Please limit your query to one page." Accepts simultaneous submissions. Responds in 4-6 weeks to queries/proposals; mss 4-8 weeks. Obtains most new clients through solicitations.

TERMS Agent receives 15% commission on domestic sales. Agent receives 25% commission on foreign sales. We offer a written contract, with 30-days notice terminate. "This agency charges for postage/messenger services only if a project is sold."

TIPS "Please review our website for the most up-to-date submission guidelines. We do not charge reading fees. We do not offer a critique service."

JOANNA PULCINI LITERARY MANAGEMENT

E-mail: info@jplm.com. **Website:** www.jplm.com. **Contact:** Joanna Pulcini.

"JPLM is not accepting submissions at this time; however, I do encourage those seeking representation to read the "Advice to Writers" essay on our website for some guidance on finding an agent."

HOW TO CONTACT Do not query this agency until they open their client list.

RECENT SALES *TV*, by Brian Brown; *The Movies That Changed Us*, by Nick Clooney; *Strange, But True*, by John Searles; *The Intelligencer*, by Leslie Silbert; *In Her Shoes* and *The Guy Not Taken*, by Jennifer Weiner.

THE PURCELL AGENCY

E-mail: TPAqueries@gmail.com. **Website:** www.thepurcellagency.com. **Contact:** Tina P. Schwartz. Estab. 2012.

REPRESENTS Considers these nonfiction areas: juvenile nonfiction. **Considers these fiction areas:** juvenile, middle grade, young adult.

This agency also takes juvenile nonfiction for MG and YA markets. At this point, the agency is not considering fantasy, science fiction or picture book submissions.

HOW TO Contact E-query. Mention if you are part of SCBWI. For fiction, send a query, the first 3 chapters, and synopsis. No attachments. For nonfiction, send table of contents + intro and sample chapter, author's credentials. Accepts simultaneous submissions. Responds in 1-3 months.

QUEEN LITERARY AGENCY

47 E. 19th St., Third Floor, New York NY 10003. (212)974-8333. **Fax:** (212)974-8347. **E-mail:** lqueen@queenliterary.com. **E-mail:** submissions@queenliterary.com. **Website:** www.queenliterary.com. **Contact:** Lisa Queen.

Prior to her current position, Ms. Queen was a former publishing executive and most recently head of IMG Worldwide's literary division.

REPRESENTS nonfiction books, novels. **Considers these nonfiction areas:** business, foods, psychology, science, sports. **Considers these fiction areas:** commercial, historical, literary, mystery, thriller.

Ms. Queen's specialties: "While our agency represents a wide range of nonfiction titles, we have a particular interest in business books, food writing, science and popular psychology, as well as books by well-known chefs, radio and television personalities, and sports figures."

HOW TO CONTACT E-query.

RECENT SALES A full list of this agency's clients and sales is available on their website.

SUSAN RABINER LITERARY AGENCY, INC., THE

315 W. 39th St., Suite 1501, New York NY 10018. (212)279-0316. **Fax:** (212)279-0932. **Website:** www.rabinerlit.com. **Contact:** Susan Rabiner.

Prior to becoming an agent, Ms. Rabiner was editorial director of Basic Books. She is also the co-author of *Thinking Like Your Editor: How to Write Great Serious Nonfiction and Get It Published* (W.W. Norton).

MEMBER AGENTS Susan Rabiner, susan@rabiner.net (well-researched, topical books written by fully credentialed academics, journalists, and recognized public intellectuals with the power to stimulate public debate on a broad range of issues including the state of our economy, political discourse, history, science, and the arts); **Sydelle Kramer,** sydellek@rabiner.net (academics, journalists, sportswriters, and memoirists);

NEW AGENT SPOTLIGHT

KATIE REED
(ANDREA HURST & ASSOCIATES)

andreahurst.com

ABOUT KATIE: Katie obtained her Bachelor's in English from California State University, Sacramento. Katie resides in the small town of Durham, California, with her incredible husband, her joyful son, and Snoodles, her loyal cat. Besides her addiction to reading, she is also a die-hard Miami Heat fan and obsessed with all things Disney.

SHE IS SEEKING: all areas of young adult, particularly: commercial (with a compelling hook and a protagonist who battles real-life teen issues), science fiction (soft), and fantasy; commercial and literary adult fiction in the genres of book club women's fiction, science fiction (soft), fantasy, suspense/thriller, and contemporary romance. For nonfiction: memoir/biography with a strong platform, self-help, crafts/how-to, inspirational, parenting.

HOW TO QUERY: Katie@andreahurst.com. Put "Query" in the subject line of your query. No attachments. Do not send proposals, sample chapters or manuscripts unless specifically requested by an agent. Please indicate if you are simultaneously submitting to other agents.

Holly Bemiss, hollyb@rabiner.net (graphic novelists, journalists, memoirists, comedians, crafters, and entertainment writers); **Eric Nelson**, ericn@rabiner.net (nationally known journalists, management consultants, academics, and people who spend a lot of time in front of TV cameras, though if a writer has an existing following and an interesting story to tell, he's always happy to hear it).

"Representing narrative nonfiction and big-idea books—work that illuminates the past and the present. I look for well-researched, topical books written by fully credentialed academics, journalists, and recognized public intellectuals with the power to stimulate public debate on a broad range of issues including the state of our economy, political discourse, history, science, and the arts."

HOW TO CONTACT Please send all queries by e-mail. Note: Because of the number of queries we receive, we cannot respond to every one. If your project fits the profile of the agency, we will be in touch within two weeks. Accepts simultaneous submissions. Obtains most new clients through recommendations from others.

TERMS Agent receives 15% commission on domestic sales. Agent receives 20% commission on foreign sales. Offers written contract; 1-month notice must be given to terminate contract.

RED SOFA LITERARY

2163 Grand Ave., #2, St. Paul MN 55105. (651)224-6670. **E-mail:** dawn@redsofaliterary.com; jennie@

redsofaliterary.com. **Website:** www.redsofaliterary.com. **Contact:** Dawn Frederick, literary agent and owner; Jennie Goloboy, agent; Laura Zats, associate agent. Red Sofa is a member of the Authors Guild and the MN Publishers Round Table. Represents 20 clients. 80% of clients are new/unpublished writers. Currently handles: nonfiction books 97%, novels 2%, story collections 1%.

Dawn Frederick: Prior to her current position, Ms. Frederick spent 5 years at Sebastian Literary Agency. In addition, Ms. Frederick worked more than 10 years in indie and chain book stores, and at an independent children's book publisher. Ms. Frederick has a master's degree in library and information sciences from an ALA-accredited institution. **Jennie Goloboy**: In Fall 2011, Jennie Goloboy joined Red Sofa Literary as an associate agent. Jennie Goloboy has a PhD in the History of American Civilization from Harvard. She is also a published author of both history and fiction, and a member of SFWA, RWA, SHEAR, OAH, the AHA, and Codex Writers Group. Her funny, spec-fic short stories appear under her pen name, Nora Fleischer. As of 2014, **Laura Zats** was the newest RS agent.

REPRESENTS nonfiction, fiction, juvenile books. **Considers these nonfiction areas:** animals, anthropology, archeology, crafts, cultural interests, current affairs, gay/lesbian, government, health, history, hobbies, humor, investigative, law, popular culture, politics, satire, sociology, true crime, women's issues, women's studies, extreme sports. **Considers these fiction areas:** erotica, fantasy, middle grade, romance, science fiction, women's, young adult.

HOW TO CONTACT Query by e-mail or mail with SASE. No attachments, please. Submit full proposal plus 3 sample chapters and any other pertinent writing samples. Accepts simultaneous submissions. Responds in 3 weeks to queries; 6 weeks to mss. Obtains most new clients through recommendations from others, solicitations.

TERMS Agent receives 15% commission on domestic sales. Agent receives 20% commission on foreign sales. Offers written contract. May charge a one-time $100 fee for partial reimbursement of postage and phone expenses incurred if the advance is below $15,000.

WRITERS CONFERENCES Madison Writers' Institute; Novel-in-Progress Bookcamp; OWFI Conference; SDSU Writers' Conference; Florida Writer's Association Conference; The Loft Literary Center; DFW Writers' Conference; MN SCBWI Conference, Bloomington Writers' Festival and Book Fair; Women of Words Retreat; ISD 196; First Pages (Hennepin County); Writer's Digest Webinar.

TIPS "Always remember the benefits of building an author platform, and the accessibility of accomplishing this task in today's industry. Most importantly, research the agents queried. Avoid contacting every literary agent about a book idea. Due to the large volume of queries received, the process of reading queries for unrepresented categories (by the agency) becomes quite the arduous task. Investigate online directories, printed guides (like *Writer's Market*), individual agent websites, and more, before beginning the query process. It's good to remember that each agent has a vision of what s/he wants to represent and will communicate this information accordingly. We're simply waiting for those specific book ideas to come in our direction."

RED TREE LITERARY AGENCY

320 7th Ave., #183, Brooklyn NY 11215. **E-mail:** elana@redtreeliterary.com. **Website:** www.redtreeliterary.com. **Contact:** Elana Roth.

Elana is a graduate of Barnard College and the Jewish Theological Seminary, where she earned degrees in English literature and Bible.

REPRESENTS **Considers these fiction areas:** juvenile, middle grade, young adult.

HOW TO CONTACT E-mail only.

RECENT SALES *Doug-Dennis and the Flyaway Fib*, by Darren Farrel; *Juniper Berry*, by M.P. Kozlowsky; *The Selection*, by Kiera Cass; *Unison Spark*, by Andy Marino.

HELEN REES LITERARY AGENCY

14 Beacon St., Suite 710, Boston MA 02108. (617)227-9014. **Fax:** (617)227-8762. **E-mail:** reesagency@reesagency.com. **Website:** reesagency.com. **Contact:** Joan Mazmanian, Ann Collette, Helen Rees, Lorin Rees. Estab. 1983. Member of AAR. Other memberships include PEN. Represents more than 100 clients. 50% of clients are new/unpublished writers. Currently handles: nonfiction books 60%, novels 40%.

MEMBER AGENTS **Ann Collette** (literary, mystery, thrillers, suspense, vampire, and women's fiction; in nonfiction, she prefers true crime, narrative nonfiction, military and war, work to do with race and class, and work set in or about Southeast Asia; Agent10702@aol.com). **Lorin Rees** (literary fiction, memoirs, business books, self-help, science, history, psychology, and narrative nonfiction; lorin@reesagency.com); **Nicole LaBombard**, nicole@reesagency.com (historical fiction, upscale commercial fiction, compelling literary fiction, young adult, narrative nonfiction, health/fitness, and business); **Rebecca Podos**, rebecca@reesagency.com (young adult fiction of all kinds, including contemporary, emotionally driven stories, mystery, romance, urban and historical fantasy, horror and sci-fi; occasionally, she considers literary and commercial adult fiction, new adult, and narrative nonfiction).

REPRESENTS nonfiction books, novels. **Considers these nonfiction areas:** business, creative nonfiction, health, history, memoirs, military, psychology, science, self-help, true crime, war. **Considers these fiction areas:** commercial, historical, horror, literary, mystery, new adult, romance, science fiction, suspense, thriller, urban fantasy, women's, young adult.

HOW TO CONTACT Consult website for each agent's submission guidelines, as they differ. Responds in 3-4 weeks to queries. Obtains most new clients through recommendations from others, conferences, submissions.

TERMS Agent receives 15% commission on domestic sales. Agent receives 20% commission on foreign sales.

RECENT SALES Recent titles include: *The Art Forger*, by B.A. Shapiro; *Busy Monsters*, by William Giraldi; *Pitch Dark*, by Steven Sidor; *You Know When the Men Are Gone*, by Siobhan Fallon; and *Death Drops*, by Chrystle Fieldler. Other titles include: *Get Your Ship Together*, by Capt. D. Michael Abrashoff; *Overpromise and Overdeliver*, by Rick Berrara; *Opacity*, by Joel Kurtzman; *America the Broke*, by Gerald Swanson; *Murder at the B-School*, by Jeffrey Cruikshank; *Bone Factory*, by Steven Sidor; *Father Said*, by Hal Sirowitz; *Winning*, by Jack Welch; *The Case for Israel*, by Alan Dershowitz; *As the Future Catches You*, by Juan Enriquez; *Blood Makes the Grass Grow Green*, by Johnny Rico; *DVD Movie Guide*, by Mick Martin and Marsha Porter; *Words That Work*, by Frank Luntz; *Stirring It Up*, by Gary Hirshberg; *Hot Spots*, by Martin Fletcher; *Andy Grove: The Life and Times of an American*, by Richard Tedlow; *Girls Most Likely To*, by Poonam Sharma.

REGAL LITERARY AGENCY

236 W. 26th St., #801, New York NY 10001. (212)684-7900. **Fax:** (212)684-7906. **E-mail:** info@regal-literary.com. **E-mail:** submissions@regal-literary.com. **Website:** www.regal-literary.com. London Office: 36 Gloucester Ave., Primrose Hill, London NW1 7BB, United Kingdom, uk@regal-literary.com Estab. 2002. Member of AAR. Represents 70 clients. 20% of clients are new/unpublished writers.

MEMBER AGENTS Michelle Andelman; Claire Anderson-Wheeler; Markus Hoffmann; Leigh Huffine; Lauren Pearson; Joseph Regal.

REPRESENTS **Considers these nonfiction areas:** creative nonfiction, memoirs, psychology, science. **Considers these fiction areas:** literary, middle grade, picture books, thriller, women's, young adult.

Actively seeking literary fiction and narrative nonfiction. "We do not consider romance, science fiction, poetry, or screenplays."

HOW TO CONTACT "Query with SASE or via e-mail. No phone calls. Submissions should consist of a 1-page query letter detailing the book in question, as well as the qualifications of the author. For fiction, submissions may also include the first 10 pages of the novel or one short story from a collection." Responds if interested. Accepts simultaneous submissions.

TERMS Agent receives 15% commission on domestic sales. Agent receives 20% commission on foreign sales. "We charge no reading fees."

RECENT SALES Audrey Niffenegger's *The Time Traveler's Wife* (Mariner) and *Her Fearful Symmetry* (Scribner), Gregory David Roberts' *Shantaram* (St. Martin's), Josh Bazell's *Beat the Reaper* (Little, Brown), John Twelve Hawks' *The Fourth Realm Trilogy* (Doubleday), James Reston, Jr.'s *The Conviction of Richard Nixon* (Three Rivers) and *Defenders of the Faith* (Penguin), Michael Psilakis' *How to Roast a Lamb: New Greek Classic Cooking* (Little, Brown), Colman Andrews' *Country Cooking of Ireland* (Chronicle) and *Reinventing Food: Ferran Adria and How He Changed the Way We Eat* (Phaidon).

TIPS "We are deeply committed to every aspect of our clients' careers, and are engaged in everything from the editorial work of developing a great book proposal or line editing a fiction manuscript to negotiating state-of-the-art book deals and working to promote and publicize the book when it's published. We are at the forefront of the effort to increase authors' rights in publishing contracts in a rapidly changing commercial environment. We deal directly with co-agents and publishers in every foreign territory and also work directly and with co-agents for feature film and television rights, with extraordinary success in both arenas. Many of our clients' works have sold in dozens of translation markets, and a high proportion of our books have been sold in Hollywood. We have strong relationships with speaking agents, who can assist in arranging author tours and other corporate and college speaking opportunities when appropriate. We also have a staff publicist and marketer to help promote our clients and their work."

THE AMY RENNERT AGENCY

98 Main St., #302, Tiburon CA 94920. **E-mail:** queries@amyrennert.com. **Contact:** Amy Rennert.

REPRESENTS nonfiction books, novels. **Considers these nonfiction areas:** biography, business, creative nonfiction, health, history, money, sports. **Considers these fiction areas:** literary, mainstream, mystery.

"The Amy Rennert Agency specializes in books that matter. We provide career management for established and first-time authors, and our breadth of experience in many genres enables us to meet the needs of a diverse clientele."

HOW TO CONTACT Cover letter and proposal for nonfiction; cover letter and first 25 pages for fiction. For picture books, cover letter and manuscript. Please use pdf attachments and please note that due to the increasing number of submissions, we can only respond if interested.

RECENT SALES Maisie Dobbs series by Jacqueline Winspear; *A Salty Piece of Land* by Jimmy Buffett; *The Prize Winner of Defiance, Ohio* by Terry Ryan; *Medical Myths That Can Kill You* by Dr. Nancy Snyderman; *Patti Lupone: A Memoir* by Patti LuPone; *Ivy +Bean* by Annie Barrows; *Goodnight, Goodnight, Construction Site* by Sherri Rinker and Tom Lichteheld.

TIPS Due to the high volume of submissions, it is not possible to respond to each and every one. Please understand that we are only able to respond to queries that we feel may be a good fit with our agency.

RICK BROADHEAD & ASSOCIATES LITERARY AGENCY

47 St. Clair Ave. W., Suite 501, Toronto ON M4V 3A5 Canada. (416)929-0516. **Fax:** (416)927-8732. **E-mail:** info@rbaliterary.com. **E-mail:** submissions@rbaliterary.com. **Website:** www.rbaliterary.com. **Contact:** Rick Broadhead, president. Estab. 2002. Membership includes Authors Guild. Represents 125 clients. 50% of clients are new/unpublished writers. Currently handles: nonfiction books 100%.

With an MBA from the Schulich School of Business, one of the world's leading business schools, Rick Broadhead is one of the few literary agents in the publishing industry with a business and entrepreneurial background, one that benefits his clients at every step of the book development and contract negotiation process. He is also a best-selling author, having authored and co-authored 35 books.

REPRESENTS nonfiction books. **Considers these nonfiction areas:** biography, business, current affairs, environment, health, history, humor, medicine, military, popular culture, politics, science, self-help.

Rick Broadhead & Associates is a leading literary agency that represents nonfiction authors to all of the top publishing houses in North America. The agency has negotiated millions of dollars in royalties for its clients with venerable American and Canadian publishing houses. Best-selling author Rick Broadhead has a proven track record for finding literary talent, developing projects with strong commercial and media potential, and matching authors with publishers. Books represented by the agency have appeared on bestseller lists, been shortlisted for literary awards, translated into multiple languages, and through its partnerships in Hollywood, optioned for film and television development. The agency's clients include accomplished journalists, historians, physicians, television personalities, bloggers and creators of popular websites, successful business executives, and experts in their respective fields. They include Yale University physician Dr. David Katz; survival skills expert and Discovery Channel host Les Stroud (*Survivorman*). The agency is actively seeking compelling proposals from experts in their fields, journalists, and authors with relevant credentials and an established media platform (tv, web, radio, print experience/exposure). Does not want to receive fiction, screenplays, children's or poetry at this time.

HOW TO CONTACT "Please send a short query letter by e-mail or via regular mail with a description of the project, your credentials, and contact info. E-mail queries are welcome. Please do not send entire mss or sample chapters unless requested. If I am interested, I will request a proposal." Accepts simultaneous submissions. Obtains most new clients through recommendations from others, solicitations.

TERMS Agent receives 15% commission on domestic sales. Agent receives 20% commission on foreign sales. Offers written contract. Charges for postage and photocopying expenses.

TIPS "Books rarely sell themselves these days, so I look for authors who have a 'platform' (media exposure/experience, university affiliation, recognized expertise, etc.). Remember that a literary agent has to sell your project to an editor, and then the editor has to sell your project internally to his/her colleagues (including the marketing and sales staff), and then the publisher has to sell your book to the book buyers at the chains and bookstores. You're most likely to get my attention if you write a succinct and persuasive query letter that demonstrates your platform/credentials, the market potential of your book, and why your book is different. I love finding great authors, pitching great book ideas, negotiating deals for my clients, and being a part of this exciting and dynamic industry."

THE RIGHTS FACTORY

P.O. Box 499, Station C, Toronto ON M6J 3P6 Canada. (416)966-5367. **Website:** www.therightsfactory.com.

MEMBER AGENTS Sam Hiyate, Ali McDonald.

"The Rights Factory is an agency that deals in intellectual property rights to entertainment products, including books, comics and graphic novels, film, television, and video games. We license rights in every territory by representing 3 types of clients."

HOW TO CONTACT There is a submission form on this agency's website.

RECENT SALES *Beauty, Pure & Simple*, by Kristen Ma; *Why Mr. Right Can't Find You*, by J.M. Kearns; *Tout Sweet: Hanging Up My High Heels for a New Life in France*, by Karen Wheeler; *The Orange Code*, by Arkadi Kuhlmann and Bruce Philp.

ANGELA RINALDI LITERARY AGENCY

P.O. Box 7877, Beverly Hills CA 90212-7877. (310)842-7665. **Fax:** (310)837-8143. **E-mail:** amr@rinaldiliterary.com. **Website:** www.rinaldiliterary.com. **Contact:** Angela Rinaldi. Member of AAR.

Prior to opening her agency, Ms. Rinaldi was an editor at NAL/Signet, Pocket Books and Bantam, and the manager of book development for *The Los Angeles Times*.

REPRESENTS nonfiction books, novels, TV and motion picture rights (for clients only). **Considers these nonfiction areas:** biography, business, cooking, current affairs, health, psychology, self-help, true crime, women's issues, wine, lifestyle, career, personal finance, prescriptive and proactive self-help books by journalists, academics, doctors and therapists, based on their research. **Considers these fiction areas:** commercial, literary, suspense, women's, upmarket women's fiction, book club women's fiction.

Actively seeking commercial and literary fiction, young adult crossovers. Does not want to receive humor, pop culture, thrillers, category romances, science fiction, fantasy, horror, film scripts, poetry, category romances, magazine articles, religion, occult, paranormal, children's or middle grade fiction.

HOW TO CONTACT E-mail queries only. For fiction, please send a brief e-mail inquiry with the first 10 pages pasted into the e-mail—no attachments unless asked for. For nonfiction, query with detailed letter or outline/proposal, no attachments unless asked for. Accepts simultaneous submissions. Responds in 2-4 weeks.

TERMS Agent receives 15% commission on domestic sales. Agent receives 25% commission on foreign sales. Offers written contract.

WRITERS CONFERENCES Writer's Digest Conference West (Los Angeles).

ANN RITTENBERG LITERARY AGENCY, INC.

15 Maiden Lane, Suite 206, New York NY 10038. **Website:** www.rittlit.com. **Contact:** Ann Rittenberg, president; Penn Whaling, associate. Member of AAR. Currently handles: fiction 75%, nonfiction 25%.

REPRESENTS Considers these nonfiction areas: memoirs, women's issues, women's studies. **Considers these fiction areas:** literary, mainstream, thriller, upmarket fiction.

This agent specializes in upmarket thrillers, literary fiction and literary nonfiction. Does not want to receive screenplays, straight genre fiction, poetry, self-help.

HOW TO CONTACT Query with SASE. Submit outline, 3 sample chapters, SASE. Query via postal mail or e-mail to info@rittlit.com. Accepts simultaneous submissions. Responds in 6 weeks to queries. Responds in 2 months to mss. Obtains most new clients through referrals from established writers and editors.

TERMS Agent receives 15% commission on domestic sales. Agent receives 20% commission on foreign sales. Offers written contract. This agency charges clients for photocopying only.

RECENT SALES *Live by Night*, by Dennis Lehane; *Leaving Haven*, by Kathleen McCleary; *Massacre Pond*, by Paul Doiron; *The Highway*, by C.J. Box; *This Is Not a Writing Manual*, by Kerri Smith Majors; *The Land of Dreams*, by Vidar Sundstol; *Behemoth*, by Ronald Tobias; and *Billboard Man*, by Jim Fusilli.

RIVERSIDE LITERARY AGENCY

41 Simon Keets Rd., Leyden MA 01337. (413)772-0067. **Fax:** (413)772-0969. **E-mail:** rivlit@sover.net. **Website:** www.riversideliteraryagency.com. **Contact:** Susan Lee Cohen.

Represents adult fiction and nonfiction.

HOW TO CONTACT Query with SASE. Accepts simultaneous submissions. Responds in 2 weeks to queries. Obtains most new clients through referrals.

TERMS Agent receives 15% commission on domestic sales. Offers written contract. Charges clients for foreign postage, photocopying large mss, express mail deliveries, etc.

RLR ASSOCIATES, LTD.

Literary Department, 7 W. 51st St., New York NY 10019. (212)541-8641. **Fax:** (212)262-7084. **E-mail:** sgould@rlrassociates.net. **Website:** www.rlrassociates.net. **Contact:** Scott Gould. Member of AAR. Represents 50 clients. 25% of clients are new/unpublished writers. Currently handles: nonfiction books 70%, novels 25%, story collections 5%.

REPRESENTS nonfiction books, novels, short-story collections, scholarly. **Considers these nonfiction areas:** creative nonfiction. **Considers these fiction areas:** commercial, literary, mainstream, middle grade, picture books, romance, women's, young adult.

"We provide a lot of editorial assistance to our clients and have connections." Actively seeking fiction, current affairs, history, art, popular culture, health and business. Does not want to receive screenplays.

HOW TO CONTACT Query by either e-mail or snail mail. For fiction, send a query and 1-3 chapters (pasted). For nonfiction, send query or proposal. Accepts simultaneous submissions. "If you do not hear from us within 3 months, please assume that your work is out of active consideration." Obtains most new clients through recommendations from others.

TERMS Agent receives 15% commission on domestic sales. Agent receives 20% commission on foreign sales. Offers written contract.

RECENT SALES Clients include Shelby Foote, The Grief Recovery Institute, Don Wade, Don Zimmer, The Knot.com, David Plowden, PGA of America, Danny Peary, George Kalinsky, Peter Hyman, Daniel Parker, Lee Miller, Elise Miller, Nina Planck, Karyn Bosnak, Christopher Pike, Gerald Carbone, Jason Lethcoe, Andy Crouch.

TIPS "Please check out our website for more details on our agency."

B.J. ROBBINS LITERARY AGENCY

5130 Bellaire Ave., North Hollywood CA 91607-2908. **E-mail:** Robbinsliterary@gmail.com. **E-mail:** angeline.bjrobbinsliterary@gmail.com. **Contact:** (Ms.) B.J. Robbins, or Amy Maldonado. Member of AAR. Represents 40 clients. 50% of clients are new/unpublished writers. Currently handles: nonfiction books 50%, novels 50%.

REPRESENTS nonfiction books, novels. **Considers these nonfiction areas:** autobiography, biography, cultural interests, current affairs, dance, ethnic, film, health, humor, investigative, medicine, memoirs, music, popular culture, psychology, self-help, sociology, sports, theater, travel, true crime, women's issues, women's studies. **Considers these fiction areas:** crime, detective, ethnic, literary, mainstream, mystery, police, sports, suspense, thriller.

HOW TO CONTACT Query with SASE. Submit outline/proposal, 3 sample chapters, SASE. Accepts e-mail queries (no attachments). Accepts simultaneous submissions. Responds in 2-6 weeks to queries. Responds in 6-8 weeks to mss. Obtains most new clients through conferences, referrals.

TERMS Agent receives 15% commission on domestic sales. Agent receives 20% commission on foreign sales. Offers written contract; 3-month notice must be given to terminate contract. This agency charges clients for postage and photocopying (only after sale of ms).

RECENT SALES *Shake Down the Stars* and *A Pinch Of Ooh La La*, by Renee Swindle (Nal); *Headhunters On My Doorstep*, by J. Maarten Troost (Gotham); *The Sinatra Club*, by Sal Polisi and Steve Dougherty (Gallery Books); *Blood Of Heroes*, by James Donovan

(Little, Brown); *Little Bighorn*, by John Hough Jr. (Arcade; *The Paris Deadline*, by Max Byrd (Turner); *Blood Brothers*, by Deanne Stillman (Simon & Schuster).

WRITERS CONFERENCES Squaw Valley Writers Workshop; San Diego State University Writers' Conference.

THE ROBBINS OFFICE, INC.

405 Park Ave., 9th Floor, New York NY 10022. (212)223-0720. **Fax:** (212)223-2535. **Website:** www.robbinsoffice.com. **Contact:** Kathy P. Robbins, owner.

MEMBER AGENTS Kathy P. Robbins; David Halpern.

REPRESENTS nonfiction books, novels. **Considers these nonfiction areas:** history, politics, journalism, regional interest, memoirs.

This agency specializes in selling serious nonfiction as well as commercial and literary fiction.

HOW TO CONTACT Accepts submissions by referral only. Do not cold query this market.

TERMS Agent receives 15% commission on domestic sales. Agent receives 15% commission on foreign sales. Agent receives 15% commission on film sales. Bills back specific expenses incurred in doing business for a client.

RODEEN LITERARY MANAGEMENT

3501 N. Southport #497, Chicago IL 60657. **E-mail:** submissions@rodeenliterary.com. **E-mail:** submissions@rodeenliterary.com. **Website:** www.rodeenliterary.com. **Contact:** Paul Rodeen. Estab. 2009.

Paul Rodeen established Rodeen Literary Management in 2009 after 7 years of experience with the literary agency Sterling Lord Literistic, Inc.

REPRESENTS nonfiction books, novels, juvenile books, illustrations, graphic novels. **Considers these fiction areas:** middle grade, picture books, young adult, graphic novels, comics.

Actively seeking "writers and illustrators of all genres of children's literature including picture books, early readers, middle grade fiction and nonfiction, graphic novels and comic books, as well as young adult fiction and nonfiction." This is primarily an agency devoted to children's books.

HOW TO CONTACT Unsolicited submissions are accepted by e-mail only to submissions@rodeenliterary.com. Cover letters with synopsis and contact information should be included in the body of your e-mail. An initial submission of 50 pages from a novel or a longer work of nonfiction will suffice and should be pasted into the body of your e-mail. Electronic portfolios from illustrators are accepted but please keep the images at 72 dpi—a link to your website or blog is also helpful. Electronic picture book dummies and picture book texts are accepted. Graphic novels and comic books are accepted. Accepts simultaneous submissions. Response time varies.

ROGERS, COLERIDGE & WHITE

20 Powis Mews, London England W11 1JN United Kingdom. (44)(207)221-3717. **Fax:** (44)(207)229-9084. **E-mail:** info@rcwlitagency.co.uk. **Website:** www.rcwlitagency.co.uk. **Contact:** David Miller, agent. Estab. 1987.

Prior to opening the agency, Ms. Rogers was an agent with Peter Janson-Smith; Ms. Coleridge worked at Sidgwick & Jackson, Chatto & Windus, and Anthony Sheil Associates; Ms. White was an editor and rights director for Simon & Schuster; Mr. Straus worked at Hodder and Stoughton, Hamish Hamilton, and Macmillan; Mr. Miller worked as Ms. Rogers' assistant and was treasurer of the AAA; Ms. Waldie worked with Carole Smith.

MEMBER AGENTS **Deborah Rogers; Gill Coleridge; Pat White** (illustrated and children's books); **Peter Straus; David Miller; Zoe Waldie** (fiction, biography, current affairs, narrative history); **Laurence Laluyaux** (foreign rights); **Stephen Edwards** (foreign rights); **Peter Robinson; Sam Copeland; Catherine Pellegrino; Hannah Westland; Jenny Hewson**.

REPRESENTS nonfiction books, novels, juvenile. **Considers these nonfiction areas:** biography, cooking, current affairs, diet/nutrition, foods, humor, satire, sports, narrative history. **Considers these fiction areas:** most fiction categories.

"YA and children's fiction should be submitted via e-mail to clairewilson@rcwlitagency.com. We do not accept any other e-mail submissions unless by prior arrangement with individual agents." Does not want to receive plays, screenplays, technical books or educational books.

HOW TO CONTACT "Submit synopsis, proposal, sample chapters, bio, SAE by mail. Submissions should include a cover letter with brief bio and the background to the book. In the case of fiction, they should consist of the first 3 chapters or approximately the first 50 pages of the work to a natural break, and a brief synopsis. Nonfiction submissions should take the form of a proposal up to 20 pages in length explaining what the work is about and why you are best placed to write it. Material should be printed out in 12 point font, in double-spacing and on one side only of A4 paper. We cannot acknowledge receipt of material nor can we accept responsibility for anything you send us, so please retain a copy of material submitted. Material will be returned only if sent with an adequately stamped and sized SASE; if return postage is not provided the material will be recycled. We do not accept e-mail submissions unless by prior arrangement with individual agents. We will try to respond within 6-8 weeks of receipt of your material, but please appreciate that this isn't always possible as we must give priority to the authors we already represent." Responds in 6-8 weeks to queries. Obtains most new clients through recommendations from others, solicitations, conferences.

TERMS Agent receives 15% commission on domestic sales. Agent receives 20% commission on foreign sales. Offers written contract.

◐ LINDA ROGHAAR LITERARY AGENCY, LLC

133 High Point Dr., Amherst MA 01002. (413)256-1921. **E-mail:** contact@lindaroghaar.com. **Website:** www.lindaroghaar.com. **Contact:** Linda L. Roghaar. Member of AAR. Represents 50 clients. 10% of clients are new/unpublished writers. Currently handles: nonfiction books 100%.

Prior to opening her agency, Ms. Roghaar worked in retail bookselling for 5 years and as a publishers' sales rep for 15 years.

REPRESENTS nonfiction books.

The Linda Roghaar Literary Agency represents authors with substantial messages and specializes in nonfiction. We sell to major, independent, and university presses. We are generalists, but we do not handle romance, horror, or science fiction.

HOW TO CONTACT We prefer e-queries. Please mention "Query" in the subject line, and do not include attachments. Accepts simultaneous submissions.

TERMS Agent receives 15% commission on domestic sales. Agent receives negotiable commission on foreign sales. Offers written contract.

◐ THE ROSENBERG GROUP

23 Lincoln Ave., Marblehead MA 01945. (781)990-1341. **Fax:** (781)990-1344. **Website:** www.rosenberggroup.com. **Contact:** Barbara Collins Rosenberg. Estab. 1998. Member of AAR. Recognized agent of the RWA. Represents 25 clients. 15% of clients are new/unpublished writers. Currently handles: nonfiction books 30%, novels 30%, scholarly books 10%, 30% college textbooks.

Prior to becoming an agent, Ms. Rosenberg was a senior editor for Harcourt.

REPRESENTS nonfiction books, novels, textbooks, college textbooks only. **Considers these nonfiction areas:** current affairs, foods, popular culture, psychology, sports, women's issues, women's studies, women's health, wine/beverages. **Considers these fiction areas:** romance, women's, chick lit.

Ms. Rosenberg is well-versed in the romance market (both category and single title). She is a frequent speaker at romance conferences. The Rosenberg Group is accepting new clients working in romance fiction (please see my Areas of Interest for specific romance subgenres), women's fiction and chick lit. Does not want to receive inspirational, time travel, futuristic or paranormal.

HOW TO CONTACT Query via snail mail. Your query letter should not exceed one page in length. It should include the title of your work, the genre and/or subgenre; the manuscript's word count; and a brief description of the work. If you are writing category romance, please be certain to let her know the line for which your work is intended. Responds in 2 weeks to queries. Responds in 4-6 weeks to mss. Obtains most new clients through recommendations from others, solicitations, conferences.

TERMS Agent receives 15% commission on domestic sales. Agent receives 15% commission on foreign sales. Offers written contract; 1-month notice must be given to terminate contract. Charges maximum of $350/year for postage and photocopying.

RECENT SALES Sold 27 titles in the last year.

WRITERS CONFERENCES RWA National Conference; BookExpo America.

NEW AGENT SPOTLIGHT

RACHAEL DILLON FRIED
(GREENBURGER ASSOCIATES)

greenburger.com

@RachDillonFried

ABOUT RACHAEL: After a stint with International Creative Management's [now ICM Partners] live appearances division in Los Angeles, Rachael embraced her love of books and relocated to New York City to pursue a career in literary representation. She landed at Sanford Greenburger. Rachael is a Rhode Island native and graduate of Brown University.

SHE IS SEEKING: both fiction and nonfiction authors, with a keen interest in unique literary voices, women's fiction, narrative nonfiction, memoir, and comedy.

HOW TO QUERY: rfried@sjga.com.

RITA ROSENKRANZ LITERARY AGENCY

440 West End Ave., #15D, New York NY 10024. (212)873-6333. **Website:** www.ritarosenkranzliteraryagency.com. **Contact:** Rita Rosenkranz. Member of AAR. Represents 35 clients. 30% of clients are new/unpublished writers. Currently handles: nonfiction books 99%, novels 1%.

Prior to opening her agency, Ms. Rosenkranz worked as an editor at major New York publishing houses.

REPRESENTS nonfiction books. **Considers these nonfiction areas:** animals, anthropology, art, autobiography, biography, business, child guidance, computers, cooking, crafts, cultural interests, current affairs, dance, decorating, economics, ethnic, film, gay, government, health, history, hobbies, how-to, humor, inspirational, interior design, language, law, lesbian, literature, medicine, military, money, music, nature, parenting, personal improvement, photography, popular culture, politics, psychology, religious, satire, science, self-help, sports, technology, theater, war, women's issues, women's studies.

"This agency focuses on adult nonfiction, stresses strong editorial development and refinement before submitting to publishers, and brainstorms ideas with authors." Actively seeks authors who are well paired with their subject, either for professional or personal reasons.

HOW TO CONTACT Send query letter only (no proposal) via regular mail or e-mail. Submit proposal package with SASE only on request. No fax queries. Accepts simultaneous submissions. Responds in 2 weeks to queries. Obtains most new clients through directory listings, solicitations, conferences, word of mouth.

TERMS Agent receives 15% commission on domestic sales. Agent receives 20% commission on foreign sales. Offers written contract, binding for 3 years; 3-month written notice must be given to terminate contract. Charges clients for photocopying. Makes referrals to editing services.

RECENT SALES Recently released and forthcoming books include *Replacement Child: A Memoir*, by Judy Mandel (Seal Press); *A Mind for Numbers: How to Excel at Math (Even if You Flunked Algebra)*, by Barbara Oakley (Tarcher); *A Century at Wrigley Field*, by Sam Pathy (Skyhorse); *Breakthrough Communication*, by Harrison Monarth (McGraw-Hill).

TIPS "Identify the current competition for your project to make sure the project is valid. A strong cover letter is very important."

ANDY ROSS LITERARY AGENCY

767 Santa Ray Ave., Oakland CA 94610. (510)238-8965. **E-mail:** andyrossagency@hotmail.com. **Website:** www.andyrossagency.com. **Contact:** Andy Ross. Member of AAR. Represents 30 clients. 20% of clients are new/unpublished writers. Currently handles: nonfiction books 100%.

REPRESENTS nonfiction books, scholarly. **Considers these nonfiction areas:** anthropology, autobiography, biography, child guidance, creative nonfiction, cultural interests, current affairs, education, environment, ethnic, government, history, language, law, literature, military, parenting, popular culture, politics, psychology, science, sociology, technology, war. **Considers these fiction areas:** commercial, juvenile, literary.

"This agency specializes in general nonfiction, politics and current events, history, biography, journalism and contemporary culture." Actively seeking literary, commercial, and young adult fiction. Does not want to receive personal memoir, poetry.

HOW TO CONTACT Queries should be less than half page. Please put the word "query" in the title header of the e-mail. In the first sentence, state the category of the project. Give a short description of the book and your qualifications for writing. Accepts simultaneous submissions. Responds in 1 week to queries.

TERMS Agent receives 15% commission on domestic sales. Agent receives 20% commission on foreign sales through a subagent. Offers written contract.

ROSS YOON AGENCY

1666 Connecticut Ave. NW, Suite 500, Washington DC 20009. (202)328-3282. **Fax:** (202)328-9162. **E-mail:** submissions@rossyoon.com. **Website:** rossyoon.com. **Contact:** Jennifer Manguera. Member of AAR. Represents 200 clients. 75% of clients are new/unpublished writers. Currently handles: nonfiction books 95%.

MEMBER AGENTS Gail Ross (represents important commercial nonfiction in a variety of areas and counts top doctors, CEOs, prize-winning journalists, and historians among her clients. She and her team work closely with first-time authors; gail@rossyoon.com); **Howard Yoon** (nonfiction topics ranging from current events and politics to culture to religion and history, to smart business; he is also looking for commercial fiction by published authors; howard@rossyoon.com); **Anna Sproul-Latimer** (nonfiction).

REPRESENTS nonfiction books.

"This agency specializes in adult trade nonfiction."

HOW TO CONTACT "We are not accepting unsolicited submissions at this time. We only consider referrals from friends of the agency and/or clients." Accepts simultaneous submissions. Responds in 4-6 weeks to queries. Obtains most new clients through recommendations from others.

TERMS Agent receives 15% commission on domestic sales. Agent receives 25% commission on foreign sales. Charges for office expenses.

JANE ROTROSEN AGENCY LLC

318 E. 51st St., New York NY 10022. (212)593-4330. **Fax:** (212)935-6985. **Website:** www.janerotrosen.com. Estab. 1974. Member of AAR. Other memberships include Authors Guild. Represents more than 100 clients.

MEMBER AGENTS Jane Rotosen Berkey (not taking on clients); **Andrea Cirillo**, acirillo@janerotrosen.com (suspense and women's fiction); Annelise Robey, arobey@janerotrosen.com (women's fiction, suspense, mystery, literary fiction and the occasional nonfiction project); **Meg Ruley**, mruley@janerotrosen.com (women's fiction as well as suspense, thrillers, and mystery); **Christina Hogrebe**, chogrebe@janerotrosen.com; **Amy Tannenbaum**, atannenbaum@janerotrosen.com (contemporary romance and new adult; Amy is particularly interested in those areas, as well as women's fiction that falls into that sweet spot between literary and commercial).

REPRESENTS nonfiction books, novels. **Considers these fiction areas:** literary, mystery, new adult, romance, suspense, thriller, women's.

HOW TO CONTACT Agent submission e-mail addresses are different. Send a query letter, a brief synopsis, and up to three chapters of your novel or the proposal for nonfiction. No attachments. Responds in 2 weeks to writers who have been referred by a client or colleague. Responds in 2 months to mss. Obtains most new clients through recommendations from others.

TERMS Agent receives 15% commission on domestic sales. Agent receives 20% commission on foreign sales. Offers written contract, binding for 3 years; 2-month notice must be given to terminate contract. Charges clients for photocopying, express mail, overseas postage, book purchase.

THE DAMARIS ROWLAND AGENCY

420 E. 23rd St., Suite 6F, New York NY 10010. **Contact:** Damaris Rowland. Member of AAR.

REPRESENTS nonfiction books, novels.

This agency specializes in women's fiction, literary fiction and nonfiction, and pop fiction.

HOW TO CONTACT Query with synopsis, SASE. Obtains most new clients through recommendations from others, solicitations, conferences.

TERMS Agent receives 15% commission on domestic sales. Agent receives 20% commission on foreign sales. Offers written contract.

THE RUDY AGENCY

825 Wildlife Lane, Estes Park CO 80517. (970)577-8500. **Fax:** (970)577-8600. **E-mail:** mak@rudyagency.com; fred@rudyagency.com. **Website:** www.rudyagency.com. **Contact:** Maryann Karinch. Adheres to AAR canon of ethics. Represents 15 clients. 50% of clients are new/unpublished writers.

Prior to becoming an agent, Ms. Karinch was, and continues to be, an author of nonfiction books—covering the subjects of health/medicine and human behavior. Prior to that, she was in public relations and marketing: areas of expertise she also applies in her practice as an agent.

MEMBER AGENTS **Maryann Karinch**; **Fred Tribuzzo** (fiction: thrillers, historical).

REPRESENTS nonfiction, novels. **Considers these nonfiction areas:** anthropology, archeology, autobiography, biography, business, child guidance, computers, cultural interests, current affairs, economics, education, ethnic, gay/lesbian, government, health, history, how-to, language, law, literature, medicine, memoirs, military, money, music, parenting, popular culture, politics, psychology, science, sociology, sports, technology, true crime, war, women's issues, women's studies. **Considers these fiction areas:** historical, thriller.

"We support authors from the proposal stage through promotion of the published work. We work in partnership with publishers to promote the published work and coach authors in their role in the marketing and public relations campaigns for the book." Actively seeking projects with social value, projects that open minds to new ideas and interesting lives, and projects that entertain through good storytelling. Does not want to receive poetry, children's/juvenile books, screenplays/plays, art/photo books, novellas, religion books, and joke books or books that fit in to the impulse buy/gift book category.

HOW TO CONTACT "Query us. If we like the query, we will invite a complete proposal (or complete ms if writing fiction). No phone queries." Accepts simultaneous submissions. Responds in 8 weeks to mss. Obtains most new clients through recommendations from others, solicitations.

TERMS Agent receives 15% commission on domestic sales. Offers written contract, binding for 1 year.

RECENT SALES *Toy Time!* by Christopher Byrne (Random House); *Lead with a Story*, by Paul Smith (Amacom); *Forging Healthy Connections*, by Trevor Crow (New Horizon Press); *The Power of Paradox*, by Deborah Schroeder-Saulnier (Career Press); *Refeathering the Empty Nest*, by Wendy Aronsson (Rowman & Littlefield); *Own Your Cancer*, by Peter Edelstein (Globe Pequot/Lyons), *The Slaughter*, by Ethan Gutmann (Prometheus Books).

TIPS "Present yourself professionally. I tell people all the time: Subscribe to *Writer's Digest* (I do), because you will get good advice about how to approach an agent."

REGINA RYAN PUBLISHING ENTERPRISES, INC.

251 Central Park W., 7D, New York NY 10024. (212)787-5589. **E-mail:** queries@reginaryanbooks.com. **Website:** www.reginaryanbooks.com. **Contact:** Regina Ryan. Currently handles: nonfiction books 100%.

Prior to becoming an agent, Ms. Ryan was an editor at Alfred A. Knopf, editor-in-chief of Macmillan Adult Trade, and a book producer.

REPRESENTS nonfiction books. **Considers these nonfiction areas:** animals, architecture, gardening, government, history, law, memoirs, parenting, politics, psychology, travel, women's issues, women's studies, narrative nonfiction; natural history (especially birds and birding); popular science, adventure, lifestyle, business, sustainability, mind-body-spirit, relationships.

HOW TO CONTACT E-query. If the agency is interested, they will request more material. Accepts simultaneous submissions. Tries to respond in 1 month to queries. Obtains most new clients through recommendations from others.

TERMS Agent receives 15% commission on domestic sales. Agent receives 15% commission on foreign sales. Offers written contract. Charges clients for all out-of-pocket expenses (e.g., long distance calls, messengers, freight, copying) if it's more than just a nominal amount.

RECENT SALES *Backyard Bird Feeding*, by Randi Minetor (Globe Pequot Press); *In Search of Sacco and Vanzetti*, by Susan Tejada (Univ. Press of New England); *What's Wrong With my Vegetable Garden?*, by David Deardorff and Kathryn Wadsworth (Timber Press); *When Johnny Comes Marching Home: What Vets Need, What They Don't Need and What All of Us Can Do to Help*, by Paula Caplan (MIT Press); *Everything Changes: The Insider's Guide to Cancer in Your 20's and 30's*, by Kairol Rosenthal (Wiley); *Angel of Death Row: My Life as a Death Penalty Defense Lawyer*, by Andrea Lyon (Kaplan Publishing).

TIPS "An analysis of why your proposed book is different and better than the competition is essential; a sample chapter is helpful."

THE SAGALYN AGENCY / ICM PARTNERS

1250 Connecticut Ave., 7th Floor, Washington DC 20036. **E-mail:** query@sagalyn.com. **Website:** www.sagalyn.com. Estab. 1980. Member of AAR. Currently handles: nonfiction books 85%, novels 5%, scholarly books 10%.

MEMBER AGENTS Raphael Sagalyn.

REPRESENTS Considers these nonfiction areas: biography, business, creative nonfiction, economics, popular culture, science, technology. **Considers these fiction areas:** commercial, upmarket fiction.

"Our list includes upmarket nonfiction books in these areas: narrative history, biography, business, economics, popular culture, science, technology." No stage plays, screenplays, poetry, science fiction, fantasy, romance, children's books.

HOW TO CONTACT Please send e-mail queries only (no attachments). Include 1 of these words in the subject line: query, submission, inquiry.

TIPS "We receive 1,000-1,200 queries a year, which in turn lead to 2 or 3 new clients. See our website for sales information and recent projects."

SALKIND LITERARY AGENCY

Part of Studio B, 734 Indiana St., Lawrence KS 66044. (785)371-0101. **E-mail:** neil@studiob.com; info@studiob.com. **Website:** www.salkindagency.com. **Contact:** Neil Salkind. Represents 200 clients. 25% of clients are new/unpublished writers. Currently handles: nonfiction books 60%, scholarly books 20%, textbooks 20%.

Prior to becoming an agent, Mr. Salkind authored numerous trade and textbooks.

MEMBER AGENTS Greg Aunapu, greg@studiob.com (nonfiction: biography, history, narrative, memoir, true-crime, adventure/true story, business/finance, current affairs, technology, pop culture, psychology, how-to, self-help, science, travel, pets/animals, relationships, parenting; fiction: commercial fiction, historical, thrillers/suspense, mystery, detective, adventure, humor, science-fiction, fantasy), **Lynn Haller**, lynn@studiob.com (technical, business, travel, self-help, health, photography, design, cooking, art, craft, politics, essays, culture, history, and textbooks); **Neil J. Salkind,** neil@studiob.com (general nonfiction).

REPRESENTS Considers these nonfiction areas: animals, art, biography, business, cooking, crafts, creative nonfiction, cultural interests, current affairs, design, health, history, how-to, memoirs, money, parenting, photography, popular culture, politics, psychology, science, self-help, technology, travel, true crime. **Considers these fiction areas:** adventure, commercial, detective, fantasy, historical, humor, mystery, science fiction, suspense, thriller.

Greg Aunapu represents both fiction and nonfiction including true crime, technology, biography, history, narrative nonfiction, memoir (by people who have accomplished something great in their fields), finance, current affairs, politics, pop-culture, psychology, relationships, science and travel. Fiction includes suspense/thrillers, mystery, detective, adventure, humor, science-fiction and modern urban fantasy. Submission guidelines can be found at www.gregaunapu.com. Nonfiction queries should be in book-proposal format; fiction queries should include a complete book synopsis and the first 25 pages of the manuscript, and an author biography. He can be reached at greg@studiob.com. **Lynn Haller** represents nonfiction authors, with a special interest in business, technology, and how-to. Queries should include a book proposal, a bio, and writing samples. She can be reached at lynn@studiob.com. **Malka Margolies** represents predominantly nonfiction. Her interests include history, current events, cultural issues, religion/spirituality, nutrition and health, women's issues, parenting and the environment. She is not interested in science fiction, fantasy, how-to or children's books. She can be reached at malka@studiob.com. **Neil J. Salkind** represents these nonfiction areas: business, cooking, crafts, health, how-to, photography and visual arts, science and self-help. He also represents textbooks and scholarly books. Does not want "to receive book proposals based on ideas where potential authors have not yet researched what has been published."

HOW TO CONTACT Query electronically. Obtains most new clients through recommendations from others.

TERMS Agent receives 15% commission on domestic sales. Agent receives 15% commission on foreign sales.

VICTORIA SANDERS & ASSOCIATES

241 Avenue of the Americas, Suite 11 H, New York NY 10014. (212)633-8811. **Fax:** (212)633-0525. **E-mail:** queriesvsa@gmail.com. **Website:** www.victoriasanders.com. **Contact:** Victoria Sanders. Estab. 1992. Member of AAR. Signatory of WGA. Represents 135 clients. 25% of clients are new/unpublished writers.

MEMBER AGENTS Tanya McKinnon, Victoria Sanders, Chris Kepner, Bernadette Baker-Baughman.

REPRESENTS nonfiction books, novels. **Considers these nonfiction areas:** autobiography, biography, cultural interests, current affairs, ethnic, film, gay/lesbian, government, history, humor, law, literature, music, popular culture, politics, psychology, satire, theater, translation, women's issues, women's studies. **Considers these fiction areas:** action, adventure, contemporary issues, crime, ethnic, family saga, feminist, lesbian, literary, mainstream, mystery, new adult, picture books, thriller, young adult.

HOW TO CONTACT Query by e-mail only. "We will not respond to e-mails with attachments or attached files."

TERMS Agent receives 15% commission on domestic sales. Agent receives 20% commission on foreign/film sales. Offers written contract. Charges for photocopying, messenger, express mail. If in excess of $100, client approval is required.

RECENT SALES Sold 20+ titles in the last year.

TIPS "Limit query to letter (no calls) and give it your best shot. A good query is going to get a good response."

SCHIAVONE LITERARY AGENCY, INC.

236 Trails End, West Palm Beach FL 33413-2135. (561)966-9294. **Fax:** (561)966-9294. **E-mail:** jendu77@aol.com; francinedelman@aol.com. **Website:** www.publishersmarketplace.com/members/profschia; blog site: www.schiavoneliteraryagencyinc.blogspot.com. **Contact:** Dr. James Schiavone, CEO, corporate offices in Florida; Jennifer DuVall, president, New York office; Francine Edelman, senior executive VP. Memberships include National Education Association. Represents 60+ clients. 2% of clients are new/unpublished writers. Currently handles: nonfiction books 50%, novels 49%, textbooks 1%.

Prior to opening his agency, Dr. Schiavone was a full professor of developmental skills at the City University of New York and author of 5 trade books and 3 textbooks. Jennifer DuVall has many years of combined experience in office management and agenting.

REPRESENTS nonfiction books, novels, juvenile, scholarly, textbooks. **Considers these nonfiction areas:** animals, anthropology, archeology, autobiography, biography, child guidance, cultural interests, current affairs, education, environment, ethnic, gay/lesbian, government, health, history, how-to, humor, investigative, juvenile nonfiction, language, law, literature, medicine, military, parenting, popular culture, politics, psychology, satire, science, sociology, spirituality, true crime. **Considers these fiction areas:** ethnic, family saga, historical, horror, humor, juvenile, literary, mainstream, science fiction, young adult.

This agency specializes in celebrity biography and autobiography and memoirs. Does not want to receive poetry.

HOW TO CONTACT Query with SASE. Do not send unsolicited materials or parcels requiring a signature. Send no e-attachments. Accepts simultaneous submissions. Responds in 2 weeks to queries. Responds in 6 weeks to mss. Obtains most new clients through recommendations from others, solicitations, conferences.

TERMS Agent receives 15% commission on domestic sales. Agent receives 20% commission on foreign sales. Offers written contract. Charges clients for postage only.

WRITERS CONFERENCES Key West Literary Seminar; South Florida Writers' Conference; Tallahassee Writers' Conference, Million Dollar Writers' Conference; Alaska Writers Conference.

TIPS "We prefer to work with established authors published by major houses in New York. We will consider marketable proposals from new/previously unpublished writers."

WENDY SCHMALZ AGENCY

402 Union St., #831, Hudson NY 12534. (518)672-7697. **E-mail:** wendy@schmalzagency.com. **Website:** www.schmalzagency.com. **Contact:** Wendy Schmalz. Estab. 2002. Member of AAR.

REPRESENTS Considers these nonfiction areas: Many nonfiction subjects are of interest to this agency. **Considers these fiction areas:** literary, mainstream, middle grade, young adult.

Actively seeking young adult novels, middle grade novels. Obtains clients through recommendations from others. Not looking for picture books, science fiction or fantasy.

HOW TO CONTACT Accepts only e-mail queries. Paste all text into the e-mail. Do not attach the ms or sample chapters or synopsis. Replies to queries only if they want to read the ms. (2014: Not currently accepting submissions of genre fiction or children's picture books.) If you do not hear from this agency within 6 weeks, consider that a no. Obtains clients through recommendations from others.

TERMS Agent receives 15% commission on domestic sales; 20% on foreign sales; 25% for Asian sales.

HAROLD SCHMIDT LITERARY AGENCY

415 W. 23rd St., #6F, New York NY 10011. **Contact:** Harold Schmidt, acquisitions. Estab. 1984. Member of AAR. Represents 3 clients.

REPRESENTS nonfiction, fiction. **Considers these fiction areas:** contemporary issues, gay, literary, original quality fiction with unique narrative voices, high quality psychological suspense and thrillers, likes offbeat/quirky.

HOW TO CONTACT Query by mail with SASE or e-mail; do not send material without being asked. No telephone or e-mail queries. We will respond if interested. Do not send material unless asked as it cannot be read or returned.

SUSAN SCHULMAN LITERARY AGENCY

454 W. 44th St., New York NY 10036. (212)713-1633. **Fax:** (212)581-8830. **E-mail:** schulmanqueries@yahoo.com. **Website:** www.publishersmarketplace.com/members/Schulman/. **Contact:** Susan Schulman. Estab. 1980. Member of AAR. Signatory of WGA. Other memberships include Dramatists Guild. 10% of clients are new/unpublished writers. Currently handles: nonfiction books 50%, novels 25%, juvenile books 15%, stage plays 10%.

REPRESENTS Considers these nonfiction areas: biography, business, cooking, ethnic, health, history, money, religious, science, travel, women's issues, women's studies. **Considers these fiction areas:** juvenile, literary, mainstream, women's.

"We specialize in books for, by and about women and women's issues including nonfiction self-help books, fiction and theater projects. We also handle the film, television and allied rights for several agencies as well as foreign rights for several publishing houses." Actively seeking new nonfiction. Considers plays. Does not want to receive poetry, television scripts or concepts for television.

HOW TO CONTACT "For fiction: Query letter with outline and three sample chapters, resume and SASE. For nonfiction: Query letter with complete description of subject, at least one chapter, resume and SASE. Queries may be sent via regular mail or e-mail. Please do not submit queries via UPS or Federal Express. Please do not send attachments with e-mail queries." Accepts simultaneous submissions. Responds in 6 weeks to queries/mss. Obtains most new clients through recommendations from others, solicitations, conferences.

TERMS Agent receives 15% commission on domestic sales. Agent receives 20% commission on foreign sales. Offers written contract; 30-day notice must be given to terminate contract.

RECENT SALES Sold 50 titles in the last year; hundred of subsidiary rights deals.

WRITERS CONFERENCES Geneva Writers' Conference (Switzerland); Columbus Writers' Conference; Skidmore Conference of the Independent Women's Writers Group.

TIPS "Keep writing!" Schulman describes her agency as "professional boutique, long-standing, eclectic."

SCOVIL GALEN GHOSH LITERARY AGENCY, INC.

276 Fifth Ave., Suite 708, New York NY 10001. (212)679-8686. **Fax:** (212)679-6710. **E-mail:** info@sgglit.com. **Website:** www.sgglit.com. **Contact:** Russell Galen. Estab. 1992. Member of AAR. Represents 300 clients. Currently handles: nonfiction books 60%, novels 40%.

MEMBER AGENTS **Jack Scovil,** jackscovil@sgglit.com; **Russell Galen**, russellgalen@sgglit.com (novels that stretch the bounds of reality; strong, serious nonfiction books on almost any subject that teach something new; no books that are merely entertaining, such as diet or pop psych books; serious interests include science, history, journalism, biography, business, memoir, nature, politics, sports, contemporary culture, literary nonfiction, etc.); **Anna Ghosh** (as of 2014 was in the process of leaving the agency to form her own agency; do not contact her at this agency anymore); **Ann Behar**, annbehar@sgglit.com (juvenile books for all ages).

REPRESENTS nonfiction books, novels. **Considers these nonfiction areas:** art, biography, business, creative nonfiction, cultural interests, foods, health, history, literature, memoirs, politics, psychology, religious, science, sports. **Considers these fiction areas:** commercial, juvenile, literary, women's.

HOW TO CONTACT E-mail queries strongly preferred. "If you prefer to mail a hard copy letter, please include your e-mail address so we can reply by e-mail. Do not send SASE or anything else." Note how each agent at this agency has their own submission e-mail. Accepts simultaneous submissions.

SCRIBBLERS HOUSE, LLC LITERARY AGENCY

P.O. Box 1007, Cooper Station, New York NY 10276-1007. (212)714-7744. **E-mail:** query@scribblershouse.net. **Website:** www.scribblershouse.net. **Contact:** Stedman Mays, Garrett Gambino. 25% of clients are new/unpublished writers.

MEMBER AGENTS Stedman Mays, Garrett Gambino.

REPRESENTS nonfiction books, occasionally novels. **Considers these nonfiction areas:** biography, business, diet/nutrition, economics, health, history, how-to, language, literature, medicine, memoirs, money, parenting, popular culture, politics, psychology, self-help, sex, spirituality, the brain; personal finance; writing books; relationships; gender issues. **Considers these fiction areas:** crime, historical, literary, suspense, thriller, women's.

HOW TO CONTACT "Query via e-mail. Put 'nonfiction query' or 'fiction query' in the subject line followed by the title of your project (send to our submissions e-mail on our website). Do not send attachments or downloadable materials of any kind with query. We will request more materials if we are interested. Usually responds in 2 weeks to 2 months to e-mail queries if we are interested (if we are not interested, we will not respond due to the overwhelming amount of queries we receive). We are only accepting e-mail queries at the present time." Accepts simultaneous submissions.

TERMS Agent receives 15% commission on domestic sales. Charges clients for postage, shipping and copying.

TIPS "If you must send by snail mail, we will return material or respond to a U.S. Postal Service-accepted SASE. (No international coupons or outdated mail strips, please.) Presentation means a lot. A well-written query letter with a brief author bio and your credentials is important. For query letter models, go to the bookstore or online and look at the cover copy and flap copy on other books in your general area of interest. Emulate what's best. Have an idea of other notable books that will be perceived as being in the same vein as yours. Know what's fresh about your project and articulate it in as few words as possible. Consult our website for the most up-to-date information on submitting."

SCRIBE AGENCY, LLC

5508 Joylynne Dr., Madison WI 53716. **E-mail:** whattheshizzle@scribeagency.com. **E-mail:** submissions@scribeagency.com. **Website:** www.scribeagency.com. **Contact:** Kristopher O'Higgins. Represents 11 clients. 18% of clients are new/unpublished writers. Currently handles: novels 98%, story collections 2%.

"With more than 15 years experience in publishing, with time spent on both the agency and editorial sides, with marketing experience to boot, Scribe Agency is a full-service literary agency, working hands-on with its authors on their projects. Check the website (scribeagency.com) to make sure your work matches the Scribe aesthetic."

MEMBER AGENTS Kristopher O'Higgins.

REPRESENTS novels, anthologies. **Considers these fiction areas:** experimental, fantasy, feminist, horror, literary, mainstream, science fiction, thriller.

Actively seeking excellent writers with ideas and stories to tell.

HOW TO CONTACT E-queries only: submissions@scribeagency.com. See the website for submission info, as it may change. Responds in 3-4 weeks to queries. Responds in 5 months to mss.

TERMS Agent receives 15% commission on domestic sales. Agent receives 20% commission on foreign sales. Offers written contract. Charges for postage and photocopying.

RECENT SALES Sold 3 titles in the last year.

WRITERS CONFERENCES BookExpo America; WisCon; Wisconsin Book Festival; World Fantasy Convention; WorldCon.

SECRET AGENT MAN

P.O. Box 1078, Lake Forest CA 92609. (949)698-6987. **E-mail:** query@secretagentman.net. **Website:** www.secretagentman.net. **Contact:** Scott Mortenson.

Selective mystery, thriller, suspense and detective fiction. Does not want to receive scripts or screenplays.

HOW TO CONTACT Query via e-mail only; include sample chapter(s), synopsis and/or outline. Prefers to read the real thing rather than a description of it. Obtains most new clients through recommendations from others.

LYNN SELIGMAN, LITERARY AGENT

400 Highland Ave., Upper Montclair NJ 07043. (973)783-3631. **Contact:** Lynn Seligman. Other memberships include Women's Media Group. Represents 32 clients. 15% of clients are new/unpublished writers. Currently handles: nonfiction books 60%, novels 40%.

Prior to opening her agency, Ms. Seligman worked in the subsidiary rights department of Doubleday and Simon & Schuster, and served as an agent with Julian Bach Literary Agency (which became IMG Literary Agency). Foreign rights are represented by Books Crossing Borders, Inc.

REPRESENTS nonfiction books, novels. **Considers these nonfiction areas:** interior, anthropology, art, biography, business, child guidance, cooking, current affairs, education, ethnic, government, health, history, how-to, humor, language, money, music, nature, photography, popular culture, psychology, science, self-help, sociology, film, true crime, women's. **Considers these fiction areas:** detective, ethnic, fantasy, feminist, historical, horror, humor, literary, mainstream, mystery, romance, contemporary, gothic, historical, regency, science fiction.

"This agency specializes in general nonfiction and fiction. I also do illustrated and photography books and have represented several photographers for books."

HOW TO CONTACT Query with SASE. Prefers to read materials exclusively. Accepts simultaneous submissions. Responds in 2 weeks to queries. Responds in 2 months to mss. Obtains most new clients through referrals from other writers and editors.

TERMS Agent receives 15% commission on domestic sales. Agent receives 25% commission on foreign sales. Charges clients for photocopying, unusual postage, express mail, telephone expenses (checks with author first).

RECENT SALES Sold 15 titles in the last year. Lords of Vice series, by Barbara Pierce; Untitled series, by Deborah Leblanc.

SERENDIPITY LITERARY AGENCY, LLC

305 Gates Ave., Brooklyn NY 11216. (718)230-7689. **Fax:** (718)230-7829. **E-mail:** rbrooks@serendipitylit.com; info@serendipitylit.com. **Website:** www.serendipitylit.com; facebook.com/serendipitylit. **Contact:**

NEW AGENT SPOTLIGHT

SHANNON HASSAN
(MARSAL LYON LITERARY AGENCY)

marsallyonliteraryagency.com

@ShannonHassan

ABOUT SHANNON: Based in Boulder, Colorado, she is also eager to hear from authors with a unique perspective on the New West. Previously, Shannon was an agent at the Warner Literary Group, and an acquisitions editor at Fulcrum Publishing. Before entering the publishing world, she was a corporate attorney at Arnold & Porter in New York, and she received her J.D. from Harvard and her B.A. from George Washington University.

SHE IS SEEKING: literary and commercial fiction, young adult fiction, and select nonfiction. For nonfiction: She is interested in memoirists with exceptional stories to tell, as well as authors with a strong platform in current affairs, history, education, or law.

HOW TO QUERY: Shannon@MarsalLyonLiteraryAgency.com and write "Query" in the subject line. In all submissions, please include a contact phone number as well as your e-mail address.

Regina Brooks. Represents 50 clients. 50% of clients are new/unpublished writers. Currently handles: nonfiction books 50%, other 50% fiction.

Prior to becoming an agent, Ms. Brooks was an acquisitions editor for John Wiley & Sons, Inc. and McGraw-Hill Companies.

MEMBER AGENTS **Regina Brooks**; **Dawn Michelle Hardy** (sports, pop culture, blog and trend, music, lifestyle and social science); **Karen Thomas** (narrative nonfiction, celebrity, pop culture, memoir, general fiction, women's fiction, romance, mystery, self-help, inspirational, Christian-based fiction and nonfiction including Evangelical); **John Weber** (unique YA and middle grade); **Folade Bell** (literary and commercial women's fiction, YA, literary mysteries & thrillers, historical fiction, African-American issues, gay/lesbian, Christian fiction, humor and books that deeply explore other cultures); **Nadeen Gayle** (romance, memoir, pop culture, inspirational/ religious, women's fiction, parenting young adult, mystery and political thrillers, and all forms of nonfiction); **Chelcee Johns** (narrative nonfiction, investigative journalism, memoir, inspirational self-help, religion/spirituality, international, popular culture, and current affairs as well as literary and commercial fiction).

REPRESENTS nonfiction books, novels, juvenile, scholarly, children's books. **Considers these nonfiction areas:** creative nonfiction, current affairs, humor, inspirational, investigative, memoirs, music, parenting, popular culture, religious, self-help, spirituality, sports. **Considers these fiction areas:** commercial, gay, historical, humor, lesbian, literary, middle grade, mystery, romance, thriller, women's, young adult.

African-American nonfiction, commercial fiction, young adult novels with an urban flair and juvenile books. No stage plays, screenplays or poetry.

HOW TO CONTACT Check the website, as there are online submission forms for fiction, nonfiction and juvenile. Accepts simultaneous submissions. Obtains most new clients through conferences, referrals.

TERMS Agent receives 15% commission on domestic sales. Agent receives 20% commission on foreign sales. Offers written contract; 2-month notice must be given to terminate contract. Charges clients for office fees, which are taken from any advance.

RECENT SALES *Putting Makeup on the Fat Boy*, by Bil Wright; *You Should Really Write a Book: How to Write Sell, and Market Your Memoir*, by Regina Brooks; *Living Color*, by Nina Jablonski; *Swirling*, by Christelyn D. Kazarin and Janice R. Littlejohn; *Red Thread Sisters*, by Carol Peacock; *Nicki Minaj: Hop Pop Moments 4 Life*, by Isoul Harris; *Forgotten Burial*, by Jodi Foster.

TIPS "See the book *Writing Great Books for Young Adults*."

SEVENTH AVENUE LITERARY AGENCY

2052-124th St., South Surrey BC Canada. (604)538-7252. **Fax:** (604)538-7252. **E-mail:** info@seventhavenuelit.com. **Website:** www.seventhavenuelit.com. **Contact:** Robert Mackwood, director. Currently handles: nonfiction books 100%.

REPRESENTS nonfiction books. **Considers these nonfiction areas:** autobiography, biography, business, computers, economics, health, history, medicine, science, sports, technology, travel.

Seventh Avenue Literary Agency is both a literary agency and personal management agency. (The agency was originally called Contemporary Management.) Actively seeking nonfiction. Does not want to receive fiction, poetry, screenplays, children's books, young adult titles, or genre writing such as science fiction, fantasy or erotica.

HOW TO CONTACT Query with SASE. Submit outline, synopsis, 1 sample chapter (nonfiction), publishing history, author bio, table of contents with proposal or query. Provide full contact information. Let us know the submission history. No fiction. Obtains most clients through recommendations from others, some solicitations. Does not add many new clients.

TIPS "If you want your material returned, please include an SASE with adequate postage; otherwise, material will be recycled. (U.S. stamps are not adequate; they do not work in Canada.)"

THE SEYMOUR AGENCY

475 Miner St., Canton NY 13617. (315)386-1831. **E-mail:** marysue@twcny.rr.com; nicole@theseymouragency.com. **Website:** www.theseymouragency.com. **Contact:** Mary Sue Seymour, Nicole Resciniti. Member of AAR. Signatory of WGA. Other memberships include RWA, Authors Guild. Represents 50 clients. 5% of clients are new/unpublished writers. Currently handles: nonfiction books 50%, other 50% fiction.

Ms. Seymour is a retired New York State certified teacher. Ms. Resciniti was recently named "Agent of the Year" by the ACFW.

MEMBER AGENTS **Mary Sue Seymour** (accepts queries in Christian, inspirational, romance, and nonfiction); **Nicole Resciniti** (accepts all genres of romance, young adult, middle grade, new adult, suspense, thriller, mystery, sci-fi, fantasy).

REPRESENTS nonfiction books, novels. **Considers these nonfiction areas:** business, health, how-to, self-help, Christian books; cookbooks; any well-written nonfiction that includes a proposal in standard format and 1 sample chapter. **Considers these fiction areas:** action, fantasy, middle grade, mystery, new adult, religious, romance, science fiction, suspense, thriller, young adult.

HOW TO CONTACT For Mary Sue: E-query with synopsis, first 50 pages for romance. Accepts e-mail queries. For Nicole: E-mail the query plus first 5 pages of the manuscript. Accepts simultaneous submissions. Responds in 1 month to queries. Responds in 3 months to mss.

TERMS Agent receives 12-15% commission on domestic sales.

RECENT SALES Sales include: *New York Times* best-selling Author Shelley Shepard Gray 8-book deal to Harper Collins; Jen Turano 3-book deal to Bethany House, Pat Trainum's 4-book deal to Revell; Jennifer Beckstrand's 6- book deal to Kensington Publishing; Amy Lillard's 3-Book Deal To Kensington Publishing; Vannetta Chapman's Multi-Book Deal to Zondervan; Jerry Eicher's

3-book deal to Harvest House; Mary Ellis's 3-Book Deal To Harvest House; NYT bestseller Julie Ann Walker's next four books in her Black Knights Inc series; Melissa Lander's YA sci-fi, *Alienated*, to Disney/Hyperion; and Kate Meader's new contemporary romance series to Pocket/Gallery.

DENISE SHANNON LITERARY AGENCY, INC.

20 W. 22nd St., Suite 1603, New York NY 10010. (212)414-2911. **Fax:** (212)414-2930. **E-mail:** info@deniseshannonagency.com. **E-mail:** submissions@deniseshannonagency.com. **Website:** www.deniseshannonagency.com. **Contact:** Denise Shannon. Estab. 2002. Member of AAR.

Prior to opening her agency, Ms. Shannon worked for 16 years with Georges Borchardt and International Creative Management.

REPRESENTS nonfiction books, novels. **Considers these nonfiction areas:** biography, business, health, narrative nonfiction; politics; journalism; memoir; social history. **Considers these fiction areas:** literary.

"We are a boutique agency with a distinguished list of fiction and nonfiction authors."

HOW TO CONTACT "Queries may be submitted by post, accompanied by an SASE, or by e-mail to submissions@deniseshannonagency.com. Please include a description of the available book project and a brief bio including details of any prior publications. We will reply and request more material if we are interested. We request that you inform us if you are submitting material simultaneously to other agencies."

RECENT SALES *My New American Life*, by Francine Prose (Harper); *Swamplandia!*, by Karen Russell (Knopf); *The Girls of No Return*, by Erin Saldin (Scholastic); *Everyone But You*, by Sandra Novack (Random House).

TIPS "Please do not send queries regarding fiction projects until a complete manuscript is available for review. We request that you inform us if you are submitting material simultaneously to other agencies."

KEN SHERMAN & ASSOCIATES

1275 N. Hayworth, Ste. 103, Los Angeles CA 90046. (310)273-8840. **Fax:** (310)271-2875. **E-mail:** kenshermanassociates@gmail.com. **Website:** www.kenshermanassociates.com/. **Contact:** Ken Sherman. Memberships include BAFTA, PEN International; signatory of WGA. Represents approximately 35 clients. clients. 10% of clients are new/unpublished writers.

Prior to opening his agency, Mr. Sherman was with The William Morris Agency, The Lantz Office and Paul Kohner, Inc. He has taught The Business of Writing For Film and Television and The Book Worlds at UCLA and USC. He also lectures extensively at writer's conferences and film festivals around the U.S. He is currently a Commissioner of Arts and Cultural Affairs in the city of West Hollywood, and is on the International Advisory Board of the Christopher Isherwood Foundation.

REPRESENTS nonfiction books, novels, movie, tv, not episodic drama, teleplays, life rights, film/TV rights to books and life rights. **Considers these nonfiction areas:** agriculture horticulture, Americana, crafts, interior, newage, young, animals, anthropology, art, biography, business, child, computers, cooking, current affairs, education, ethnic, gardening, gay, government, health, history, how to, humor, language, memoirs, military, money, multicultural, music, nature, philosophy, photography, popular culture, psychology, recreation, regional, religion, science, self-help, sex, sociology, software, spirituality, sports, film, translation, travel, true crime, women's, creative nonfiction. **Considers these fiction areas:** glitz, new age, psychic, adventure, comic, confession, detective, erotica, ethnic, experimental, family, fantasy, feminist, gay, gothic, hi lo, historical, horror, humor, literary, mainstream, military, multicultural, multimedia, mystery, occult, picture books, plays, poetry, poetry translation, regional, religious, romance, science, short, spiritual, sports, thriller, translation, western, young adult. **Considers these script areas:** action, biography, cartoon, comedy, contemporary, detective, erotica, ethnic, experimental, family, fantasy, feminist, gay, glitz, historical, horror, mainstream, multicultural, multimedia, mystery, psychic, regional, religious, romantic comedy, romantic drama, science, sports, teen, thriller, western.

HOW TO CONTACT Contact by referral only. Reports in approximately 1 month to mss. Obtains most new clients through recommendations from others.

TERMS Agent receives 15% commission on domestic sales. Agent receives 15% commission on foreign sales. Agent receives 10-15% commission on film sales. Offers written contract. Charges clients for reasonable office expenses (postage, photocopying, etc.).

RECENT SALES Sold more than 20 scripts in the last year. *Back Roads*, by Tawni O'Dell with Adrian Lyne set to direct; *Priscilla Salyers Story*, produced by Andrea Baynes (ABC); *Toys of Glass*, by Martin Booth (ABC/Saban Entertainment); *Brazil*, by John Updike (film rights to Glaucia Carmagos); *Fifth Sacred Thing*, by Starhawk (Bantam), with Starhawk adapting her book into a screenplay; *Questions From Dad*, by Dwight Twilly (Tuttle); *Snow Falling on Cedars*, by David Guterson (Universal Pictures); *The Witches f Eastwick—The Musical*, by John Updike (Cameron Macintosh, Ltd.); *Rabbit/HBO-1-Hr Series*, John Updike.

WRITERS CONFERENCES Maui Writers' Conference; Squaw Valley Writers' Workshop; Santa Barbara Writers' Conference; Screenwriting Conference in Santa Fe; Aspen Summer Words Literary Festival (The Aspen Institute and the San Francisco Writer's Conference); San Francisco Writers' Conference; Chautaq UA Writers' Conference.

WENDY SHERMAN ASSOCIATES, INC.

27 W. 24th St., Suite 700B, New York NY 10010. (212)279-9027. **E-mail:** wendy@wsherman.com. **E-mail:** submissions@wsherman.com. **Website:** www.wsherman.com. **Contact:** Wendy Sherman; Kim Perel. Member of AAR. Represents 50 clients.

Prior to opening the agency, Ms. Sherman served as vice president, executive director, associate publisher, subsidiary rights director, and sales and marketing director for major publishers.

MEMBER AGENTS Wendy Sherman (board member of AAR), Kim Perel.

REPRESENTS Considers these nonfiction areas: creative nonfiction, foods, humor, memoirs, parenting, popular culture, psychology, self-help, narrative nonfiction. **Considers these fiction areas:** mainstream fiction that hits the sweet spot between literary and commercial.

"We specialize in developing new writers, as well as working with more established writers. My experience as a publisher has proven to be a great asset to my clients."

HOW TO CONTACT Query via e-mail only. "We ask that you include your last name, title, and the name of the agent you are submitting to in the subject line. For fiction, please include a query letter and your first 10 pages copied and pasted in the body of the e-mail. We will not open attachments unless they have been requested. For nonfiction, please include your query letter and author bio. Due to the large number of e-mail submissions that we receive, we can only reply to e-mail queries in the affirmative. We respectfully ask that you do not send queries to our individual e-mail addresses." Accepts simultaneous submissions. Responds in 1 month to queries. Obtains most new clients through recommendations from other writers.

TERMS Agent receives standard 15% commission. Offers written contract.

RECENT SALES *Z, A Novel of Zelda Fitzgerald*, by Therese Anne Fowler; *The Silence of Bonaventure Arrow*, by Rita Leganski; *Together Tea*, by Marjan Kamali; *A Long Long Time Ago and Essentially True*, by Brigid Pasulka; *Illuminations*, by Mary Sharratt; *The Accounting*, by William Lashner; *Lunch in Paris*, by Elizabeth Bard; *The Rules of Inheritance*, by Claire Bidwell Smith; *Love in Ninety Days*, by Dr. Diana Kirschner; *The Wow Factor*, by Jacqui Stafford; *Humor Memoirs*, by Wade Rouse.

TIPS "The bottom line is: Do your homework. Be as well prepared as possible. Read the books that will help you present yourself and your work with polish. You want your submission to stand out."

ROSALIE SIEGEL, INTERNATIONAL LITERARY AGENCY, INC.

1 Abey Dr., Pennington NJ 08534. (609)737-1007. **Fax:** (609)737-3708. **E-mail:** rosalie@rosaliesiegel.com. **Website:** rosaliesiegel.com. **Contact:** Rosalie Siegel. Member of AAR. Represents 35 clients. 10% of clients are new/unpublished writers.

HOW TO CONTACT "Please note that we are no longer accepting submissions of new material." Obtains most new clients through referrals from writers and friends.

TERMS Agent receives 15% commission on domestic sales. Agent receives 20% commission on foreign sales. Offers written contract; 2-month notice must be given to terminate contract. Charges clients for photocopying.

RECENT SALES *Mud Season*, by Ellen Stimson (Norton).

JEFFREY SIMMONS LITERARY AGENCY

15 Penn House, Mallory St., London NW8 8SX England. (44)(207)224-8917. **E-mail:** jasimmons@unicombox.co.uk. **Contact:** Jeffrey Simmons. Represents 43 clients. 40% of clients are new/unpublished writers. Currently handles: nonfiction books 65%, novels 35%.

Prior to becoming an agent, Mr. Simmons was a publisher. He is also an author.

REPRESENTS nonfiction books, novels. **Considers these nonfiction areas:** autobiography, biography, current affairs, film, government, history, language, memoirs, music, popular culture, sociology, sports, translation, true crime. **Considers these fiction areas:** action, adventure, confession, crime, detective, family saga, literary, mainstream, mystery, police, suspense, thriller.

"This agency seeks to handle good books and promising young writers. My long experience in publishing and as an author and ghostwriter means I can offer an excellent service all around, especially in terms of editorial experience where appropriate." Actively seeking quality fiction, biography, autobiography, showbiz, personality books, law, crime, politics, and world affairs. Does not want to receive science fiction, horror, fantasy, juvenile, academic books, or specialist subjects (e.g., cooking, gardening, religious).

HOW TO CONTACT Submit sample chapter, outline/proposal, SASE (IRCs if necessary). Prefers to read materials exclusively. Responds in one week to queries. Responds in one month to mss. Obtains most new clients through recommendations from others, solicitations.

TERMS Agent receives 10-15% commission on domestic sales. Agent receives 15% commission on foreign sales. Offers written contract, binding for lifetime of book in question or until it becomes out of print.

TIPS "When contacting us with an outline/proposal, include a brief biographical note (listing any previous publications, with publishers and dates). Preferably tell us if the book has already been offered elsewhere."

BEVERLEY SLOPEN LITERARY AGENCY

131 Bloor St. W., Suite 711, Toronto ON M5S 1S3 Canada. (416)964-9598. **E-mail:** beverly@slopenagency.ca. **Website:** www.slopenagency.ca. **Contact:** Beverley Slopen. Represents 70 clients. 20% of clients are new/unpublished writers.

Prior to opening her agency, Ms. Slopen worked in publishing and as a journalist.

REPRESENTS nonfiction books, novels, scholarly. **Considers these nonfiction areas:** anthropology, archeology, autobiography, biography, business, creative nonfiction, current affairs, economics, investigative, psychology, sociology, true crime. **Considers these fiction areas:** commercial, literary, mystery, suspense.

"This agency has a strong bent toward Canadian writers." Actively seeking serious nonfiction that is accessible and appealing to the general reader. Does not want to receive fantasy, science fiction, or children's books.

HOW TO CONTACT Query by e-mail. Returns materials only with SASE (Canadian postage only). To submit a work for consideration, e-mail a short query letter and a few sample pages. Submit only one work at a time. If we want to see more, we will contact the writer by phone or e-mail. Accepts simultaneous submissions. Responds in 2 months to queries.

TERMS Agent receives 15% commission on domestic sales. Agent receives 10% commission on foreign sales. Offers written contract, binding for 2 years; 3-month notice must be given to terminate contract.

RECENT SALES *Solar Dance*, by Modris Eksteins (Knopf Canada, Harvard University Press); *The Novels*, by Terry Fallis; *God's Brain*, by Lionel Tiger & Michael McGuire (Prometheus Books); *What They Wanted*, by Donna Morrissey (Penguin Canada, Premium/DTV Germany); *The Age of Persuasion*, by Terry O'Reilly & Mike Tennant (Knopf Canada, Counterpoint US); *Prisoner of Tehran*, by Marina Nemat (Penguin Canada, Free Press US, John Murray UK); *Race to the Polar Sea*, by Ken McGoogan (HarperCollins Canada, Counterpoint US); *Transgression*, by James Nichol (HarperCollins US, McArthur Canada, Goldmann Germany); *Midwife of Venice* and *The Harem Midwife*, by Roberta Rich; *Vermeer's Hat*, by Timothy Brook (HarperCollins Canada, Bloomsbury US); *Distantly Related to Freud*, by Ann Charney (Cormorant).

TIPS "Please, no unsolicited manuscripts."

SLW LITERARY AGENCY

4100 Ridgeland Ave., Northbrook IL 60062. (847)509-0999. **Fax:** (847)509-0996. **E-mail:** shariwenk@swenkagency.com. **Contact:** Shari Wenk. Currently handles: nonfiction books 100%.

REPRESENTS nonfiction books. **Considers these nonfiction areas:** sports.

"This agency specializes in representing books written by sports celebrities and sports writers."

HOW TO CONTACT Query via e-mail, but note the agency's specific specialty.

VALERIE SMITH, LITERARY AGENT

1746 Route 44-55, Box 160, Modena NY 12548. **Contact:** Valerie Smith. Represents 17 clients. Currently handles: nonfiction books 2%, novels 75%, story collections 1%, juvenile books 20%, scholarly books 1%, textbooks 1%.

REPRESENTS nonfiction books, novels, juvenile, textbooks. **Considers these nonfiction areas:** agriculture horticulture, cooking, how-to, self-help. **Considers these fiction areas:** fantasy, historical, juvenile, literary, mainstream, mystery, science, young, women's/chick lit.

"This is a small, personalized agency with a strong long-term commitment to clients interested in building careers. I have strong ties to science fiction, fantasy and young adult projects. I look for serious, productive writers whose work I can be passionate about." Does not want to receive unsolicited mss.

HOW TO CONTACT Query with synopsis, bio, 3 sample chapters, SASE. Contact by snail mail only. Obtains most new clients through recommendations from others.

TERMS Agent receives 15% commission on domestic sales. Agent receives 20% commission on foreign sales. Offers written contract; 6-week notice must be given to terminate contract.

ROBERT SMITH LITERARY AGENCY, LTD.

12 Bridge Wharf, 156 Caledonian Rd., London NI 9UU England. (44)(207)278-2444. **Fax:** (44)(207)833-5680. **E-mail:** robertsmith.literaryagency@virgin.net. **Contact:** Robert Smith. Other memberships include AAA. Represents 40 clients. 10% of clients are new/unpublished writers. Currently handles: nonfiction books 80%, syndicated material 20%.

Prior to becoming an agent, Mr. Smith was a book publisher (Ebury Press, Sidgwick & Jackson, Smith Gryphon).

REPRESENTS nonfiction books, syndicated material. **Considers these nonfiction areas:** autobiography, biography, cooking, diet/nutrition, film, foods, health, investigative, medicine, memoirs, music, popular culture, self-help, sports, theater, true crime, entertainment.

"This agency offers clients full management service in all media. Clients are not necessarily book authors. Our special expertise is in placing newspaper series internationally." Actively seeking autobiographies.

HOW TO CONTACT Submit outline/proposal, SASE (IRCs if necessary). Prefers to read materials exclusively. Responds in 2 weeks to queries. Obtains most new clients through recommendations from others, direct approaches to prospective authors.

TERMS Agent receives 15% commission on domestic sales. Agent receives 20% commission on foreign sales. Offers written contract, binding for 3 months; 3-month notice must be given to terminate contract. Charges clients for couriers, photocopying, overseas mailings of mss (subject to client authorization).

RECENT SALES *The Last Torpedo Flyers*, by Arthur Aldridge with Mark Ryan (Simon & Schuster); *Shamed*, by Sarbjit Kaur Athwal (Virgin Books); *Many a True Word*, by Richard Anthony Baker (Headline); *The Ghosts of Happy Valley*, by Juliet Barnes (Aurum Press); *Fast Exercise*, by Peta Bee (and Dr. Michael Mosley) (Short Books); *The Food Swap Diet*, by Peta Bee (Piatkus); The *Complete and Essential Jack the Ripper*, by Paul Begg and John Bennett (Penguin); *The Complete Jack The Ripper A-Z*, by Paul Begg, Martin Fido, and Keith Skinner (John Blake Publishing); *My James*, by Ralph Bulger with Rosie Dunn (Macmillan); *The Autobiography Of Jack the Ripper*, by James Carnac (Transworld); *Seven Years with Banksy*, by Robert Clarke (Michael O'Mara); *The Best Medicine*, by Georgie Edwards (Ebury Press); *Confessions of an Essex Girl*, by Becci Fox (Macmillan); *The News Is Read*, by Charlotte Green (The Robson Press); *Bad Girl*, by Roberta Kray (Sphere); *Streetwise*, by Roberta Kray (Sphere); *Hitler's Valkyrie*, by David R.L. Litchfield (The History Press); *Down But Not Out*, by Maurice Mayne with Mark Ryan (The History Press); *History's Narrowest Escapes*, by James Moore and Paul Nero (The History Press); *All Of Me*, by Kim Noble (Piatkus); *Enter the Dragon*, by Theo Paphitis (Orion).

MICHAEL SNELL LITERARY AGENCY

P.O. Box 1206, Truro MA 02666-1206. (508)349-3718. **E-mail:** patricia@michaelsnellagency.com. **Website:** michaelsnellagency.com. **Contact:** Michael Snell. Represents 200 clients. 25% of clients are new/unpublished writers.

Prior to opening his agency in 1978, Mr. Snell served as an editor at Wadsworth and Addison-Wesley for 13 years.

MEMBER AGENTS **Michael Snell** (business, leadership, entrepreneurship, pets, sports); **Patricia Snell**, (business, business communications, parenting, relationships, health).

REPRESENTS nonfiction books. **Considers these nonfiction areas:** business (all categories, all levels), creative nonfiction, health, how-to, self-help, women's issues, fitness.

This agency specializes in how-to, self-help, and all types of business, business leadership, entrepreneurship, and books for small-business owners from low-level how-to to professional and reference. Especially interested in business management, strategy, culture building, performance enhancement, marketing and sales, finance and investment, career development, executive skills, leadership, and organization development. Actively seeking strong book proposals in any area of business where a clear need exists for a new business book. Does not want to receive fiction, children's books, or complete mss (considers proposals only).

HOW TO CONTACT Query by mail with SASE, or e-mail. Visit the agency's website for Proposal Guidelines. Only considers new clients on an exclusive basis. Responds in 1 week to queries. Responds in 2 weeks to mss. Obtains most new clients through unsolicited mss, word of mouth, *Literary Market Place*, *Guide to Literary Agents*.

TERMS Agent receives 15% commission on domestic sales. Agent receives 15% commission on foreign sales.

TIPS "Send a maximum 1-page query with SASE. Brochure on 'How to Write a Book Proposal' is available on request with SASE. We suggest prospective clients read Michael Snell's book, *From Book Idea to Bestseller* (Prima, 1997), or visit the company's website for detailed information on how to write a book proposal plus a downloadable model proposal.

SPECTRUM LITERARY AGENCY

320 Central Park W., Suite 1-D, New York NY 10025. **Fax:** (212)362-4562. **Website:** www.spectrumliteraryagency.com. **Contact:** Eleanor Wood, president. Estab. 1976. Member of SFWA. Represents 90 clients. Currently handles: nonfiction books 10%, novels 90%.

MEMBER AGENTS **Eleanor Wood** (referrals only), **Justin Bell** (science fiction, mysteries, nonfiction).

REPRESENTS nonfiction books, novels. **Considers these fiction areas:** mystery, science fiction.

HOW TO CONTACT Snail mail query with SASE. Submit author bio, publishing credits. No unsolicited mss will be read. Responds in 1-3 months to queries. Obtains most new clients through recommendations from authors.

TERMS Agent receives 15% commission on domestic sales. Deducts for photocopying and book orders.

TIPS "Spectrum's policy is to read only book-length manuscripts that we have specifically asked to see. Unsolicited manuscripts are not accepted. The letter should describe your book briefly and include publishing credits and background information or qualifications relating to your work, if any."

SPENCERHILL ASSOCIATES

P.O. Box 374, Chatham NY 12037. (518)392-9293. **Fax:** (518)392-9554. **E-mail:** submissions@spencerhillassociates.com. **Website:** www.spencerhillassociates.com. **Contact:** Karen Solem or Nalini Akolekar. Member of AAR. Represents 96 clients. 10% of clients are new/unpublished writers.

Prior to becoming an agent, Ms. Solem was editor-in-chief at HarperCollins and an associate publisher.

MEMBER AGENTS Karen Solem; Nalini Akolekar.

REPRESENTS novels. **Considers these fiction areas:** commercial, erotica, literary, mainstream, mystery, paranormal, romance, thriller.

"We handle mostly commercial women's fiction, historical novels, romance (historical, contemporary, paranormal, urban fantasy), thrillers, and mysteries. We also represent Christian fiction only—no nonfiction." No nonfiction, poetry, science fiction, children's picture books, or scripts.

HOW TO CONTACT "We accept electronic submissions and are no longer accepting paper queries. Please send us a query letter in the body of an e-mail, pitch us your project and tell us about yourself: Do you have prior publishing credits? Attach the first three chapters and synopsis preferably in .doc, rtf or txt format to your e-mail. Send all queries to submission@spencerhillassociates.com. We do not have a preference for exclusive submissions, but do appreciate knowing if the submission is simultaneous. We receive thousands of submissions a year and each query receives our attention. Unfortunately, we are unable to respond to each query individually. If we are interested in your work, we will contact you within 8 weeks." Accepts simultaneous submissions.

TERMS Agent receives 15% commission on domestic sales. Agent receives 20% commission on foreign sales. Offers written contract; 3-month notice must be given to terminate contract.

RECENT SALES A full list of sales and clients is available on the agency website.

THE SPIELER AGENCY

27 W. 20 St., Suite 305, New York NY 10011. **E-mail:** thespieleragency@gmail.com. **Contact:** Joe Spieler. Represents 160 clients. 2% of clients are new/unpublished writers.

Prior to opening his agency, Mr. Spieler was a magazine editor.

MEMBER AGENTS **Eric Myers**, eric@TheSpielerAgency.com (pop culture, memoir, history, thrillers, young adult, middle grade, new adult, and picture books (text only); **Victoria Shoemaker**, victoria@TheSpielerAgency.com (environment and natural history, popular culture, memoir, photography and film, literary fiction and poetry, and books on food and cooking); **John Thornton**, john@TheSpielerAgency.com (nonfiction); **Joe Spieler**, joe@TheSpielerAgency.com (nonfiction and fiction and books for children and young adults).

REPRESENTS novels, juvenile books. **Considers these nonfiction areas:** cooking, environment, film, foods, history, memoirs, photography, popular culture. **Considers these fiction areas:** literary, middle grade, New Age, picture books, thriller, young adult.

HOW TO CONTACT Before submitting projects to the Spieler Agency, check the listings of our individual agents and see if any particular agent shows a general interest in your subject (e.g. history, memoir, YA, etc.). Please send all queries either by e-mail or regular mail. If you query us by regular mail, we can only reply to you if you include a self-addressed, stamped envelope. Accepts simultaneous submissions. Cannot guarantee a personal response to all queries. Obtains most new clients through recommendations, listing in *Guide to Literary Agents*.

TERMS Agent receives 15% commission on domestic sales. Charges clients for messenger bills, photocopying, postage.

WRITERS CONFERENCES London Book Fair.

TIPS "Check www.publishersmarketplace.com/members/spielerlit/."

PHILIP G. SPITZER LITERARY AGENCY, INC

50 Talmage Farm Lane, East Hampton NY 11937. (631)329-3650. **Fax:** (631)329-3651. **E-mail:** Luc.Hunt@spitzeragency.com. **Website:** www.spitzeragency.com. **Contact:** Luc Hunt. Member of AAR. Represents 60 clients. 10% of clients are new/unpublished writers. Currently handles: nonfiction books 35%, novels 65%.

Prior to opening his agency, Mr. Spitzer served at New York University Press, McGraw-Hill, and the John Cushman Associates literary agency.

REPRESENTS nonfiction books, novels. **Considers these nonfiction areas:** biography, current affairs, history, politics, sports, travel. **Considers these fiction areas:** juvenile, literary, mainstream, suspense, thriller.

This agency specializes in mystery/suspense, literary fiction, sports and general nonfiction (no how-to).

HOW TO CONTACT E-mail or mail query containing synopsis of work, brief biography, and two sample chapters. Responds in 2 weeks to queries. Responds in 6 weeks to mss. Obtains most new clients through recommendations from others.

TERMS Agent receives 15% commission on domestic sales. Agent receives 20% commission on foreign sales. Charges clients for photocopying.

RECENT SALES *Creole Belle* by James Lee Burke (Simon & Schuster), *Never Tell* by Alafair Burke (HarperCollins), *Townie*, by Andre Dubus III (Norton), *The Black Box*, by Michael Connelly (Little, Brown & Co), *Headstone*, Ken Bruen (Mysterious Press/Grove-Atlantic), *Mean Town Blues* by Sam Reaves (Pegasus Books), *The Fifth Season*, by Donald Honig (Ivan Dee Publisher), *The Big Town*, by Monte Schulz (Fantagraphics Books), *Assume Nothing*, Gar Anthony Haywood (Severn House), *Midnight Alley* (Oceanview Publishing), *My Brother's Keeper*, by Keith Gilman (Severn House), *Fontana*, by Joshua Martino (Bold Stroke Books), *Everything Beautiful Began After*, by Simon Van Booy (HarperPerennial).

WRITERS CONFERENCES London Bookfair, Frankfurt, BookExpo America.

NANCY STAUFFER ASSOCIATES

P.O. Box 1203, Darien CT 06820. (203)202-2500. **E-mail:** nancy@staufferliterary.com. **Website:** publishersmarketplace.com/members/nstauffer. **Contact:** Nancy Stauffer Cahoon. Other memberships include Authors Guild. Currently handles: nonfiction books 10%, novels 90%.

"Over the course of my more than 20 year career, I've held positions in the editorial, marketing, business, and rights departments of *The New York Times*, McGraw-Hill, and Doubleday. Before founding Nancy Stauffer Associates, I was Director of Foreign and Performing Rights then Director, Subsidiary Rights, for Doubleday, where I was honored to have worked with a diverse range of internationally known and bestselling authors of all genres."

HOW TO CONTACT Accepts simultaneous submissions. Obtains most new clients through referrals from existing clients.

TERMS Agent receives 15% commission on domestic sales. Agent receives 20% commission on foreign sales.

RECENT SALES *Blasphemy*, by Sherman Alexie; *Benediction*, by Kent Haruf; *Bone Fire*, by Mark Spragg; *The Carry Home*, by Gary Ferguson.

STEELE-PERKINS LITERARY AGENCY

26 Island Ln., Canandaigua NY 14424. (585)396-9290. **Fax:** (585)396-3579. **E-mail:** pattiesp@aol.com. **Contact:** Pattie Steele-Perkins. Member of AAR. Other memberships include RWA. Currently handles: novels 100%.

REPRESENTS novels. **Considers these fiction areas:** romance, women's, category romance, romantic suspense, historical, contemporary, multicultural, and inspirational.

HOW TO CONTACT Submit query along with synopsis and one chapter via e-mail (no attachments) or snail mail. Snail mail submissions require SASE. Accepts simultaneous submissions. Obtains most new clients through recommendations from others, queries/solicitations.

TERMS Agent receives 15% commission on domestic sales. Offers written contract, binding for 1 year; 1-month notice must be given to terminate contract.

RECENT SALES Sold 130 titles last year. This agency prefers not to share specific sales information.

TIPS "Be patient. E-mail rather than call. Make sure what you are sending is the best it can be."

STERLING LORD LITERISTIC, INC.

65 Bleecker St., 12th Floor, New York NY 10012. (212)780-6050. **Fax:** (212)780-6095. **E-mail:** info@sll.com. **Website:** www.sll.com. Estab. 1987. Member of AAR. Signatory of WGA. Represents 600 clients. Currently handles: nonfiction books 50%, novels 50%.

MEMBER AGENTS **Philippa Brophy** (represents journalists, nonfiction writers and novelists, and is most interested in current events, memoir, science, politics, biography, and women's issues); **Laurie Liss** (represents authors of commercial and literary fiction and nonfiction whose perspectives are well developed and unique); **Sterling Lord**; **Peter Matson**; **Douglas Stewart** (primarily fiction and memoir, running the gamut from the innovatively literary to the unabashedly commercial); **Neeti Madan** (memoir, journalism, popular culture, lifestyle, women's issues, multicultural books and virtually any intelligent writing on intriguing topics); **Robert Guinsler** (literary and commercial fiction [including YA], journalism, narrative nonfiction with an emphasis on pop culture, science and current events, memoirs and biographies); **George Nicholson**; **Jim Rutman**; **Celeste Fine** (expert, celebrity, and corporate clients with strong national and international platforms, particularly in the health, science, self-help, food, business, and lifestyle fields); **Judy Heiblum** (literary fiction, narrative nonfiction, history, and popular science); **Erica Rand Silverman** (specializes in representing authors and illustrators of children's literature, picture books through YA, and adult nonfiction, with a special interest in parenting, DIY, emotional health and education); **Caitlin McDonald**; **Mary Krienke**.

REPRESENTS **Considers these nonfiction areas:** biography, creative nonfiction, current affairs, education, history, memoirs, multicultural, parenting, popular culture, politics, science, women's issues. **Considers these fiction areas:** commercial, juvenile, literary, middle grade, picture books, young adult.

HOW TO CONTACT Query via snail mail. "Please submit a query letter, a synopsis of the work, a brief proposal or the first three chapters of the manuscript, a brief bio or resume, and a stamped self-addressed envelope for reply. Original artwork is not accepted. Enclose sufficient postage if you wish to have your materials returned to you. We do not respond to unsolicited e-mail inquiries." Responds in approximately 1 month.

TERMS Agent receives 15% commission on domestic sales; 20% commission on foreign sales. Offers written contract.

STERNIG & BYRNE LITERARY AGENCY

2370 S. 107th St., Apt. #4, Milwaukee WI 53227. (414)328-8034. **Fax:** (414)328-8034. **E-mail:** jackbyrne@hotmail.com. **Website:** www.sff.net/people/jackbyrne. **Contact:** Jack Byrne. Memberships include SFWA, MWA. Represents 30 clients. 10% of clients are new/unpublished writers. Currently handles: nonfiction books 5%, novels 90%, juvenile books 5%.

REPRESENTS nonfiction books, novels, juvenile. **Considers these fiction areas:** fantasy, horror, mystery, science fiction, suspense.

"Our client list is comfortably full, and our current needs are therefore quite limited." Actively seeking science fiction/fantasy and mystery by established writers. Does not want to receive romance, poetry, textbooks, or highly specialized nonfiction.

HOW TO CONTACT Query with SASE. Prefers e-mail queries (no attachments); hard copy queries also acceptable. Responds in 3 weeks to queries. Responds in 3 months to mss.

TERMS Agent receives 15% commission on domestic sales. Agent receives 20% commission on foreign sales. Offers written contract; 2-month notice must be given to terminate contract.

TIPS "Don't send first drafts, have a professional presentation (including cover letter), and know your field. Read what's been done—good and bad."

STIMOLA LITERARY STUDIO

308 Livingston Ct., Edgewater NJ 07020. **E-mail:** info@stimolaliterarystudio.com. **Website:** www.stimolaliterarystudio.com. **Contact:** Rosemary B. Stimola. Estab. 1997. Member of AAR. Represents 45 clients. 15% of clients are new/unpublished writers. Currently handles: 10% novels, 90% juvenile books.

Agency is owned and operated by a former educator and children's bookseller with a PhD in Linguistics.

MEMBER AGENTS Rosemary B. Stimola.

Actively seeking remarkable young adult fiction and debut picture book author/illustrators. No institutional books.

HOW TO CONTACT Query via e-mail. "No attachments, please!" Accepts simultaneous submissions. Responds in 3 weeks to queries "we wish to pursue further." Responds in 2 months to requested mss. While unsolicited queries are welcome, most clients come through editor, agent, client referrals.

TERMS Agent receives 15% commission on domestic sales. Agent receives 20% (if subagents are employed) commission on foreign sales. Offers written contract, binding for all children's projects. 60 days notice must be given to terminate contract.

RECENT SALES *The Vanishing Season*, by Jodi Lynn Anderson (Harper Collins); *A Year In The Jungle* by Suzanne Collins and James Proimos; *Hello! Hello!* by Matt Cordell; *Better Off Friends* by Elizabeth Eulberg (Scholastic); *Scare Scape* by Sam Fisher (Scholastic); *The Secret Hum Of A Daisy* by Tracy Holczer (Putnam/Penguin); *Vasya's Noisy Paintbox* by Barb Rosenstock and Mary Grand Pre; *Chengdu Would Not Could Not Fall Asleep* by Barney Saltzberg (Hyperion); *Courage Has No Color* by Tanya Lee Stone.

TIPS Agent is hands-on, no-nonsense. May request revisions. Does not line edit but may offer suggestions for improvement. Well-respected by clients and editors. "A firm but reasonable deal negotiator."

STONESONG

270 W. 39th St. #201, New York NY 10018. (212)929-4600. **Fax:** (212)486-9123. **E-mail:** editors@stonesong.com. **E-mail:** submissions@stonesong.com. **Website:** stonesong.com.

MEMBER AGENTS Alison Fargis, Ellen Scordato, Judy Linden, Emmanuelle Morgen, Sarah Passick.

Does not represent plays, screenplays, or poetry.

HOW TO CONTACT Accepts electronic queries for fiction and nonfiction. Submit query addressed to 1 agent. Include first chapter or first 10 pages of ms.

RECENT SALES *Revolutionary*, by Alex Myers; *Reboot*, by Amy Tintera; *Dangerous Curves Ahead*, by Sugar Jamison; *Sweet Paul Eat and Make*, by Paul Lowe; *Smitten Kitchen*, by Deb Perelman.

ROBIN STRAUS AGENCY, INC.

229 E. 79th St., Suite 5A, New York NY 10075. (212)472-3282. **Fax:** (212)472-3833. **E-mail:** info@robinstrausagency.com. **Website:** www.robinstrausagency.com. **Contact:** Ms. Robin Straus. Estab. 1983. Member of AAR.

Prior to becoming an agent, Robin Straus served as a subsidary rights manager at Random House and Doubleday and worked in editorial at Little, Brown.

REPRESENTS **Considers these nonfiction areas:** biography, cooking, creative nonfiction, current affairs, history, memoirs, parenting, popular culture, psychology, science. **Considers these fiction areas:** commercial, literary, mainstream, women's.

Does *not* represent juvenile, young adult, science fiction/fantasy, horror, romance, Westerns, poetry or screenplays.

HOW TO CONTACT E-query or query via snail mail with SASE. "Send us a query letter with contact information, an autobiographical summary, a brief synopsis or description of your book project, submission history, and information on competition. If you wish, you may also include the opening chapter of your manuscript (pasted). Please let us know if you are showing the manuscript to other agents simultaneously."

TERMS Agent receives 15% commission on domestic sales. Agent receives 20% commission on foreign sales. Offers written contract. Charges for photocopying, express mail services, messenger and foreign postage, galleys and books for submissions, etc. as incurred.

PAM STRICKLER AUTHOR MANAGEMENT

P.O. Box 505, New Paltz NY 12561. (845)255-0061. **E-mail:** pamstrickleragency@gmail.com. **Website:** www.pamstrickler.com. **Contact:** Pamela Dean Strickler. Member of AAR. Also an associate member of the Historical Novel Society and member of RWA.

Prior to opening her agency, Ms. Strickler was senior editor at Ballantine Books.

REPRESENTS novels. **Considers these fiction areas:** historical, romance, women's.

Does not want to receive nonfiction or children's books.

HOW TO CONTACT This agency is currently closed to queries.

THE STRINGER LITERARY AGENCY, LLC

E-mail: stringerlit@comcast.net. **Website:** www.stringerlit.com. **Contact:** Marlene Stringer.

REPRESENTS **Considers these fiction areas:** fantasy, middle grade, mystery, romance, thriller, women's, young adult.

This agency specializes in fiction. This agency is seeking all kinds of romance, except inspirational or erotic. Does not want to receive picture books, plays, short stories, or poetry. The agency is also seeking nonfiction as of this time (2014).

HOW TO CONTACT Electronic submissions through website submission form only. Accepts simultaneous submissions.

RECENT SALES *The Secret History*, by Stephanie Thornton (NAL); The Night Prowlers Series, by J.T. Geissinger (Montlake); *Wisp of a Thing*, by Alex Bledsoe (Tor); *Breath of Frost*, by Alyxandra Harvey (Walker); *Housewitch*, by Katie Schickel (Forge); *The Paper Magician*, by Charlie Holmberg (47 North); *Fly by Night*, by Andrea Thalasinos (Forge); *Duty of Evil*, by April Taylor (Carina).

TIPS "If your ms falls between categories, or you are not sure of the category, query and we'll let you know if we'd like to take a look. We strive to respond as quickly as possible. If you have not received a response in the time period indicated on website, please re-query."

REBECCA STRONG INTERNATIONAL LITERARY AGENCY

235 W. 108th St., #35, New York NY 10025. (212)865-1569. **E-mail:** info@rsila.com. **Website:** www.rsila.com. **Contact:** Rebecca Strong. Estab. 2004.

Prior to opening her agency, Ms. Strong was an industry executive with experience editing and licensing in the US and UK. She has worked at Crown/Random House, Harmony/Random House, Bloomsbury, and Harvill.

REPRESENTS nonfiction books, novels. **Considers these nonfiction areas:** biography, business, health, history, memoirs, science, travel.

"We are a consciously small agency selectively representing authors all over the world." Does not want to receive poetry, screenplays or any unsolicited mss.

HOW TO CONTACT E-mail submissions only; subject line should indicate "submission query"; include cover letter with proposal. For fiction, include 1-2 complete chapters only pasted into e-mail. Accepts simultaneous submissions. Responds in 6-8 weeks to queries. Obtains most new clients through recommendations from others, conferences.

TERMS Agent receives 15% commission on domestic sales. Agent receives 20% commission on foreign sales. Offers written contract, binding for 10 years; 30-day notice must be given to terminate contract.

TIPS "I represent writers with prior publishing experience only: journalists, magazine writers or writers of fiction who have been published in anthologies or literary magazines. There are exceptions to this guideline, but not many."

THE STROTHMAN AGENCY, LLC

P.O. Box 231132, Boston MA 02123. **E-mail:** info@strothmanagency.com. **Website:** www.strothmanagency.com. **Contact:** Wendy Strothman, Lauren MacLeod. Member of AAR. Other memberships include Authors' Guild. Represents 50 clients.

Prior to becoming an agent, Ms. Strothman was head of Beacon Press (1983-1995) and executive vice president of Houghton Mifflin's Trade & Reference Division (1996-2002).

MEMBER AGENTS Wendy Strothman; Lauren MacLeod.

REPRESENTS novels, juvenile books. **Considers these nonfiction areas:** business, current affairs, environment, government, history, language, law, literature, politics, travel. **Considers these fiction areas:** literary, middle grade, young adult.

"Because we are highly selective in the clients we represent, we increase the value publishers place on our properties. We specialize in narrative nonfiction, memoir, history, science and nature, arts and culture, literary travel, current affairs, and some business. We have a highly selective practice in literary fiction, young adult and middle grade fiction, and nonfiction. We are now opening our doors to more commercial fiction but from authors who have a platform. If you have a platform, please mention it in your query letter. The Strothman Agency seeks out scholars, journalists, and other acknowledged and emerging experts in their fields. We are now actively looking for authors of well-written young adult fiction and nonfiction. Browse the Latest News to get an idea of the types of books that we represent. For more about what we're looking for, read Pitching an Agent: The Strothman Agency on the publishing website www.strothmanagency.com." Does not want to receive commercial fiction, romance, science fiction or self-help.

HOW TO CONTACT Accepts queries only via e-mail at strothmanagency@gmail.com. See submission guidelines online. Accepts simultaneous submissions. Responds in 4 weeks to queries. Responds in 6 weeks to mss. Obtains most new clients through recommendations from others.

TERMS Agent receives 15% commission on domestic sales. Agent receives 20% commission on foreign sales. Offers written contract; 30-day notice must be given to terminate contract.

THE STUART AGENCY

260 W. 52 St., #24C, New York NY 10019. (212)586-2711. **Fax:** (212)977-1488. **E-mail:** andrew@stuartagency.com. **Website:** stuartagency.com. **Contact:** Andrew Stuart. Estab. 2002.

Prior to his current position, Mr. Stuart was an agent with Literary Group International for five years. Prior to becoming an agent, he was an editor at Random House and Simon & Schuster.

REPRESENTS nonfiction books, novels.

Seeking history, science, narrative nonfiction, business, current events, memoir, psychology, sports, and literary fiction.

HOW TO CONTACT Query via online submission form on the agency website.

RECENT SALES Projects and clients include former Congressman Ron Paul's New York Times #1 Bestseller *The Revolution*, legendary publisher and free speech advocate Larry Flynt, Pulitzer Prize-winning journalists Kathleen Parker, William Dietrich and Carl Cannon, political scientist Alan Wolfe, Hollywood studio mogul Mike Medavoy, Mark Bauerlein, author of the national bestseller *The Dumbest Generation*, Christopher Ryan, author of the New York Times bestseller *Sex at Dawn*, renowned child psychiatrist Bruce Perry, New York Times bestselling novelist Mary Monroe, and the *New York Times* bestseller *The Darwin Awards: Evolution in Action*.

EMMA SWEENEY AGENCY, LLC

245 E 80th St., Suite 7E, New York NY 10075. **E-mail:** queries@emmasweeneyagency.com. **Website:** www.emmasweeneyagency.com. Member of AAR. Other memberships include Women's Media Group. Represents 80 clients. 5% of clients are new/unpublished writers. Currently handles: nonfiction books 50%, novels 50%.

Prior to becoming an agent, Ms. Sweeney was director of subsidiary rights at Grove Press. Since 1990, she has been a literary agent.

MEMBER AGENTS **Emma Sweeney**, president; **Noah Ballard**, rights manager and agent.

REPRESENTS nonfiction books, novels. **Considers these nonfiction areas:** biography, business, history, religious. **Considers these fiction areas:** literary, mainstream, mystery.

Does not want to receive romance, Westerns or screenplays.

HOW TO CONTACT "We accept only electronic queries, and ask that all queries be sent to queries@emmasweeneyagency.com rather than to any agent directly. Please begin your query with a succinct (and hopefully catchy) description of your plot or proposal. Always include a brief cover letter telling us how you heard about ESA, your previous writing credits, and a few lines about yourself. We cannot open any attachments unless specifically requested, and ask that you paste the first 10 pages of your proposal or novel into the text of your e-mail."

TERMS Agent receives 15% commission on domestic sales. Agent receives 10% commission on foreign sales.

RECENT SALES *Equal Of The Sun* by Anita Amirrezvani to Scriber; *The Cottage At Glass Beach* by Heather Barbieri to Harper Collins; *The Thinking Woman's Guide To Real Magic* by Emily Croy Barker to Pam Dorman Books; *Where Rivers Run Sand* by Julene Bair to Viking; *My First Coup D'etat* by John Dramani Mahama to Bloomsbury; *The Day My Brain Exploded* by Ashok Rajamani to Algonquin.

THE SWETKY AGENCY

2150 Balboa Way, No. 29, St. George UT 84770. (435)313-8006. **E-mail:** fayeswetky@amsaw.org. **Website:** www.amsaw.org/swetkyagency/index.html. **Contact:** Faye M. Swetky. Other memberships include American Society of Authors and Writers. Represents 20+ clients. 90% of clients are new/unpublished writers. Currently handles: nonfiction books 45%, novels 45%, movie scripts 10%, TV scripts 20%.

Prior to becoming an agent, Ms. Swetky was an editor and corporate manager. She has also raised and raced thoroughbred horses.

REPRESENTS nonfiction books, novels, short story collections, juvenile, movie, TV, movie scripts, feature film, MOW, sitcom, documentary. **Considers these nonfiction areas:** All major genres. **Considers these fiction areas:** All major genres. **Considers these script areas:** action, biography, cartoon, comedy, contemporary, detective, erotica, ethnic, experimental, family, fantasy, feminist, gay, glitz, historical, horror, juvenile, mainstream, multicultural, multimedia, mystery, psychic, regional, religious, romantic comedy, romantic drama, science, sports, teen, thriller, Western.

"We handle only book-length fiction and nonfiction and feature-length movie and television scripts. Please visit our website before submitting. All agency-related information is there, including a sample contract, e-mail submission forms, policies, clients, etc." Actively seeking marketable full-length material. Do not send unprofessionally prepared mss and/or scripts.

HOW TO CONTACT See website for submission instructions. Accepts e-mail queries only. Accepts simultaneous submissions. Response time varies. Obtains most new clients through queries.

TERMS Agent receives 15% commission on domestic sales; 20% commission on foreign sales; 20% commission on film sales. Offers written contract, binding for 6 months; 30-day notice must be given to terminate contract.

RECENT SALES *Pointman; For Men and for Gods; Boozehound; Sorry, I Thought I Loved You; Beating Bipolar; Message to My Butterfly; 101 Incredible Moments in Golf; Youth Pen; From Cocaine to Coconuts; The Last Warlord; They Call Me Doc; From Container to Kitchen.*

TIPS "Be professional. Have a professionally prepared product."

STEPHANIE TADE LITERARY AGENCY

P.O. Box 235, Durham PA 18039. (610)346-8667. **Contact:** Stephanie Tade.

Prior to becoming an agent, Ms. Tade was an executive editor at Rodale Press. She was also an agent with the Jane Rotrosen Agency.

MEMBER AGENTS Stephanie Tade.

REPRESENTS nonfiction.

"Mostly commercial nonfiction, especially in categories of health/diet, spirituality and Eastern philosophy, relationships/dating, self-improvement, psychology, science, and women's issues.

HOW TO CONTACT Query by e-mail or mail with SASE.

TALCOTT NOTCH LITERARY

2 Broad St., Second Floor, Suite 10, Milford CT 06460. (203)876-4959. **Fax:** (203)876-9517. **E-mail:** editorial@talcottnotch.net. **Website:** www.talcottnotch.net.

Contact: Gina Panettieri, President. Represents 35 clients. 25% of clients are new/unpublished writers.

Prior to becoming an agent, Ms. Panettieri was a freelance writer and editor.

MEMBER AGENTS Gina Panettieri, gpanettieri@talcottnotch.net (history, business, self-help, science, gardening, cookbooks, crafts, parenting, memoir, true crime and travel, women's fiction, paranormal, urban fantasy, horror, science fiction, historical, mystery, thrillers and suspense); **Paula Munier**, pmunier@talcottnotch.net (mystery/thriller, SF/fantasy, romance, YA, memoir, humor, pop culture, health & wellness, cooking, self-help, pop psych, New Age, inspirational, technology, science, and writing); **Rachael Dugas**, rdugas@talcottnotch.net (young adult, middle grade, romance, and women's fiction); **Jessica Negron**, jnegron@talcottnotch.net (commercial fiction, sci fi and fantasy [and all the little subgenres], psychological thrillers, cozy mysteries, romance, erotic romance, YA).

REPRESENTS Considers these nonfiction areas: business, cooking, crafts, gardening, health, history, humor, inspirational, memoirs, parenting, popular culture, psychology, science, self-help, technology, travel, true crime. **Considers these fiction areas:** commercial, fantasy, historical, horror, mainstream, middle grade, mystery, New Age, paranormal, romance, science fiction, suspense, thriller, urban fantasy, women's, young adult.

HOW TO CONTACT Query via e-mail (preferred) with first 10 pages of the ms within the body of the e-mail, not as an attachment. Accepts simultaneous submissions. Responds in 1 week to queries. Responds in 4-6 weeks to mss.

TERMS Agent receives 15% commission on domestic sales. Agent receives 20% commission on foreign sales. Offers written contract, binding for 1 year.

RECENT SALES Sold 36 titles in the last year. *Delivered From Evil*, by Ron Franscell (Fairwinds) and *Sourtoe* (Globe Pequot Press); *Hellforged*, by Nancy Holzner (Berkley Ace Science Fiction); *Welcoming Kitchen; 200 Allergen- and Gluten-Free Vegan Recipes*, by Kim Lutz and Megan Hart (Sterling); *Dr. Seteh's Love Prescription*, by Dr. Seth Meyers (Adams Media); *The Book of Ancient Bastards*, by Brian Thornton (Adams Media); *Hope in Courage*, by Beth Fehlbaum (Westside Books) and more.

TIPS "Know your market and how to reach them. A strong platform is essential in your book proposal. Can you effectively use social media/Are you a strong networker? Are you familiar with the book bloggers in your genre? Are you involved with the interest-specific groups that can help you? What can you do to break through the 'noise' and help present your book to your readers? Check our website for more tips and information on this topic."

PATRICIA TEAL LITERARY AGENCY

2036 Vista Del Rosa, Fullerton CA 92831-1336. **Phone/Fax:** (714)738-8333. **Contact:** Patricia Teal. Member of AAR. Other memberships include RWA, Authors Guild. Represents 20 clients. Currently handles: nonfiction books 10%, 90% fiction.

REPRESENTS nonfiction books, novels. **Considers these nonfiction areas:** animals, autobiography, biography, child guidance, health, how-to, investigative, medicine, parenting, psychology, self-help, true crime, women's issues, women's studies. **Considers these fiction areas:** glitz, mainstream, mystery, romance, suspense, women's.

This agency specializes in women's fiction, commercial how-to, and self-help nonfiction. Does not want to receive poetry, short stories, articles, science fiction, fantasy, or regency romance.

HOW TO CONTACT Published authors only should submit. Query with SASE. Accepts simultaneous submissions. Obtains most new clients through conferences, recommendations from authors and editors.

TERMS Agent receives 10-15% commission on domestic sales. Agent receives 20% commission on foreign sales. Offers written contract, binding for 1 year. Charges clients for ms copies.

RECENT SALES Sold 30 titles in the last year. *Texas Rose*, by Marie Ferrarella (Silhouette); *Watch Your Language*, by Sterling Johnson (St. Martin's Press); *The Black Sheep's Baby*, by Kathleen Creighton (Silhouette); *Man With a Message*, by Muriel Jensen (Harlequin).

WRITERS CONFERENCES RWA Conferences; Asilomar; BookExpo America; Bouchercon; Maui Writers Conference.

TIPS "Include SASE with all correspondence. I am taking on published authors only."

TESSLER LITERARY AGENCY, LLC

27 W. 20th St., Suite 1003, New York NY 10011. (212)242-0466. **Fax:** (212)242-2366. **Website:** www.tessleragency.com. **Contact:** Michelle Tessler. Estab.

2004. Member of AAR. Currently handles: 90% nonfiction books, 10% novels.

Prior to forming her own agency, Ms. Tessler worked at the prestigious literary agency Carlisle & Company (now Inkwell Management) and at the William Morris Agency.

REPRESENTS **Considers these nonfiction areas:** biography, business, creative nonfiction, foods, memoirs, science, travel. **Considers these fiction areas:** commercial, literary, women's.

"Our list is diverse and far-reaching. In nonfiction, it includes narrative, popular science, memoir, history, psychology, business, biography, food, and travel. In many cases, we sign authors who are especially adept at writing books that cross many of these categories at once. In fiction, we represent literary, women's, and commercial. We do not take on genre fiction or children's books. If your project is in keeping with the kind of books we take on, we want to hear from you."

HOW TO CONTACT Submit query through online query form only. Accepts simultaneous submissions. New clients by queries/submissions through the website and recommendations from others.

TERMS Receives 15% commission on domestic sales; 20% on foreign sales. Offers written contract.

RECENT SALES *Underwater Puppies* by Seth Casteel (Little, Brown); *Blood and Ivy* by Paul Collins (WW Norton); *Girl Waits With Gun* by Amy Stewart (Houghton Mifflin Harcourt); *The Sleepwalker's Guide to Dancing* by Mira Jacob (Random House); *Darpa* by Sharon Weinberger (Knopf); *Are We Smart Enough to Know How Smart Animals Are?* by Frans de Waal (WW Norton); *Shanghai Grand* by Taras Grescoe (St. Martin's); *Breaking the Standard* by Peter Doran (Viking); *Homecoming* by Amanda Eyre Ward (Random House); *Part Time Paleo* by Leanne Ely (Plume).

THE TFS LITERARY AGENCY

P.O. Box 46-031, Park Ave., Lower Hutt 5044 New Zealand. **E-mail:** tfs@elseware.co.nz. **Website:** www.elseware.co.nz. **Contact:** Chris Else, Barbara Else. Other memberships include NZALA.

General fiction, nonfiction, and children's books from New Zealand authors only. No poetry, individual short stories, or articles.

HOW TO CONTACT Send query and brief author bio via e-mail.

THREE SEAS LITERARY AGENCY

P.O. Box 8571, Madison WI 53708. (608)834-9317. **E-mail:** queries@threeseaslit.com. **Website:** threeseasagency.com. **Contact:** Michelle Grajkowski, Cori Deyoe. Estab. 2000. Member of AAR. Other memberships include RWA (Romance Writers of America), SCBWI. Represents 55 clients. 10% of clients are new/unpublished writers. Currently handles: nonfiction books 5%, novels 80%, juvenile books 15%.

Since its inception, 3 Seas has sold more than 500 titles worldwide. Ms. Grajkowski's authors have appeared on all the major lists including *The New York Times*, *USA Today* and *Publishers Weekly*. Prior to joining the agency in 2006, Ms. Deyoe was a multi-published author. She represents a wide range of authors and has sold many projects at auction.

MEMBER AGENTS Michelle Grajkowski; Cori Deyoe.

REPRESENTS nonfiction, novels, juvenile.

3 Seas focuses primarily on romance (including contemporary, romantic suspense, paranormal, fantasy, historical and category), women's fiction, mysteries, nonfiction, young adult, and children's stories. "Currently, we are looking for fantastic authors with a voice of their own." 3 Seas does not represent poetry or screenplays.

HOW TO CONTACT E-mail queries only. For fiction titles, query with first chapter and synopsis embedded in the e-mail. For nonfiction, query with complete proposal and first chapter. For picture books, query with complete text. One sample illustration may be included. Accepts simultaneous submissions. Responds in 1 month to queries. Obtains most new clients through recommendations from others, conferences.

TERMS Agent receives 15% commission on domestic sales. Agent receives 20% commission on foreign sales. Offers written contract.

RECENT SALES Jennifer Brown and Alexis Morgan, both of whom are bestselling authors. Also: Laura Marie Altom, Lindsey Brookes, Carla Capshaw, P.A. DePaul, Anna DeStefano, Heather Doherty, Molly Evans, K.M. Fawcett, R. Barri Flowers, Kristi Gold, Winnie Griggs, Susan Gee Heino, Timothy Lewis, Lesli Muir Lytle, Donna MacMeans, Tracy Madison, Lori McDonald, Elizabeth Michels, Trish Milburn, Keri

Mikulski, Tricia Mills, Lisa Mondello, Natalie Richards, Liz Talley and Norah Wilson.

TRACY BROWN LITERARY AGENCY

P.O. Box 88, Scarsdale NY 10583. (914)400-4147. **Fax:** (914)931-1746. **E-mail:** tracy@brownlit.com. **Contact:** Tracy Brown. Represents 35 clients. Currently handles: nonfiction books 90%, novels 10%.

Prior to becoming an agent, Mr. Brown was a book editor for 25 years.

REPRESENTS Considers these nonfiction areas: biography, current affairs, health, history, psychology, travel, women's issues, travel, popular history. **Considers these fiction areas:** literary.

Specializes in thorough involvement with clients' books at every stage of the process from writing to proposals to publication. Actively seeking serious nonfiction and fiction. Does not want to receive YA, sci-fi or romance.

HOW TO CONTACT Submit outline/proposal, synopsis, author bio. Accepts simultaneous submissions. Responds in 2 weeks to queries. Obtains most new clients through referrals.

TERMS Agent receives 15% commission on domestic sales. Agent receives 20% commission on foreign sales. Offers written contract.

RECENT SALES *Why Have Kids?* by Jessica Valenti (HarperCollins); *Tapdancing to Work*, by Carol J. Loomis (Portfolio); *Mating in Captivity* by Esther Perel.

TRANSATLANTIC LITERARY AGENCY

2 Bloor St., Suite 3500, Toronto ON M4W 1A8 Canada. (416)488-9214. **E-mail:** info@transatlanticagency.com. **Website:** transatlanticagency.com. Represents 250 clients. 10% of clients are new/unpublished writers.

MEMBER AGENTS **Trena White** (nonfiction); **Amy Tompkins** (fiction, nonfiction, juvenile); **Stephanie Sinclair** (fiction, nonfiction); **Patricia Ocampo** (juvenile/illustrators); **Fiona Kenshole** (juvenile, illustrators); **Samantha Haywood** (fiction, nonfiction, graphic novels); **Jesse Finkelstein** (nonfiction); **Marie Campbell** (middle grade fiction); **Shaun Bradley** (referrals only); **Jennifer Starkman**; **Barb Miller**; **Lynn Bennett**; **David Bennett**.

REPRESENTS nonfiction books, novels, juvenile. **Considers these nonfiction areas:** business, creative nonfiction, cultural interests, current affairs, environment, how-to, investigative, memoirs, politics, religious, technology, true crime, women's issues. **Considers these fiction areas:** commercial, historical, juvenile, literary, middle grade, new adult, picture books, romance, women's, young adult.

"In both children's and adult literature, we market directly into the United States, the United Kingdom and Canada." Actively seeking literary children's and adult fiction, nonfiction. Does not want to receive picture books, poetry, screenplays or stage plays.

HOW TO CONTACT Always refer to the website, as guidelines will change, and only various agents are open to new clients at any given time. Obtains most new clients through recommendations from others.

TERMS Agent receives 15% commission on domestic sales. Agent receives 20% commission on foreign sales. Offers written contract; 45-day notice must be given to terminate contract. This agency charges for photocopying and postage when it exceeds $100.

RECENT SALES Sold 250 titles in the last year.

S©OTT TREIMEL NY

434 Lafayette St., New York NY 10003. (212)505-8353. **E-mail:** general@scotttreimelny.com. **Website:** ScottTreimelNY.blogspot.com; www.ScottTreimelNY.com. Estab. 1995. Member of AAR. Other memberships include Authors Guild, SCBWI. 10% of clients are new/unpublished writers. Currently handles: 100% juvenile/teen books.

Prior to becoming an agent, Mr. Treimel was an assistant to Marilyn E. Marlow at Curtis Brown, a rights agent for Scholastic, a book packager and rights agent for United Feature Syndicate, a freelance editor, a rights consultant for HarperCollins Children's Books, and the founding director of Warner Bros. Worldwide Publishing.

REPRESENTS nonfiction books, novels, juvenile, children's, picture books, young adult.

This agency specializes in tightly focused segments of the trade and institutional markets.

HOW TO CONTACT No longer accepts simultaneous submissions. Wants queries only from writers he has met at conferences.

TERMS Agent receives 15% commission on domestic sales. Agent receives 20% commission on foreign sales. Offers verbal or written contract. Charges clients for photocopying, express postage, messengers, and books needed to sell foreign, film and other rights.

NEW AGENT SPOTLIGHT

PETER KNAPP

(PARK LITERARY GROUP)

parkliterary.com

@petejknapp

ABOUT PETER: Prior to joining Park Literary, he was the story editor at Floren Shieh Productions, where he consulted on book-to-film adaptations for Los Angeles-based film and TV entities. He graduated from New York University with a B.A. in Art History.

HE IS SEEKING: middle grade and young adult fiction, as well as suspense and thrillers for all ages. He does not represent picture books or nonfiction.

HOW TO SUBMIT: queries@parkliterary.com. Put "Query for Peter: [Title]" in the subject line. All materials must be in the body of the e-mail.

RECENT SALES *The Hunchback Assignments*, by Arthur Slade (Random House, HarperCollins Canada; HarperCollins Australia); *Shotgun Serenade*, by Gail Giles (Little, Brown); *Laundry Day*, by Maurie Manning (Clarion); *The P.S. Brothers*, by Maribeth Boelts (Harcourt); *The First Five Fourths*, by Pat Hughes (Viking); *Old Robert and the Troubadour Cats*, by Barbara Joosse (Philomel); *Ends*, by David Ward (Abrams); *Dear Canada*, by Barbara Haworth-Attard (Scholastic); *Soccer Dreams*, by Maribeth Boelts (Candlewick); *Lucky Me*, by Richard Scrimger (Tundra); *Play, Louie, Play*, by Muriel Harris Weinstein (Bloomsbury).

WRITERS CONFERENCES SCBWI NY, NJ, PA, Bologna; The New School; Southwest Writers' Conference; Pikes Peak Writers' Conference.

TIPS "We look for dedicated authors and illustrators able to sustain longtime careers in our increasingly competitive field. I want fresh, not derivative story concepts with overly familiar characters. We look for gripping stories, characters, pacing, and themes. We remain mindful of an authentic (to the age) point-of-view, and look for original voices. We spend significant time hunting for the best new work, and do launch debut talent each year. It is best *not* to send manuscripts with lengthy submission histories already."

TRIADA U.S. LITERARY AGENCY, INC.

P.O. Box 561, Sewickley PA 15143. (412)401-3376. **E-mail:** uwe@triadaus.com. **Website:** www.triadaus.com. **Contact:** Dr. Uwe Stender. Member of AAR. Represents 65 clients. 20% of clients are new/unpublished writers.

REPRESENTS fiction, nonfiction. **Considers these nonfiction areas:** biography, business, cooking, diet/nutrition, economics, education, foods, health, how-to, memoirs, popular culture, science, sports, advice, relationships, lifestyle. **Considers these fiction areas:** action, adventure, crime, detective, ethnic, historical, horror, juvenile, literary, mainstream, mystery, occult, police, romance, women's, especially young adult, women's fiction, and mysteries.

"We are looking for great writing and story platforms. Our response time is fairly unique. We recognize that neither we nor the authors have time to waste, so we guarantee a 5-day response time. We usually respond within 24 hours. " Actively looking for both fiction and nonfiction in all areas.

HOW TO CONTACT E-mail queries preferred; otherwise query with SASE. "We do not respond to postal submissions that aren't accompanied by SASE." Accepts simultaneous submissions. Obtains most new clients through recommendations from others, conferences.

TERMS Agent receives 15% commission on domestic sales. Agent receives 20% commission on foreign sales. Offers written contract; 30-day notice must be given to terminate contract.

RECENT SALES *The Man Whisperer*, by Samantha Brett and Donna Sozio (Adams Media); *Whatever Happened to Pudding Pops*, by Gael Fashingbauer Cooper and Brian Bellmont (Penguin/Perigee); *86'd*, by Dan Fante (Harper Perennial); *Hating Olivia*, by Mark SaFranko (Harper Perennial); *Everything I'm Not Made Me Everything I Am*, by Jeff Johnson (Smiley Books).

TIPS "I comment on all requested manuscripts that I reject."

TRIDENT MEDIA GROUP

41 Madison Ave., 36th Floor, New York NY 10010. (212)333-1511. **E-mail:** press@tridentmediagroup.com; info@tridentmediagroup.com. **E-mail:** ellen.assistant@tridentmediagroup.com. **Website:** www.tridentmediagroup.com. **Contact:** Ellen Levine. Member of AAR.

MEMBER AGENTS **Kimberly Whalen**, ws.assistant@tridentmediagroup (commercial fiction and nonfiction, women's fiction, suspense, paranormal, and pop culture); **Scott Miller**, smiller@tridentmediagroup.com (thrillers, crime fiction, women's and book club fiction, and a wide variety of nonfiction, such as military, celebrity and pop culture, narrative, sports, prescriptive, and current events); **Alex Glass,** aglass@tridentmediagroup (literary fiction, crime fiction, pop culture, sports, health and wellness, narrative nonfiction, and children's books); **Melissa Flashman**, mflashman@tridentmediagroup.com (pop culture, memoir, wellness, popular science, business and economics, and technology—also fiction in the genres of mystery, suspense or YA); **Alyssa Eisner Henkin**, ahenkin@tridentmediagroup.com (juvenile, children's, young adult); **Don Fehr**, dfehr@tridentmediagroup.com (literary and commercial fiction, narrative nonfiction, memoirs, travel, science, and health); **John Silbersack**, silbersack.assistant@tridentmediagroup.com (commercial and literary fiction, science fiction and fantasy, narrative nonfiction, young adult, thrillers); **Erica Spellman-Silverman; Ellen Levine**, levine.assistant@tridentmediagroup.com (popular commercial fiction and compelling nonfiction—memoir, popular culture, narrative nonfiction, history, politics, biography, science, and the odd quirky book); **Mark Gottlieb**, mgottlieb@tridentmediagroup.com; **MacKenzie Fraser-Bub**, MFraserBub@tridentmediagroup.com (many genres of fiction—specializing in women's fiction).

REPRESENTS **Considers these nonfiction areas:** biography, business, creative nonfiction, current affairs, economics, health, history, memoirs, military, popular culture, politics, science, sports, technology, travel. **Considers these fiction areas:** commercial, crime, fantasy, juvenile, literary, middle grade, mystery, paranormal, science fiction, suspense, thriller, women's, young adult.

Actively seeking new or established authors in a variety of fiction and nonfiction genres.

HOW TO CONTACT Preferred method of query is through the online submission form on the agency website. Query only one agent at a time.

RECENT SALES Recent sales include: *Sacred River*, by Syl Cheney-Coker; *Saving Quinton*, by Jessica Sorensen; *The Secret History of Las Vegas*, by Chris Abani; *The Summer Wind*, by Mary Alice Munroe.

TIPS "If you have any questions, please check FAQ page before e-mailing us."

THE UNTER AGENCY

23 W. 73rd St., Suite 100, New York NY 10023. (212)401-4068. **E-mail:** Jennifer@theunteragency.com. **Website:** www.theunteragency.com. **Contact:** Jennifer Unter. Estab. 2008.

Ms. Unter began her book publishing career in the editorial department at Henry Holt & Co. She later worked at the Karpfinger Agency while she attended law school. She then became an associate at the entertainment firm of Cowan, DeBaets, Abrahams & Sheppard LLP where she practiced primarily in the areas of publishing and copyright law.

REPRESENTS **Considers these nonfiction areas:** biography, environment, foods, health, memoirs, popular culture, politics, travel, true crime, nature subjects. **Considers these fiction areas:** commercial, mainstream, middle grade, picture books, young adult.

This agency specializes in children's and nonfiction, but does take quality fiction.

HOW TO CONTACT Send an e-query. There is also an online submission form. If you do not hear back from this agency within 3 months, consider that a no.

RECENT SALES A full list of recent sales/titles is available on the agency website.

UPSTART CROW LITERARY

244 Fifth Avenue, 11th Floor, New York NY 10001. **E-mail:** danielle.submission@gmail.com; alexandra.submission@gmail.com. **Website:** www.upstartcrowliterary.com. **Contact:** Danielle Chiotti, Alexandra Penfold. Estab. 2009.

MEMBER AGENTS **Michael Stearns** (not accepting submissions); **Danielle Chiotti** (books ranging from contemporary women's fiction to narrative nonfiction, from romance to relationship stories, humorous tales, and YA fiction); **Ted Malawer** (accepting queries only through conference submissions and client referrals); **Alexandra Penfold** (children's—picture books, middle grade, YA; illustrators and author/illustrators).

REPRESENTS **Considers these nonfiction areas:** cooking, foods. **Considers these fiction areas:** middle grade, picture books, women's, young adult.

HOW TO CONTACT Upstart Crow agents that are currently accepting submissions are Danielle Chiotti and Alexandra Penfold.

VAN DIEST LITERARY AGENCY

P.O. Box 1482, Sisters OR 97759. **Website:** www.christianliteraryagency.com.

MEMBER AGENTS David Van Diest, Sarah Van Diest.

REPRESENTS **Considers these fiction areas:** inspirational.

Christian books. "We are actively looking to discover and bring to market a few authors with fresh perspectives on timely subjects."

HOW TO CONTACT "Before submitting a proposal or manuscript, we ask that you submit an online query found on the 'Contact Us' page. We will contact you if we would like to receive a full proposal. Or you can snail mail a query to our address, ATTN: Acquisitions Editor."

VENTURE LITERARY

2683 Via de la Valle, G-714, Del Mar CA 92014. (619)807-1887. **Fax:** (772)365-8321. **E-mail:** submissions@ventureliterary.com. **Website:** www.ventureliterary.com. **Contact:** Frank R. Scatoni. Represents 50 clients. 40% of clients are new/unpublished writers. Currently handles: nonfiction books 80%, novels 20%.

Prior to becoming an agent, Mr. Scatoni worked as an editor at Simon & Schuster.

MEMBER AGENTS Frank R. Scatoni (general nonfiction, biography, memoir, narrative nonfiction, sports, serious nonfiction, graphic novels, narratives).

REPRESENTS nonfiction books, novels, graphic novels, narratives. **Considers these nonfiction areas:** anthropology, biography, business, cultural interests, current affairs, dance, economics, environment, ethnic, government, history, investigative, law, memoirs, military, money, multicultural, music, popular culture, politics, psychology, science, sports, technology, true crime, women's issues, women's studies. **Considers these fiction areas:** action, adventure, crime, detective, literary, mainstream, mystery, police, sports, suspense, thriller, women's.

Specializes in nonfiction, sports, biography, gambling, and nonfiction narratives. Actively seeking nonfiction, graphic novels and narratives. Does not want fantasy, sci-fi, romance, children's picture books, or Westerns.

HOW TO CONTACT Considers e-mail queries only. *No unsolicited mss* and no snail mail whatsoever. See website for complete submission guidelines. Obtains most new clients through recommendations from others.

TERMS Agent receives 15% commission on domestic sales. Agent receives 20% commission on foreign sales. Offers written contract.

RECENT SALES *The 9/11 Report: A Graphic Adaptation*, by Sid Jacobson and Ernie Colon (FSG); *Having a Baby* by Cindy Margolis (Perigee/Penguin); *Phil Gordon's Little Blue Book*, by Phil Gordon (Simon & Schuster); *Atomic America*, by Todd Tucker (Free Press); *War as They Knew It*, by Michael Rosenberg (Grand Central); *Game Day*, by Craig James (Wiley); *The Blueprint* by Christopher Price (Thomas Dunne Books).

VERITAS LITERARY AGENCY

601 Van Ness Ave., Opera Plaza, Suite E, San Francisco CA 94102. (415)647-6964. **Fax:** (415)647-6965. **E-mail:** submissions@veritasliterary.com. **Website:** www.veritasliterary.com. **Contact:** Katherine Boyle.

Member of AAR. Other memberships include Author's Guild and SCBWI.

MEMBER AGENTS Katherine Boyle, Michael Carr.

REPRESENTS nonfiction books, novels. **Considers these nonfiction areas:** current affairs, memoirs, popular culture, politics, true crime, women's issues, narrative nonfiction, art and music biography, natural history, health and wellness, psychology, serious religion (no New Age) and popular science. **Considers these fiction areas:** commercial, fantasy, literary, middle grade, mystery, science fiction, young adult.

Does not want to receive poetry or Christian fiction.

HOW TO CONTACT This agency accepts short queries or proposals via e-mail only. "If you are sending a proposal or a manuscript after a positive response to a query, please write 'requested material' on the subject line and include the initial query letter."

RECENT SALES *Hedwig and Berti* by Frieda Arkin (St. Martin's); *Shadowdance* by David Dalglish (Orbit); *Sickened: A Memoir of a Lost Childhood* by Julie Gregory (Bantam); *If I Am Missing or Dead* by Janine Latus (Simon & Schuster); *Free Burning* by Bayo Ojikutu (Crown).

RALPH M. VICINANZA LTD.

303 W. 18th St., New York NY 10011. (212)924-7090. **Fax:** (212)691-9644. Member of AAR.

MEMBER AGENTS Ralph M. Vicinanza; Chris Lotts; Christopher Schelling.

HOW TO CONTACT This agency takes on new clients by professional recommendation only.

TERMS Agent receives 15% commission on domestic sales. Agent receives 20% commission on foreign sales.

VICKY BIJUR LITERARY AGENCY

333 West End Ave., Suite 5B, New York NY 10023. **E-mail:** queries@vickybijuragency.com. **Website:** www.vickybijuragency.com. Estab. 1988. Member of AAR.

Vicky Bijur worked at Oxford University Press and with the Charlotte Sheedy Literary Agency. Books she represents have appeared on *the New York Times Bestseller List, in the New York Times Notable Books of the Year, Los Angeles Times Best Fiction of the Year, Washington Post Book World Rave Reviews of the Year.*

MEMBER AGENTS Vicky Bijur; Shelby Sampsel.

REPRESENTS nonfiction books, novels. **Considers these nonfiction areas:** cooking, government, health, history, psychology, psychiatry, science, self-help, sociology, biography; child care/development; environmental studies; journalism; social sciences. **Considers these fiction areas:** commercial, literary, mystery, thriller.

We do not represent children's books, poetry, science fiction, fantasy, horror, or romance.

HOW TO CONTACT "You can query us via e-mail to queries@vickybijuragency.com, or by regular mail. If you query by hard copy, please include an SASE for our response. If you want your material returned, include an SASE large enough to contain pages. To query us with fiction, please send a synopsis and the first chapter of your manuscript with your query letter (if e-mailed, please paste the chapter into body of e-mail, as we don't open attachments from unfamiliar senders). For nonfiction, please send a query letter and proposal. No phone or fax queries. We generally respond to all queries within six weeks of receipt."

RECENT SALES *Louise's Dilemma*, by Sarah Shaber; *After I'm Gone*, by Laura Lippman; *The Sleeping Dictionary*, by Sujata Massey.

WADE & CO. LITERARY AGENCY, LTD

33 Cormorant Lodge, Thomas Moore St., London E1W 1AU England. (44)(207)488-4171. **Fax:** (44) (207)488-4172. **E-mail:** rw@rwla.com. **Website:** www.rwla.com. **Contact:** Robin Wade. Estab. 2001.

Prior to opening his agency, Mr. Wade was an author.

MEMBER AGENTS Robin Wade.

REPRESENTS fiction and nonfiction, including children's books.

"We are young and dynamic, and actively seek new writers across the literary spectrum." Does not want to receive poetry, plays, screenplays or short stories. Is also currently closed to picture books.

HOW TO CONTACT New proposals for full-length adult and young adult books (excluding children's picture books or poetry) are always welcome. We much prefer to receive queries and submissions by e-mail, although we do, of course, accept proposals by post. There is no need to telephone in advance. Please provide a few details about yourself, a synopsis (i.e. a clear narrative summary of the complete story, of between say 1 and 6 pages in length) and the first 10,000 words or so (ideally as Word doc or PDF attachments) over e-mail. Responds in 1 week to queries. Responds in 1 month to mss.

TERMS Agent receives 10% commission on domestic sales. Agent receives 20% commission on foreign sales. Offers written contract; 1-month notice must be given to terminate contract.

TIPS "We seek manuscripts that are well written, with strong characters and an original narrative voice. Our absolute priority is giving the best possible service to the authors we choose to represent, as well as maintaining routine friendly contact with them as we help develop their careers."

WALES LITERARY AGENCY, INC.

P.O. Box 9426, Seattle WA 98109. (206)284-7114. **E-mail:** waleslit@waleslit.com. **Website:** www.waleslit.com. **Contact:** Elizabeth Wales; Neal Swain. Member of AAR. Other memberships include Authors Guild, Pacific Northwest Writers Association. Represents 60 clients. 10% of clients are new/unpublished writers. Currently handles: nonfiction books 60%, novels 40%.

Prior to becoming an agent, Ms. Wales worked at Oxford University Press and Viking Penguin.

MEMBER AGENTS Elizabeth Wales; Neal Swain.

This agency specializes in quality fiction and nonfiction. Does not handle screenplays, children's picture books, genre fiction, or most category nonfiction.

HOW TO CONTACT Accepts queries sent with cover letter and SASE, and e-mail queries with no attachments. No phone or fax queries. Guidelines and client list available on website. Accepts simultaneous submissions. Responds in 2 weeks to queries, 2 months to mss.

TERMS Agent receives 15% commission on domestic sales. Agent receives 20% commission on foreign sales.

RECENT SALES *Growing A Feast: The Chronicle Of A Farm To Table Meal*, by Kurt Timmermeister (W.W. Norton, Jan 2014); *Badluck Way: A Year On TheRagged Edge Of The West* By Bryce Andrews (Atria/Simon & Schuster, Jan 2014); *American Savage: Insights, Slights, Fights On Faith, Sex, Love, and Politics*, by Dan Savage (Penguin, 2013).

WRITERS CONFERENCES AWP; Chuckanut Writers Conference; Missoula Writers Conference, and others.

TIPS "We are especially interested in work that espouses a progressive cultural or political view, projects a new voice, or simply shares an important, compelling story. We also encourage writers living in the Pacific Northwest, West Coast, Alaska, and Pacific Rim countries, and writers from historically underrepresented groups, such as gay and lesbian writers and writers of color, to submit work (but does not discourage writers outside these areas). Most importantly, whether in fiction or nonfiction, the agency is looking for talented storytellers."

WATERSIDE PRODUCTIONS, INC.

2055 Oxford Ave., Cardiff CA 92007. (760)632-9190. **Fax:** (760)632-9295. **E-mail:** admin@waterside.com. **Website:** www.waterside.com. Estab. 1982.

MEMBER AGENTS **Bill Gladstone** (big nonfiction books); **Margot Maley Hutchinson** (computer, health, psychology, parenting, fitness, pop-culture, and business); **Carole Jelen**, carole@jelenpub.com (innovation and thought leaders especially in business, technology, lifestyle and self-help); **Neil Gudovitz** (neilg@earthlink.net); **David Nelson**; **Jill Kramer**, WatersideAgentJK@aol.com (quality fiction with empowering themes for adults and YA [including crossovers]; she also represents nonfiction books in the areas of: mind-body-spirit, self-help, celebrity memoirs, relationships, sociology, finance, psychology, health and fitness, diet/nutrition, inspiration, business, family/parenting issues, and more); **Brad Schepp** (e-commerce, social media and social commerce, careers, entrepreneurship, general business, health and fitness).

REPRESENTS **Considers these nonfiction areas:** business, computers, diet/nutrition, health, inspirational, money, parenting, psychology, self-help, sociology, technology. **Considers these fiction areas:** mainstream, young adult.

Specializes in computer books, how-to, business, and health titles. Note that most agents here are nonfiction only, so target your query to the appropriate agent.

HOW TO CONTACT "Please read each agent bio [on the website] to determine who you think would best represent your genre of work. When you have chosen your agent, please write his or her name in the subject line of your e-mail and send it to admin@waterside.com with your query letter in the body of the e-mail, and your proposal or sample material as an attached Word document." Obtains most new clients through referrals from established client and publisher list.

TIPS "For new writers, a quality proposal and a strong knowledge of the market you're writing for goes a long way toward helping us turn you into a published author. We like to see a strong author platform. Two foreign rights agents on staff—Neil Gudovitz and Kimberly Brabec—help us with overseas sales."

WATKINS LOOMIS AGENCY, INC.

P.O. Box 20925, New York NY 10025. (212)532-0080. **Fax:** (646)383-2449. **E-mail:** assistant@watkinsloomis.com. **Website:** www.watkinsloomis.com. Estab. 1980. Represents 50+ clients.

MEMBER AGENTS Gloria Loomis, president; Julia Masnik, junior agent.

REPRESENTS nonfiction, novels. **Considers these nonfiction areas:** autobiography, biography, cultural interests, current affairs, environment, ethnic, history, popular culture, technology, investigative journalism. **Considers these fiction areas:** literary, short story collections.

This agency specializes in literary fiction and nonfiction.

HOW TO CONTACT *No unsolicited mss.* This agency does not guarantee a response to queries.

TERMS Agent receives 15% commission on domestic sales. Agent receives 20% commission on foreign sales.

RECENT SALES *The Wrong Enemy*, by Carlotta Gall (nonfiction); *Debbie Doesn't Do It Anymore*, by Walter Mosley (fiction); *China's Second Continent*, by Howard W. French (nonfiction); *Why I Read: The Serious Pleasure of Books*, by Wendy Lesser (nonfiction). Entire list of sales is available on the agency website.

WAXMAN LEAVELL LITERARY AGENCY, INC.

443 Park Ave. S, Suite 1004, New York NY 10016. (212)675-5556. **Fax:** (212)675-1381. **E-mail:** scottsubmit@waxmanleavell.com; byrdsubmit@waxmanleavell.com; hollysubmit@waxmanleavell.com; rachelsubmit@waxmanleavell.com; and larrysubmit@waxmanleavell.com; taylorsubmit@waxmanleavell.com. **Website:** www.waxmanleavell.com. **Contact:** Scott Waxman; Byrd Leavell; Holly Root; Rachel Vogel; Larry Kirshbaum; Taylor Haggerty. Represents 60 clients. 50% of clients are new/unpublished writers. Currently handles: nonfiction books 50%, novels 50%.

Prior to founding the Scott Waxman Agency in 1997, Mr. Waxman was an editor at HarperCollins.

REPRESENTS Considers these nonfiction areas: prescriptive, historical, sports, narrative, pop culture, humor, memoir, biography, celebrity. **Considers these fiction areas:** historical, literary, mainstream, middle grade, mystery, paranormal, romance, thriller, women's, young adult.

"We're looking for new novelists with non-published works."

HOW TO CONTACT Please visit our website. Accepts simultaneous submissions.

TERMS Agent receives 15% commission on domestic sales. Agent receives 10% commission on foreign sales. Offers written contract; 2-month notice must be given to terminate contract.

WEED LITERARY

55 E. 65th St., Suite 4E, New York NY 10065. **E-mail:** info@weedliterary.com. **Website:** www.weedliterary.com. **Contact:** Elisabeth Weed. Estab. 2007.

Prior to forming her own agency, Ms. Weed was an agent at Curtis Brown and Trident Media Group.

REPRESENTS fiction, novels. **Considers these fiction areas:** literary, women's.

This agency specializes in upmarket women's fiction. Does not want to receive picture books, YA, middle grade, or romance.

HOW TO CONTACT Send a query letter. "Please do not send queries or submissions via snail, registered, certified mail, or by FedEx or UPS requiring signature."

RECENT SALES *Life Without Summer*, by Lynne Griffin (St. Martin's Press); *Time of My Life*, by Allison Winn Scotch (Shaye Areheart Books); and *The Last Will of Moira Leahy*, by Therese Walsh (Shaye Areheart Books).

WRITERS CONFERENCES Muse and the Marketplace (Boston, annual).

CHERRY WEINER LITERARY AGENCY

925 Oak Bluff Ct., Dacula GA 30019. (732)446-2096. **Fax:** (732)792-0506. **E-mail:** cherry8486@aol.com. **Contact:** Cherry Weiner. Represents 40 clients. 10% of clients are new/unpublished writers. Currently handles: nonfiction books 10-20%, novels 80-90%.

REPRESENTS nonfiction books, novels. **Considers these nonfiction areas:** self-help. **Considers these fiction areas:** action, adventure, contemporary issues, crime, detective, family saga, fantasy, frontier, historical, mainstream, mystery, police, psychic, romance, science fiction, supernatural, thriller, westerns.

This agency is currently not accepting new clients except by referral or by personal contact at writers' conferences. Specializes in fantasy, science fiction, westerns, mysteries (both contemporary and historical), historical novels, Native-American works, mainstream, and all genre romances.

HOW TO CONTACT Query with SASE. Prefers to read materials exclusively. Does not accept e-mail queries. Responds in 1 week to queries. Responds in 2 months to mss that I have asked for.

TERMS Agent receives 15% commission on domestic sales. Agent receives 15% commission on foreign sales. Offers written contract. Charges clients for extra copies of mss, first-class postage for author's copies of books, express mail for important documents/mss.

RECENT SALES Sold 70 titles in the last year. This agency prefers not to share information on specific sales.

TIPS "Meet agents and publishers at conferences. Establish a relationship, then get in touch with them and remind them of the meeting and conference."

THE WEINGEL-FIDEL AGENCY

310 E. 46th St., 21E, New York NY 10017. (212)599-2959. **Contact:** Loretta Weingel-Fidel. Currently handles: nonfiction books 75%, novels 25%.

Prior to opening her agency, Ms. Weingel-Fidel was a psychoeducational diagnostician.

REPRESENTS nonfiction books, novels. **Considers these nonfiction areas:** art, autobiography, biography, dance, memoirs, music, psychology, science, sociology, technology, women's issues, women's studies, investigative journalism. **Considers these fiction areas:** literary, mainstream.

This agency specializes in commercial and literary fiction and nonfiction. Actively seeking investigative journalism. Does not want to receive genre fiction, self-help, science fiction, or fantasy.

HOW TO CONTACT Accepts writers by referral only. *No unsolicited mss.*

TERMS Agent receives 15% commission on domestic sales. Agent receives 20% commission on foreign sales. Offers written contract, binding for 1 year with automatic renewal. Bills sent back to clients are all reasonable expenses, such as UPS, express mail, photocopying, etc.

TIPS "A very small, selective list enables me to work very closely with my clients to develop and nurture talent. I only take on projects and writers about which I am extremely enthusiastic."

LARRY WEISSMAN LITERARY, LLC

526 8th St., #2R, Brooklyn NY 11215. **E-mail:** lwsubmissions@gmail.com. **Contact:** Larry Weissman. Represents 35 clients. Currently handles: nonfiction books 80%, novels 10%, story collections 10%.

REPRESENTS nonfiction books, novels, short story collections. **Considers these fiction areas:** literary.

"Very interested in established journalists with bold voices. Interested in anything to do with food. Fiction has to feel 'vital' and short stories are accepted, but only if you can sell us on an idea for a novel as well." Nonfiction, including food and lifestyle, politics, pop culture, narrative, cultural/social issues, journalism. No genre fiction, poetry or children's.

HOW TO CONTACT "Send e-queries only. If you don't hear back, your project was not right for our list."

TERMS Agent receives 15% commission on domestic sales. Agent receives 20% commission on foreign sales.

WELLS ARMS LITERARY

E-mail: info@wellsarms.com. **Website:** www.wellsarms.com. **Contact:** Victoria Wells Arms. Estab. 2013.

Prior to opening her agency, Victoria was a children's book editor for Dial Books.

REPRESENTS Considers these fiction areas: juvenile, middle grade, picture books, young adult.

We focus on books for readers of all ages, and we particularly love board books, picture books, readers, chapter books, middle grade, and young adult fiction—both authors and illustrators. We do not represent to the textbook, magazine, adult romance or fine art markets.

HOW TO CONTACT E-query. Put "Query" in your e-mail subject line. No attachments.

WERNICK & PRATT AGENCY

E-mail: info@wernickpratt.com. **Website:** www.wernickpratt.com. **Contact:** Marcia Wernick; Linda Pratt. Member of AAR, SCBWI.

Prior to co-founding Wernick & Pratt Agency, Ms. Wernick worked at the Sheldon Fogelman Agency, in subsidiary rights, advancing to director of subsidiary rights; Ms. Pratt also worked at the Sheldon Fogelman Agency.

MEMBER AGENTS Marcia Wernick, Linda Pratt.

"Wernick & Pratt Agency specializes in children's books of all genres, from picture books through young adult literature and everything in between. We represent both authors and illustrators. We do not represent authors of adult books." Wants people who both write and illustrate in the picture book genre; humorous young chapter books with strong voice, and which are unique and compelling; middle grade/YA novels, both literary and commercial. No picture book mss of more than 750 words, or mood pieces; work specifically targeted to the educational market; fiction about the American Revolution, Civil War, or World War II unless it is told from a very unique perspective.

HOW TO CONTACT Submit via e-mail only. "Please indicate to which agent you are submitting." Detailed submission guidelines available on website. Responds in 6 weeks.

WHIMSY LITERARY AGENCY, LLC

49 North 8th St., G6, Brooklyn NY 11249. (212)674-7161. **E-mail:** whimsynyc@aol.com. **Website:** whimsyliteraryagency.com/. **Contact:** Jackie Meyer. Memberships include Center for Independent Publishing Advisory Board. Represents 30 clients. 20% of clients are new/unpublished writers. Currently handles: nonfiction books 100%.

Prior to becoming an agent, Ms. Meyer was with Warner Books for 19 years; Ms. Vezeris and Ms. Legette have 30 years' experience at various book publishers.

MEMBER AGENTS **Jackie Meyer**; **Olga Vezeris** (fiction and nonfiction); **Nansci LeGette**, senior associate in LA.

REPRESENTS nonfiction books. **Considers these nonfiction areas:** art, biography, business, child guidance, cooking, education, health, history, horticulture, how-to, humor, interior design, memoirs, money, New Age, popular culture, psychology, self-help, true crime, women's issues, women's studies. **Considers these fiction areas:** mainstream.

"Whimsy looks for projects that are concept- and platform-driven. We seek books that educate, inspire and entertain." Actively seeking experts in their field with good platforms.

HOW TO CONTACT Send a query letter via e-mail. Send a synopsis, bio, platform, and proposal. No snail mail submissions. Responds "quickly, but only if interested" to queries. *Does not accept unsolicited mss.* Obtains most new clients through recommendations from others, solicitations.

TERMS Agent receives 15% commission on domestic sales. Agent receives 20% commission on foreign sales. Offers written contract.

WM CLARK ASSOCIATES

186 Fifth Ave., Second Floor, New York NY 10010. (212)675-2784. **Fax:** (347)-649-9262. **E-mail:** general@wmclark.com. **Website:** www.wmclark.com. Estab. 1997. Member of AAR. 50% of clients are new/unpublished writers. Currently handles: nonfiction books 50%, novels 50%.

Prior to opening WCA, Mr. Clark was an agent at the William Morris Agency.

REPRESENTS nonfiction books, novels. **Considers these nonfiction areas:** architecture, art, autobiography, biography, cultural interests, current affairs, dance, design, ethnic, film, history, inspirational, memoirs, music, politics, popular culture, religious, science, sociology, technology, theater, translation, travel memoir, Eastern philosophy. **Considers these fiction areas:** contemporary issues, ethnic, historical, literary, mainstream, Southern fiction.

William Clark represents a wide range of titles across all formats to the publishing, motion picture, television, and new media fields on behalf of authors of first fiction and award-winning, best-selling narrative nonfiction, international authors in translation, chefs, musicians, and artists. Offering individual focus and a global presence, the agency undertakes to discover, develop, and market today's most interesting content and the talent that create it, and forge sophisticated and innovative plans for self-promotion, reliable revenue streams, and an enduring creative career. Referral partners are available to provide services including editorial consultation, media training, lecture booking, marketing support, and public relations. Agency does not respond to screenplays or screenplay pitches. It is advised that before querying you become familiar with the kinds of books we handle by browsing our Book List, which is available on our website.

HOW TO CONTACT Accepts queries via online form only at www.wmclark.com/query-form.html. We respond to all queries submitted via this form. Responds in 1-2 months to queries.

TERMS Agent receives 15% commission on domestic sales. Agent receives 20% commission on foreign sales. Offers written contract.

TIPS "WCA works on a reciprocal basis with Ed Victor Ltd. (UK) in representing select properties to the US market and vice versa. Translation rights are sold directly in the German, Italian, Spanish, Portuguese, Latin American, French, Dutch, and Scandinavian territories in association with Andrew Nurnberg Associates Ltd. (UK); through offices in China, Bulgaria, Czech Republic, Latvia, Poland, Hungary, and Russia; and through corresponding agents in Japan, Greece, Israel, Turkey, Korea, Taiwan, and Thailand."

WOLF LITERARY SERVICES, LLC

Website: wolflit.com. Estab. 2008.

MEMBER AGENTS **Kirsten Wolf** (no queries); **Adrianna Ranta** (all genres for all age groups with a penchant for edgy, dark, quirky voices, unique settings, and everyman stories told with a new spin; she loves gritty, realistic, true-to-life stories with conflicts based in the real world; women's fiction and nonfiction; accessible, pop nonfiction in science, history, and craft; and smart, fresh, genre-bending works for children); **Kate Johnson** (literary fiction, particularly character-driven stories, psychological investigations, modern-day fables, and the occasional high-concept plot; she also represents memoir, cultural history and narrative nonfiction, and loves working with journalists); **Allison Devereux** (magical realism, literary fiction, stories featuring picaresque characters, and books on art and design).

REPRESENTS **Considers these nonfiction areas:** art, crafts, creative nonfiction, history, memoirs, science, women's issues. **Considers these fiction areas:** literary, women's, young adult, magical realism.

HOW TO CONTACT To submit a project, please send a query letter along with a 50-page writing sample (for fiction) or a detailed proposal (for nonfiction) to queries@wolflit.com. Samples may be submitted as an attachment or embedded in the body of the e-mail. Responds if interested.

RECENT SALES *Hoodoo*, by Ronald Smith (Clarion); *Edible*, by Daniella Martin (Amazon Publishing); *Not a Drop to Drink*, by Mandy McGinnis (Katherine Tegen Books); *The Empire Striketh Back*, by Ian Doescher (Quirk Books).

WOLFSON LITERARY AGENCY

P.O. Box 266, New York NY 10276. **E-mail:** query@wolfsonliterary.com. **Website:** www.wolfsonliterary.com/. **Contact:** Michelle Wolfson. Estab. 2007. Adheres to AAR canon of ethics.

Prior to forming her own agency in December 2007, Ms. Wolfson spent two years with Artists & Artisans, Inc. and two years with Ralph Vicinanza, Ltd.

Actively seeking commercial fiction: young adult, mainstream, mysteries, thrillers, suspense, women's fiction, romance, practical or narrative nonfiction (particularly of interest to women).

HOW TO CONTACT E-queries only! Accepts simultaneous submissions. Responds only if interested. Positive response is generally given within 2-4 weeks. Responds in 3 months to mss. Obtains most new clients through queries or recommendations from others.

TERMS Agent receives 15% commission on domestic sales. Agent receives 25% commission on foreign sales. Offers written contract; 30-day notice must be given to terminate contract.

WRITERS CONFERENCES SDSU Writers' Conference; New Jersey Romance Writers of America Writers' Conference; American Independent Writers Conference in Washington DC.

TIPS "Be persistent."

WORDSERVE LITERARY GROUP

7061 S. University Blvd., Suite 307, Centennial CO 80122. **Website:** www.wordserveliterary.com. **Contact:** Greg Johnson. Represents 100 clients. 20% of clients are new/unpublished writers. Currently handles: nonfiction books 50%, novels 35%, juvenile books 10%, multimedia 5%.

Prior to becoming an agent in 1994, Mr. Johnson was a magazine editor and freelance writer of more than 20 books and 200 articles.

MEMBER AGENTS Greg Johnson, Alice Crider, Sarah Freese.

REPRESENTS **Considers these nonfiction areas:** biography, inspirational, memoirs, parenting, self-help.

Considers these fiction areas: historical, inspirational, mainstream, spiritual, suspense, thriller, women's.

Materials with a faith-based angle. No fantasy or sci-fi. Please do not send mss that are more than 120,000 words.

HOW TO CONTACT Please address queries to: admin@wordserveliterary.com. In the subject line, include the word "query." All queries should include the following three elements: a pitch for the book, information about you and your platform (for nonfiction) or writing background (for fiction), and the first 5 (or so) pages of the manuscript pasted into the e-mail. More submission guidelines available online. Accepts simultaneous submissions. Responds in 4 weeks to queries. Responds in 2 months to mss. Obtains most new clients through recommendations from others.

TERMS Agent receives 15% commission on domestic sales. Agent receives 10-15% commission on foreign sales. Offers written contract; up to 60-day notice must be given to terminate contract.

TIPS "We are looking for good proposals, great writing and authors willing to market their books, as appropriate. Also, we're only looking for projects with a faith element bent. See the website before submitting."

WRITERS HOUSE

21 W. 26th St., New York NY 10010. (212)685-2400. **Fax:** (212)685-1781. **Website:** www.writershouse.com. **Contact:** Michael Mejias. Estab. 1973. Member of AAR. Represents 440 clients. 50% of clients are new/unpublished writers.

MEMBER AGENTS Amy Berkower; Stephen Barr, sbarr@writershouse.com; Susan Cohen; Dan Conaway; Lisa DiMona; Susan Ginsburg; Leigh Feldman; Merrilee Heifetz; Brianne Johnson; Daniel Lazar; Simon Lipskar; Steven Malk; Jodi Reamer, Esq.; Robin Rue; Rebecca Sherman; Geri Thoma; Albert Zuckerman.

REPRESENTS nonfiction books, novels, juvenile. **Considers these nonfiction areas:** animals, art, autobiography, biography, business, child guidance, cooking, decorating, diet/nutrition, economics, film, foods, health, history, humor, interior design, juvenile nonfiction, medicine, military, money, music, parenting, psychology, satire, science, self-help, technology, theater, true crime, women's issues, women's studies. **Considers these fiction areas:** adventure, cartoon, contemporary issues, crime, detective, erotica, ethnic, family saga, fantasy, feminist, frontier, gay, hi-lo, historical, horror, humor, juvenile, literary, mainstream, middle grade, military, multicultural, mystery, New Age, occult, picture books, police, psychic, regional, romance, spiritual, sports, thriller, translation, war, women's, young adult.

This agency specializes in all types of popular fiction and nonfiction. Does not want to receive scholarly, professional, poetry, plays, or screenplays.

HOW TO CONTACT Query with SASE. Do not contact two agents here at the same time. While snail mail is OK for all agents, some agents do accept e-queries. Check the website for individual agent bios. "Please send us a query letter of no more than 2 pages, which includes your credentials, an explanation of what makes your book unique and special, and a synopsis. (If submitting to Steven Malk: Writers House, 7660 Fay Ave., #338H, La Jolla, CA 92037. Note that Malk only accepts queries on an exclusive basis.)" Accepts simultaneous submissions. Obtains most new clients through recommendations from authors and editors.

TERMS Agent receives 15% commission on domestic sales. Agent receives 20% commission on foreign sales. Offers written contract, binding for 1 year. Agency charges fees for copying mss/proposals and overseas airmail of books.

TIPS "Do not send mss. Write a compelling letter. If you do, we'll ask to see your work. Follow submission guidelines and please do not simultaneously submit your work to more than 1 Writers House agent."

WRITERS' REPRESENTATIVES, LLC

116 W. 14th St., 11th Floor, New York NY 10011-7305. **E-mail:** transom@writersreps.com. **Website:** www.writersreps.com. Represents 100 clients. Currently handles: nonfiction books 90%, novels 10%.

Prior to becoming an agent, Ms. Chu was a lawyer; Mr. Hartley worked at Simon & Schuster, Harper & Row and Cornell University Press.

MEMBER AGENTS Lynn Chu, Glen Hartley.

REPRESENTS nonfiction books, novels. **Considers these fiction areas:** literary.

Serious nonfiction and quality fiction. No motion picture or television screenplays.

HOW TO CONTACT Query with SASE. Prefers to read materials exclusively. Considers simultaneous queries, but must be informed at time of submission. Consult website section "FAQ" for detailed submission guidelines.

TERMS Agent receives 15% commission on domestic sales. Agent receives 20% commission on foreign sales.
TIPS "Always include an SASE; it will ensure a response from the agent and the return of your submitted material."

YATES & YATES

1100 Town & Country Road, Suite 1300, Orange CA 92868. (714)480-4000. **Fax:** (714)480-4001. **E-mail:** submissions@yates2.com. **Website:** www.yates2.com. Represents 60 clients.

REPRESENTS nonfiction books. **Considers these nonfiction areas:** autobiography, biography, business, current affairs, memoirs, politics, sports, religious.
RECENT SALES *No More Mondays*, by Dan Miller (Doubleday Currency).

ZACHARY SHUSTER HARMSWORTH

1776 Broadway, Suite 1405, New York NY 10019. (212)765-6900. **Fax:** (212)765-6490. **Website:** www.zshliterary.com. **Contact:** Kathleen Fleury. Alternate address: 535 Boylston St., 11th Floor, Boston MA 02116. (617)262-2400. **Fax:** (617)262-2468. Represents 125 clients. 20% of clients are new/unpublished writers. Currently handles: nonfiction books 45%, novels 45%, story collections 5%, scholarly books 5%.

"Our principals include two former publishing and entertainment lawyers, a journalist and an editor/agent. Lane Zachary was an editor at Random House before becoming an agent."

MEMBER AGENTS **Lane Zachary** (memoir, current events, history, biography and psychology); **Todd Shuster** (current affairs, biography, true-crime, popular science, adventure, politics and civil rights, history, memoir, business, health, parenting, and psychology; his fiction list is comprised primarily of literary and "crossover" commercial novels, including mysteries and thrillers); **Esmond Harmsworth** (fiction and nonfiction); **Jennifer Gates** (a range of nonfiction, as well as literary and commercial fiction and children's); **Mary Beth Chappell**; **Eve Bridburg** (fiction and nonfiction); **Janet Silver** (literary fiction and nonfiction, including memoir, biography, history, science, philosophy, and poetry); **Bridget Wagner Matzie** (nonfiction and commercial fiction); **Natasha Alexis** (literary and commercial fiction and nonfiction, YA, narrative nonfiction, pop science); **Jacob Moore** (currently looking for journalists, bloggers, academics, sci-fi/fantasy writers, playwrights, and memoirists contemplating relevant social and philosophical issues in new and creative ways); **Lana Popovic** (a wide range of both fiction and nonfiction projects); **Jane Von Mehren**.
REPRESENTS nonfiction books, novels.

Check the website for updated info.

HOW TO CONTACT *Cannot accept unsolicited submissions.* If you are invited to send material, use the online agency submission form. Obtains most new clients through recommendations from others.
TERMS Agent receives 15% commission on domestic sales. Agent receives 20% commission on foreign sales. Offers written contract, binding for 1 work only; 30-day notice must be given to terminate contract.

KAREN GANTZ ZAHLER LITERARY MANAGEMENT AND ATTORNEY AT LAW

860 Fifth Ave., Suite 7J, New York NY 10065. (212)734-3619. **E-mail:** karen@karengantzlit.com. **Website:** www.karengantzlit.com. **Contact:** Karen Gantz Zahler. Currently handles: nonfiction books 95%, novels 5%, film, TV scripts.

Prior to her current position, Ms. Gantz Zahler practiced law at two law firms, wrote two cookbooks, *Taste of New York* (Addison-Wesley) and *Superchefs* (John Wiley & Sons). She also participated in a Presidential Advisory Committee on Intellectual Property, U.S. Department of Commerce. She currently chairs Literary and Media Committee at Harmone Club NYC.

REPRESENTS nonfiction books, novels, very selective.

"We are hired for two purposes, one as lawyers to negotiate publishing agreements, option agreements and other entertainment deals, and two as literary agents to help in all aspects of the publishing field. Ms. Gantz is both a literary agent and a literary property lawyer. Thus, her firm involves themselves in all stages of a book's development, including the collaboration agreement with the writer, advice regarding the book proposal, presentations to the publisher, negotiations including the legal work for the publishing agreement and other rights to be negotiated, and work with the publisher and public relations firm so that the book gets the best possible media coverage. We do extensive manuscript reviews for a few." Actively seeking nonfiction. "We assist with speaking engagements and publicity."

HOW TO CONTACT Accepting queries and summaries by e-mail only. Check the website for complete submission information, because it is intricate and specific. Responds in 4 weeks to queries. Obtains most new clients through recommendations from others, solicitations.

RECENT SALES *Extraordinary Hearts: A Journey of Cardiac Medicine and the Human Spirit* by Dr. John Elefteriades (Berkley Books); *Transplant* by Dr. John Elefteriades (Berkley Books); *The Lost Khrushchev: A Journey into the Gulag of the Russian Mind* by Nina L. Khrushcheva (Tate Publishing); *The Magic of Math: Solving for x and Figuring Out Why* by Arthur Benjamin (Basic Books); more sales can be found online.

TIPS "Our dream client is someone who is a professional writer and a great listener. What writers can do to increase the likelihood of our retainer is to write an excellent summary and provide a great marketing plan for their proposal in an excellent presentation. Any typos or grammatical mistakes do not resonate well. If we want to review your project, we will ask you to send a copy by snail mail with an envelope and return postage enclosed. We don't call people unless we have something to report."

HELEN ZIMMERMANN LITERARY AGENCY

New Paltz NY 12561. **E-mail:** submit@ZimmAgency.com. **Website:** www.zimmermannliterary.com. **Contact:** Helen Zimmermann. Estab. 2003. Currently handles: nonfiction books 80%, other 20% fiction.

Prior to opening her agency, Ms. Zimmermann was the director of advertising and promotion at Random House and the events coordinator at an independent bookstore.

REPRESENTS Considers these nonfiction areas: diet/nutrition, health, memoirs, music, popular culture, sports, women's issues, relationships. **Considers these fiction areas:** literary.

"As an agent who has experience at both a publishing house and a bookstore, I have a keen insight for viable projects. This experience also helps me ensure every client gets published well, through the whole process." Actively seeking memoirs, pop culture, women's issues, and accessible literary fiction. Does not want to receive horror, science fiction, poetry or romance.

HOW TO CONTACT Accepts e-mail queries only. E-mail should include a short description of project and bio, whether it be fiction or nonfiction. Accepts simultaneous submissions. Responds in 2 weeks to queries. Responds in 1 month to mss. Obtains most new clients through recommendations from others, solicitations.

TERMS Agent receives 15% commission on domestic sales. Offers written contract; 30-day notice must be given to terminate contract.

WRITERS CONFERENCES BEA/Writer's Digest Books Writers' Conference; Portland, ME Writers Conference; Berkshire Writers and Readers Conference; La Jolla Writers Conference; The New School Writers Conference; Vermont Writers Conference; ASJA Conference; Books Alive! Conference; Southeast Writers Conference; Kansas Writers Conference.

RENÈE ZUCKERBROT LITERARY AGENCY

115 West 29th St., 3rd Floor, New York NY 10001. (212)967-0072. **Fax:** (212)967-0073. **E-mail:** renee@rzagency.com. **E-mail:** submissions@rzagency.com. **Website:** rzagency.com. **Contact:** Renèe Zuckerbrot. Represents 30 clients. Currently handles: 30% nonfiction and 70% fiction.

Prior to becoming an agent, Ms. Zuckerbrot worked as an editor at Doubleday as well as in the editorial department at Putnam.

REPRESENTS Considers these nonfiction areas: creative nonfiction. **Considers these fiction areas:** commercial, literary, mystery, short story collections, thriller, women's.

Literary and commercial fiction, short-story collections, mysteries, thrillers, women's fiction, slipstream/speculative, narrative nonfiction (focusing on science, history and pop culture). "Looking for writers with a unique voice." No business books, self-help, spirituality or romance. No screenplays.

HOW TO CONTACT Query by e-mail: submissions@rzagency.com. Include a synopsis, publication history and a brief personal bio. You may include a sample chapter. Responds in approximately 4-6 weeks.

TERMS Agent receives 15% commission on domestic sales. Agent receives 25% commission on foreign sales (10% to RZA; 15% to foreign rights co-agent).

CONFERENCES

Attending a writers' conference that includes agents gives you the opportunity to learn more about what agents do and to show an agent your work. Ideally, a conference should include a panel or two with a number of agents to give writers a sense of the variety of personalities and tastes of different agents.

Not all agents are alike: Some are more personable, and sometimes you simply click better with one agent versus another. When only one agent attends a conference, there is a tendency for every writer at that conference to think, "Ah, this is the agent I've been looking for!" When the number of agents attending is larger, you have a wider group from which to choose, and you may have less competition for the agent's time.

Besides including panels of agents discussing what representation means and how to go about securing it, many of these gatherings also include time—either scheduled or impromptu—to meet briefly with an agent to discuss your work.

If they're impressed with what they see and hear about your work, they will invite you to submit a query, a proposal, a few sample chapters, or possibly your entire manuscript. Some conferences even arrange for agents to review manuscripts in advance and schedule one-on-one sessions during which you can receive specific feedback or advice regarding your work. Such meetings often cost a small fee, but the input you receive is usually worth the price.

Ask writers who attend conferences and they'll tell you that, at the very least, you'll walk away with new knowledge about the industry. At the very best, you'll receive an invitation to send an agent your material!

Many writers try to make it to at least one conference a year, but cost and location can count as much as subject matter when determining which one to attend. There are conferences in almost every state and province that can provide answers to your questions about writing and the publishing industry. Conferences also connect you with a community of other writers. Such connections help you learn about the pros and cons of different agents, and they can also give you a renewed sense of purpose and direction in your own writing.

SUBHEADS

Each listing is divided into subheads to make locating specific information easier. In the first section, you'll find contact information for conference contacts. You'll also learn conference dates, specific focus, and the average number of attendees. Finally, names of agents who will be speaking or have spoken in the past are listed along with details about their availability during the conference. Calling or e-mailing a conference director to verify the names of agents in attendance is always a good idea.

> At the beginning of some listings, you will find one or more of the following symbols:
>
> - ⊕ Conference new to this addition
> - Canadian Conference
> - International Conference
>
> Find a pull-out bookmark with a key to symbols on the inside cover of this book.

Costs: Looking at the price of events, plus room and board, may help writers on a tight budget narrow their choices.

Accommodations: Here conferences list overnight accommodations and travel information. Often conferences held in hotels will reserve rooms at a discount rate and may provide a shuttle bus to and from the local airport.

Additional Information: This section includes information on conference-sponsored contests, individual meetings, the availability of brochures, and more.

ALASKA WRITERS CONFERENCE

Alaska Writers Guild, PO Box 670014, Chugiak AK 99567. **E-mail:** bahartman@me.com; alaskawriters guild.awg@gmail.com. **Website:** alaskawritersguild.com. **Contact:** Brooke Hartman. Annual event held in the fall—usually September. Duration: 2 days. There are many workshops and instructional tracks of courses. This event sometimes teams up with SCBWI and Alaska Pacific University to offer courses at the event. Several literary agents are in attendance each year to hear pitches and meet writers.

COSTS 2013 costs: Up to $275, though discounts for different memberships brings down that number.

ACCOMMODATIONS Crowne Plaza Hotel in Anchorage. Conference room rates available. Several scholarships are available (see the website).

ALGONKIAN FIVE DAY NOVEL CAMP

2020 Pennsylvania Ave. NW, Suite 443, Washington DC 20006. **E-mail:** algonkian@webdelsol.com. **Website:** fwwriters.algonkianconferences.com. Conference duration: 5 days. Average attendance: 12 students maximum per workshop. "During 45+ hours of actual workshop time, students will engage in those rigorous narrative and complication/plot exercises necessary to produce a publishable manuscript. Genres we work with include general commercial fiction, literary fiction, serious and light women's fiction, mystery/cozy/thriller, SF/F, young adult, and memoir/narrative nonfiction. The three areas of workshop emphasis will be PREMISE, PLATFORM, and EXECUTION. Site: "The Algonkian Park is located 30 miles from Washington, D.C. A good map and directions can be found here. It is 12 miles from Dulles International Airport (the perfect place to fly into—cab fares from Dulles to Algonkian are about $25). The cottages are fully furnished with TV, phones, linens, dishes, central air and heat. All cottages feature fireplaces, decks with grills, equipped kitchens, cathedral ceilings, and expansive riverside views of the Potomac. Participants each have their own room in the cottage. The address of the Algonkian Park Management headquarters is 47001 Fairway Drive, Sterling, Virginia, and their phone number is 703-450-4655. If you have any questions about the cottages or facilities, ask for Lawan, the manager."

AMERICAN CHRISTIAN WRITERS CONFERENCES

P.O. Box 110390, Nashville TN 37222-0390. (800)219-7483. **Fax:** (615)834-7736. **E-mail:** acwriters@aol.com. **Website:** www.acwriters.com. **Contact:** Reg Forder, director. Estab. 1981. ACW hosts dozens of annual two-day writers conferences and mentoring retreats across America taught by editors and professional freelance writers. These events provide excellent instruction, networking opportunities, and valuable one-on-one time with editors. Annual conferences promoting all forms of Christian writing (fiction, nonfiction, scriptwriting). Conferences are held between March and November during each year.

COSTS Costs vary based on conference. Prices also depend on whether it is a conference or a mentoring retreat.

ACCOMMODATIONS Special rates are available at the host hotel (usually a major chain like Holiday Inn).

ADDITIONAL INFORMATION Send an SASE for conference brochures/guidelines.

ANTIOCH WRITERS' WORKSHOP

c/o Antioch University Midwest, 900 Dayton St., Yellow Springs OH 45387. (937)769-1803. **E-mail:** info@antiochwritersworkshop.com. **Website:** www.antiochwritersworkshop.com. **Contact:** Sharon Short, director. Estab. 1986. Average attendance: 80. Programs are offered year-round; see the website for details. The dates of the 2014 conference are July 12-18. Workshop concentration: fiction, poetry, personal essay, memoir. Workshop located at Antioch University Midwest in the Village of Yellow Springs. 2014 summer program keynoter and Sunday morning craft class leader is Andre Dubus III. Faculty for morning classes and afternoon seminars through rest of the week include Hallie Ephron, Marly Youmans, Gayle Brandeis, Tara Ison, Mike Mullin, and many other authors as well as visiting literary agents. Writers of all levels (beginner to advanced) of fiction, memoir, personal essay, and poetry are warmly welcomed to discover their next steps on their writing paths—whether that's developing craft or preparing to submit for publication. An agent and an editor will be speaking and available for meetings with attendees.

COSTS (registration fee plus tuition) Full week: $735, non-local, first time attendees; $675, alumni/locals; $575 for Ohio College/University students and faculty. Optional ms critique is $75[$85] for Full Week attendees. A la carte: $125 [$150], Saturday Seminar; $375, Morning Only classes; $375, Afternoon Only Focus on Form seminar.

ACCOMMODATIONS Accommodations are available at local hotels and bed & breakfasts.

ART WORKSHOPS IN GUATEMALA

4758 Lyndale Ave. S, Minneapolis MN 55419-5304. (612)825-0747. **E-mail:** info@artguat.org. **Website:** www.artguat.org. **Contact:** Liza Fourre, director. Estab. 1995. Annual. Workshops held year-round. Maximim class size: 10 students per class.

COSTS See website. It includes tuition, lodging, breakfast, ground transportation.

ACCOMMODATIONS All transportation and accommodations included in price of conference.

ADDITIONAL INFORMATION Conference information available now. For brochure/guidelines visit website, e-mail or call. Accepts inquiries by e-mail, phone.

ASPEN SUMMER WORDS LITERARY FESTIVAL & WRITING RETREAT

Aspen Writers' Foundation, 110 E. Hallam St., #116, Aspen CO 81611. (970)925-3122. **Fax:** (970)925-5700. **E-mail:** info@aspenwriters.org. **Website:** www.aspenwriters.org. **Contact:** Natalie Lacy, programs coordinator. Estab. 1976. 2014 dates: June 14-18. ASW is one part laboratory and one part theater. It is comprised of two tracks—the Writing Retreat and the Literary Festival—which approach the written word from different, yet complementary angles. The Retreat features introductory and intensive workshops with some of the nation's most notable writing instructors and includes literature appreciation symposia and professional consultations with literary agents and editors. The Writing Retreat supports writers in developing their craft by providing a winning combination of inspiration, skills, community, and opportunity. The Literary Festival is a booklover's bliss, where the written word takes center stage. Since 2005, each edition of the Festival has celebrated a particular literary heritage and culture by honoring the stories and storytellers of a specific region. Annual conference held the fourth week of June. Conference duration: 5 days. Average attendance: 150 at writing retreat; 300+ at literary festival.

COSTS Check website each year for updates.

ACCOMMODATIONS Discount lodging at the conference site will be available. 2014 rates to be announced (see website). Free shuttle around town.

⊕ ATLANTA WRITERS CONFERENCE

E-mail: awconference@gmail.com. **E-mail:** gjweinstein@yahoo.com. **Website:** atlantawritersconference.com. **Contact:** George Weinstein. The Atlanta Writers Conference happens twice a year (every 6 months) and invites several agents, editors and authors each time. There are instructional sessions, and time to pitch professionals.

ACCOMMODATIONS Westin Airport Atlanta Hotel.

ADDITIONAL INFORMATION There is a free shuttle that runs between the airport and the hotel.

BALTIMORE COMIC-CON

Baltimore Convention Center, One West Pratt St., Baltimore MD 21201. (410)526-7410. **E-mail:** general@baltimorecomiccon.com. **Website:** www.baltimorecomiccon.com. **Contact:** Marc Nathan. Estab. 1999. Annual. September 5-7, 2014. Conference "promoting the wonderful world of comics to as many people as possible." The Baltimore Comic-Con welcomes the return of The Harvey Awards: "The Harvey Awards are one of the comic book industry's oldest and most respected awards. The Harveys recognize outstanding achievements in over 20 categories, ranging from Best Artist to The Hero Initiative Lifetime Achievement Award. They are the only industry awards both nominated by and selected by the full body of comic book professionals."

ACCOMMODATIONS Does not offer overnight accommodations. Provides list of area hotels or lodging options.

ADDITIONAL INFORMATION For brochure, visit website.

BALTIMORE WRITERS' CONFERENCE

English Department, Liberal Arts Building, Towson University, 8000 York Rd., Towson MD 21252. (410)704-3695. **E-mail:** prwr@towson.edu. **Website:** baltimorewritersconference.org. Estab. 1994. "Annual conference held in November at Towson University. Conference duration: 1 day. Average attendance: 150-200. Covers all areas of writing and getting published. Held at Towson University. Session topics include fiction, nonfiction, poetry, magazine and journals, agents and publishers. Sign up the day of the conference for quick critiques to improve your stories, essays, and poems."

COSTS 2013 costs: $75-95 (includes all-day conference, lunch and reception). Student special rate of $35 before mid-October, $50 thereafter.

ACCOMMODATIONS Hotels are close by, if required.

ADDITIONAL INFORMATION Writers may register through the BWA website. Send inquiries via e-mail.

BAY TO OCEAN WRITERS' CONFERENCE

P.O. Box 544, St. Michaels MD 21663. (443)786-4536. **E-mail:** info@baytoocean.com. **Website:** www.baytoocean.com. Estab. 1998. Contacts include Diane Marquette, Mala Burt, Judy Reveal (coordinators).

COSTS Adults $155, students $55. A paid manuscript review is also available—details on website. Includes continental breakfast and networking lunch.

ADDITIONAL INFORMATION Mail-in registration form available on website in December prior to the conference. Pre-registration is required, no registration at door. Conference usually sells out one month in advance. Conference is for all levels of writers.

BIG SUR WRITING WORKSHOP

Henry Miller Library, Highway One, Big Sur CA 93920. (831)667-2574. **Website:** bigsurwriting.wordpress.com. Annual workshops focusing on children's and young adult writing (picture books, middle grade, and young adult). (2014 dates: both March 7-9 and Dec. 5-7.) Workshop held in Big Sur Lodge in Pfeiffer State Park. Cost of workshop: $770; included meals, lodging, workshop, Saturday evening reception; $600 if lodging not needed. www.henrymiller.org. This event is helmed by the literary agents of the Andrea Brown Literary Agency, which is the most successful agency nationwide in selling kids books. All attendees meet with at least 2 faculty members, so work is critiqued.

BLOCKBUSTER PLOT INTENSIVE WRITING WORKSHOPS (SANTA CRUZ)

Santa Cruz CA **E-mail:** contact@blockbusterplots.com. **Website:** www.blockbusterplots.com. **Contact:** Martha Alderson M.A. (also known as the Plot Whisperer), instructor. Estab. 2000. Held 4 times per year. Conference duration: 2 days. Average attendance: 20. Workshop is intended to help writers create an action, character, and thematic plotline for a screenplay, memoir, short story, novel, or creative nonfiction. Site: Conference hall.

COSTS $95 per day.

ACCOMMODATIONS Provides list of area hotels and lodging options.

ADDITIONAL INFORMATION Brochures available by e-mail or on website. Accepts inquiries by e-mail.

BLOODY WORDS MYSTERY CONFERENCE

E-mail: 2014.bloodywords.com/contact. **E-mail:** chair@bloodywords.com. **Website:** www.2014.bloodywords.com. **Contact:** Cheryl Freedman, chair. Estab. 1999. 2014 info: June 6-8 in Toronto. Theme: Danse Macabre: Historical Mysteries and the Dance of Death. "This is a conference for both readers and writers of mysteries, the only one of its kind in Canada. Programming includes presentations by experts in forensics, criminology, and publishing; panels with authors discussing a range of topics; workshops; Friday night special event; and more. See About Us on our website for details."

COSTS $190 Canadian (includes the opening reception, special event and banquet, all panels, readings, dealers' room, workshops, chance to meet with an agent, and more).

ACCOMMODATIONS Offers block of rooms at the Hyatt Regency on King. Check website for details.

ADDITIONAL INFORMATION Sponsors short mystery story contest (blind judging)—5,000 word limit; judges are experienced editors of anthologies; fee is $5 (entrants must be registered for conference). Also sponsors The Bony Blithe Award for light mysteries; see website for details. Conference information is available now on our website. Agents and editors participate in conference.

BLUE RIDGE CHRISTIAN "AUTUMN IN THE MOUNTAINS" NOVELISTS RETREAT

(800)588-7222. **E-mail:** ylehman@bellsouth.net. **Website:** www.lifeway.com/novelretreat. **Contact:** Yvonne Lehman, director. Estab. 2007. Annual retreat held in October at Ridgecrest/LifeWay Conference Center near Asheville NC. (2014 dates: October 19-22, 2014.) For beginning and advanced novelists. Site: LifeWay/Ridgecrest Conference Center, 20 miles east of Asheville, NC. Faculty: Yvonne Lehman (director, over 50 novels, editor Lighthouse Publishing of Carolinas), Lynette Eason (best-selling suspense, 20 books), Ann Tatlock (two-time Christy winner), Diana Flegal (Hartline Literary Agent), Edie Melson (novelist, social media expert), Ron & Janet Benrey (Mystery/suspense, Greenbrier publishers/editors).

COSTS Before April 1 tuition: $275. After April 1: $325. Lodging $69-$89 per night. To register: 1-800-588-7222.

BOOKS-IN-PROGRESS CONFERENCE

Carnegie Center for Literacy and Learning, 251 West Second Street, Lexington KY 40507. (859)254-4175. **E-mail:** ccll1@carnegiecenterlex.org; lwhitaker@carnegiecenterlex.org. **Website:** carnegiecenterlex.org/events/books-in-progress-conference/. **Contact:** Laura Whitaker. Estab. 2010. This is an annual writing conference at the Carnegie Center for Literacy and Learning in Lexington, KY. "The conference will offer writing and publishing workshops and includes a keynote presentation." Literary agents are flown in to meet with writers and hear pitches. Website is updated several months prior to each annual event.

COSTS As of 2013, costs were $175.

ACCOMMODATIONS Several area hotels are nearby.

BOOMING GROUND ONLINE WRITERS STUDIO

Buch E-462, 1866 Main Mall, UBC, Vancouver BC V6T 1Z1 Canada. **Fax:** (604)648-8848. **E-mail:** contact@boomingground.com. **Website:** www.boomingground.com. **Contact:** Robin Evans, director. Writer mentorships geared toward beginner, intermediate, and advanced levels in novel, short fiction, poetry, nonfiction, and children's writing, and more. **Open to students.** Online mentorship program—students work for 6 months with a mentor by e-mail, allowing up to 120-240 pages of material to be created. Program cost: $500 (Canadian). Site: Online and by e-mail.

BREAD LOAF IN SICILY WRITERS' CONFERENCE

Middlebury College, Middlebury VT 05753. (802)443-5286. **Fax:** (802)443-2087. **E-mail:** ncargill@middlebury.edu; BLSICILY@middlebury.edu. **Website:** www.middlebury.edu/blwc/SICILY. **Contact:** Michael Collier, Director. Estab. 2011. Annual conference held in September. Conference duration: 7 days. Offers workshops for fiction, nonfiction, and poetry. Agents and editors will be in attendance. 2014 dates: Sept. 21-27. Average attendance: 32.

COSTS $2,790—includes tuition, housing.

ACCOMMODATIONS Hotel Villa San Giovanni in Erice, Sicily (western coast of the island).

BREAD LOAF ORION ENVIRONMENTAL WRITERS' CONFERENCE

Middlebury College, Middlebury VT 05753. (802)443-5286. **Fax:** (802)443-2087. **E-mail:** ncargill@middlebury.edu; BLORION@middlebury.edu. **Website:** www.middlebury.edu/blwc/BLOrion. **Contact:** Michael Collier, Director. Estab. 2014. Annual conference held in June. Conference duration: 7 days. Offers workshops for fiction, nonfiction, and poetry. Agents and editors will be in attendance. 2014 dates: June 9-15. Average attendance: 60.

COSTS $1,995—includes tuition, housing.

ACCOMMODATIONS Mountain campus of Middlebury College.

BREAD LOAF WRITERS' CONFERENCE

Middlebury College, Middlebury College, Middlebury VT 05753. (802)443-5286. **Fax:** (802)443-2087. **E-mail:** ncargill@middlebury.edu. **E-mail:** blwc@middlebury.edu. **Website:** www.middlebury.edu/blwc. **Contact:** Michael Collier, Director. Estab. 1926. Annual conference held in late August. Conference duration: 10 days. Offers workshops for fiction, nonfiction, and poetry. Agents and editors will be in attendance.

COSTS $2,935 (includes tuition, housing).

ACCOMMODATIONS Bread Loaf Campus in Ripton, Vermont.

ADDITIONAL INFORMATION 2014 Conference Dates: August 13-23. Location: Mountain campus of Middlebury College. Average attendance: 230.

THE BUSINESS OF PET WRITING CONFERENCE

The Pet Socialite, Prince Street Station, PO Box 398, New York NY 10012. (212)631-3648. **E-mail:** info@petwritingconference.com. **Website:** www.petwritingconference.com. **Contact:** Charlotte Reed, director. Estab. 2008. Conference duration: 1 day. Next workshop held spring 2014. Average attendance: 100. Annual conference caters to authors and journalists with interest in writing about animals. Offers seminars and workshops that "help pet writers increase their visibility with better blogging, column writing, and hosting internet radio shows; learning more about narrative and creative nonfiction; building their freelance portfolio with newspaper, magazine, and blog clips; and creating successful book marketing campaigns. Offers opportunity to meet with two top agents and editors on an individualized basis. Also welcomes a variety of notable veterinarians and prominent representatives from the pet food industry who are eager to assist pet writers with their research, book and article ideas, contact information, additional educational opportunities, and access to materials (studies, reports, press releases, newsletters, etc). Featured agents have included Kate Epstein, Jeffrey Kleinman, and Meredith Hays.

COSTS Varies by year. 2014 costs not yet clear.

ADDITIONAL INFORMATION Brochures and guidelines available on website.

BYRON BAY WRITERS FESTIVAL

Northern Rivers Writers' Centre, P.O. Box 1846, 69 Johnson St., Byron Bay NSW 2481 Australia. 040755-2441. **E-mail:** jeni@nrwc.org.au. **Website:** www.byronbaywritersfestival.com. **Contact:** Jeni Caffin, director. Estab. 1997. Annual festival held the first weekend in August at Byron's Bay Belongil Fields. Festival duration: 3 days. Celebrate and reflect with over 100 of the finest writers from Australia and overseas. Workshops, panel discussions, and literary breakfasts, lunches, and dinners will also be offered. The Byron Bay Writers Festival is organised by the staff and Committee of the Northern Rivers Writers' Centre, a member-based organisation receiving core funding from Arts NSW.

COSTS See costs online under Tickets. Early bird, NRWC members and students, kids.

ADDITIONAL INFORMATION "2014 Festival dates are August 1-3 with workshops beginning July 28 and discounted Early Bird passes are on sale from April 4 at our website or 02 6685 6262. Full program on sale June 9."

CALIFORNIA CRIME WRITERS CONFERENCE

Co-sponsored by Sisters in Crime/Los Angeles and the Southern California Chapter of Mystery Writers of America, **E-mail:** sistersincrimela@gmail.com. **Website:** www.ccwconference.org. Estab. 1995. Biennial. Conference held in June. Average attendance: 200. Two-day conference on mystery and crime writing. Offers craft, forensic and career-buildings sessions, 2 keynote speakers, author, editor, and agent panels and book signings. Breakfast and lunch both days included.

ADDITIONAL INFORMATION Conference information is available at www.ccwconference.org.

CAPE COD WRITERS CENTER ANNUAL CONFERENCE

P.O. Box 408, Osterville MA 02655. **E-mail:** writers@capecodwriterscenter.org. **Website:** www.capecodwriterscenter.org. **Contact:** Nancy Rubin Stuart, executive director. Duration: 3 days; first week in August. Offers workshops in fiction, commercial fiction, nonfiction, poetry, writing for children, memoir, pitching your book, screenwriting, digital communications, getting published, ms evaluation, mentoring sessions with faculty. Held at Resort and Conference Center of Hyannis, Hyannis, MA.

COSTS Vary, depending on the number of courses selected.

CAPON SPRINGS WRITERS' WORKSHOP

2836 Westbrook Drive, Cincinnati OH 45211-0627. (513)481-9884. **E-mail:** beckcomm@fuse.net. Estab. 2000. No conference scheduled for 2014. There is a tentative 2015 event; check the website often for updates. Conference duration: 3 days. Covers fiction, creative nonfiction, and publishing basics. Conference is held at Capon Springs and Farms Resort, a secluded 5,000-acre mountain resort in West Virginia.

COSTS Check in 2015.

ACCOMMODATIONS Facility has swimming, hiking, fishing, tennis, badminton, volleyball, basketball, ping pong, etc. A 9-hole golf course is available for an additional fee.

ADDITIONAL INFORMATION Brochures available for SASE. Inquire via e-mail.

CELEBRATION OF SOUTHERN LITERATURE

Southern Lit Alliance, 3069 S. Broad St., Suite 2, Chattanooga TN 37408-3056. (423)267-1218. **Fax:** (866)483-6831. **E-mail:** srobinson@southernlitalliance.org. **Website:** www.southernlitalliance.org. **Contact:** Susan Robinson. "The Celebration of Southern Literature stands out because of its unique collaboration with the Fellowship of Southern Writers, an organization founded by towering literary figures like Eudora Welty, Cleanth Brooks, Walker Percy, and Robert Penn Warren to recognize and encourage literature in the South. The 2015 celebration marked 26 years since the Fellowship selected Chattanooga for its headquarters and chose to collaborate with the Celebration of Southern Literature. More than 50 members of the Fellowship will participate in the 2015 event, discussing hot topics and reading from their latest works. The Fellowship will also award 11 literary prizes and induct new members, making this event the place to discover up-and-coming voices in Southern literature. The Southern Lit Alliance's Celebration of Southern Literature attracts more than 1,000 readers and writers from all over the U.S. It strives to maintain an informal atmosphere where conversations will thrive, inspired by a common passion for the written word. The Southern Lit Alliance (formerly The Arts & Education Council) started as 1 of 12 pilot agencies founded by a Ford Foundation grant in 1952. The Alliance is the only organization of the 12 still in existence. The Southern Lit Alliance celebrates Southern writers and readers through community education and innovative literary arts experiences."

⊕ CHICAGO WRITERS CONFERENCE

E-mail: ines@chicagowritersconference.org; mare@chicagowritersconference.org. **E-mail:** ines@chicagowritersconference.org; mare@chicagowritersconference.org. **Website:** chicagowritersconference.org. **Contact:** Mare Swallow. Estab. 2011. This conference happens every year in the fall. 2014 dates: Oct 24-26. Find them on Twitter at @ChiWritersConf. The conference brings together a variety of publishing professionals (agents, editors, authors) and brings together several Chicago literary, writing, and bookselling groups.

CLARION WEST WRITERS WORKSHOP

P.O. Box 31264, Seattle WA 98103-1264. (206)322-9083. **E-mail:** info@clarionwest.org. **Website:** www.clarionwest.org. "Contact us through our webform." **Contact:** Nelle Graham, workshop director. Clarion West is an intensive 6-week workshop for writers preparing for professional careers in science fiction and fantasy, held annually in Seattle WA. Usually goes from mid-June through end of July. Conference duration: 6 weeks. Average attendance: 18. Held near the University of Washington. Deadline for applications is March 1. Instructors are well-known writers and editors in the field.

COSTS $3,600 (for tuition, housing, most meals). Limited scholarships are available based on financial need.

ACCOMMODATIONS Workshop tuition, dormitory housing and most meals: $3,600. Students stay on-site in workshop housing at one of the University of Washington's sorority houses. "Students write their own stories every week while preparing critiques of all the other students' work for classroom sessions. This gives participants a more focused, professional approach to their writing. The core of the workshop remains speculative fiction, and short stories (not novels) are the focus." Conference information available in Fall. For brochure/guidelines send SASE, visit website, e-mail or call. Accepts inquiries by e-mail, phone, SASE. Limited scholarships are available, based on financial need. Students must submit 20-30 pages of ms with 4-page biography and $40 fee ($30 if received prior to February 10) for applications sent by mail or e-mail to qualify for admission.

ADDITIONAL INFORMATION This is a critique-based workshop. Students are encouraged to write a story every week; the critique of student material produced at the workshop forms the principal activity of the workshop. Students and instructors critique mss as a group. Conference guidelines are available for an SASE. Visit the website for updates and complete details.

CLARKSVILLE WRITERS CONFERENCE

1123 Madison St., Clarksville TN 37040. (931)551-8870. **E-mail:** artsandheritage@cdelightband.net; burawac@apsu.edu. **E-mail:** artsandheritage@cdelightband.net; burawac@apsu.edu. **Website:** www.artsandheritage.us/writers/. **Contact:** Ellen Kanervo. Annual conference held in the summer. The conference features a variety of presentations on fiction, nonfiction and more. Past attendees include: Darnell Arnoult, Earl S. Braggs, Christopher Burawa, Susan Gregg Gilmore, James & Lynda O'Connor, Katharine Sands, George Singleton, Bernis Terhune, p.m. terrell. Our presentations and workshops are valuable to writers and interesting to readers. This fun, affordable, and talent-laden conference is presented at Austin Peay State University and the Clarksville Country Club.

COSTS Costs available online; prices vary depending on how long attendees stay and if they attend the banquet dinner.

ADDITIONAL INFORMATION Multiple literary agents are flown in to the event every year to meet with writers and take pitches.

CONFERENCE FOR WRITERS & ILLUSTRATORS OF CHILDREN'S BOOKS

Book Passage, 51 Tamal Vista Blvd., Corte Madera CA 94925. (415)927-0960, ext. 239. **E-mail:** bpconferences@bookpassage.com. **Website:** www.bookpassage.com. Contact Kathryn Petrocelli, conference coordinator. Writer and illustrator conference geared toward beginner and intermediate levels. Sessions cover such topics as the nuts and bolts of writing and illustrating, publisher's spotlight, market trends, developing characters/finding voice in your writing, and the author/agent relationship. Four-day conference held each summer. Includes opening night dinner, 3 lunches and a closing reception.

CRESTED BUTTE WRITERS CONFERENCE

P.O. Box 1361, Crested Butte CO 81224. **E-mail:** coordinator@conf.crestedbuttewriters.org. **Website:** www.crestedbuttewriters.org/conf.php. **Contact:** Barbara Crawford or Theresa Rizzo, co-coordinators. Estab. 2006.

COSTS $330 nonmembers; $300 members; $297 Early Bird; The Sandy Writing Contest Finalist $280; and groups of 5 or more $280.

ACCOMMODATIONS The conference is held at The Elevation Hotel, located at the Crested Butte Mountain Resort at the base of the ski mountain (Mt. Crested Butte, CO). The quaint historic town lies nestled in a stunning mountain valley 3 short miles from the resort area of Mt. Crested Butte. A free bus runs frequently between the 2 towns. The closest airport is 30 miles away, in Gunnison CO. Our website lists 3 lodging options besides rooms at the event facility. All condos, motels and hotel options offer special conference rates. No special travel arrangements are made through the conference; however, information for car rental from Gunnison airport or the Alpine Express shuttle is listed on the conference FAQ page.

ADDITIONAL INFORMATION "Our conference workshops address a wide variety of writing craft and business. Our most popular workshop is Our First Pages Readings—with a twist. Agents and editors read opening pages volunteered by attendees—with a few best selling authors' openings mixed in. Think the A/E can identify the bestsellers? Not so much. Each year one of our attendees has been mistaken for a bestseller and obviously garnered requests from some on the panel. Agents attending: Carlie Webber—CK Webber Associates and TBDs. The agents will be speaking and available for meetings with attendees through our Pitch and Pages system. Editors attending: Christian Trimmer, senior editor at Disney Hyperion Books, and Jessica Williams of Harper Collins. Award-winning authors: Mark Coker, CEO of Smashwords; Kristen Lamb, social media guru, Kim Killion, book cover designer; Jennifer Jakes; Sandra Kerns; and Annette Elton. Writers may request additional information by e-mail."

DESERT DREAMS CONFERENCE: REALIZING THE DREAM

P.O. Box 27407, Tempe AZ 85285. **E-mail:** desertdreams@desertroserwa.org; desertdreamsconference@gmail.com. **Website:** www.desertroserwa.org. **Contact:** Conference coordinator. Estab. 1986. Last conference held April 2012. Next conference April 4-6, 2014. Average attendance: 250. Desert Dreams Writers' Conference provides authors of all skill levels, from beginner to multi-published, with the tools necessary to take their writing to the next level. Sessions will include general writing, career development, genre-specific, agent/publisher spotlights, as well as an agent/editor panel. There will also be one-on-one appointments with editors or agents, a book signing, and keynote addresses. Site: Tempe Mission Palms Resort & Hotel, Tempe, AZ.

COSTS Vary each year; approximately $200-235 for full conference.

ACCOMMODATIONS Hotels may vary for each conference; it is always a resort location in the Phoenix area.

ADDITIONAL INFORMATION Sponsors contest as part of conference, open to conference attendees only. For brochure, inquiries, contact by e-mail, phone, fax, mail or visit website. Agents and editors participate in conference.

⊕ DETROIT WORKING WRITERS ANNUAL WRITERS CONFERENCE

Detroit Working Writers, Box 82395, Rochester MI 48308. **E-mail:** conference@detworkingwriters.org. **Website:** dww-writers-conference.org/. Estab. 1961. 2014 dates: May 17. The theme in 2014 is "A Writer's Worth." Location is the main branch of the Clinton-Macomb Public Library in Clinton Twp, MI. Conference is one day, with breakfast, luncheon and keynote speaker, 4 breakout sessions, and three choices of workshop session. Much more info available online. Detroit Working Writers was founded on June 5, 1900, as the Detroit Press Club, The City of Detroit's first press club. Today, more than a century later, it is a 501 (c)(6) organization, and the State of Michigan's oldest writer's organization. In addition to the Conference, DWW hold quarterly workshops on craft-related topics such as the elements of poetry, finding the perfect agent, and memoir development.

COSTS $60-150, depending on early bird registration and membership status within the organization.

ERMA BOMBECK WRITERS WORKSHOP

University of Dayton, 300 College Park, Dayton OH 45469. **E-mail:** erma@udayton.edu. **Website:** humorwriters.org. **Contact:** Teri Rizvi. This is a specialized writing conference for writers of humor (books, articles, essays, film/TV). It happens every two years. The 2014 conference is from April 10-12. The Bombeck Workshop is the only one in the country devoted to both humor and human interest writing. Through the workshop, the University of Dayton and the Bombeck family honor one of America's most celebrated storytellers and humorists. Over the past decade, the workshop has attracted such household names as Dave Barry, Art Buchwald, Nancy Cartwright, Don Novello, Garrison Keillor, Gail Collins, Connie Schultz, Adriana Trigiani and Alan Zweibel. The workshop draws approximately 350 writers from around the country and typically sells out very quickly, so don't wait once registration opens.

FESTIVAL OF FAITH AND WRITING

Department of English, Calvin College, 1795 Knollcrest Circle SE, Grand Rapids MI 49546. (616)526-6770. **E-mail:** ffw@calvin.edu. **Website:** festival.calvin.edu. Estab. 1990. Biennial festival held in April. Conference duration: 3 days. The festival brings together writers, editors, publishers, musicians, artists, and readers to discuss and celebrate insightful writing that explores issues of faith. Focuses on fiction, nonfiction, memoir, poetry, drama, children's, young adult, academic, film, and songwriting. Past speakers have included Katherine Paterson, Wally Lamb, Eugene Patterson, Marilynne Robinson, Joyce Carol Oates, Salman Rushdie and Michael Chabon. Agents and editors attend the festival.

COSTS Consult festival website.

ACCOMMODATIONS Shuttles are available to and from local hotels. Shuttles are also available for overflow parking lots. A list of hotels with special rates for conference attendees is available on the festival website. High school and college students can arrange on-campus lodging by e-mail.

ADDITIONAL INFORMATION Online registration is open up to approx. 1 month before the event. (2014 online registration is open through March 14.) Accepts inquiries by e-mail and phone. Next festival is April 10-12, 2014.

FLATHEAD RIVER WRITERS CONFERENCE

P.O. Box 7711, Kalispeil MT 59904-7711. (406)881-4066. **E-mail:** answers@authorsoftheflathead.org. **Website:** www.authorsoftheflathead.org/conference.asp. Estab. 1990. Two-day conference packed with energizing speakers. After a focus on publishing the past two years, this year's focus is on writing, getting your manuscripts honed and ready for your readers. Highlights include two literary agents who will review 12 manuscripts one-on-one with the first 24 paid attendees requesting this opportunity, a synopsis writing workshop, a screenwriting workshop, poetry, and more.

COSTS Check the website for updated cost information.

ACCOMMODATIONS Rooms are available at a discounted rate.

ADDITIONAL INFORMATION Watch website for additional speakers and other details. Register early as seating is limited.

FLORIDA CHRISTIAN WRITERS CONFERENCE

530 Lake Kathryn Circle, Casselberry FL 32707. (386)295-3902. **E-mail:** FloridaChristianWritersConf@gmail.com. **Website:** floridacwc.net. **Contact:** Eva Marie Everson, Mark Hancock. Estab. 1988. Annual conference held in February/March. Conference duration: 4 days. Average attendance: Limited to 250 people. "The Florida Christian Writers Conference 2014 meets under the stately oaks of Lake Yale Conference Center near Leesburg, Florida. The conference is designed to meet the needs of beginning writers to published authors. This is your opportunity to learn more about the publishing industry, to build your platform, and to follow God's leading to publish the message He has given you. We offer 90 one-hour workshops and 9 or more six-hour classes."

COSTS $675 (includes tuition, meals).

ACCOMMODATIONS We provide a shuttle from the Orlando airport. $725/double occupancy; $950/single occupancy.

ADDITIONAL INFORMATION "Each writer may submit 2 works for critique. We have specialists in every area of writing. Brochures/guidelines are available online or for a SASE."

FUN IN THE SUN

Florida Romance Writers, P.O. Box 550562, Fort Lauderdale FL 33355. **E-mail:** FRWfuninthesun@yahoo.

com. **Website:** frwfuninthesunmain.blogspot.com. Estab. 1986. Biannual conference held in January/February on a cruise ship. (2015 details: Jan. 22-26, on the Liberty of the Seas by Royal Carribean.) Features intensive workshops on the craft of writing taught by an array of published authors; a marketing and publicity boot camp; an open-to-the-public book signing for all attending published authors; one-on-one editor/agent pitch sessions; and special events.

COSTS See website for updates, depending on membership status and registration date. Early bird discounts is before Feb. 14, 2014.

ADDITIONAL INFORMATION Ours is the longest-running conference of any RWA chapter. Brochures/registration are available online, by e-mail, or for a SASE.

GENEVA WRITERS CONFERENCE

Geneva Writers Group, Switzerland. **E-mail:** info@GenevaWritersGroup.org. **Website:** www.genevawritersgroup.org. Estab. 1993. Biennial conference (even years) held at Webster University in Bellevue/Geneva, Switzerland. (The 2014 dates were Jan. 31–Feb. 2.) Conference duration: 2.5 days, welcoming more than 200 writers from around the world. Speakers and presenters have included Peter Ho Davies, Jane Alison, Russell Celyn Jones, Patricia Hampl, Robert Root, Brett Lott, Dinty W. Moore, Naomi Shihab Nye, Jo Shapcott, Wallis Wilde Menozzi, Susan Tiberghien, Jane Dystel, Laura Longrigg, and Colin Harrison.

GREAT LAKES WRITERS FESTIVAL

Lakeland College, P.O. Box 359, Sheboygan WI 53082-0359. **E-mail:** elderk@lakeland.edu. **Website:** www.greatlakeswritersfestival.org. Estab. 1991. Annual. Last conference held November 7-8, 2013. Conference duration: 2 days. "Festival celebrates the writing of poetry, fiction, and creative nonfiction." Site: "Lakeland College is a small, 4-year liberal arts college of 235 acres, a beautiful campus in a rural setting, founded in 1862." No themes or panels; just readings and workshops. 2013 faculty included Nick Lantz and Allyson Goldin Loomis.

COSTS Free and open to the public. Participants may purchase meals and must arrange for their own lodging.

ACCOMMODATIONS Does not offer overnight accommodations. Provides list of area hotels or lodging options.

ADDITIONAL INFORMATION All participants who would like to have their writing considered as an object for discussion during the festival workshops should submit it to Karl Elder electronically by October 15. Participants may submit material for workshops in 1 genre only (poetry, fiction, or creative nonfiction). Sponsors contest. Contest entries must contain the writer's name and address on a separate title page, typed, and be submitted as clear, hard copy on Friday at the festival registration table. Entries may be in each of 3 genres per participant, yet only 1 poem, 1 story, and/or 1nonfiction piece may be entered. There are 2 categories—high school students on 1 hand, all others on the other—of cash awards for first place in each of the 3 genres. The judges reserve the right to decline to award a prize in 1 or more of the genres. Judges will be the editorial staff of *Seems* (a.k.a. Word of Mouth Books), excluding the festival coordinator, Karl Elder. Information available in September. For brochure, visit website.

GREEN MOUNTAIN WRITERS CONFERENCE

47 Hazel St., Rutland VT 05701. (802)236-6133. **E-mail:** ydaley@sbcglobal.net. **E-mail:** yvonnedaley@me.com. **Website:** vermontwriters.com. **Contact:** Yvonne Daley, director. Estab. 1999. "Annual conference held in the summer. Covers fiction, creative nonfiction, poetry, journalism, nature writing, essay, memoir, personal narrative, and biography. Held at The Mountain Top Inn and Resort, a beautiful lakeside inn located in Chittenden, VT. Speakers have included Grace Paley, Ruth Stone, Howard Frank Mosher, Chris Bohjalian, Yvonne Daley, David Huddle, David Budbill, Jeffrey Lent, Verandah Porche, Tom Smith, and Chuck Clarino."

COSTS $500 before May 1; $550 and up after May 1. Partial scholarships are available.

ACCOMMODATIONS Dramatically reduced rates at The Mountain Top Inn and Resort for attendees. Close to other area hotels, b&bs in Rutland County, Vermont.

ADDITIONAL INFORMATION Participants' mss can be read and commented on at a cost. Sponsors contests. Conference publishes a literary magazine featuring work of participants. Brochures available on website or e-mail. "We offer the opportunity to learn from some of the nation's best writers at a small, supportive conference in a lakeside setting that allows one-to-one feedback. Participants often continue to correspond and share work after conferences."

GULF COAST WRITERS CONFERENCE

P.O. Box 35038, Panama City FL 32412. (850)628-6028. **E-mail:** PottersvillePress@mchsi.com. **Website:** www.gulfcoastwritersconference.com/. Estab. 1999. Annual conference held in September in Panama City, Fla. Conference duration: 2 days. Average attendance: 100+. This conference is deliberately small and writer-centric with an affordable attendance price. (The 2013 event was the first time the conference was completely free.) Speakers include writers, editors and agents. Cricket Freeman of the August Agency is often in attendance. A former keynote speaker was mystery writer Michael Connelly.

⊕ HAMPTON ROADS WRITERS CONFERENCE

P.O. Box 56228, Virginia Beach VA 23456. **E-mail:** hrwriters@cox.net. **Website:** hamptonroadswriters.org. Workshops cover fiction, nonfiction, screenplays, memoir, poetry, and the business of getting published. A bookshop, book signings, and many networking opportunities will be available. Multiple literary agents are in attendance each year to meet with writers. Much more information available on the website.

COSTS Up to $255. Costs vary. There are discounts for members, for early bird registration, for students and more.

HEDGEBROOK

PO Box 1231, Freeland WA 98249-9911. (360)321-4786. **Fax:** (360)321-2171. **Website:** www.hedgebrook.org. **Contact:** Vito Zingarelli, residency director. Estab. 1988. "Hedgebrook is a retreat for women writers on Whidbey Island on 48 beautiful acres, near Seattle, where writers of diverse cultural backgrounds working in all genres, published or not, come from around the globe to write, rejuvenate, and be in community with each other. Located on beautiful Whidbey Island near Seattle, Hedgebrook offers one of the few residency programs in the world exclusively dedicated to supporting the creative process of women writers, and bringing their work to the world through innovative public programs."

ADDITIONAL INFORMATION Go online for more information.

HOLLYWOOD PITCH FESTIVAL

Fade In Magazine, P.O. Box 2699, Beverly Hills CA 90213. (800)646-3896. **E-mail:** inquiries@fadeinonline.com. **Website:** hollywoodpitchfestival.com/. Estab. 1996. 2014: August 1-3, Los Angeles. Register online or call to register (800) 646-3896. Conference duration: Three days. This is a pitch event that provides non-stop pitch meetings over a two-day period—with 200 of Hollywood's top buyers/representatives under one roof. HPF only has one class—a pitch class taught by a professional A-list filmmaker on Saturday morning, and it is optional. Each attendee will receive by e-mail a list of the companies/industry representatives attending, what each company is currently looking to produce (i.e., genre, budget), along with each company's credits. We also post a genre list at each event for cross-reference.

COSTS Our ticket prices are flat fees that cover each attendee's entire weekend (including food and drink). There are no other extra, added costs (i.e., no per pitch meeting fees) involved (unless you're adding hotel rooms).

⊕ HOUSTON WRITERS GUILD CONFERENCE

HOUSTON WRITERS GUILD CONFERENCE 31160, Houston TX 77231. (713)721-4773. **E-mail:** HoustonWritersGuild@Hotmail.com. **E-mail:** HoustonWritersGuild@Hotmail.com. **Website:** houstonwritersguild.org. 2014 date: Saturday, April 12. This annual conference, organized by the Houston Writers Guild, has concurrent sessions and tracks on the craft and business of writing. Each year, multiple agents are in attendance taking pitches from writers.

COSTS Costs are different for members and non-members. 2014 costs: $100 members, $125 non-members.

ADDITIONAL INFORMATION There is a writing contest at the event. There is also a for-pay pre-conference workshop the day before the conference.

HOW TO BE PUBLISHED WORKSHOPS

P.O. Box 100031, Irondale AL 35210-3006. **E-mail:** mike@writing2sell.com. **Website:** www.writing2sell.com. **Contact:** Michael Garrett. Estab. 1986. Workshops are offered continuously year-round at various locations. Conference duration: 1 session. Average attendance: 10-15. Workshops to "move writers of category fiction closer to publication." Focus is not on how to write, but how to get published. Site: Workshops held at college campuses and universities. Themes include marketing, idea development, characterization, and ms critique. Special critique is offered, but advance submission is not required. Workshop information available on website. Accepts inquiries by e-mail.

COSTS $79-99.

INTERNATIONAL MUSIC CAMP CREATIVE WRITING WORKSHOP

111-11th Ave. SW, Minot ND 58701. (701)838-8472. **Fax:** (701)838-1351. **E-mail:** info@internationalmusiccamp.com. **Website:** www.internationalmusiccamp.com. **Contact:** Christine Baumann and Tim Baumann, camp directors. Estab. 1956. Annual. Conference held in June. Average attendance: 35. "The workshop offers students the opportunity to refine their skills in thinking, composing, and writing in an environment that is conducive to positive reinforcement. In addition to writing poems, essays, and stories, individuals are encouraged to work on their own area of interest with conferencing and feedback from the course instructor." Site: International Peace Garden on the border between the US and Canada. "Similar to a university campus, several dormitories, classrooms, lecture halls, and cafeteria provide the perfect site for such a workshop. The beautiful and picturesque International Peace Garden provides additional inspiration to creative thinking." Instructor: Melissa Cournia & Andrea Nell.

COSTS $395, includes tuition, room and board. Early bird registration (postmarked by May 1) $370.

ACCOMMODATIONS Airline and depot shuttles are available upon request. Housing is included in the fee.

ADDITIONAL INFORMATION Conference information is available on the website. Welcomes questions via e-mail.

INTERNATIONAL WOMEN'S FICTION FESTIVAL

Via Cappuccini 8E, Matera 75100 Italy. (39)0835-312044. **Fax:** (39)0835-312093. **E-mail:** e.jennings@womensfictionfestival.com. **Website:** www.womensfictionfestival.com/. **Contact:** Elizabeth Jennings. Estab. 2004. Annual conference usually held in September. 2014 dates: Sept. 25-28, 2014. Conference duration: 3.5 days. Average attendance: 100. Sessions on fiction, nonfiction, screenwriting, writing for children, poetry, etc. International writers conference with a strong focus on fiction and a strong focus on marketing to international markets.

COSTS 220 euros.

ACCOMMODATIONS Le Monacelle, a restored 17th century convent. A paid shuttle is available from the Bari Airport to the hotel in Matera.

JAMES RIVER WRITERS CONFERENCE

ArtWorks Studios 136, 320 Hull St., #136, Richmond VA 23224. (804)433-3790. **Fax:** (804)291-1466. **E-mail:** info@jamesriverwriters.com; fallconference@jamesriverwriters.com. **Website:** www.jamesriverwriters.com. **Contact:** Katharine Herndon, exec. director. Estab. 2003.

COSTS In 2013, the cost was up to $240, though less expensive options were available. See the website for all pricing options.

ACCOMMODATIONS Richmond is easily accessible by air and train. Provides list of area hotels or lodging options. "Each year we arrange for special conference rates at an area hotel."

ADDITIONAL INFORMATION Workshop material is not required; however, we have offered an option for submissions: the first pages critique session in which submissions are read before a panel of agents and editors who are seeing them for the first time and are asked to react on the spot. No additional fee. No guarantee that a particular submission will be read. Details posted on the website, www.jamesriverwriters.com. Information available in June. For brochure, visit website. Agents participate in conference. Editors participate in conference. Both meet with writers to take pitches. Previous agents in attendance include April Eberhardt, Deborah Grosvenor, Victoria Skurnick, and Paige Wheeler.

JOURNEY INTO THE IMAGINATION: A FIVE-DAY WRITING RETREAT

995 Chapman Rd., Yorktown NY 10598. (914)962-4432. **E-mail:** emily@emilyhanlon.com. **Website:** www.thefictionwritersjourney.com/Spring_Writing_Retreat.html. **Contact:** Emily Hanlon. PO Box 536 Estab. 2004. Annual. 2014 dates: May 6-11. Average attendance: 8-12. "Purpose of workshop: fiction, memoir, short story, creativity, and the creative process." Site: Pendle Hill Retreat Center in Wallingford, PA (just north of Philadelphia). "Excellent food and lovely surroundings and accommodations. The core of this weekend's work is welcoming the unknown into your writing. We will go on a magical mystery tour to find and embrace new characters and to deepen our relationship to characters who already may people our

stories. Bring something on which you are already working or simply bring along your Inner Writer, pen and a journal, and let the magic unfold!"

COSTS 2014: 5 nights—$1150 if you register before March 1. $1250 after March 1. All rooms are private with shared bath.

ADDITIONAL INFORMATION For brochure, visit website.

KACHEMAK BAY WRITERS CONFERENCE

Kenai Peninsula College - Kachemak Bay Campus, 533 East Pioneer Ave., Homer AK 99603. **E-mail:** iyconf@uaa.alaska.edu. **Website:** writersconference.uaa.alaska.edu. Annual writers conference held in the summer (usually June). 2014 dates: June 13-17; keynote speaker is Alice Sebold. Sponsored by Kachemak Bay Campus - Kenai Peninsula College /UAA. This nationally recognized writing conference features workshops, readings and panel presentations in fiction, poetry, nonfiction, and the business of writing. There are "open mic" sessions for conference registrants; evening readings open to the public; agent/editor consultations, and more.

COSTS Some scholarships available; see the website.

ACCOMMODATIONS Homer is 225 miles south of Anchorage, Alaska, on the southern tip of the Kenai Peninsula and the shores of Kachemak Bay. There are multiple hotels in the area.

KENTUCKY WOMEN WRITERS CONFERENCE

University of Kentucky College of Arts & Sciences, 232 E. Maxwell St., Lexington KY 40506. (859)257-2874. **E-mail:** kentuckywomenwriters@gmail.com. **Website:** womenwriters.as.uky.edu/. **Contact:** Julie Wrinn, director. Estab. 1979. Conference held in second or third weekend of September. The 2014 dates are Sept. 12-13. The 2014 location is the Carnegie Center for Literacy in Lexington, Ky. Conference duration: 2 days. Average attendance: 150-200. Conference covers all genres: poetry, fiction, creative nonfiction, playwriting. Writing workshops, panels, and readings featuring contemporary women writers. The 2014 conference will feature Pulitzer Prize-winning poet Tracy K. Smith as its keynote speaker.

COSTS $175 early bird discount before Aug 1, $195 thereafter; $30 for undergraduates and younger; includes boxed lunch on Friday; $20 for Writers Reception. Other meals and accommodations are not included.

ADDITIONAL INFORMATION Sponsors prizes in poetry ($200), fiction ($200), nonfiction ($200), playwriting ($500), and spoken word ($500). Winners also invited to read during the conference. Pre-registration opens May 1.

KENTUCKY WRITERS CONFERENCE

Western Kentucky University and the Southern Kentucky Book Fest, Western Kentucky University Libraries, 1906 College Heights Blvd., Bowling Green KY 42101. (270)745-4502. **E-mail:** kristie.lowry@wku.edu. **Website:** www.sokybookfest.org/KYWritersConf. **Contact:** Kristie Lowry. This event is entirely free to the public. (2014 dates: April 25-26.) Duration: 1 day. Precedes the Southern Kentucky Book Fest the next day. Authors who will be participating in the Book Fest on Saturday will give attendees at the Writers Conference the benefit of their wisdom on Friday. Free workshops on a variety of writing topics will be presented during this day-long event. Sessions run for 75 minutes and the day begins at 9 a.m. and ends at 3:30 p.m. The conference is open to anyone who would like to attend including high school students, college students, teachers, and the general public.

KENYON REVIEW WRITERS WORKSHOP

Kenyon College, Gambier OH 43022. (740)427-5207. **Fax:** (740)427-5417. **E-mail:** kenyonreview@kenyon.edu; writers@kenyonreview.org. **Website:** www.kenyonreview.org. **Contact:** Anna Duke Reach, director. Estab. 1990. Annual 8-day workshop held in June. Participants apply in poetry, fiction, creative nonfiction, literary hybrid/book arts or writing online, and then participate in intensive daily workshops which focus on the generation and revision of significant new work. Held on the campus of Kenyon College in the rural village of Gambier, Ohio. Workshop leaders have included David Baker, Ron Carlson, Rebecca McClanahan, Meghan O'Rourke, Linda Gregorson, Dinty Moore, Tara Ison, Jane Hamilton, Lee K. Abbott, and Nancy Zafris.

COSTS $1,995; includes tuition, room and board.

ACCOMMODATIONS The workshop operates a shuttle to and from Gambier and the airport in Columbus, Ohio. Offers overnight accommodations. Participants are housed in Kenyon College student housing. The cost is covered in the tuition.

ADDITIONAL INFORMATION Application includes a writing sample. Admission decisions are made on a rolling basis. Workshop information is available online at www.kenyonreview.org/workshops in November. For brochure send e-mail, visit website, call, fax. Accepts inquiries by SASE, e-mail, phone, fax.

KEY WEST LITERARY SEMINAR

718 Love Lane, Key West FL 33040. (888)293-9291. **E-mail:** mail@kwls.org. **Website:** www.kwls.org. "The mission of KWLS is to promote the understanding and discussion of important literary works and their authors; to recognize and support new voices in American literature; and to preserve and promote Key West's literary heritage while providing resources that strengthen literary culture." The annual seminar and writers' workshop program are held in January. Scholarships are available to teachers, librarians, and students. Awards are given to emerging writers. See website for details.

COSTS $575/seminar; $450/writers' workshops.

ACCOMMODATIONS A list of nearby lodging establishments is made available.

KILLER NASHVILLE

P.O. Box 680759, Franklin TN 37068-0686. (615)599-4032. **E-mail:** contact@killernashville.com. **Website:** www.killernashville.com. Jaden Terrell, Exec. Dir. **Contact:** Clay Stafford, founder. Estab. 2006. Annual. Next events: Aug. 21-24, 2014. Conference duration: 3 days. Average attendance: 400+. Conference designed for writers and fans of mysteries and thrillers, including fiction and nonfiction authors, playwrights, and screenwriters. There are many opportunities for authors to sign books. Killer Nashville's 2014 writers conference will have over 60 sessions, 2 guests of honor, agent/editor/publisher roundtables, 5 distinct session tracks (general writing, genre specific writing, publishing, publicity & promotion, and forensics), breakout sessions for intense study, special sessions, manuscript critiques (fiction, nonfiction, short story, screenplay, marketing, query), realistic mock crime scene for guests to solve, networking with bestselling authors, agents, editors, publishers, attorneys, publicists, representatives from law and emergency services, mystery games, authors' bar, wine tasting event, two cocktail receptions, guest of honor dinner and awards program, prizes, free giveaways, free book signings, and more.

COSTS Early Bird Registration: $210 (February 15); Advanced Registration: $220 (April 30); $230 for three day full registration.

ACCOMMODATIONS The Hutton Hotel has all rooms available for the Killer Nashville Writers' Conference.

ADDITIONAL INFORMATION Additional information about registration is provided online.

KINDLING WORDS EAST

VT **Website:** www.kindlingwords.org. Annual retreat held in late January near Burlington, Vermont. A retreat with three strands: writer, illustrator and editor; professional level. Intensive workshops for each strand, and an open schedule for conversations and networking. Registration limited to approximately 70. Hosted by the 4-star Inn at Essex (room and board extra). Participants must be published by a CCBC listed publisher, or if in publishing, occupy a professional position. Registration opens August 1 or as posted on the website, and fills quickly. Check website to see if spaces are available, to sign up to be notified when registration opens each year, or for more information.

LA JOLLA WRITERS CONFERENCE

P.O. Box 178122, San Diego CA 92177. (858)467-1978. **E-mail:** akuritz@san.rr.com. **Website:** www.lajollawritersconference.com. **Contact:** Jared Kuritz, director. Estab. 2001. Annual conference held in October/November. Conference duration: 3 days. Average attendance: 200. The LJWC covers all genres and both fiction and nonfiction as well as the business of writing. We take particular pride in educating our attendees on the business aspect of the book industry and have agents, editors, publishers, publicists, and distributors teach classes. There is unprecedented access to faculty at the LJWC. Our conference offers lecture sessions that run for 50 minutes, and workshops that run for 110 minutes. Each block period is dedicated to either workshop or lecture-style classes, with 6-8 classes on various topics available each block. For most workshop classes, you are encouraged to bring written work for review. Literary agents from prestigious agencies such as The Andrea Brown Literary Agency, The Dijkstra Agency, The McBride Agency and Full Circle Literary Group, the Zimmerman Literary Agency, the Van Haitsma Literary Agency, the Farris Literary Agency and more have participated in the past, teaching workshops in which they are familiarized with attendee work. Late night and early bird sessions are also available. The conference creates a strong sense of community, and it has seen many of its attendees successfully published.

COSTS Information available online at website.

LAS VEGAS WRITERS CONFERENCE

Henderson Writers' Group, 614 Mosswood Dr., Henderson NV 89015. (702)564-2488; or, toll-free, (866)869-7842. **E-mail:** marga614@mysticpublishers.com. **Website:** www.lasvegaswritersconference.com. Annual. Held in April. Conference duration: 3 days. Average attendance: 150 maximum. "Join writing professionals, agents, industry experts, and your colleagues for 3 days in Las Vegas as they share their knowledge on all aspects of the writer's craft. While there are formal pitch sessions, panels, workshops, and seminars, the faculty is also available throughout the conference for informal discussions and advice. Plus, you're bound to meet a few new friends, too. Workshops, seminars, and expert panels will take you through writing in many genres including fiction, creative nonfiction, screenwriting, journalism, and business and technical writing. There will be many Q&A panels for you to ask the experts all your questions." Site: Sam's Town Hotel and Gambling Hall in Las Vegas.

COSTS $425 until 1/14/14; $475 starting 1/15/14; $500 at door; $300 for one day.

ADDITIONAL INFORMATION Sponsors contest. Agents and editors participate in conference.

LAURA THOMAS JUNIOR WRITERS AUTHORS CONFERENCE

Laura Thomas Communications, Delta British Colombia V6X 2M9 Canada. (604)307-4971. **E-mail:** laura@laurathomascommunications.com. **Website:** laurathomascommunications.com/conference/. **Contact:** Laura Thomas. Estab. 2013. New conference held in the fall and spring each year. Conference duration: 1 day, 9-5. Covers poetry and writing for children and young adults, ages 9-21. Fall 2013 conference held in Richmond at Sandsman Signature Hotel & Resort. Spring 2014 conference held at the Manor House Hotel, Guildford, Surrey, UK, in May. Speakers have included Michelle Barker (author and editor), Deneka Michaud (journalist and communications professional), Lois Peterson (author), Darlene Foster (author), and George Opacic (author and publisher).

COSTS $89 single ticket and $79 sibling rate. Includes workshops and meals, scholarships are available.

ADDITIONAL INFORMATION Writers may request information by e-mail.

THE MACDOWELL COLONY

100 High St., Peterborough NH 03458. (603)924-3886. **Fax:** (603)924-9142. **E-mail:** admissions@macdowellcolony.org. **Website:** www.macdowellcolony.org. Estab. 1907. Open to writers, playwrights, composers, visual artists, film/video artists, interdisciplinary artists and architects. Applicants submit information and work samples for review by a panel of experts in each discipline. Application form submitted online at www.macdowellcolony.org/apply.html.

COSTS Travel reimbursement and stipends are available for participants of the residency, based on need. There are no residency fees.

MENDOCINO COAST WRITERS CONFERENCE

1211 Del Mar Dr., second address is P.O. Box 2087, Fort Bragg CA 95437. (707)485-4032. **E-mail:** info@mcwc.org. **Website:** www.mcwc.org. Estab. 1988. Annual conference held in July. Average attendance: 80. Provides workshops for fiction, nonfiction, and poetry. Held at a small community college campus on the northern Pacific Coast. Workshop leaders have included Kim Addonizio, Lynne Barrett, John Dufresne, John Lescroart, Ben Percy, Luis Rodriguez, Peter Orner, Judith Barrington and Ellen Sussman. Agents and publishers will be speaking and available for meetings with attendees.

COSTS $525+ (includes panels, meals, 2 socials with guest readers, 4 public events, 3 morning intensive workshops in 1 of 6 subjects, and a variety of afternoon panels and lectures).

ACCOMMODATIONS Information on overnight accommodations is made available.

ADDITIONAL INFORMATION Emphasis is on writers who are also good teachers. Registration opens March 15. Send inquiries via e-mail.

MIDWEST WRITERS WORKSHOP

Ball State University, Department of Journalism, Muncie IN 47306. (765)282-1055. **E-mail:** midwestwriters@yahoo.com. **Website:** www.midwestwriters.org. **Contact:** Jama Kehoe Bigger, director. Annual workshop held in late July in eastern Indiana. Writer workshops geared toward writers of all levels. Topics include most genres. Faculty/speakers have included Joyce Carol Oates, George Plimpton, Clive Cussler, Haven Kimmel, James Alexander Thom, William Zinsser, Phillip Gulley, Lee Martin, and numerous bestselling mystery, literary fiction, young adult, and children's authors. Workshop also includes agent pitch sessions, ms evaluation and a writing contest. Registration tentatively limited to 200.

COSTS $150-375. Most meals included.

ADDITIONAL INFORMATION Offers scholarships. See website for more information.

MISSOURI WRITERS' GUILD CONFERENCE

St. Louis MO **E-mail:** mwgconferenceinfo@gmail.com. **Website:** www.missouriwritersguild.org. **Contact:** Tricia Sanders, vice president/conference chairman. Writer and illustrator workshops geared to all levels. **Open to students.** Annual conference held early April or early May each year. Annual conference "gives writers the opportunity to hear outstanding speakers and to receive information on marketing, research, and writing techniques." Agents, editors, and published authors in attendance.

ACCOMMODATIONS 2014: Ramada Plaza Hotel downtown.

ADDITIONAL INFORMATION The primary contact individual changes every year, because the conference chair changes every year. See the website for contact info.

MONTROSE CHRISTIAN WRITERS' CONFERENCE

218 Locust St., Montrose PA 18801. (570)278-1001 or (800)598-5030. **Fax:** (570)278-3061. **E-mail:** mbc@montrosebible.org. **Website:** montrosebible.org. Estab. 1990. "Annual conference held in July. Offers workshops, editorial appointments, and professional critiques. We try to meet a cross-section of writing needs, for beginners and advanced, covering fiction, poetry, and writing for children. It is small enough to allow personal interaction between attendees and faculty. Speakers have included William Petersen, Mona Hodgson, Jim Fletcher, and Terri Gibbs." Held in Montrose, from July 20-25, 2014.

COSTS Tuition is $180.

ACCOMMODATIONS Will meet planes in Binghamton, NY, and Scranton, PA. On-site accommodations: room and board $325-370/conference; $75-80/day including food (2014 rates). RV court available.

ADDITIONAL INFORMATION "Writers can send work ahead of time and have it critiqued for a small fee." The attendees are usually church related. The writing has a Christian emphasis. Conference information available in April. For brochure, visit website, e-mail or call. Accepts inquiries by phone or e-mail.

JENNY MCKEAN MOORE COMMUNITY WORKSHOPS

English Department, George Washingtion University, 801 22nd St. NW, Rome Hall, Suite 760, Washington DC 20052. (202) 994-6180. **Fax:** (202) 994-7915. **E-mail:** lpageinc@aol.com. **Website:** www.gwu.edu/~english/creative_jennymckeanmoore.html. **Contact:** Lisa Page, Acting Director of creative writing. Estab. 1976. Workshop held each semester at the university. Average attendance: 15. Concentration varies depending on professor—usually fiction or poetry. The Creative Writing department brings an established poet or novelist to campus each year to teach a writing workshop for GW students and a free community workshop for adults in the larger Washington community. Details posted on website in June, with an application deadline at the end of August or in early September.

ADDITIONAL INFORMATION Admission is competitive and by ms.

MUSE AND THE MARKETPLACE

Grub Street, 160 Boylston St., 4th Floor, Boston MA 02116. (617)695.0075. **E-mail:** info@grubstreet.org. **Website:** grubstreet.org/. The conferences are held in the late spring, such as early May. (2014 dates are May 2-4.) Conference duration: 3 days. Average attendance: 400. Dozens of agents are in attendance to meet writers and take pitches. Previous keynote speakers include Jonathan Franzen. The conference has workshops on all aspects of writing.

COSTS Varies, depending on if you're a member or non-member (includes 6 workshop sessions and 2 Hour of Power sessions with options for the Manuscript Mart and a Five-Star lunch with authors, editors and agents). Other passes are available for Saturday-only and Sunday-only guests.

NAPA VALLEY WRITERS' CONFERENCE

Napa Valley College, 1088 College Ave., St. Helena CA 94574. (707)967-2900, x1611. **E-mail:** writecon@napavalley.edu. **Website:** www.napawritersconference.org. **Contact:** John Leggett and Anne Evans, program directors. Estab. 1981. Established 1981. Annual weeklong event, 2014 dates: July 27 - Aug. 1. Location: Upper Valley Campus in the historic town of St. Helena, 25 miles north of Napa in the heart of the valley's

wine growing community. Excellent cuisine provided by Napa Valley Cooking School. Average attendance: 48 in poetry and 48 in fiction. "Serious writers of all backgrounds and experience are welcome to apply." Offers poets workshops, lectures, faculty readings, ms critiques, and meetings with editors. "Poetry session provides the opportunity to work both on generating new poems and on revising previously written ones."
COSTS Total participation fee is $900. More cost info (including financial assistance info) is online.
ADDITIONAL INFORMATION The conference is held at the Upper Valley Campus of Napa Valley College, located in the heart of California's Wine Country. During the conference week, attendees' meals are provided by the Napa Valley Cooking School, which offers high-quality, intensive training for aspiring chefs. The goal of the program is to provide each student with hands-on, quality, culinary and pastry skills required for a career in a fine-dining establishment. The disciplined and professional learning environment, availability of global externships, low student-teacher ratio and focus on sustainability make the Napa Valley Cooking School unique.

⊕ NASHVILLE SCREENWRITERS CONFERENCE

(615)254-2049. **E-mail:** info@nashscreen.com. **Website:** www.nashscreen.com. 2014 dates: May 30–June 1. The entire lineup of speakers and panelists is online. This is a three-day conference dedicated to those who write for the screen. Nashville is a city that celebrates its writers and its creative community, and every writer wants to have a choice of avenues to increase their potential for success. In this memorable weekend, conference participants will have the opportunity to attend various writing panels led by working professionals and participate in several special events.

NATCHEZ LITERARY AND CINEMA CELEBRATION

P.O. Box 1307, Natchez MS 39121-1307. (601)446-1208. **Fax:** (601)446-1214. **E-mail:** carolyn.smith@colin.edu. **Website:** www.colin.edu/nlcc. Estab. 1990. Annual conference held in February. Conference duration: 5 days. Conference focuses on all literature, including film scripts. Each year's conference deals with some general aspect of Southern history. Speakers have included Eudora Welty, Margaret Walker Alexander, William Styron, Willie Morris, Ellen Douglas, Ernest Gaines, Elizabeth Spencer, Nikki Giovanni, Myrlie Evers-Williams, and Maya Angelou.

NATIONAL WRITERS ASSOCIATION FOUNDATION CONFERENCE

10940 S. Parker Rd., #508, Parker CO 80138. (303)841-0246. **E-mail:** natlwritersassn@hotmail.com. **Website:** www.nationalwriters.com. **Contact:** Sandy Whelchel, executive director. Estab. 1926. Annual conference held the second week of June in Denver. Conference duration: 1 day. Average attendance: 100. Focuses on general writing and marketing.
COSTS Approximately $100.
ADDITIONAL INFORMATION Awards for previous contests will be presented at the conference. Brochures/guidelines are online, or send an SASE.

NETWO WRITERS CONFERENCE

Northeast Texas Writers Organization, P.O. Box 411, Winfield TX 75493. (469)867-2624 or Paul at (903)573-6084. **E-mail:** jimcallan@winnsboro.com. **Website:** www.netwo.org. Estab. 1987. Annual conference held in April. (2014 dates are April 25-26.) Conference duration: 2 days. Presenters include agents, writers, editors, and publishers. Agents in attendance will take pitches from writers. The conference features a writing contest, pitch sessions, critiques from professionals, as well as dozens of workshops and presentations.
COSTS $60+ (discount offered for early registration).
ACCOMMODATIONS Online, we have posted information on lodging—motels and hotels. As the conference has moved to the Mount Pleasant Civic Center, we no longer have the "dorm accommodations" available in 2011 and before. The NETWO Writers Conference is at the Mount Pleasant Civic Center, in Mt. Pleasant, Texas. Located on U.S. Business 271 just one block south of Interstate 30, it is easily accessible from north, south, east and west. It offers excellent facilities: climate control, large rooms, excellent sound systems, ability to handle Power Point presentations, ample room for the on-site lunch which is part of the conference, improved restroom facilities, and private rooms for the one-on-one interviews with agents, editor and publisher. There is ample parking available. Several motels are within two blocks.
ADDITIONAL INFORMATION Conference is cosponsored by the Texas Commission on the Arts. See website for current updates.

⊕ NEW JERSEY ROMANCE WRITERS PUT YOUR HEART IN A BOOK CONFERENCE

P.O. Box 513, Plainsboro NJ 08536. **E-mail:** dmcomfort@aol.com. **Website:** www.njromancewriters.org. Estab. 1984. Annual conference held in October. Average attendance: 500. Workshops are offered on various topics for all writers of romance, from beginner to multi-published. Speakers have included Nora Roberts, Kathleen Woodiwiss, Patricia Gaffney, Jill Barnett and Kay Hooper. Appointments are offered with editors/agents.

ACCOMMODATIONS Special rate available for conference attendees at the Sheraton at Renaissance Woodbridge Hotel in Iselin, New Jersey.

ADDITIONAL INFORMATION Conference brochures, guidelines, and membership information are available for SASE. Massive book fair is open to the public with authors signing copies of their books.

NIMROD ANNUAL WRITERS' WORKSHOP

800 S. Tucker Dr., Tulsa OK 74104. (918)631-3080. **E-mail:** nimrod@utulsa.edu. **Website:** www.utulsa.edu/nimrod. **Contact:** Eilis O'Neal, editor-in-chief. Estab. 1978. Annual conference held in October. Conference duration: 1 day. Offers one-on-one editing sessions, readings, panel discussions, and master classes in fiction, poetry, nonfiction, memoir, and fantasy writing. Speakers have included Ted Kooser, Colum McCann, Molly Peacock, Peter S. Beagle, Aimee Nezhukumatathil, Philip Levine, and Linda Pastan. Full conference details are online in August.

COSTS Approximately $50. Lunch provided. Scholarships available for students.

ADDITIONAL INFORMATION *Nimrod International Journal* sponsors *Nimrod* Literary Awards: The Katherine Anne Porter Prize for fiction and The Pablo Neruda Prize for poetry. Poetry and fiction prizes: $2,000 each and publication (1st prize); $1,000 each and publication (2nd prize). Deadline: must be postmarked no later than April 30.

NORTH CAROLINA WRITERS' NETWORK FALL CONFERENCE

P.O. Box 21591, Winston-Salem NC 27120. (336)293-8844. **E-mail:** mail@ncwriters.org. **Website:** www.ncwriters.org. Estab. 1985. Annual conference held in November in different NC venues. Average attendance: 250. This organization hosts 2 conferences: 1 in the spring and 1 in the fall. Each conference is a weekend full of workshops, panels, book signings, and readings (including open mic). There will be a keynote speaker, a variety of sessions on the craft and business of writing, and opportunities to meet with agents and editors.

COSTS Approximately $250 (includes 4 meals).

ACCOMMODATIONS Special rates are usually available at the Conference Hotel, but conferees must make their own reservations.

ADDITIONAL INFORMATION Available at www.ncwriters.org.

NORTHERN COLORADO WRITERS CONFERENCE

108 East Monroe Dr., Fort Collins CO 80525. (970)556-0908. **E-mail:** kerrie@northerncoloradowriters.com. **Website:** www.northerncoloradowriters.com. Estab. 2006. Annual conference held in the spring (usually March or April) in Colorado. Conference duration: 2-3 days. The conference features a variety of speakers, agents and editors. There are workshops and presentations on fiction, nonfiction, screenwriting, children's books, staying inspired, and more. Previous agents who have attended and taken pitches from writers include Jessica Regel, Kristen Nelson, Rachelle Gardner, Andrea Brown, Ken Sherman, Jessica Faust, Jon Sternfeld, and Jeffrey McGraw. Each conference features more than 30 workshops from which to choose from. Previous keynotes include Chuck Sambuchino, Andrew McCarthy and Stephen J. Cannell.

COSTS $295-445, depending on what package the attendee selects, and whether you're a member or nonmember.

ACCOMMODATIONS The conference is hosted at the Fort Collins Hilton, where rooms are available at a special rate.

ODYSSEY FANTASY WRITING WORKSHOP

P.O. Box 75, Mont Vernon NH 03057. **E-mail:** jcavelos@sff.net. **Website:** www.odysseyworkshop.org. Saint Anselm College, 100 Saint Anselm Drive, Manchester, New Hampshire 03102. Estab. 1996. Annual workshop held in June (through July). Conference duration: 6 weeks. Average attendance: 15. A workshop for fantasy, science fiction, and horror writers that combines an intensive learning and writing experience with in-depth feedback on students' mss. Held on the campus of Saint Anselm College in Manchester, New Hampshire. Speakers have included George R.R. Martin, Elizabeth Hand, Jane Yolen, Harlan Ellison, Melissa Scott and Dan Simmons.

COSTS In 2014: $1,965 tuition, $812 housing (double room), $1,624 (single room); $35 application fee, $450-600 food (approximate), $550 processing fee to receive college credit.

ADDITIONAL INFORMATION Students must apply and include a writing sample. Application deadline April 8. Students' works are critiqued throughout the 6 weeks. Workshop information available in October. For brochure/guidelines, send SASE, e-mail, visit website, or call. Accepts inquiries by SASE, e-mail, phone.

OKLAHOMA WRITERS' FEDERATION, INC. ANNUAL CONFERENCE

3800 Bonaire Place, Edmond OK 73013. **Website:** www.owfi.org. **Contact:** Christine Jarmola, president. Annual conference held just outside Oklahoma City. Held first weekend in May each year. Writer workshops geared toward all levels. Oklahoma Writers Federation, Inc. is open and welcoming to writers of all genres and all skill levels. Our goal is to help writers become better and to help beginning writers understand and master the craft of writing. The theme of our conference is to create good stories with strong bones. We will be exploring cultural writing and cultural sensitivity in writing. This year we will also be looking at the cutting edge of publishing and the options it is producing.

COSTS $175 before April; $200 after April. Cost includes awards banquet and famous author banquet. Three extra sessions are available for an extra fee. Visit our website for a complete faculty list and conference information.

⊕ OREGON CHRISTIAN WRITERS SUMMER CONFERENCE

Red Lion Hotel on the River, 909 N. Hayden Island Dr., Portland OR 97217-8118. **E-mail:** summerconf@oregonchristianwriters.org. **Website:** www.oregonchristianwriters.org. **Contact:** Lindy Jacobs, OCW Summer Conference Director. Estab. 1989. Held annually in August at the Red Lion Hotel on the River, a full-service hotel. Conference duration: 4 days. 2014 dates: August 4-7; 2015 dates: August 10-13. Average attendance: 225 (175 writers, 50 faculty). Top national editors, agents, and authors in the field of Christian publishing teach 12 intensive coaching classes and 30 workshops plus critique sessions. Published authors as well as emerging writers have opportunities to improve their craft, get feedback through manuscript reviews, meet one-on-one with editors and agents, and have half-hour mentoring appointments with published authors. Classes include fiction, nonfiction, memoir, young adult, poetry, magazine articles, devotional writing, children's books, and marketing. Daily general sessions include worship and an inspirational keynote address. Each year contacts made during the OCW summer conference lead to publishing contracts. 2014 conference theme will be "Writing with God: Take Heart," based on Psalm 27:14. 2014 Keynote speakers: Allen Arnold and Dan Walsh. Agents: Chip MacGregor, Mary Sue Seymour, Sue Brower, Bill Jensen, and Sandra Bishop. Other speakers/teachers: Susan May Warren, James Rubart, Randy Ingermanson, Jeff Gerke, Mary DeMuth, Jill Williamson, Leslie Gould, Susan Meissner, Joanna Echols, and Susan King. Past speakers have included: Liz Curtis Higgs, Francine Rivers, Bill Myers, Jeff Gerke, Angella Hunt, James L. Rubart, Susan May Warren, and James Scott Bell.

COSTS $475 for OCW members, $495 for nonmembers. Registration fee includes all classes, workshops, and 2 lunches and 3 dinners. Lodging additional. Full-time registered conferees may also pre-submit three proposals for review by an editor through the conference, plus sign up for a half-hour mentoring appointment with an author.

ACCOMMODATIONS Conference is held at the Red Lion on the River Hotel. Conferees wishing to stay at the hotel must make a reservation through the hotel. Some conferees commute. A block of rooms has been reserved at the hotel at a special rate for conferees and held until mid-July. The hotel reservation link will be posted on the website in late spring. Shuttle bus transportation will be provided by the hotel for conferees from Portland Airport (PDX) to the hotel, which is 20 minutes away.

ADDITIONAL INFORMATION Conference details will be posted online beginning in January. All conferees are welcome to attend the Cascade Awards ceremony, which takes place Wednesday evening during the conference. For more information about the Cascade Writing Contest, please check the website.

OUTDOOR WRITERS ASSOCIATION OF AMERICA ANNUAL CONFERENCE

615 Oak St., Suite 201, Missoula MT 59801. (406)728-7434. **E-mail:** info@owaa.org. **Website:** owaa.org.

Contact: Jessica Pollett, conference and membership coordinator. Outdoor communicator workshops geared toward all levels. Annual three-day conference. Craft improvement seminars; newsmaker sessions. 2014 conference to be held in McAllen, TX. Cost of workshop: $425-449; includes attendance at all workshops and most meals. Visit owaa.org/2014conference for additional information

OZARK CREATIVE WRITERS, INC. CONFERENCE

P.O. Box 424, Eureka Springs AR 72632. **E-mail:** ozarkcreativewriters@gmail.com. **Website:** www.ozarkcreativewriters.org. Open to professional and amateur writers, workshops are geared to all levels and all forms of the creative process and literary arts. Sessions sometimes include songwriting, with presentations by best-selling authors, editors, and agents. The OCW Conference promotes writing by offering competition in all genres. The annual event is held in October at the Inn of the Ozarks, in the resort town of Eureka Springs, Arkansas. Approximately 200 attend each year; many also enter the creative writing competitions.

PACIFIC COAST CHILDREN'S WRITERS WHOLE-NOVEL WORKSHOP: FOR ADULTS AND TEENS

P.O. Box 244, Aptos CA 95001. (831)684-2042. **Website:** www.childrenswritersworkshop.com. Estab. 2003. 2014 dates: Oct. 17-19. "Our seminar offers semi-advanced through published adult writers an editor and/or agent critique on their full novel or 15-30 page partial. (Mid-book and synopsis critique may be included with the partial.) A concurrent workshop is open to students age 13 and up, who give adults target-reader feedback. Focus on craft as a marketing tool. Team-taught master classes (open clinics for manuscript critiques) explore such topics as "Story Architecture and Arcs." Continuous close contact with faculty, who have included Andrea Brown, agent, and Simon Boughton, VP/executive editor at 3 Macmillan imprints. **Past seminars**: Oct. 10-12, 2013. Registration limited to 16 adults and 10 teens. For the most critique options, submit sample chapters and synopsis with e-application by mid May; open until filled. **Content:** Character-driven novels with protagonists ages 11 and older. Collegial format; 90 percent hands-on. Our pre-workshop anthology of peer manuscripts maximizes learning and networking. Several enrollees have landed contracts as a direct result of our seminar. **Details:** Visit our website and e-mail Director Nancy Sondel via the contact form.

PACIFIC NORTHWEST WRITER ASSN. SUMMER WRITER'S CONFERENCE

PMB 2717, 1420 NW Gilman Blvd., Ste. 2, Issaquah WA 98027. (425)673-2665. **E-mail:** pnwa@pnwa.org. **Website:** www.pnwa.org. Writer conference geared toward beginner, intermediate, advanced and professional levels. Meet agents and editors. Learn craft from renowned authors. Uncover new marketing secrets. PNWA's 59th Annual Conference will be held July 17-20, 2014, at the Hilton Seattle Airport & Conference Center, at the Hyatt Regency, Bellevue, WA 98004. This event usually has 10-20 literary agents in attendance taking pitches from writers.

PENNWRITERS CONFERENCE

RR #2, Box 241, Middlebury Center PA 16935. **Website:** www.pennwriters.org/prod/. Estab. 1987. The Mission of Pennwriters Inc. is to help writers of all levels from the novice to the award-winning and multi-published, improve and succeed in their craft. The annual Pennwriters conference is held every year in May in Pennsylvania, switching between locations —Lancaster in even years and Pittsburgh in odd years. 2014 event: May 16-18 at Eden Resort in Lancaster.

ACCOMMODATIONS See website for current information.

ADDITIONAL INFORMATION Sponsors contest. Published authors judge fiction in various categories. Agent/editor appointments are available on a first-come, first serve basis.

PHILADELPHIA WRITERS' CONFERENCE

P.O. Box 7171, Elkins Park PA 19027-0171. (215) 619-7422. **E-mail:** info@pwcwriters.org. **E-mail:** info@pwcwriters.org. **Website:** pwcwriters.org. Estab. 1949. Annual. Conference held in June. Average attendance: 160-200. Conference covers many forms of writing: novel, short story, genre fiction, nonfiction book, magazine writing, blogging, juvenile, poetry.

ACCOMMODATIONS Wyndham Hotel (formerly the Holiday Inn), Independence Mall, Fourth and Arch Streets, Philadelphia, PA 19106-2170. "Hotel offers discount for early registration."

ADDITIONAL INFORMATION Accepts inquiries by e-mail. Agents and editors attend conference. Visit us on the web for further agent and speaker details. Many questions are answered online.

PIKES PEAK WRITERS CONFERENCE

Pikes Peak Writers, PO Box 64273, Colorado Springs CO 80962. (719)244-6220. **E-mail:** info@pikespeakwriters.com. **Website:** www.pikespeakwriters.com. Estab. 1993. Annual conference held in April. Conference duration: 3 days. Average attendance: 300. Workshops, presentations, and panels focus on writing and publishing mainstream and genre fiction (romance, science fiction/fantasy, suspense/thrillers, action/adventure, mysteries, children's, young adult). Agents and editors are available for meetings with attendees on Saturday.

COSTS $300-500 (includes all meals).

ACCOMMODATIONS Marriott Colorado Springs holds a block of rooms at a special rate for attendees until late March.

ADDITIONAL INFORMATION Readings with critiques are available on Friday afternoon. Also offers a contest for unpublished manuscripts; entrants need not attend the conference. Deadline: November 1. Registration and contest entry forms are online; brochures are available in January. Send inquiries via e-mail.

POETRY WEEKEND INTENSIVES

40 Post Ave., Hawthorne NJ 07506. (973)423-2921. **Fax:** (973)523-6085. **E-mail:** mariagillan@verizon.net. **Website:** www.mariagillan.com; www.mariagillan.blogspot.com. **Contact:** Maria Mazziotti Gillan, executive director. Estab. 1997. Usually held 2 times/year in June and December. Average attendance: 26.

COSTS $425, including meals. Offers a $25 early bird discount. Housing in on-site facilities included in the $425 price.

ACCOMMODATIONS Location: generally at St. Marguerite's Retreat House, Mendham, NJ; also several other convents and monasteries.

ADDITIONAL INFORMATION Individual poetry critiques available. Poets should bring poems to weekend. Registration form available for SASE or by fax or e-mail. Maria Mazziotti Gillan is the director of the Creative Writing Program of Binghamton University- State University of New York, exec. director of the Poetry Center at Passaic County Community College, and edits *Paterson Literary Review*. Laura Boss is the editor of *Lips* magazine. Fifteen professional development credits are available for each weekend.

ROCKY MOUNTAIN FICTION WRITERS COLORADO GOLD

Rocky Mountain Fiction Writers, P.O. Box 735, Conifer CO 80433. **E-mail:** conference@rmfw.org. **Website:** www.rmfw.org. Estab. 1982. Annual conference held in September. Conference duration: 3 days. Average attendance: 350. Themes include general novel-length fiction, genre fiction, contemporary romance, mystery, science fiction/fantasy, mainstream, young adult, screenwriting, short stories, and historical fiction. Speakers have included Margaret George, Jodi Thomas, Bernard Cornwell, Terry Brooks, Dorothy Cannell, Patricia Gardner Evans, Diane Mott Davidson, Constance O'Day, Connie Willis, Clarissa Pinkola Estes, Michael Palmer, Jennifer Unter, Margaret Marr, Ashley Krass, and Andren Barzvi. Approximately 8 editors and 5 agents attend annually.

COSTS Available online.

ACCOMMODATIONS Special rates will be available at conference hotel.

ADDITIONAL INFORMATION Editor-conducted workshops are limited to 8 participants for critique, with auditing available. Pitch appointments available at no charge. Friday morning master classes available. Craft workshops include beginner through professional levels. New as of 2013: Writers' retreat available immediately following conference; space is limited.

ROMANCE WRITERS OF AMERICA NATIONAL CONFERENCE

14615 Benfer Road, Houston TX 77069. (832)717-5200. **Fax:** (832)717-5201. **E-mail:** info@rwa.org. **Website:** www.rwa.org/conference. Estab. 1981. Annual conference held in July. (2014 conference: July 23-26 in San Antonio.) Average attendance: 2,000. More than 100 workshops on writing, researching, and the business side of being a working writer. Publishing professionals attend and accept appointments. The keynote speaker is a renowned romance writer. "Romance Writers of America (RWA) is a nonprofit trade association, with a membership of more than 10,000 romance writers and related industry professionals, whose mission is to advance the professional interests of career-focused romance writers through networking and advocacy."

COSTS $385-610 depending on your membership status as well as when you register.

ADDITIONAL INFORMATION Annual RTA awards are presented for romance authors. Annual Golden Heart awards are presented for unpublished writers. Numerous literary agents are in attendance to meet with writers and hear book pitches.

RT BOOKLOVERS CONVENTION

55 Bergen St., Brooklyn NY 11201. (718)237-1097 or (800)989-8816, ext. 12. **Fax:** (718)624-2526. **E-mail:** jocarol@rtconvention.com. **E-mail:** nancy@rtbookreviews.com. **Website:** rtconvention.com. Annual conference held May 13-18. 2014 Convention will be in New Orleans at the Marriott Center on Canal Street. Features 125 workshops, agent and editor appointments, a book fair, and more.

COSTS See website for pricing and other information.

ACCOMMODATIONS Rooms available nearby.

SALT CAY WRITERS RETREAT

Salt Cay Bahamas. (732)267-6449. **E-mail:** admin@saltcaywritersretreat.com. **Website:** www.saltcaywritersretreat.com. **Contact:** Karen Dionne and Christopher Graham. 5-day retreat held in the Bahamas in October. "The Salt Cay Writers Retreat is particularly suited for novelists (especially those writing literary, upmarket commercial fiction, or genre novelists wanting to write a break-out book), memoirists and narrative nonfiction writers. However, any author (published or not-yet-published) who wishes to take their writing to the next level is welcome to apply." Speakers have included or will include editors Chuck Adams (Algonquin Books), Amy Einhorn (Amy Einhorn Books); agents Jeff Kleinman, Michelle Brower, Erin Niumata, Erin Harris (Folio Literary Management); authors Robert Goolrick, Jacquelyn Mitchard.

COSTS $2,450 through May 1; $2,950 after.

ACCOMMODATIONS Comfort Suites, Paradise Island, Nassau, Bahamas.

SAN DIEGO STATE UNIVERSITY WRITERS' CONFERENCE

SDSU College of Extended Studies, 5250 Campanile Dr., San Diego State University, San Diego CA 92182-1920. (619)594-2517. **Fax:** (619)594-8566. **E-mail:** sdsuwritersconference@mail.sdsu.edu. **Website:** ces.sdsu.edu/writers. Estab. 1984. Annual conference held in January/February. Conference duration: 2.5 days. Average attendance: 350. Covers fiction, nonfiction, scriptwriting and e-books. Held at the Doubletree Hotel in Mission Valley. Each year the conference offers a variety of workshops for the beginner and advanced writers. This conference allows the individual writer to choose which workshop best suits his/her needs. In addition to the workshops, editor reading appointments and agent/editor consultation appointments are provided so attendees may meet with editors and agents one-on-one to discuss specific questions. A reception is offered Saturday immediately following the workshops, offering attendees the opportunity to socialize with the faculty in a relaxed atmosphere. Last year, approximately 60 faculty members attended.

COSTS Approximately $399-435.

ACCOMMODATIONS Attendees must make their own travel arrangements. A conference rate for attendees is available at the Doubletree Hotel.

SAN FRANCISCO WRITERS CONFERENCE

1029 Jones St., San Francisco CA 94109. (415)673-0939. **Fax:** (415)673-0367. **E-mail:** Barbara@sfwriters.org. **Website:** sfwriters.org. **Contact:** Barbara Santos, marketing director. Estab. 2003. "Annual conference held President's Day weekend in February. Average attendance: 400+. Top authors, respected literary agents, and major publishing houses are at the event so attendees can make face-to-face contact with all the right people. Writers of nonfiction, fiction, poetry, and specialty writing (children's books, cookbooks, travel, etc.) will all benefit from the event. There are important sessions on marketing, self-publishing, technology, and trends in the publishing industry. Plus, there's an optional 4-hour session called Speed Dating for Agents where attendees can meet with 20+ agents. Speakers have included Jennifer Crusie, Richard Paul Evans, Jamie Raab, Mary Roach, Jane Smiley, Debbie Macomber, Firoozeh Dumas, Zilpha Keatley Snyder, Steve Berry, Jacquelyn Mitchard. More than 20 agents and editors participate each year, many of whom will be available for meetings with attendees."

COSTS Check the website for pricing on later dates. 2014 pricing was $650-795 depending on when you signed up and early bird registration, etc.

ACCOMMODATIONS The Intercontinental Mark Hopkins Hotel is a historic landmark at the top of Nob Hill in San Francisco. The hotel is located so that everyone arriving at the Oakland or San Francisco airport can take BART to either the Embarcadero or Powell Street exits, then walk or take a cable car or taxi directly to the hotel.

ADDITIONAL INFORMATION "Present yourself in a professional manner and the contact you will make will be invaluable to your writing career. Brochures and registration are online."

SAN FRANCISCO WRITING FOR CHANGE CONFERENCE

1029 Jones St., San Francisco CA 94109. (415)673-0939. **E-mail:** Barbara@sfwriters.org. **Website:** SFWritingforChange.org. **Contact:** Barbara Santos, marketing director; Michael Larsen, co-director. Estab. 2004. Annual conference to be held September 6, 2014 at Unitarian Universalist Center in San Francisco. Average attendance: 100. Early discounts available. Includes panels, workshops, keynote address, editor and agent consultations.

COSTS Costs to be announced. Please visit the website.

ACCOMMODATIONS Check website for event details, accommodations, directions, and parking.

ADDITIONAL INFORMATION "The limited number of attendees (150 or fewer) and excellent presenter-to-attendee ratio make this a highly effective and productive conference. The presenters are major names in the publishing business, but take personal interest in the projects discovered at this event each year." Guidelines available on website [sfwritingforchange.org].

SASKATCHEWAN FESTIVAL OF WORDS

217 Main St. N., Moose Jaw SK S6J 0W1 Canada. **Website:** www.festivalofwords.com. Estab. 1997. Annual 4-day event, third week of July (2014 dates: July 17-20). Location: Moose Jaw Library/Art Museum complex in Crescent Park. Average attendance: about 4,000 admissions. "Canadian authors up close and personal for readers and writers of all ages in mystery, poetry, memoir, fantasy, graphic novels, history, and novel. Each summer festival includes more than 60 events within 2 blocks of historic Main Street. Audience favorite activities include workshops for writers, audience readings, drama, performance poetry, concerts, panels, and music."

ACCOMMODATIONS Information available at www.templegardens.sk.ca, campgrounds, and bed and breakfast establishments. Complete information about festival presenters, events, costs, and schedule also available on website.

SCBWI—CANADA EAST

Canada. **E-mail:** canadaeast@scbwi.org. **Website:** www.canadaeast.scbwi.org. **Contact:** Lizann Flatt, regional advisor. Writer and illustrator events geared toward all levels. Usually offers one event in spring and another in the fall. Check website Events pages for updated information.

SCBWI COLORADO/WYOMING (ROCKY MOUNTAIN) EVENTS

E-mail: denise@rmcscbwi.org; todd.tuell@rmcscbwi.org. **Website:** www.rmc.scbwi.org. **Contact:** Todd Tuell and Denise Vega, co-regional advisors. SCBWI Rocky Mountain chapter (CO/WY) offers special events, schmoozes, meetings, and conferences throughout the year. Major events: Fall Conference (annually, September); Summer Retreat, "Big Sur in the Rockies" (bi- and triannually). More info on website.

SCBWI—MIDATLANTIC, ANNUAL FALL CONFERENCE

P.O. Box 3215, Reston VA 20195. **E-mail:** teaganek@hotmail.com; valopttrsn@verizon.net. **Website:** midatlantic.scbwi.org/. **Contact:** Erin Teagan and Valerie Patterson, conference co-chairs; Ellen R. Braff, advisor. For updates and details visit website. Registration limited to 275. Conference fills quickly. Cost: $145 for SCBWI members; $175 for nonmembers. Includes continental breakfast and boxed lunch. Optional craft-focused workshops and individual consultations with conference faculty are available for additional fees.

SCBWI WINTER CONFERENCE ON WRITING AND ILLUSTRATING FOR CHILDREN

8271 Beverly Blvd., Los Angeles CA 90048. (323)782-1010. **Fax:** (323)782-1892. **E-mail:** scbwi@scbwi.org. **Website:** www.scbwi.org. **Contact:** Stephen Mooser. Estab. 2000 (formerly SCBWI Midyear Conference). Society of Children's book Writers and Illustrators. Annual. Conference held in February. Average attendance: 1,000. Conference is to promote writing and illustrating for children: picture books; fiction; nonfiction; middle grade and young adult; network with professionals; financial planning for writers; marketing your book; art exhibition; etc. Site: Manhattan.

COSTS See website for current cost and conference information.

ADDITIONAL INFORMATION SCBWI also holds an annual summer conference in August in Los Angeles. Visit website for details.

THE SCHOOL FOR WRITERS FALL WORKSHOP

The Humber School for Writers, Humber Institute of Technology & Advanced Learning, 3199 Lake Shore Blvd. W., Toronto ON M8V 1K8 Canada. (416)675-6622. **E-mail:** antanas.sileika@humber.ca; hilary.higgins@humber.ca. **Website:** www.humber.ca/scapa/programs/school-writers. The School for Writers Workshop has moved to the fall with the International Festival of Authors. The workshop runs during the last week in October. Conference duration: 1 week. Average attendance: 60. New writers from around the world gather to study with faculty members to work on their novels, short stories, poetry, or creative nonfiction. Agents and editors participate in the conference. Include a work-in-progress with your registration. Faculty has included Martin Amis, David Mitchell, Kevin Barry, Rachel Kuschner, Peter Carey, Roddy Doyle, Tim O'Brien, Andrea Levy, Barry Unsworth, Edward Albee, Ha Jin, Julia Glass, Mavis Gallant, Bruce Jay Friedman, Isabel Huggan, Alistair MacLeod, Lisa Moore, Kim Moritsugu, Francine Prose, Paul Quarrington, Olive Senior, and D.M. Thomas, Annabel Lyon, Mary Gaitskill, M. G. Vassanji.

COSTS Around $850 (in 2014). Some limited scholarships are available.

ADDITIONAL INFORMATION Accepts inquiries by e-mail, phone, and fax.

SCHOOL OF THE ARTS AT RHINELANDER UW-MADISON CONTINUING STUDIES

21 N Park St., 7th Floor, Madison WI 53715-1218. (608)262-7389. **E-mail:** lkaufman@dcs.wisc.edu. **Website:** continuingstudies.wisc.edu/lsa/soa/. Estab. 1964. "Each summer for 50 years, more than 250 people gather in northern Wisconsin for a week of study, performance, exhibits, and other creative activities. More than 50 workshops in writing, body/mind/spirit; food and fitness; art and folk art; music; and digital media are offered. Participants can choose from any and all 1-, 2-, 3- and 5-day classes to craft their own mix for creative exploration and renewal." Dates: July 19-23, 2014. Location: James Williams Middle School and Rhinelander High School, Rhinelander, WI. Average attendance: 250.

COSTS Ranges from $20-$300 based on workshops.

ACCOMMODATIONS Informational available from Rhinelander Chamber of Commerce.

SEWANEE WRITERS' CONFERENCE

735 University Ave., 119 Gailor Hall, Stamler Center, Sewanee TN 37383-1000. (931) 598-1654. **E-mail:** allatham@sewanee.edu. **Website:** www.sewaneewriters.org. **Contact:** Adam Latham. Estab. 1990. Annual conference. 2014 dates: July 22–Aug. 3. Average attendance: 150. "The University of the South will host the 25th session of the Sewanee Writers' Conference. Thanks to the generosity of the Walter E. Dakin Memorial Fund, supported by the estate of the late Tennessee Williams, the Conference will gather a distinguished faculty to provide instruction and criticism through workshops and craft lectures in poetry, fiction, and playwriting. During an intense twelve-day period, participants will read and critique each other's manuscripts under the leadership of some of our country's finest fiction writers, poets, and playwrights. All faculty members and fellows give scheduled readings; senior faculty members offer craft lectures; open-mic readings accommodate many others. Additional writers, along with a host of writing professionals, visit to give readings, participate in panel discussions, and entertain questions from the audience. Receptions and mealtimes offer opportunities for informal exchange. This year's faculty includes fiction writers John Casey, Tony Earley, Adrianne Harun, Randall Kenan, Margot Livesey, Jill McCorkle, Alice McDermott, Christine Schutt, Allen Wier, and Steve Yarbrough; and poets Claudia Emerson, B.H. Fairchild, Debora Greger, William Logan, Maurice Manning, Charles Martin, Mary Jo Salter, and A.E. Stallings. Daisy Foote and Dan O'Brien will lead the playwriting workshop. Diane Johnson and Wyatt Prunty will read from their work. The Conference will offer its customary Walter E. Dakin Fellowships and Tennessee Williams Scholarships, as well as awards in memory of Stanley Elkin, Horton Foote, Barry Hannah, John Hollander, Donald Justice, Romulus Linney, Howard Nemerov, Father William Ralston, Peter Taylor, Mona Van Duyn, and John N. Wall. Additional scholarships have been made possible by Georges and Anne Borchardt and Gail Hochman. Every participant—whether contributor, scholar, or fellow—receives assistance. The Conference fee reflects but two-thirds of the actual cost to attend. Additional funding is awarded to fellows and scholars."

COSTS $1,000 for tuition and $800 for room, board, and activity costs.

ACCOMMODATIONS Participants are housed in single rooms in university dormitories. Bathrooms are shared by small groups.

SOCIETY OF CHILDREN'S BOOK WRITERS & ILLUSTRATORS ANNUAL SUMMER CONFERENCE ON WRITING AND ILLUSTRATING FOR CHILDREN

8271 Beverly Blvd., Los Angeles CA 90048-4515. (323)782-1010. **Fax:** (323)782-1892. **E-mail:** scbwi@scbwi.org. **Website:** www.scbwi.org. Estab. 1972. Annual conference held in early August. Conference duration: 4 days. Average attendance: 1,000. Held at the Century Plaza Hotel in Los Angeles. Speakers have included Andrea Brown, Steven Malk, Ashley Bryan, Bruce Coville, Karen Hesse, Harry Mazer, Lucia Monfried, and Russell Freedman. Agents will be speaking and sometimes participate in ms critiques.

COSTS Approximately $450 (does not include hotel room).

ACCOMMODATIONS Information on overnight accommodations is made available.

ADDITIONAL INFORMATION Ms and illustration critiques are available. Brochure/guidelines are available in June online or for SASE.

⊕ SOUTH CAROLINA WRITERS WORKSHOP

4840 Forest Drive, Suite 6B: PMB 189, Columbia SC 29206. **E-mail:** scwwliaison@gmail.com; scww2013@gmail.com. **Website:** www.myscww.org/. Estab. 1991. Conference in October held at the Hilton Myrtle Beach Resort in Myrtle Beach, SC. Held almost every year. (2014 dates: Oct. 24-26.) Conference duration: 3 days. The conference features critique sessions, open mic readings, presentations from agents and editors and more. The conference features more than 50 different workshops for writers to choose from, dealing with all subjects of writing craft, writing business, getting an agent and more. Agents will be in attendance.

ACCOMMODATIONS Hilton Myrtle Beach Resort.

SOUTH COAST WRITERS CONFERENCE

Southwestern Oregon Community College, P.O. Box 590, 29392 Ellensburg Ave., Gold Beach OR 97444. (541)247-2741. **Fax:** (541)247-6247. **E-mail:** scwc@socc.edu. **Website:** www.socc.edu/scwriters. Estab. 1996. Annual conference held Presidents Day weekend in February. Conference duration: 2 days. Covers fiction, poetry, children's, nature, songwriting, and marketing. Melissa Hart is the next scheduled keynote speaker, and presenters include Robert Arellano, Bill Cameron, Tanya Chernov, Heidi Connolly, Kelly Davio, Tawna Fenske, Kim Cooper Findling, Stefanie Freele, and songwriter Chuck Pyle.

ADDITIONAL INFORMATION See website for cost and additional details.

SOUTHEASTERN WRITERS ASSOCIATION- ANNUAL CONFERENCE

161 Woodstone, Athens GA 30605. **E-mail:** purple@southeasternwriters.org. **Website:** www.southeasternwriters.com. **Contact:** Amy Munnell & Sheila Hudson, presidents. Estab. 1975. **Open to all writers.** (2014 dates: June 13-17.) Contests with cash prizes. Instruction offered for novel and short fiction, nonfiction, writing for children, humor, inspirational writing, and poetry. Manuscript deadline April 1st, includes free evaluation conference(s) with instructor(s). Agent in residence. Annual 4-day workshop held in June. Cost of workshop: $445 for 4 days or lower prices for daily tuition. (See online.) Accommodations: Offers overnight accommodations on workshop site. Visit website for more information and cost of overnight accommodations. E-mail or send SASE for brochure.

ACCOMMODATIONS Multiple hotels available in St. Simon's Island, GA.

SPACE COAST WRITERS GUILD ANNUAL CONFERENCE

(321)956-7193. **E-mail:** scwg-jm@cfl.rr.com; stilley@scwg.org. **Website:** www.scwg.org/conference.asp. Annual conference held last weekend of January along the east coast of central Florida. Conference duration: 2 days. Average attendance: 150+. This conference is hosted each winter in Florida and features a variety of presenters on all topics writing. Critiques are available for a price, and agents in attendance will take pitches from writers. Previous presenters have included Debra Dixon, Davis Bunn (writer), Ellen Pepus (agent), Jennifer Crusie, Chuck Sambuchino, Madeline Smoot, Mike Resnick, Christina York, Ben Bova, Elizabeth Sinclair.

COSTS $180-220. Agent and editor appointments cost more.

ACCOMMODATIONS The conference is hosted on a beachside hotel, with special room rates available.

ADDITIONAL INFORMATION Agents are in attendance taking pitches every year.

SPACE (SMALL PRESS AND ALTERNATIVE COMICS EXPO)

Back Porch Comics, P.O. Box 20550, Columbus OH 43220. **E-mail:** bpc13@earthlink.net. **Website:** www.backporchcomics.com/space.htm. Next conference/trade show to be held April 12-13, 2014. Conference duration: 2 days. "The Midwest's largest exhibition of small press, alternative, and creator-owned comics." Site: Held at Ramada Plaza Hotel and Conference Center, 4900 Sinclair Rd., Columbus, OH 43229. Over 150 small press artists, writers, and publishers.

COSTS Admission: $5 per day or $8 for weekend.

ADDITIONAL INFORMATION For brochure, visit website. Editors participate in conference.

SQUAW VALLEY COMMUNITY OF WRITERS

P.O. Box 1416, Nevada City CA 95959-1416. (530)470-8440. **E-mail:** info@squawvalleywriters.org. **Website:** www.squawvalleywriters.org. **Contact:** Brett Hall Jones, executive director. Estab. 1969.

COSTS Tuition is $995, which includes 6 dinners.

ACCOMMODATIONS The Community of Writers rents houses and condominiums in the Valley for participants to live in during the week of the conference. Single room (1 participant): $700/week. Double room (twin beds, room shared by conference participant of the same sex): $465/week. Multiple room (bunk beds, room shared with 2 or more participants of the same sex): $295/week. All rooms subject to availability; early requests are recommended. Can arrange airport shuttle pick-ups for a fee.

ADDITIONAL INFORMATION Admissions are based on submitted ms (unpublished fiction, 1 or 2 stories or novel chapters); requires $35 reading fee. Submit ms to Brett Hall Jones, Squaw Valley Community of Writers, P.O. Box 1416, Nevada City, CA 95959. Brochures are available online or for an SASE in February. Send inquiries via e-mail. Accepts inquiries by SASE, e-mail, phone. Agents and editors attend/participate in conferences.

STORY WEAVERS CONFERENCE

Oklahoma Writer's Federation, (405)682-6000. **E-mail:** president@owfi.org. **Website:** www.OWFI.org. **Contact:** Linda Apple, president. Oklahoma Writer's Federation, Inc. is open and welcoming to writers of all genres and all skill levels. Our goal is to help writers become better and to help beginning writers understand and master the craft of writing.

COSTS Cost is $150 before April. $175 after April. Cost includes awards banquet and famous author banquet. Three extra sessions are available for an extra fee: How to Self-Publish Your Novel on Kindle, Nook, and iPad (and make more money than being published by New York), with Dan Case; When Polar Bear Wishes Came True: Understanding and Creating Meaningful Stories, with Jack Dalton; How to Create Three-Dimensional Characters, with Steven James.

ACCOMMODATIONS The site is at the Embassy Suite using their meeting halls. There are very few stairs and the rooms are close together for easy access.

ADDITIONAL INFORMATION "We have 20 speakers, five agents, and nine publisher/editors. For a full list and bios, please see website."

SUMMER WRITING PROGRAM

Naropa University, 2130 Arapahoe Ave., Boulder CO 80302. (303)245-4862. **Fax:** (303)546-5287. **E-mail:** swpr@naropa.edu. **Website:** www.naropa.edu/swp. **Contact:** Kyle Pivarnik, special projects manager. Estab. 1974. Annual. 2014 Workshops held June 1-28. Workshop duration: 4 weeks. Average attendance: 250. Offers college credit. Accepts inquiries by e-mail, phone. With 13 workshops to choose from each of the 4 weeks of the program, students may study poetry, prose, hybrid/cross-genre writing, small press printing, or book arts. Site: All workshops, panels, lectures and readings are hosted on the Naropa University main campus. Located in downtown Boulder, the campus is within easy walking distance of restaurants, shopping, and the scenic Pearl Street Mall.

COSTS In 2013: $500/week, $2,000 for all 4 weeks (non-credit students).

ACCOMMODATIONS Housing is available at Snow Lion Apartments. Additional info is available on the housing website: naropa.edu/student-life/housing/.

ADDITIONAL INFORMATION Writers can elect to take the Summer Writing Program for noncredit, graduate, or undergraduate credit. The registration procedure varies, so consider whether or not you'll be taking the SWP for academic credit. All participants can elect to take any combination of the first, second, third, and/or fourth weeks. To request a catalog of upcoming programs or to find additional information, visit naropa.edu/swp. Naropa University also welcomes participants with disabilities. Contact Andrea Rexilius at (303)546-5296 or arexilius@naropa.edu before May 15 to inquire about accessibility and disability accommodations needed to participate fully in this event.

SURREY INTERNATIONAL WRITERS' CONFERENCE

SIWC, P.O. Box 42023 RPO Guildford, Surrey BC V3R 1S5 Canada. **E-mail:** kathychung@siwc.ca. **Website:** www.siwc.ca. **Contact:** Kathy Chung, proposals contact and conference coordinator. Annual writing conference outside Vancouver, CA, held every October. Writing workshops geared toward beginner, intermediate, and advanced levels. More than 70 workshops and panels, on all topics and genres. Blue Pencil and Agent/Editor Pitch sessions included. Different conference price packages available. Check our website for more information. This event has many literary agents in attendance taking pitches.

TAOS SUMMER WRITERS' CONFERENCE

Department of English Language and Literature, MSC 03 2170, 1 University of New Mexico, Albuquerque NM 87131-0001. (505)277-5572. **Fax:** (505)277-2950. **E-mail:** taosconf@unm.edu. **Website:** www.unm.edu/~taosconf. **Contact:** Sharon Oard Warner. Estab. 1999. Annual conference held in July. Offers workshops and master classes in the novel, short story, poetry, creative nonfiction, memoir, prose style, screenwriting, humor writing, yoga and writing, literary translation, book proposal, the query letter and revision. Participants may also schedule a consultation with a visiting agent/editor.

COSTS Weeklong workshop registration $650, weekend workshop registration $350, master classes between $1,250 and $1,525.

ACCOMMODATIONS Held at the Sagebrush Inn and Conference Center.

TEXAS CHRISTIAN WRITERS' CONFERENCE

7401 Katy Freeway, Houston TX 77092. (713)686-7209. **E-mail:** dannywoodall@yahoo.com. **Contact:** Danny Woodall. Estab. 1990. Open conference for all interested writers, held the first Saturday in August. "Focus on all genres." Sponsors a contest for short fiction; categories include articles, devotionals, poetry, short story, book proposals, drama. Fees: $8-15. Conference information available with SASE or e-mail to Danny Woodall. Agents participate in conference. Senior discounts available.

COSTS $65 for members of IWA, $80 nonmembers, discounts for seniors (60+) and couples, meal at noon, continental breakfast and breaks.

ACCOMMODATIONS Offers list of area hotels or lodging options.

ADDITIONAL INFORMATION Open conference for all interested writers. Sponsors a contest for short fiction; categories include articles, devotionals, poetry, short story, book proposals, drama. Fees: $8-15. Conference information available with SASE or e-mail to Danny Woodall. Agents participate in conference. (For contest information, contact patav@aol.com.)

TEXAS WRITING RETREAT

Grimes County, TX. **E-mail:** PaulTCuclis@gmail.com. **E-mail:** PaulTCuclis@gmail.com. **Website:** www.texaswritingretreat.com. **Contact:** Paul Cuclis, coordinator. Estab. 2013. The Texas Writing Retreat is an intimate event with a limited number of attendees. Held on a private residence ranch an hour outside of Houston, it has an agent and editor in attendance teaching. All attendees get to pitch the attending agent. Meals and excursions and amenities included. This is a unique event that combines craft sessions, business sessions, time for writing, relaxation, and more.

COSTS Costs vary per year. Check the website for latest updates. There are different pricing options for those staying onsite vs. commuters.

ACCOMMODATIONS Private ranch residence in Texas.

THRILLERFEST

P.O. Box 311, Eureka CA 95502. **E-mail:** infocentral@thrillerwriters.org. **Website:** www.thrillerfest.com. **Contact:** Kimberley Howe, executive director. Grand Hyatt New York, 109 E. 42nd St., New York, NY 10017. Estab. 2006. Annual. 2014: July 8-12 in Manhattan. Conference duration: 5 days. Average attendance: 900. Workshop/conference/festival. "A great place to learn the craft of writing the thriller. Classes taught by NYT best-selling authors. A fabulous event for fans/readers to meet and spend a few days with their favorite authors and packed with terrific programming." Speakers have included David Morrell, James Patterson, Sandra Brown, Ken Follett, Eric Van Lustbader, David Baldacci, Brad Meltzer, Steve Martini, R.L. Stine, Steve Berry, Kathleen Antrim, Douglas Preston, Gayle Lynds, Harlan Coben, Lee Child, Lisa Scottolini,

Katherine Neville, Robin Cook, Andrew Gross, Kathy Reichs, Brad Thor, Clive Cussler, Donald Maass, M.J. Rose, and Al Zuckerman. Two days of the conference are CraftFest, where the focus is on the craft of writing, and 2 days are ThrillerFest, which showcase the author-fan relationship. Also featured: AgentFest—a unique event where authors can pitch their work face-to-face to 50 top literary agents, and the International Thriller Awards and Banquet.

COSTS Price will vary from $300-1,100, depending on which events are selected. Various package deals are available offering savings, and Early Bird pricing is offered beginning September of each year.

ACCOMMODATIONS Grand Hyatt in New York City.

TMCC WRITERS' CONFERENCE

Truckee Meadows Community College, 5270 Neil Rd., Reno NV 89502. (775)829-9010. **Fax:** (775)829-9032. **E-mail:** wdce@tmcc.edu. **Website:** wdce.tmcc.edu. Estab. 1991. Annual conference held April 27. Average attendance: 150. Conference focuses on strengthening mainstream/literary fiction and nonfiction works and how to market them to agents and publishers. Site: Truckee Meadows Community College in Reno, Nevada. "There is always an array of speakers and presenters with impressive literary credentials, including agents and editors." Speakers have included Chuck Sambuchino, Sheree Bykofsky, Andrea Brown, Dorothy Allison, Karen Joy Fowler, James D. Houston, James N. Frey, Gary Short, Jane Hirschfield, Dorrianne Laux, and Kim Addonizio.

COSTS $119 for a full-day seminar; $32 for a 10-minute one-on-one appointment with an agent or editor.

ACCOMMODATIONS Contact the conference manager to learn about accommodation discounts.

ADDITIONAL INFORMATION "The conference is open to all writers, regardless of their level of experience. Brochures are available online and mailed in January. Send inquiries via e-mail."

TONY HILLERMAN WRITER'S CONFERENCE

1063 Willow Way, Santa FE NM 87505. (505)471-1565. **E-mail:** wordharvest@wordharvest.com. **Website:** www.wordharvest.com. **Contact:** Jean Schaumberg, co-director. Estab. 2004. Annual event held in November. Conference duration: 3 days. Average attendance: 100. Site: Hilton Santa Fe Historic Plaza. First day: Pre-Conference Workshops, hands-on and interactive, taught by published authors who are also wonderful teachers. Second day: The New Book/New Author Breakfast where author attendees have a chance to talk about their new books. A full day of presentations on the craft of writing. We honor the winner of the $10,000 Tony Hillerman Prize for best first mystery at the Hillerman luncheon. A flash critique session—Writing With the Stars—is open to any interested attendee and adds to the fun and information. Third day: A full day of presentations on the business of writing. A book signing/reception is followed by the keynote dinner.

COSTS Previous year's costs: $395 per registration.

ACCOMMODATIONS Hilton Santa Fe Historic Plaza offers $119 single or double occupancy. November 6-10. Book online with the hotel.

ADDITIONAL INFORMATION Sponsors a $10,000 first mystery novel contest with St. Martin's Press. Submission deadline for the Hillerman Mystery Competition is June 1. Visit the website for more guidelines.

UMKC WRITING CONFERENCE

5300 Rockhill Rd., Kansas City MO 64110. (816)235-2736. **Fax:** (816)235-5279. **E-mail:** wittfeldk@umkc.edu. **Website:** www.newletters.org/writers-wanted/nl-weekend-writing-conference. **Contact:** Kathi Wittfeld. New Letters Weekend Writing Conference will be held June 27-29, 2014, at Diastole. New Letters Writer's Conference is geared toward all levels—beginner, intermediate, advanced and professional levels. Conference open to students and community. Annual workshops. Workshops held in Summer. Cost of workshop varies. Write for more information. Mark Twain Writers Workshop will not be held in 2014.

⊕ UNICORN WRITERS CONFERENCE

P.O. Box 176, Redding CT 06876. (203)938-7405. **E-mail:** bookings@unicornwritersconference.com; unicornwritersconference@gmail.com. **Website:** www.unicornwritersconference.com. This writers conference draws upon its close proximity to New York City and pulls in many literary agents and editors to pitch each year. There are sessions, tracks, pitch gatherings, query/manuscript review sessions, and more.

ACCOMMODATIONS Held at Saint Clements Castle in Connecticut. Directions available on event website.

UNIVERSITY OF NORTH DAKOTA WRITERS CONFERENCE

Department of English, 110 Merrifield Hall, 276 Centennial Drive, Stop 7209, Grand Forks ND 58202.

(701)777-2393. **Fax:** (701)777-2373. **E-mail:** crystal.alberts@email.und.edu. **Website:** und.edu/orgs/writers-conference/. **Contact:** Crystal Alberts, director. Estab. 1970. Annual conference. 2014 dates: April 2-4. Offers panels, readings, and films focused around a specific theme. Almost all events take place in the UND Memorial Union, which has a variety of small rooms and a 1,000-seat main hall. Past speakers include Art Spiegelman, Truman Capote, Sir Salman Rushdie, Allen Ginsberg, Alice Walker, and Louise Erdrich.

COSTS All events are free and open to the public. Donations accepted.

ACCOMMODATIONS All events are free and open to the public. Accommodations available at area hotels. Information on overnight accommodations available on website.

ADDITIONAL INFORMATION Schedule and other information available on website.

UW-MADISON WRITERS' INSTITUTE

21 North Park St., Room 7331, Madison WI 53715. (608)265-3972. **Fax:** (608)265-2475. **E-mail:** lscheer@dcs.wisc.edu. **Website:** www.uwwritersinstitute.org. **Contact:** Laurie Scheer. Estab. 1989. Annual. Conference usually held in April. Site: Madison Concourse Hotel, downtown Madison. Average attendance: 350-500. Conference speakers provide workshops and consultations. For information, send e-mail, visit website, call, fax. Accepts inquiries by SASE, e-mail, phone, fax. Agents and editors participate in conference.

COSTS $160-260; includes materials, breaks.

ACCOMMODATIONS Provides a list of area hotels or lodging options.

ADDITIONAL INFORMATION Sponsors contest.

VIRGINIA CENTER FOR THE CREATIVE ARTS

154 San Angelo Dr., Amherst VA 24521. (434)946-7236. **Fax:** (434)946-7239. **E-mail:** vcca@vcca.com. **Website:** www.vcca.com. Estab. 1971. Offers residencies year-round, typical residency lasts 2 weeks to 2 months. Open to originating artists: composers, writers, and visual artists. Accommodates 25 at one time. Personal living quarters include 22 single rooms, 2 double rooms, bathrooms shared with one other person. All meals are served. Kitchens for fellows' use available at studios and residence. The VCCA van goes into town twice a week. Fellows share their work regularly. Four studios have pianos. No transportation costs are covered. "Artists are accepted into the VCCA without regard for their ability to contribute financially to their residency. Daily cost is $180 per fellow. We ask fellows to contribute according to their ability."

COSTS Application fee: $30. Deadline: May 15 for October-January residency; September 15 for February-May residency; January 15 for June-September residency. Send SASE for application form or download from website. Applications are reviewed by panelists.

WESTERN RESERVE WRITERS & FREELANCE CONFERENCE

7700 Clocktower Dr., Kirtland OH 44094. (440) 525-7812. **E-mail:** deencr@aol.com. **Website:** www.deannaadams.com. **Contact:** Deanna Adams, director/conference coordinator. Estab. 1983. Biannual. Last conference held September 28, 2013. Conference duration: 1 day or half-day. Average attendance: 120. "The Western Reserve Writers Conferences are designed for all writers, aspiring and professional, and offer presentations in all genres—nonfiction, fiction, poetry, essays, creative nonfiction, and the business of writing, including Web writing and successful freelance writing." Site: "Located in the main building of Lakeland Community College, the conference is easy to find and just off the I-90 freeway. The Fall 2013 conference featured top-notch presenters from newspapers and magazines, along with published authors, freelance writers, and professional editors. Presentations included developing issues in today's publishing and publishing options, turning writing into a lifelong vocation, as well as workshops on plotting, creating credible characters, writing mysteries, romance writing, and tips on submissions, getting books into stores, and storytelling for both fiction and nonfiction writers. Included throughout the day are one-on-one editing consults, Q&A panel, and book sale/author signings."

COSTS Fall all-day conference includes lunch: $95. Spring half-day conference, no lunch: $69.

ADDITIONAL INFORMATION Brochures for the conferences are available by January (for spring conference) and July (for fall). Also accepts inquiries by e-mail and phone. Check Deanna Adams' website for all updates. Editors and agents often attend the conferences.

WHIDBEY ISLAND WRITERS' CONFERENCE

P.O. Box 1289, Langley WA 98260. **E-mail:** admin@nila.edu; wiwc@nila.edu. **Website:** www.nila.edu/wiwc/. This is an annual writing conference in the Pacific Northwest. There are a variety of sessions on topics such as fiction, craft, poetry, platform, agents, screenwriting, and much more. Topics are varied, and there is something for all writers. Multiple agents and editors are in attendance. The schedule and faculty change every year, and those changes are reflected online.

WILLAMETTE WRITERS CONFERENCE

2108 Buck St., West Linn OR 97068. (503)305-6729. **Fax:** (503)344-6174. **Website:** www.willamettewriters.com/wwc/3/. Estab. 1981. Annual conference held in August. (2014 dates: Aug. 1-3.) Conference duration: 3 days. Average attendance: 600. "Willamette Writers is open to all writers, and we plan our conference accordingly. We offer workshops on all aspects of fiction, nonfiction, marketing, the creative process, screenwriting, etc. Also, we invite top-notch inspirational speakers for keynote addresses. We always include at least 1 agent or editor panel and offer a variety of topics of interest to both fiction and nonfiction writers and screenwriters." Agents will be speaking and available for meetings with attendees.

COSTS Pricing schedule available online.

ACCOMMODATIONS If necessary, arrangements can be made on an individual basis through the conference hotel. Special rates may be available. 2014 location is the Lloyd Center DoubleTree Hotel.

ADDITIONAL INFORMATION Brochure/guidelines are available for a catalog-sized SASE.

WINCHESTER WRITERS' CONFERENCE, FESTIVAL AND BOOKFAIR, AND IN-DEPTH WRITING WORKSHOPS

University of Winchester, Winchester Hampshire WA S022 4NR United Kingdom. 44 (0) 1962 827238. **E-mail:** judith.heneghan@winchester.ac.uk. **Website:** www.writersfestival.co.uk. The 34th Winchester Writers' Festival will be held on June 20-22 at the University of Winchester, Winchester, Hampshire S022 4NR. Joanne Harris, internationally acclaimed author of *Chocolat*, will give the Keynote Address and will lead an outstanding team of 60 best-selling authors, commissioning editors and literary agents offering day-long workshops, 40 short talks and 500 one-to-one appointments to help writers harness their creative ideas, turn them into marketable work and pitch to publishing professionals. Participate by entering some of the 12 writing competitions, even if you can't attend. Over 120 writers have now reported major publishing successes as a direct result of their attendance at past conferences. This leading international literary event offers a magnificent source of support, advice, inspiration and networking opportunities for new and published writers working in all genres. Enjoy a creative writing holiday in Winchester, the oldest city in England and only one hour from London. To view Festival programme, including all the competition details, go to: writersfestival.co.uk.

WISCONSIN BOOK FESTIVAL

Madison Public Library, 201 W. Mifflin St., Madison WI 53703. (608)266-6300. **E-mail:** bookfest@mplfoundation.org. **Website:** www.wisconsinbookfestival.org. Estab. 2002. Annual festival held in October. Conference duration: 5 days. The festival features readings, lectures, book discussions, writing workshops, live interviews, children's events, and more. Speakers have included Isabel Allende, Jonathan Alter, Paul Auster, Michael Chabon, Billy Collins, Phillip Gourevitch, Ian Frazier, Tim O'Brien, Elizabeth Strout.

COSTS All festival events are free.

WOMEN WRITERS WINTER RETREAT

Homestead House B&B, 38111 West Spaulding, Willoughby OH 44094. (440)946-1902. **E-mail:** deencr@aol.com. **Website:** www.deannaadams.com. Estab. 2007. Annual—always happens the last weekend in February. Conference duration: 3 days. Average attendance: 35-40. Retreat. "The Women Writers' Winter Retreat was designed for aspiring and professional women writers who cannot seem to find enough time to devote to honing their craft. Each retreat offers class time and workshops facilitated by successful women writers, as well as allows time to do some actual writing, alone or in a group. A Friday night dinner and keynote kick-starts the weekend, followed by Saturday workshops, free time, meals, and an open mic to read your works. Sunday wraps up with 1 more workshop and fellowship. All genres welcome. Choice of overnight stay or commuting." Site: Located in the heart of downtown Willoughby, this warm and attractive bed and breakfast is easy to find, around the corner from the main street, Erie Street, and behind a popular Arabica coffee house. Door prizes and book sale/author signings throughout the weekend.

COSTS Single room: $315; shared room: $235 (includes complete weekend package, with B&B stay and all meals and workshops); weekend commute: $165; Saturday only: $125 (prices include lunch and dinner).

ADDITIONAL INFORMATION Brochures for the writers retreat are available by December. Accepts inquiries and reservations by e-mail or phone. See Deanna's website for additional information and updates.

WOMEN WRITING THE WEST

8547 E. Araphoe Rd., Box J-541, Greenwood Village CO 80112-1436. **E-mail:** conference@womenwritingthewest.org. **Website:** www.womenwritingthewest.org. 2014 dates: Oct 16-20 in Denver, Colo. "Women Writing the West is a nonprofit association of writers, editors, publishers, agents, booksellers, and other professionals writing and promoting the women's West. As such, women writing their stories in the American West in a way that illuminates them authentically. In addition, the organization provides support, encouragement, and inspiration to all women writing about any facet of the American West. Membership is open to all interested persons worldwide. Open to students. Cost of membership: Annual membership dues $65. Publisher dues are $65. International dues are $70. In addition to the annual dues, there is an option to become a sustaining member for $100. Sustaining members receive a WWW enamel logo pin, prominent listing in WWW publications, and the knowledge that they are assisting the organization. Members actively exchange ideas on a list e-bulletin board. WWW membership also allows the choice of participation in our marketing marvel, the annual WWW Catalog of Author's Books. An annual conference is held every fall. Our blog, Facebook and ListServ publish current WWW activities; features market research, and experience articles of interest pertaining to American West literature and member news. Sponsors annual WILLA Literary Award, which is given in several categories for outstanding literature featuring women's stories, set in the West. The winner of a WILLA literary Award receives a cash award and a trophy at the annual conference. Contest open to non-members. Annual conference held in third weekend in October. Covers research, writing techniques, multiple genres, marketing/promotion, and more. Agents and editors will be speaking and available for one-on-one meetings with attendees. Conference location changes each year."

COSTS See website. Discounts available for members, and for specific days only.

ACCOMMODATIONS See website for location and accommodation details.

WORDS & MUSIC

624 Pirate's Alley, New Orleans LA 70116. (504)586-1609. **Fax:** (504)522-9725. **E-mail:** info@wordsandmusic.org. **Website:** www.wordsandmusic.org. Estab. 1997. Annual conference held in November. 2014 conference: 20-24. Conference duration: 5 days. Average attendance: 300. Presenters include authors, agents, editors and publishers. Past speakers included agents Deborah Grosvenor, Judith Weber, Stuart Bernstein, Nat Sobel, Jeff Kleinman, Emma Sweeney, Liza Dawson and Michael Murphy; editors Lauren Marino, Webster Younce, Ann Patty, Will Murphy, Jofie Ferrari-Adler, Elizabeth Stein; critics Marie Arana, Jonathan Yardley, and Michael Dirda; fiction writers Oscar Hijuelos, Robert Olen Butler, Shirley Ann Grau, Mayra Montero, Ana Castillo, H.G. Carrillo. Agents and editors critique manuscripts in advance; meet with them one-on-one during the conference.

COSTS See website for a costs and additional information on accommodations. Website will update closer to date of conference.

ACCOMMODATIONS Hotel Monteleone in New Orleans.

WRITE-BY-THE-LAKE WRITER'S WORKSHOP & RETREAT

21 N. Park St., 7th Floor, Madison WI 53715. (608)262-3447. **E-mail:** cdesmet@dcs.wisc.edu. **Website:** www.dcs.wisc.edu/lsa/writing. **Contact:** Christine DeSmet, director. Open to all writers and students; 12 workshops for all levels. Includes 2 Master Classes for full-novel critique. Held the third week of June on UW-Madison campus. Registration limited to 15; fewer in Master Classes. Writing facilities available; computer labs, wi-fi in all buildings and on the outdoor lakeside terrace.

COSTS $365 before May 20; $415 after May 20. Additional cost for Master Classes and college credits. Cost includes instruction, welcome luncheon, and pastry/coffee each day.

ADDITIONAL INFORMATION E-mail for more information. "Registration opens every December for following June. See web pages online."

WRITE CANADA

The Word Guild, P.O. Box 1243, Trenton ON K8V 5R9 Canada. **E-mail:** info@thewordguild.com. **E-mail:** writecanada@rogers.com. **Website:** www.writecanada.org. Conference duration: 3 days. Annual conference. 2014 dates: June 12-14 in Guelph, Ontario, for writers who are Christian of all types and at all stages. Offers solid instruction, stimulating interaction, exciting challenges, and worshipful community.

WRITERS@WORK CONFERENCE

P.O. Box 711191, Salt Lake City UT 84171-1191. (801)996-3313. **E-mail:** jennifer@writersatwork.org. **Website:** www.writersatwork.org. Estab. 1985. Annual conference held in June. (The 2014 conference is June 4-8.) Conference duration: 5 days. Average attendance: 250. Morning workshops (3-hours/day) focus on novel, advanced fiction, generative fiction, nonfiction, poetry, and young adult fiction. Afternoon sessions will include craft lectures, discussions, and directed interviews with authors, agents, and editors. In addition to the traditional, one-on-one manuscript consultations, there will be many opportunities to mingle informally with agents/editors. Held at the Alta Lodge in Alta Lodge, Utah. Speakers have included Steve Almond, Bret Lott, Shannon Hale, Emily Forland (Wendy Weil Agency), Julie Culver (Folio Literary Management, Chuck Adams (Algonquin Press), and Mark A. Taylor (Juniper Press).

COSTS $690-1,005, based on housing type and consultations.

ACCOMMODATIONS Onsite housing available. Additional lodging and meal information is on the website.

WRITER'S DIGEST CONFERENCES

F+W Media, Inc., 10151 Carver Road, Suite 200, Blue Ash OH 45242. **E-mail:** jill.ruesch@fwmedia.com. **E-mail:** phil.sexton@fwmedia.com. **Website:** www.writersdigestconference.com. Estab. 1995. The Writer's Digest conferences feature an amazing lineup of speakers to help writers with the craft and business of writing. Each calendar year typically features multiple conferences around the country. In 2014, the New York conference will be Aug. 1-3, while the Los Angeles conference will be Aug. 15-17. The most popular feature of the east coast conference is the agent pitch slam, in which potential authors are given the ability to pitch their books directly to agents. For the 2014 conference, there will be more than 50 agents in attendance. For more details, see the website.

COSTS Cost varies by location and year. There are typically different pricing options for those who wish to stay for the entire event vs. daylong passes.

ACCOMMODATIONS A block of rooms at the event hotel is reserved for guests.

WRITERS' LEAGUE OF TEXAS AGENTS CONFERENCE

Writers' League of Texas, 611 S. Congress Ave., Suite 200 A-3, Austin TX 78704. (512)499-8914. **Fax:** (512)499-0441. **E-mail:** conference@writersleague.org. **E-mail:** jennifer@writersleague.org. **Website:** www.writersleague.org. Estab. 1982. Established in 1981, the Writers' League of Texas is a nonprofit professional organization whose primary purpose is to provide a forum for information, support, and sharing among writers, to help members improve and market their writing skills, and to promote the interests of writers and the writing community. The Writers' League of Texas Agents & Editors Conference is for writers at every stage of their career. Beginners can learn more about this mystifying industry and prepare themselves for the journey ahead. Those with completed manuscripts can pitch to agents and get feedback on their manuscripts from professional editors. Published writers can learn about market trends and network with rising stars in the world of writing. No matter what your market, genre, or level, our conference can benefit you.

COSTS Rates vary based on membership and the date of registration. The starting rate (registration through January 15) is $309 for members and $369 for nonmembers. Rate increases through later dates. See website for updates.

ACCOMMODATIONS 2013 event was at the Hyatt Regency Austin, 208 Barton Springs Road, Austin, TX 78704. Check back often for new information.

ADDITIONAL INFORMATION 2014 event held from June 27-29, 2014. Contests and awards programs are offered separately. Brochures are available upon request.

WRITERS WEEKEND AT THE BEACH

P.O. Box 877, Ocean Park WA 98640. (360)262-0160. **E-mail:** pelkeyjc@hotmail.com. **E-mail:** bobtracie@hotmail.com; pelkeyjc@hotmail.com. **Contact:** John Pelkey. Estab. 1992. Annual conference held in April. Conference duration: 2 days. Average attendance:

45. A retreat for writers with an emphasis on poetry, fiction, and nonfiction. Held at the Ocean Park Methodist Retreat Center & Camp. Speakers have included Miralee Ferrell, Leslie Gould, Linda Clare, Birdie Etchison, Colette Tennant, Gail Dunham, and Marion Duckworth.

COSTS $200 for full registration before March 1 and $215 after March 1.

ACCOMMODATIONS Offers on-site overnight lodging.

WRITE ON THE RIVER

8941 Kelsey Lane, Knoxville TN 37922. **E-mail:** bob@bobmayer.org. **Website:** www.bobmayer.org. **Contact:** Bob Mayer. Estab. 2002. Held several times a year. Conference duration: 2 days. Held at a private residence.

COSTS Varies; depends on venue. Please see website for any updates.

ADDITIONAL INFORMATION Limited to 4 participants, and focused on their novel and marketability.

THE WRITERS' WORKSHOP

387 Beaucatcher Rd., Asheville NC 28805. (828)254-8111. **E-mail:** writersw@gmail.com. **Website:** www.twwoa.org. Estab. 1984. Biannual writing retreat at Folly Beach, SC. 2014 dates: May 15-18. Kurt Vonnegut said: "God bless The Writers' Workshop of Asheville!" He and Don De Lillo, Peter Matthiessen, E.L. Doctorow, Eudora Welty, John le Carre and many other distinguished authors have given benefit readings for us. We offer classes, contests, retreats, and other events. Workshops in all genres of writing, for beginning or experienced writers, are held in Asheville and Charlotte, NC. Our in-house Renbourne Editorial Agency offers the highest quality editing and revising services for writers of all genres.

COSTS Vary. Financial assistance available to low-income writers. Information on overnight accommodations is made available.

ADDITIONAL INFORMATION We also sponsor these contests, open to all writers: Annual Poetry Contest, Prizes from $100-300 (Deadline: Feb. 28); Hard Times Writing Contest, Prizes from $100-300, (Deadline: May 30); Fiction Contest, Prizes from $150-350 (Deadline: Aug. 30); Annual Memoirs Competition, Prizes from $150-350 (Deadline: Nov. 30). Contests for young writers are posted at our website.

WRITE-TO-PUBLISH CONFERENCE

WordPro Communication Services, 9118 W. Elmwood Dr., Suite 1G, Niles IL 60714-5820. (847)296-3964. **Fax:** (847)296-0754. **E-mail:** lin@writetopublish.com. **Website:** www.writetopublish.com. **Contact:** Lin Johnson, director. Estab. 1971. Annual. Conference held June 4-7, 2014. Average attendance: 200. Conference is focused for the Christian market and includes classes on writing for children. Writer workshops geared toward all levels. Open to students. Site: Wheaton College, Wheaton, IL (Chicago).

COSTS approximately $475; includes conference and banquet.

ACCOMMODATIONS In campus residence halls. Cost is approximately $280-360.

ADDITIONAL INFORMATION Optional ms evaluation available. College credit available. Conference information available in January. For details, visit website, or e-mail brochure@writetopublish.com. Accepts inquiries by e-mail, fax, phone.

WRITING AND ILLUSTRATING FOR YOUNG READERS CONFERENCE

1480 East 9400 South, Sandy UT 84093. **E-mail:** staff@wifyr.com. **Website:** www.wifyr.com. Estab. 2000. Annual workshop held in June 2014. Conference duration: 5 days. Average attendance: 100+. Learn how to write, illustrate, and publish in the children's and young adult markets. Beginning and advanced writers and illustrators are tutored in a small-group workshop setting by published authors and artists and receive instruction from and network with editors, major publishing house representatives, and literary agents. Afternoon attendees get to hear practical writing and publishing tips from published authors, literary agents, and editors. Held at the Waterford School in Sandy, UT. Speakers have included John Cusick, Stephen Fraser, Alyson Heller, and Ruth Katcher.

COSTS Costs available online.

ACCOMMODATIONS A block of rooms are available at the Best Western Cotton Tree Inn in Sandy, UT at a discounted rate. This rate is good as long as there are available rooms.

THE HELENE WURLITZER FOUNDATION

P.O. Box 1891, Taos NM 87571. (575)758-2413. **Fax:** (575)758-2559. **E-mail:** hwf@taosnet.com. **Website:** www.wurlitzerfoundation.org. **Contact:** Michael A. Knight, executive director. Estab. 1953.

ACCOMMODATIONS "Provides individual housing in fully furnished studio/houses (casitas), rent and utility free. Artists are responsible for transportation to and from Taos, their meals and materials for their work. Bicycles are provided upon request."

⊕ WYOMING WRITERS CONFERENCE

Various cities in Wyoming **E-mail:** pfrolander@rangeweb.net. **Website:** wyowriters.org. **Contact:** Patricia Frolander. This is a statewide writing conference for writers of Wyoming and neighboring states. Last conference: June 6-8, 2014, in Sheridan, WY. Each year, multiple published authors, editors and literary agents are in attendance. The city/location of the conference varies from year to year around the state. Locations have included Sheridan, Casper, Cody, and more.

AGENTS INDEX

LITERARY AGENTS SPECIALTIES INDEX

FICTION

ACTION

ADVENTURE

COMMERCIAL

CRIME

DETECTIVE

EROTICA

ETHNIC

EXPERIMENTAL

FAMILY SAGA

FANTASY

FEMINIST

GLITZ

HISTORICAL

HORROR

HUMOR

INSPIRATIONAL

JUVENILE

LESBIAN

LITERARY

MAINSTREAM

MIDDLE GRADE

MULTICULTURAL

MYSTERY

NEW ADULT

PARANORMAL

PICTURE BOOKS

POLICE

REGIONAL

RELIGIOUS

ROMANCE

SATIRE

SCIENCE FICTION

SHORT STORY COLLECTIONS

SUSPENSE

THRILLER

URBAN FANTASY

WESTERN

WOMEN'S

YOUNG ADULT

NONFICTION

ANIMALS

ANTHROPOLOGY

ARCHEOLOGY

ARCHITECTURE

ART

AUTOBIOGRAPHY

BIOGRAPHY

BUSINESS

CHILD GUIDANCE

COMPUTERS

COOKING

CRAFTS

CREATIVE NONFICTION

CULTURAL INTERESTS

CURRENT AFFAIRS

DANCE

DESIGN

DIET/NUTRITION

ECONOMICS

EDUCATION

ENVIRONMENT

ETHNIC

FILM

FOODS

GARDENING

GAY/LESBIAN

GOVERNMENT

HEALTH

HISTORY

HOBBIES

HOW TO

HOW-TO

HUMOR

INSPIRATIONAL

INVESTIGATIVE

LANGUAGE

LAW

LESBIAN

LITERATURE

MEDICINE

MEMOIRS

MILITARY

MONEY

MULTICULTURAL

MUSIC

NATURE

NEW AGE

PARENTING

PHILOSOPHY

PHOTOGRAPHY

POLITICS

POPULAR CULTURE

PSYCHOLOGY

RELIGIOUS

SATIRE

SCIENCE

SELF-HELP

SEX

SOCIOLOGY

SPIRITUALITY

SPORTS

TECHNOLOGY

THEATER

TRANSLATION

TRAVEL

TRUE CRIME

WAR

WOMEN'S ISSUES

WOMEN'S STUDIES